COSMIC COMMUNION

Cosmic Communion

Star Wisdom, volume 4
2022

EDITOR
Joel Matthew Park

ADVISORY BOARD
Brian Gray ~ Claudia McLaren Lainson ~ Robert Powell, PhD
Lacquanna Paul ~ Robert Schiappacasse

Lindisfarne Books

Lindisfarne Books
an imprint of Steinerbooks/Anthroposophic Press, Inc.
402 Union Street, No. 58, Hudson, NY 12534
www.steinerbooks.org

Cosmic Communion: Star Wisdom, vol. 4 © 2022 by Joel Park and Robert Powell (from 2011 to 2018 this series was published as *Journal for Star Wisdom*). All contributions are published with permission from the authors. All rights reserved. No part of this publication may be reproduced, stored in a retrieval system, or transmitted in any form or by any means, electronic, mechanical, photocopying, recording, or otherwise without the prior written permission of the publisher.

With grateful acknowledgment to Peter Treadgold (1943–2005), who wrote the Astrofire program (available from the Sophia Foundation), with which the ephemeris pages in *Star Wisdom* are computed each year.

Disclaimer: The views expressed by the contributors in *Star Wisdom* do not necessarily reflect those of the editorial board of *Star Wisdom* or Lindisfarne Books/Anthroposophic Press, Inc.

Design by William Jens Jensen

ISBN: 978-1-58420-900-3 (paperback)

CONTENTS

Astrosophy 6

Preface
   by Robert Powell, PhD 7

The Seven Ideals of the Rose of the World
   by Robert Powell, PhD 12

Editorial Foreword
   by Joel Matthew Park 13

A Letter to the Editor 25

Grail Chronology: Classics in Astrosophy, Part V
   by Robert Powell, PhD 31

The Sacrifices of Jesus and Christ, Part I
   by Joel Matthew Park 44

Rudolf Steiner and the Christmas Conference:
   Astrological Aspects of the Laying of the Foundation Stone, Part II
   by Krisztina Cseri 68

The Archetypal Language: Returning to the Origin of the Houses, Part III
   by Joel Matthew Park 95

Tone Art
   by Amber Wolfe Rounds 111

Working with the *Star Wisdom* Calender
   by Robert Powell, PhD 131

Symbols Used in Charts / Time 133

Commentaries and Ephemerides, January – December 2022
   by Joel Matthew Park
   Monthly Stargazing Preview and Astronomical Sky Watch
   by Julie Humphreys 136

Sophia Star Calendar 2022
   by Kathleen Baiocchi 191

Glossary 244

Bibliography and Related Reading 251

About the Contributors 254

ASTROSOPHY

The Sophia Foundation was founded and exists to help usher in the new age of Sophia and the corresponding Sophianic culture, the Rose of the World, prophesied by Daniel Andreev and other spiritual teachers. Part of the work of the Sophia Foundation is the cultivation of a new star wisdom, *Astro–Sophia* (*astrosophy*), now arising in our time in response to the descent of Sophia, who is the bearer of Divine Wisdom, just as Christ (the Logos, or the Lamb) is the bearer of Divine Love. Like the star wisdom of antiquity, astrosophy is sidereal, which means "of the stars." Astrosophy, inspired by Divine Sophia, descending from stellar heights, directs our consciousness toward the glory and majesty of the starry heavens, to encompass the entire celestial sphere of our cosmos and, beyond this, to the galactic realm—the realm that Daniel Andreev referred to as "the heights of our universe"—from which Sophia is descending on her path of approach into our cosmos. Sophia draws our attention not only to the star mysteries of the heights, but also to the cosmic mysteries connected with Christ's deeds of redemption wrought two thousand years ago. To penetrate these mysteries is the purpose of the annual volumes of *Star Wisdom*.

For information about Astrosophy/Choreocosmos/Cosmic Dance workshops
Contact the Sophia Foundation:
4500 19th Street, #369, Boulder, CO 80304
Phone: (303) 242-5388; sophia@sophiafoundation.org;
www.sophiafoundation.org

PREFACE

Robert Powell, PhD

This is the fourth volume of the annual *Star Wisdom* (formerly *Journal for Star Wisdom*), intended to help all people interested in the new star wisdom of astrosophy and in the cosmic dimension of Christianity, which began with the Star of the Magi. The calendar comprises an ephemeris page for each month of the year, computed with the help of Peter Treadgold's *Astrofire* computer program, with a monthly commentary by Joel Park. The monthly commentary relates the geocentric and heliocentric planetary movements to events in the life of Jesus Christ.

Jesus Christ united the levels of the earthly personality (*geocentric* = Earth-centered) and the higher self (*heliocentric* = Sun-centered) insofar as he was the most highly evolved earthly personality (Jesus) embodying the higher self (Christ) of all existence, the Divine "I AM." To see the life of Jesus Christ in relation to the world of stars opens the door to a profound experience of the cosmos, giving rise to a new star wisdom (astrosophy) that is the Spiritual Science of Cosmic Christianity.

Star Wisdom is scientific, resting on a solid mathematical–astronomical foundation and a secure chronology of the life of Jesus Christ, while it is also spiritual, aspiring to the higher dimension of existence, expressed outwardly in the world of stars. The scientific and the spiritual come together in the sidereal zodiac that originated with the Babylonians and was used by the three magi who beheld the star of Bethlehem and came to pay homage to Jesus a few months after his birth.

In continuity of spirit with the origins of Cosmic Christianity with the three magi, the sidereal zodiac is the frame of reference used for the computation of the geocentric and heliocentric planetary movements that are commented upon in the light of the life of Jesus Christ in *Star Wisdom*.

Thus, all zodiacal longitudes indicated in the text and presented in the following calendar are in terms of the sidereal zodiac, which needs to be distinguished from the tropical zodiac widely used in contemporary astrology in the West. The tropical zodiac was introduced into astrology in the middle of the second century AD by the Greek astronomer Claudius Ptolemy. Prior to this, the sidereal zodiac was used. Such was the influence of Ptolemy on the Western astrological tradition that the tropical zodiac replaced the sidereal zodiac used by the Babylonians, Egyptians, and early Greek astrologers. Yet the astrological tradition in India was not influenced by Ptolemy, and so the sidereal zodiac is still used to this day by Hindu astrologers.

The sidereal zodiac originated with the Babylonians in the sixth to fifth centuries BC and was defined by them in relation to certain bright stars. For example, Aldebaran ("the Bull's Eye") is located in the middle of the sidereal sign–constellation of the Bull at 15° Taurus, while Antares ("the Scorpion's heart") is in the middle of the sidereal sign–constellation of the Scorpion at 15° Scorpio. The sidereal signs, each 30° long, coincide closely with the twelve astronomical zodiacal constellations of the same name, whereas the signs of the tropical zodiac—since they are defined in relation to the vernal point—now have little or no relationship to the corresponding zodiacal constellations. This is because the vernal point, the zodiacal location of the Sun on March 20–21, shifts slowly backward through the sidereal zodiac at a rate of 1° every seventy-two years ("the precession of the equinoxes"). When Ptolemy introduced the tropical zodiac into astrology, there was a nearly exact coincidence between the tropical and the sidereal zodiac, as the vernal point, which is defined as 0° Aries in the tropical zodiac, was at 1° Aries in the sidereal zodiac in the middle of the second century AD. Thus, there was only 1° difference between the two zodiacs. Thus, it made hardly any difference to Ptolemy or his contemporaries to use the tropical zodiac instead of the sidereal zodiac. Now, however—the vernal point having shifted back from 1° Aries to 5° Pisces owing to precession—there is a 25° difference, and thus there is virtually no correspondence between the two. Without going into further detail concerning the complex issue of the zodiac (as shown in the *Hermetic Astrology* trilogy), the sidereal zodiac is the zodiac used by the three magi, who were the last representatives of the true star wisdom of antiquity. For this reason, the sidereal zodiac is used throughout the texts in *Star Wisdom*.

Readers interested in exploring the scientific (astronomical and chronological) foundations of Cosmic Christianity are referred to the works listed here under "Literature." The *Chronicle of the Living Christ: Foundations of Cosmic Christianity* (listed on the following page) is an indispensable reference source (abbreviated *Chron.*) for *Star Wisdom*. The chronology of the life of Jesus Christ rests upon Robert Powell's research into the description of Christ's daily life by Anne Catherine Emmerich in her three-volume work, *The Visions of Anne Catherine Emmerich* (abbreviated *ACE*).

Further details concerning *Star Wisdom* and how to work with it on a daily basis may be found in the general introduction to the *Christian Star Calendar*. The general introduction explains all the features of *Star Wisdom*. The new edition, published in 2003, includes sections on the megastars (stars of great luminosity) and on the 36 decans (10° subdivisions of the twelve signs of the zodiac) in relation to their planetary rulers and to the extra-zodiacal constellations, or the constellations above or below the circle of the twelve constellations–signs of the zodiac. Further material on the decans, including examples of historical personalities born in the various decans, as well as a wealth of other material on the signs of the sidereal zodiac, can be found in *Cosmic Dances of the Zodiac* (listed below). Also foundational is *History of the Zodiac,* published by Sophia Academic Press (listed under "Works by Robert Powell").

LITERATURE

(See also "References" section)

General Introduction to the Christian Star Calendar: A Key to Understanding, 2nd ed. Palo Alto, CA: Sophia Foundation, 2003.

Bento, William, Robert Schiappacasse, and David Tresemer, *Signs in the Heavens: A Message for our Time.* Boulder: StarHouse, 2000.

Emmerich, Anne Catherine, *The Visions of Anne Catherine Emmerich* (new edition, with material by Robert Powell). Kettering, OH: Angelico Press, 2015.

Paul, Lacquanna, and Robert Powell, *Cosmic Dances of the Planets.* San Rafael, CA: Sophia Foundation Press, 2007.

———, *Cosmic Dances of the Zodiac.* San Rafael, CA: Sophia Foundation Press, 2007.

Smith, Edward R., *The Burning Bush: Rudolf Steiner, Anthroposophy, and the Holy Scriptures* (3rd ed.). Great Barrington, MA: SteinerBooks, 2020.

Steiner, Rudolf, *Astronomy and Astrology: Finding a Relationship to the Cosmos.* London: Rudolf Steiner Press, 2009.

Sucher, Willi, *Cosmic Christianity and the Changing Countenance of Cosmology.* Great Barrington, MA: SteinerBooks, 1993. *Isis Sophia* and other works by Willi Sucher are available from the Astrosophy Research Center, PO Box 13, Meadow Vista, CA 95722.

Tidball, Charles S., and Robert Powell, *Jesus, Lazarus, and the Messiah: Unveiling Three Christian Mysteries.* Great Barrington, MA: SteinerBooks, 2005. This book offers a penetrating study of the Christ mysteries against the background of *Chronicle of the Living Christ* and contains two chapters by Robert Powell on the Apostle John and John the Evangelist (Lazarus).

Tresemer, David (with Robert Schiappacasse), *Star Wisdom and Rudolf Steiner: A Life Seen Through the Oracle of the Solar Cross.* Great Barrington, MA: SteinerBooks, 2007.

Astrosophical Works by Robert Powell, PhD

Starcrafts (formerly Astro Communication Services, or ACS):
History of the Houses (1997)
History of the Planets (1989)
The Zodiac: A Historical Survey (1984)
www.acspublications.com
www.astrocom.com
Business Address:
Starcrafts Publishing
334 Calef Hwy.
Epping, NH 03042
Phone: 603-734-4300
Fax: 603-734-4311
Contact maria@starcraftseast.com

SteinerBooks:

Orders: (703) 661-1594; www.steinerbooks.org
By email: service@steinerbooks.org

The Astrological Revolution: Unveiling the Science of the Stars as a Science of Reincarnation and Karma, coauthor Kevin Dann (Great Barrington, MA: SteinerBooks, 2010). After reestablishing the sidereal zodiac as a basis for astrology that penetrates the mystery of the stars' relationship to human destiny, the reader is invited to discover the astrological significance of the totality of the vast sphere of stars surrounding the Earth. This book points to the astrological significance of the entire celestial sphere, including all the stars and constellations beyond the twelve zodiacal signs. This discovery is revealed by the study of megastars, illustrating how they show up in an extraordinary way in Christ's healing miracles by aligning with the Sun at the time of those events. This book offers a spiritual, yet scientific, path toward a new relationship to the stars.

Christian Hermetic Astrology: The Star of the magi and the Life of Christ (Hudson, NY: Anthroposophic Press, 1998). Twenty-five discourses set in the "Temple of the Sun," where Hermes and his pupils gather to meditate on the Birth, the Miracles, and the Passion of Jesus Christ. The discourses offer a series of meditative contemplations on the deeds of Christ in relation to the mysteries of the cosmos. They are an expression of the age-old hermetic mystery wisdom of the ancient Egyptian sage, Hermes Trismegistus. This book offers a meditative approach to the cosmic correspondences between major events in the life of Christ and the heavenly configurations at that time 2,000 years ago.

Chronicle of the Living Christ: Foundations of Cosmic Christianity (Hudson, NY: Anthroposophic Press, 1996). An account of the life of Christ, day by day, throughout most of the 3½ years of his ministry, including the horoscopes of conception, birth, and death of Jesus, Mary, and John the Baptist, together with a wealth of material relating to the new star wisdom focused on the life of Christ. This work provides the chronological basis for *Christian Hermetic Astrology* and *Star Wisdom*.

Elijah Come Again: A Prophet for our Time: A Scientific Approach to Reincarnation (Great Barrington, MA: SteinerBooks, 2009). By way of horoscope comparisons from conception–birth–death in one incarnation to conception–birth–death in the next, this work establishes scientifically two basic astrosophical research findings. These are: the importance 1) of the sidereal zodiac and 2) of the heliocentric positions of the planets. Also, for the first time, the identity of the "saintly nun" is revealed, of whom Rudolf Steiner spoke in a conversation with Marie von Sivers about tracing Novalis's karmic background. The focus throughout the book is on the Elijah individuality in his various incarnations, and is based solidly on Rudolf Steiner's indications. It also can be read as a karmic biography by anyone who chooses to omit the astrosophical material.

Star Wisdom (2019–); *Journal for Star Wisdom* (2010–2018) (Great Barrington, MA: Lindisfarne Books, edited by Joel Matthew Park, Robert Powell and others engaged in astrosophic research. A guide to the correspondences of Christ in the stellar and etheric world. Includes articles of interest, a complete geocentric and heliocentric sidereal ephemeris, and an aspectarian. According to Rudolf Steiner, every step taken by Christ during his ministry between the baptism in the Jordan and the resurrection was in harmony with, and an expression of, the cosmos. The journal is concerned with these heavenly correspondences during the life of Christ. It is intended to help provide a foundation for Cosmic Christianity, the cosmic dimension of Christianity. It is this dimension that has been missing from Christianity in its 2,000-year history. A starting point is to contemplate the movements of the Sun, Moon, and planets against the background of the zodiacal constellations (sidereal signs) today in relation to corresponding stellar events during the life of Christ. This opens the possibility of attuning to the life of Christ in the etheric cosmos in a living way.

Sophia Foundation Press and Sophia Academic Press Publications

Books available from Amazon.com
JamesWetmore@mac.com
www.logosophia.com

History of the Zodiac (San Rafael, CA: Sophia Academic Press, 2007). Book version of Robert Powell's PhD thesis, *The History of the Zodiac*. This penetrating study restores the sidereal zodiac to its rightful place as the original zodiac, tracing it back to fifth-century-BC Babylonians. Available in paperback and hardcover.

Hermetic Astrology: Volume 1, Astrology and Reincarnation (San Rafael, CA: Sophia Foundation Press, 2007). This book seeks to give the ancient science of the stars a scientific basis. This new foundation for astrology based on research into reincarnation and karma (destiny) is the primary focus. It includes numerous reincarnation examples, the study of which reveals the existence of certain astrological "laws" of reincarnation, on the basis of which it is evident that the ancient sidereal zodiac is the authentic astrological zodiac, and that the heliocentric movements of the planets are of great significance. Foundational for the new star wisdom of astrosophy.

Hermetic Astrology: Volume 2, Astrological Biography (San Rafael, CA: Sophia Foundation Press, 2007). Concerned with karmic relationships and the unfolding of destiny in seven-year periods through one's life. The seven-year rhythm underlies the human being's astrological biography, which can be studied in relation to the movements of the Sun, Moon, and planets around the sidereal zodiac between conception and birth. The "rule of Hermes" is used to determine the moment of conception.

Sign of the Son of Man in the Heavens: Sophia and the New Star Wisdom (San Rafael, CA: Sophia Foundation Press, 2008). Revised and expanded with new material, this edition deals with a new wisdom of stars in the light of Divine Sophia. It was intended as a help in our time, as we were called on to be extremely wakeful up to the end of the Maya calendar in 2012.

Cosmic Dances of the Zodiac (San Rafael, CA: Sophia Foundation Press, 2007), coauthor Lacquanna Paul. Study material describing the twelve signs of the zodiac and their forms and gestures in cosmic dance, with diagrams. Includes a wealth of information on the twelve signs and the 36 decans (the subdivision of the signs into decans, or 10° sectors, corresponding to constellations above and below the zodiac).

Cosmic Dances of the Planets (San Rafael, CA: Sophia Foundation Press, 2007), coauthor Lacquanna Paul. Study material describing the seven classical planets and their forms and gestures in cosmic dance, with diagrams, including much information on the planets.

American Federation of Astrologers (AFA) Publications (currently not in print)

www.astrologers.com

The Sidereal Zodiac, coauthor Peter Treadgold (Tempe, AZ: AFA, 1985). A *History of the Zodiac* (sidereal, tropical, Hindu, astronomical) and a formal definition of the sidereal zodiac with the star Aldebaran ("the Bull's Eye") at 15° Taurus. This is an abbreviated version of *History of the Zodiac*.

Rudolf Steiner College Press Publications

9200 Fair Oaks Blvd., Fair Oaks, CA 95628

The Christ Mystery: Reflections on the Second Coming (Fair Oaks, CA: Rudolf Steiner College Press, 1999). The fruit of many years of reflecting on the Second Coming and its cosmological aspects. Looks at the approaching trial of humanity and the challenges of living in apocalyptic times, against the background of "great signs in the heavens."

The Sophia Foundation

4500 19th Street, #369, Boulder, CO 80304; distributes many of the books listed here and other works by Robert Powell.
Tel: (303) 242-5388
sophia@sophiafoundation.org
www.sophiafoundation.org

Computer program for charts and ephemerides, with grateful acknowledgment to Peter Treadgold, who wrote the computer program

Preface

Astrofire (with research module, star catalog of over 4,000 stars, and database of birth and death charts of historical personalities), capable of printing geocentric and heliocentric–hermetic sidereal charts and ephemerides throughout history. The hermetic charts, based on the astronomical system of the Danish astronomer Tycho Brahe, are called "Tychonic" charts in the program. This program can:

- compute birth charts in a large variety of systems (tropical, sidereal, geocentric, heliocentric, hermetic);
- calculate conception charts using the hermetic rule, in turn applying it for correction of the birth time;
- produce charts for the period between conception and birth;
- print out an "astrological biography" for the whole of lifework with the geocentric, heliocentric (and even lemniscatory) planetary system;
- work with the sidereal zodiac according to the definition of your choice (Babylonian sidereal, Indian sidereal, unequal-division astronomical, etc.);
- work with planetary aspects with orbs of your choice.

The program includes eight house systems and a variety of chart formats. The program also includes an ephemeris program with a search facility. The geocentric–heliocentric sidereal ephemeris pages in the annual volumes of *Star Wisdom* are produced by the software program *Astrofire*, which is compatible with Microsoft Windows.

Those interested in obtaining the *Astrofire* program should contact:

The Sophia Foundation
4500 19th Street, #369
Boulder, CO 80304
Tel: (303) 242-5388
sophia@sophiafoundation.org
www.sophiafoundation.org

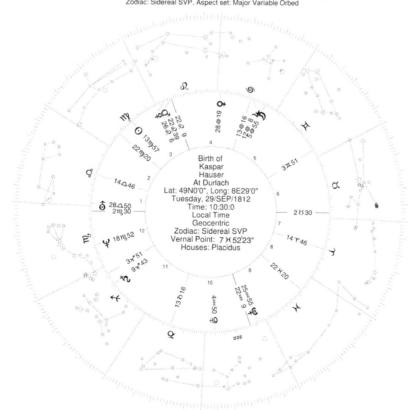

A horoscope generated by the Astrofire *program*

THE SEVEN IDEALS OF THE ROSE OF THE WORLD
Robert Powell, PhD

In gratitude to Daniel Andreev (1906–1959), the Russian prophet of the Rose of the World as the coming world culture, inspired by Sophia—a culture based on Love and Wisdom.

The Rose of the World is arising through the approach of Divine Sophia toward the Earth. Her approach is calling forth the following basic qualities or attributes of the new world culture that She is creating and inspiring:

1. First and foremost: *interreligion*. For Sophia all true religious and spiritual traditions are different layers of spiritual reality, which She seeks to weave together as petals of the Rose of the World. Sophia is not founding a new world religion as She approaches, descending from cosmic heights, and drawing ever closer to our solar system. On Her path of descent, approaching our planet to incarnate into the Earth's aura during the Age of Aquarius, She is bestowing insight concerning each religion and spiritual tradition, thus awaking interreligiosity, signifying a heartfelt interest in religious and spiritual traditions other than one's own. This signifies the blossoming and unfolding of the petals of the Rose of the World, creating brother–sisterhood between all peoples.

2. Sophia's approach toward our planet is bringing about an awaking of social conscience on a global scale, inspiring active compassion combined with unflagging practical efforts on behalf of social justice around the world.

3. Through Sophia a framework for understanding the higher dimension of historical processes is coming about: metahistory, illumining the meaning of historical processes of the past, present, and future in relation to humankind's spiritual evolution. This entails glimpses into the mystical consciousness of humanity such as may be found in the book of Revelation.

Daniel Andreev, c. 1957

4. On the national sociopolitical level, Sophia's inspiration is working to transform the state into a community. The community of Italy, the community of France, etc., is the ideal for the future, rather than the political entity of the state representing (or misrepresenting) the people. And on the global scale Sophia is seeking to bring about the unification of the planet as a world community through bringing the different country communities into a harmonious relationship with one another on a religious, cultural, and economic level.

5. This world community, the Rose of the World, inspired by Sophia, will seek to establish the economic wellbeing of every man, woman, and child on the planet, to ensure that everyone has a roof over their heads and sufficient food to live on. Here it is a matter of ensuring a decent standard of living for all peoples of the Earth.

6. A high priority of the Rose of the World will be the ennobling of education. New methods of education are being inspired by Sophia to help bring out everyone's creative talents. To ennoble education so that each person's creativity can unfold is the goal here.

7. Finally, Sophia is working for the transformation of the planet into a garden and, moreover, for the spiritualization of nature. Humanity and nature are to live in cooperation and harmony, with human beings taking up their responsibility toward nature, which is to work for the spiritualization and redemption of the kingdoms of nature.

EDITORIAL FOREWORD

Joel Matthew Park

The year 2022 is upon us, and with it we commemorate the 100-year anniversary of the founding of the Movement for Religious Renewal—more popularly known in the English-speaking world as the Christian Community—as well as the burning of the first Goetheanum on December 31, 1922. As the first flames were going up in the modern "Temple of Man," Rudolf Steiner was speaking these words (emphasis mine, in bold):

> But now that we have set before us the true nature of man, let us see what results follow. We have seen that man cannot be understood unless he is regarded as bearing within him, as it were, a piece of Nature, in such a manner that the counteracting natural forces cancel one another; and if we examine this piece of Nature in man with the eyes of Spiritual Science, we find it to be penetrated as to the physical and etheric bodies during sleep by mineral and vegetable modes of activity, which are seen to be in the summer condition. If we are now able to observe in the right way this budding, sprouting life, we may learn to understand its real significance.
>
> When does this budding and sprouting take place? When the "I" and astral body are not present, when they are away during sleep. And whence comes this budding and sprouting process? That is precisely what spiritual vision shows us. Let us picture man asleep. His physical and etheric bodies lie in the bed. Spiritual vision sees them as soil, as mineral matter, out of which plant life is sprouting. It is a different form of plant life, of course, from the one we see around us, but recognizable as such by spiritual sight. Above gleam the "I" and astral body like a flame, unable to approach the physical and etheric. Sleeping man therefore is a sort of budding, sprouting plot of ground, with a gleaming "I" and astral body belonging to it, but detached.
>
> And when man is awake? I must describe this state as follows. **The mineral and vegetable portions are seen to be withering and collapsing, while the "I" and astral body gleam down into them, and as it were, burn them up.** This is waking man, with the mineral matter crumbling within him. The mineral element of man crumbles during his waking hours. There is a sort of plant-like activity that, although quite different in appearance, gives a general and universal impression of autumn foliage, of drooping, withering leaves that are dying and vanishing; and **all through this fading substance, big and little flames are gleaming and glowing. These big and little flames are the astral body and the "I," which are now living in the physical and etheric bodies.** And then the question arises: What happens to these gleaming and glowing flames during sleep, when they are separated from the physical and etheric bodies?
>
> When this problem is attacked by the methods of occult science we find the solution to be a consequence you could yourselves draw from a comparison of various descriptions that I have given from time to time. The power that drives away the flame and gleam of the "I" and astral body, and that is then actively at work in the budding and sprouting vegetative life of the summer-like, sleeping physical body, and also in its mineral element, causing even that too to evolve a kind of life, so that in the course of its infinitesimal subdividing, it looks like a mass of melting atoms, a continuous mobile mass, everywhere active, fluid- mineral and yet air-like, at all points permeated by sprouting life—what *is* this inner power? It is the reverberating wave of our life before birth, whose pulsations beat upon our physical and etheric bodies during sleep. When we are awake during earthly life, we still the pulsating vibrations. **So long as the flame and gleam of the "I" and astral body are united with the physical and etheric bodies, we annul those impulses that spring from an existence preceding our earthly life and that we experience during sleep, we bring**

them to quiescence. And now we learn for the first time, from an inspection of ourselves, how to regard external Nature in the right way. For all natural laws and energies affecting external vegetable and mineral Nature resemble what is mineral and vegetable in ourselves, permeated with sprouting life, during sleep. And so this means that as our sleeping physical and etheric bodies point to our own past, to a spiritual life in which we lived before birth, so does all external Nature that is vegetable or mineral point to a *past*. As a matter of fact, if we are to comprehend aright the natural laws and forces of our external environment, exclusive of the animal element and physical man, we must recognize that they point to the Earth's past, to the dying-away of the Earth. And the thoughts we entertain about external Nature are really directed to the dying element in Earth existence.

Now if this decaying Earth nature is to be brought to life so that it can receive impulses for the *future*, this can come about in no other way than it does in man, that is to say, by the insertion of soul and spirit into mineral and vegetable. In the case of the animals, the *soul* element enters in, and then with man, *spirit* enters in.[1]

We can feel a great awe and wonder at the mystery of these powerful words being spoken at the very times that flames were rising up within the body of the Goetheanum! Who can say how conscious Rudolf Steiner was as to the fate of the Goetheanum leading up to this moment? The most I can say with any certainty is that his Angel—well aware of the intertwined karma of Rudolf Steiner, the Anthroposophical Movement, and their center in the Goetheanum—inspired him directly to speak these words at this particular moment.

Out of these words the tragedy of the burning of the first Goetheanum takes on a very different perspective. We are able to see this magnificent structure as a kind of sleeping being, a being of mineral and vegetable life, flourishing and flowing with the powers of high Summer—but primarily as a gift of grace from the life between death and rebirth, a gift from another world, a world holding sway over the *past—Ex Deo Nascimur*. So far at this point in time, the Anthroposophical Movement was lacking the free initiative of its members—the flame of the "I" and the astral body had to descend into this sleeping etheric and physical body, to awaken it, by *destroying it—In Christo Morimur*—potentially allowing the soul and spirit to enter in and receive impulses from the *future—Per Spiritum Sanctum Reviviscimus*.

He continues later on in this same lecture with the following words:

> If we observe the Earth's crust and its vegetation aright, we shall look upon all the life of the Earth and say: You crystals, you mountains, you budding and sprouting plants, I see in you monuments of a living, creative past that is now in process of dying. But in man himself, if we are able to have the right insight into this dying element that draws its energy from pre-earthly existence and exhausts itself and dies away in the physical and etheric bodies—in man we see this physical and etheric organism permeated by an astral body and "I" throwing light across into the future and able to unfold freely, on a plane of balanced natural energies, a life of thought and ideation. It may be said that we see in man *past and future side by side*. In Nature on the other hand, so far as she is mineral or vegetable, we see only the past. That element that already functions as future during man's present, is the element that confers *freedom* upon him; and this freedom is not to be found in external Nature. If external Nature were doomed to remain just what her mineral and vegetable kingdoms make her, she would be doomed to die, in the same way that the mere physical and etheric organism of man perishes. Man's physical and etheric organisms die, but man does not, because the nature of the astral and "I" within him carries within it, not death but an *arising*, a *coming into being*.
>
> If therefore external Nature is not to perish, she must be given what man has through his astral body and his "I." This means that as man through his astral body and his "I" has self-conscious ideas, he must, in order to

---

1 Steiner, *Man and the World of Stars,* lect. 12 (with edits).

ensure a future to the Earth, insert into the Earth too, the supersensible and invisible that he has within himself. Even as man must derive his reincarnation in another earth-life from that in him that is supersensible and invisible, since his dying physical and etheric bodies are powerless to confer it, so can no future arise for the Earth from the mineral and vegetable globe that surrounds us. Only when we place into the Earth what she has not herself, only then can an Earth of the Future arise. And what is not there of itself on the Earth is principally the *active thoughts of man*, as they live and weave in his own Nature-organism, which holds always a balance and is on this account self-dependent. If he brings these independent thoughts to a real existence, he confers a future on the Earth. But he must first have them. Thoughts that we make in our ordinary knowledge of Nature—thoughts about what is dying away, are mere reflections—not realities. But thoughts we receive from spiritual research are quickened in Imagination, Inspiration, and Intuition. If we accept them they become forms having independent existence in the life of the Earth.

Concerning these creative thoughts, I once said in my book entitled *A Theory of Knowledge Implicit in Goethe's World Conception*, that such thinking represents the spiritual form of communion among mankind. For as long as man gives himself up to his mirror-thoughts about external Nature, he does nothing but repeat the past. He lives in corpses of the Divine. When he himself brings life into his thoughts, then, giving and receiving communion through his own being, he allies himself with the element of Divine Spirit that permeates the world and assures its future.

Spiritual knowledge is thus a veritable communion, the beginning of a cosmic ritual that is right and fitting for the man of today, who is then able to grow because he begins to realize how he permeates his own physical and etheric organism with his astral body and "I," and how, as he quickens the spirit in himself, he charms it also into the dead and dying matter that surrounds him. And a new experience is then his.

When he looks upon his own organism in its *solid* condition, he feels that it links him to the starry universe. Insofar as the starry universe is a being at rest, maintaining—e.g., in the signs of the Zodiac a position at rest in relation to the Earth, man is connected in his physical organism with these constellations in space. But by allowing his powers of soul and spirit to pour into this 'form picture' in space, he himself changes the world.

Man is also traversed in like manner by streams of *fluid*. The etheric organism lives in the fluids and juices of the body. It is the etheric body that causes the blood to circulate and that brings into movement the other fluids and juices in man. Through this etheric organism he is brought into touch, if I may so express it, with the *deeds* of the stars, with the *movements* of the planets. Just as the resting pictures in the heaven of the fixed stars act upon, or stand in relation to, the solid structure of the human organism, so do the planetary movements of the system to which we belong stand in relation to the fluids in man.

But as the world presents itself to our immediate vision, it is a dead world. Man transforms it by means of his own spirit, when he shares his spirit with the world, by quickening his thoughts to Imagination, Inspiration, and Intuition, thus fulfilling the spiritual Communion of mankind. It is important that man should become *conscious* of this. The livelier and more alert this consciousness becomes, the more easily does man find the way to this spiritual Communion. I should like to give you today some words that may serve as a foundation for this consciousness, words that, when allowed to act rightly upon the soul—and this means, they must be made to live over and over again in the soul until the soul experiences to the full their moving, living meaning—will then bring something into existence in the human soul that transforms the dead environment with which man is connected into a living one, and quickens the past to life in order that from out of its death may arise the life of the future. This can only happen when man becomes aware of his connection with the Cosmos in the following way:

In Earth-activity (I am imagining the earthly matter that I take into myself with what fashions the solid structure of my organism.)

> In Earth-activity draws near to me,
> Given to me in substance-imaged form,
> The Heavenly Being of the Stars.

For it is a fact that when we take something that serves us as food and look upon its form, then we find in it a copy of the constellations of the fixed stars. We take it into ourselves. With the substance of the Earth that is contained in Earth-activity, we take into us the being of the stars, the being of the heavens. But we must be conscious that we as human beings, by a deliberate, loving act of human will, transform what has become matter, back again into spirit. In this manner we perform a real act of *transubstantiation*. We become aware of our own part in the world and so the spiritual thought-life is quickened within us.

> In Earth-activity draws near to me,
> Given to me in substance-imaged form,
> The Heavenly Being of the Stars.
> In Willing I see them transformed with Love!

And when we think of what we take into ourselves to permeate the fluid part of our organism, the circulation of the blood and juices, then that, in so far as it originates on Earth, is a copy not of the heavens or of the stars but of the *deeds* of the stars, that is to say, the movements of the planets. And I can become conscious how I spiritualize that, if I stand rightly in the world; and I can speak the following formula:

> In Watery life stream into me,
> Forming me through with power of
>   substance-force,
> The Heavenly Deeds of the Stars

—that is, the deeds of the planetary movements. And now:

> In Feeling I see them transformed with
>   Wisdom!

While I can see how in *will* the being of the stars changes lovingly into the spiritual content of the future, I can also see how in *feeling* a wise change takes place when I receive into me, in what permeates my fluid organism, a copy of heavenly deeds. Man can experience in this way in his will and in his feeling how he is placed into the world. Surrendering himself to the supreme direction of the universe that is all around him, he can carry out in living consciousness the act of transubstantiation in the great temple of the Cosmos—standing within it as one who is celebrating a sacrifice in a purely spiritual way.

What would otherwise be mere abstract knowledge achieves a relationship of will and feeling to the world. The world becomes the Temple, the House of God. When man as *knowing* man summons up also powers of *will* and *feeling*, he becomes a sacrificing being. His fundamental relationship to the world rises from knowledge into *cosmic ritual*.

The first beginning of what must come to pass if Anthroposophy is to fulfil its mission in the world is that man's whole relationship to the world must be recognized to be one of cosmic ritual or cult.[2]

Rudolf Steiner powerfully and poetically expresses here the nature of a true Cosmic Communion, a theme he was to revisit over and over again in the last 3 years of his life: the spiritual world was once directly active in Nature; in order to give humanity the possibility of acquiring freedom, they withdrew from Nature's activity—what we perceive is the semi-mechanical remnant of what was once living, flowing, becoming. It is now up to *human activity* if our grand inheritance of Nature is to be re-enlivened with the Spirit. In ancient times, the Gods spoke directly to humanity through the stars...the stars are now silent—it is *we* who must speak to *them*.

SATURN ENTERS AQUARIUS

In addition to the 100-year anniversary of the burning of the first Goetheanum, the year 2022 sees the entry of heliocentric Saturn into Aquarius, on November 24. As Robert Powell has pointed out before, we can bring the Saturn rhythm into relation with the rhythm of the astral body of Christ, each

---

2 Ibid.

Editorial Foreword

"Saturn year" of 29.5 Solar years being an expression of one day of the life of Christ—now playing out on the historical plane for all of humanity. The life of Jesus Christ planted the seeds for thousands of years of future human history.

As Saturn entered Sagittarius in 1929, it marked humanity's entry into the 37th day of temptation in the wilderness—the confrontation with the Luciferic temptation to bow down before him and be given all the kingdoms of this world. This is the temptation of the "will to power." Heliocentric Saturn was in Sagittarius and Capricorn from February 23, 1929, through July 18, 1934, when Saturn entered Aquarius. It was precisely these years that saw the Great Depression and the rise of fascism throughout Europe—particularly in Nazi Germany. The coming to power of the Adolf Hitler and the political ideology of fascism were the woeful expression for all of humanity of the temptation of Lucifer to the *will to power*.

This confrontation with the 37th day in the wilderness lasted all through World War II and into its aftermath, until 1958, when heliocentric Saturn once again entered Sagittarius. This marked the start of the 38th day in the wilderness, when Christ confronted the dual temptation of Lucifer and Ahriman in the enticement to cast himself from the pinnacle of the Temple. This is the temptation to relinquish conscience and conscious self-direction, instead submitting to the urges of animal instinct—to dive down into the subconscious.

Heliocentric Saturn was in Sagittarius and Capricorn once again, from August 10, 1958 through January 3, 1964, when it entered Aquarius. Over the course of World War II, fascism was defeated from the West by capitalist democracies, and from the East by communist nations. During the years 1958-64, this defeat was marked by the splitting of Germany between these two powers, into Western and Eastern Germany—one capitalist, the other communist—with the Berlin Wall harshly maintaining the division in the years to come. This split marked the conflict that would end up characterizing the 38th day of temptation—the Cold War between the West, represented particularly by the United States, and the East, represented particularly by the USSR—but also China and Vietnam.

Indeed, the Vietnam War was the awful expression of a country savagely torn in two between capitalist and communist forces, the war that represented this descent into the heart of darkness of the second day of temptation, just as World War II represented the first day of temptation. It was during the years 1958 to '64 that, under the leadership of the young John F. Kennedy, the United States and therefore the world briefly had a chance to take another path. It was John F. Kennedy's unwillingness to allow the CIA to bait him into conflict with Cuba, or to escalate the conflict in Vietnam into full-blown war, that resulted in his assassination at the hands of his own government (among other things, such as his urge to dismantle the CIA as well as the Federal Reserve). The assassination of John F. Kennedy marked the beginning of a global descent into madness. The drug culture exploded in the ensuing years—an obvious expression of "casting oneself from the pinnacle." But even communism itself—removing self-responsibility and putting it into the hands of the "collective unconscious" of the State—is an ideology that perfectly expresses the second temptation: an ideology so enticing on its surface, with promises of utopia, but utterly destructive in its application, particularly toward the unique individual. And surely, the military doctrine of Mutually Assured Destruction (a phrase coined in 1962) that held sway during this time period says it all—MAD.

In the end, by the grace of God—or perhaps more specifically the grace of the Virgin Mary—communism was overthrown by the capitalist, social-democratic cultures of the West, through an act of "sublimation through contact" in the spirit of the Letter–Meditations on Force and the Tower of Destruction (see *Meditations on the Tarot*) rather than outright confrontation—which to be sure, would have brought an end to *everything*, not just the threat of global communist takeover. And it was precisely at the beginning of the 39th day of temptation that this defeat of communism occurred: Saturn was in Sagittarius and Capricorn from January 17, 1988, through June 8, 1993.

During these years, the Berlin Wall fell, and the USSR dissolved. The formerly communist nations were virtually all converted to social-democratic governments with capitalist economies.

While the defeat of communism was a blessing to the Earth, it came at an awful cost: a Faustian bargain with Mephistopheles himself. These years marked the beginning of the confrontation with Ahriman, and the temptation to turn stones into bread—to mechanize all existence. The years 1988-93 saw the rise of the internet and home computing—the particular brand of capitalist economics that now held sway in the world wedded itself ever more closely to science and technology, which increasingly began to infiltrate all aspects of life. These years also saw the ascendency of the former head of the CIA—a man who very likely was deeply involved with the assassination of John F. Kennedy—to the presidency: George H. W. Bush. This was the beginning of the Ahrimanic treatment of the American people and the entire globe: the executive government was from now on nothing less than an extension of the intelligence agencies, and the ultimate goal of the proliferation of communication technology was not for the sake of promoting the social life and education, but in order to set up a global mass surveillance network, with citizens worldwide increasingly delighted to make available all psychological and biometric data to anyone who might be looking for it.

It was also during these years that the "new battlefield" was created, as the United States invaded Iraq during the Gulf War. Without the looming threat of communism, the Imperial West needed a new justification for its existence. The strategy was to enter into conflict with the very attack dogs they had used in prior conflicts. Saddam Hussein's Iraq had been heavily supported by the United States in the early 1980s during the Iraq-Iran War. At exactly the same time, Osama bin Laden and the Mujahideen were being supported by the United States in the Soviet-Afghan War. This strategy of planting the seed of a new enemy in order to fight a fully-blossomed one would continue all the way through the Obama Administration, when the rise of ISIS/Al-Qaida was welcomed as a way to destabilize Syria. The principal of an endless War on Terror, in which the imperial forces of the West pit controlled oppositions against each other in order to justify endless surveillance of the global populace and artificially prop up a capitalist shell of an economy was the enlightened strategic replacement of MAD.

This came to a head under the Obama administration, which expanded the military engagements of the United States from Iraq and Afghanistan to include Libya, Syria, Yemen, Somalia, and Pakistan—at least seven countries total; which worked hand in hand with Silicon Valley from day one; which increased the powers of mass surveillance begun under the Patriot Act; which punished and suppressed more whistle blowers than any other administration—including high-profile individuals such as Chelsea Manning, Edward Snowden, and most of all Julian Assange, and yet could present itself with such class, sophistication, and style—with the aid of a fawning media—that the public presented very little resistance to such unprecedented technocratic overreach. This is the legacy that the Obama administration leaves.

And now, just as it was during the years 1929 to 1934, 1958 to 1964, and 1988 to 1993, we have entered another day in the wilderness—but a day very unlike those that preceded it. This is the 40th day of temptation, the last before the ministry of Christ can properly begin. During this day on November 30 AD 29, Christ was confronted with the *fourth temptation*—which is that of megalomania, the combined force of all three prior temptations (see the Letter–Meditation on the Chariot in *Meditations on the Tarot*). This temptation attacks all three members of the soul simultaneously: the will is tempted to power; the feelings are tempted to abdicate responsibility; and thinking is tempted to materialism, to order the world through mechanization. Only after having overcome this fourth temptation was Christ "ministered unto by Angels."

Heliocentric Saturn entered Sagittarius July 1, 2017 and will leave Capricorn for Aquarius this year—on November 24, 2022. Similar to the previous three time periods outlined above, we are in the midst of a breakdown of the dominant paradigm from the previous day of temptation: global capitalism. The years 1929 to '34 saw the rise of three beasts which then went to war with each other: fascism, capitalism, and communism. The latter two defeated fascism in the ensuing years, and during the years 1958 to 1964 the conflict between these conquerors came to the fore. Then between 1988 and '93, communism was put to rest by global capitalism—this system then became dominant, seemingly with no contender. What will come into its place as it inevitably self-destructs?

There are several possibilities. Before laying those out, it is important to clarify what exactly is meant by the term "global capitalism," which is the system that became dominant increasingly over the past 93 years. This particular form of capitalism has been given the more accurate name of the "British system" of economics by the author Matthew Ehret in his book *The Clash of Two Americas, vol I: The Unfinished Symphony*. He contrasts this system of economics, which finds its origins in the work of Adam Smith's *Wealth of Nations*, with what has come to be known as the "American system" of economics—although to be fair, this system could also be called the "German-American system," as it has its roots primarily in the works of the well-known American Founding Father Alexander Hamilton, but also in that of Friedrich List, a German-American political economist contemporaneous with Friedrich Schelling.

In a review of Ehret's book,[3] David William Pear summarizes the two systems in no uncertain terms:

> The American System promotes economic development, industrialization, and trade tariffs to protect developing domestic industries against foreign dumping of cheap products. It also proactively promotes large infrastructure projects such as railroads. The federal government finances them with a national bank. The federal government's authority and duty to "coin money and regulate the value thereon" is proclaimed in the U.S. Constitution. A national bank can best provide funding for infrastructure projects and industrialization. Matthew Ehret calls lending for infrastructure "creative debt," because it produces value. The results of an American System are shared prosperity.
>
> The foil of the American System is the "British System" of slavery, exploitation, imperialism, war and scarcity. The British System is based on Adam Smith's laissez-faire "magic" hand, private banking, debt-slavery, Malthusianism zero-sum economics, social Darwinism, survival of the fittest, and eugenics. The British System is enforced with soul-destroying violence, to which it becomes addicted.
>
> The American System is a win–win system. The British System is the rich getting richer and the poor getting poorer. The American System promotes liberty. The British system promotes authoritarianism. The American System honors human rights. The British System is dehumanizing. Some of the champions of the American System were George Washington, Benjamin Franklin, Alexander Hamilton, Abraham Lincoln, and later Franklin Delano Roosevelt, John F. Kennedy, and Martin Luther King.
>
> The American Revolution sparked an international movement in Russia, France, Germany, Prussia, Spain, Italy and even India and Morocco! It motivated Czar Alexander II to free the serfs and begin developing Russia. The American system inspired Otto von Bismarck to consolidate Germany, and develop Germany's industry and technology. The American System held out the possibility of uniting the U.S. with Russia and China in a global system of cooperation. The American System was Alexander Hamilton's and Abraham Lincoln's vision of Manifest Destiny, which was to be for the benefit of all humanity.
>
> Alas, the American System was sabotaged by the British Empire, domestic subversive elements and elitists. Every U.S. president who backed the American System and a national bank was assassinated or died in office under mysterious circumstances. William Harrison was assassinated in 1841, Zachary Taylor died mysteriously in 1850, Abraham Lincoln was assassinated in 1865, James A. Garfield in 1881, William McKinley in 1901, Warren Harding died mysteriously in 1923, Franklin Delano

---

[3] See https://countercurrents.org/2021/07/the-clash-of-two-americas-the-unfinished-symphony-a-book-by-matthew-ehret/

Roosevelt died under suspicious circumstances in 1945, and John F. Kennedy was assassinated by a conspiracy in 1963.

And other opponents of the "British System" were assassinated in this 200-year bloodbath of the 19th and 20th century. Alexander Hamilton was killed in a duel by Aaron Burr in 1804. The "Great Liberator" Czar Alexander II was assassinated in 1881. Louis XVI who favored a constitutional monarchy and the American System was executed in 1793, as was French President Sadi Carnot in 1894. Spanish Prime Minister Antonio Canovas in 1897. King Umberto I of Italy in 1900. Mahatma Gandhi in 1948. Martin Luther King, Jr. and Robert F. Kennedy were assassinated in 1968.

The goal of the Western lodges for centuries has been the Anglicanization of the globe through mercantilism, through economics.[4] In the twentieth century, this goal was realized. By the time the stock market crashed in 1929, the world was primed and ready for the British system to become ubiquitous. As the quote above makes clear, anyone who stood in the way of this system was swiftly dealt with, and those individuals became fewer and farther between from 1929 on—and virtually non-existent after the 1960s. Therefore, very few of us have any notion that there is any form of capitalism besides the British system that has "cornered the market" on Western economics.

What we have witnessed since March of 2020 is this rapacious system coming to its horrible, self-annihilating end. As this British system fell apart in the past year and a half, it metamorphosed—or, rather, devolved—into an awful mixture of the three beasts that fought for world dominance in the 20th century: British system capitalism combined with the worst aspects of both communism and fascism. The Great Reset envisioned by the likes of Klaus Schwab and Bill Gates—a world where self-proclaimed experts manage the health, finances, movements, and speech of everyone else, in the name of safety and environmental protection—is the dreadful spawn of the unholy union of the three rival parents. In a way, we might say that fascism, communism, and global capitalism were three masks worn by a single monstrous entity, each helping it to achieve its aims unrecognized—and now the masks have come off, and we get to see it in its complete and awful form. This monstrous entity is imperialism—it has been with us, gestating, all through the age of the consciousness soul, and now is the time to come to terms with it.[5]

But it is not yet a foregone conclusion that the awful pseudo-utopia envisioned by the Great Resetters will come about. There is in reality a vacuum left by the dismantling of the dominant system; if many nations of the world would engage in rehabilitating something like the American system of economics, this would be a good step in the right direction. A modern proponent of such a system in the United States is Peter Navarro. Japan is an example of the successful implementation of the American system.[6]

I consider the above two options—Imperialism or the American system—to be the most likely contenders for a dominant system over the course of the last day of temptation, which will last until 2047. A third scenario is that—for a time, and for those of us who are unwilling to engage in a Great Reset form of society—social structures decentralize all the way into anarchy and a struggle to survive on a day-to-day basis. A less likely, but much more desirable outcome would be for the world to increasingly turn to ideas born of the authentic spiritual image of the Threefold Social Organism. A very positive potential scenario would be the return to something relatively familiar such as the American system as a start, and with the tending and cultivation of the proper gardeners, helping it to evolve into a true system of associative, fraternal economy.

It is very likely, even in a best-case scenario that many turn to the Threefold Social Order, that the external battlefield on the historical plane during

---

4 For a more on this, see for example Rudolf Steiner's *The Karma of Untruthfulness*, vols. 1 & 2.

5 See, for example, Ingraham, *The Modern Anglo-Dutch Empire: Its Origins, Evolution, and Anti-Human Outlook*.

6 See Bradeen Spannaus, *Hamilton Versus Wall Street: The Core Principles of the American System of Economics*.

this time period will involve the United States and China in particular. As G. A. Bondarev points out:

> During a course of lectures held in June 1924 on the estate of wealthy landowner Count Carl Keyserlinck in Koberwitz near Breslau (its theme was the possibility of a renewal of agriculture on a biodynamic basis), Rudolf Steiner uttered a warning which has a direct bearing on our own time: "The true antithesis is not between America and Russia—that is only apparent. The real conflict comes between China and America. Whether this is across Europe or across the Pacific Ocean, that is the question. Europe would justifiably hope that it would happen across the Pacific Ocean."[7]

The 100th anniversary of these words is just over two years away; it would be prudent to take their warning to heart (I hope to go somewhat more deeply into this theme in *Star Wisdom*, volume 5, next year). We can turn our hearts and minds, our prayers and meditations to the Hierarchies, that we avoid the disastrous "Empire vs. anarchy" world, and can find our way ever closer to the form of culture aching to emerge—the Threefold Social Organism. This is a form of "Cosmic Communion"—to offer up the reality of the world situation to the Hierarchies. We can pray that we resist the fourth temptation, and are ministered unto by Angels.

Jupiter and Uranus

There are two major alignments occurring this year which are not addressed in the commentaries (see the explanation for this in the introductory paragraphs of "Commentaries and Stargazing"). The first is the conjunction of Jupiter and Neptune, which occurs about every thirteen years (a little less to be precise, about every 12.75 years). This year they conjoin at 28° Aquarius: first geocentrically on April 12, then heliocentrically on June 6. The second major alignment is that of Uranus and the Node, which conjoin about every fifteen years (again, to be precise, a little more than that—more like 15.25 years). They are conjunct on July 31 geocentrically at 23° Aries, and tychonically at 21° Aries on August 27.

When Jupiter and Neptune come together, their combined influence can bring about a renewed focus on high ideals and nobility; on the other hand, along with this can come calls for the refinement of culture and renewal of values that are empty displays—only words, with no follow through in deed. The meeting of Uranus and the Node, on the other hand, can bring with it highly original thinking and expressions of personality—often brilliant or eccentric, sometimes rather aloof, as though coming from another world altogether.

There are a number of modern politicians born during a Uranus-Node conjunction—in fact, all four American Presidential administrations prior to the Biden administration. Barack Obama was born during the conjunction of 1961–62; Donald Trump, George W. and Laura Bush, and Bill and Hillary Clinton were all born in 1946, during the 1946–47 conjunction. One might wonder what the fate of such individuals (or associates like Ghislaine Maxwell, also born during the 1961–62 conjunction) might hold in the coming year? Clearly there is a dark side to this alignment, expressing the will to power, intrigue, ruthlessness, and even downright debauchery.

Uranus and Node were within close orb with each other in 1976 and 1977. Saturn was square to both Uranus and Node at this time—Saturn was square Uranus last year, and is square Node this year, so the time period of 1976 to 1977 is being remembered strongly from 2021 to 2022. It was from October 1976 through January of 1977 that Robert Powell—who was born with Uranus and Node just past conjunction in 1947—had a meeting with the Novalis individuality, who may have been born around this time. After this encounter, Powell had an awakening of karmic clairvoyance—first to his own past lives, gradually broadening to those of friends and acquaintances, and then to historical personalities. This is an example of Uranus and Node in their highest expression—perhaps enhanced due to their square alignment with Saturn.

---

7 Bondarev, *Events in the Ukraine and a Possible Future Scenario*, book 1, p. 101.

Similarly, Uranus and Node were conjunct, square Saturn, in early 1931—around the time that Valentin Tomberg (who was also born with a conjunction of Uranus and Node in 1900) was first publishing his early anthroposophical articles, many of them political in nature. We might imagine that a shift in consciousness was occurring for this young man akin to what occurred for Robert Powell in 1976–77. Each of these young men were around 30 years of age at the time of the Uranus-Node-Saturn alignment—one might wonder whether a similar shift of consciousness could lie in store for individuals born close to the Uranus-Node conjunction of 1991–'92, who are around 30 years of age right now?

The time period from 1931 to 1934 is particularly remembered this year, as there was a Jupiter-Neptune conjunction soon after the Uranus–Node alignment: on October 26, 1932, opposite this year's alignment, at 14° Leo. By this point, Saturn was in Capricorn, as it is for most of this year, where it would continue to be until 1934. Out of all of the prior time periods in the past century during which Saturn was in Capricorn, it is the time period from 1931 to 1934 in particular that is remembered this year, as the threat of pharmaceutical tyranny and techno-fascism rears its ugly head.

The last time that Jupiter and Neptune met in Aquarius was on April 3, 1856, at 25°14'—just a few degrees shy of their meeting at 28° Aquarius this year. Just over a year prior, on February 20, 1855, Uranus and the Node met at 23° Aries (from the tychonic perspective), two degrees away from where they meet this year. The years 1855 to 1856 was the period that saw the beginning of "Bleeding Kansas," the confrontations between pro-slavery and anti-slavery forces in the newly acquired territory. These were the confrontations that preceded the all-out American Civil War that began in 1861. The Republican Party had just formed in 1854 out of dissatisfaction with both the Whigs and the Democrats, and Abraham Lincoln was beginning to emerge into the limelight.

The second Opium War was in full swing. Cocaine was being derived for the first time. Mass media began in the Great Britain. Gregor Mendel began his experiments in hereditary characteristics and genetics. Many of the specters that haunt us today can find their roots in this time period.

On the more spiritual level, this was the time of Victor Hugo, Charles Dickens, Walt Whitman, Henry David Thoreau, and the first writings of Leo Tolstoy. Richard Wagner was just beginning to compose his *Ring* cycle. Eliphas Levi was in the process of releasing his works on the *Dogma and Ritual of Occult Magic*. Had he survived, Kaspar Hauser would have been in his early '40s—we can only imagine what the Grail Knighthood of Central Europe would have appeared as during this time period, as it could only manifest itself in the spiritual world as inspiration to a humanity most deeply entrenched in materialism.

Going further back, the first time since 2022 that we find a Jupiter–Neptune conjunction occurring the same year as a Uranus–Node conjunction is 1779. The end of the 18th century was the last time period when Pluto was in Capricorn, which it just entered again in 2021. Once again, we are brought to a very pivotal time period: Goethe's career was just beginning—this was the start of a Golden Age of German culture that would last for the next seventy years. At the same time, this was the heart of the American Revolutionary War, which lasted from 1775 to 1783.

Usually, Jupiter–Neptune conjunctions make their way from one sign of the zodiac to the next—e.g., in 1958 they met in Libra, in 1971 in Scorpio, in 1984 in Sagittarius, etc. Something that is unique about this year's conjunction in Aquarius is that it is in the same sign as last time: the two met—just barely—in Aquarius on September 19, 2009, at 0°24'. The last time that there were two Aquarian conjunctions of Jupiter and Neptune in a row were in the 6th century. The two conjoined at 0°16' Aquarius on December 5 AD 526, and at 28°12' Aquarius (the same as this year) on August 23 AD 539. According to legend, this second conjunction was just a few years after the death of the historical King Arthur at the legendary Battle of Camlann in 537.

This was occurring at the same time that work was completed on the Hagia Sofia (Dec. 27, 537), overseen by the great Emperor Justinian. It was under Justinian that a major reform of Byzantine law was undertaken, one which laid the foundations for the practice of law for a thousand years and more afterward. Justinian's views on law can be summarized by the words of Ulpian, a famous Roman jurist who lived in the 1st to 2nd centuries AD: *jus est ars boni et aequi* (law is the art of the good and the just), while his views on jurisprudence are likewise contained in the words of Ulpian: *juris prudent est divinarum atque humanarum rerum notitia, justi atque injusti scientia* (jurisprudence is the knowledge of divine and human things, the science of justice and also of injustice). The rehabilitation of Justinian law was attempted in the years 1946 to '47—during a conjunction of Uranus and Node—in the form of Valentin Tomberg's doctoral thesis, recently republished under the title *The Art of the Good: On the Regeneration of Fallen Justice*.[8]

It was in the year 540 that St. Benedict wrote his monastic rules—the "Rule of St. Benedict," which can be summed up in the words *pax* (peace) and *ora et labora* (work and pray). These rules laid the foundation for Western monasticism as a whole, and have been in use ever since then. And so, in the years 2009 to '22, we have had a recollection of these pivotal years in the history of the West from 526 to 539—years that saw great leaders of the "Pauline" Britons (King Arthur), of the "Petrine" Romans (St. Benedict) and of the "Johannine" Byzantines (Emperor Justinian), each leaving his mark indelibly into the present day. Pray that we have such leadership in the West, the Center, and the East in the years to come!

And so, we have many archetypal recollections flowing into the year 2022: from the 6th century, to the time of the American Revolution, the times leading up to both the American Civil War and World War II, as well as the spiritual events of 1976–77. I hope to focus on some of these themes more closely in *Star Wisdom*, volume 5.

INTRODUCING THE AUTHORS

This year's edition begins with a fantastic "Letter to the Editor" from reader René Bastien, in which the two of us write back and forth addressing some of the intricacies of the timeline of the Holy Grail and the life of Parzival that can be discovered through a close reading of Estelle Isaacson's *The Grail Bearer* and *The Younger Kyot*. We then feature another "Classics in Astrosophy" on the theme of Grail Chronology—of understanding history through spiritual knowledge, specifically via the faculty of Intuition. It is this practice of Grail Chronology in which René and I dabble in our email exchange; Robert Powell brings it to clarity in the "Classics…" article. I then continue this practice of Grail Chronology in my "Sacrifices of Jesus and Christ," which sets the stage for the further investigation of modern ecosophical practice that will be featured in the second part of this article next year.

Krisztina Cseri then offers us the follow up to last year's article on "Rudolf Steiner and the Christmas Conference"—whereas last year she focused more on the macrocosmic aspects which made the end of 1923 the most potent time to lay the Foundation Stone, this year she hones in on microcosmic aspects contained in Rudolf Steiner's astrological biography that equally set the stage for this sacrificial deed. This deed is perhaps the archetype of the Cosmic Communion of which Rudolf Steiner was speaking as the flames began to consume the first Goetheanum.

In both my article on the houses, "The Archetypal Language," as well as Amber Wolfe Rounds' article, "Tone Art," the focus comes even more directly to the radiating out from human activity and Mother Earth toward the starry heavens—to the new form of cosmic ritual which is our theme for this year.

As I forewarned the reader last year in my introduction to the "Commentaries and Ephemerides 2021," there has been a change to the way I have approached the commentaries this year. This is laid out in more detail in my introduction to the "Commentaries and Ephemerides 2022" later in this volume; briefly, this year I have

---

8 See pages 21–25 and 45–50 in particular for his picture of Justinian law or "True Jurisprudence."

made an appendix or concordance through which one is directed to whatever passages in the three volumes of *The Visions of Anne Catherine Emmerich* are remembered by the stellar alignment for that particular day. This complete, three volume addition has been available from Angelico Press since 2015: it is strongly recommended the reader purchase a copy of the entire set in order to follow this year's commentaries. It may seem like quite a bit of money to spend, but these are volumes that everyone should have—I could, and probably will, spend the rest of my life poring over them. They are of much greater value to you than the volume you hold in your hand, I assure you!

Finally, the volume ends with a true labor of love: the "Sophia Star Calendar 2022" from new contributor Kathleen Baiocchi. Kathleen has been a longtime reader and supporter of the work of the Sophia Foundation, and offers this calendar as a gift to all, but in particular to Robert Powell, Laquanna Paul, and the Sophia Foundation, in gratitude for their work. She brings our attention each day to the powerful megastars with which the Sun is in conjunction—may we bring the meditation of Rudolf Steiner to bear on the fixed stars and wandering stars alike as we draw our attention to them repeatedly this year:

In Earth-activity draws near to me,
Given to me in substance-imaged form,
The Heavenly Being of the Stars.
In Willing I see them transformed with Love

In Watery life stream into me,
Forming me through with power of
    substance-force,
The Heavenly Deeds of the Stars—
In Feeling I see them transformed with Wisdom!

As always, I extend my gratitude to each of the contributors who made this fourth volume possible; to the editorial board for their ongoing support; to Jens Jensen and Stephan O'Reilly at SteinerBooks for their hard work getting this into print form every year; to the several anonymous proofreaders at SteinerBooks who are finding all the typos; and, of course, to you the reader. If you have any questions or concerns—or perhaps are interested in contributing next year—please reach out to me at joelmpark77@gmail.com.

Pax et Bonum,
Joel Matthew Park

A LETTER TO THE EDITOR
René Bastien

January 19, 2021:
Dear Robert and Joel,

I have read with great interest the article of Joel, "First Steps toward a Grail Timeline," in *Cosmology Reborn: Star Wisdom*, vol. I. I want to share with you my reflections after having read *The Grail Bearer* and *The Younger Kyot* (in English and in German in Angelika Jenal's translation) and *Parzival,* from Wolfram von Eschenbach.

See the attached document, "Some Steps toward a Grail Timeline." I hope that you can answer the question of the year of the birth of Repanse.

                Best greetings,
                René Bastien

SOME STEPS TOWARD A GRAIL TIMELINE

by René Bastien

[editorial responses from JMP in brackets]

I have read with great interest the article of Joel Park, "First Steps toward a Grail Timeline," in *Cosmology Reborn: Star Wisdom*, vol. I.

After reading *The Grail Bearer* (in bold below) and *The Younger Kyot* from Estelle Isaacson, I want to give you following reflections.

The Grail Bearer

p. 42 **Conception of Repanse. Estelle believes she saw Jupiter, Venus and the Sun all together in Gemini.**
The Sun is in Gemini in the month June at that time [Edit—i.e., if we assume she was born in the 8th century AD—JMP].
For Jupiter, 1 year from 12 is possible.

p. 44 **The Dark Death. Repanse appeared to be about 3 years old.**

p. 45 **The knight, the lady and the child took what possessions they could carry.**
No mention is made of another child.
Trevizent and Anfortas are not born.
Trevizent is older than Anfortas—see *The Younger Kyot*.

p. 52 **Repanse is about 7, her brothers Trevizent and Anfortas play nearby.**
Trevizent could be 3—he was not born when Repanse was 3. Anfortas could be 2.

p. 57 **Clairsonnet was at this time pregnant with a girl. Repanse, about 9 years old, had only just become aware of this.**

p. 58 **Come, give me your hand, that you may feel the baby move within me.**
I suppose it is Herzeloyde.

p. 71 **Repanse has been presented as a woman in celebration of her fourteenth year.**
Schoysiane must be at least 14 when she becomes Grail Bearer. [Edit—Or, perhaps she must be 14 before she can marry Kyot—JMP]

p. 95 **Repanse's youngest sister, Herzeloyde, has just discovered she is pregnant.**

p. 97 **Only one—all ears—stayed by Gwaharedd's side, and she a little girl, perhaps nine years old, by name Sigune.**
This was in June 788, about 8 months before the birth of Perceval, Feb. 14, 789.
So, Sigune was born 779. And Schoysiane married Kyot 778.

p. 104 **The Grail chose Schoysiane. Now, sixteen months later, Schoysiane was to be married.**
Joel wrote "shortly after having married Kyot, Schoysiane became pregnant with Sigune."
It could be that Repanse became Grail Bearer and Anfortas Grail King shortly after Easter 778. And Schoysiane became Grail Bearer

shortly before Christmas 776. Why Easter and Christmas? Repanse as reincarnation of Mary Magdalene and Anfortas as reincarnation of Joseph of Arimathea [Edit—Anfortas is the reincarnation of Nicodemus, Trevrizent is the reincarnation of Joseph of Arimathea—JMP] are intimately involved with the mystery of Golgotha.

So Schoysiane married Kyot, the reincarnation of Melchior/Mensor, the Gold King.

There are exactly 4 months between December 6 (the birth of the Nathan Jesus) and April 5 (the resurrection of Jesus Christ). 4 months and 1 year is 16 months.

We could imagine that Schoysiane became Grail Bearer in December 776—a few days after December 6 in relationship with the mystery of the birth—and Repanse became Grail Bearer a few days after April 5 778 in relationship with the mystery of Golgotha. Perceval became Grail King 7 days after Pentecost 810 in relationship with the Mystery of Mary Sophia and the Holy Spirit.

The Grail Family

p. 215 Frimutel admonished his son "One day you will be King"..."Yes, you must choose wisely" your knights.

Anfortas needed some time to choose wisely his knights. So, I think he was 18 when he became Grail king. He could be born 760. And I think Schoysiane was 15 or 16. She could be born 762 or 763.

Repanse is 7 when Anfortas is about 2. Repanse could be born 755. [Edit—Sun, Jupiter and Venus were together in Gemini June 756; this would put Repanse's birth around March 757. See more below.—JMP]

Trevizent is about 3 when Repanse is 7. He could be born 758/759. [760]

Repanse is 9 when Herzeloyde is born. She could be born 764. [765–66]

So, we could have:

June 754 conception of Repanse [June 756]
March 755 birth of Repanse [March 757]
End of 758 birth of Trevizent [760]
760 birth of Anfortas [762]
762 or 763 Birth of Schoysiane [763-64]
764 birth of Herzeloyde. [765–66]

Estelle's indications for the conception of Repanse give you the possibility to confirm or correct the date of her birth and the other dates.

Take notice that Repanse was 23 [21] when she became Grail Bearer and 55 [53] when she decided to go to India and to marry Feirefiz. At the birth of Prester John, she was at least 56 [54].

Kyot—Guillaume de Toulouse

The Younger Kyot gives little possibilities for dating. I suppose that the chronology is respected. So we could have:

755, birth of Guillaume de Toulouse (Wikipedia—see both the English and French pages)

Spring 777, Kyot (22) meets Flegetanis—the Virgin is high in the night sky (*The Younger Kyot*, pp. 32-48)

Summer or Fall 777, Kyot meets Trevrizent - Schoysiane is Grail Bearer for some moons (*The Younger Kyot*)

Winter 777/778, Kyot comes to the Grail castle and meets Schoysiane

April 778, Kyot (23) marries Schoysiane

779, Birth of Sigune, Schoysiane dies. Herzeloyde is looking for Sigune.

780s, Kyot marries Cunegonde

End of 780s? Kyot is under captivity, marries Arabel (a.k.a. Giburg), becomes Guillaume d'Orange. Many "chansons de gestes" tell this story, one of them is *Willehalm* from Wolfram von Eschenbach. See the article on the German Wikipedia.

790, Guillaume (35) is named count of Toulouse by Charlemagne (Wikipedia)

804, Guillaume (49) retires at Gellone (Wikipedia)

May 21, 804, Kyot of Catalonia is in Belrapeire when Parzival meets Condwiramurs, his niece. The "old men" are no longer knights and can go through the lines of the enemies.

See *Parzival*, W. v. Eschenbach, in Prosa übertragen von W. Stapel, p. 97 "Kyot von

Katelangen und der edle Manpliyot geleiten ihres Bruders Kind" Kondwiramurs.

Fall 809, Parzival comes to Gellone – St. Guilhelm le Désert and becomes ill (*The Grail Bearer,* Chapter 22).

Winter 809/810, Kyot instructs Parzival (*The Grail Bearer,* Chapter 22).

May 28, 812, Guillaume dies at Gellone (Wikipedia).

❉

January 20, 2021:
Dear René,

This is wonderful! What you have written here is very much in line with additional work I have done myself around this timeline, although what you have written goes well beyond it in some parts. I came to very similar conclusions surrounding the birth years of the "Grail family," as well as the biography of Kyot. It may be, however, that Kyot's captivity—when he met and married Arabel—was in the late 790's/early 800's, after he became Count of Toulouse. I need to check on that. But somewhere in the back of my mind this was in a way his last deed as a Knight before founding the Abbey, that meeting Arabel was a turning point for him.

What strikes me about Repanse de Shoye giving birth to Prester John in her mid-fifties, is that this may be a similar "miraculous birth" as to Isaac from Sarah or John the Baptist from Elizabeth. I believe there are also portions of *The Grail Bearer* in which Estelle emphasizes the fact that Repanse embodied a kind of "eternal youth" or "eternal purity." And perhaps this had something to do with why her younger sister became Grail Bearer before Repanse herself did—in some sense, Repanse was "younger," although 7 to 8 years older than Schoysiane.

Would it be possible for me to publish our exchange and your research as a "Letter to the Editor" in *Star Wisdom, vol. 4,* to be published Nov 2021?

Many thanks,
Joel

❉

January 24, 2021:
Dear Joel,

I am very happy to hear from you so fast. Of course you can publish our exchange in Star Wisdom.

I have read the articles on Wikipedia on Guillaume de Gellone and his son Bernard de Septimanie (*795) in French and German. It is difficult: in the French article, Bernard is the son of Cunegonde and has 6 brothers/sisters; in the German article, Cunegonde dies before 795, Bernard is the son of Arabel/Guiburg and has 6 brothers/sisters. Guillaume was named Count of Toulouse by Charlemagne in 790 instead of Chorson.

In *Willehalm* and the other "chansons de gestes," Willehalm meets Arabel and is in captivity before he is Count—of Toulouse, of Orange.... I think it takes some years—the three battles of Alyscans—until living together in Orange and/or Toulouse and having children. The first son would be Bernard if the German article is true—and if Wolfram von Eschenbach's *Willehalm* respects the chronology.

Best greetings
René

❉

Correspondence between Joel Matthew Park and Estelle Isaacson from 2016, when the *The Grail Bearer* was first issued, addressing some of the same observations/reflections shared above by René:

October 6, 2016:
Dear Estelle,

Yes, I know it's a bit weird for Repanse to be that old. Your visions indicate Sun, Venus, and Jupiter in Gemini at her conception. Based on this, at first I thought her conception was in 768, rather than 756. However, let's lay out some pieces of the puzzle and see how they fit together:

1. Parzival is supposedly 15 at the time he sets out for the Grail, according to Chretien de Troyes. I am confidant that he did this in the year 804; this means he was born in 789. [Edit—It later became clear to me that he was 15 when he left home in 804, and he sets out

on what becomes the "Grail quest" a year later, in AD 805 —JMP].
2. According to your visions, Sigune is about 9 years older than Parzival, meaning she was born in 780.
3. In other visions, it's indicated that Repanse de Shoye is the oldest of the five, about 7 years older than Schoysiane, Sigune's mother.

That means, if we assume 769 as the birth year for Repanse, that makes 776 the birth year for Schoysiane—she would only be 4 years old when she has Sigune! A fatal birth indeed…

If we assume, rather, that Repanse was born in 757, then Schoysiane was born in 764, making her 16 when she gave birth to Sigune. That seems to work a bit better!

Admittedly, though, it is a bit strange for Repanse to be in her 50s when she gives birth to Prester John. Here's my take: I believe there's a section of visions dedicated to Repanse being blessed in a quite special way with youthfulness and beauty. I think there's a possibility that there's a kind of Sarah and Isaac situation with Repanse and Prester John; that due to being Grail Bearer, her youthfulness was maintained in a special way in order to be able to have Prester John at such an advanced age.

As for the order of Kyot's wives, I get the impression, based on when his children were born (and to whom), that he married Schoysiane as a relatively young man (late 770s–780), then married Cunegunde prior to setting out on his campaigns (late 780s or so). He then met Arabel and married her while abroad (turn of the century). This might seem a bit untoward of Kyot, but we can see the same thing with Gahmuret, marrying Herzeloyde while still technically married to Feirfiz's mother abroad.

So… he then returns from his campaigns with Arabel, and soon after retires from warfare and founds St. Guilhem in 804. Arabel dies by 806, according to Kyot's updated will from that year. I haven't looked at the will recently, but I think there's a good chance that she already had children prior to marrying Kyot, possibly from a deceased first husband, who Kyot took in as his own, at least in terms of his will and passing on his possessions.

Yours,
Joel

❊

A Partial Timeline of Grail Events, created by Joel Matthew Park, from August 2016:

755, birth of Kyot (according to the Wikipedia article on William of Gellone).

Around March, 757 – Birth of Repanse de Schoye (this is based on Isaacson's indication of her conception with Jupiter, Sun, and Venus in Gemini. This would have occurred in June, 756; hence, the birth would be around March 757).

Ca. 758-765, births of Anfortas, Trevrizent, Schoysiane, and Herzeloyde (this is based on an article on Hugo de Tours, the historical Trevrizent, from the French Wikipedia, which places his birth around 765).

Ca. 780, births of Sigune and Condwiramurs (according to Eschenbach's *Titurel*, Sigune was born when Condwiramurs was an infant; according to Isaacson, Sigune was born 9 years before Parzival).

– Death of Schoysiane (first wife of Kyot, who died giving birth to Sigune. We can assume the marriage of Schoysiane and Kyot was about a year prior).

– Coronation of Repanse de Schoye and Anfortas (Isaacson).

– Kyot becomes Paladin of Charlemagne (Wikipedia).

Ca. 789, Kyot marries Cunegunde, his second wife (this is based on records of Kyot's will, from the French Wikipedia article on Guillaume d'Orange)

– Birth of Parzival (based on Chretrien de Troyes' indication that he is about 15 when he leaves home)

Turn of the century, Kyot battles the Saracens (based on Wikipedia). He marries his third wife Arabel and comes into contact with Star Wisdom.

Early 803, Parzival sets out to become a knight, and soon after marries Condwiramurs (based on an interpretation of Eschenbach's astronomical indications).
– Death of Herzeloyde and Schionatulander (Eschenbach).
– The wounding of Anfortas (Isaacson).
zMichaelmas 804, First grail castle visit; Parzival fails to ask the question (Eschenbach).
804-806, Kyot founds St. Guilhem, writes his will (French Wikipedia).
– Parzival trains under Kyot (Isaacson).
– Arabel dies around 806 (French Wikipedia).
Eastertide 809, Parzival meets Trevrizent and learns of his task (Eschenbach).
– Gawain rescues Castle Marveile, defeats Klingsor (Eschenbach)
Pentecost-St. John's 809, The second visit of Parzival to the Grail Castle. He asks the question, healing Anfortas and becoming the Grail King (Eschenbach).
– Death of Sigune (Eschenbach).
– Wedding of Repanse and Ferfeiz. They move to India (Eschenbach).
– Kyot takes on the instruction of Parzival's son Kardeiz (Eschenbach).
May 28, 812, Death of Kyot (Wikipedia).

❋

An updated timeline, based on the investigations of René Bastien in his "Some Steps Towards a Grail Timeline," and Joel Matthew Park's article "First Steps Towards a Grail Timeline":

755, Birth of Guillaume de Toulouse (Wikipedia – see both the English and French pages).
Around March, 757, Birth of Repanse de Schoye (this is based on Isaacson's indication of her conception with Jupiter, Sun, and Venus in Gemini. This would have occurred in June, 756; hence, the birth would be around March 757).
Ca 758-765, Births of Anfortas, Trevrizent, Schoysiane, and Herzeloyde (this is based on an article on Hugo de Tours, the historical Trevrizent, from the French Wikipedia, which places his birth around 765).
Christmas, 776, Schoysiane becomes Grail Bearer, around the age of 12-13.
Spring 777, Kyot (22) meets Flegetanis – the Virgin is high in the night sky (*The Younger Kyot*, pp. 32-48).
Summer or Fall 777, Kyot meets Trevrizent. Schoysiane is Grail Bearer for some moons (*The Younger Kyot*)
Winter 777/778, Kyot comes to the Grail castle and meets Schoysiane.
April 778, Kyot (23) marries Schoysiane (14). Repanse de Schoye (21) becomes Grail Bearer and Anfortas (16) becomes Grail King.
779, Birth of Sigune, Schoysiane dies in childbirth. Herzeloyde is looking for Sigune.
Ca 780, Birth Condwiramurs (according to Eschenbach's *Titurel*, Sigune was born when Condwiramurs was an infant; according to Isaacson, Sigune was born 9 years before Parzival). Kyot becomes Paladin of Charlemagne (Wikipedia).
780s, Kyot marries Cunegonde.
End of 780s, Kyot is under captivity, marries Arabel (a.k.a. Giburg), becomes Guillaume d'Orange. Many "chansons de gestes" tell this story, one of them is *Willehalm* from Wolfram von Eschenbach. See the article on the German Wikipedia.
Ca 789, Birth of Parzival (based on Chretrien de Troyes' indication that he is about 15 when he leaves home).
790, Guillaume (35) is named count of Toulouse by Charlemagne (Wikipedia).
Turn of the Century, Kyot goes on his final campaign against the Saracens. He has a transformative experience with the True Cross which inspires him to found St. Guilhem-le-Desert.
804, Guillaume (49) retires at Gellone (Wikipedia).
Spring 804, Parzival leaves home. His mother, Herzeloyde, dies after his departure. He disturbs the relationship of Jeschute and Orilus, and comes upon his cousin Sigune and

her dead love Schionatulander. He kills Ither at King Arthur's Court, and lives for a time under the tutelage of Gurnemanz.

May 21, 804, Kyot of Catalonia is in Belrapeire when Parzival meets Condwiramurs, his niece. The "old men" are no longer knights and can go through the lines of the enemies.
See *Parzival,* W. v. Eschenbach, in Prosa übertragen von W. Stapel, p. 97 "Kyot von Katelangen und der edle Manpliyot geleiten ihres Bruders Kind" Kondwiramurs.

April 805, Here Saturn reaches its moving exaltation, and the Sun, the Moon, Mars, and Jupiter all approach their fixed (or archetypal) exaltations. It is very likely that around this time Anfortas was wounded by the Lance. Estelle Isaacson indicates in her book *The Grail Bearer* that this occurred in the late winter/early spring, shortly before Parzival set out on his quest that would lead him to the Grail King.

September 25, 805, Parzival, who has recently left Condwiramurs in search of adventure, stumbles upon Monsalvaesche. He fails to ask the question. The next day, he reunites Jeschute and Orilus. Soon after this, he confronts the Knights of the Round Table, and is made to feel the shame of his actions by Cundrie. He wanders for many years.

804-806, Kyot writes his will. Arabel dies around 806 (French Wikipedia).

Fall 809, Parzival comes to Gellone (St. Guilhem le Désert) and becomes ill (*The Grail Bearer,* Chapter 22).

Winter 809/810, Kyot instructs Parzival (*The Grail Bearer,* Chapter 22).

March 29, 810 (Good Friday), Parzival comes upon the hermit Trevrizent (his uncle) and learns of the true nature of the Grail and of his mission. He stays with him for a time and sets out with a repentant fervor to make good out of his errors. Soon afterward, over the course of Eastertide, Gawain rescues Castle Marveile, defeating Klingsor (Eschenbach).

May 26, 810 (Festival of the Holy Trinity), Parzival and Feirefiz ride to Monsalvaesche. Parzival heals Anfortas, becoming the Grail King. Death of Sigune (Eschenbach). Wedding of Repanse and Ferfeiz. They move to India (Eschenbach). Kyot takes on the instruction of Parzival's son Kardeiz (Eschenbach).

Late Winter/Early Spring 811, birth of Prester John in India.

May 28, 812, Guillaume dies at Gellone (Wikipedia).

GRAIL CHRONOLOGY
CLASSICS IN ASTROSOPHY, PART V

Robert Powell, PhD

Editorial Foreword
Midsummer, 1979
Mercury Star Journal

In this Midsummer issue of volume 5 (1979) of the *Mercury Star Journal* we shall seek to look at Grail Christianity—and its associated star wisdom—in a historical context, and in the first place we shall begin to lay the foundations for a Grail chronology. Indeed, chronology could be called a "Grail science"—a science belonging to the pre-Christian Grail Tradition inaugurated by Zoroaster.[1]

Zoroaster founded a "mystery school" in Babylon in the sixth century BC, into which—among others—Pythagoras was initiated. The mystery teachings taught in this school could be grouped under three headings: (1) the mysteries of Saturn; (2) the mysteries of the Sun; and (3) the mysteries of the Moon.[2] The mysteries of the Moon were concerned especially with *meteorology*, i.e., with how the weather is influenced by what takes place in the cosmos, where the Moon is the most important factor to be taken into consideration. The mysteries of the Sun were concerned with *astrology*, i.e., with how the human soul descends from the cosmos to the Earth, to incarnate in a physical body; it is from these mysteries that the science of casting horoscopes originated.[3] Lastly, the mysteries of Saturn were concerned above all with *chronology* (the connection is apparent through consideration of the Greek name for Saturn, which is "Chronos"). For these chronological mysteries cultivated within Zoroaster's school in Babylon, a definition of the Zodiac was formulated in scientific terms, which definition we shall make use of in laying the foundation for a (new) Grail chronology.

We have discussed the definition of the Babylonian zodiac in the previous issue of the *Mercury Star Journal*, and a diagram of this zodiac is given in the present issue (cf. figure 2 in Part II of the series on the "Sidereal Zodiac"). As is shown in this diagram, and as may be determined from the definition of the Babylonian zodiac given in the previous issue of this journal, the present location of the vernal point—for the year 1979—is exactly 5.5°—in the Babylonian fixed-star sign of Pisces. Since the vernal point regresses through the zodiac at the rate of 1° in 72 years, it is evident that in 396 years (= 5.5 x 72) the vernal point will pass over from the sign of Pisces into that of Aquarius—i.e., the Age of Aquarius, according to this Grail chronology (which has its roots in Chaldean star wisdom), will commence in just under 400 years time, in AD 2375. How is it to be explained that so many people of the present time feel that a New Age—which they identify with the Age of Aquarius—has already begun? With the help of the science of the Grail we shall endeavor to arrive at some clarity with regard to this question.

In the first place, since each sign of the zodiac is 30° in length, it is apparent that 2,160 years (= 30 x 72) are required for the vernal point to retrogress through one zodiacal sign (the present rate of regression of the vernal point is 1° in ca. 71.5 years, but when long-term fluctuations are taken into consideration the average regression of the vernal point is almost exactly 1° in 72 years).

---

1 Cf. *The Bundahisn* xxxiv, trsl. E. W. West, *Sacred Books of the East* v, Oxford, 1880, p. 149 for an outline of Zoroastrian chronological ideas

2 For a summary of Chaldean mystery teachings preserved in the so-called "Chaldean Oracles," which are generally attributed to Zoroaster, see Wilhelm Kroll, "De Oraculis Chaldaicis," *Breslau Philologische Abhandlungen*, vii (1894), pp. 76ff.

3 Cf. my article, "The Origin of Horoscopic Astrology," MSJ, IV, pp. 4–10

Thus, the Age of Pisces began in AD 215, since 215 + 2,160 = 2,375. Similarly, the Age of Aries began in −1945—i.e., in 1946 BC, since 2,160 − 1,945 = 215. The dates 1946 BC, AD 215 and AD 2375 are thus key dates in Grail chronology, coinciding with the commencement of new ages in humankind's spiritual history.[4]

The first of these dates coincided with the founding of the Jewish nation, since "Abraham lived and worked....between 2000 and 1950 BC"[5] The slaying of the Passover lamb, which cult evoked the memory of Abraham's sacrifice of a ram instead of his son Isaac (cf. Gen. 22:13), expresses symbolically that the Hebrew nation sought to embody the impulse of the Age of Aries (the Ram).

Within each zodiacal age spiritual impulses of a specific kind are at work, which have a positive and a negative side. It is characteristic of these impulses that the positive side can manifest only when it is received with a certain degree of consciousness. Thus it is the task of the great leaders of humanity—those who are conscious of such factors—to ensure that in each age a community of people is founded who can receive and manifest the positive mission to be fulfilled in a particular age. Initially it is necessary that *one* person embodies this impulse—and thus acts as a "seed" for the transmission of this impulse to the community that he founds. That Abraham was such a "seed" for the community that he founded is expressed in the words of the Lord: "....I will indeed bless you, and I will multiply your descendants as the stars of heaven..." (Gen. 22:17); and in the words "By your descendants shall all the nations of the earth be blessed" (Gen. 22:18) is indicated that this community, the recipients of the positive side of the impulse of the Age of Aries, would be a blessing to the rest of mankind by virtue of their upholding the cosmic-appointed task for that age. For if no community of people, however small, were to uphold the positive mission of a given zodiacal age, the whole course of historical evolution would go astray. Thus, those who do uphold the positive impulse during a given age are a blessing to the rest of mankind, whether or not they are regarded as such.

The positive side of the impulse for the Age of Aries was the development of the "I"-force, achieved by way of developing a "spiritual backbone" through moral uprightness. This is expressed in the esoteric name "Israel" that was given to the community founded to take up the positive impulse of the Age of Aries, as "Israel" (according to one interpretation) means "upright." In order to develop the force of consciousness embodied in the words "I am," the Israelites had to be true to the Lord of Yahweh, the "I AM." This meant sacrificing the old form of consciousness, which was a kind of instinctive clairvoyance, and beginning the development of thought—the clear consciousness of self associated with the faculty of thought. Abraham was an initiate—one of the great leaders of humanity—who was able to make this step, shown by his leaving the star-worshipping people of Mesopotamia and setting out on his own to a new land. In a certain sense, Abraham could be thought of as the world's first "thinker." Later in the Age of Aries it is apparent how this faculty of thought became developed on a widespread scale, but in it seed form it was embodied in one human being who lived at the beginning of the age—namely Abraham.

The negative side of the impulse at work in the Age of Aries is conveyed by the Biblical word "fornication." The most serious sin within the community of Israel was to turn away from Yahweh to other gods. To turn away from the "I AM"— to forsake the development of the "I-force"—was to commit fornication—i.e., to give oneself up to gods whose sphere of activity lies not in the clear light of consciousness of the "I am," but in the

---

4 These dates are in harmony with the Indian chronological reckoning for the Kali Yuga period and with Sir Isaac Newton's chronological researches (allowing for a slight correction). They are also in harmony with the dates of the major periods of cultural development known as "cultural epochs" in Spiritual Science, as I have shown in my book *Newton's Chronology* (no fixed date of publication, as yet).

5 Heinze Genge, "Versuch einer Abraham-Datierung," *In memoriam Eckhard Unger, Beitrage zu Geschichte, Kultur und Religion des alten Orients,* Baden-Baden, 1971, p. 94

human subconscious. Fornication was to worship "Baal" or "Asherah," or to go to the "high places" and worship any of the innumerable star gods. To remain upright and true to Yahweh—the "I AM"—was the spiritual mission of Israel, and fornication with the gods who work in the sphere of subconsciousness was to forsake this mission. This expresses the positive and negative sides of the Age of Aries: on the one side the development of the "I"-force through maintaining moral uprightness and unfolding the faculty of thought, and on the other side to forsake moral uprightness and to return to the old instinctive clairvoyance. The two sides also came to expression later in the Age of Aries in the polarity between the Greek philosophers on the one hand, and the sibyls on the other hand. The positive impulse of the Age of Aries reached its highest peak of expression in the Hebrew prophets and in the Greek philosophers, whilst the negative side can be seen in the "fornication" practiced in the numerous cults devoted to gods that work in subconscious regions of the human being.

However, a clear distinction must be drawn between the popular cults that were devoted to deities such as "Baal," and the mystery cults such as that of Zoroaster's mystery school in Babylon. Zoroaster and his pupils could in no way be described as adherents to the principle of "fornication." Rather, they—like the Hebrew prophets—were concerned with maintaining strict standards of moral uprightness and also, in their own way, with unfolding the faculty of thought. However, whereas the Greek philosophers unfolded the faculty of thought in the sphere of philosophy (characteristic of the Age of Aries) the tendency in Zoroaster's mystery school was to direct the faculty of thought in the direction of science (characteristic of the Age of Pisces).

The teachings and practices in this Chaldean mystery school—comprising Saturn, Sun and Moon mysteries—were a synthesis of the very highest cosmic wisdom of the past with the "scientific faculty"; a reflection of this synthesis can be glimpsed in Pythagorean teachings. Indeed, as with all true mystery schools, whose function is to prepare the impulses for a future age "ahead of time," Zoroaster's mystery school was a "seed center" within the Age of Aries with the task of preparing for the Age of Pisces. Zoroaster, who had developed the highest wisdom attainable to mankind in the pre-Christian era, had the mission of summarizing the wisdom of the past—which could then be classified in terms of Saturn, Sun and Moon mysteries—and "translating" this wisdom of the past into an intellectual-conceptual form that would be appropriate for the future—e.g., in such forms as what we nowadays understand by the terms: chronology, astrology and meteorology.

Thus, the Chaldean mystery school founded by Zoroaster in Babylon in the sixth century BC can be regarded as a kind of "spiritual repository" containing seed impulses for the future. Looking back across history it is possible, here and there, to see brief manifestations of this Chaldean star wisdom—e.g., in the astrology of the Three Magi, and in the Grail Events of the ninth century AD It is in this sense, moreover, that the Babylonian zodiac—taken from the spiritual repository of Chaldean mystery wisdom—is used here to provide a "Grail chronology" of the zodiacal ages, in a form that is suitable for modern scientifically-oriented consciousness of the present age, the Age of Pisces.

As outlined in the previous issue of MSJ, this journal is dedicated to the task of cultivating a modern Grail star wisdom—which may be classified under the three headings: Astronomy, Astrology and Astrosophy. This star wisdom is seen as appropriate—and as necessary—for the present age. Its roots are to be found in Zoroaster's mystery school, and historical instances of it are to be found in the astrology of the Three Kings, and in the Grail star wisdom of the ninth century AD The full blossoming of modern Grail star wisdom began, however, with the work of Elisabeth Verde—born exactly one hundred years ago, who was the first leader of the Mathematical-Astronomical Section of the School of Spiritual Science, centered at the Goetheanum, Dornach, Switzerland—and with the work of Willi Sucher, to whom this journal owes its origin. Elisabeth

Vreede and Willi Sucher are representatives of the modern Grail star wisdom that is coming to birth in the twentieth century, which, in the spirit of the star wisdom of the Three Kinds, is dedicated to the service of the Messiah, whose Second Coming—in an etheric form ("in the clouds")—is now under way. The meaning of the New Age that more and more people are coming to experience *is* the Second Coming. How this falls in relation to the Age of Pisces, and in relation to the approaching Aquarian age, will be outlined in a future issue of this journal. For the present it suffices to say that the emergence of the New Age, owing to the Second Coming of Jesus Christ, is both a *fulfilment* of the Age of Pisces and a *preparation* for the Age of Aquarius. To open one's heart and mind to the grace of the presence of the Son of Man is to take the first step toward fulfilling the mission of the present age and toward preparing for the age to come. Such is the sign of the times in which we live, which could be designated by the words: MANKIND ON THE WAY TO DAMASCUS.

Editorial Foreword
Michaelmas, 1979
Mercury Star Journal

In a recent review of the *Mercury Star Journal*,[6] the review writes, "the theme that has long underlain the *Mercury Star Journal*'s foundation (is) to be a bearer of the living wisdom of reincarnation and karma into the consciousness of modern men in accordance with the inherent quest of the western world for a true COSMOLOGY..." The Grail science of Astrosophy is indeed a vehicle for the Christian teachings of reincarnation and karma, and the spread of these teachings—which may at first be confined to small groups of spiritual seekers in the western world—will gradually bring about far-reaching changes in modern culture, working as a community-building impulse in the sphere of human relationships.

The widespread awakening to Astrology that is now underway in the West is symptomatic of the awakening—from the sleep of materialism—to the reality of the *human soul*... with its passions, desires, yearning for love, and longing for fulfilment on the physical plane. Yet a further level of awakening is possible, however, where the human being becomes aware of a level of being that lies beyond the ebb and flow of impulses at work within the soul. This second awakening is the awakening to the reality of the *human spirit:* at first on the level of ideas—where, for example, the idea of the immortality of the self may light up within—and then as concrete experience, in which the individual knows by direct experience that he has passed through former incarnations on the earth and that, therefore, as an individuality his existence reaches out beyond the confines of birth and death. Just as Astrology is (or at least endeavors to be) a science of the soul, the reemergence of which is symptomatic of the reawakening of mankind to the reality of the soul, so is Astrosophy a science of the spirit—of the individuality that passes through successive incarnations of the earth, and of his destiny (karma) the emergence of which in the twentieth century is a sign of the awakening to the reality fo the human spirit, which indwells the soul as its immortal kernel. Thus, the Grail science of Astrosophy does not in any way compete with or seek to replace Astrology, in the sense of concerning itself not so much with the nature of the human soul but rather with the relationship of the human individuality to the starry world, and with how karma is "carried over" by the planets—in their mutual relationships (aspects) and positions in the zodiac—from one earthly incarnation to the next. Indeed, Astrosophy can fructify Astrology, shedding new light up on the ancient mystery science of the Chaldeans.

One of the central problems with which Astrosophy is concerned is *freedom*. If man has a destiny, how can he be free? If his destiny is linked to the starry world in some mysterious way, does this imply that he is subject to "cosmic mechanism"? In the Gospel of St. John, it is written: "If you continue in my word, you are truly my disciples, and you will know the truth, and the truth will make you free" (John 8:31–32). Thus, those who enter

---
[6] Cf. Charles Lawrie, "*Mercury Star Journal* 78/79," *Mercury Arts Newsletter* 67, Christmas/New Year 1979, p. 19.

upon the Grail path, a path of discipleship following the master—Jesus Christ—and who begin to receive the knowledge of the Grail ("the truth"), will become ever more free. From this perspective a key to the problem of freedom lies in the sequence: Christian discipleship—truth (knowledge)—freedom. That is to say, by becoming a disciple of Jesus Christ—who is, since Golgotha, the Lord of karma—knowledge of truth will be transmitted to a person concerning his own destiny, which will bring him stage by stage to ever-higher levels of freedom. In this sense, an individual's true freedom does not lie in the freedom to do whatever he wants to do; rather, he is free to the extent that he knows that he is doing, i.e., to the extent that he knows his own destiny. Thus, for the Christian esotericist freedom grows along the path of discipleship—it grows from incarnation to incarnation—so that freedom is actually a goal, the realization of which is a guiding principle for the human individuality from life to life. Jorgen Smit's article on this theme, concerning freedom as an essential principle in the development of a new star wisdom, illumines the role of the Archangel Michael—the "countenance of Christ"—as the being who brings man into relationship with the stars in a free way; and we have included it in this Michaelmas issue of the *Mercury Star Journal*—at the time of year dedicated to St. Michael—to serve as a starting point for meditation on this fundamental problem (i.e., that of freedom) in the sphere of Astrosophy.

In the previous issue of the *Mercury Star Journal*, the 100th anniversary of the birth of Elisabeth Vreede—founder-leader of the Mathematical-Astronomical Section of the School of Spiritual Science—who dedicated herself to the task of developing a new, Christian form of star wisdom, was commemorated. The year 1979 has witnessed another important anniversary; it is the 250th anniversary of the birth of the German poet, playwright and philosopher *Lessing* (b. Jan. 22, 1729; d. Feb. 15, 1781), who is remembered also as being the first thinker in the West to arrive for himself at the idea of reincarnation. In fact, it was almost exactly two hundred years ago that the thought of reincarnation became introduced into the Christian world through Lessing's work *The Education of the Human Race* (written toward the end of his life, ca. 1778). At the end of this work, which provides a summary of his philosophy, he writes:

> It is so! The very same Way by which the Race reaches its perfection must every individual man—one sooner, another later—have travelled over. Have travelled over in one and the same life? Can he have been, in one and the self-same life, a sensual Jew and a spiritual Christian? Can he in the self-same life have over-taken both? Surely not that! But why should not every individual man have existed more than once upon this World?...Why should I not come back as often as I am capable of acquiring fresh knowledge, fresh expertise? Do I bring away so much from once that there is nothing to repay the trouble of coming back? Is this a reason against it? Or, because I forget that I have been here already? Happy it is for me that I do forget. The recollection of my former condition would permit me to make only a bad use of the present. And what I must forget *now*, is that necessarily forgotten forever?[7]

Here Lessing arrived with intensity and clarity at the *idea* of reincarnation. Now, some 250 years later, an increasing number of individuals are awakening to the *concrete experience* of reincarnation—as if in answer to Lessing's question, "what I must forget *now* (i.e., forget as an experience), is that necessarily forgotten forever?" What is important here—in this spiritual awakening—is that first the awakening is on the idea level, and this is then followed by awakening on the level of experience. The idea precedes the experience and thereby human freedom is protected. For in the awakening to an idea, the possibility is present, also, of rejecting the idea—in which case the experience corresponding to the idea is suppressed. Thus, the idea of reincarnation was introduced into the western world, first by Lessing and subsequently by others, as preparation for the New Age of Christianity arising in the twentieth century, in which—along the path of discipleship—awakening

---

7 Lessing, *The Education of the Human Race: The Harvard Classics,* vol. 32, pp. 195–220.

to the living experience of reincarnation occurs at a definite stage.

Grail Christianity—the Christianity of the New Age—does not make a dogma of reincarnation or of any other teachings from the sphere of esotericism, but rather points reincarnation as an idea that can become actual experience. Openness to the idea is the key principle here, and it is this attitude that distinguishes Grail Christianity from Catholicism. Although, in all fairness, it must be said that the Church has not been open to the idea of reincarnation for a very good reason. For there are grave spiritual dangers attached to the idea of reincarnation, perhaps the most serious of which is the turning of man's spiritual gaze away from the kingdom of heaven to the earthly realm. When man's attention becomes focused upon his earthly incarnations, and correspondingly turned away from the heavenly realm, there is the danger that he will lose sight of his true spiritual goal—"the holy city, new Jerusalem" (Rev. 21:2)—which is being built in the heavenly kingdom, and is not of this world. Thus, accounts of series of incarnations where the earthly realm alone is referred to, and that do not contain an uplifting moral impulse, can actually contribute to a kind of materialism that is even more potent in its spiritual effect that the soulless and spiritless scientific materialism of the present day. And it is against this danger that the Church has guarded western culture by excluding the idea of reincarnation, and by directing man's spiritual gaze to his true home—to the kingdom of heaven.

Thus, the second fundamental problem that belongs to the sphere of Astrosophy—the Grail science of reincarnation and karma—is, alongside the problem of freedom, the problem of *balance*—i.e., of finding a harmonious balance between occupation with the mysteries of man's life on earth and the mysteries of the kingdom of heaven. To live in balance between heaven and earth is the ideal—neither to forsake the earth and man's mission here, nor to become too strongly bound (in the sense of becoming spiritually chained) to this world. Thus, to counterbalance the earth-oriented spiritual impulse that is awakened through knowledge of reincarnation and karma, an increasingly intensive occupation with the mysteries of the cosmos is necessary—i.e., with the mysteries of the spiritual cosmos—the kingdom of heaven—and the coming into being of the heavenly city of Jerusalem. Expressed in terms of the quest for the Grail, balance is preserved by directing the inner gaze toward the goal of the future—the heavenly city—so that occupation with man's spiritual history does not become a one-sided beholding of the past and of sequences of incarnations lying in the past. The Grail seeker's quest is analogous, spiritually, to the quest that the Three Magi undertook physically, when they set off to seek the Child Jesus in Jerusalem. For Jesus Christ is the temple in the heavenly city of Jerusalem, as referred to in the Apocalypse, where he is called by the esoteric name of "the Lamb": "And I saw no temple in the city, for its temple is the Lord God the Almighty and the Lamb" (Rev. 21:22).

We have taken the step in this Michaelmas 1979 issue of the *Mercury Star Journal* of publishing Hans Gsanger's research leading to the identity of the Three Magi. This identification should be considered in the light of Rudolf Steiner's karma research, where he identified the Child Jesus whom the Three Magi sought out as the reincarnated Zaratas, or Zoroaster, who lived in Babylon in the sixth century BC, and who had lived earlier, in prehistoric times, as Zarathustra, the founder of the Zoroastrian religion in Persia.[8] As Rudolf Steiner always stressed—and as may be repeated with regard to Hans Gsanger's research—the reader is obliged to test the results of karma research for himself, and not simply to accept them. As with scientific research, the responsibility lies with the reader to evaluate for himself the result for karma research when they are published, which process of evaluation may take time—perhaps decades—and can be accomplished along the path of meditation in conjunction with knowledge that may be

---

8   For details of Rudolf Steiner's karma research concerning the mysteries of the being of Jesus Christ, which are much more comprehensive than the one aspect referred to here—in connection with Zoroaster—see, for example, Steiner, *The Spiritual Guidance of the Individual and Humanity*.

acquired from historical sources. Again, an attitude of openness is important here, and a dedication to Christ—the Lord of karma—as the ultimate source of truth in the sphere of knowledge concerning reincarnation and karma. There may be readers who feel that they cannot accept the karma research findings that appear in this issue of the *Mercury Star Journal*, but this is all the more an opportunity to exercise the faculty of enquiry that is the Grail seeker's way: to put the question to the Risen One—in the light of the Grail—and to await that answer that follows—sooner or later—either as certainty conveyed by the clear, still voice of conscience, or in some other way. "Ask, and it will be given you; seek, and you will find; knock, and it will be opened to you. For everyone who asks receives, and he who seeks finds, and to him who knows it will be opened" (Matt. 7:7).

GRAIL CHRONOLOGY
MICHAELMAS 1979
MERCURY STAR JOURNAL

Grail star wisdom comprises three mutually complementary sciences—Astronomy, Astrology and Astrosophy—the development of which depend on the unfolding of three faculties latent within every human being, namely the faculties of Imagination (spiritual seeing), Inspiration (spiritual hearing) and Intuition (the spiritual sense of direct knowing). With respect to the theme under consideration—Grail chronology—it is especially the latter faculty that is relevant.

Through Intuition the essence of another being can be known, and it is thus that knowledge concerning the individuality of a human being—the passage of the immortal spirit from one earthly incarnation to another—can be attained by means of this spiritual faculty. Astrosophy—the Grail science of reincarnation and karma—thus depends on the development of the faculty of Intuition, which faculty will arise more and more, to the extent with which human beings unite themselves with Christ, thereby bringing themselves into relationship with the source of eternal love. The formula given by the Master for the development of this spiritual faculty runs as follows: "A new commandment I give to you, that you love one another—even as I have loved you, that you also love one another. By this all men will know that you are my disciples, if you have love for one another" (John 13:34–35).

It is the power of love—the love exemplified by Jesus Christ—that unfolds the faculty of Intuition and, correspondingly, knowledge of reincarnation. The emergence of Grail Christianity on the Earth could be described as a "phenomenon of love"—i.e., as a realization of the above formula given by the Master. For example, two people who have never met before are introduced through a mutual acquaintance and inwardly "recognize" one another by means of a deep feeling of sympathy and love. This is a stage on the way toward intuition. When this "recognition" is intensified to a heightened degree it leads to *knowing*, a direct knowing of the identity of the other (which need not—on a conscious level—be mutual, however).

What is important in this "phenomenon of love," which is the essence of Grail Christianity, is "that you are my disciples" and—at the same time—"that you love one another." The basis of Grail Christianity is *union* with Jesus Christ—i.e., "that you are my disciples," and the outer sign of this discipleship is "that you love one another." Needless to say, the development of higher spiritual faculties entails the moral responsibility conveyed by the word "disciple"—i.e., not just dedication to the ideals of Truth, Beauty and Goodness but also the will to cultivate certain virtues belonging to this path of discipleship—such as, for example, humility, reverence, compassion and obedience to conscience.

The Three Magi who came from the Orient to pay homage to the Child were precursors of Grail Christianity. They came as "Kings," but came in the spirit of love and humility. By means of Intuition they knew of the identity of the Child. They *knew* that this Child—although in outward appearance like any other child—was the incarnation of the Bodhisattva *Zoroaster*, the great spiritual leader of mankind who had lived in Babylon over 500 years previously, at the time of *Daniel* and *Cyrus the Great*, as the teacher of the Chaldean priesthood and, among others, *Pythagoras*.

They knew that this Child would fulfil a destiny of eternal significance for the human race; they knew—not in words, but in silent contemplation—that the one before them had the potential (as a Bodhisattva) to "receive the religion" at the age of thirty, as he had done so before when (in a former life) around the age of thirty he had come to the "conference" with the highest God—Ahura Mazda or Ormuzd. Hidden behind the figure of the Child Jesus before them was the one who, as the founder of the Zoroastrian religion, had proclaimed the spirit of the Sun, Ahura Mazda, and who now was on the Earth to fulfil the incarnation of the same spirit (whom we know as Christ), whose cosmic existence he had taught previously. Whereas previously, as the founder of the Zoroastrian religion, he had brought to humanity the *message* of Christ (under the name "Ahura Mazda" or "Ormuzd"), in his incarnation as Jesus he was to enable *Christ Himself* to speak and live on the Earth. Formerly, Christ spoke through Zoroaster as his messenger on Earth; this time Christ Himself was to live on the Earth in the physical body of Jesus.

The faculty whereby the Three Magi were able to recognize the reincarnated Zoroaster was the fruit of love—the love that they had toward their spiritual teacher. But as an "auxiliary aid"—to help raise to consciousness what they intuitively recognized—they made use of the Grail sciences of chronology and astrology, which (together with meteorology) were cultivated in Zoroaster's mystery school in Babylon, and evidently continued to be cultivated by the Chaldean priesthood over the centuries, until the time of the Three Magi. It is especially the Grail science of chronology that is of interest to us here—i.e., how did the stars reveal to the Magi that the "time of fulfilment" was at hand?

In my article "Grail Research at the Goetheanum" (MSJ v, pp. 13–26),[9] reference was made to the "trigon" formed by conjunctions of Saturn and Jupiter, which rotates through the sidereal zodiac in ca. 2,562 years, so that after 854 years (one third of the rotation period) each corner of the trigon has progress to the next (see figure):

Reference was made also the Persian-Sasanian tradition associated with the occurrence of Saturn-Jupiter conjunctions, namely that important religious and political changes are indicated by conjunctions of these planets. Evidence that the Chaldean priesthood were transmitters of this tradition appears in the writings of Berosus, a Chaldean priest who left Babylon and founded a mystery school during the early part of the third century BC—for Greek seekers after the Chaldean wisdom—on the Greek island of Cos. Thus, Berosus's *Babyloniaca* contains an astrological world history based on 60-year conjunctions (the exact astronomical period is actually closer to 59 years). This theory pertaining to Saturn-Jupiter conjunctions ties in closely with Zoroastrian chronological ideas, as pointed out by David Pingree in his discussion of the use by the Arabic astrologer Masha'allah of this theory, where he says that "the influence of Zoroastrian ideas will be immediately apparent..."[10] Hence, it is not so far removed from the bounds of possibility that it was Zoroaster himself in his Babylonian incarnation, who originally formulated the principle of Saturn-Jupiter conjunctions as the primary indicators of turning points in spiritual history, and that this became transmitted within the Chaldean priesthood until the time of the Three Magi (and was evidently taken up later by sages in the Sasanian empire).

The decisive Saturn–Jupiter conjunction for the Three Magi was what took place near the middle of sidereal Pisces in 7 BC. With this conjunction a definite stage was reached in the descent to earthly life of the incarnating soul of Zoroaster, which latter knowledge, i.e., concerning the life of the human being in spiritual spheres prior to birth,

---

9 Republished in 2021's *As Above, So Below: Star Wisdom vol III,* as "Classics in Astrosophy, pt IV"

10 E.S. Kennedy and David Pingree, *The Astrological History of Masha'allah*, p. 74.

belongs to the secrets of astrology. The Magi knew that the time was at hand—the birth of Zoroaster was approaching. But where were they to seek for his birth?

The quest of the Magi to locate the birthplace of their reincarnating teacher was a "quest for the Grail" on the physical plane—on the Earth.[11] One of the Magi, the reborn Cyrus the Great had (in his incarnation as Cyrus) not only knowledge of the mission of the Jews, as Daniel also had, but also took an active part in enabling this mission to be accomplished. Thus, he had an intimation of the mission to prepare a physical body for the Messiah, which mission was symbolized in the building of the temple in Jerusalem, i.e., the temple—the house of God at Jerusalem—was the outer sign of the "house" (physical body) to be built by the Jewish folk for the incarnation of the Messiah. In Cyrus's first year as king of Babylon—in 538 BC—he issued a decree for the rebuilding of the temple, and released the Jewish people from their Babylonian captivity, allowing them to return to Jerusalem. As stated in the book of Ezra, a record of Cyrus's decree for the rebuilding of the temple at Jerusalem, which Nebuchadnezzar had destroyed in 586 BC (or 587 BC according to some historians), was kept in the archives at Ecbatana. "A record. In the first year of Cyrus the king, Cyrus the king issued a decree: Concerning the house of God at Jerusalem, let the house be rebuilt..." (Ezra 6:3). Knowledge of this record may well have been transmitted within the Chaldean priesthood and thus could have returned to the reborn Cyrus, who—as one of the Three Magi—may thereby have become awoken to his own destiny from his former incarnation. In some such way the Three Magi became alerted to the city of Jerusalem as the place where the birth of their reincarnating teacher—as "king of the Jews"—was to be expected. Knowing that the "house of God" was built in Jerusalem, and being able to perceive what this symbolized—or in some similar way—they came to the realization that the "house" (physical body) of the Messiah was to be found in Jerusalem.

Alas, the Magi did not have more exact knowledge; for if they had known the birthplace more exactly (Bethlehem, and not Jerusalem), the tragic slaughter of children by Herod the Great could have been avoided. However, a lesson can be learnt from the experience of the Three Magi, a lesson that every Christian esotericist has to learn sooner or later—namely the lesson of *silence*. By way of their spiritual faculties, combined with what they were able to receive from the Chaldean mystery tradition, the Three Magi were entrusted with deeply esoteric knowledge relating to the birth of the Savior. With this birth the whole future of mankind was at stake. Whilst veiled in secrecy, the birth of Jesus could take place undisturbed, in peace and quiet, but as soon as knowledge of the birth became spoken out (outside of the esoteric circle formed by the Magi)—which it did when the Three Magi came to Herod—Jesus's mission became threatened. It was only through compensatory divine intervention—the appearance of an Angel to warn Joseph—that the threatening danger (that the Child Jesus be slain) could be avoided, by means of the flight of the holy family to Egypt.

The lesson to be learnt from the slaughter of children at Bethlehem is the necessity for silence with regard to the esoteric truths with which one is entrusted—especially when these truths are from the domain of knowledge of reincarnation (and most especially when this knowledge concerns living [i.e., incarnated] people). The speaking out of occult knowledge of this kind can only occur within a circle of "disciples," where the atmosphere is blessed by the presence of Christ, either directly or via one of his mediators. The Three Magi formed such a circle—a circle that was blessed by the "star"—i.e., by the Bodhisattva Zoroaster ("golden star"), the messenger of Christ.[12] Through their karmic bond, in the ser-

---

11 Nowadays, the Grail quest—the search for Christ Jesus—has to be directed to the plane above the physical Earth; namely, it is in the elemental world, in the sphere bounded by the Moon's orbit, where—since World War II—the Risen One is to be found

12 A bodhisattva is a human being who has attained a high level of union with Christ and who, thereby, is entrusted with a specific aspect of Christ's mission for the redemption of Man, of Nature, and of other (fallen) beings.

vice of white occultism, the Three Magi formed a holy circle of "disciples" able to be recipients of concrete esoteric knowledge concerning Zoroaster's reincarnation.

Through the emergence of Grail Christianity (in wider circles from the twentieth century onward) such circles will again be possible, in which groups of "disciples" come together in the service of the Risen One and form together a "knowledge organism"—to be recipients of the "hidden knowledge of the Grail" (to use Rudolf Steiner's expression, cf. *Occult Science,* p. 306). However, it is only *"in nomine Christi"* that concrete knowledge of reincarnation—e.g., of the former incarnations of fellow "disciples" may be spoken of—otherwise the speaking out of knowledge of this kind entails the risk of ensuing tragedy.

The Three Magi, on account of the destiny that led them to him, believed that they could trust Herod. However, their belief was mistaken, and the speaking out of their occult knowledge concerning the birth of the "king of the Jews" was actually a betrayal, a breach of the golden rule of silence. Consequently, a terrible tragedy—the slaughter of the innocents—ensued. This example can help to awaken the necessary sense of moral responsibility that knowledge of reincarnation entails, and also points to the *absolute protection* of this knowledge—which is, quite simply, the law of silence. One who resolves to maintain silence (and keeps to his resolution) *cannot* betray.

But to return to the theme of Grail chronology: as a Saturn-Jupiter conjunction occurs every twenty years, how did the Magi know that it was with the conjunction in Pisces—in 7 BC—that the decisive moment, the approach of the "fulfilment of time," had come? How did they know that this particular conjunction (which was actually a triple conjunction) signified the start of the twenty-year period within which the birth of Jesus would fall?

This question can be answered from an inner standpoint—i.e., from the perspective of the consciousness of the Three Magi in relation to the incarnating Zoroaster, or from an outer standpoint, i.e., from the perspective of history (meaning spiritual history). Although the former perspective is of considerable interest, belonging as it does to the domain of concrete occultism, it is the latter perspective that can help most especially in the endeavor to gain some insight into the nature of Grail chronology and its general applications. With respect to this latter perspective, the above question can be rephrased as follows: In terms of mankind's spiritual history, what was "special" about the period of time when Jesus was born?

Clearly this question can be answered in a multitude of ways. However, for our purposes it makes sense to look at this question only from a very specific point of view, namely that of the Chaldean mystery tradition that came down to the Three Magi. Although this tradition was already in existence when Zoroaster (Zaratas) began his teaching activity—ca. 569 BC, according to Hans Gsanger—it was through Zoroaster that real esoteric content was given to the tradition cultivated by the Chaldean priesthood. This esoteric content consisted of three kinds of mysteries: the Saturn mysteries, to which category Zoroastrian–Chaldean chronological teachings belong, the Sun mysteries, to which sphere the astrological teachings can be assigned, and the mysteries of the Moon, under which heading the teachings concerning meteorology fall. All three categories of mysteries in Zoroaster's Babylonian mystery school were dependent upon *astronomy,* however—moreover, an astronomy that (unlike earlier astronomy) was of an exact—i.e., what we may justifiably call "scientific" nature. Thus, following on the tremendous impulse given by Zoroaster in his Babylonian incarnation, the very first scientific definition of the zodiac was formulated, which zodiac was used in Babylonian astronomy down until the time of the Three Magi (and with the conquest of Babylon by Alexander the Great, the Babylonian sidereal zodiac became transmitted to Greece, Egypt and even as far afield as India).

The earliest recorded use of the Babylonian zodiac that has been found to date is from a cuneiform text giving a list of solar eclipses, in terms of the sidereal signs of the Babylonian zodiac, from 475 to 457 BC. As shown in Part I of the series of articles on the "Sidereal Zodiac" in this volume of the *Mercury Star Journal,* the basis for the definition of the Babylonian zodiac is the Aldebaran-Antares axis, which divides the zodiacal belt more or less exactly in two. Thus, the Babylonian zodiac was defined—with twelve equal 30° sidereal signs—so that Aldebaran lies at 15° Taurus (the midpoint of the sign of Taurus) and Antares at 15° Scorpio (the midpoint of the sign of Scorpio). The definition of the remaining signs of the Babylonian zodiac in terms of fixed stars lying in the zodiacal belt follows form this primary definition—e.g., Leo is defined in relation to the first magnitude star Regulus, with Regulus at 5° Leo; Virgo is defined in relation to the first magnitude star Spica at 29° Virgo, etc.[13]

Thus, the Three Magi came to know of the Babylonian zodiac, which remained in use in Babylonian astronomy until the beginning of the Christian Era (until the first century AD). This zodiac, applied in the sense of Grail chronology, can give a key to understanding that the "time of fulfilment"—in a historical sense—was near (at the time of the Magi). Thus, in his book *Der Stern Der Weisen* (Vienna–Munich, 1969), the erstwhile professor of theoretical astronomy at the University of Vienna, Conrad Ferrari d'Occhieppo, has endeavored to reconstruct the journey of the Three Magi from Babylon to Jerusalem under the guidance of the "star," which he identifies with the threefold Saturn-Jupiter conjunction in the sidereal sign of Pisces in 7 BC. He points out that this threefold conjunction was reckoned in advance—the dates on which the three conjunctions were to occur were reckoned—and the computation showed that the conjunction would take place in the Babylonian zodiacal sign of Pisces; this much is known from a record of this reckoning that was excavated from a Babylonian site. This excavated cuneiform text is purely the astronomical trace of something that occurred spiritually to the Three Magi. Through their spiritual faculties they were in a position to decipher the meaning of what otherwise appears as a routine astronomical calculation amidst thousands of other similar computations. Whatever the occult details underlying this deciphering may have been, the astronomical facts are clear. The question is: How may these astronomical facts be interpreted?

In the light of the Zoroastrian–Chaldean tradition (remembering that it was possibly Zoroaster himself who inaugurated this teaching in the sixth century BC) *every* Saturn-Jupiter conjunction signifies a new spiritual impulse in history. A *triple* Saturn-Jupiter conjunction, however, on account of its relatively infrequent occurrence, is especially impressive, and thus may have signified in the Zoroastrian–Chaldean tradition a quite special new impulse. The fact that this conjunction occurred in Pisces points to its significance for the future—i.e., for the future Age of Pisces.

In a chronological sense the conjunctions of Saturn and Jupiter, recurring every twenty years, can be likened to the motion of the "minute hand"—whilst the passage of the zodiacal ages, each lasting 2,160 years, can be thought of as the "hour hand"—of the "cosmic clock" of spiritual history. Around the time of the birth of Jesus the "hour hand" was drawing near to the end of an age—signified by the precession of the spring equinoctial point drawing near to the end of the sign of Aries. In the sense of Grail chronology, this latter fact indicates the special nature of the time at which Jesus was born. Although the Magi may not have been aware (at least, not consciously) of the meaning of the time in which they lived—i.e., the twilight of the Age of Aries, this is nevertheless a factor that we—as modern seekers of the Grail—may raise to consciousness. The Christ Sun shines at the dawn and twilight of each age—to give its initial impulse, and to bless its fruits "at the end of the day." Christ shone at the beginning of the Age of Aries through Abraham, Isaac, Jacob and his twelve sons—as the founders of Israel, the "people of the Ram." The Aries impulse was thus inaugurated and grounded in the twelve tribes of Israel. This does not mean to say that it was *only* in the people of Israel that the Aries impulse manifested—as it certainly manifested strongly in other cultures also—but that the people of Israel came into existence specifically as bearers of the Aries impulse. This impulse was

---

13 These articles were later published as a collected booklet called *The Sidereal Zodiac* in 1984, and greatly expanded upon in Robert Powell's doctoral thesis *The History of the Zodiac*, published in 2005.

carried further, receiving a tremendous renewal through Moses and—later—through David. It was maintained, against attacks from outside the Hebrew nation, as well as betrayal from within, until the time of the Three Magi, when the Christ Sun shone again—this time in full glory through the being of Jesus, but also through John the Baptist, the twelve disciples, the apostle Paul, and other members of the Hebrew race who participated in the founding of Christianity. Thus, the Christ Sun shone at the beginning—at the dawn—of the Age of Aries, with the founding of Israel, and also at the beginning of the twilight period at the end of the Age of Aries, with the coming of the Messiah as the fruit of the mission of the Hebrew Nation. How exactly is this twilight period to be reckoned in the sense of Grail chronology? The location of the vernal point in the Babylonian zodiac for 1979 is 5.5° Pisces (5.5 in the Babylonian sidereal sign of Pisces)—i.e., the vernal point has still 5.5° to travel before it enters the sign of Aquarius. The rate of precession of the vernal point (averaged out over history) is 1° in 72 years; thus the entry of the vernal point into Aquarius—the beginning of the Aquarian age—will take place in 396 years (5.5 × 72)—i.e., in AD 2375. A zodiacal age lasts 2,160 years (30 × 72), which is the length of time required for the vernal point to retrogress through one sign, 30° in length, of the Babylonian zodiac. Hence the Age of Pisces commenced in AD 215 (215 + 2,160 = 2,375). Similarly, the Age of Aries began in -1945—i.e., in 1946 BC (since 2,160 − 1,945 = 215).

In the Indian sacred book known as *The Laws of Manu*, written down probably about the second century AD, the following indication is given as to how the twilight period at the end of an age is to be reckoned: "They declare that the Krita age (consists of) four thousand years (of the gods); the twilight preceding it consists of as many hundreds, and the twilight following of the same number."[14] Thus, the twilight period at the end of the Krita age is 400 years long—i.e., it is one-tenth of the 4,000-year period.[15] Taking one-tenth of a zodiacal age of 2,160 years, we have a twilight period of 216 years. According to this reckoning the Christ Sun began to shine in the year -1—i.e., 2 BC, which lies 216 years before AD 215 (the start of the Age of Pisces). Amongst the Church fathers, the year 2 BC was indeed the year in which they reckoned the birth of Jesus to have taken place. Thus, this simple chronological reckoning—of the precession of the vernal point in relation to the Babylonian zodiac—yields exactly the time at which the birth of Jesus, in the sense of Grail Chronology, could have been expected to fall. This does not mean to imply that the Three Magi made such a reckoning, but rather shows that the Babylonian zodiac has a chronological validity—i.e., that Grail chronology is a science according to which the working of the cosmic impulse of Christ can be reckoned. And this reckoning by no means diminishes the glory of the shining of the Christ Sun—no more than reckoning the time of sunrise and sunset diminishes the beauty and majesty of the rising and setting Sun.

It is more likely that rather than making any reckoning of the zodiacal ages—and their dawn and twilight periods—the Magi knew intuitively that the twilight of the age was beginning—i.e., they were attuned to the cosmic reality of the phenomenon of the shining of the Christ Sun. As modern seekers of the Grail, we are in a position to reckon—through the faculty of human intelligence—what former Grail seekers knew intuitively. And in this fact a challenge is thrown open to us: to so unite ourselves with the Christ impulse that the way back (or rather forward) to this kind of intuitive knowledge can be found again. Then it may be said that the reckonings of Grail chronology, which can serve as a guideline for orientation in the unfolding of spiritual

---

14 The Laws of Manu I, 69; trsl G. Buhler in *Sacred Books of the East* vol xxv, Oxford, 1886, p. 19

15 Note that taking the two twilight periods as additional to the 4,000-year period, thus making a 4,800-year period, implies that the 400-year twilight period is one-twelfth of the whole. One-twelfth of a zodiacal age is 180 years, and 180 years from the year of the Crucifixion—AD 33—yields the date AD 213—almost exactly the start of the Age of Pisces

history, will begin to be realized in their higher reality, through union with the being of Christ. Thereby Grail Christianity will begin to find its realization upon the Earth, as the complementary working of what is attainable through the unfolding of spiritual faculties—through an every-increasing union with Jesus Christ—and of what can be deduced by the faculty of human intelligence. Thus human intelligence is not to be despised; rather, it is to be lifted up in service of the Christ Mystery, in the endeavor to understand His activity as the guide, friend, helper and server of the human race on the path following His "star"—the Grail seekers' "star"—toward the "new heaven and new earth...the holy city, *new Jerusalem*" (Rev. 21:1–2)—i.e., spiritual Jerusalem, just as those Grail seekers of antiquity—the Three Kings—followed His "star" from Babylon to the holy city, physical Jerusalem.

"Every earthly condition during a certain period of time is to be explained as a weaving and interplay of those forces that come into flower and those that die away, those that belong to the rising and those that belong to the falling line—sunrise and sunset—and in between, the zenith at noon, where the two forces unite and become one.

Seen from one's horizon, a person beholds the stars in the sky, rising in the east and climbing ever higher until they reach their highest point in the south. From then onward, they sink until they set in the west. And though the stars disappear from sight in the west, one must nevertheless say to oneself: The real place of setting lies in the south and coincides with the zenith, just as the true place of rising is in the north and coincides with the nadir.

Rising starts from the nadir. Through that, a circular motion is described that can be divided into two halves by a vertical line running south to north. In the part containing the eastern point, the rising forces are active. In the part containing the western point, the sinking forces are present. The eastern and western points cut the semicircle through the center. They are the two points in which, for our physical eye, vision of the forces begins and ends. They are one's horizon."

—Rudolf Steiner, *"Freemasonry" and Ritual Work*, p. 387

THE SACRIFICES OF JESUS AND CHRIST, PART I
Joel Matthew Park

THE FIRST SACRIFICE

Around May 2020, something that had been bubbling for a long time began to take form within me. This was the result of a deep engagement with some friends of mine—fellow "itinerant hermits" or "grail knights"—on the topic of the biography of our mutual friend Robert Powell. It has also been formed due to an engagement with Valentin Tomberg's essays on the pre-earthly sacrifices of Christ (available in English in the book *Christ and Sophia*) as part of my journey through Tomberg's *Lord's Prayer Course*. A further element was provided during my exploration of the Suit of Swords of the Minor Arcana of the Tarot of Marseilles with my friend and colleague Phillip Malone. And finally, in teaching a course on Philosophical Perspectives for the Camphill Academy in Camphill Village Copake in spring 2020, many new insights came to light.

I want to begin these considerations by pointing to the first portion of the 16th Letter–Meditation from *Meditations on the Tarot*, on the Arcanum of the Tower of Destruction. Here, the Anonymous Author contextualizes what exactly the "Fall of Humanity" involved. A Manichaean–Anthroposophical interpretation of the Fall would say that humanity was tempted by the Luciferic spirits to turn its gaze toward the physical material world rather than maintaining a strictly spiritual–sensory orientation. From an Anthroposophical perspective, the human being bears seven bodies that interpenetrate each other: physical body, etheric body, astral body, ego, spirit self, life spirit, and spirit body.[1] However, what is significant in Anthroposophy is Rudolf Steiner makes it clear that the physical body *as such* is not necessarily *material*. It is a "phantom," a body of *physical forces,* not necessarily of *material substance.*[2]

What occurred at the time of the Fall according to a surface understanding of Anthroposophy or Manichaeism is that in turning their gaze toward the material–sensory world, human beings absorbed material substance—they were in a sense "poisoned" by materiality. Like a drop of milk into a glass of water, the milk permeates the entirety of the water, making the whole of it cloudy. The two become impossible to separate—at least, without the intense procedure of distillation. So it was with the clear, diamond-like physical body being "infected" with materiality.

But this is a one-sided and therefore inaccurate perspective to take. The Anonymous Author makes clear to us in the 16th Letter–Meditation of *Meditations on the Tarot*, on the Tower of Destruction, that the Fall of Humanity occurred on the level of the *soul* first; it is not the poison of materiality entering the physical body that hampers the human being. It is the poison of *desire for illicit knowledge,* to make oneself like gods, that has poisoned the human's overall organization—a poisoning of the astral body primarily, one might say, which then opens the gateway to infection in the rest of the human being.

And so let us take our gaze back to the time of ancient Lemuria. The human being has fallen due to a desire for illicit knowledge—a desire inspired within it through an attentiveness to Luciferic spirits (i.e., the "Hierarchies of the Left"). The original state of the human being was rather to maintain obedience, poverty, and chastity toward the nine Hierarchies of the Right. Due to this inordinate attention given to the Luciferic spirits, the human being subsequently "falls" out of Paradise (a sphere in between the lunar sphere and Earth) and incarnates in a physical body. But it isn't

---

1 For a fuller elaboration, see Steiner, *Theosophy,* chap. 1.

2 See, for example, Steiner, *From Jesus to Christ*.

strictly a physical body, at least not in the way we understand the physical body currently. How can we come to a better understanding of this primal physical state?

We might say that while the body of the human being at that time was certainly physical, it was actually a kind of homogenous mixture of all seven bodies listed above: physical, etheric, and astral bodies; ego; spirit self, life spirit, and spirit man. There was no differentiation; all flowed together. The human being existed at an extremely dim level of intuitive consciousness, with a body that could be extended and transformed more or less at will—and the will of the human being, at this point, was entirely merged with and flowed into whatever will surrounded and came in contact with it. The human body was at the whim of the human soul; and the human soul in turn was at the whim of the cosmos, for good or ill.

An extreme danger presented itself here—the human sense organs, at this point, were totally alive, utterly receptive and engaged with whatever was confronting them. It was through the physical senses that spiritual beings—some with extremely dark intentions—could find their way into the human organism, more or less possessing and overtaking it completely. In the region of Paradise, a kind of hole had opened in the cosmos; where once the absolute purity of the human being dwelt in relation to the guiding spirits, a sphere of lies and delusion began to open up, the so called "Belt of Lies" or "Luciferic Sphere." This sphere allowed Ahrimanic spirits to dedicate themselves to robbing human beings of their physicality, which would turn the human race into a group of ghosts, imprisoned in between life and death. A decision was made at this point. An archangelic being, the archangel Jesus, in union with Christ, sacrificed his ego—his body of conscious intention, conscious will—in order to bring about a protection of the human organization.

This sacrifice of ego resulted in two things: first of all, the Moon was extruded from the Earth and entered the lunar sphere; along with this, the Elohim Yahweh left the sphere of the Sun (and the other six Elohim) to take up his abode in the Lunar Sphere. This Lunar Sphere took on a dense materiality—this dense materiality, up to the present day, acts as a kind of shield or barrier from the attempts on the part of Ahrimanic spirits to rob human beings of their physicality. It is like the skull protecting the brain. Yahweh is the cosmic cross-bearer, bearing the cross of the Moon for the sake of humanity.[3]

The second result took place within the human organization itself: the physical body took on materiality, and for the first time a distinct, concrete physical body coalesced or precipitated out of the homogenous mass of seven bodies of the human being. This resulted in changes to our organization: the senses "died," they no longer participated in such a dangerously intimate way with the phenomena they present to the human soul. In dying, they were able to be integrated into a harmonious whole—sensory integration became possible, rather than an overwhelming and overpowering collage of sensory input. This is reflected in the sensory integration that occurs in the normally developing child around age one. Notice that at the age of one the child normally attains

---

3 See Steiner, *The Occult Movement in the Nineteenth Century*, lect. 5.

uprightness and the ability to walk, to have some control of its movements.[4]

This is exactly what happened during this time of the first sacrifice of Jesus and Christ. *The seed of the ego's formation* was planted within the human being. This drew the human being upright, creating the basis for the skull and spinal cord, and the skin—the primal barrier between outside and inside—was in a way poured out over the human form from above to below. The attainment of dense materiality is therefore not a poisoning of the physical body—on the contrary, it is the shield, the barrier that has allowed the human being to develop into a free spiritual being (i.e., a being endowed with an ego).

And so to be clear in describing this first sacrifice: the first or "lowest" body of the human being coalesced into a distinct entity, precipitated out as it were by the other six. In the meantime, the other six bodies remained as a homogenous "flowing together," albeit with the *seed of the ego's eventual formation* planted within it by Jesus and Christ. This seed would take many ages to come to fruition. While the physical, material body was the immediate gift of these two beings, a *potential* and a *promise* was planted within the developing human being. While the physical body could immediately be put to use, the developing member of the human being (the ego) had to be *properly cultivated*—and this is the origin of *rite*, of religious ritual. Certain rituals had to be performed, in exact ways, so that the development of the Ego could take its proper course.

The first sacrifice of archangel Jesus and Christ occurred sometime around the middle of the Lemurian epoch, more or less in conjunction with the Fall.[5] At this moment, human beings were given the *immediate gift* of the organized mineral–physical body, due to the *developing seed* of the ego being planted within them. From this point onward, the human being's primal, intuitive clairvoyance began to dim; they began to have the first inklings of a division between subject and object, but in the form of *primal inspirations*. Increasingly, they no longer felt completely at one with the spiritual world. Instead, they began to feel this world to be outside of them, yet still made up of concrete spiritual beings. None of this was in any way occurring in full consciousness, but in a dim, almost hypnotic state.

It is my conviction that the first sacrifice of Jesus and Christ went hand in hand with the events described in Genesis involving Cain and Abel. As we will see, the seed of the ego that had been planted within humanity *by* the spiritual world needed to be met with a corresponding action on the part of humanity *toward* the spiritual world.

---

4 For further elaboration on the sacrifices of Jesus and Christ, see Tomberg, *Christ and Sophia* (the appendix), as well as Steiner, *Approaching the Mystery of Golgotha*.

5 The Mystery of Golgotha (the Fourth Sacrifice of Jesus and Christ) took place when the Sun's vernal point was at 2° Aries, around one-third of the way through the fourth post-Atlantean epoch. On the other hand, Robert Powell hypothesizes that the Sun's vernal point was at 19° Capricorn during the *Second* Sacrifice of Jesus and Christ (at the end of the first Atlantean epoch). This would put the Third Sacrifice somewhere around the time that the Sun's vernal point was 26° Leo, in the middle of the sixth Atlantean epoch, and the First Sacrifice close to the time that the Sun's vernal point was 12° Gemini, at the start of the fourth Lemurian epoch.

In essence, the ego that had been provided was a *sacrifice* on the part of archangel Jesus—he sacrificed a fully formed portion of his being to act as a substitute, and a guide, until the human being could have a fully individualized personality. And so, what was required from humanity as sacred magical rite was a corresponding sacrifice, a properly performed sacrificial ritual.

We might say that the story of Cain and Abel shows us humanity's tragic discovery of what is *true ritual* (i.e., sacred magic) vs. what is *arbitrary* or *fallen ritual* (ceremonial or black magic). The shepherd Abel properly mirrored the sacrifice enacted by Archangel Jesus, by sacrificing the best of his lambs. The *animal sacrifice*, from the time of Abel, carried on through the entire history of the Hebrew people, becoming ever more codified and precise, until the time of Christ. It was at the moment of the Mystery of Golgotha that the need for the sacrificial lamb ceased (we will return to this later in the article).

Cain, on the other hand, first attempted an arbitrary-ceremonial magical rite—one inspired out of his own misguided whim and creativity rather than accurately reflecting a higher spiritual reality—symbolized by the burning of vegetation. Then in his frustration, he performed a black magical rite—inspired by rage, jealousy, and lust for power—symbolized in the human sacrifice of his brother Abel. The seed was already planted here, at the beginning of all ritual, for three paths to open up: one to the sacred, another to the arbitrary, and a third to the debased.

THE SECOND SACRIFICE

The attention of Jesus and Christ then turned to the etheric body of the human being. At this point in time, the etheric body (body of life forces) of the human being was completely permeated by the other five members, particularly the astral body. Our organic functions at this point in time were not just keeping us alive, they were deeply *felt* and *experienced*, as a content of soul. We only experience our etheric body in such a way in modern times when we feel ill—our astral body sinks down into our etheric at such times. At the dawn of the Atlantean age, human beings constantly felt *unwell*—and due to the existence of arbitrary and debased magical practices, constantly ran the risk of becoming even more ill and out of balance, and sunken within themselves.

Archangel Jesus, toward the beginning of the Atlantean epoch, sacrificed his astral body for the sake of the human being. The sacrifice of this pure *astral* body resulted in the coalescing, the birthing of the fully formed *etheric* body—precipitated out by the other five members of the human being, just as the physical body had been during ancient Lemuria. And at the same time, due to the sacrifice of the astral body of archangel Jesus, the seed was planted for the eventual unfolding and distinct formation of the human being's *astral body*.

The etheric body and the physical body now existed as two distinct members, active in the material earthly plane. Both the astral body and the ego had now been potentized due to the first two sacrifices of Jesus and Christ, yet they remained essentially united and blended with the other three higher members of the human being (spirit self or *manas*, life spirit or *buddhi*, and spirit body or *atman*). They were, in a sense, "hovering above" the other two externalized members. The ego and the astral body each demanded a different sort of ritual in order to continue to develop within the "flowing together" of the higher human being (i.e., higher than the etheric body).

With the astral body now separated from the etheric body, the possibility for vocalization, and a kind of song language based in vowel sounds could develop. This is reflected in human development at the age of 2, when the first attempts at speech are made. In this sounding, the human being now developed in the horizontal, toward other human beings and nature, in juxtaposition to its vertical development during the first sacrifice. Just as the twelve senses had begun to integrate and harmonize in the aftermath of the first sacrifice, likewise now the seven life processes could properly unfold and come into harmony with each other.

The rituals for the development of the astral body consisted in the rites of the ancient Atlantean oracles. It is entirely possible that these rites consisted in part in the "vegetable sacrifice," the ceremonial or nature magic that Cain attempted to establish at too early a period, but that now had found its rightful place. Abel's animal sacrifice created smoke that rose vertically, relating it to the development of the uprightness of the ego, while the vegetable sacrifice created smoke that spread out horizontally, relating it to the community- and nature-oriented development of the astral body.

The human being at this point had entirely entered a stage of dim inspirational clairvoyance, and with the second sacrifice of Jesus and Christ, began to feel even more distinctly the split between subject and object. Inspirational clairvoyance, direct contact with spiritual beings, very gradually faded—over the course of thousands of years and many lifetimes—into imaginative clairvoyance, a dreamlike awareness of flowing pictures that represented the spiritual world to the human being.

THE THIRD SACRIFICE

Eventually, the astral body reached its full gestation. At the same time, it ran the risk of overwhelming the higher members of the human being, particularly the still-developing ego, with which it was still united. And so archangel Jesus sacrificed his pure *etheric body* to Christ to facilitate the birth of the fully formed *astral body* in the human being, separating it from the other four higher members that continued to operate as a single conglomeration.

The astral body could now begin to differentiate into its three faculties of thinking, feeling, and willing. The human being at this stage had entirely lost the inspirational clairvoyance that had gradually faded since the second sacrifice at the beginning of the age of Atlantis, living entirely in the dream pictures of imaginative clairvoyance. Out of this imaginative clairvoyance, the human being had experienced a continuity of consciousness from life to life, its memory extending back thousands of years. The speech of human beings had had a magical effect on the natural world—a creative force had lived within it.

These faculties now began to fade. As humanity transitioned from Atlantis into the post-Atlantean period, picture-clairvoyance began to fade away. The human being very gradually began to experience *thoughts*—but as *perceptions*, not yet as independent creations of the ego. By the time of ancient Greece, the human being was fully experiencing the world as subject and object—as soul and world, but an outer world permeated with thoughts, like the residue of a once perceptible spiritual world.

This third sacrifice at the end of Atlantis, the event that began this transition from picture-consciousness to thought-consciousness, also brought with it the development of consonantal speech, and of allowing *ideas* to incarnate in language, and not just *feeling and will* through songlike vowel sounds as it had been after this second sacrifice. This third sacrifice is reflected in the third year of child development, when the child begins to be able to *think*—albeit at a very rudimentary, imaginative level.

Take note that the development and cultivation of the *astral body* took place between the second and third sacrifices of Jesus and Christ—during the heart of the Atlantean period.[6] Whatever rituals had been properly attached to the development of the astral body thereafter either died away or lived on in a decadent (and therefore unnecessary and potentially hazardous) form. However—particularly *after* the third sacrifice of Christ, when the Manu (Noah) laid the foundation for the coming post-Atlantean culture—the ritual animal sacrifice for the sake of the development of the ego (the content of the ancient Hebrew religion) only took on greater form and significance.

We might say that the subsequent ages of humanity—after the third sacrifice of Jesus and Christ, as humanity transitioned from ancient Atlantis to the post-Atlantean world—were a kind of recapitulation of what had come before. The Age of Cancer (8426–6266 BC) straddled the end of Atlantis and the beginning of the ancient Indian culture. This time period recapitulated the transition from Paradise: the Fall and the first sacrifice of Jesus and Christ that gave the human being the upright physical body. The Age of Gemini (6266–4106 BC) straddled the ancient Indian culture and the ancient Persian culture. This time period recapitulated the transition from the end of Lemuria (the first sacrifice) to the beginning of Atlantis (the second sacrifice). Then the Age of Taurus (4106–1946 BC) straddled the end of the Persian culture and the start of ancient Egyptian/Assyrian/Babylonian culture, recapitulating the heart of ancient Atlantis, between the second and third sacrifices of Jesus and Christ.

All of this culminated in the time period of the Hebrew Patriarchs: Abraham, Isaac and Jacob, at the dawn of the Age of Aries (1946 BC). This was the point in history when the true preparation for the pivotal fourth sacrifice—the Mystery of Golgotha—could begin in earnest.

THE BEING PHILOSOPHIA

Let's briefly recap before going further. The first sacrifice of Archangel Jesus was the offering of his ego in order to organize and bring to manifestation the physical body of the human being at the end of ancient Lemuria. The offering of his archangelic ego planted the seed for the eventual unfolding of the purely human "I," the earthly personality, at the time of the Mystery of Golgotha, thousands of years later. The cultivation of this developing ego was performed primarily by the ancient Hebrew culture through the Hebrew religious rites, beginning with Abel's sacrifice of a Lamb to Yahweh, all the way through to the time of Jesus Christ.

However, at the beginning of the age of Atlantis, archangel Jesus also sacrificed his astral body in order to facilitate the birthing of the human being's etheric body. While the full manifestation of the human being's etheric body was the immediate gift of this sacrifice, it also planted the seed for the eventual and similar full development of the astral body, at the end of the Atlantean era. In between, certain ancient rituals—ceremonial magical rites—were enacted in order to cultivate this developing astral body. These occurred alongside the ongoing Hebrew rituals meant to develop the ego. At the culmination of Atlantis, with the birth of the astral body in the human being, these rituals were no longer necessary. Any remnant of

---

6 See footnote 5.

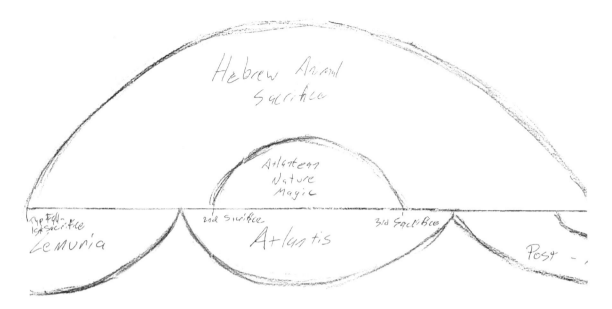

them was decadent and potentially harmful—in fact, in their most decadent form, they led to the Great Deluge that ended ancient Atlantis. At best, this ceremonial magic was merely ineffective. On the other hand, the ancient Hebrew rite carried on, and continued to take on a more and more codified form.

We can put before our mind's eye a larger cycle of development, extending from the first sacrifice in the middle of ancient Lemuria through the fourth sacrifice at the Mystery of Golgotha, consisting of the ancient Hebrew religion. Embedded within this cycle is a smaller one, which only unfolded between the second and third sacrifices of Jesus and Christ during the heart of the Atlantean age.

As the post-Atlantean era unfolded, the zodiacal ages of Cancer, Gemini, and Taurus recapitulated the time period laid out above, from the end of Lemuria to the end of Atlantis. It was the Age of Aries that properly brought something—or *Someone*—new to birth, and finally saw the concrete codification of the Hebrew rituals that had existed in a more organic sense for many generations, through the patriarchs and Moses. When I say "birth," the reader may very well ask: what exactly—or *Who* exactly—was it that was born at the beginning of the Age of Aries, around 1946 BC?

In a lecture from January 10, 1915, Rudolf Steiner paints a vivid picture of a being named Philosophia.[7] He characterizes Her unfolding biography as the remnant or expression of the ancient Sun evolution in our current Earthly world. Whereas the normal human being's biography unfolds over a series of seven-year cycles, Philosophia's biography, according to Steiner, unfolds in a series of approximately *seven hundred-year* cycles.

For the human being, these seven-year cycles are as follows:

0–7 = birth of physical body, development of etheric body. Related to the Moon Sphere.

7–14 = birth of the etheric body, development of the astral body. Related to the Mercury Sphere.

14–21 = birth of the astral body, development of the sentient soul. Related to the Venus Sphere.

21–28 = birth of the sentient soul, development of the intellectual soul. Related to the Sun Sphere.

28–35 = birth of the intellectual soul, development of the consciousness soul. Related to the Sun Sphere.

---

[7] See Steiner, *Artistic Sensitivity as a Spiritual Approach to Knowing Life and the World*, lect. 2.

- 35–42 = birth of the consciousness soul, development of *manas* or spirit self. Related to the Sun Sphere.

- 42–49 = birth of *manas*, development of life spirit or *buddhi*. Related to the Mars Sphere.

- 49–56 = birth of *buddhi*, development of spirit body or *atman*. Related to the Jupiter Sphere.

- 56–63 = birth of *atman*, development of the "Zodiacal Man," the karma-free human being. Related to the Saturn Sphere.

- 63–70 = birth of the Zodiacal Man. Related to the Zodiac.[8]

In this fascinating and complex lecture, Rudolf Steiner describes the evolution of this being Philosophia in terms related to the above unfolding of human biography. He points to the historical evolution of human consciousness as an indication of the evolution of this being. Oddly enough, he begins his description of the biography of this being at her third life cycle—that of the astral body, related to the Venus sphere. He makes only very vague remarks regarding the first two life cycles (we will return to this later).

The third life cycle (the equivalent of ages 14 to 21 for the human being) of Philosophia began around the time of the pre-Socratic philosophers. These pre-Socratic philosophers represented the bridge from the old elemental picture consciousness that understood the cosmos via myth, to the newly arising consciousness that revealed itself to the human soul in the form of *thought*. This new capacity of the thought-perceiving soul only fully revealed itself in Socrates, Plato, and Aristotle. For these three most representative Greek philosophers, the activity of human thinking did not proceed as it does for the modern human being, as though thoughts were created by the ego's own activity. Rather, these thinkers *perceived thoughts* as being given to them like any other perception, out of the nature of the very phenomena to which they gave their attention. The divide between soul (subject) and world (object) had become clear; yet this divide was bridged through *thoughts* that were given to the human soul, like words whispered in one's ear.

Steiner indicates that this third cycle lasted from around the 6th century BC up to the early days of the Church. He indicates that while the development of a world conception based on thought was coming from ancient Greece, something else was arising in human evolution in connection with the Hebrew people. Their entire mission was tied up with the birth of the individual human ego, the "I." This was born toward the end of this 700-year period, in AD 33, at the Mystery of Golgotha.

The next approximately 700-year life cycle in the biography of Philosophia began during the days of the early Church Fathers and extended through the late 9th century AD—Steiner explicitly refers to John Scotus Eriugena as representing the end of this cycle.[9] This time period was typified by a revisiting of the world conceptions that had been born in ancient Greece—Platonism in particular, through the Neoplatonists—but at the same time recognizing the limitation of human thinking. It began to be recognized that human thinking does not encapsulate the *entirety* of the soul's experience of the world. The thought conceptions of Plato were put to use in order to understand and bring to full consciousness (gnosis) the primal, mystical religious experience of the soul, and the content of religious traditions (primarily Judaism and Christianity).

This was followed by a crucial time period: the approximately 700-year time period of the development of the intellectual soul of Philosophia. For human beings, the heart of the intellectual soul years from ages 28 to 35 contains the "Christ years" of the one's biographical unfolding (ages 30 to 33). The time period equivalent to the "Christ years" for Philosophia lasted from the 9th century through the 16th to 17th centuries. It was precisely during this time historically that the philosophical/religious movement of Scholasticism began to

---

8 See Powell, *Hermetic Astrology* vol 2 for more information.

9 John Scotus Eriugena (ca. 800–ca. 877), Irish-Catholic Neoplatonist philosopher and theologian.

unfold. Just as the prior time period, from the early Church Fathers up through John Scotus Eriugena, was a revisiting of *Platonism,* now through the burgeoning forces of the ego bestowed upon the human being through the Mystery of Golgotha, the Scholastic period saw a revisiting and revival of *Aristotelianism*. Through Thomas Aquinas, Aristotle was Christianized. It was at this point in human history that, for the first time on a completely conscious level, thought was experienced as being produced *by* the human soul, rather than as a perception coming toward it from without. The task of Scholasticism was to form a truce between the thinking produced out of the *reason* of the human soul on the one hand, and the content of religious experience and tradition (*faith* or dogma) on the other hand. Religious experience was understood to be a matter of grace, as a gift from another world that could only be perceived through the capacity of faith. It was fundamentally based on a trans-subjective experience, and therefore could not become universal. On the other hand, the activity of reason, of the thinking soul, was the effort of the human being to bring this religious content into a conceptual structure and justification that had a universal, objective value.

This time period ended around the 16th/17th centuries, with the Copernican and Cartesian revolutions. The human self began to be felt very strongly as an independent, thought-creating entity. Scientists and philosophers began to feel ever more acutely the lack of the ego's self-justification, a deeper and deeper confusion in regards to the fundamental accuracy of human thinking and sense observation, and a loss of the sense of the human personality's place in the cosmos. World conceptions based on natural science and observation seemed to have no room left for the human soul. More and more the ego had to struggle to find its place in the world conceptions that were being forced upon the human being due to the inevitable and necessary rise of materialism. It is in the midst of this struggle that we currently stand.

THE AGE OF ARIES

In spring 2020, I had the great opportunity to teach a course on Philosophical Perspectives in the Camphill Academy. I used the lecture from *Artistic Sensitivity* that I have only briefly summarized here as my point of departure, in conjunction with the book *Riddles of Philosophy*, one that Rudolf Steiner began in 1900 and completed in 1914. As I worked over this material with my students over the course of three months, it helped me to strike upon what I believe is the exact timing of the unfolding of this being Philosophia.

The first three life cycles of Philosophia took place over the course of the Age of Aries (1946 BC–AD 215), each one lasting 720 years—this is why Steiner said the life cycles of Philosophia were *approximately* seven hundred years in length:

Physical body/Moon Sphere: 1946–1226 BC
Etheric body/Mercury Sphere: 1226–506 BC
Astral body/Venus Sphere: 506 BC–AD 215

The Mystery of Golgotha in this schema would coincide with the equivalent (for Philosophia) of what would be age 19 in a human biography. We might imagine the life of Christ as related to the extremely potent time period between the first return of the Moon's Node (18.61 years old) and the end of the first metonic cycle (19 years old). A window opens for the human being at this time, when one so to speak "renews one's vows" in relation to decisions made prior to incarnating.

The next three life cycles are taking place over the course of the Age of Pisces (AD 215–2375), and the final three will take place over the course of the Age of Aquarius (AD 2375–4535). We will look more closely at these time periods, but first, we will turn our gaze to the mystery of the first two life cycles of the being Philosophia, which took place between 1946–506 BC (the development of her "physical" and "etheric bodies"). Did Rudolf Steiner give any indications as to the nature of these two life cycles outside of his lecture from *Artistic Sensitivity*, since he makes no explicit mention of them there? Why did the birth of Philosophia coincide with this time period: the start of the Age of Aries? And what developed during that time period that had directly to do with the Mystery of Golgotha, the fourth Sacrifice of Jesus and Christ?

Aries is related to the human head. The Age of Aries was a time period when the human head became particularly active. We can see this first of all in that the human being's pictorial consciousness totally faded, and was eclipsed by a perception of *thoughts* rather than *pictures*. This development reached its apotheosis in the Greek philosophers. On the other hand, the Age of Aries culminated in the birth of the human personality, which felt itself as centered in the head.

Can we try to understand the nature of these first two cycles, the "Moon years" and "Mercury years" of Philosophia, which Rudolf Steiner barely goes into during the actual lecture on the biography of Philosophia from 1915? The closest he comes to doing so is an allusion to pre-Socratic philosophers such as Thales and Anaxagoras who grasped their world philosophy in an elemental, temperamental form: for them, the origin of the world was found in a primal Water or a primal Fire. These philosophers were active when Philosophia was equivalent to the age of 12 to 14 years old (700–500 BC), transitioning out of the "Mercury years" of primary school into the "Venus years" of the teenage adolescent.

We can find an answer to the mystery of these first two "life cycles" of Philosophia by looking to two other lectures given by Rudolf Steiner five years previously, in 1910: the second lecture on the "True Nature of the Second Coming," from March 6 and the second lecture from the series on the Gospel of St. Matthew on September 2.[10]

From the first of these two lectures, we get the clearest indication as to why exactly the start of the Age of Aries marked the birth of the being Philosophia in the history of mankind. This is related to the Hebrew Patriarch Abraham, who was born and lived around the start of the Age of Aries, 1946 BC (emphasis mine in bold, editorial in brackets):

> ...at the conclusion of the first millennium of Kali Yuga [i.e., around the year 2000 BC], a kind of substitute was given for vision of the spiritual worlds. This substitute was made possible through the fact that a particular individual—Abraham—was chosen out because **the special organization of his physical brain enabled him to have consciousness of the spiritual world** *without* the old faculties. That is why in Spiritual Science we call the first millennium of Kali Yuga the Abraham epoch; it was the epoch when man did, it is true, lose the direct vision of the spiritual worlds, but when there unfolded in him something like a consciousness of the Divine that gradually made its way more and more deeply into his ego, with the result that **he came to conceive of the Deity as related to human ego-consciousness**. In the first millennium of Kali Yuga—which at its conclusion we can call the Abraham epoch—the Deity is revealed as the *World-Ego*.

So, we see that with Abraham, we have the birth of thinking that is attached specifically to the physical brain. The spiritual world is no longer perceived in a pictorial sense as something outside the human being; it now begins to be grasped as an internal reality of *World-Ego*. This new development in human evolution, this birth of Philosophia, is represented in the sacrificial lamb appearing to spare Isaac from the sacrifice. The lamb, Aries—the human head—sacrifices its perception of the spiritual world as an objective reality, and begins to turn itself to the perception of thoughts, so that the individual human personality (Isaac) can arise within the human soul.

This first cycle in the biography of Philosophia—the Moon cycle, the years equivalent to those related to the physical body in human development (0–7)—is consequently born with Abraham. In the three Hebrew Patriarchs Abraham, Isaac, and Jacob we might see an image of the first three years of child development, and the gifts of uprightness (Abraham), speech (Isaac), and thought (Jacob). The second half of these years, the equivalent of 3.5 to 7, are then spent in Egypt.

---

10 "True Nature of the Second Coming" is currently available from SteinerBooks as a CD audiobook, *The Second Coming of Christ*. Steiner's lectures on the Gospel of Matthew are available from SteinerBooks as *According to Matthew: The Gospel of Christ's Humanity*.

It is the departure from Egypt back into the Holy Land that marks the "change of teeth" of Philosophia. Moses is the figure who marks the end of the "Moon years," transitioning to the "Mercury years" of 1226 to 506 BC (equivalent to 7 to 14 in a human biography).

The story of the "Moon years" is the gradual establishment, the "codifying" so to speak, of the religious rite of the ancient Hebrews. Up until this point it had existed as a kind of golden thread, organically flowing from generation to generation through more or less direct perception and/or memory of the spiritual world. But with the life of Abraham this direct perception and memory is sundered. With the time in history between the lives of Abraham and Moses, we see the rise of the first alphabets—picture-writing to begin with, hieroglyphics. Writing came about in order to preserve the knowledge that was no longer accessible through direct perception. This process culminated in the Pentateuch, the first five books of the Bible written by Moses.

Here we see that the picture-consciousness of the spiritual world became *mythology,* a remnant of what was once perceivable. At the same time, we see written in exact detail the rites of the Hebrew people that, up until that time, had not been codified. What existed previously as direct inspiration from the spiritual world needed to be transmitted to, and codified by, a chosen individual for the sake of the many.

And so, although Rudolf Steiner first speaks of the ancient Greeks in relation to the development of Philosophia, it is in the ancient Hebrew peoples that we find her origin and her birth. Further confirmation of this is found in the second lecture mentioned above, from the series on the Gospel of St. Matthew. Steiner is here speaking of Zarathustra's incarnation in ancient Persia, some 5,000 years before Christ. At this time, Zarathustra had two pupils. To one of them he passed on his astral body, which bore within it all the mysteries of Space. This individual reincarnated as Thoth or Hermes Trismegistus, around the year 2500 BC. He originated the Osiris cult and much of the external culture of ancient Egypt. The other pupil received the etheric body of Zarathustra, which bore all the mysteries of Time. This individual reincarnated as Moses, who, along with the rest of the ancient Hebrews from Joseph onward, was immersed in the Hermetic culture of ancient Egypt:

> Now imagine the meeting between Hermetic wisdom and Mosaic wisdom in the ancient Egyptian Mystery centers. According to our spiritual–scientific cosmology, this event was comparable to one that took place in the cosmos. After the original separation of the Earth from the Sun, the Earth remained united with the Moon for a time. Later, part of the Earth moved out into space to form what is now the Moon. In other words, the Earth sent part of itself back out into space toward the Sun. We find a similar process in the strange encounter in Egypt between Mosaic Earth wisdom and Hermetic Sun wisdom.
>
> As Mosaic wisdom continued to develop after its separation from Sun wisdom, it developed into a science of the Earth and the human being—that is, earthly wisdom. In the course of this development, Mosaic wisdom grew outward to meet the Sun. To a certain extent, it received and absorbed the wisdom coming directly from the Sun, after which it continued to develop independently. Hence Moses remained in Egypt only long enough to receive what he needed. Then the Exodus occurred, so that his Earth wisdom could digest and further develop the Sun wisdom it had absorbed. We must therefore distinguish two stages in Mosaic wisdom: one stage when it developed in the womb of Hermetic wisdom, which it absorbed from all sides, and a post-separation stage, when it continued to develop independently after the Exodus from Egypt.
>
> Moses was born with the wisdom Zarathustra had given to him as the Earth initiate, and he was meant to find the way back to the Sun after imbuing this legacy with Hermetic wisdom. We are told that Hermes Trismegistus (later known as Mercury or Thoth) introduced art and science—exoteric knowledge and worldly art—in forms appropriate to his people. The wisdom Moses implanted in worldly culture also had to reach a certain level of development in ways

appropriate to the ethnic group that harbored it, but Moses was to achieve the Hermes–Mercury perspective in a different, even opposite way that developed Hermetic wisdom on its way back to the Sun. In a direct way (as if radiated from the Sun), Moses had received something of what Hermes had to offer, but he then had to redevelop it independently and imbue it with the Sun element.[11]

And so we can discover from the above quotation that the "Moon years" center around the meeting of the Hebraic Earth wisdom with the Egyptian Solar wisdom, like the Moon reaching out to the Sun from the Earth. Next, we come to the description of the second life phase, the Mercury phase, of the being Philosophia. This life phase centers on the time of King David, who is an image of the "nine-year change" in the life of Philosophia. At this time the Hebrew people transitioned to an age of Kings, to the "Solomon era," which comes after the "Moses era." Mythology slowly transformed into epic poetry. The law established by theocratic, initiate priest–kings transitioned into a monarchy: the roles of king, priest and prophet each separated, specialized and mutually influenced one another. We can see in the Psalms of David, in the Song of Songs, Proverbs, and Ecclesiastes a kind of proto-philosophy—part philosophy, part poetry.

Steiner describes the time periods of the "Mercury years" (1226–506 BC) and the "Venus years" (506 BC–AD 215) as such:

> Hermes Trismegistus (later known as Mercury, or Thoth) introduced art and science—exoteric knowledge and worldly art—in forms appropriate to his people. The wisdom Moses implanted in worldly culture also had to reach a certain level of development in ways appropriate to the ethnic group that harbored it, but Moses was to achieve the Hermes–Mercury perspective in a different, even opposite way that developed Hermetic wisdom on its way back to the Sun. In a direct way (as if radiated from the Sun), Moses had received something of what Hermes had to offer, but he then had to redevelop it independently and imbue it with the Sun element.

The independent development of Mosaic wisdom occurred in three distinct steps that are best portrayed in terms of cosmic processes. When events on Earth radiate back into space, they encounter first Mercury, then Venus, and then the Sun. (We know that the Venus of conventional astronomy is called Mercury in esoteric terminology, while what is commonly known as Mercury is the Venus of esotericism.) The first of these three steps is shown in the development of the Hebrews up to the time and reign of David. He is described as the royal psalmist, a divine prophet who was not only a man of God but also a sword bearer and a musician. He is portrayed as the Hermes, or Mercurius, of the Hebrews. In David, the Hebrew ethnic stream had advanced to the stage of producing an independent Hermes. In other words, Hermetic wisdom had reached the region of Mercury on its return to the Sun.

Anything that radiates from Earth toward the Sun encounters Venus at a certain point. Similarly, the centuries-old Mosaic wisdom of the Hebrews encountered a completely different element that flowed into it from the other side, from Asia, during the Babylonian captivity. At this stage in its development, Hebrew wisdom encountered a weakened form of Zarathustra's wisdom, which had persisted in esoteric schools of the Chaldeans and Babylonians. During the Babylonian captivity, Mosaic wisdom united with the esoteric knowledge that had found its way to Mesopotamia.

This event was different from the Mercury stage in that Moses directly encountered an element that had once proceeded from the Sun itself. In the centers that housed Hebrew wisdom during the Babylonian captivity, Moses (not the person, but the wisdom he left to his people) merged directly with the Sun aspect of his wisdom. At that time, the reincarnated Zarathustra was teaching in the Mesopotamian Mystery centers, which were available to Hebrew sages. Around the time of the Babylonian captivity, Zarathustra, who had relinquished some of his wisdom, was teaching in order to regain part of it. Zarathustra had reincarnated repeatedly, and in this particular incarnation as Zarathas, or Nazarathos, he became the teacher of the

---

11 Steiner, *According to Matthew*, pp. 41–42.

captive Jews, who were familiar with the holy places of the region.

Thus, as the current of Mosaic wisdom continued to flow, it encountered what Zarathustra himself had become after moving from the more distant Mystery schools to the Mesopotamian centers, where he taught the initiated Chaldean teachers and fructified the ancestral Mosaic wisdom of the Hebrews in his incarnation as Zarathas, or Nazarathos. Such was the destiny of Mosaic wisdom. It originated with Zarathustra but later traveled to a foreign land. The reunion during the Babylonian captivity was like a blindfolded Sun being carried down to Earth and having to retrace its steps and rediscover what it had lost.

Zarathustra, like all initiates, depended on the bodily instrument into which he incarnated. In his earlier incarnation, Zarathustra had expressed the full essence of the Sun and communicated it to Hermes and Moses. But in the Mesopotamian Mystery schools, where he was also Pythagoras's teacher, he taught in the only way possible in that particular body. In the sixth century BC, he needed a Mesopotamian body in order to teach Pythagoras and the Hebrew scholars as well as the Chaldean and Babylonian sages who had the capacity to hear him. Zarathustra's teachings as Zarathas were like the Sun's light reflected to Earth by Venus. Thus, Zarathustra's wisdom had to appear in a diluted version instead of its original form. Although it would reappear later in its original form, Zarathustra first had to acquire a suitable body...[12]

So, we see that the Venus years were inaugurated at the time of the reincarnated Zarathustra (Nazarathos) in the 6th century AD. Both the ancient Hebrew and the ancient Greek streams were given a kind of infusion of life at this time: Nazarathos taught both Pythagoras and the prophet Daniel. Yet each stream carried a different mission. The ancient Hebrews had the mission of cultivating a physical body that could actually bring to birth the individualized ego—the *promise* of the *first* sacrifice of Jesus and Christ finding its *fulfillment* in the *fourth* sacrifice, the Mystery of Golgotha, the birth of the human "I":

> We said yesterday that there were three different ethnic soul types in Asia: the Indians in the south, the Iranians, and the Turanians in northern Asia. We pointed out that these three types arose because the northern current of Atlantean migration settled in Asia and then spread out in various directions. But another current, which passed through Africa, also reached as far as the Turanian region. The conflux of the northern and African currents gave rise to a unique ethnic mixture, from which the Hebrews later emerged as the result of very specific events. We also described how decadent, superficial, and atavistic astral–etheric clairvoyance became evil in certain ethnic groups. Among the people who became the Hebrews, however, this clairvoyance was turned inward and took a completely different direction. Instead of working outwardly in the form of lower astral remnants of ancient Atlantean clairvoyance, in the Hebrews it developed in the right way and became an active, organizing force within the human being. Among the Hebrews, this force, rather than being expressed in decadent, atavistic clairvoyance, as it was in the Turanians, became productive and transformative. It reorganized and perfected the physical body in relation to consciousness.
>
> Thus, we can say that the forces at work in the physical nature of the Hebrews—reproduced from generation to generation through heredity—were no longer useful for external perception and had to enter a different arena if they were to remain in their correct element. The forces that had once given the Atlanteans the power of spiritual perception of space and spiritual realms and later declined among the Turanians into a remnant of clairvoyance were now directed inwardly in the Hebrew people. The divine–spiritual aspects of Atlantean culture now worked internally in the Hebrews, developing organs and shaping the body. In the blood of the Hebrews, this element flared up as divine consciousness within the human being. It was as if the Atlantean clairvoyant perception of the cosmos was turned completely inward and became the organ-based consciousness of

---

12 Steiner, *According to Matthew*, lect. Sept. 2, 1910, pp. 41–44.

Yahweh, the God within. The members of this little ethnic group felt imbued and impregnated by the God who pervaded space; they recognized this indwelling God united in the pulsing of their blood.

Yesterday we contrasted the Iranians and Turanians. If we now contrast the Turanians and Hebrews, we realize that the decadent element in the Turanians later became progressive when it pulsed in the blood of the Hebrews. Atlantean clairvoyant perception had perceived the divinity behind all beings. This divinity now became concentrated in a single point, so to speak, and was passed down through the blood of generations, through Abraham, Isaac, Jacob, and so on, guiding their destinies. A formerly outer element assumed a completely different form; it was turned inward, no longer seen but sensed and experienced. Instead of various individual names, it was called by a single name: "I AM the I AM." During Atlantean times, people experienced it anywhere that they were not—that is, in the world outside them. Now, however, they experienced it within, in the "I," and in the flow of their bloodline. The great god of the world had become the God of generations of Hebrew people, the God of Abraham, Isaac, and Jacob.

This was the beginning of Hebrew culture. Today we simply made a preliminary point about the blood of this people, which internalized all the spiritual factors that had previously pervaded human beings from outside. Tomorrow we will consider this culture's unique esoteric mission in human evolution. We will see the mysterious events that unfolded during its early stages and learn about the unique character of this ethnic group, from which Zarathustra received the body for the being we know as Jesus of Nazareth.[13]

THE FOURTH SACRIFICE

In contrast to the ancient Hebrews, it was the mission of the ancient Greeks to bring to absolute perfection the human astral body that had been born at the end of the Atlantean age. Their goal was to allow perception of thought to fully eclipse the ancient picture-consciousness. This perfected astral body could then be the solid foundation upon which the individualized ego could stand. The ancient Hebrews brought to realization the promise of the Ego given to them at the time of the first sacrifice of Jesus and Christ; but they would have been unable to do this without the perfecting of the astral body on the part of the ancient Greeks.

We see this perfecting and offering of the astral body brought to a single point—an individual, representative, sacrificial activity—at the time of Christ. The archangel Jesus once again offered his astral body to the Nathan Jesus, the vessel for Christ.[14] He had offered this astral body at the dawn of the Atlantean age in order to allow its force to flow down into the human etheric body, organizing and elaborating it, allowing it to separate off from the higher conglomeration of "bodies." During the fourth sacrifice at the time of the Mystery of Golgotha, the archangel Jesus once again offered this astral body—but this time in order to lay the foundation for something higher to be born: the human ego. Keeping in mind that Rudolf Steiner indicated that archangel Jesus was the same as the Apollo of the ancient Greeks, we could say that the Apollonian wisdom of Greece was offered to the representative Hebrew—indeed, the representative of all Humanity—in order to facilitate the birth of the individual human "I," the promise of the first sacrifice of Jesus and Christ.

At the time of the Baptism in the Jordan, the astral body of the archangel Jesus—in unity with the astral body of Gautama Buddha—offered a chalice into which the ego of Christ could descend. The descent of this ego—the *Eje asher Eje*, the Self of Selves—brought to fulfillment the promise of the first sacrifice of Jesus and Christ eons earlier during the Lemurian epoch, during which the physical, material body of the human being was formed and organized, and the seed was planted for the eventual unfolding of the personal, individual human ego.

Christ was the "first fruit" of the manifestation of the Ego—something that over the course of the next years would grow to become the common

---

13 Steiner, *According to Matthew*, pp. 44–46.

14 See Tomberg, *Christ and Sophia*, chap. 12, pp. 149–56.

property of all humanity. For the first time in history, each human being would feel themselves to be a unique, individual personality, with a unique, individual biography.

Once again we have a new formation of the human being, who now has a fully externalized and individualized physical body; a fully individualized etheric body; a fully individualized astral body; and the personal, "lower" ego has precipitated out from the three higher members of the human being—manas, buddhi, atman—which continue to be a kind of undifferentiated conglomeration, still in formation. They were—and up to the present, are—the transcendental and collective fifth member of the human being.

This separation of the fourth member expresses itself in the presence of two "eyes" in the human being. The lower self, the personality, is an eye directed below to the sense-perceptible world for the sake of the development of the self-conscious intellect. Increasingly since the Mystery of Golgotha, human beings have begun to feel that their thoughts are produced out of their own inner activity, not given to them as perceptions akin to sense perceptions. Meanwhile, the higher self, the conscience, is the eye directed above. The dim, intuitive stirrings of conscience are the expression of the higher self—the mixture of manas, buddhi, atman.

At the moment of Golgotha, with the unfolding of the individual, personal ego, the mission of the Hebrew people was fulfilled. Hand in hand with this, the fulfillment of the ancient Hebrew sacrificial rite had also come—the animal sacrifice, no longer being necessary, is done away with. The "old Law" is replaced by the "new Law" of the Love of Christ. It is this Love of Christ that maintains the unity and connection between the lower "eye" below and the higher "eye" above. A new goal and mission comes to humanity—for the life of Christ represents the beginning of a process that is the complete inversion of that initiated by the first sacrifice of Christ. Whereas at the first sacrifice, the seed of the Ego was planted as *future potential* so that the physical body could be *immediately organized*, the fourth sacrifice performed the counter-operation. Here, the seed of the transformed physical body—the Resurrection Body—was planted so that the *ego* could be immediately organized.

After the first sacrifice, an individual material physical body became the common property of each incarnating human being. In the meantime, a sacrificial rite had to be performed, in preparation for the time of the Mystery of Golgotha, when the individual personality would be born. During the fourth sacrifice, the individual personality—the Ego—now became the common property of each incarnating human being. And analogously, a *new rite* had to be initiated in order to prepare for the *seventh* sacrifice of Christ, when the transformed physical body—atman, the Resurrection Body—will become the common property of all humanity. It was the Holy Eucharist, the Mass of Bread and Wine that was instituted at this time. The Mass can never fundamentally be altered or replaced by any other rite—it is valid until the seventh sacrifice, until the Resurrection Body becomes the common property of all humanity, after which physical incarnation will no longer be necessary; i.e., it is valid until the "end of time," or "end of the age."

And so the religious ritual of humanity can be divided into two clear sections: the time from ancient Lemuria through the Mystery of Golgotha—until the Last Supper—when the Hebrew sacrifice was the most fundamental rite; and the time from the Last Supper until the beginning of the American cultural age, the "end of time"—when *material* incarnation (reincarnation, birth and death) will cease.

In the midst of the first portion, from ancient Lemuria through the Mystery of Golgotha (what could be broadly termed the ancient Hebrew era), we see the emergence of the ancient Atlantean rituals, in the heart of the Atlantean era between the second and third sacrifices of Jesus and Christ that book-ended this time period. We noted that at the time of the first sacrifice, Cain attempted to bring the Atlantean rituals too soon, while Abel brought the sacrifice of the Lamb—one that was appropriate then and until the Last Supper.

It is interesting that Cain attempted to institute the Atlantean rituals before their time—in a sense, you could say he played the role of a forerunner, giving a foretaste of the Atlantean rituals that were to come in a subsequent time. Now, if we turn our attention back to the being Philosophia, we see something similar occurring at the time of her birth, at the dawn of the Age of Aries in 1946 BC. We see there that Abraham met with Melchizedek, the Manu or spiritual guide in the transition from Atlantis to the post-Atlantean era. Together they shared an Agape (Love) Feast of Bread and Wine. Similar to Cain laying the foundation for ancient Atlantis in his sacrifice of the vegetable harvest, here Abraham lays the foundation for the institution of the Eucharist with Melchizedek some 2000 years prior to the Last Supper. But it was not yet time for this rite to become widespread—it was only preparation. Rather, it was time for the further codification of the sacrifice of the Lamb, shown to us in the story of Isaac's sacrifice being prevented by the appearance of a Ram in the bushes.

THE AGE OF PISCES

Returning to the biography of Philosophia at the time of the Mystery of Golgotha: if the "Moon years" of her biography lasted from the time of Abraham to Moses–Joshua (1946–1226 BC) and her "Mercury years" lasted from the time of Moses/Joshua to the Babylonian captivity (1226–506 BC), then the Mystery of Golgotha and the gift of the human personality occurred toward the end of her "Venus years" (506 BC–AD 215). In fact, we see that the life of Christ approximately corresponds to the time of the first Nodal return (18.61 years) and the end of the first Metonic cycle (19 years) in the normal human biography. The end of a Metonic cycle marks the time when the Earth, Moon and Sun have been in every possible relationship to each other, whereas the Nodal return indicates that the pathways of the Sun and Moon intersect at the place they did at birth. The human being is given a reminder at this time of pre-heavenly purposes and intentions—we might say that the ego flashes up at this point, and begins to express itself more and more strongly over the following years of the individual's biography.

This is precisely what occurred during the biography of Philosophia. The first three of her life cycles took place over the course of the Age of Aries. Aries is related to the human head, to the development of human thinking and the personality centered in the head. During the last third of this time—the Venus years, from 506 BC to AD 215—this development came to fruition. We saw the full flowering of human thought capacity in Plato and Aristotle: Plato's world conception directed vertically, to the realm of the eternal archetypes—to the One—and Aristotle's world conception directed horizontally, to elaborating every branch of science based out of a perception of those same archetypes as *immanent* in every aspect of external reality—to the Multiplicity.

However, after Aristotle, Greek Philosophy petered out. No one could top Aristotle. He had investigated and elaborated everything more thoroughly than any successor could hope to contribute any further. They could only pore over his work, trying to develop a complete systematism out of what he had brought. Aristotle's work was, through the life of Alexander the Great, transmitted to the Middle East, where it was preserved for a later time.

Afterward, and around the life of Christ, the decadence of the Greco–Roman era reached its height. It was as though the cultural flame had burned brightest in the Michaelic era of Plato, Aristotle, and Buddha, only to burn out completely. The entire culture devolved on the one hand into a hedonist paganism, devoid of any true relationship to the Spirit, and on the other hand to a martial law and order, an all-too-rigid Roman empire. It was into this compost heap of culture that the Christ-Ego was planted, to spring up and flourish mightily over the next 2,000 years. The Mystery of Golgotha marked the "flashing in" of the eternal mission—the pre-Earthly intention, the ego—of Philosophia.

Now we will look closely at the continuing biography of the being Philosophia. She has transitioned from the development of the head and thought perception in the Age of Aries (1946 BC–AD 215) into the Age of Pisces. Here she experiences the three Solar cycles of development, encompassing the equivalent of the years 21 to 42 in a normal human biography. Here the three realms of the ego—sentient soul, intellectual soul, and consciousness soul—unfold in turn. And what is at stake here? There is a movement, gradually, out of thought *perception* in the realm of the *head*, into thought *experience* in the realm of the *will*. We are now in the realm of the Fish: the feet, the will, the ocean of the subconscious depths. Human beings gradually came to feel thought as something produced out of their own depths, and not given to them by the cosmos as direct perception. Really, this is a coming to terms with the reality of the individualized ego, standing alone in the cosmos, in contrast to the experience of the Age of Aries, when thought perception simply built the stage on which the ego could eventually unfold. Human beings increasingly have to grapple with what this means in terms of the ego's place in the cosmos, and the true, fundamental nature of the ego itself.

The first solar cycle of the human being, from ages 21 to 28, marks the unfolding of the sentient soul, the lowest layer of the human ego. At this point, the human ego, the individual personality, is still relatively subconscious. One's personality is still very determined by and reliant on family, social group, etc, and not determined from within. This corresponds, in Philosophia's biography, to the years AD 215 to 935, the first third of the Age of Pisces. This time period sees a revisiting of the philosophy of Plato in the form of Neoplatonism. The striving of individuals such as Origen, Porphyry, Plotinus, St. Augustine, Hypatia, and many others is to bring the Platonic mode of conception into another, more mysterious realm of human soul experience. These philosophers noted that the entirety of human soul experience could not be encapsulated in mere thinking; there was another realm, the mystical or religious realm, that had equal or even greater validity to them, which could not be adequately accessed by human thought. And so Platonic philosophy was used in order to elaborate and understand Christian theology, the content of religious experience.[15]

It was also put into concrete practice by individuals such as Dionysius the Areopagite in the 6th century in a process called *henosis*, whereby what is not God, the One, is bit by bit negated within the soul. Thoughtful reflection is put to use to realize inwardly what is *not* God within the human soul until one is brought gradually higher and higher up Jacob's Ladder to the One—to the inexpressible Godhead of the World within the human soul. Whereas the Greek philosophers felt that the microcosmic perception of thought was an adequate reflection of the macrocosm within the human soul, the Neoplatonists and early Church Fathers saw thought as an inadequate reflection of the macrocosm. Religious, mystical experience in union with thinking more adequately expressed the wholeness of the world within the human soul. This time period was brought to its fulfillment by John Scotus Eriugena in the 9th century AD.

---

15 Much of what is in this paragraph and those that follow in this section is drawn from Steiner, *Riddles of Philosophy*.

The second solar cycle in a human biography is that of the intellectual soul. Here the human personality settles into itself, via the first Saturn return at approximately age 29.5 and the subsequent "Christ years" between ages 30 and 33. A balance begins to emerge between self and world, individual and surroundings. One no longer feels so merged with one's environment, heredity, and social group. One strives to establish one's profession and persona (mask) of adulthood, typically by finding one's career, partner, children, etc.

In the biography of Philosophia, this corresponded to the second third of the Age of Pisces, the years AD 935 to 1655. During this time period, there was renewed contact between Europe and the Middle East due to the Crusades. The Aristotelian world conception, which had been preserved in the Arabian courts, was transmitted back to the West from which it had sprung. It fell into the lap of the Scholastics—of the Franciscans and Dominicans in particular—exactly during the equivalent of the "Christ years" in Philosophia's biography (approximately the 13th to 16th centuries AD).

It was only during this time period of the intellectual soul development of Philosophia that mankind as a whole began to strongly and consciously experience the individual ego as the source of thinking rather than thought as a more or less outer perception coming toward the soul. Thomas Aquinas in particular took up the task of bringing into harmony *reason*, which is the product of human thinking (work), and *faith*, which comes to us from religious experience and dogma (grace). Human thinking cannot, out of itself, discover or create truth, but has been brought about as a faculty of the human soul that is able to *justify* the given truths of the spiritual world offered through religious dogma. Thomas Aquinas and the Scholastics subsequently christened Aristotelianism just as the Neoplatonists had christened Platonism some 700 years prior.

The aftermath of the Scholastics was twofold. On the one hand the German mystics such as Nicolaus Cusanus arose. The methodology of these mystics had a kinship to the *henosis* of Dionysius, but with a key difference. With Dionysius, the aim was to access a hidden part of the human soul that revealed more of the world than was accessible to human thought. The German mystics no longer sought this realm within the human soul itself; they wished to utilize and transform the thinking ego in order to access an *objective spiritual world* transcending the human ego. The ego was seen as separate from an objective spiritual world, rather than immersed in and interwoven with it.

Similarly, and subsequently, arose the scientific revolution of the 16th century, with Leonardo da Vinci, Giordano Bruno, and Copernicus. They too no longer perceived the outer world as though interwoven with a thought structure embedded within it, and likewise interwoven with the content of the human soul. They saw thought as something produced out of their own rigorous inner activity, and the sense world as something totally separate and objective over and against their individual, thinking subject (the ego).

Within the Age of Aries, the transition out of the Egyptian/Babylonian cultural epoch—and into the Greco-Roman epoch—took place in the 8th century BC. It was after this that the full flowering of thought perception, devoid of picture consciousness, took place—in ancient Greece rather than Egypt or Israel. Similarly, around this time in the biography of Philosophia, we see the transition out of the Greco-Roman epoch into the Anglo-Germanic epoch, in the early 15th century AD. And just as the last third of the Age of Aries (506 BC–AD 215) saw the full flourishing of ancient Greek philosophy, so the last third of the Age of Pisces has seen the full flourishing of what we might call consciousness of the Ego.

The third and last solar cycle in a human biography takes place from the ages of 35 to 42. It is the unfolding of the consciousness soul. Here the individual human being feels completely alone, yet (ideally) fully established in their proficiencies, conscious of their weaknesses, self-determining, creative, and capable. If not, a deep dissatisfaction, an existential ennui can become ever stronger. Here the choice is made whether to rise to higher levels of development out of one's own will and work, or to stagnate and devolve, to remain more or less a teenager for life. They may also increasingly feel the external pressures of life, may be increasingly wrapped up in, acutely aware of, and concerned by external affairs over which they wish they had more control. It is an intense time of life.

This time period was marked in the biography of Philosophia in the year 1655, when she transitioned into the development of her consciousness soul. We can see this as a kind of "mini-consciousness soul age" within the wider one of 1414 to 3574 (the Anglo–Germanic epoch referred to above)—the loneliest loneliness, the self completely thrown back upon itself. The year 1655 came right on the heels of the life of Descartes, who coined the *cogito ergo sum*, "I think, therefore I am." The keynote of Cartesianism was doubt: all that is not the thinking ego must be met with doubt and skepticism in order to discover its true nature, its lawfulness according to reason. The fundamental experience that cannot be doubted *is* this very doubting itself—I think, i.e., I *doubt*, therefore I am. Cartesianism increasingly came to split the world into two pieces: an extendable (i.e., measurable) outer world, and an unmeasurable/subjective inner world. Only what was measurable—i.e., sense perceptible and/or able to be described by reason—could be considered objective, and therefore true and real.

Notice that this Cartesian split went hand in hand with the transition from geocentrism to heliocentrism. Under a geocentric model, there was hierarchy and order intrinsic to the Universe. The spiritual world operated in the heights above, as expressed by the movements of the stellar bodies; the Earth was the center of this creative activity, and Man was the center of the Earth. There was a hierarchy of angelic beings expressed in the planetary spheres above; this hierarchy was reflected in that of Nature (man, animal, plant, mineral) and Culture (priest, knight, merchant, peasant) below. Reason and faith lived together under a happy marriage.

After Kepler, all of this changed. Kepler had a choice. He had before him the work of both Copernicus and Tycho Brahe. The Copernican model is the heliocentrism that we all know today. What this model subconsciously reinforced for the human being is: "You cannot trust appearances. You must abstract the mathematically accurate reality out of the sense perceptions that are deceiving you. The Earth has no special place in the world, and therefore you are not part of a hierarchy. You are not special; on the other hand, you are *free*—free to engage in self-determination and discovery through doubt and research." In contrast to Copernicus, Tycho Brahe had rediscovered the ancient Egyptian model of a universe with two centers: the Sun and Moon revolving around the Earth, while the rest of the planets (and the cosmos) revolve around the Sun. The acceptance of the Tychonic perspective would have led to a delicate interweaving between the Enlightenment mood of discovery without casting off the immanent order of the cosmos. Man would have been free to investigate and discover, to create and to question, but still would have felt himself an integral part of a whole. For a time these two cosmologies competed; it was Kepler's decision to adhere to and popularize the Copernican model that led to the "Cartesian split," and ultimately to the entire materialistic scientism in which our culture has been increasingly immersed ever since.

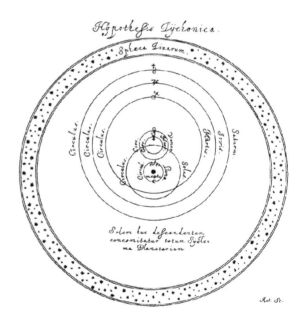

During the *last third* of the Age of Aries, we saw the emergence of Platonism, Aristotelianism, and the Mystery of Golgotha. These three together determined the course of the subsequent 2000 years, with the Christening of first Platonism (by the Neoplatonists) and then Aristotelianism (by the Scholastics). Have we yet, over the course of this *last third* of the Age of Pisces, experienced something analogous to Platonism, Aristotelianism, and the Mystery of Golgotha? Where are we *now*?

Let's recall that the life cycle of the being Philosophia first passed through the Age of Aries:

1946–1226 BC = Moon cycle (0–7). Physical body. The time of the Hebrew Patriarchs through the Exodus.

1226–506 BC = Mercury cycle (7–14). Etheric body. The time of the Exodus through the Babylonian captivity.

506 BC–AD 215 = Venus cycle (14–21). Astral body. Babylonian captivity, and the flowering of Greek philosophy, through the Fourth Sacrifice (the Mystery of Golgotha), up to the beginnings of Neoplatonism.

Notice that the first two thirds of the Age of Aries are building up to, and culminate in, the last third. Within the first two hundred years of this last third, both Platonism and then Aristotelianism are born and make their indelible mark on the world. They burn brightly but then fade away, subsumed by Roman decadence, transplanted to Egypt and the Middle East, and preserved for later times.

Then, in the last two hundred years or so of the Age of Aries, the Mystery of Golgotha occurs. The Fourth Sacrifice seems to come out of nowhere, from a totally different sphere than the world conceptions of Greek philosophy, and begins to upend and renew all European culture. While Greek philosophy—hand in hand and contemporaneous with Buddhism—represented the fullest realization of the human astral body that had been born at the time of Christ's third sacrifice at the end of the Age of Atlantis, the Mystery of Golgotha allowed the human personality, the crown jewel of Creation, to be placed *within* this astral body—the birth of the distinct Ego, the "I," the personality.

The Age of Pisces then proceeds to reconfigure what had been given as the fruit of the Age of Aries:

AD 215–935 = First Sun cycle (21–28). Sentient Soul. Platonism is revisited, sublimated, and christened through Neoplatonism and the early Church Fathers.

AD 935–1655 = Second Sun cycle. Intellectual Soul. Aristotelianism is revisited, sublimated, and christened through Scholasticism, the Renaissance, and the first Scientific Revolution.

This revisitation was necessary due to the fact that the human being no longer experienced world conception as a *perceiving of thought*, but as the product of *thought activity of the ego*. Just as *thought perception*, becoming more and more vivid, gradually occulted the picture-consciousness of the distant past during the Age of Aries, so now *ego experience*, becoming more and more vivid, gradually occulted the objective perception of thought that was common during the Greco-Roman Era, replacing it eventually with our modern—and highly accentuated—perception of the "I" as a unique, totally subjective core of our being, which *creates* thoughts through thinking activity, rather than *perceives* thoughts as an objective aspect of reality akin to sense perception.

This is a path initially of a feeling of independence, liberation, and freedom; and then doubt and skepticism; and then utter loneliness and lack of all meaning—an existential crisis *en masse*—unless one can discover, through inner activity, in what way the personality, the ego, is a member of the cosmos—and not an arbitrary member, but instead one that is vitally *necessary*. This is the mission of the Age of Pisces—to discover the place of the personal ego in the cosmos.

During the last third of the Age of Aries, we saw the sequence: Platonism—Aristotelianism—Christianity. On the one hand, this was the fulfillment and close of the mission of the Age of Aries; but, as we have seen, it also set the stage for the mission of the Age of Pisces. We can ask ourselves: do we see something similar developing during the last third of the Age of Pisces, the time period we are almost exactly in the middle of? Is there something analogous to Platonism that has developed? To Aristotelianism? And what about the Mystery of Golgotha?

The equivalent to Platonism for the Age of Pisces is, in its purest form, *Goetheanism*. It was Goethe more than any other who *experienced the ego properly,* as expressed in his essay, *Nature:*

> Nature! We are surrounded and enveloped by her, incapable of leaving her domain, incapable of penetrating deeper into her. She draws us into the rounds of her dance, neither asking nor warning, and whirls away with us until we fall exhausted from her arms...all men are in her and she is in them.... Even the most unnatural is Nature; even the clumsiest pedantry has something of her genius.... We obey her laws even when we resist them; we are working *with* her even when we mean to work *against* her.... Nature is everything.... She rewards and punishes, delights and tortures herself.... She has placed me into life, she will also lead me out of it. I trust myself to her care. She may hold sway over me. She will not hate her work. It was not I who spoke of her. Nay, it was Nature who spoke it all, true and false. Nature is the blame for all things; hers is the merit.
>
> When a man's healthy nature acts in its entirety, when he feels himself in the world as in a great, beautiful, worthy and cherished whole, when inner harmony fills him with pure and free delight, then the universe, if it could become aware of itself, would rejoice as having reached its destination and would admire the peak of its own becoming and being.

Goethe did not *express* or *elaborate* his worldview; he *lived* it, for this is what is intrinsic *to* this worldview. It has nothing anymore to do with the abstraction of the self for the sake of reflection and discursive argument; it is radically *immersed* into whatever is experienced, whether in the act of sensing or conceiving, until it is fully *brought to life again* within the ego itself. Goethe felt the ego to be the portion of Creation that has become aware of itself, and, along with Schiller, saw in science, art, and religion merely the human being carrying on the activity of Nature *consciously*, whereas all that had led up to the human being was this same human activity operating *unconsciously*. The human ego is Nature, aware of herself.

Whereas Platonism was a philosophical movement spearheaded by one individuality, one cannot properly say that Goethe or Goetheanism contains the whole of the Platonic equivalent of our time. It is not only Goethe but Schiller, Hegel, Fichte, Shelling, Novalis. The French and German Enlightenment, Weimer Classicism, and German and English Romanticism are all part and parcel of this grand Platonic flourishing at the beginning of this consciousness soul cycle of the being Philosophia.

But this Goetheanism could not last. Like Platonism, subsumed by Roman decadence and preserved in Alexandria until a later age, Goetheanism has been driven into the catacombs, subsumed by the modern, ultra-materialistic, Western mode of existence. And there it will remain until its time has come.

Platonism found its partner and counterbalance in Aristotelianism in the Age of Aries. The modern equivalent of Aristotelianism is Anthroposophy—the activity of Goetheanism vigorously and rigorously applied to each field of life. The contrast between Platonism, which seeks original wholeness, and Aristotelianism, which attends to the particulars of the present, is expressed in a modern form in the contrast of holistic Goetheanism versus thorough Anthroposophy. And just as Aristotle was *so* thorough in his application of philosophy to life that he left virtually zero room for the development and growth of his school of thought for thousands of years, Rudolf Steiner has left us a similar banquet feast and roadblock. It will take us a very long time to work through all that Rudolf Steiner has left us before we can truly, creatively, bring it to its fulfillment.

And why? Why was humanity not ready to work with Platonism and Aristotelianism until hundreds and thousands of years later? Because we were not actually *equipped* to yet. We needed the Mystery of Golgotha—we needed the ego, provided from an entirely different cultural and spiritual stream to the Greco–Roman—in order to properly *digest* and work with Platonism and Aristotelianism. It is the same with Goetheanism and Anthroposophy—it was impossible to work with them properly in the late 18th, 19th, and early 20th centuries, because we were not actually *equipped* to do so. What is it that human beings require in order to work with Goetheanism and Anthroposophy?

What we need is *manas consciousness*, the spirit self of the human being, which begins to experience the world in *living, imaginative pictures*. In other words, what we require is the *return, in full consciousness* of the picture consciousness that, between the Atlantean cataclysm and the rise of Greek philosophy, entirely faded. That is, this picture-consciousness must return *without* occulting the experience of the independent ego. We descended into the Hell of the completely isolated and dark ego—now must come the freeing of the prisoners and the Resurrection out of the tomb.

And here we come to the modern equivalent of the Mystery of Golgotha. Whereas that event—the Fourth Sacrifice of Jesus and Christ—involved archangel Jesus sacrificing his astral body for the sake of the birth of the ego, in our time the archangel Jesus sacrifices his *ego* for the sake of the birth of our manas consciousness. This presents itself as a kind of "swooning" in the spiritual world. The archangel Jesus has become a being with a twilight-consciousness, who can only awaken at the direct request of human beings who have become aware of his activity. As Valentin Tomberg states in a lecture in Rotterdam, January, 1939:

> An angel loses consciousness in the world of spirit; in selflessness, he sacrifices himself to humankind in such a way that his consciousness can be rekindled only when it lights up in the inner human being, in the conscience...the consciousness of the angel is lost, somewhat like fainting spiritually. And on Earth, humankind's moral life must be quickened as a means of preparation. There must be awareness of this moral stream that flows down. It will resurrect in human consciousness only when the deep-seated moral questions of human beings come to meet it.[16]

And as Rudolf Steiner stated on May 2, 1913:

> By means of what has been necessary since the sixteenth century for the Earth's evolution—specifically the ever-increasing triumph of science—something that is also significant for the invisible worlds has intervened in the whole evolution of humanity. With the triumph of science, materialistic and agnostic feelings (of greater intensity than had previously been the case) penetrated humanity. Materialistic tendencies had existed even earlier, but never of the intensity that became predominant in the sixteenth century. More and more, when human beings entered the spiritual worlds through the portals of death, they brought with them the result of their materialistic ideas on Earth, so that after the sixteenth century more and more seeds of earthly materialism were constantly carried over. These seeds developed in a particular way.
>
> Although Christ entered the ancient Hebrew race and was led to his death there, the angelic being who has been the external form of Christ has suffered a dissolution of consciousness in the course of the nineteenth century as a result of the opposing materialistic forces that rose into the spiritual worlds consequent upon materialistic human souls passing through the portals of death. And the emergence of unconsciousness in the spiritual worlds as the result of materialism in the manner just described will lead to the resurrection of Christ consciousness in the twentieth century in the souls of human beings on Earth between birth and death.
>
> In a certain sense, one can predict from this that, from the twentieth century onward, what humanity has lost in consciousness will certainly arise again for clairvoyant perception. In the beginning only a few, then a constantly increasing number of human beings in the twentieth century will be capable of perceiving the appearance of the etheric Christ, that is, Christ in the form of an angel. For the sake of humanity, something that can be called a destruction of consciousness occurred in the worlds lying

---

16 Tomberg, *Christ and Sophia*, p. 400.

directly above our earthly worlds, in which Christ has been visible between the Mystery of Golgotha and the present day.

One can say that, at the time of the Mystery of Golgotha, something happened in a little-known corner of Palestine that was in fact the greatest event that ever happened to all of humanity, but of which little notice was taken by people of the time. If something like that can happen, can we be surprised when we hear what happened in the nineteenth century when those who had passed through the portals of death since the sixteenth century encountered Christ?

"The seeds of earthly materialism"—which souls stepping through the portals of death since the sixteenth century have carried up to the spiritual world in ever-greater proportion, creating more and more darkness—make up the "black sphere of materialism." This black sphere was taken up by the Christ into his being in the sense of the Manichaean principle, effecting a "spiritual death by suffocation" in the angelic host among whom the Christ being has manifested himself since the Mystery of Golgotha. This sacrifice of Christ in the nineteenth century is comparable to the sacrifice on the physical level in the Mystery of Golgotha and can be designated as the second crucifixion of Christ on the etheric level. The spiritual death by suffocation that accompanied the dissolution of consciousness of the angelic being is a repetition of the Mystery of Golgotha in the worlds lying directly behind ours, so that a resurrection of the previously hidden Christ consciousness can take place in the souls of human beings on Earth. This return to life is in the process of becoming the clairvoyant vision of humanity in the twentieth century.

Christ consciousness can thus be united with the earthly consciousness of humanity from the twentieth century on, because the dying out of Christ consciousness in the angelic sphere in the nineteenth century means the resurrection of direct Christ consciousness in the sphere of the Earth. That is, the life of Christ will, from the twentieth century on, be felt increasingly in the souls of human beings as a direct personal experience.

At the time of Christ, a few people existed who could read the signs of the time and were able to understand the Mystery of Golgotha. They could grasp how a great and powerful being had descended from the spiritual worlds to live on Earth, passing through death, so that, through his death, his being's substances could be incorporated into the Earth. Similarly, today some of us can perceive that in certain worlds lying directly behind ours, a kind of spiritual death, a dissolution of consciousness, took place so that a rebirth of the earlier hidden Christ consciousness could take place in the souls of human beings on Earth.

Since the Mystery of Golgotha took place, many people can proclaim the name of Christ, and from the twentieth century on there will be a constantly increasing number of people who can communicate the knowledge of the Christ being given in spiritual science. Twice already Christ has been crucified: the first time physically in the physical world at the beginning of our era, and a second time in the nineteenth century spiritually, I have described. One could say that humanity experienced the resurrection of the Christ being's body then; from the twentieth century on, it will experience the resurrection of Christ consciousness.[17]

---

17 Steiner, *Approaching the Mystery of Golgotha*, pp. 27–30

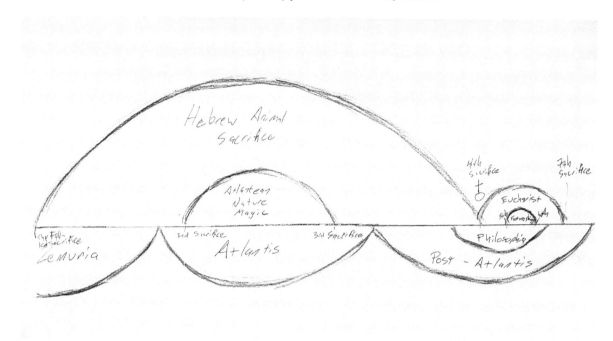

In Part II, in next year's *Star Wisdom*, we will try to understand what the equivalent in the Age of Pisces was to the Hebrew stream in the Age of Aries and, along with this, what marked the culmination of this stream in the 20th century in relation to the Fifth Sacrifice, Christ's return in the etheric. We will also look to the future, to see when and where we might experience the fulfillment of Goetheanism and Anthroposophy, the modern forms of Platonism and Aristotelianism.

Alongside of this, we will return to looking at the Sacrifices of Jesus and Christ from the point of view of *religious rite* and *preparation* for the developing members of the human being (buddhi and atman).

> *A star is above my head.*
> *Christ speaks from the star:*
> *"Let your soul be borne*
> *Through my strong force.*
> *I am with you.*
> *I am in you.*
> *I am for you.*
> *I am your 'I.'"*
> —Rudolf Steiner

RUDOLF STEINER AND THE CHRISTMAS CONFERENCE
ASTROLOGICAL ASPECTS OF THE LAYING OF THE FOUNDATION STONE, PART II

Krisztina Cseri

As we are approaching the 100-year anniversary of the Christmas Conference held from December 25, 1923, until January 1, 1924, by Rudolf Steiner in Dornach, new gates are gradually opening for our deeper understanding of the event. I hope that with my study I can give some additional inspiration to further individual research or spiritual deepening.

As I wrote in the first part of my study[1], there are two main issues on which I suggest meditating. One is the cosmic background of the Laying of the Foundation Stone as an "astro–psychological process"—a "cosmic initiation through the head" (to which I refer as a "Sirian initiation" in Part 1) brought to a close by the death of Rudolf Steiner; the other is the preparation of the individuality of Rudolf Steiner for the Laying of the Foundation Stone.

As I indicated in Part I as well, I can emphasize only a few moments out of the complex total picture, therefore my interpretation may suggest one-sidedness. On the one hand, however, the elaboration of the details may drive away the attention from the main thought-line; on the other hand, I cannot include the interpretation of all the details into a short article. Therefore, I will indicate only a few important points in Rudolf Steiner's life, where I see important correspondences. My assumptions will join in a way also to the ongoing issue of house systems, though not with the aim of a full elaboration of my own view.

II. THE PREPARATION OF RUDOLF STEINER FOR THE LAYING OF THE FOUNDATION STONE

In the first part of the study, I called attention to my view according to which the cosmic background of the Laying of the Foundation Stone was strongly related to the movement of Pluto around the perihelion of the Earth, which was (and is) also in conjunction with the meridian of Sirius. I regarded the Pluto–Sun–Earth–Sirius relationship as a quite unique and rare event. The other aspect of the issue was the examination of Rudolf Steiner's death in relation with the movement of Pluto. I stated that I think Steiner's death is strongly related to Pluto's last return to its positions at the Christmas Conference.

Maybe the reader could find other ways which could add further meaning to the described images. For example, if we appeal to the meditations on the Major Arcana of the Tarot,[2] the striking role of Pluto and Sirius as celestial sources of *intuition* can be meditated on also by means of the 19th Letter–Meditation on The Sun. The image of the *elliptic movement* of the Earth around the Sun can be associated with the 22nd Arcanum (the elliptic wreath on The World), and also to the 10th Arcanum (The Wheel of Fortune) which latter points to the Fall as an apside of the elliptical wheel (please recognize that the center of the wheel is not in the middle of the vertical spoke of the wheel on the image).

In this second part, in the first section my aim is to concentrate on the individuality of Rudolf Steiner through the correspondence of his embryonic life and actual life, as I recognize important etheric imprints in his time-organism which might

---

1 See *As Above, So Below: Star Wisdom*, vol 3.

2 Anon., *Meditations on the Tarot*.

indicate points of sensitivity in his personal preparation for the Laying of the Foundation Stone; this section will be introduced by a few thoughts on the hermetic rule and the house system. In the second section—taking the result of the first section as its point of departure—I am going to call the attention to the possible influence of a star, Dubhe, which seems not only to produce a linkage between St. Thomas Aquinas, Rudolf Steiner and the event of the Laying of the Foundation Stone, but may also point to a possible cooperative effect of Dubhe and Sirius in the background of the events in Rudolf Steiner's life. Hopefully, this second article can also provide an additional certainty about the significance of the leading participants in the first article (Sirius and Pluto), and that the Laying of the Foundation Stone is remarkably bound to the turn of 1923/24.

The hermetic rule and the relationship of the prenatal period with actual life

There is a very remarkable discovery about the relationship of the embryonic period and the life between birth and death, which was elaborated first by Willi Sucher and then by Robert Powell. The core points are the following:

- The hermetic rule specifies the importance of the Ascendant [ASC in what follows] and the Moon, stating that the zodiacal locations of the ASC and the Moon at birth become interchanged with the zodiacal locations (or their opposites) of the ASC and the Moon at conception.[3]
- New application of the hermetic rule: The ten lunar sidereal months of the embryonic period, during which the embryo is formed, prefigure ten seven-year periods of life.[4]

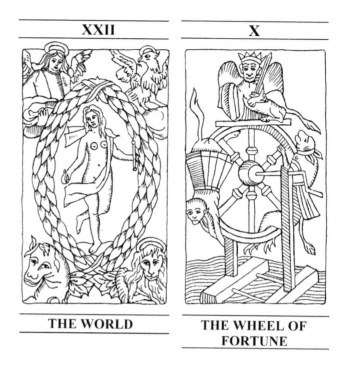

THE WORLD   THE WHEEL OF FORTUNE

This new method of examination entails the necessity of a completely new thinking method, since we compare a time period consisting of many snapshots to another time period consisting of many snapshots. We try to identify the background of an occurrence by taking into consideration the snapshots of the two periods, saying that the snapshots of the embryonic period provide archetypal images of the emerging events in the life between birth and death. This comparison between time dimensions of two types (i.e., two different quantities of time) means at the same time that the snapshots are not necessarily snapshots in the usual astrological sense (i.e., they are not classical horoscopes) between which a comparison could be made. Thus, it is not evident that two horoscopes (one taken from the prenatal period and one taken from the corresponding period of the life between birth and death) will show recognizable correspondences or that there are correspondences between them at all.

---

3 "There is an alignment of the Ascendant–Descendant axis at birth with the zodiacal location of the Moon at conception, and there is an alignment of the Ascendant–Descendant axis at conception with the zodiacal location of the Moon at birth" (Powell, *Hermetic Astrology*, vol. 2., p. 64).

4 Discovery of Willi Sucher in the 1930s (ibid., p. 105). "The implication of Willi Sucher's discovery of the deeper significance of the hermetic rule is that it is not just the stars at the moment of birth which are important for the destiny of the human being, but also the movements of the planets against the background of the stars throughout the entire period of incarnation between conception and birth" (ibid., p. 64).

These preliminary images as seeds come into being during the prenatal life in the etheric organism, and emerge during life—quite mysteriously—such that the dynamics of one day in the prenatal life corresponds to the dynamics of approximately ninety-three days in life between birth and death. That is, in four days of the prenatal period we can find the seed, or preliminary image of about one year of life. We must therefore know very precisely the prenatal period to receive any accurate inspiration regarding life between birth and death, as a few degrees (or even minutes) inaccuracy of the ASC (and thereby the whole framework of the horoscope) can distort the expected correspondences with life events by months or even years. It is quite a crucial point which makes difficult the decision about the usage of this method at all.

When we study transits projected to horoscopes or when we compare the horoscopes of individualities in synastry, we say that certain sensitive points are activated, primarily in one's astral body, by the celestial event or by the preserved and carried celestial condition in the aura of the other individuality. When we project the embryonic period to life between birth and death, in this dimension there is no actual transit or actual partner to activate the astral body of the individuality, but there is a program (or essence) brought from the past which evolves its effect independently from the actual transits.[5] And this program has a *framework*, which is determined by the birth intention at the midnight hour and set by the phenomenon of the relationship between the Moon and the ASC. *We know the birth ASC by the position of the Moon at the conception already(!), which is a momentous thing: the ASC has already a function at conception, and it is a secondary phenomenon—in the sense of time—what the human being sees at the horizon at birth.*

Therefore, the framework which can be seen in the birth chart is, in fact, already fixed at conception, offering a base for the coming into being of the program. This framework is called "house system" in astrology, but generally only in the sense of a planet-filled framework of the birth chart. I think it is advisable—in certain investigations—to separate the dimensions or developmental stages of the house system, which I will call here "will-pattern-framework" and "will-pattern-essence" (the former, therefore, is fixed at conception and the latter is a dimension of the birth chart) differentiating them from the concept of the "house system" which generally has its base only in the birth chart—i.e., takes into account the human being who has fully arrived on Earth.

It is important from the viewpoint of the structure of the framework that the soul is born to earthly life on the basis of the Moon ASC rule (hermetic rule), which *does not mention a criterion for the earthly location* of conception and birth. A particular time–space *intention* for birth is associated with a shift of a few minutes or degrees in the positions of the ASC/DESC and the Moon according to different conception–birth location–pairs. For example, if Rudolf Steiner's conception had taken place in Helsinki (Finland), then he would have been conceived on June 1, 1860, 11:59 (LT) in Helsinki and would have been born on February 25, 1861, 23:22 (LT) in Kraljevec. The same with a more extreme example, if his conception had taken place in Anchorage (Alaska, USA), then he would have been conceived—without an interchange of the ASC/DESC—on June 1, 1860, 11:58 (LT) in Anchorage and would have been born on February 25, 1861, 23:59 (LT) in Kraljevec according to the hermetic rule. Certainly, to different times there belong different positions of the ASC/DESC and Moon. At the same time, it is important to emphasize, that in the case of the house systems produced by means of the equatorial grid (see Placidus), the IC/MC axis *does not shift to the same extent* as the ASC/DESC axis for the different conception–birth pairs. In my examples I never found the same extent of shifting, even if the difference is very slight. Thus, in the case

---

5 Obviously, the actual transits also have effects on the soul, and furthermore these effects promote the manifestation of the seeds from the past. However, we do not necessarily find angular aspects from the transiting planets to the constellations belonging to the embryonic seeds (this applies to an actual partner, as well).

of the different conception–birth pairs the will-pattern-framework not only shifts on the zodiac, but it becomes different in its inner structure (i.e., houses of different angles come into being in it) in the case of a framework produced by the equatorial grid.[6]

I suppose that if the soul's intention for conception and birth can not be realized *altogether* (i.e., for both events) perfectly, then the soul chooses the closest solution, as a result of which the positions of the ASC/DESC axis and the Moon will shift on the zodiac. The question arises: *In addition to this shift* how could the soul adjust herself *also* to a house system with altered structure?

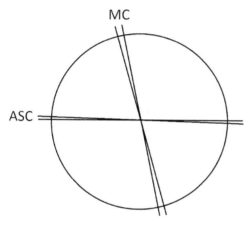

If everything happens according to the soul's preliminary plan—i.e., the soul arrives to Earth according to the circumstances of the planned conception and birth (including the locations as well), which is obviously the main rule, then the question still exists: What kind of force can determine for him an IC/MC axis—which belongs to his birth's time–space constellation—at the time of conception? In the case of the ASC/DESC axis the Moon constitutes such a force; however, I do not know another force for the other parts of the framework. It is not a question for someone who thinks of the house system only from the time of birth onward. However, in my understanding, the hermetic rule refers to the coming into being of the framework at conception. It does not say—for example—that where the Moon is at conception there will be the Sun at birth, it says that the ASC/DESC axis will be there, which is *the basis of the house system*. Although the IC/MC axis could hypothetically be known in advance if we assume "everything happened precisely according to the plan," nevertheless I cannot see any cosmic force attaching somehow to the IC/MC axis at conception. I can think only in the cross consisting of four right angles (in the context of the ecliptic) or the four equally sized segments of the sphere (in the context of the ecliptic grid) as an underlying space-force-system for the will-pattern-framework (of twelve segments), which are in harmony with the universal prototypes and forces, and which can be deduced from the Moon ASC/DESC situation already at conception, based on equal angles. The question has similarity to the question of the sidereal zodiac, where the axis of Aldebaran and Antares in itself determines the whole structure of the zodiac.

This is *partly* the reason why I do not use a will-pattern-framework of Placidus type in order to examine the relationship between the embryonic period and the life between birth and death (nor for other investigations). Summarizing briefly: on the one hand, the soul cannot keep the proportional structure of the framework for different conception–birth pairs in addition to the bilateral fulfillment of the hermetic rule, and on the other hand, I do not know what would determine the IC/MC axis of birth at conception (in the case of the ASC/DESC axis the Moon does so). At the same time, the vertical axis in right angle to the ASC/DESC is a given thing. I have to add that I think that the significance of the vertical axis is no less than the significance of the ASC/DESC axis—at

---

6 **Comparison for conception** (Kraljevec–Helsinki): ASC 24°48' Leo – ASC 24°46' Leo = 0°02' difference. MC 21°56' Taurus – MC 18°40' Taurus = 3°16' difference. **Comparison for birth** (Kraljevec – Kraljevec [conception in Helsinki]: ASC 19°35' Libra – ASC 19°09' Libra = 0°26' difference. MC 1°49' Leo – MC 1°14' Leo = 0°35' difference. **Comparison for conception** (Kraljevec – Anchorage): ASC 24°48' Leo – ASC 25°09' Leo = 0°21' difference. MC 21°56' Taurus – MC 18°55' Taurus = 3°01' difference. **Comparison for birth** (Kraljevec – Kraljevec [conception in Anchorage]: ASC 19°35' Libra – ASC 25°55' Libra = 6°20' difference. MC 1°49' Leo – MC 10°44' Leo = 8°55' difference (data by Astrofire software).

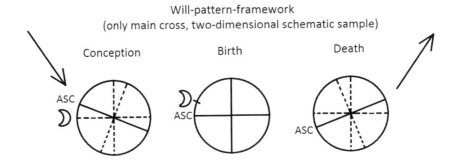

least concerning the framework appearing in the birth chart.

As to my understanding, the fixation is a postulate, for if the framework could be changeable, there would be no sense of the program that is written on the fixed framework. And there would be no sense of the projection of the embryonic period to actual life—assuming obviously that the will-pattern-framework is as important to the life of the human being as the starry background. (What I say here does not exclude the possibility of the examination of the relation of the elements of the will-pattern-essence at birth and the former "stage essences"—i.e., the examination of embryonic transits to the birth chart and studying their projection to actual life. That is, I make a differentiation between the meaning of the framework and the meaning of the dynamics of forces.)

In my interpretation, the soul remains in contact with the spiritual world from her conception till her death through the ecliptic grid, and she steps down on Earth only at the ASC/DESC, where the earthly horizon intersects the ecliptic. She is with one foot on Earth and with one foot in Heaven, which situation accompanies her whole earthly life. I think the "entity" of the will-pattern-framework is between Heaven and Earth—but rather on the part of Heaven, as conception means the first encounter between Heaven and Earth in preparing for actual life, and the ASC/DESC is fixed only by the Moon and not by the act of birth of the individuality.

As it turns out from the previous thoughts, I separate the will-pattern-framework and the will-pattern-essence. The former entity is born at conception (assuming that the hermetic rule is a reality) and the latter entity is born at birth when the human being has already evolved an etheric organism and his body has absorbed mineral substances. The will-pattern-essence is a much fuller or a much more earthly phase in comparison to its framework-like form, however we cannot set aside the existence of the framework-like form and its history between conception and birth.

This approach also points to the separation of a *dynamic* and a *static* viewpoint. We can study the relation of the embryonic period and actual life via the development of/in the will-pattern-framework, and we can study the general character of a person via the will-pattern-essence of the birth chart. An extended version of the latter viewpoint can be the investigation of the "preliminary will-pattern-essences" at stages in the embryonic life in order to differentiate certain "stage–characters" of a person in his actual life (see later in Steiner's case).[7]

Horoscope as an imperfect means of astrology

I think the clarification of the above thoughts would be necessary to begin the large and lifelong work on the theme of the houses.

---

[7] This also means that, in my opinion, there is no sense of a house system in a conception chart, as there is only a will-pattern-framework at that time without the essence. During the embryonic period there are preliminary will-pattern-essences that reach their full evolution at birth as a first step and during the corresponding life phases as a second step. (The framework cast for conception and measured from the ASC belonging to conception I cannot interpret at all, neither as a will-pattern-framework nor a house system—not excluding the significance of its few elements [see e.g., ASC/DESC]. I think the same of a death chart.)

As I also mentioned in the first part of this study, the circle of the horoscope on a plane is a necessary means for our researches, but can hide many perspectives that might contribute to the wholeness of the understanding of an individuality or an event. *Regarding time*: one horoscope can show a constellation for only one date, and it requires some effort to see through it (or through horoscopes cast for more dates) the past and the future relations in the case of a dynamic investigation. But at least, time is time, and there is no distortion in a horoscope regarding time. *Regarding space*: the form of the circle hides the real forms of movements and the real (i.e., proportionally real) distances of the planets and stars from the Earth or the Sun. Projecting the paths of the planets to the ecliptic hides the structural points as well, where the spheres encounter each other (at the so-called nodes of the planets). These are distortions of reality, even if we know why these distortions are necessary.

The largest structural distortion that can be done regarding space, and whose rationale stands on weak legs, is the house system. If the Poles of the azimuthal grid (Zenith and Nadir) are not on the ecliptic—that is, if something other than a point of the ecliptic was above the head or under the feet of the individual at birth—the distortion of reality by projection is unavoidable, and the further the Zenith and Nadir are away from the ecliptic the greater the distortion is. If someone is born under one of the Ecliptic Poles, he/she has no Ascendant at all, as the horizon is equal with the ecliptic. I think it is a fundamental problem regarding any issue of the houses, even though we assume that the plane of the Sun and the Earth (and the planetary spheres being roughly in that plane) has a kind of sucking force regarding the stellar influences and plays a role of a kind of cosmic heart meridian in right angle to the ecliptic meridians. Stellar forces lay down to the ecliptic plane to reach us (and our will-pattern-framework) and we (and our will-pattern-framework) also lay down to the ecliptic plane to receive them. I think that in the future we will investigate reality in more layers than the two-dimensional plane.

The investigations of the effects of the stars rising or setting at the horizon or being above our head or under our feet (or being at any angle in relation with us) leads to spherical trigonometry.

This structural establishment and consequent distortion of the real house system is why I think that there is *no ultimate solution* for the system that we interpret as house system today. I do not say that the two-dimensional house system has not got meaning for us or we do not need to deal with the two-dimensional house system at all, but I think we must be very cautious with *ultimate* conclusions regarding any content or direction of currents of forces in this framework or the structure of the system itself.

The reader might feel that there is a tension between researchers in this whole issue, which comes up in this publication periodically. I think a part of this tension comes from unclarified principles and the complexity of the question itself. The clarification would need a kind of round table conference where our questions (including the readers' questions) would stimulate each other for further elaboration and clarification of our views. This kind of mutual endeavor might lead to a synthesis on another level.

For my part—remaining with the two-dimensional horoscopes—regarding the structure, I have not been able to find a better approach than the equal-sized segments of the will-pattern-framework that is directed by the Poles of the ecliptic.

Regarding the content and the direction of currents of forces—I would elevate the question out of the "clockwise vs. counterclockwise" problem. I would think in *metamorphosis* of forces (and metamorphosis of content) instead of any antimony, and *viewpoints of examinations*. As there was/is both a transformation in the content of the houses and a transformation in the interpretation of the houses throughout history, a complex change cannot be identified only with a "change in direction," invoking the danger that someone would clearly and completely reverse the houses as they are interpreted in our time.[8] As the houses are

---

8 There is an author whose book is sometimes referred to in this question. He is Jacques Dorsan

the battlefields of our spiritual and material existence, where our "I" experiences these two aspects of life, we should see clearly how our material will (i.e., our will manifesting itself through our limbs and in the material world) goes through spiritualization in the vessel of the houses and in the mirror of the house contents.

My understanding is that there are only *transformations of contents* and *viewpoints of examinations* regarding the house system. However, it would lead out of the scope of this study to elaborate these questions. Nevertheless, taking into account the difficulty of this issue I would be quite satisfied if the structure of the framework could be determined for further investigations. In the following—through the case of Rudolf Steiner—I might add a finding to this issue which probably can help to get closer to a possible solution.

Rudolf Steiner and his vertical axis

The higher significance of the axis of initiative indicated by the Midheaven—considered from the standpoint of the zodiacal man—is the realization of God's will on Earth. "Not my will, but thy will be done" is the keynote of the zodiacal man in taking initiative. The significance of the Midheaven for the zodiacal man is that it is an axis connecting Heaven and Earth, whereby the connection is made through initiative taken freely but in accordance with the Being of God the Father. The initiatives taken are free, and they are creative deeds for the good of the Earth and humankind; they are deeds of sacrifice.[9]

When I studied the connection of the Christmas Conference and Rudolf Steiner's death, it came into my mind that there must be something also in his birth chart and in his embryonic period which indicates his preparation for his cosmic deed; if his death is in relation with this deed, it must be so important that his birth should also

be in relation with it. Obviously, there were many events which were important in his life and it is difficult to say what was more or less important. However, viewing from a larger perspective it is evident that the Laying of the Foundation Stone was Rudolf Steiner's main deed in the unfolding of his mission.

I think there is a basic line in his embryonic period, which can be seen as a main line of preparation of his individuality for the Laying of the Foundation Stone. This line is connected mainly with the Sun and Mercury. I will focus on these two celestial bodies in the following and do not take into account the effects of the other planets here.

The most striking moment in Rudolf Steiner's embryonic period was the time when, after 4 meetings (conjunctions) of the *Sun and Mercury, they met one last time on a day which is in correspondence with August 25, 1923 in projection. Then Mercury crossed the Ecliptic Nadir on October 9, 1923, and the Sun on November 10, 1923.*[10] These two phenomena—i.e., the Sun–Mercury conjunction and the crossing of the Ecliptic Nadir by the Sun and Mercury—are *separately* important.

It is a generally accepted view that Rudolf Steiner around the age of 63 could make a deeper contact with the starry world according to the seven-year cycles of biography—a contact which helped him to accomplish the Laying of the Foundation Stone. *On the other hand, there is a 1:360 probability that Mercury and the Sun reach the Ecliptic Nadir during the embryonic period precisely before this event in projection.* This crossing of the vertical axis at the Nadir point constitutes the *main point of departure and key to this study.*

What we describe here (concerning the Ascendant and Midheaven axis, with respect to the zodiacal man) comes to expression in the human being already long before the zodiacal period of life begins, but it does so in a much weaker and less far-reaching form...from around the age of twenty-one onward, with the emergence of

---

and he gave the title to his book: *The Clockwise House System*. Dorsan did not reverse the direction of the houses with their "original" meaning, which would mean a clear reversal. He made a mixture of the generally known house contents, which is not identical with a clear reversal.

9 Powell, *Hermetic Astrology* vol. 2. "Astrological Biography," p. 176.

10 This projection supposes that Rudolf Steiner's conception and birth data are correct and his ASC was really at 19°35' Libra, otherwise the dates shift according to the extent of the inaccuracy of the conception and birth data.

the self, the human being becomes increasingly capable of self-initiative—i.e., initiative born out of his self, and not instilled into him from without by others.[11]

At the other end of the vertical axis, we can see the passage of the Sun in 1877 in projection, then *the turn of Mercury touching the vertical axis (in a 21' orb) on the Ecliptic Zenith side.* Mercury was retrograde till August 20, 1860, 6:32 a.m. (Kraljevec) and turned at 19°56' Cancer.[12] *The projection of turning direct to life between birth and death indicates August 17, 1881, which is only half a year earlier than the date when he was 21 years of age, and when the "self-initiatives" could have begun.*

The significant events that occurred in Rudolf Steiner's life around 18 to 21 years of age (e.g., the experience of the start of the age of Archangel Michael, the meeting with his Master and the assignment by Karl Julius Schröer) are generally associated to his Moon's nodal axis return (18.6 years) and the start of his awakening Sun period (21 years). However, I think they are also in relation with the loop of Mercury in the embryonic period, which *touched the vertical axis* in connection with this actual life period. Here it is important again that most people reach 18.6 and 21 years of age, but the probability is very little that Mercury turns at the Ecliptic Zenith in the embryonic period in connection with the mentioned events.

The passing of the vertical axis by Sun and Mercury at the Ecliptic Zenith side shows a more complex picture than their movement at the Ecliptic Nadir side, owing to the loop movement of Mercury, the inferior Sun–Mercury conjunction in the loop and the turning direct of Mercury at the Ecliptic Zenith, which movements in turn deepened the stellar influences (the effects of the stars will be discussed later). Summarizing shortly, it seems that the inferior conjunction meant a preliminary seed, an "opening gate" toward Steiner's—probably most important—encounter with his Master, that was organized by Felix Koguzki. Responding to Rudolf Steiner's questions, the Master directed him to study Fichte's thought, to transform the dragon of materialism that had overtaken natural science and to take the bull of public opinion by the horns. It is remarkable that the spiritual flow of Steiner's Ecliptic Zenith point went into the sign of Cancer, about which he himself said that it is in connection with *materialism*. Arriving at the axis of initiative in projection, he got to know the "Rosicrucian will" through his Master and then he "put on the dragon's skin"—for the time being (as a young man) in the field of thinking and setting aims. At the other side, at the Ecliptic Nadir, the sign of Capricorn can be found, which is bound to *spiritism* and means at the same time *initiation*. Arriving here in projection—in opposition to his own initiation by his Master—he himself became the initiator of humanity at the peak of his lifework, at the turn of 1923/1924. Since the Sun crossed the Ecliptic Zenith in projection *before* the age of 21 of Rudolf Steiner, the power of this crossing can appear more weightless in the field of the will (in self-initiatives), than in the later period, at the Ecliptic Nadir. In my opinion, here the interplay of the celestial bodies (Sun and Mercury) and the stellar influence belonging to the vertical axis could leave a stronger imprint in the etheric body.

Another interesting point is that St. Thomas Aquinas died with a nodal axis of the Moon in alignment with Rudolf Steiner's vertical axis, with North Node (19°40' Cancer) in conjunction with the Ecliptic Zenith of Rudolf Steiner (19°35' Cancer).[13]

The Moon's nodes are in a special position among the other nodes of the planets since the Moon produces an intersection with the Sun–Earth sphere orbiting around the Earth and thus they are the closest to the Earth. The Moon's nodes

---

11 Powell, *Hermetic Astrology,* vol. 2. "Astrological Biography," p. 175.

12 It means that it did not touch exactly the axis which is at 19°35' Cancer, but was in a 21' orb.

13 It has to be added that Rudolf Steiner also died with nearly the same Moon's nodal axis, North Node being at 18°12' Cancer. I think that there is a strong emphasis on this point of the zodiac, and also on the stars along the nearby ecliptic meridians which run toward the constellation of Cancer.

constitute the nearest points of communication between the great universe and the Earth, i.e., the last step and "gate" from the solar cosmos toward the Earth and the same way back again. According to Rudolf Steiner they constitute gates between the astral realms of the cosmos and the Earth.

For me the question arises that since the Sun–Earth plane (the ecliptic) constitutes a kind of plane of communication not only for the whole Sun system but for the forces streaming from the starry world, and at the same time the Moon's nodes have quite a special position due to the closeness of the Moon to the Earth, how can we interpret the operation of the Moon's nodes in a narrower or in a wider sense. In my experience (as well as in some astrological literature), there is more emphasis on the interpretation of the Moon's nodes in the houses (narrower sense) than their interpretation in the zodiacal signs (wider sense).

In astrological literature, the main focus is on the life fields, which are bound together by the head and tail (its aim and its point of departure) of the life-stream (nodal axis) represented by the dragon or snake, and thus on the direction of striving or development of the soul (a karmic direction). According to the general interpretation, summarizing briefly, the Ascending node shows the desired aim, the mission of the soul, and the Descending node is in connection with the essence of the experiences of the past life.

Since the Moon has a great role in establishing and forming the will-pattern-framework (or the house system) according to the hermetic rule, it is not surprising that the interpretation of the nodes belonging to the Moon are highly connected to their positions in the houses (or along the axes). However, this does not exclude the wider interpretation either, according to which the Moon's nodes constitute gates to any kind of cosmic activity and impulse which come from the starry world and arrive to the sphere of the Earth through the plane of the ecliptic. And this is also obvious from the fact that the Moon itself brings the house system into harmony with the sphere of the stars through the points of ASC/DESC—i.e., the determination of the will-pattern-framework itself fits primarily to the stars and not to the planets. The spiritual interpretation also allows us to infer the orientations of the soul's sphere passages in the cosmos (its need to come into contact with the stellar effects).

In the case of Rudolf Steiner, the special situation is that the Moon's nodal axis at the death of St. Thomas Aquinas indicates a stellar orientation toward Dubhe (the Ascending Moon's node in the death chart probably points to *a dimension* of the aim of birth in the next life), which then returns in the vertical axis of Rudolf Steiner's will-pattern-framework at the next birth. (Certainly, we can deduce the alignment of the two axes only according to the sidereal interpretation, which is independent from precession.)

A few conclusions on the basis of the previous thoughts

On the basis of the study of Rudolf Steiner's vertical axis with the help of his embryonic period—and taking into account the alignment of the Moon's nodal axis of St. Thomas Aquinas—I arrive at three conclusions:

- I assume that Rudolf Steiner was well prepared for the Laying of the Foundation Stone as Mercury and the Sun implanted into him—into his "axis of initiative"—a receptivity to perceive the "word of the time" in his actual life.
- The study also provides a proof for me, that the vertical axis connected to the ecliptic grid *has* significance even if there can be another meaning of the IC/MC axis and there can be another framework belonging to it; otherwise, we could not see these remarkable occurrences. This finding provides a confirmation for the employment of the equal segment based will-pattern-framework (house system).
- Since the Moon's nodal axis at the death of St. Thomas Aquinas was aligned with the vertical axis of Rudolf Steiner at birth (and for his whole embryonic period) the question arises: Can there be other laws of astrological reincarnation, which take into account the house system (at least its main cross axes), in addition to the laws discovered by Robert Powell,

Rudolf Steiner and the Christmas Conference

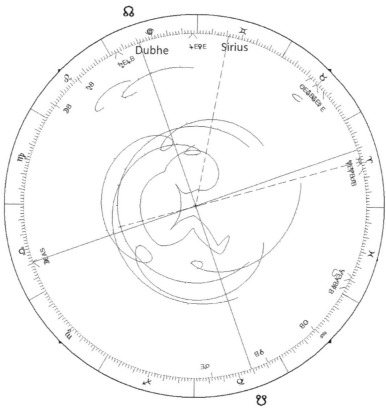

Birth of Rudolf Steiner - Prenatal Geocentric Planetary Distances
At Kraljevec, Latitude 46N22', Longitude 16E39'
Date: Monday, 25/FEB/1861, Gregorian
Time: 23:25, Local Time

vertical axis = Moon's nodal axis
at the death of St. Thomas Aquinas

which mainly take into account the planets' stellar positions and their angles?[14]

14 The evolution of the house system is in connection with the Moon and the Earth–Moon relation to a large extent, as the location of the embryonic period and the hermetic rule itself suggest. Based on my studies so far, the significance of the Moon-related structural points—i.e., the Moon's Nodes and the Lilith/Priapus (or points of apogee/perigee) also appear primarily in relation with the houses and their interpretation in the signs seems secondary. Therefore, in the case of the house-related reincarnation specialties, I suppose that these specialties may play a role in the alignments to certain positions (e.g., Lilith in a certain birth house at death and at the next birth, or Moon's nodal axis at death in alignment with one of the axes of the cross at next birth), however I have not got any experience. It is a great difficulty for this kind of research that most of the time we do not know the hour and minute of the birth or death *within the day*.

This issue leads to other questions regarding the "freedom degrees" of horoscopic dimensions and investigations. What can be the significance of the structural points and the planets in the houses at all? How different is their significance? What is more important for the soul: to have Saturn in a given house or Mercury in a given house? Knowing the discovered astrological reincarnation laws and the significance of the sign of the ASC and the Sun, there is quite little opportunity to have certain planet–house positions at free choice at birth. For example, if someone would like to be born with Leo ASC and Saturn in the 1st house (and with a given Sun position), he can be born roughly three times in a century, during the time when Saturn is in Leo (or in Virgo). Or thinking, for example, of a Virgo–Pluto generation, everyone with Leo ASC will have a 2nd house (or 1st house) Pluto position, he has no choice. (The direction of numbering of the houses here does not matter.) Obviously, it is also a question how the emphasis in astrological laws of reincarnation may change throughout human evolution.

Continuing with the issue of the passage of the Sun and Mercury at the Ecliptic Nadir. The classical interpretation of the Nadir and the belonging house can be summarized under the terms of family, nation, humanity and the Earth as our homeland, which is under our feet and which is our source of physical life. Rudolf Steiner took the free initiative at the Christmas Conference when the "karmic seed" at his vertical axis began to pulsate most strongly, which must have been—according to the introductory quote from Robert Powell—a "creative deed for the good of the Earth and mankind; it was a deed of sacrifice." At the same time there was another meaning of the Christmas Conference, a more personal one, which I think is strongly connected to the Nadir end of the axis. As Valentin Tomberg says: "Rudolf Steiner had made a deep karmic resolution to connect himself with this karmic community of human beings even more closely than before. By this deed he uttered the words that Christ Jesus once spoke to his disciples, namely, 'I will remain with you always, even until the end of the Earth.' This is the inner meaning of the Christmas Conference: that Rudolf Steiner remains with the human stream, which he had formerly borne as a cross, and into which he now entered. That is the *crucifixion*."[15]

This is why I stated in the first part of my study that the time of Rudolf Steiner's death is strongly related to the reception process of the Foundation Stone by his followers. He was like a good shepherd who had to wait, "until it is fulfilled"—which process I associate with the direct–retrograde movement of Pluto around the perihelion of the Earth and the meridian of Sirius from the astrological point of view.

For me the personality of Rudolf Steiner was a parental figure for humanity, who is a good mother or father, who accompanies his children on Earth and who made a new connection between Heaven and Earth during the Christmas Conference for the sake of our human evolution. He was an artist and a philosopher (as his birth Sun was interpreted in the 5th or 9th house in this Journal previously), but according to the "extended version of the static viewpoint of the will-pattern-essence of the birth chart" mentioned above, his "stage character" corresponding to this stage in his embryonic period indicates a member of the family, who took deeply on his heart the issue of his largest family—i.e., humankind, making a sacrifice for it. For me, personally, this "stage character" of him is even more important than his "general character."

I regard it also remarkable that Steiner held many lectures on reincarnation and karmic relationships between the Christmas Conference and his death, which can be associated with the spiritual dimension of the "family-related" house.

Sun and Mercury in the embryonic period

The direct and retrograde motions of the planets were partly discussed in the first part of this study in last year's edition of *Star Wisdom*, where the movement of Pluto showed remarkable significance. Though there are essential differences in the movements and effects of the inner planets and the outer planets, yet there are similarities, which are also true for the study of the movements of Mercury. For example, the extroverted attitude of the soul, the world of deeds, is characteristic of the direct phase, and the introverted attitude of the soul, the possibility for conscious processing of experience, the world of contemplation, is characteristic of the retrograde phase. In spiritual terms, in the direct phase the limbs of the human being grow, as it were, into the cosmos, while his head shrinks; thus, he encounters cosmic substances in an unconscious way in the spiritual realm of the will (an impulse is born in the unconscious out of the cosmos), while the human being gives his deeds arising from the seed of the spiritual impulse received in the previous direct phase and integrated (became conscious seed) in the retrograde phase. In the retrograde phase the limbs shrink back and the head grows; thus it is then when the impulses brought from the cosmic spiritual space can become conscious and can be integrated in the thinking of the human being (i.e., a seed is born in the head out of the unconscious). In a way similar to the outer planets, the inner planet

---

15 Valentin Tomberg, *Inner Development* (Anthroposophic Press, 1992), p. 112.

gathers sidereal substances in the direct phase, and the transmission of the sidereal effects toward the Earth occurs in the retrograde phase. However, in the case of the inner planets, it is not the conjunction and opposition with the Sun, which indicate the cornerstones of the cycle, but rather the superior and inferior conjunctions with the Sun.

In the case of the inferior conjunction of the Sun and Mercury the planet is between the Sun and the Earth: it is in the state of "New Mercury." In this dark time a new seed can be planted in consciousness. In the case of the superior conjunction, Mercury is farthest from the Earth and is behind the Sun: it is in the state of "Full Mercury." In this brightness can the fruits which evolved from the seed in the consciousness be manifested in their fullness. The result that is apparent here is a reflection of the action taken in the direct phase, based on the contemplation that was engaged in during the preceding retrograde phase. The result then remains in focus until the next "sowing."[16]

All those who experience the passage of the Sun (or Mercury) through the Ecliptic Nadir in the embryonic period, may experience a kind of deep union with the Earth in the corresponding time. We all experience the "Full Mercury" situation in the embryonic period, and this can gain expression in deeds of complete creative freedom during the actual life. *However, it is a rare case that the "Full Mercury" situation takes place in the immediate proximity of the Ecliptic Nadir.* In this case, symbolically speaking, the limbs of the human being (especially the legs) expand to the cosmic space in such a way that they—as it were—penetrate through the Earth. At such a time Mercury is not only furthest from the Earth in its orbit, but is below the Earth. This state of Sun–Mercury may represent a kind of pulling force for the spiritual space of the will to and from the depths of the Earth.

The sphere of Mercury culminates at superior conjunction and gets opened toward cosmic substances, which it then transmits toward the Earth. Rudolf Steiner could experience this in his embryonic period in terms of his will-pattern-framework as what the Earth completely obscured, that is, as if a fulfillment or opening had taken place deep in the Earth, or beyond the Earth. That is, for him, Mercury could draw impulses from the cosmic substances below the Earth at this point, which Steiner sensed through the Earth.

Concerning the embryonic life of Rudolf Steiner, therefore, the Christmas Conference took place at his "axis of self-initiative," and at its Nadir point (from the viewpoint of the movement of the Sun and Mercury), i.e., on the Earthly side and not on the Heavenly side. On the basis of the occurrences in the embryonic period I have two readings on this: on the one hand, the *sacrifice of union with humanity (entering the Society),* and on the other hand, the execution of deeds arising from impulses *penetrating deep into the Earth* and/or coming up from there (*renewing the Earth–Heaven relationship*).

While we can regard the Sun as the star of the "I," the activity of its nearest helpmate—i.e., Mercury, has a strong relationship with our astral body, which is the bearer of the soul. At the same time the activity of the sphere of Mercury is very complex and here I can mention only a few features. For example, it advances the plan of destiny evolved in the sphere of Saturn to become more human in us—i.e., the mysteries of destiny can manifest at the level of our thinking, feeling, and will. It has great significance in the transformation of cosmic intelligence into human intelligence—i.e., it induces sensitivity/receptivity in our soul so that cosmic intelligence can appear in our individual intelligence and initiatives, reaching the actions of the limbs. It further develops

---

16 This is an oversimplification. The process should be elaborated into four periods: from inferior conjunction to stationary direct, from stationary direct to superior conjunction, from superior conjunction to stationary retrograde and from stationary retrograde to inferior conjunction. I highly recommend the book by Erin Sullivan, *Retrograde Planets,* to work further on the spiritual dimensions of this issue with some psychological support, with special attention to the relation of the Mercurial movement to the switches between the left and right brain, to the turns or crossings at the threshold of the unconscious and conscious mind, and to the other image of the Mercurial movement which is called the Caduceus.

the philosophical way of thinking associated with Jupiter in the direction of rational, combinatorial thinking, which is a key factor to our participation in the material world. Through all these activities, the beings of this sphere greatly assist the present work of Archangel Michael, whose intention is that man shall have discerning ability in his intellectual understanding (in his thoughts and concepts) toward the revelations of the spiritual world and consciously grasp them.

Ultimately, regarding his intermediary role Mercury helps the work of the World Soul (or Holy Soul) so that cerebral intellectuality may unite with wisdom—i.e., Sophia, which union has then an effect on all areas of our life: the balance in our thinking appears in our world of feelings and will, thus the operation of the human soul and the World Soul can get into harmony.

Mercury traces a hexagram as seen from the Earth during its yearly orbit. The hexagram is the seal of Solomon, the symbol of Sophia or the Temple of Sophia.[17] The inferior conjunctions assist the process in which wisdom becomes conscious, becomes intellectualized (Mercury's triangle drawn near the Earth) and the superior conjunctions mean the unconscious encounter with cosmic wisdom in the embracing arms of the Divine Mother (Mercury's triangle drawn away from the Earth). The collaboration of these two triangles live in the work of the World Soul, which keeps the two in balance.

In the embryonic period of Rudolf Steiner—according to my understanding—it is the reverse of the classical (archetypal) interpretation of the seal of Solomon which appears, that is, one of the superior conjunctions points downward, toward the Earth (Mother), and one of the inferior conjunctions points upward, toward Heaven (Father).[18] This means that while Rudolf Steiner absorbed cosmic intelligence in his thoughts around 18 to 21 years of age (he embraced cosmic wisdom for his own development from the direction of Heaven—a Sophia impulse), at the time of the Laying of the Foundation Stone he performed a deed as a messenger of Heaven toward Earth for the sake of the evolution of others (Christ impulse).

He experienced two inferior conjunctions in his embryonic life: one in a tight orb in the direction of the Ecliptic Zenith, which is in connection with the end of 1878, the other in the 1st and 2nd segments under the ASC, which is in connection with the beginning of 1907. Interpreting the effect of the inferior conjunction up to the beginning of the direct phase, these times were characterized by seeking the path and planting seeds. The experience of the fight of Archangel Michael, the encounter with the Master and the assignment by K. J. Schröer may have initiated a process in Rudolf Steiner, which may have led to his doctoral dissertation as a primary fruit (1891), which is also considered as a prelude to *The Philosophy*

---

17 In fact, the symbol has a complex meaning. In a lecture, Steiner called the hexagram a symbol of the Holy Grail (*The Temple Legend*, Jan. 2, 1906).

18 In my understanding, the inferior conjunctions constitute the *archetypal* triangle pointing downward. If someone regards the superior conjunctions as the peaks of the archetypal triangle pointing downward, then he must modify the interpretation in the way that he interprets the encounter of the triangle of Mother–Daughter–Holy Soul with the point of the vertical axis pointing to the Mother. I have not found the exact association of the Luminous Holy Trinity with the Mercury hexagram anywhere so far. In fact, the interpretation of the phases of the pulsating, breathing process is nowhere linked *evidently* to Christ or Sophia (or the corresponding Holy Trinities).

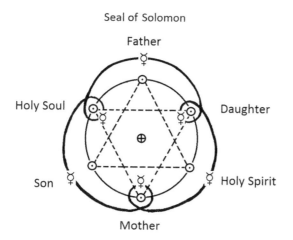
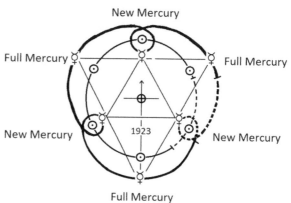

of Freedom,[19] and to the Christmas Conference itself as a secondary, more distant fruit. After the passage of the Sun and Mercury through the ASC and the beginning of the lecturing activity as a consequence of the events, the unsustainability of the compulsion to adapt to the worldview in the Theosophical Society (despite his authorization to form a Western esoteric section in 1907) may have been the next point of departure for him, which led—as if after a dissolution of the chained Prometheus—to his independent path, to the founding of the Anthroposophical Society, and finally to the events of the Christmas Conference.

It is important to see, that in the second case the superior conjunction—which means the experience of full creative freedom, seizing all possible circumstances for growth and expansion, personally, professionally and creatively—almost coincided with the passage through his "axis of initiative" as well, which makes this possibility even more unique, since the mobilization of the will is the strongest at the vertical axis (this "axis of initiative" is the main axis of the will in the will-pattern-framework). The crucifixion that Steiner may have experienced in his embryonic period at "Full Mercury," must have been living as a fundamental impulse in him to recognize the appropriate time for the initiation of humanity, for the establishing of a new connection between Heaven and Earth, and to decide to unite himself with the baptism of this new connection.

As I wrote in the first part of my study on the bases of Willi Sucher's researches, I regard the Apsides of the Earth pointing to the meridian of Sirius as quite significant from the viewpoint of the timing of the Laying of the Foundation Stone, where Pluto's mediation may have helped the cosmic turning point of time. Based on what I described there, I would say that the line of the Apsides is a kind of axis of initiative of the Sun–Earth relation, and therefore the personal initiation and initiative of Rudolf Steiner encounters at this point the initiation and initiative of humanity. From the viewpoint of humanity the initiation took place through the Head, while from the personal viewpoint of Rudolf Steiner it took place through the Limbs, by his free creative deed. In my reading, both Rudolf Steiner's destiny line imprinted in his etheric body and the possibility of connection of the Sun–Earth relation with Sirius through Pluto, points to the end of 1923. Thus, the event of the Laying of the Foundation Stone is remarkably *bound to a given date* both from the viewpoint of the actual cosmic situation and the individual preparation of Rudolf Steiner.

Rudolf Steiner took with him in his etheric body the will impulse that at the end of 1923 he had to do something concrete for human evolution. The effect of Mercury in the embryonic period (or rather the product of the period of Mercury from "New Mercury" to "Full Mercury") and at the

---

19 See Steiner, *Truth and Knowledge: Introduction to "The Philosophy of Spiritual Activity."*

25.12.1923 – 03.01.1924

(+ cosmic influx through Pluto from ca. 14.10.1923)

Sirius

Perihelion

Tree of knowledge

Tree of life

Aphelion

Path of Sun and Mercury during the embryonic life of Rudolf Steiner

Sun and Mercury at the Ecliptic Nadir in relation with 1923

Ecliptic Zenith

1890, 1881, 1878, 1862

ASC — DESC

1909, 1907

1923

Ecliptic Nadir

Laying of the Foundation Stone to the Jupiter existence in a Mercurial sense (see *Studies on the Foundation Stone Meditation*).

Here, because of the lowest peak of the hexagram (i.e., in Steiner's case, the forces of Christ pointing to the Mother) I would like to recall that the Laying of the Foundation Stone is also a key to the redemption of the entire Natural Realm (realms of the minerals, plants and animals), which is a task alongside the present and the forthcoming stages of Earth evolution. However, since the first great cosmic task is to accomplish the Jupiter existence, at first we have to redeem the numbness in the mineral world through the redemption of numbness in our own being. Rudolf Steiner gave the 12-sided Foundation Stone so that our "I" can awaken from its numbness and get into a new condition, to a living contact with the 12 currents of the zodiac. Mercury is in connection with our whole astral body, but within that, the thought life and the will life is most emphasized. Mercury can help us by its mobility both as an ideal and as a concrete influence of forces in promoting multidisciplinary thinking in thought life, which is the key for overcoming numbness that will ultimately result in external changes in Nature, and eventually lead to Jupiter existence. Mercury is the closest planet to the Sun. As the closest companion to the Sun, it is a constant pulling or driving force for us throughout the ages to reach the final stages of Earth evolution, the Spirit Man. "Mercury works from the unfathomable depths of human will–future up into the head of a human being" says Willi Sucher.[20] In the etheric body of Rudolf

same time the building stone of Sophia's Temple directing toward the Earth unfolded in 1923 in the fact that he recognized the need to build the spiritual temple in the human hearts. He recognized that the *heart* is the key to the *balance* between the cosmic realms and the Earth, on which balance the future is based.

As a preparation for the Jupiter phase of Earth evolution he planted the Foundation Stone into the Heart so that by the accomplishment of heart-thinking the human being may get closer to his higher "I," that is to Christ, and through the fusion of wisdom and intellectuality to intuitive thinking, which can constitute the proper thought-web to the base of our Jupiter existence, and at the same time can result in the development of our higher bodies.

The works by Valentin Tomberg can be of great help, on the one hand, in understanding the seal of Solomon drawn by Mercury—i.e., the essence of the Luminous Holy Trinity, and associating it with Steiner's aspirations (see, for example, *Meditations on the Tarot*, Letter XIX), and, on the other hand, in understanding the relation of the

---

20 Sucher, *Isis Sophia I*, p. 119.

Steiner this Sun–Mercury conjunction, referring to Earth evolution, may have contributed to the background for recognizing the actual cosmic time and to the mobilizing of his will for the Laying of the Foundation Stone, *precisely in 1923*. He himself became the "Messenger of Gods."

The significance of the final awakening of Ita Wegman in August 1923 may also be relevant. She represented the healing art of Mercury as well and gave impetus and strength—correspondingly to the imprint of the Sun–Mercury union in the etheric body—to Rudolf Steiner up to the Christmas Conference, which then was accomplished by Steiner *individually* (in parallel with the *independent* passage of Sun and Mercury through the vertical axis after their conjunction).[21] It would be interesting to know Ita Wegman's conception and birth time, and this way the movements in her embryonic period. When she was born (February 22, 1876), Mercury was retrograde at about 22° Capricorn, close to a 3° orb of Rudolf Steiner's Ecliptic Nadir—therefore also in conjunction with Mercury in Steiner's "stage-horoscope" corresponding to the Laying of the Foundation Stone (!). The appearance of the two *healers* in Steiner's life—at the two opposite points of the vertical axis—is also interesting: in 1879 Felix Koguzki appeared to lead Steiner to his Rosicrucian Master and in 1923 Ita Wegman helped Steiner to his initiatory deed.

---

21 Ita Wegman first turned to Rudolf Steiner with a question in 1904 after one of his lectures (Mercury is retrograde from 1904 in projection). After the Theosophical Conference in Munich in 1907 she had a conversation with Steiner when she said that she would "remain with him" (Mercury–Sun inferior conjunction in 1907 in projection). It was in August, 1923, in Penmaenmawr, when their karmic connection was revealed entirely for Ita Wegman and raised the question regarding the foundation of new mysteries. "It was Ita Wegman's destiny, to put this question which Rudolf Steiner then spoke of as the decisive question, a true Parsifal question, which made it possible for him to perform the deed." (Kirchner-Bockholt, *Rudolf Steiner's Mission and Ita Wegman*, p. 113)

Other remarkable moments in the embryonic period

If we focus on the other axis, the ASC/DESC axis of Rudolf Steiner's birth chart, we can see that during the embryonic period the two main participants who planted the seeds of the Christmas Conference at the axis of initiative, i.e., the Sun and Mercury, passed through the ASC around 1900 in projection. Mercury intersected it at the end of 1896 and the Sun at the end of 1900.

Rudolf Steiner wrote his doctoral dissertation *Truth and Science* (1891) and then *The Philosophy of Freedom* (1894) in connection with the Sun–Mercury superior conjunction. The passage of the Sun through the ASC was preceded by a "descent into hell," that is, an experience of the dragon's realm and an exhausting trial of soul following the work and fate of Haeckel and Nietzsche, which at the same time meant the profound test of the *Philosophy of Freedom* (the principles of Michaelic perception). This test corresponds to the general experience characteristic of the second phase of the direct movement. The inner struggle with the demonic forces and the direct experience of death forces may be closely related to the last segment before the ASC according to the classical interpretation of astrology—thus the "afterthought about the fruit" was associated with the deepest soul experiences.

The inner union with Michael not only helped Steiner in the inner struggle with Ahrimanic forces, but also led him to a concrete encounter with Christ at the end of 1899, after which a new phase began in his life on a more elevated level. The Sun reached opposition with Pluto in projection to January 4, 1900—which I will write about in the next section—when the Sun was in a 4° orbital conjunction with the ASC, which can be regarded as a conjunction, from the side of the last segment. The Sun passed through the ASC in December 1900 in projection, and Steiner began his esoteric lecturing activity around that time under the auspices of the Theosophical Society in Berlin.[22]

---

22 First esoteric lecture, Michaelmas day 1900, on Goethe's "Fairy Tale."

As for Mercury, after its first turning to direct motion in 1881, the second turn to direct motion took place in 1909 in projection, when Steiner withdrew from the Theosophical Society. So far, he had managed to smooth out the differences between the different views in the Society. He tried to bring Christ light into the oriental wisdom traditions, but as the anti-Christian attitude grew stronger, his efforts came to an end. He had to leave the movement to form his own group, where his teachings on Christ could be accepted.

Remarkable in the embryonic period is the passage of Sun and Mercury through Scorpio during this period. The two periods of Mercury from stationary retrograde to inferior conjunction (1904–1907) and from inferior conjunction to stationary direct (1907–1909) would require further elaboration—with particular attention to the appearance of the *artistic* elements in Steiner's work, which can be regarded as a feature of the retrograde period.

By November 1912 in projection, although the Sun was already in Sagittarius—and at the same time, according to classical astrology, in the 2nd segment under the ASC which is in relation with material stabilization of values—Mercury had reached only its third conjunction with the meridian of Antares coming out of its loop. By September 1913 in projection, it was still in a wide orb of Antares—just entering the 2nd segment under the ASC. On the basis of his fetal impulses Rudolf Steiner also had to raise the possibility of destructive forces against his works during this period that includes the laying of the foundation stone of the First Goetheanum. The forces of Scorpio usually provoke the destruction of the material plane, thus diverting humanity's attention from the physical plane toward the spiritual plane. Steiner's great etheric strength may have been taken away by the subsequent burning down of the Goetheanum, yet the fundamental impulse of Scorpio–Mercury inscribed in his etheric organism suggests the creation of spiritual frameworks without casting them into material form or with the danger of unsustainability of casting into matter. Taking into account the forces of Mercury alone—absorbed in his etheric body—they suggest an endeavor for this period which is aimed at creating a "spiritual skeleton" (with the awareness of the temporality of the material plane).

Connections with Sirius during the embryonic period

During the embryonic period, only the Sun and Mercury could touch the meridian of Sirius from a geocentric point of view. Mercury was in conjunction with the meridian of Sirius on June 19, 1860, which can be projected into Steiner's life at about the age of four, which is difficult to interpret.

The Sun was in conjunction with the meridian of Sirius on July 4, 1860, which can be projected at the age of eight years and five months (July 18, 1869). However, it is important to note that it is customary to interpret an orb of 1 to 2° regarding the meridian of Sirius (as I referred to it in Part I), therefore the period between the ages of seven and eight may also come into consideration.

Rudolf Grosse writes in his book *The Christmas Foundation: Beginning of a New Cosmic Age* about the correspondence of the events in 869 and the Christmas Conference. He adds that the anniversary of the events in 869 was in 1869, which was dealt with by Steiner, as well.

> ...even the free human being must have his place within the laws of history. Even he must take into account the possibilities offered by the situation in which he finds himself. Consciously and thoughtfully, he must consider how he stands with his own impulses at the present moment in history.

Some entries made in a notebook in 1924 reveal how Steiner looked back on certain rhythms of his life. On the first page we find the following calculation:

$$1869 = 8$$
$$869$$

The thought contained in these figures might be formulated as follows: A thousand years after the Council of Constantinople, in the year 1869, I was a child of eight. *My biography is linked to this thousand-year cycle.*[23]

---

23 Grosse, *The Christmas Foundation: Beginning of a New Cosmic Age*, p. 118.

It is difficult to find out how in the eight-year-old Rudolf Steiner would have emerged the need for continuation in relation with the events of 869 (the discussions in the supersensible world) after 1000 years had elapsed. Nevertheless, from Valentin Tomberg we can read in *Inner Development* that "it is a profound and remarkable fact that the childhood experiences of great personalities often foreshadow in abbreviated form what lies before them in the way of personal destiny" and he associates the event which appeared at about the age of seven, when Steiner saw a train coming in flames to the railway station, to the burning down of the First Goetheanum.[24] Perhaps the abbreviated form has an even more abbreviated foreshadowing in the embryonic period? Perhaps the encounter with Sirius in the embryonic period already brought two events that left a sharp imprint in childhood, which then reappeared at another level in the burning of the Goetheanum and the Christmas Conference?

In any case, Steiner writes in his *Autobiography* that the burning of the train had a great effect on him and left many unanswered questions. He was comforted for this mood when he found a geometry book in his teacher's room at the age of eight, which opened up a new world. "…and the theorem of Pythagoras fascinated me. I derived a deep feeling of contentment from the fact that one could live with the soul in building forms that are seen wholly inwardly, independent of the outer senses…The ability to grasp something purely through the spirit brought me an inner joy." "I can look back objectively to…using geometry to justify my talk of an 'invisible' world."[25]

It was probably at this time that Rudolf Steiner first encountered in his actual life the individuality of Pythagoras by means of the Pythagorean theorem. Pythagoras was a Sirian initiate (a disciple of Zarathustra), and it was then through him that Steiner was able to connect with the cosmic laws associated with Sirius. The Pythagorean theorem penetrates the mystery of the trinity of divine forces underlying the manifested world while revealing the quantitative relationship between the three sides of a right triangle.

The essence of geometry may have its basis in the implications of the orbit of one body around another body (as in the case of the Earth around the Sun), because this orbit suggests a circle and, consequently, all sorts of angular relationships, the basis of geometrical figures. These angular relations result in archetypal forms, and contemplation on them draws the consciousness deeply into the nature of the formative world, which precedes the manifestation of the material world and at the same time leads to cognition of divine creative processes.

The forces of Sirius are quite powerful in promoting expansions of consciousness and grasping infinite cosmic relationships. As a star of Zarathustra and a cosmic heart center, it embodies forces of mediation between spirit and matter. In this mediation between the two worlds, contemplation on geometry may have provided Steiner with confirmation of the relationship between the formative world and the spiritual world. This formative world became the home of the eight-year-old Rudolf Steiner at that time. The encounter of the two Suns (Sun and Sirius) may have served as a background for him to take the first steps in understanding the rhythms of the solar system in its cosmic context, which later led to a broad understanding of cosmic laws and to the Christmas Conference as a Sirian initiation. The triangle of Pythagoras became a dodecahedral-shaped spiritual temple.

It also happened in Steiner's eighth year of age (that is in an orb of conjunction of Sun and Sirius in the embryonic period) that he had his first occult experience, when he met in the waiting room his dead aunt asking for help. It was then that he began to consciously perceive the spiritual world, and this experience may have been the first gateway to the occultism which he later called "the occultism of the white path." This occultism for humanity and not for egoistic purposes appeared later in its highest level of development in the sacrifice of the Christmas Conference.

As I wrote in the first part of this study, I think that Sirius and Pluto (and the Pluto–Earth–Sun

---

24 Tomberg, *Inner Development*, p. 103.
25 Steiner, *Autobiography*, pp. 22–23.

constellation) played an important role in the Laying of the Foundation Stone. As a result, I sought not only the etheric traces of Sirius, but also the etheric imprint of forces inherent in the Pluto–Sun opposition. At this point, I found a seemingly complex phenomenon that emerges from the geocentric embryonic examination and calls attention to studies from the heliocentric point of view.

Pluto was retrograde for about 5.5 months in the embryonic period of Rudolf Steiner. *During this time it was only on October 31, 1860 in opposition with the Sun, which is in conformity with January 4, 1900.* Here we are faced (again) with the question of the orbs, on the one hand, and with the relations of the "stage essences" to the final essence appearing in the birth chart, on the other hand. According to the latter, the Sun was in opposition to birth-Pluto on October 30, 1860, which is in conformity with October 30, 1899. It seems that both dates refer to the end of 1899 when Rudolf Steiner had his decisive experience standing in the presence of Golgotha.

And just before this time, Venus was in conjunction with the meridian of Sirius from the heliocentric point of view (on October 30, 1860 in the embryonic period and on October 19, 1899 in projection). That is, the preliminary picture of the events occurring at the end of 1899 can be seen in the embryonic period in a Pluto–Sun opposition, together with a Venus–Sirius heliocentric conjunction. Since Rudolf Steiner stood at the presence of Golgotha at the end of 1899, the force relations ingrained in the etheric body may have veiled references to the memories of Golgotha, which may have reappeared in another form—in very similar force relations at the Laying of the Foundation Stone in actual life.

Robert Powell in his book *Elijah Come Again* (in the chapter *Holy Saturday—A Venus Mystery*, p. 105) explains that heliocentric Venus was in conjunction with the Moon at the descent of Christ into the Earth on Holy Saturday (which is at the same time a complementary image of the heliocentric Venus–Moon opposition at the Transfiguration). In relation to Venus, he highlights Christ's love for Earth and his love for the mysteries hidden in the depths, for which he sacrificed himself and descended into the heart of Mother Earth. The role of the Moon also stands out as the Moon is closest to the Earth and represents the karma and former wisdom of the Earth. The question arises as to how "Sirius (or the heart of Zarathustra) being present in the depths of the Earth" has a relation with the event of Golgotha, with the redemption of Mother Earth within, and what kind of impulses Venus invokes for us today from this relation when she is in conjunction with physical Sirius during the year.[26] In any case, this heliocentric constellation can be projected to Autumn 1899 from the embryonic period of Rudolf Steiner.

> During the period when my statements about Christianity seemingly contradict my later ones, a conscious knowledge of true Christianity began to dawn within me. Around the turn of the century this knowledge grew deeper. The inner test described above occurred shortly before the turn of the century. This experience culminated in my standing in the spiritual presence of the Mystery of Golgotha in a most profound and solemn festival of knowledge.[27]

The opposition of Pluto and the Sun took place just before the Sun could reach the horizontal axis (ASC), which could mean that after crossing the ASC Rudolf Steiner could add a completely new color to his teachings: his worldview was penetrated by the consequences of his meeting with Christ. From 1900 on, he began lecturing about concrete details of the spiritual world.

Dubhe and Sirius

Returning back to the vertical axis, which I interpret as being in a right angle to the ASC (i.e., the real Zenith point of the place of birth is projected to the ecliptic by the ecliptic grid and not by the equatorial grid, resulting in the Ecliptic Zenith), I recognized that if I follow the ecliptic line toward the Zenith point above Kraljevec I reach Dubhe (within 1° conjunction). I observed several times how the azimuthal grid and the ecliptic

---

26 For example, Venus was heliocentrically in conjunction with the meridian of Sirius within 2° orb at the time of Peter Deunov's birth.

27 Steiner, *Autobiography*, p. 188.

grid moved "on each other" around the birth time of Rudolf Steiner; that is how the Zenith above Rudolf Steiner approached the ecliptic meridian of Dubhe.²⁸ It became a grandiose picture for me, how the Pole of the azimuthal grid reached the meridian of the α-star of the Great Bear (Dubhe) (20°27' Cancer projected to the ecliptic) and how the horizon reached the α-star of Libra (Zubenelgenubi) (20°21' Libra projected to the ecliptic).

It is a remarkable thing that the two stars were (and are) in a right angle (89.7°) *in reality* (i.e., not in any projection) seen from the Earth, which again gives a new aspect. If we interpret the will-pattern-framework as a cross (i.e., the axes are in right angles), then the axes work together on the basis of their right angles in themselves, thus on the basis of the angle called "square" in astrology. The planes of the axes have immediate influence on each other—i.e., there is an immediate impact of any initiative (vertical axis) to the plane of contemplation (ASC/DESC), and vice versa, even if we can and must differentiate the effects. The two α-stars in right angle, very close to the ecliptic lines, which transmit the spiritual streams to Rudolf Steiner's cross, might mean a *strengthened stellar source for* his will-pattern-framework for his whole life, being incorporated to his will-pattern-essence.

Remaining with the crosses (right angles) there is also a remarkable connection of Rudolf Steiner's *ecliptic will-pattern-framework*. Maybe we can speak of another cross with which Rudolf Steiner was in connection? Concerning Hindu esoteric astrology, one author says that Sirius is *"technically the reflecting star of pointer star Dubhe."*²⁹ From the perspective of the birth chart of Rudolf Steiner it only appears that Sirius is in quite precise angles with the points of the ecliptic cross: it is at 19°22' Gemini, trine to the Ascendant at 19°35' Libra and in semi-sextile to the Ecliptic Zenith at 19°35' Cancer. However, in addition, it is close to square in its relation with Dubhe *in reality* (i.e. not in projection to the ecliptic).

When I was pondering on the striking role of Dubhe as a kind of directing star in Rudolf Steiner's life (and its striking role at the death of St. Thomas Aquinas), and simultaneously the role of Sirius in the seed experiences in the embryonic period, and the role of Sirius in the Laying of the Foundation Stone, I made contact with books on the mystery of Nabta Playa in Africa,³⁰ where again Dubhe is "a partner star of Sirius."³¹

Nabta Playa is regarded as the "oldest astronomical megalithic site" or the "oldest astronomical device" in the world.³² There are whole chapters about the connections of Dubhe, Sirius and the megalith lines and about the relationship of Dubhe and Sirius in themselves in *Black Genesis*. Although there are different calculations and hypotheses about the exact alignments and the purposes of the alignments of these "buildings" and the stars, it seems that every scholar emphasizes the mentioned connections with Dubhe and Sirius. "Sirius also coordinated simultaneously with the star Dubhe in the Big Dipper so that their alignments formed an approximate 90° angle. (This curious connection also had been noted by Wendorf and Malville; they commented that the megalith builders of Nabta Playa had a fascination with right angles.)"³³ "Indeed, any architect or designer will readily agree that right angles are universally recognized by humans, not least because they define, among many other things,

---

28 By the software Stellarium [available on www.stellarium.org] and then in my imagination.

29 Vaid, *The Secrets of Astrology*, p. 20.

30 Bauval and Brophy, *Black Genesis*.

31 "At first thought it might seem awkward for naked-eye astronomer–priests to simultaneously note a star (Sirius) breaking the horizon and its partner star (Dubhe) 90 degrees to the north and up in the sky..." (Pye and Dalley, *Lost Cities and Forgotten Civilizations*, p. 225).

32 "We are not proposing that the Calendar Circle was constructed eighteen thousand years ago, but rather that it commemorates two important dates in the precession cycle of Orion—4900 BCE and 16,500 BCE—with the former date being the actual date of its construction and use as indicated by radiocarbon dating and the latter date being some sort of memorial of an important event, perhaps a beginning in the history of those Sub-Saharan herders who came to Nabta Playa in prehistoric times" (Bauval and Brophy, *Black Genesis: The Prehistoric Origins of Ancient Egypt*, p. 53).

33 Pye and Dalley, *Lost Cities and Forgotten Civilizations*, p. 225.

the four cardinal directions of Earth. Sirius rising may have been marked by the star Alkaid in the Big Dipper from the seventh millennium BCE to about 4800 BCE, but after that date and until 3500 BCE the star Dubhe in the Big Dipper replaced Alkaid, and it was noticed that *Dubhe and Sirius always formed a right angle*. After that date, Nabta Playa and the ceremonial complex were abandoned."[34] "Today the precise angular separation of Dubhe and Sirius is *93.4 degrees*."[35]

The authors of *Black Genesis* constrained themselves in their conclusions to the significance of the right angle as a universal symbol and to a ritual called "stretching of the cord" in which the king and the priestess signed the foundation stones of a new temple.[36]

---

34 Bauval and Brophy, *Black Genesis*, p.63.

35 Ibid., p.130. Note: "Today the precise angular separation of Dubhe and Sirius is 93.4 degrees. Yet both Sirius and Dubhe are relatively close to our solar system, about 8.6 lightyears distant and 124 light years distant, respectively. Thus, they have a fairly large proper motion (the apparent motion of individual stars against the backdrop of distant "fixed stars"). Combining the best recent measures of their proper motions, we can calculate that Sirius and Dubhe are moving away from each other at a rate of about 0.34 degree per thousand years. About 4500 BCE, then, they were separated by 91.2 degrees, and they formed a perfect 90 degrees (a right angle) in the sky around 8160 BCE."

36 "Exactly how was this stellar alignment ritual performed? Was the king aiming his gaze at a star in the Big Dipper while, simultaneously, the priestess announced the moment of the rising of Sirius, after which the cord between them was stretched and the rods were hammered into the soil, thus fixing the axis of the future temple? A further clue to the ritual is that the pharaoh observed carefully the motion of a star in real time. Inscriptions on the Temple of Horus at Edfu, accompanying portrayals of the ritual, quote the pharaoh: 'I take the measuring cord in the company of Seshat. I consider the progressive movement of the stars. My eye is fixed on the Bull's Tigh constellation. I count off time, scrutinizing the clock.'… This is also what might have happened at the ceremonial center of Nabta Playa thousands of years earlier.… Then, when the alignment was achieved, the first observer was to fix the rod in the soil. Later, a row of megaliths would be set along this alignment. On another day, this ritual was repeated to set an alignment toward the rising spot of Sirius on the horizon as seen from CSA

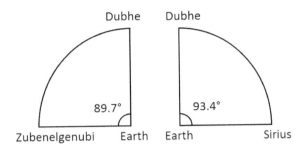

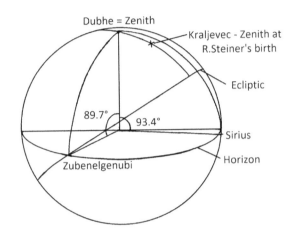

Dubhe and Zubenelgenubi have an approximately 89.7° angular direct effect on the human being, which is felt also in an approximate right angle by the ecliptic grid (Zubenelgenubi is on the ecliptic)—especially when the individual will-cross is aligned with the ecliptic meridians. On the contrary, the forces along the right angle of Sirius and Dubhe cannot also influence man in a right angle via the ecliptic grid, for Sirius and Dubhe are not in right angle in projection to the ecliptic. It means that if we assume that *the plane of the ecliptic is the essential factor* in transmitting forces toward man from the cosmos, the two stars cannot influence man in a right-angle effect. It is an interesting thing, since certain aspects

---

[Complex Structure A]. Thus, the two lines of stone work together, one going north (line A) and the other southeast (line B). This interpretation is consistent with the ancient texts that describe that the Dubhe alignment required realtime observing of the star in the sky, whereas Sirius rising on the horizon is more easily set. These two lines also form a rough right angle, a feature that surely would have been noticed and intriguing" (Bauval and Brophy, *Black Genesis*, pp. 128–129).

of sacred buildings were oriented to Dubhe (or other stars of the Great Bear) and Sirius parallelly, which can mean an intention of receiving forces from these directions at one and the same time—true, we don't know if they were only looking for the combined effect of the stars or the effect of the *angle* of the star forces, as well. Nevertheless, for the builders the ecliptic did not play a role in the transmission of the forces, the forces could be received directly (or also directly). In other words, the temples were oriented not to the ecliptic degrees where the stars are projected in human horoscopes but to the stars themselves. And if they sought for forces associated with the axis of the Earth, then they sought for *real* directions (North–South), and not the Poles projected to the ecliptic.

In spite of the fact that—in terms of his axis of initiative—Rudolf Steiner's perception could have been oriented either to the Dubhe direction or to the Sirius direction of the right angle at one and the same time *via the ecliptic* (and was oriented to Dubhe), it is imaginable that he searched for the connection with this angular relationship of Dubhe and Sirius through which significant forces are perhaps streaming toward the Earth (see later and in Part I).

As a consequence of the preceding, the question also arises as to whether there can exist other crosses (or other angles) in our microcosm in correspondence with the macrocosm (in correspondence with the Earth's relations to the stars), which have relevance even without the transmission of the ecliptic grid (or any other grid). When we examine the conjunctions of the planets and the stars, it is obvious that the ecliptic can play the role of the common ground (denominator), since the planets move along the ecliptic, and can "meet" with the stars on the plane of the ecliptic. On the other hand when we examine a will-pattern-framework (or individual cross, or house system, if you like), the question can arise how this dimension *really works*. I do not say that the vertical axis projected to the ecliptic is not a valid dimension; I say that there can be additional geometric forms (I think now mainly in crosses, but other angles cannot be excluded) in the human being, which do not appear in the ecliptic-based horoscopes, but can have relevance in man's totality and could be described only with the help of spherical drawings. And obviously it can be a question how these geometric forms can be activated by the movements of the planets or without the movements of the planets. In the case of the movements of the planets most probably along the ecliptic meridians—i.e., the ecliptic grid would be the bridge in our being to these angular effects when we speak of the activation of them by planets. Otherwise, depending on the revolution of the Earth and the place on the Earth, the rising, setting and other angular relations of the stars (and consequently their stronger or weaker effect) can get into direct connection to the will-pattern-framework living within us (which is the structure of our relations to the starry world basically without the planets).

In other words, the crosses (or other geometric forms) are existing in the relations of the Earth and the stars, but the question is how we can stand in the center of them, how the influences streaming toward the Earth in the right angles (or other angles) can affect us (with the help of the ecliptic grid or without the help of the ecliptic grid).

For example, remaining with Rudolf Steiner, the closest star above his head at his birth was HIP 48861-SA043117-HD86166-HR3929 with 9h49m09 right ascension and +46°04'34" declination. It was his "most real" directing star "at the top" of his vertical axis. If we see the azimuthal grid with this star as its pole, there are very significant stars along the horizon, which are in a rough right angle with this point. For example, the angular distance of Hamal, the α-star of Aries and HIP 48861 was 90.9° at the time of Rudolf Steiner's birth. In his horoscope we can see Hamal's projection only in a 7° orb of the Descendant, thus we can not recognize the right angle in the horoscope. Deneb and Vega were also along the horizon line, Deneb being closer to it at a 87.8° angle with HIP 48861. Deneb can be seen close to the Ecliptic Nadir in the birth chart in a 21° orb, which can not reflect the real angular distance of the stars (square with only 2.2° orb), due to the projection to the ecliptic. It means that if we imagine Rudolf Steiner opening his arms on the horizontal plane (in right angle with his upright standing), he is affected in the dimension of the crosses (in right angles) not only by Zubenelgenubi at his ASC, but these other stars as well (in reality and not by projection to the ecliptic).

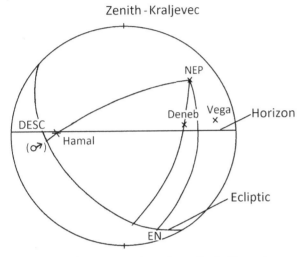

Again, I do not say that the ecliptic lines do not transmit the forces from the stars, I say that certain horoscopically invisible angles exist—formed by our relation to significant stars—and have an effect in themselves or can be activated by the planets in the human being, which can have an impact on the structure of the whole being of man—from the viewpoint of this article, on Rudolf Steiner. (Now in this view I fixed the vertical axis, and man can "revolve" only around his vertical axis, thus we examine the stars on the horizon—those in right angle to the Zenith point.)

Dubhe as transmitter of the Divine Will

Aside from the actual mapping corresponding to the azimuthal grid, it also follows from the preceding that I consider the location of the actual Zenith point on the meridian going through the Ecliptic Poles to be more important than the equatorial meridian on which this point is located in considering the will-pattern-framework.

If we combine the study of Rudolf Steiner's will-pattern-framework with the study of the forces flowing from the constellation of the Great Bear toward the ecliptic, we see that, while the meridian coming from the Celestial (Equatorial) Pole and going through the Zenith point are not related to any star of the Great Bear, the one coming from the Ecliptic Pole and going through the Zenith point also passes through Dubhe within 1° orb. Meanwhile, it is also in a 5° orb with Merak, while the equatorial meridian passing through the Zenith point is not so closely related to any of the stars of the Great Bear.

Here, of course, the question arises as to how important we consider the influence of the stars of the Great Bear to be (compared to other stars) and how important we consider the conjunction of the axis of the framework with the meridian of any star.

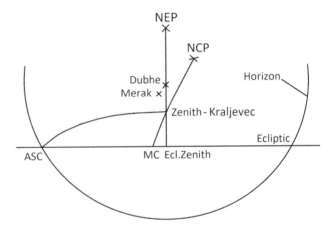

Since experience shows that the passages of the planets through the corner points of the framework (i.e., house cusps which include the main axes of the framework) have great importance, I assume that for the soul it is also important what star is the source of the forces that the planets transmit at these points during their passage. Furthermore, it is also probably important what kind of star forces flow from what angle toward the soul in the will-pattern-framework without planets.

Concerning the Great Bear, we are faced with a mysterious phenomenon. It is one of the three constellations that play a central role in oriental culture (Great Bear, Sirius, Pleiades). In ancient Indian culture, the seven Holy Rishis were associated with the seven stars of the Great Bear, which also means that the seven stars had different, yet extremely significant roles. In the 2008 spring edition of *Starlight,* we can find the statements of Valentin Tomberg and Robert Powell about the relationship between the seven Rishis and the seven chakras—i.e., the work of the seven sages on the development of the seven chakras. There is also a list of the modern representatives of the seven Rishis, associated with the seven stars—but emphasizing that the correspondence "is of a schematic nature and should be treated as such rather than something absolute" (p. 18).

This is an extremely interesting thing, as no other constellation can be found with such a resolution and association to sages or chakras.

We can read in Steiner's lecture: "If we, in the post-Atlantean time, look back into the ancient sacred Indian culture, we see the seven holy Rishis, in whose souls there lived something of an immediate perception of the spiritual worlds. Had one of the seven holy Rishis been asked about the fundamental mood of his soul, he would have said: 'We look up to the spiritual powers from whom all human development has proceeded. This reveals itself to us in *seven rays*'" (CW 143).

So Rudolf Steiner mentions seven rays, however I could not find these seven rays in another context outside the Rishis in his lectures. On the other hand, the seven rays have extensive literature from antiquity through Christianity to modern Rosicrucian and Theosophical literature, including deep psychology and works on various metaphysical healing techniques. These can be found by the reader at several places.

I found the characterization of the seven rays associated with the stars of the Great Bear only by modern theosophist Alice Bailey and her followers, and by a Hindu esoteric astrologer with whom I assume a relationship with Alice Bailey.

The modern occult literature following Alice Bailey seems to have the same order for the stars from the left to the right as appears in *Starlight*—and associates the rays to them in this order. I found the association of the Fifth ray to Dubhe at two places.[37]

Alice Bailey handles the Pointer stars (i.e., Dubhe and Merak) prominently in the evolutionary process, saying that they have an extreme role in transmitting the *Divine Will* toward the Earth, and the fusion of their energies is in line with the ultimate goal of evolution. They represent different aspects of the divine will, but, together with the Pole star (and through intermediary planetary and star forces), they form an interlocking directorate, potently effective in the evolution of consciousness.[38] It is interesting at the same time how the two stars are moving away physically from each other.[39]

According to the Alice Bailey literature, the main meaning of the Fifth ray is: "The Ray of Concrete Knowledge and Science" and "The Revealer of Truth." I do not have the experience to voice an opinion on the literature dealing with the seven rays, but for me it is quite clear that both the general characteristics of the Pointers and the meaning of the Fifth ray are consistent with Rudolf Steiner's activity. It is enough to think of his whole work and the Laying of the Foundation Stone as a culmination (transmission of the Divine Will—Great Bear, Pointers) or specifically of the establishment of spiritual science (Fifth ray—Dubhe).

I also suppose that the Great Pointer Generation, that is, those around whose birth Pluto visited the ecliptic meridians of the Pointers in the years around 1950, could and can relate to the teachings of Rudolf Steiner at a very deep level. At the same time, perhaps the cause of the tension in the spiritual communities lies in the distancing or in the different qualities of the two stars? In any case, it is those born in 1947 who can get to know the effect of Dubhe (separated from Merak) by means of Pluto as clearly as possible, since it is in their embryonic period when Pluto could first touch the vicinity of Dubhe (in

---

37 "Star V: Dubhe...there is strong reason to think that the seven rays should be associated with the stars in the order given above." (Robbins, *Tapestry of the Gods*, vol. 1, p. 20) "Dubhe is the emanatory of Fifth Cosmic Ray [Kratu Maharishi's manifested body]" (Vaid, *The Secrets of Astrology*, p. 51).

38 Bailey, *Esoteric Astrology*, p. 483.

39 Rudolf Steiner also speaks about the movement of the stars of the Great Bear, and in his drawings, we can see the moving away of Dubhe as well (*Interdisciplinary Astronomy: Third Scientific Course*, Jan. 11, 1921).

the last 248-year cycle).⁴⁰ And the Pointer Generation is most likely to tell what cosmic forces Rudolf Steiner incorporated into his etheric body by the motion of the planets (see Mercury's first loop at the Ecliptic Zenith, ca. between Merak and Dubhe, turning direct at the vertical axis connected to Dubhe), which in its final development (at the other end of the axis) led to the Christmas Conference.⁴¹

The question might arise as to whether the first loop of Mercury in the embryonic period projected to the end of the first third of Steiner's life, and the superior conjunction of Mercury and Sun projected to August 1923 *in themselves* are sufficient to signal the significant events, and in this case there is no need for any passage through the vertical axis of the will-pattern-framework (consequently, the mentioned events do not allow us to infer an equal house system).

According to my reading, the exact transmission of forces flowing from the Great Bear constellation through the ecliptic meridians toward the vertical axis can be very important for both the embryonic and the actual life, therefore I regard the stellar contact of the axis of initiative important (in case of the Placidus system this connection cannot be applied to any of the stars of the Great Bear); on the other hand, I consider the axis of initiative itself to be so important that it seems to me that an act of such a magnitude as the Christmas Conference had required the presence of the deepest impulse of initiative ingrained in the etheric organism, in addition to the Sun–Mercury conjunction. (The Mercury–Sun

---

40 In the scientific academic life, I found one prominent personality in connection with Pluto and the "Ray of Concrete Knowledge and Science" who was born on July 30, 1947, and thus the Dubhe impulse may have entered her embryonic life via Pluto early. She is Françoise Barré-Sinoussi, French virologist professor, who was awarded the Nobel Prize in 2008 for the discovery of HIV.

41 I regard it important to highlight a book by Dr. Dann titled *Masquerade* for further investigation of the forces flowing from Dubhe and Merak. In this book Dr. Dann compares the birth and death charts of the previous incarnations of Mr. X in Part 3 ("Signatures of Satan"). He calls the attention to the alignment of certain planets of Caracalla, Fernando Valdés, Joseph Stalin and Mr. X on the Cancer–Capricorn axis in a range extending from 20°16' to 21°51' (i.e., around the meridian of Dubhe) on page 82. He calls attention to the alignment of certain planets of Stalin and Mr. X on the Cancer–Capricorn axis in a range extending from 25°00' to 26°43' (i.e., around the meridian of Merak) on page 86.

I would add that the Moon's nodal axis was at 23°49' Cancer–Capricorn (in conjunction with the meridian of Merak) at the birth of Mr. X. And according to my calculation for the birth chart of Mr. X (February 5, 1962, 06:48 or 06:50 LT, Tobruk, Libya, corresponding to conception in Tobruk or Honolulu on May 7, 1961), the Ascendant of Mr. X is in conjunction with Rudolf Steiner's vertical axis within 1°orb. It is worth comparing Rudolf Steiner's embryonic "stage character" chart most relevant to the Christmas Conference (Feb. 1, 1861) with Mr. X's birth chart to perceive the possible opposite extremes of forces manifested through their individualities.

In the same way, it might be worth considering Mr. X's embryonic period for possible cornerstones of his life. For example, the *Sun passed only once through his vertical axis*, at its Zenith point, in the embryonic period. It corresponds with the *beginning of November 2008* in projection, which must have meant a decisive moment concerning his initiatives (vertical axis) and a possible growth of his publicity in larger scales (Zenith). In addition, reaching the conjunction of the Ecliptic Zenith and Neptune ("God of the Seas") may have symbolic significance for us. Another very highlighted point may have been the passage of the Sun across the meridian of Antares, forming at the same time a square with Pluto in the middle of Leo, which can be projected to July–Aug. 2015, which time was very crucial regarding Pluto's crossing of the aphelion of the Earth, as I wrote about this issue in the first part of this study last year.

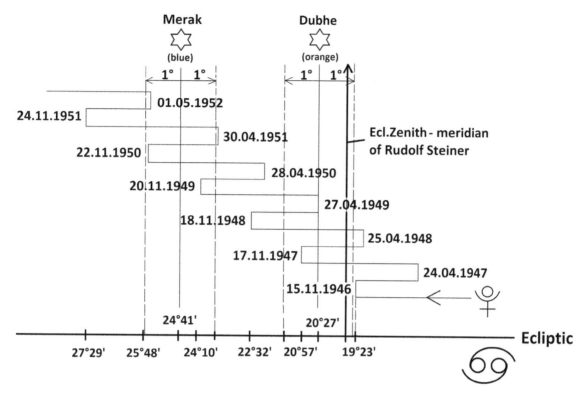

Schematic drawing. The movement of Pluto between 1946 and 1952.

conjunction may also refer to the relationship between Rudolf Steiner and Ita Wegman. After their ultimate "spiritual encounter" in August 1923, Rudolf Steiner laid the Foundation Stone *individually*.) It may also be of great significance that the Moon's nodal axis of St. Thomas Aquinas at his death coincided with this same axis. It requires further engrossment to detect the stellar nature of the seed which was sown in Rudolf Steiner at the Mercury–Sun inferior conjunction at the ecliptic meridian of *Merak* on the Zenith side of the axis, and what kind of forces exactly the whole loop represented for him in projection to the beginning of the era of Archangel Michael.

As I wrote at the beginning of this article, this study can provide only a few viewpoints for further elaboration regarding the content of the Laying of the Foundation Stone and our knowledge of Rudolf Steiner. It might be continued by the observation of the movements of the other planets and taking into account the heliocentric viewpoint in the embryonic period—or by elaborating the mentioned viewpoints further. My aim is to inspire

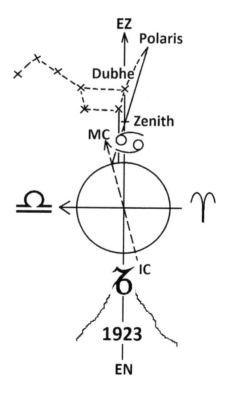

further studies regarding the spiritual aspects of this exceptional event and individuality from an astrological/astrosophical viewpoint.

I would like to express my acknowledgements and gratitude to Joel Matthew Park, who allowed me to publish my thoughts here, and who helped with the correction of my English writing to make the text more understandable.

> "When the Christ impulse entered the evolution of humanity in the way known to us, one result was that the chaotic forces of the sibyls were thrust back for a time, as when a stream disappears below ground and reappears later on. These forces were indeed to reappear in another form, a form purified by the Christ impulse.... Yes, a time is coming when the old astrology will live again in a new form, a Christ-filled form, and then, if one can practice it properly so that it will be permeated with the Christ impulse, one may venture to look up to the stars and question them about their spiritual script."
>
> —Rudolf Steiner (*Christ and the Spiritual World and the Search for the Holy Grail*, pp. 94, 122)

THE ARCHETYPAL LANGUAGE

RETURNING TO THE ORIGIN OF THE HOUSES, PART III

Joel Matthew Park

In the first part of this series of articles, "Saturn in Cancer" (published in *Saturn–Mary–Sophia: Star Wisdom, vol II* in 2019), I made the case that Rudolf Steiner implicitly promoted the use of a clockwise house system throughout his career. While he never explicitly described this system or called it by that name, he repeatedly 1) drew the twelve signs of the zodiac in clockwise order, even though they appear in a counterclockwise order when one actually looks at the ecliptic, and 2) referred to the Sun's *diurnal* passage through the twelve signs, even though it takes almost an entire year for the Sun to pass through the entirety of the zodiac. The only astrological framework which makes sense of both 1 and 2 above is a clockwise house system, where the names of the twelve signs of the zodiac are being used interchangeably with the twelve houses, such that Aries = first house, Taurus = second house, etc.

While most readers may have only heard of a clockwise house system via the relatively recent work of Jacques Dorsan (his *Clockwise House System* was published in French in 1984, and translated into English only some ten years ago), and might consider such a reversal of the "traditional" counterclockwise arrangement a trifling novelty at best, and a disruptive misunderstanding at worst, I also pointed out in this first article that in fact the oldest recorded treatment on the twelve houses promotes just such a clockwise ordering. Manilius describes a clockwise house system in his *Astronomica*, published in the first century AD.

In the follow up to this article, "The Tree of Life" (published in *As Above, So Below: Star Wisdom, vol III* in 2020), I expanded on this theme by attempting to flesh out my own intuitively perceived cosmological picture of the coming-into-being of the houses. My understanding is that the spiritual beings and forces within the twelve signs of the zodiac accompanied the Logos on his gradual descent into Earthly incarnation as Jesus Christ, radiating from the periphery into the heart of the Earth. Through the Deed of Golgotha, the twelve signs of the zodiac were concentrated, via Christ, into the very center of the Earth, to an infinitesimally small point—the realm of the Father in the heights returned to the Mother in the depths. At the moment of the Resurrection (approximately 5:45 a.m. [local time], April 5 AD 33), this concentrated, infinitesimally small point burst open, and in doing so the twelve signs inverted themselves around the axis of Aries–Libra. What once were ordered counterclockwise, radiating *into* the Earth *from* the periphery—the twelve signs of the zodiac—were now ordered clockwise, radiating *from* the Earth, *outward* into the cosmic periphery. I proposed naming the systematic study of and practical engagement with this *Earth*–cosmos "ecosophy," as the complement to the systematic study of and practical engagement with the *Stellar*–cosmos we know of as "astrosophy."

Ever since the time of Christ, there has been a great deal of confusion around both of these systems. Especially for ecosophy (i.e., the house system), it could seem as though it were stillborn, in that it was only understood in its proper clockwise arrangement for a century or two before the system of Porphyry developed in the second century AD. Astrosophy, over the past three millennia, has developed a strong archetypal language to describe itself and make itself alive for one's imagination. Thus far, ecosophy has had to borrow from this archetypal language, and while at times this can clarify certain features of the houses through analogy, it can also confuse the issue (e.g., Rudolf Steiner referring to the houses by the names of the twelve signs, thereby making it totally unclear initially that he is referring to houses).

In what follows, I will attempt to bring some further understanding to the genesis of the house system. First of all, we will again look at the descent of the Logos, the incarnation of Christ, and His Ascension in order to bring clarity to the birth, death, and resurrection of both astrosophy and ecosophy. Second of all, and out of the picture painted in the first part, I will suggest the archetypal language that is proper to ecosophy, one that has been gestating since the dawn of the age of the consciousness soul, but can only be properly recognized now, at the time of the Second Coming of Christ.

The Expansion and Contraction of Christ's Etheric Body

In the second part of this article series, "The Tree of Life," I drew attention to the fact that, hand in hand with Christ's gradual descent into incarnation, there was an increasing clarification of the science of sidereal astrology. As Christ descended from the sphere of Fixed Stars during ancient India, to the Sun during ancient Persia, to the Moon during ancient Egypt, to the Earth's elemental sphere during ancient Israel, and finally incarnated into the body of Jesus of Nazareth in the River Jordan on September 23 AD 29, the consciousness of human beings "descended" to Earth as well, out of lofty spiritual heights.

At the dawn of ancient India, humanity as a whole enjoyed a vivid pictorial consciousness of the spiritual world, while the perception of the physical world was hazy and dreamlike. These two forms of perception gradually traded places—clairvoyance became less and less intense, as well as less common, while perception of the physical world clarified and became more widespread. During the ancient Egyptian epoch, the Initiate–Priests who retained the clairvoyant perception of the spiritual world were able to "read" the stars directly. When they looked up to the starry heavens, they did not see bare constellations as we do today—instead they saw the activity of the gods.

By the time of Zarathustra in the 6th century BC, this clairvoyance had almost entirely faded, even for the Initiate–Priests (or Magi). It was Zarathustra's task to codify and structure that which had been an organically developed and intuitive "science" up until that point. Incidentally, mathematics was developed out of this science, so that the Magi could calculate the positions of the planets and stars in reference to the circle of the ecliptic. This science of sidereal astrology was put in place by Zarathustra in the 6th century BC so that his pupils (the future Three Kings) would be able to follow the star to his birth on March 6, 6 BC.

This science of Babylonian sidereal astrology made its way through ancient Greece over the next 300 years; along with Aristotelian science, it made its way to Alexandria due to the travels and conquests of Alexander the Great. Babylonian astrology and Aristotelian science thereby became dominant features of the culture of the civilized world for hundreds of years—that is, until the Muslim conquest of Alexandria in the 7th century AD.

Already before this time period, the Church after the time of Constantine in the 4th century AD had done their best to subdue and suppress the pagan knowledge stored in the Library of Alexandria. In spite of this, the writings of Ptolemy made their way to the Muslim peoples of Arabia; while Europe entered the time of the Dark Ages (5th–10th centuries AD) after the fall of the Roman Empire, the treasures of the Greco–Roman culture were preserved—albeit in a static, caricatured form—in the Middle East, waiting like a seed for the right conditions to begin germinating. Besides a brief interaction between the European and Arabian worlds in the realm of astrology in the time of Parzival (between Kyot and Arabel, while Kyot was in captivity by the Saracens), this science more or less died to the West until the time of the Crusades in the 11th century.

The situation is similar in the case of the newly born science of ecosophy: the original house system comes into being in the work of Manilius in the first century AD (his *Astronomica* was written between AD 30 and 40). Soon afterward, however, there are already distortions in the dominant house system: the astrologer Vettius Valens proposes a counterclockwise house system in the 2nd century (one that is later attributed to the Neoplatonic philosopher Porphyry of Tyros). This becomes the dominant house system up through the time of the Dark Ages, when the houses are forgotten in Europe along with the rest of the "pagan sciences."

It is most illuminating to look at this history of astrology in the West in the light of Robert Powell's indications concerning the etheric body of Christ after his Ascension on May 14 AD 33:

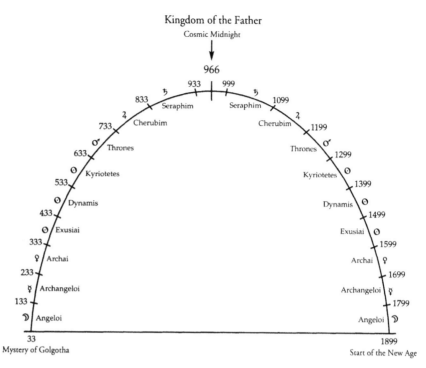

...The 100-year rhythm is the length of time needed for three phases of the Christ impulse to unfold, namely on the levels of thought, feeling, and will, each phase lasting 33⅓ years. The 100-year rhythm is thus the key rhythm relating to the expansion of Christ's etheric body through the cosmos, through the nine ranks of the spiritual hierarchies, and through the planetary spheres.

The expansion started after the Mystery of Golgotha in AD 33. Without following it in detail, the expansion through the Moon sphere—the lowest planetary sphere, that of the Angels—took place in the period AD 33 to 133. And the expansion through the Saturn sphere—the highest planetary sphere, that of the Seraphim—took place between 833 and 933. In the following 33⅓-year period, from 933 to 966, the life of Jesus Christ—inscribed in his etheric body—was imprinted into the zodiacal realm of the fixed stars beyond the planetary spheres, this imprint serving as the highest archetype of human biography. The year 966 signified the turning point in the expansion of Christ's etheric body. It denotes the "midnight hour" of his existence between First and Second Comings.

The period 966 to 999 in the fixed-star world mirrored the period between 933 and 966, and in the year 999 there began the descent through the planetary spheres, through the nine ranks of the spiritual hierarchies, following the 100-year rhythm. The period 999 to 1099 signified the descent through the Saturn sphere, that of the Seraphim. And the interval from 1799 to 1899 was the time of the descent of Christ's etheric body through the Moon sphere, that of the Angels. There is thus a perfect mirroring between the stages of ascent and descent of the Christ (see figure).

A study of the dates of the stages of ascent and descent of Christ's etheric body reveals that they frequently coincide with important turning points in the history of Christianity. For example, Rudolf Steiner spoke repeatedly of the significance of the year 333, when the Christ impulse entered the Sun sphere. This was preceded by the expansion of Christ's etheric body through the Moon sphere (33–133), the Mercury sphere (133–233), and the Venus sphere (233–333). The First Ecumenical Council, held in Constantinople in the year 325 (after which Christianity became more and more the state religion of the Roman Empire after severe persecution during the first three centuries), coincided closely with AD 333. The Ecumenical Council in 325 was a more outward event; Rudolf Steiner referred to a more hidden event that took place around the year 333: a council of Christian initiates at the Black Sea, which was decisive for esoteric Christianity.

The expansion of Christ's etheric body through the Sun sphere, with its three hierarchies of spiritual beings, lasted 300 (3×100) years, from 333 to 633. This was followed by the passage through the Mars sphere, from 633 to 733. This period was characterized by the conflict with Islam. Mohammed died in 632 and Islam began to expand rapidly, spreading to Spain and threatening to penetrate into France across the Pyrenees. However, the tide of Islamic expansion was turned in 732, when Charles Martel defeated the invading Arabs at the battle of Poitiers. This decisive moment coincided with the end of the Mars period in the expansion of Christ's etheric body.

Further expansion took place through the Jupiter sphere between 733 and 833. This was the time of the Carolingian renaissance, during which Charlemagne was crowned Holy Roman Emperor. However, the power of the Carolingian dynasty began to wane when Charlemagne's son, Louis the Pious, was forced to divide the kingdom between his four sons in 833. Coinciding with the outer event, at least one researcher dates another event—of great significance for esoteric Christianity—the crowning of Parzifal as Grail King.[1]

A few more "interesting coincidences" are worth mentioning. In 966, the year mentioned above as the "midnight hour" or turning point between the expansion and contraction of Christ's etheric body, Poland became Christian. In 1099, with the transition from the Saturn to the Jupiter sphere on the path of descent of Christ's etheric body, the Crusaders reconquered Jerusalem from the Saracens and Godfrey of Bouillon was crowned king of Jerusalem. Around the year 1799, the transition from the Mercury to the Moon sphere on the path of descent, the Romantic movement was born in Germany through the poet Novalis, whose "Hymns to the Night" and "Spiritual Songs," written at that time, rank as great works of Romantic poetry. In 1899–1900, as already mentioned, the "Knights of Divine Sophia"—Andrei Belyi, Aleksandr Blok, and Sergei Soloviev—came together in Russia to herald the birth of the New Age, coinciding with the reentry of Christ's etheric body from the Moon sphere into the Earth's etheric aura.[2]

Notice that shortly after the life of Christ, we have the work of Hellenistic astrologers like Manilius or Ptolemy who are still working with the authentic forms: Manilius with the clockwise house system, and Ptolemy with sidereal astrology. Christ's etheric body is still close to the Earth. But as it begins to drift away, human beings begin to forget the truth concerning both the starry Heavens and the inner Earth. Certainly, for a good part of European society at this point, the interest in these things seems to disappear almost entirely from outer culture, whereas that which is retained in the Middle East—Ptolemaic astrology and the house system of Porphyry, both of which originated in the 2nd century AD—become distorted and fixed versions of what was once a living reality.

It is during the time period that Christ's etheric is in the Sun sphere—from 333 to 633—that the fall of the Roman Empire occurs, and much of the wisdom of Alexandria is gradually destroyed or forgotten. With the entry of Christ's etheric into the Mars sphere, between AD 633 and 733, this storehouse of wisdom is stolen away to the Middle East. Only briefly, during the Jupiter years of 733 through 833 is there any contact between the West and the Middle East in terms of astrology, as described in the legends of Kyot and Arabel by Wolfram von Eschenbach.

Christ's etheric finished its journey back to the Father between AD 933 and 999—this is the point of deepest forgetting on humanity's part of both the outer (cosmic) and inner (earthly) stars. Yet even during its journey through the Saturn sphere on either side of this time period—between 833

---

[1] Note: This proposed dating of the crowning of Parzifal as Grail King in 833 has been challenged by my own research, published in *Cosmology Reborn: Star Wisdom, vol I* in 2018 under the title "First Steps Toward a Grail Timeline." My research points to the year AD 810 as the time of Parzifal's coronation. This would coincide rather closely with Charlemagne's crowning of his son Louis the Pious as co-Emperor in AD 813, and his death shortly thereafter in 814—JMP.

[2] Powell, *Most Holy Trinosophia*, pp. 87–90.

and 933 on the ascent, and 999 and 1099 on the descent—there is already a total forgetting of both sidereal astrology and the houses for European culture. This is why the houses seemed to experience a kind of stillbirth—they were like grass sown before winter, only just sprouting before killed by the frost and snow, yet to return in full vibrancy in the spring. Unlike the discipline of Babylonian astrology, they had not enjoyed centuries of being an established discipline prior to Christ's incarnation—indeed, they only came into existence as a *consequence* of this incarnation!

Just as there was a "touching in" of Europe with Middle Eastern astrology during the Jupiter years of ascent from 733 until 833, so during the descent of Christ's etheric through the Jupiter sphere in 1099 to 1199, the return of astrology to European culture begins. Due to the journeys of the Knights Templar in the Crusades, much of the ancient pagan wisdom that was stored away in the Muslim cultures of North Africa and the Middle East began to come back to Europe. The writings of Ptolemy were first translated into Latin by Plato de Tivoli in 1138.

During the ascent of the etheric body of Christ through the Mars sphere, from 633 to 733, the death knell was dealt to astrology, the houses, and Aristotelianism in Europe—all of these sciences were transferred to Islamic nations. Similarly, it was during the years of the descent of Christ's etheric body through the Mars sphere in 1199 through 1299 that a reversal came about. All of the primeval wisdom that had been preserved in Arabia began to pour back into Europe due to the contact established between the two during the Crusades. This began, of course, during the "Jupiter years" of 1099 to 1199, but didn't become a widespread cultural phenomenon in Europe until the "Mars years" of the following century.

During the next few centuries—the passage of Christ's etheric through the Sun sphere from 1299 through 1599, mirroring its ascent through this same sphere from 333 through 633—Aristotelianism became integrated into Christian theology and philosophy through the Scholastics (particularly Thomas Aquinas), several house systems were created in competition with the Porphyry system (e.g., Campanus and Regiomantanus), and Ptolemaic astrology became widespread. Unfortunately, this Ptolemaic astrology was a pale reflection of the sidereal astrology of the Babylonians. It retained the mythical, prophetic, and spiritual character of ancient astrology, but had lost any connection to the actual (sidereal) stars in the heavens. This was due to a loss of understanding of the precession of the equinoxes: when Ptolemy wrote that the Sun entered Aries at the Spring Equinox, he was more or less correct for his time period of the 2nd century AD. By the time his work was rediscovered by the Europeans, the vernal point had precessed backward some 12° into Pisces. But the Europeans had not yet resurrected the *astronomical* aspect of Babylonian astrology—they did not yet observe the precession of the equinox, and therefore treated Ptolemy's astrological information as something fixed like an eternal law, rather than something subject to change over time due to *deeper* laws.

As Christ's etheric left the Sun sphere for the sphere of Venus in 1599, the first Scientific Revolution was well underway—the time of Galileo, Copernicus, Tycho Brahe, and Johannes Kepler. The "other half" of ancient Babylonian astrology comes into being as the relatively modern science of astronomy. Unfortunately, the science of astronomy was lacking in the mythical/archetypal essence of astrology, and only became more so over time. It increasingly treated the cosmos as a kind of mechanism, especially after the time of Copernicus, who was the first to propose the theory of heliocentrism. At the same time that Copernicus was proposing the Sun as the center of gravity of the Solar System in order to explain the apparent movement of the planets (i.e., retrogression), Tycho Brahe was proposing his "Tychonic" system, which saw the Sun and Moon revolving around the Earth, while the rest of the planets circled around the Sun. This twofold center of Sun *and* Earth would explain both retrogression as well as the elliptical orbits of the planets.

Unfortunately, Johannes Kepler—the successor of both Copernicus and Brahe—chose the heliocentric system of Copernicus over that of Tycho

Brahe. In doing so, he set the stage for the meteoric rise of materialism over the past 400 years. (What is interesting is that this first Scientific Revolution, which occurred as Christ's etheric body *descended* from the Sun sphere to the Venus sphere, was fought against as relentlessly by the established Church as was the "pagan wisdom" that was done away with when Christ's etheric body *ascended* from the Venus sphere to the Sun sphere, around AD 333.)

And so the descent of Christ's etheric body through the Venus, Mercury and Moon spheres from 1599 to 1899 was accompanied by evermore precise observations of the starry heavens on the part of astronomers, along with an increasingly mechanistic picture of the universe, devoid of spirit, soul, or even life. On the other hand, tropical astrology became evermore detached from the actual positions of the planets in the starry heavens due to turning a blind eye to the reality of precession—and therefore, by the 20th century, was viewed as a pseudoscientific discipline, offering snake oil solutions born out of a combination of superstition, psychology, and tradition. Needless to say, a great deal of confusion accumulated in these two realms, although the adherents of each would argue with absolute certainty and dedication to their fields. Paradoxically, the confused, partial perspective held by each made the two fields *appear* totally irreconcilable, when their reconciliation is exactly what is needed in order to resolve the confusion!

The burgeoning field of ecosophy fared no better during this same time period (from 1599 to the present). During the 13th to 17th centuries, the Campanus, Regiomantanus, Morinus, and Placidus systems had been added to the Porphyry system, with the complicated Placidus system becoming dominant. Since then, many others have been developed: Carter's Poly Equatorial, Meridian, Sinusoidal, Goelzer, Koch, Topocentric, etc.—all of them, of course, counterclockwise, and never very clear about what exactly underlies the houses as a phenomenon.[3] To be sure, if tropical astrology is setting the example, one does not need a particular concrete reality (such as the actual positions of the stars in the heavens) to ground and anchor one's psycho–mythological "science"!

In summary: as Christ's etheric began to descend once again to humanity from the 10th century onward, glimmers of enlightenment gradually fell—yet compared to the time before his Ascension, all is now very confused. For example, it is in the subsequent centuries after his return to the Father that dozens of different house systems begin to be devised, each more elaborate and complicated than the prior. Similarly, it is during these years that at first a resurgence or rediscovery of astrology takes place—but it has frozen in the form that it took in the 2nd century with Ptolemy. Precession has been forgotten, and tropical astrology (i.e. the tropical calendar) is born. By the 16th century, further confusion is added by the investigation of *astronomy*, divorced from *astrology*. Out of this investigation, scientists come to the conclusion that the Earth revolves around the Sun, and *not* the Sun around the Earth, as had been believed since the time of Pythagoras. Briefly, the world sees Tycho Brahe's revival of the ancient Egyptian system, in which *both* the Sun and Earth are treated as centers of the Solar System, but it is quickly drowned out by the Copernican system promoted and popularized by Kepler.

And so, confusion is everywhere, as none of these various systems seem to harmonize at all. Only glimmers, bits and pieces of the truth descend gradually on humanity as Christ's etheric comes back into the Earth's aura. There is an inkling through Tycho Brahe that there is both a Mother *and* a Father, and that somehow *both* the Earth *and* the Sun are centers of our Solar System—but this is abandoned. The heliocentric, Father-centric approach is left to the new, outer, materialistic science, while the geocentric, Mother-centric approach is left to an old, illusory pseudo-science. On the other hand, there is an inkling that the houses mean *something*, and somehow are determined by the ascendent or horoscope, but it is not clear why. It is entirely

---

3 For a good summary of different house systems, see here: https://www.astro.com/faq/fq_fh_owhouse_e.htm

forgotten that they follow the clockwise motion of the day, the motion counter to that of the cosmos—instead, they are cast in imitation of the counterclockwise zodiac. The houses become reflectors or imitators of the cosmos, rather than significators of the Inner Earth.

Thus, during the centuries leading up to the return of Christ's etheric to the Earth sphere, we find all of the elements that made up the emergent discipline of ecosophy as well as the established discipline of astrosophy as they existed at the time of the Mystery of Golgotha, but torn asunder, detached from the whole, and specialized into idiosyncratic and imbalanced forms.

THE CONSEQUENCES OF THE RETURN OF CHRIST'S ETHERIC BODY

According to the research of Robert Powell, the etheric body of Christ returned to our Earth's sphere in 1899, and spent a century there with us. It is only since then, through the Parousia (Presence) of Christ, that the various threads described above could begin to be woven together into a comprehensible tapestry. This began with the work of Rudolf Steiner, who strove to re-enliven astrology (among virtually every other discipline) by bringing it into connection with a living perception of the spiritual world. Central to the activity of the spiritual world is Jesus Christ, and his deed on Golgotha. Christ is the central Sun—the center of gravity—in the cosmos of spiritual beings. Therefore a renewed astrology—an *astrosophy*—would have the life and spirit of Christ as its center. Rudolf Steiner worked closely with Elisabeth Vreede to bring this astrosophy about, and in turn she worked with the young Willi Sucher, who made enormous strides in this direction in the first half of the 20th century.

The work of tying together the frayed strands continued from another side with the Irish astrologer Cyril Fagan around the middle of the 20th century. He was the one to return sidereal (observational) astrology to the West. India had been the only culture to retain the authentic sidereal astrology of the Babylonians in the form of Vedic Astrology. We might think of this Vedic Astrology as a kind of Nathan Jesus, held back in purity until the right time. Cyril Fagan and his coworker Donald Bradley returned the reality of this ancient, sidereal astrology to the West in the first half of the 20th century. This brought together two of the threads above: it took the archetypal approach of tropical astrology, with its twelve 30° signs, and reunited it with the actual observation of the stars and planets (astronomy). Along with the anthroposophical work of Rudolf Steiner in the first part of the 20th century, Fagan's work laid the foundation for the new Astrosophy to be born.[4]

And this brings us to the work of Robert Powell. What is crucial with Robert's work is that it has always had two goals: 1) to re-establish as nearly as possible the original, Babylonian sidereal astrology and 2) to make Christ the new center of this astrology. In terms of the former, he expanded on the work begun by Cyril Fagan, and spent approximately 30 years studying the origins of the Zodiac, culminating in the publication of his PhD thesis *The History of the Zodiac* in 2005. In terms of the latter, he built upon the foundation established by Rudolf Steiner, Elizabeth Vreede, and Willi Sucher to create a completely Christ-centric astrology. With the accomplishment of these two goals, he has made available to the world the path to the Father—Astrosophy. In addition to reuniting astronomy and astrology in the name of Christ, he resurrected the lost Tychonic system of understanding the Solar System. This system is helio-geocentric: the Sun and Moon revolve around the Earth, while the remaining planets—Mercury, Venus, Mars, Jupiter, and Saturn—revolve around the Sun. When one brings this motion to life inwardly, one can see an elegant, complex, lemniscatory movement. One can feel this inner imagination awakening a connection between head and heart. We so often feel divided in ourselves—"should I allow my head to be the center of my consciousness and decision making, or my heart?" The Tychonic

---

4 For some excellent information on Cyril Fagan as well as the unearthing of Babylonian sidereal astrology during the 19th to 20th centuries, see here: http://www.radical-astrology.com/irish/fagan/bowser.html

system encourages us to allow the *flow between the two* to be the determinant and motivator of our actions (see image of Tychonic system):

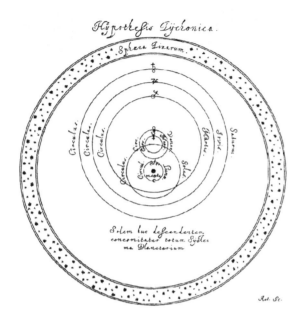

Rudolf Steiner indicated the Tychonic system was the correct one, and that due to Kepler promoting the Copernican system over the Tychonic, humanity was driven into a totally materialistic science. He predicted that humanity would revisit the Tychonic system, and a struggle or conflict between the two—Copernican and Tychonic—would continue into the future.[5] What is so powerful about the Tychonic system is that it recognizes *two centers*, both Sun and Earth. It "honors thy Father and Mother," as the Sun is our Father and the Earth is our Mother. In addition to reconciling astronomy and astrology, Robert Powell has also reunited the heliocentric and geocentric perspectives.

Through that which has been made possible by the Presence of Christ in the 20th Century, Robert Powell completed the work—begun and informed by many others—of fusing together that which had separated in terms of astrosophy. What about ecosophy—the study of the Earth's houses? What steps are left to be taken here?

---

5 For more information, see my introduction to the Commentaries in 2020's *As Above, So Below: Star Wisdom*, vol 3.

The Renewal of Ecosophy in the 20th Century

The houses could only just make their appearance around the time of the Mystery of Golgotha, before the light illuminating their mystery began to return to the Father. At the Ascension, Christ returned to the Father in order to share the good news with him—the formation of the Resurrection Body, and the reopening of the portal to the Mother in the heart of the underworld, below the nine subearthly spheres. But as he returns to the Father, he receives a new mission. His First Coming consisted in opening a door or building a bridge—descending to the Mother in the depths, who had withdrawn there with Paradise (the "golden realm of Shambhala") at the time of the Fall and the fratricide of Cain. Now, the mission of his Second Coming has to do with establishing a flow of traffic back and forth through this door and over this bridge—not just reopening the gateway to the Mother, but leading individual human beings *through* this gateway. In his First Coming, he set the example and showed the way to the Mother and the Father; in his Second Coming, he is with us as we actually *walk the path with him.*

Similar to its role in the resurrection of astrosophy during the 20th century, it is the work of Rudolf Steiner that brings new, living spiritual insights and impulses to the field of ecosophy. There are, of course, his somewhat veiled indications pointing in the direction of a clockwise house system. But more than that, he seemed to inhabit a consciousness that experienced direct perception not only of *cosmic* realities of the spiritual world and the angelic hierarchies "above" mankind, but of *chthonic* realities of the inner Earth and the elemental beings "below" mankind as well. This comes to expression perhaps most concretely in his 1924 agriculture course in Koberwitz, and carried forward into the present day as biodynamic agriculture. This is the practice *par excellence* through which humanity serves to transform the natural and elemental kingdoms below him, transforming the Earth into a Star.

Another important step in the renewal of ecosophy in the 20th century was taken by French psychologists Michel and Françoise Gauquelin and the pioneering French sidereal astrologer Jacques Dorsan. In 1967, after almost twenty years of rigorous research, the Gauquelins published *The Cosmic Clocks*, which laid the foundation for the work of Jacques Dorsan. In 1984, after nearly 50 years of casting horoscopes and in-depth study of their implications, he published his work *The Clockwise House System,* in which he proposed that the true direction of the houses is *clockwise* and not *counterclockwise*. Another step to a practical ecosophy had been taken.

Similar to the renewal of astrosophy, the work of Rudolf Steiner supplies the actual living content for ecosophy, whereas the *Clockwise House System* developed (or properly speaking *rediscovered*) by Gauquelin and Dorsan supply the conceptual framework through which this living content could be put to use—similar to the sidereal astrology rediscovered by Cyril Fagan, which also supplied the conceptual framework through which a Christ-centered astrosophy could operate. We might think of all of anthroposophy as playing the role of Solomon Jesus in relation to the advent of the Etheric Christ. It is a fount of living, experiential wisdom and rich, counterintuitive practical advice. On the other hand, sidereal astrology and the clockwise house system are like Nathan Jesus, treasures of the past that have somehow been preserved in their purity, ready to be filled with the "new wine" of anthroposophy. The work of Robert Powell has been analogous to the entry of the Zarathustra Ego from the Solomon Jesus into the pure sheaths of the Nathan Jesus in the year AD 12—he has taken the "pure sheath" of sidereal astrology and filled it with the mighty Ego of anthroposophy.

But there is another aspect to the practice of ecosophy that began to unfold in a new way during the 20th century that has yet to be recognized; this has to do with the question of the "archetypal language" that belongs to ecosophy. Astrosophy has a well-established archetypal language that is based out of Greco-Roman mythology (the gods and goddesses of Saturn, Jupiter, Venus, etc. express the multivalent reality of a psycho–spiritual being in a much more vivid and living way than mere adjectives could do). But it also comes with a set of *sigils* or symbols, which in and of themselves communicate the being of the different signs of the zodiac and planets in a more direct way than conceptual language is able to do—in a way, these sigils are like hieroglyphic remnants from ancient Egypt, somewhere between picture and letter; they remind us of a time period when "the stars once spoke to man."

Thus far, ecosophy has either gone without an archetypal language, or at best it has borrowed one from astrosophy. The houses are typically numbered one through twelve, and described using bare concepts (e.g. the second house is that of material possessions), and/or the language of astrosophy is used analogously in order to illumine their meaning (e.g., the second house is related to the sign of Taurus). But as we have seen over the course of this investigation into the houses, they have a totally different origin than the signs of the zodiac—they are based around the cross of the cardinal points radiating out of the center of the Earth, laid there by Christ almost 2000 years ago, whereas the signs of the zodiac are an ancient reality, the accumulation of several stages of cosmic evolution, radiating from the periphery toward the Earth and humanity. The language of astrosophy, based as it is in pre-Christian, pagan symbolism and mythology, is proper to it—it is not necessarily proper to its "child" discipline, ecosophy. Is there an archetypal language that *belongs* to ecosophy? In order to answer this question, we will have to look back at another theme from last year's article.

Remember that in addition to the fully crystallized and accurate system of astrology finding its form at the time of Christ's First Coming as an *outer* discipline, the mysteries of the Mother had descended to the level of the Hebrew alphabet and the Kabbalistic Sephiroth Tree, the Tree of Life. The Egyptian mysteries of Hermes Trismegistus—of Isis and Osiris—were once perceived within the constellations of Orion and

Lepus. When Moses (who had been raised as an Egyptian and initiated into their rites) left with the Hebrew peoples, he brought the hidden "treasures of Egypt" along with him—what once was perceived within the stars in the form of Hermeticism became codified within the Sephiroth Tree, with its ten Sephiroth, four planes, and twenty-two paths of wisdom—the twenty-two letters of the Hebrew alphabet. At the time of Christ, the reality of the Sephiroth condensed even further, and became the etheric body of Christ. This body was to be brought to the Mother in the depths as a seed, in order to grow once again the Tree of Life—reopening the gates of Paradise, the way to the Mother in the depths. It was this very Sephiroth Tree that began to radiate out of the center of the Earth at the moment of the Resurrection on Easter Sunday.

These mysteries of the inner Earth were best understood by Lazarus. It has always been the destiny of this individuality—whether in his incarnation as Tubal-Cain, or Hiram Abiff, or Lazarus—to investigate the inner Earth mysteries in order to contribute to the creation of the Philosopher's Stone, the Resurrection Body. Lazarus was the one who cleared the path for Christ *prior to* the Deed of Golgotha. He descended, albeit ill prepared and inadequate to the task, into the inner Earth during a failed initiation ritual led by his sister, Mary Magdalene. Just as Peter, with all the faith and courage he could muster, attempted to walk on the water to Christ and still sank, so did Lazarus "sink" into the subearthly spheres. No mere human can lift the veil of Isis.

In order to rescue Lazarus from being lost in the underworld, Christ brought him back to life with the power of the *Word*—"Lazarus, Come Forth!"—and thereby bestowed on him a *copy of his etheric body*. Ever since then, the individuality who was Lazarus has borne the etheric body of Christ—and the living content of this body has been the raw material from which the Rosicrucian mysteries—the mysteries of the inner Earth—have been derived ever since, beginning with the Gospel of St. John and John's Apocalypse. Remarkably, just after Lazarus's incarnation as Christian Rosenkreuz in the 14th to 15th centuries—simultaneously with the appearance of dozens of house systems, a heliocentric astronomy, and geocentric tropical astrology—a new archetypal language was born. This new language was the resurrection of the Hebrew alphabet in its Christian form—the twenty-two paths of wisdom of the Sephiroth Tree and the twenty-two letters of the Hebrew alphabet now become the twenty-two Major Arcana of the Tarot of Marseilles.

The Tarot of Marseilles are the picture language of the Rosicrucian mysteries. They are Arcana, sacred images—they are at once symbols of spiritual realities, yet at the same time they *are* that which they *symbolize*. Therefore, although they *symbolize* the etheric body of Christ, in a mysterious sense they also *are* this etheric body made manifest. They contain within them "all that has been and is and shall be"—and the time has now come when, through them, *all* mortals can lift the veil of Isis.

Whereas the sigils and archetypes that make up the language of astrosophy are carried over directly from the Egyptian, Babylonian and Hellenic time periods which gave birth to the authentic sidereal astrology, the Major Arcana are a christening and resurrection of the picture language of hieroglyphics. They, too, have taken their time to gestate ever since the "forgetting" of AD 833 to 1099, during which Christ's etheric had expanded to the Saturn sphere and the "Midnight Hour" of the Father God. Somehow, a portion of the occult wisdom of the Hebrews (what is contained primarily in the *Sepher Yetzirah*), was in the possession of the Mamluk dynasty in Egypt in the 13th century—but it had been transformed into a *card game*. This card game had four suits (representing the four planes of the Sephiroth), and each suit had ten numbered cards (representing the ten Sephiroth) and four royal cards (again representing the four planes, as well as the four letters of the divine name YHVH). However, none of the royal suits had images of humans or animals, due to the iconoclastic injunction whereby Muslims avoid accidentally creating a representation of Muhammad.

And so, while Christ's etheric body was in the Mars sphere, from 1199 to 1299, the Templars came in contact with the Mamluks, and like Moses brought the hidden treasures out of Egypt. Once back in Europe, the card game evolved to the point that the royal cards bore the likeness of human figures; and eventually, twenty-two Major Arcana (or Trumps) were added to the fifty-six Minor Arcana already in existence. The "letters of the alphabet" were now added to the "numbers." As alluded to above, this was all happening in Italy, Switzerland, and in particular Marseilles, France during the "Sun years" of 1299 to 1599. There are a number of designs of Tarot decks still in existence today that can be traced back all the way to the "Venus years" of 1599 to 1699.

In the "Mercury years" of 1699 to 1799, the occult author Antoine Court de Gebelin—inspired by the individuality of Lazarus, who was incarnated at that time as the Comte de St. Germaine—was the first to propose that the Tarot were a repository of ancient wisdom, and more than just a card game. It was at this point that they began to be used for divinatory purposes (pointing to their true nature as the sigils of one's "fortune" as presented in the placement of the planets in the houses of the birth horoscope). It was not until the 19th century, during the "Moon years" of 1799 to 1899 that the French occultist Eliphas Levi presented the Tarot as an even deeper reality—as symbols meant for both meditation and for magical ritual. He brought the Tarot even more concretely into relationship with Egyptian Hermeticism, the *Book of Thoth*, and the Kabbala.

All of this was leading up to the true "incarnation" of the Tarot of Marseilles, in all of their true depth, through the agency of Valentin Tomberg—once Christ had returned to the sphere of the Earth in the 20th century. Between 1957 and 1967, he penned his magnum opus, *Meditations on the Tarot*. He intended for this work to be published anonymously and posthumously, which it was in the 1980s (the English translation by Robert Powell was first published in 1985, just one year after Dorsan's *Clockwise House System*). This work finally performed the task of unveiling the *true nature* and *true purpose* of the Tarot of Marseilles. Prior to this time, they had more or less been understood as divinatory tools, a gypsy's fortune telling game. For the first time they could be properly and publicly understood as spiritual ferments or seeds which, when properly digested, lead to an awakening of a new form of consciousness—one that leads to the Etheric Christ and the Mother in the depths. And so, in addition to the work of Gauquelin and Dorsan in rediscovering the original clockwise house system, another step toward a functional ecosophy in the 20th century was taken by Valentin Tomberg. The biodynamic work of Rudolf Steiner should inform the living content and practice of this discipline; the work of Dorsan in rediscovering the clockwise house should provide the structural orientation; and the work of Tomberg, the archetypal language.

THE ARCHETYPAL LANGUAGE OF ECOSOPHY

If we accept the suggestion that the Tarot of Marseilles are the symbolic language of ecosophy, it then becomes a question of *how* specifically that works. There are twenty-two Major Arcana—in what way is each one related to an ecosophical aspect?

According to Robert Powell's intuitive research, seven of the Arcana are related to the classical planets; twelve of them are related to the signs of the zodiac; and three are related to the outer planets (including Pluto). In practice, he has used these Arcana to represent the astrosophical phenomena directly; here, we will rather propose that this division of seven, twelve, and three Arcana *directly* represent ecosophical (i.e., inner Earth) phenomena, and are only *analogously* related to the cosmic stars and planets—in the same way that the signs of the zodiac are only *analogously* related to the twelve houses.

For Robert, the following system of comparison has presented itself to him:

The Magician (or Juggler) — The Sun
The High Priestess — Saturn
The Empress — The Moon

The Emperor — Jupiter
The Pope — Mercury
The Lover — Venus
The Chariot — Mars
Justice — Libra
The Hermit — Sagittarius
Wheel of Fortune — Leo
Force — Virgo
The Hanged Man — Pisces
Death (Nameless) — Scorpio
Temperance — Aquarius
The Devil — Pluto
Tower of Destruction (or House of God) — Uranus
The Star — Capricorn
The Moon — Cancer
The Sun — Gemini
Judgement — Taurus
The Fool — Aries
The World — Neptune

Based on this, we would no longer refer to the first house as being analogous to Aries; we would simply call this the house of The Fool. Similarly, the second house would be called the house of Judgement. The twelve houses—or rather *temples* as Manilius originally called them—in order from the first at the ascendent, and running clockwise (to the zenith, the descendent, the nadir, and back toward the ascendent) would then be:

1. Temple of the Fool (straddling the ascendent)
2. Temple of Judgement
3. Temple of the Sun
4. Temple of the Moon (straddling the zenith)
5. Temple of the Wheel of Fortune
6. Temple of Force
7. Temple of Justice (straddling the descendent)
8. Temple of Death (or the Nameless Temple)
9. Temple of the Hermit
10. Temple of the Star (straddling the nadir)
11. Temple of Temperance
12. Temple of the Hanged Man

And the "inner planets" that arrange themselves within these twelve temples would then be:

The Magician (or Juggler), The Lover, The Pope, The Chariot, The Emperor, The High Priestess, The Empress;
Tower of Destruction (of House of God), The World, The Devil

The twelve temples begin to take on much more life, as they are now not only indicators of mundane fortune in different realms like health, family, career, etc., but are entire archetypal worlds with manifold, multivocal qualities. To begin to grasp the fullness of each of these twenty-two archetypes, I strongly recommend the reader investigate *Meditations on the Tarot*; one could also begin to investigate the images of the Arcana themselves, along the lines of Hermetic conversation: see, for example, www.the-unknown-friends.com. We can bring yet another layer of depth to these twelve temples by bringing them into relation with the clockwise wheel of world outlooks which Rudolf Steiner outlined on January 22, 1914. Seven of the inner planets can be brought into connection with the "seven moods," and three of them with the "three tones" from the same lecture. Here I list below once again the twelve temples, first with each one's traditional role, and second of all its world outlook according to Rudolf Steiner. I then list the seven "classical planets" and their soul moods, and the three "outer planets" and their soul tones.

Temple of the Fool: The temple of the personality, and of idealism
Temple of Judgement: The temple of resources, and of rationalism
Temple of the Sun: The temple of communication, and of mathematism
Temple of the Moon: The temple of heritage, and of materialism
Temple of the Wheel of Fortune: The temple of play, and of sensationalism
Temple of Force: The temple of health, and of phenomenalism
Temple of Justice: The temple of partnerships, and of realism
Temple of Death: The temple of death, and of dynamism

The Archetypal Language

Resurrection of Jesus Christ - Geocentric
At Jerusalem, Latitude 31N46', Longitude 35E13'
Date: Sunday, APR 5, 33, Julian
Time: 5:48 am, Local Time
Sidereal Time 18:33:16, Vernal Point 2♈35'46", House System: Equal
Zodiac: Sidereal SVP, Aspect set: Conjunction/Square/Opposition

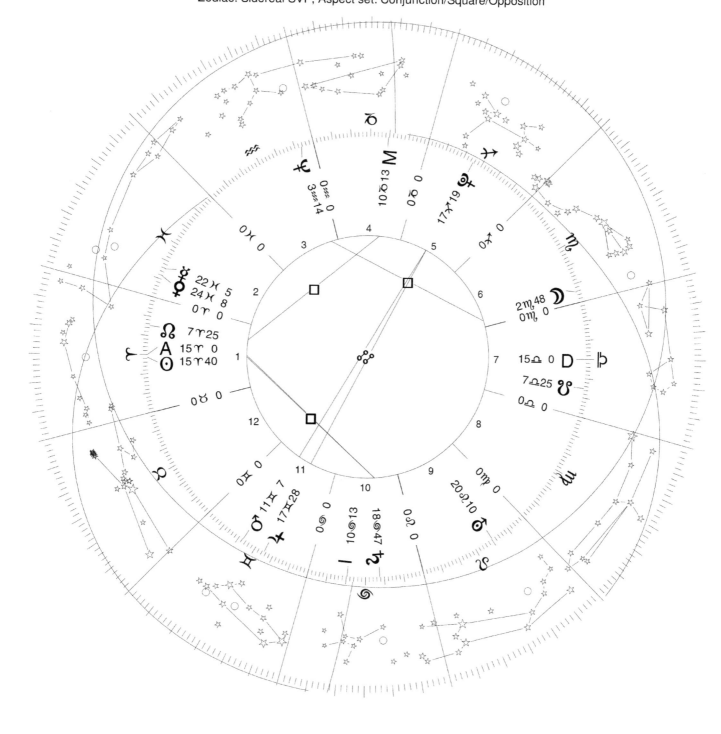

Temple of the Hermit: The temple of philosophy, and of monadism
Temple of the Star: The temple of vocation, and of spiritism
Temple of Temperance: The temple of friendships, and of pneumatism
Temple of the Hanged Man: The temple of self-sacrifice, and of psychism
The Magician: The mood of empiricism
The Lover: The mood of mysticism
The Pope: The mood of transcendentalism
The Chariot: The mood of volunteerism
The Emperor: The mood of logicism

The High Priestess: The mood of gnosis
The Empress: The mood of occultism
Tower of Destruction: The tone of theism
The World: The tone of intuitionism
The Devil: The tone of naturalism

To give a vivid example of what an inner Earth horoscope would look like if written in the archetypal language of the Tarot, I include both the standard, astrosophical horoscope for the Resurrection of Christ (page 107), as well as the Tarot-based, ecosophical horoscope (page 108). It is remarkable how much can be expressed in this collection of twenty-two sacred images that cannot adequately be expressed in words—and how different it is to gaze upon such a collage vs the normal horoscope of the Resurrection, which to be sure expresses so much, but not what we see here. Some readers may be unfamiliar with how to work with the Tarot of Marseilles; primarily it is through observing the details closely, and then asking questions—what does it indicate that the Chariot (in motion) and the Emperor (stationary) have joined forces in service to Temperance? What relationship do they have to her two flowing vases, or her two wings? Has the Tower of Destruction become the lamp of the Hermit? What force is released at the break of dawn—when the Magician has "broken free" of the state of the Hanged Man and become Wandering Fool? Is the Devil now trapped in the revolving Wheel of Fortune? Or is he being flung out of it—toward the Chariot and the Emperor? Perhaps of greatest significance here is the presence of the High Priestess in the depths with The Star... more on this configuration will come in the next part of this article series.

In the fourth part of this series, my intention is to return to the work of both Rudolf Steiner and Manilius in order to get further clarity around how to put the temples into *practice*, in order to "walk in cosmic time"—to say the right words, and perform the right deeds, at the right time. I hope to include a practical example from the work of the Healing Plant Garden in Camphill Village Copake.

As a preparation for this, I include here a little-known essay written by R. S. W. Bobette in 1998, which reiterates my own initial questions around Steiner's use of a clockwise zodiac and points the reader in the direction of the specific instances of Steiner's use of said zodiac.

THE DAILY-ROUND ZODIAC: A LITTLE COSMIC MYSTERY

R. S. W. Bobbette, 1998

Scattered throughout his career, Dr. Rudolf Steiner gave peeks at what is for me as yet, a little cosmic mystery. That is, he pointed to the idea that the sun traverses the zodiac (or its "equivalent" or "echo"?) daily. If I present the pertinent quotes, you will see what I mean.

On the 6th Dec. 1910, Dr. Steiner explained: "If you follow the course of the Sun in the daytime from the constellation of Aries, through Taurus, Gemini and so on, to Virgo, you must follow its progress at night from Libra on to Aquarius and Pisces. This is the direction of the Spiritual Sun."[6]

A few days later, on December 18, the point was made again:

> John the Baptist had necessarily to receive an Aquarius Initiation, the expression indicating that the Sun was standing in the constellation of Aquarius. Try to understand it this way: On the day or light side of the Zodiac lie Aries, Taurus, Gemini, Cancer, Leo, Virgo, then Libra. The constellations on the night or dark side of the Zodiac are Scorpio, Sagittarius, Capricorn, Aquarius and Pisces. Since the last two lie on the night side, the Sun's rays coming from them must not only traverse physical space but they must send the spiritual light of the Sun, which passes *through* the Earth, through spiritual space.
>
> If we trace the course of the Sun in the heavens, we find that as the physical Sun sets the spiritual Sun begins to rise. In its day or summer course the Sun progresses from Taurus to Aries, and so on; in its night or winter course it will reveal to us the secrets of the Initiation of Aquarius or Pisces. Physically, the Sun's course is from Virgo to Leo, Cancer, Gemini, Taurus, Aries; spiritually its course is from Virgo to Libra, Scorpio, Sagittarius, Capricorn and Aquarius to Pisces. The spiritual counterpart of the course of the physical Sun is the passage from Aquarius to Pisces.

As I said, Steiner gave us only "peeks" (insofar as I've found) at this idea of a daily round related to or comparable to the zodiac. The next one I've found was given Apr. 17, 1917:

> Constantine therefore embarked upon the ambitious plan to found Constantinople, and the work was completed in AD 326. He intended that the foundation of the city should

---

6 Steiner, *Background to the Gospel of St. Mark*, p. 73.

coincide with this turning point in world history. He therefore chose to lay the foundation stone at the moment when the Sun stood in the sign of the Archer and the Crab ruled the hour. He followed closely the indications of the cosmic signs.[7]

Indications of this daily round are few and far between; the last I know include, on January 20, 1924:

> Now, you can look at the vernal point of the zodiac, where the sun rises every spring. This point is not stationary; it is advancing. In the Egyptian epoch, for example, it was in the constellation of Taurus. It has advanced through Taurus and Aries, and is today in the constellation of Pisces; and it is still advancing. It moves in a circle and will return after a certain time. Though this point where the sun rises in the spring describes a complete circle in the heavens in 25,920 years, the sun describes this circle every day. It rises and sets, thereby describing the same path as the vernal point. Let us contemplate, on the one hand, the long epoch of 25,920 years, which is the time taken by the vernal point to complete its path; and on the other hand, the short period of twenty-four hours in which the sun rises, sets and rises again at the same point. The sun describes the same circle.[8]

A little later, on June 14, 1924:

> We should really speak of Aries–Sun, Taurus–Sun, Cancer–Sun, Leo–Sun, and so on. For the Sun is a different being in each case. Moreover, the resultant influence depends both on the daily course and on the yearly course of the Sun, as determined by its position in the vernal point.[9]

The terse 1917 reference to "and the Crab ruled the hour" is also reflected in a predictive discussion given later in that year, on November 25, 1917:

> What will matter will be whether one carries out a certain process in the morning, evening, or at noon, or whether one allows what one did in the morning to be somehow further influenced by active forces of the evening, or whether the cosmic influences from morning until evening is excluded, paralyzed....
>
> It will be the task of the good, healing science to find certain cosmic forces that, through the working together of two cosmic streams, are able to arise on the earth. These two cosmic streams will be those of Pisces and Virgo.... The good will be that one will discover how, from the two directions of the cosmos, morning and evening forces can be placed at the service of humanity: on the one side from the direction of Pisces and on the other side from the direction of Virgo.
>
> Those who seek to achieve everything through the dualism of polarity, through positive and negative forces, will not concern themselves with these forces. The spiritual mysteries that allow the spirituality to stream forth from the cosmos—with the help of the twofold forces of magnetism, from the positive and the negative—emerge in the universe from Gemini; these are the forces of midday.[10]

The long passage from which the above was extracted also indicates Sagittarius as "the forces of midnight."

When I first noticed this reference to "day constellations" and "night constellations," I thought of an allegory to the yearly passage through them, but there is definite reference to daily passage. The equally definite indications of practical importance mean that this is a "little mystery" worth pursuing.[11]

---

7 Steiner, *Building Stones for an Understanding of the Mystery of Golgotha*, pp. 138–139
8 Steiner, *Anthroposophy and the Inner Life*, p. 29
9 Steiner, *Agriculture*, p. 115.
10 Steiner, *The Reappearance of Christ in the Etheric*, pp. 195–200.
11 From https://wn.rsarchive.org/RelArtic/BobbetteRSW/steiner2_010.html. See also Steiner, *Toward Imagination*, for another of Rudolf Steiner's references to a clockwise zodiacal wheel.

TONE ART

Amber Wolfe Rounds

In my previous piece for *Star Wisdom*, I provided historical examples of experimental musicians who composed from Anthroposophy as a means of analyzing new musical impulses that have arisen in the last century. I discussed how Rudolf Steiner encouraged musicologist Kathleen Schlesinger and composer Elsie Hamilton to create avant-garde music that corresponded to the seven planets of antiquity. Astrological perspective on the modern planets Uranus, Neptune, and Pluto was offered as a framework for understanding massive musical changes that occurred in the 20th century, specifically the creation of electronic instruments. I reviewed the work of Anthroposophist and experimental musician, David Tudor, who pioneered electronic instrument creation and inspired two new genres: noise and sound art. Lastly, I introduced my own research in Anthroposophical sound art, which proposes to heal the schism between the material and spiritual approaches in modern music composition.

In this essay, I will detail how the cosmic modes of Schlesinger and Hamilton plus the chthonic tones of Tudor inspired me to conduct action research in anthroposophical sound art. My research proposes a methodology of anthroposophical sound art best described as "tone art." In my previous piece for *Star Wisdom*, I stated that tone art:

- Acknowledges the soul and spirit, as well as the physical properties of sound.
- Strives for transdisciplinary holism by working with art, science, and spirituality.
- Reveres nature and collaborates with subnature to strive toward music creation that reflects extra-earthly super-nature.
- Invites transformation of the composer-performer through cultivation of the higher faculties of imagination, inspiration, and intuition.

The action research I conducted for my master's project was motivated by the question: *How does one create contemporary sound art from anthroposophy?* My action research involved two components. First, I collected feedback from listeners at a series of concerts that my group, Zizia, performed. Next, I composed music based on the natal charts of 21 individuals and asked participants to share their experiences listening to melodies created from astrology. I will provide my methods, present my findings, and discuss how my action research inspired my definition of tone art.

MATERIALS AND METHODS

Zizia

I first began to explore the interconnections between anthroposophy, astrology and music through collaborations with ecological sound artist and pollinator conservationist, Jarrod Fowler. My background in astrology connected naturally with Fowler's work with phenology, "nature's calendar."[1] Our musical practice unfolded accordingly: Fowler offered organic wisdom; I provided cosmic insight. We called our project Zizia, after *Zizia*, a North American native plant genus in the carrot family and host for butterflies and pollen specialist bees.[2] Zizia creates contemporary sound art inspired by anthroposophy.

Zizia[3] performed a series of ten concerts across the United States from September 2018 to February 2019. In these performances, Zizia acknowledged

---

1 National Phenology Network, n.d., p. 1.
2 Fowler, *Specialist Bees of the Northeast*.
3 See https://zizia.xyz.

the traditional connections between astrology and music, while collaborating with nature and sub-nature to create an experience of extra earthly, super-nature. Materials and methods of Zizia performances will be described below following a fourfold elemental schema. I will begin with the element of earth to describe the physical context of performances and then move to fire to describe our actions and intuitions. Next, the element of air will introduce our conceptual framework and inspirations, and lastly, I will provide imaginations of our concert experience with the feeling of water.

Earth. The physical body of the human being is associated with the element of earth. Earth symbolizes the material context that forms a necessary structure for spiritual consciousness to grow. Zizia performed ten concerts at art galleries and organizations during the fall and winter of 2018–19. In sequence, the cities we visited were: Somerville, Massachusetts; Brooklyn; Philadelphia; Takoma Park, Maryland; Asheville, North Carolina; Chicago; Seattle; Los Angeles; Dallas; and Houston. Concerts were booked in collaboration with local artists and musicians; Zizia shared almost every concert with at least one other performer. Zizia brought our own amplification, sometimes used PA systems provided by venues, and on two occasions, performed acoustic sets. The sizes of audiences ranged from ten to fifty people. Zizia improvised with the environment of each concert venue for flexible and site-specific performances.

Fire. The "I," or ego, of the human being is associated with the element of fire. Fire symbolizes both the activities and the spiritual potential of performance, as well as the capacity for intuition. Zizia rattled, rubbed, struck, and scraped percussion instruments comprised of plants and other natural objects sourced from the environments surrounding the venues. Stringed instruments were plucked with fingers and vibrated using an electronic bow (Heet Sound EBow Plus). Electronic instruments were manipulated, programmed, and triggered. Insect recordings sourced from the Borror Lab of Bioacoustics at the Ohio State University[4] were broadcast from at least four amplifiers in different areas of each room. Zizia performed with awareness of the spiritual origin of tone, and collaborated with electronic instruments as agents of indeterminacy in order to cultivate intuitive capacities.

Air. The astral body is associated with the element of air. Air symbolizes the conceptual framework of composition, the social context of performance, and the capacity for inspiration. Zizia organized our compositions according to seven-minute segments resulting in performances that lasted from 28 to 35 minutes. Musical scores were performed at roughly the rate of 72 beats per minute, and natural object percussion occurred according to a thirteen count circular breathing pattern. Dynamics ranged from triple *pianississimo* to triple *fortississimo*. Zizia remained on stage or near tables during the majority of our first concerts. By the last two concerts of the tour, we continually moved around the venue, percussing natural objects or shifting the positions of portable cassette tape recorders. Astrology determined the notes and tunings performed on guitar, while melodies followed a 5:7 polyrhythm. Zizia composed from astrology, synchronizing performances with cosmic rhythms to inspire performers and audiences.

Water. The etheric body is associated with the element of water. Water symbolizes the feeling of the performance and the capacity for imagination. Imagine:

You are sitting in a dark, quiet room. You are surrounded by other people, most of whom are strangers. You are waiting for a performance to begin. You feel slightly anxious due to the extended silence. You hear soft crackling, popping, rattling, rustling, and snapping sounds intermittently percussing around you. You imagine that something is creeping toward you through leaf litter on the forest floor. You hear sounds from people and places inside and outside the venue between the susurrations. You realize that the rhythmic crepitations and stridulations of night insects have

---

4 Fowler sampled one and a half day's worth of insect field recordings from an archive of "over 40,000 animal sound recordings" recorded by the Borror Lab (https://osuc.biosci.ohio-state.edu/blb/).

slowly been growing louder without you noticing, amplifying from the corners of the room...

You hear a warm tone begin to resonate. You notice that the frequency gradually amplifies, eventually filling the entire space. You listen to the depth of overtones and undertones that seemingly phase back and forth between your ears. You feel your stomach rumbling from a low-frequency that has gradually amplified. You notice how the tone transforms, distorting then compressing, hissing softly under the sounds of night insects and rustling plants. You hear the measured twanging of strings, whose frequencies are synchronically harmonizing with stridulating crickets. You lose track of time, lost in a phasing melody that seems more circular than linear, impossible to memorize. You observe the notes metamorphose, filtered as though underwater...

You listen to noises, sounds, and tones amplify to an immersive cacophony. You are alarmed to sense the presence of some super-natural organism, no more benevolent than malevolent. You imagine a creature profoundly of this earth, yet unlike anything you have observed in waking life. You feel an inexplicable relief as the organism vanishes while the noises gradually decay and echo. You notice the songs of night insects are still present, although their calls seem more melodious, somehow. You ponder: are these the sounds of insects inside or outside of the venue? You question: are these tones from the performers or the environment? You sit, perplexed yet calm, listening for an extended duration, finally quietly meditating. You do not applaud...

In summary, Zizia created sound environments from concepts of Anthroposophy, including the elemental world and the fourfold human. The mineral world awakened us to observe and collaborate with our living chthonic environments surrounding each performance. The human world strengthened and warmed our intuitive explorations of the spiritual nature of tone. The animal world inspired us to create and harmonize with our living cosmic contexts during each performance. The plant world formed our imaginative investigations of health through restorative musical performances.

Thus, Zizia enlivened body, soul, and spirit by performing with awareness of our physical body, etheric body, astral body, and "I."

Concert Composition

Zizia composed from fourfold elemental principles to create an experience where the microcosm of terrestrial ecology met the macrocosm of extra-terrestrial astrology. Astrology provided a means of incorporating a space-specific and time-specific component to our performances, which used cosmic rhythms to both create indeterminate melodies and to connect with the moods of our audiences. In this next section, I will explain my method of composing music according to the practice of astrological indeterminacy in greater detail. Three types of indeterminacy will be distinguished, each of which parallel one of the three modalities of astrology. I will then discuss my experience with the Planetary Modes, explain how I linked the modes to a zodiacal tone spiral, and finally, elaborate on how the indeterminate processes using the modes and tones were connected to create unique musical performances.

In my last essay, I shared how British musicologist Kathleen Schlesinger (1862–1953) dedicated her career to pursuing the interrelations between the planets and music through comprehensive study of musical modes across ancient cultures. Australian pianist and composer Elsie Hamilton (1880–1965) joined Schlesinger in her studies, helping the research come alive by creating unique compositions that highlighted the microtonal subtlety of these ancient scales. Schlesinger and Hamilton shared seven aulos[5] modes from ancient Greece, each one corresponding to one of the seven classical planets. Steiner championed their research, for their studies illuminated the ancient link between cosmos, human, and music while also contributing to the modern field of microtonal music composition.[6]

---

5 A double-reed instrument similar in design to an oboe or Armenian duduk and thought to sound like a bagpipe.

6 Lee, B. *Kathleen Schlesinger and Elsie Hamilton: Pioneers of just intonation.*

Due to my interest in the Modes, I enrolled in *Musical Experience as Light On the Path*, a course taught by Gotthard Killian at the Center for Anthroposophy in Wilton, New Hampshire. Killian, who has written extensively about Schlesinger and Hamilton, guided us through demonstrations of the Planetary Modes on cello. The richness of hearing the Modes performed in person inspired me to conduct further research into the application of this unique musical system. I found that while Hamilton composed beautiful and unique pieces with the Planetary Modes, there was no indication of her or others using astrology to guide what mode to perform at a given time or place.

Zizia imagined ways of linking the Modes to actual astrology, inspired by the experiments conducted by David Tudor and John Cage. In my previous essay, I discuss how David Tudor (1926–1996) created music from Anthroposophy, a fact that he kept private throughout his life.[7] Whereas Hamilton and Schlesinger revitalized cosmic influences to compose avant-garde music accepted by Steiner, Tudor transfigured chthonic inspirations to collaborate with electronic instruments rejected by anthroposophists. Tudor investigated *musica humana*, that point at which the musicality of the human being allowed him to be a bridge between macro and microcosm. He referenced the anthroposophical concept of the human as divine instrument frequently in his personal notes. Tudor recognized himself as nerve man, a human instrument of the cosmos, with electronic instruments forming his extended nervous system.

Tudor is best known for his long standing collaboration with revolutionary composer John Cage (1912–1992). Cage and Tudor shared interests in both Eastern and Western forms of occult traditions. Cage coined the term "chance operations" to describe the practice of linking musical notes to divination tools such as the I-Ching. Chance operations used the results of divination to determine musical compositions, a practice that has become known as *indeterminacy*.[8] Tudor was inspired by the astrological symbolism of the Tarot and used the Major Arcana as his chance operation composition tool of choice.[9] Cage and Tudor sought to remove subjective preferences of the composer through indeterminacy, allowing themselves to be surprised by the outcomes.

Cage was one of the first composers to describe his own musical practice as *experimental*, a term that has since been associated with unorthodox approaches to music composition and performance. The practice of indeterminacy has since become a key component of experimental music.[10] Tudor and Cage experimented with three categories of indeterminacy, herein defined as *fixed*, *cardinal*, and *mutable*. Tudor worked extensively with the Tarot and with electronics as agents of indeterminacy, however Cage provided more documentation of composition using each type of indeterminacy. Therefore, pieces by Cage will be provided as examples of each category of indeterminacy.

The first category, *fixed indeterminacy*, connects haphazard or random chance operations with musical parameters to generate scores, which can then be performed. *Music of Changes* is an example of fixed indeterminacy, wherein musical parameters were created using I-Ching based chance operations.[11] The fixed modality corresponds to the capacity of *thinking*. Composers use their intellect to methodically link musical components to all possible outcomes from a chance operation.

In the second category, *cardinal indeterminacy*, composers note certain performance parameters and performers interpret the manifestations of parameters within compositions. Examples of cardinal indeterminacy include *Child of Tree* and *Branches*, which instruct performers to improvise with a stopwatch using amplified plant materials and other chance determined instruments.[12] The cardinal modality corresponds to the

---

7 Nakai, Y. *David Tudor and the Occult Passage of Music*.
8 Marshall, *John Cage's I- Ching Chance Operations*.
9 Smigel, 2003, p. 218
10 Marshall, n.d.
11 Cage, *Music of Changes*.
12 Cage, *Branches,* and Cage, *Child of Tree*.

Planet	String					
	E	A	D	G	B	E
Sun	C	F#	C	G/G#	A#	C
Venus	B	G#	D	F#	B	E
Mercury	D	A#	C	F#	A#	E
Moon	C	G#	C	E	G#	C
Saturn (+Capo 2nd Fret)	E (F#)	A# (C)	C (D)	E (F#)	A (B)	E (F#)
Jupiter	E	A#	D	G	B	E
Mars	D	G#	C	F#	A#	D

Table 1: Seven planetary tunings for guitar. Guitar tunings were inspired by the Planetary Modes of Hamilton and Schlesinger. The strings correspond to the notes in standard tuning.

capacity of *willing*. Performers strengthen the will through intuiting interpretations of compositional parameters.

Lastly, *mutable indeterminacy* involves the use of non-standard notation, wherein musical acts are represented entirely by illustrations or symbols, which are thus archetypally interpreted and controlled by the performer. *Concert for Piano and Orchestra* is one example of mutable indeterminacy: in the score, space and time are relative and notes are presented in three different sizes, which the performers can interpret as either amplitudes or durations.[13] The mutable modality is associated with the capacity of *feeling*. Mutable indeterminacy evokes feelings through imaginative interpretations from archetypal symbols.

Zizia created music with the Planetary Modes by using three categories of Cagean indeterminacy, herein defined: *fixed, cardinal,* and *mutable*. First, I linked the Planetary Modes with local apparent astrological occurrences to create a unique system of *fixed indeterminacy*. I created seven unique guitar tunings inspired by the Planetary Modes, which are illustrated in Table 1. My guitar was tuned at C = 128 Hz to the mode that corresponded with the planetary ruler of the astrological sign where the Moon was located on a given night.[14] The Moon transits each zodiac sign in ~2.5 days, thus cycling through the 12 zodiac signs in ~27.5 days or one lunar month. For example, if the Moon appeared in Virgo on the night of an event, my guitar would be tuned to the mode that corresponds to Mercury, ruler of Virgo. Thus, local apparent Moon rhythms provided cyclical space-time-specific qualities for fixed indeterminacy.

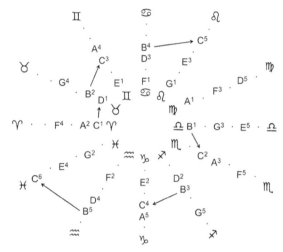

Figure 1: Zodiacal tone spiral adapted from Maria Renold (2004)

Fixed indeterminacy from Moon rhythms produced tuning systems from which melodies based on the zodiacal tone spiral could be performed, now demonstrating *cardinal indeterminacy*. I performed chord shapes and melodies according to the zodiacal tone spiral illustrated by Maria Renold and created a unique system of cardinal indeterminacy. Steiner provided this zodiacal tone spiral to the first Eurythmists, a group that included Lucy Neuscheller, mother of Renold. The tone spiral starts with a low C^1 for Aries, the sign that initiates the astrological year, and moves in upward, spiraling intervals through the signs of the zodiac. To continue with my Planetary Mode example, if the Moon were in Virgo, then I would perform $A^1 F^3 D^5$ or A, F, and D chord shapes on guitar. The cardinal indeterminate practice of performing what would be an A chord in standard

---

13 Cage, *Concert for Piano and Orchestra*.

14 Renold, *Intervals, Scales, Tones: And the Concert Pitch c = 128 Hz*.

tuning on a guitar tuned to a planetary tuning created surprising melodies. Thus, cardinal indeterminacy allowed me to interpret the manifestations of musical parameters based on the astrological symbolism of each concert.

The qualities of each planet and zodiac sign offered symbolic suggestions for musical interpretations of emotions and feelings. Archetypal symbols of local apparent astrology provided unique opportunities for *mutable indeterminacy*. The Moon is associated with water, the etheric body, and the collective unconscious, which governs emotions and feelings. Moods, or the ebbs and flows of emotional life, cycle during and across months. Composing and performing from tuning systems based on the locations of the Moon afforded attunement to the moods of our environments and audiences through mutable indeterminacy. Resulting "meaningful coincidences" between audience reactions and the position of the Moon illustrated the phenomena Carl Jung termed synchronicity.[15] Continuing with my example, if the Moon were in Virgo, then Zizia might percuss natural objects associated with the element of *earth* such as stones and plant roots, while expressing modality of *mutability* by adapting or modifying components of the score. Thus, mutable indeterminacy allowed me to interpret and control the feel of my performances based on the astrological archetypes of each concert.

Zizia composed and performed from cosmic and chthonic rhythms to create indeterminate music that attuned with the moods of our audiences. First, fixed indeterminacy offered inspirational chance-based compositional structures from local apparent astrology and ecology, akin to the fixed modality of astrology. Next, cardinal indeterminacy provided intuitional interpretations of compositional parameters within the structures of local astro-ecology, comparable to the cardinal modality of astrology. Lastly, mutable indeterminacy allowed imaginative presentations of astro-ecological symbols, similar to the mutable modality in astrology. Henceforth, simultaneous employment of these three types of indeterminacy will be referred to as *threefold indeterminacy*.

Concert Survey

The simultaneous fourfold (elements) and threefold (modalities) structuring provided a compelling compositional framework for Zizia concerts. In order to assess the audience responses to Zizia performances, I designed and sent a survey to all of the attendees of performances from September 2018–February 2019. The survey responses provided valuable insight into how Zizia performances were received by those with no knowledge of the anthroposophical component of our compositional strategy. The survey also provided a valuable opportunity to utilize scientific methods to analyze an art practice informed by spirituality.

The survey was created using the website Survey Monkey. The link was shared with all of the audience members for whom I had contact information. I sent a survey request to a total of 30 individuals who had attended one of the ten Zizia concerts. The first part of the survey sought to draw out responses from an anthroposophical framework to determine which of the capacities the Zizia concerts impacted most strongly. In anthroposophical terminology, the physical body corresponds to the earth element, without which none of the three capacities can be actualized. Therefore, the survey began by asking about the level of physical comfort during the listening experience. The questions offered five multiple-choice questions from "very uncomfortable" to "very comfortable." The survey then addressed the feeling aspect in a similar manner. Lastly, the willing capacity was addressed. After each of the above multiple-choice questions, respondents were asked to elaborate on their feelings, ideas, and desired actions in an open-ended comment box.

The survey asked respondents whether they were surprised by anything in the Zizia concert, and whether they had ever experienced anything similar, in a concert context or otherwise. The survey concluded with several demographic questions. Respondents were asked to select one of the following age groups: 14–20; 21–27; 28–34;

---

15 Tarnas, *Cosmos and Psyche*.

35–40; 41–48; 49–55; 56–62; 63–69; 70–77. Respondents were asked whether they were musicians or not. Lastly, the survey asked respondents to select how familiar they were with the work of Rudolf Steiner.

The use of both multiple choice and open-ended comment boxes was designed to solicit both quantitative and qualitative data. Materials and methods of surveys that assessed Zizia concerts followed a similar elemental framework as Zizia performances and compositions. Surveys were designed to provide a framework for meaningful exchange between audience and performer after the concert had concluded.

Concert Study Findings

Respondents reported that Zizia concerts impacted their feelings, ideas, and desired actions. The most common response regarding feelings evoked while listening to Zizia was that respondents felt as though they were in nature. One respondent said, "recording and playing back sounds in the room, as well as not playing over the room sound, made me feel as if I was constantly a part of the performance. The use of negative space in particular demanded my concentration." This respondent likely attended one of the last concerts that Zizia performed, during which the performers moved continuously around the room, changing the placement of cassette players and playing various natural objects in various locations. The respondent also discusses the use of "negative space," likely referring to the amount of silence present throughout the performance.

One respondent felt "wonder, confusion, joy, amusement, intrigue," while another reported feeling "challenged, tense, dreamy." Both comments reflect a complex range of emotional responses from a single concert experience. Another respondent "felt that it helped me to concentrate, to slow down everything around me, and to explore an unfamiliar ecosystem of complexity." This sentiment was echoed by a respondent, who reflected that, "the set seemed very organic, sonically and physically. I felt immersed and involved in what was happening in the room at times, and also felt intense moments of introspection. TM [transcendental meditation] like."

Despite the tendency to view experimental music as intellectual, rather than emotion-based, concert attendees reported fewer ideas than feelings. Some of the ideas that respondents remembered were highly imaginative, for instance "visual landscapes and stories of creatures roaming." Another respondent said, "I kept thinking about the relations between recorded sounds of the natural environment and electronic and processed sounds. I was drawn to closer listening through understanding it as a kind of environmental listening." A different respondent had similar thoughts "about nature vs. technology and nature in tandem with technology." These responses suggest that the conscious use of natural and sub-natural sounds was one of the more thought-provoking aspects of the Zizia concerts. While respondents expressed an interest in the complexity of the electronics, their comments emphasized the natural and organic components of the sounds produced.

Ideas often implied inspiration toward action. For example, "it made me think of the untapped potential of incorporating space, smell and sound source variation into performance over all. That is a lot to think about." In general, respondents reported they were motivated to create their own art after listening to Zizia. Several respondents also said that the Zizia concert made them wish to listen more to everything around them. Respondents reported being surprised by the Zizia concerts in the following ways:

- "I was surprised by the content. It was wild and abstract and very out there. But I was also surprised that it brought out/up some emotional energy in me."
- "Some aural effects like sounds travelling in a strange way."
- "I hadn't predicted something so sparse after seeing the gear table. I also don't usually see anyone use so much of a venue as part of the performance."
- "The complexity of the signal chain. The real-time aspect of the performance."

- "The audience's reactions were surprising, especially toward the end."
- "The short length, expected a longer performance / more segmented moments rather than one singular culminating crescendo."
- "The use of things not traditionally considered musical instruments - the boxes of nature, the wildlife scares, the room itself."[16]

Composing from indeterminacy seemed to allow for more moments of synchronicity to appear, or at the very least, for me to notice moments of synchronicity that are always present but often overlooked. For example, the first note that I play on my guitar in a concert is often the same as the tone that is coming from a Borror Lab recording. This is not planned: we use different tapes for each concert, and my tunings are also unique to each concert.

The high (80%) response rate to the Zizia concert feedback discussion was one of the most important overall findings. Also noteworthy was the discovery that only one respondent was "very familiar" with the work of Rudolf Steiner. This finding may indicate that experimental music audiences do not have much familiarity with Anthroposophy, but further research is needed to support that assertion. In conclusion, findings show that listeners felt a range of feelings, experienced creative inspirations, and most often had imaginations of nature while listening to Zizia concerts.

Natal Chart Composition

The next portion of action research utilized both the Planetary Modes and the tone spiral to create musical compositions derived from the natal charts of a group of individuals. The natal chart composition study further utilized fixed, cardinal, and mutable indeterminacy in a practice that was even more specific to astrology. The template of a natal chart generated rhythmic notation, thus utilizing fixed indeterminacy. Notes were selected from the tone spiral, demonstrating the will of cardinal indeterminacy. Finally, mutable indeterminacy occurred through astrological interpretations of the compositional symbolism. My practice of threefold indeterminacy was further refined over the course of the natal chart composition study.

Precedents for using astronomy and astrology as indeterminate compositional tools exist. For example, in *Atlas Elipticalis*, "Cage superimposed music paper on top of star charts and plotted musical compositions as though they were constellations," demonstrating another example of fixed indeterminacy.[17] An example of mutable indeterminacy is *Tierkreis* (1974–75), twelve compositions that Karheinz Stockhausen composed based on the astrological associations of each zodiac sign. My practice used natal charts to generate fixed indeterminacy to compose structured scores; cardinal indeterminacy in selection of notes and instruments; and mutable indeterminacy by embracing the qualitative traditions of astrological symbolism.

First, I derived a method of *fixed indeterminacy* to translate natal charts into rhythmic notation. Each house is represented by one beat in the system of notation developed. The beat is subdivided into a triplet to represent three 10° segments, and the appearance of each planet occupies one count. A 360° degree chart was translated into three 12-beat measures for a total of 36 beats. Thus, the time signature was 12:8. Scores were then written in musical notation using the program MuseScore 3.3. For example, in the chart illustrated by *Figure 2*, the phrase begins with the ascendant, shown by the AC in the middle of the left portion of the circle. Two eighth rests are given, and then the appearance of Pluto at 21° signifies the first note on beat three.

Next, I selected notes based on the zodiacal tone spiral. The zodiac sign of each planet indicated what notes would be selected from the tone spiral. In the chart below, Pluto is in Libra, therefore the notes $B^1\ G^3\ D^5$ are played. The rhythmic progression is played three times through, so that each of the three notes for the zodiac sign of each

---

[16] Concert study respondents, personal communication, May 15–Sept. 12, 2019

[17] Smigel, *Alchemy of the Avant-garde: David Tudor and the New Music of the 1950s*.

Tone Art

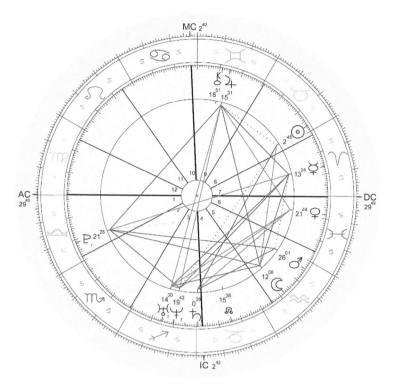

Figure 2. Astrological chart example two: a participant in the natal chart study born at 5:00 p.m., May 18, 1990, in Nycosia, Cyprus.

Figure 3. A score composed from the astrological chart illustrated by Figure 2. The position of each planet determines the rhythm, as indicated by the planetary glyph above each note. The zodiac symbols below the notes indicate the sign of the planet and thus, what notes would be selected from Figure 1, the zodiacal tone spiral.

planet are sounded. However, by only illustrating the rhythmic notation and the corresponding zodiac signs, I left the score open to interpretation. I did not write the score using a full clef. Instead, I allowed for *cardinal indeterminacy,* leaving performers free to choose from any system of correspondence between tones and zodiac signs.

Natal Chart Analysis

I translated the natal charts of 20 individuals, including my own, into musical notation for my case study. My breath determined the tempo: a full inhalation and exhalation equaled an eighth note, approximately 72 bpm.[18] I selected participants who had some familiarity with astrology, anthroposophy, and/or experimental music. Each participant provided date, time, and place of birth in order to calculate an exact astrological chart. While some participants knew each other, most did not, and two were strangers to me. The possibility of composing music based on actual natal charts added a unique component of *mutable indeterminacy*; a richness of archetypal symbolism would be revealed through astrological analysis of each participant.

Natal charts were calculated using the website astro.com, hosted by Astrodienst. The chart was calculated using the "extended chart options" page on astro.com. The house system was "Fagan-Bradley" using the sidereal zodiac. The natal chart of every participant was analyzed according to classical and anthroposophical astrology. The charts were also analyzed as a group in order to understand the overall character of the respondents. A composite chart was derived from the natal charts of all 21 participants using astro.com.

The planetary ruler of each natal chart and the house where it resided were identified for every participant. The planetary archetype of every participant was identified based on the planetary ruler of the chart. The sign and house placement of all of the planets were documented. From that information, the elements and qualities of each participant were tallied, first based on the sign where each planet appeared and second based on the house where each planet appeared.

One of the four temperaments (melancholic, phlegmatic, sanguine, choleric) was identified as the dominant temperament based on the overall

---

18 Renold, *Intervals, Scales, Tones: And the Concert Pitch c = 128 Hz.*

elemental distribution for each participant. For example, if a participant had the majority of planetary placements in air signs, they would be classified as sanguine temperament. In cases where the distribution of elements was tied, a mean value was provided, for example "sanguine-choleric." The temperaments and the chart rulers of all participants in the natal chart study were characterized to predict the quality of responses and the content of comments from astrology and limit my interpretive bias. After each participant characterization was performed, the previously mentioned factors were averaged to show a characteristic participant of the study. Averages were calculated using Microsoft Excel.

Predictions of how participants would respond to each part of the survey were made based on the placements of planets. Associations between various planets and the capacities for feeling, thinking, and willing were drawn from classical and anthroposophical astrology. Predictions for the temperament of comments in the feeling section of the feedback sheet were made by looking at the elements of the signs in which Venus, North Node, and Neptune were located. Predictions for the temperament of comments in the thinking section of the feedback sheet were made based on the placement of Mercury, Jupiter, and Uranus. Predictions for the temperament of the comments in the willing section of the feedback sheet were made based on where Mars, Sun, and Pluto were located. Finally, predictions for where participants might feel the melodies in their body were made based on the physical body and organ system associations with the zodiacal signs of their Ascendant, Moon, and Saturn.

I analyzed and predicted temperaments in order to observe any interconnections between natal chart composition and musical composition responses. One precedent for my analysis of temperament based on astrological charts has been set by an anecdotal study by Greenbaum. Greenbaum identified temperaments for 35 Waldorf students based solely on their natal charts, and then compared the results with the temperament selected by their teachers.[19] Similarly, I analyzed temperament based on averaged and composite astrological features, and then looked for synchronicity in the temperament of responses. The practice of mutable indeterminacy inspired the observation of synchronic moments through astrological symbolism.

Natal Chart Study

Natal chart compositions were played on a Roosebeck "Heather" 22-string lever harp tuned to a scale based on the frequencies for the Planetary Modes as provided by Hamilton. Since my harp only spanned three octaves, I adapted the tone spiral such that once the third octave had been reached, the notes returned to low C and repeated the cycle. As composer and performer, I demonstrated *cardinal indeterminacy* by adapting my original score to suit the limitations of my instrument. The Hamilton frequency chart that I consulted is sourced from Talisha Goh and is reproduced in Table 2. My harp was recorded to digital at Studio B+ in College Park, MD by Tommy Sherrod, using Sennheiser 421, Beyerdynamic m160, and Neumann U87 microphones.

Participants were given three musical tracks to listen to: one track corresponded to their own natal chart, another was composed from the chart of someone they knew, and a third was derived from the natal chart of a stranger. The three tracks were given random alphanumeric code names to eliminate bias. Participants were instructed to pay attention to whether the notes impacted any particular parts of the body. The majority of participants listened to recordings and filled out surveys online. I conducted the study for several participants in person: I performed the three tracks live on harp and was present while participants filled out feedback forms.

Natal chart composition study participants were instructed to listen to the first recording and then fill out a Survey Monkey feedback form. The process was repeated two more times for the other two tracks. The final form included a reflection on the overall experience and participants guessed

---

19 Greenbaum, *Temperament: Astrology's Forgotten Key*, pp. 57-72

Mode	Tone and Hertz							
Sun/Dorian	C 256	D 281.6	E 312.89	F# 352	G 375.46 / G# 402.28	A# 433.24	B 469.22	C 512
Venus/Phrygian	B 234.67	C 256	D 281.6	E 312.89	F# 352	G 375.46 / G# 402.28	A# 433.24	B 469.22
Mercury/Lydian	A# 216.62	B 234.67	C 256	D 281.6	E 312.89	F# 352	G 375.46 / G# 402.28	A# 433.24
Moon/Mixolydian	G# 201.14	A# 216.62	B 234.67	C 256	D 281.6	E 312.89	F# 352	G# 402.28
Saturn/Hypodorian	F# 176	G 187.73	A# 216.62	B 234.67	C 256	D 281.6	E 312.89	F# 352
Jupiter/Hypophrygian	E 156	F# 176	G 187.73	A# 216.62	B 234.67	C 256	D 281.6	E 312.89
Mars/Hypolydian	D 140.8	E 156	F# 176	G 187.73	A# 216.62	B 234.67	C 256	D 281.6

Table 2. *Hamilton Frequencies arranged by Mode,* adapted from Goh, 2014.*

* *The names of the Planetary Modes are specific to the Greek aulos modes. Musicians still refer to modes with the same names, but these are distinct from the ancient Greek modes and correspond to scales that originated within church traditions during the Middle Ages (Renold, p. 46).*

which track corresponded to their natal chart. The survey began with the same questions as the Zizia Concert Feedback form to address the feeling, thinking, and willing capacities. The question about physical comfort was omitted because the instructions in the introduction to the feedback form included the directive to find a comfortable place to listen.

All comments from each respondent were analyzed according to temperament. For example, a response such as "my mind wandered and I had difficulty focusing on the sounds" would be classified as sanguine. A response such as "I got up and danced" would be categorized as choleric. The response "I felt a wave of melancholy" would be melancholic, and "I felt at peace" would be characterized as phlegmatic. The associations of the respondents' individual temperament and the temperaments displayed in the written responses were compared to show patterns. I compared the temperaments displayed by each participant's responses versus the temperaments indicated by people listening to their track. Each respondent's preferred track was also characterized by temperament. These were identified to show connections between the natal chart and the respondent's interpretation of the musical composition. I also looked at the planetary ruler to try and predict the temperament of comments.

The small number of participants allowed me to carefully observe nuances in listening styles. Qualitative data was more important than quantitative data for this survey, which prioritized individual responses. Compositional methods of fixed,

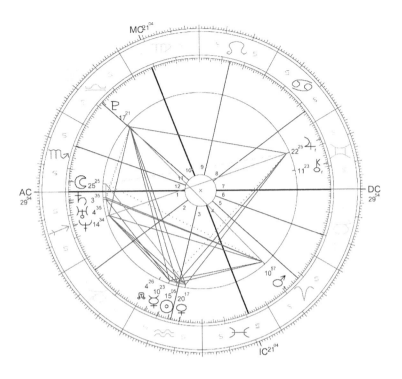

Figure 4: Multi-composite astrological chart for 16 respondents in the natal chart study and myself. The multi-composite shows a Sun in Aquarius, Moon in Scorpio, and Scorpio Ascendant.

Figure 5: A score created from the multi-composite astrological chart illustrated in Figure 3.

cardinal, and mutable indeterminacy continued to be explored. Thus, the interactive listening process initiated through the Zizia musical composition survey deepened through the more intimate natal chart composition study.

Natal Chart Study Findings

The natal chart study had an 80% response rate, the same percentage as the Zizia concert survey. Responses to the natal chart case study were highly individualized. Overall, the responses were affirming and useful for my work as both an astrologer and composer. As an astrologer, I appreciated the opportunity to closely work with the astrology of a large group of individuals. As a composer, I valued the opportunity to hear direct feedback about melodies. I will first discuss an overview of themes across all responses and then provide detailed summaries of three respondents' survey feedback.

My initial astrological approach of averaging the placements of all planets across all charts was a valuable experience, but the later technique of analyzing based on a multi-composite chart provided deeper insight and more accurate response predictions. Averaged placement of planets across all houses and signs predicted a choleric temperament for listening styles and responses, which was inaccurate. The multi-composite chart creates an average based around a circular, rather than linear scale, which is difficult to achieve using standard methods of averaging data. Although averaging individual charts was not accurate, the practice helped me appreciate the nuance in each respondent's experience, and recognize the importance of using a circular, rather than linear method of averaging in astrology.

Initial calculations using a multi-composite chart predicted overall choleric responses. However, I realized that the multi-composite included data for participants who had not responded to the study. I omitted the birth data of participants who had not actually responded to the study and instead cast a multi-composite chart with only respondent data. The respondent multi-composite chart predicted overall sanguine responses, which proved to be highly accurate. Due to the accuracy of the multi-composite chart, I will highlight some noteworthy features of the multi-composite chart.

The multi-composite chart for all participants in the study had Sun in Aquarius, Moon in Scorpio, and Ascendant in Scorpio. Uranus rules Aquarius in contemporary astrology, joining the classical ruler, Saturn. Aquarians are associated with forward-thinking, progressive, and utopian ideals. The multi-composite ascendant in the fixed, water sign of Scorpio suggests that the purpose and orientation of the study was to communicate hidden emotional truths. Scorpio Moon shows that the emotional responses to the survey were transformative and functioned on an occult level.

The majority of participants were born within the same generation, resulting in coherence among outer planet placement. Most participants had Uranus in Sagittarius, Neptune in Sagittarius, and Pluto in Libra. Uranus and Neptune in the mutable, fire sign of Sagittarius suggests that participants shared a strong spiritual intuition that motivates them toward self-directed higher knowledge while rejecting the orthodoxy of religion. Pluto in the cardinal, air sign of Libra indicates that respondents shared an interest in creating a new, balanced, and egalitarian relationship to power. The placements of Uranus, Neptune, and Pluto together suggest that the majority of respondents work with sub-nature in an intuitive and unconventional manner.

The planetary ruler of the ascendant and thus the multi-composite chart was Mars. The element of fire was emphasized due to the placement of the ruling planet in a fire sign (Aries), but its location in a water house (the Fourth) dampened the fiery impulse. The most recurrent element for the multi-composite was air, suggesting sanguine tendencies. Earth was notably lacking in the multi-composite, implying that the melancholic responses would be underrepresented. Air was indeed represented when responses were analyzed by temperament: both the feeling and thinking responses were a majority of sanguine and the willing section was characterized as phlegmatic-sanguine. The averaged majority of planets in mutable signs and cadent houses could also have contributed to the sanguinity in responses.

The element of air was further emphasized when the angles between planets were analyzed. Astrologers refer to the angles between planets as aspects and analyze them in order to understand challenging and favorable karmic influences in a natal chart. Planets that are 30° or 60° from each other form favorable aspects, while planets that are 90° or 180° indicate tension within the chart. In the multi-composite chart, Venus, Jupiter, and Pluto are each roughly 60° from each other, forming what astrologers call a *grand trine*. Grand trines indicate harmonious relationships between the planets involved. In the case of the multi-composite, the grand trine occurred within air signs, further emphasizing communication, music, and sanguinity.

Despite the emphasis on sanguinity, respondents tended to prefer tracks that they perceived as phlegmatic. Images evoked by the tracks were also decidedly phlegmatic, with a majority describing scenes associated with water (thirteen mentions) and/or plants (twelve mentions). Examples of responses having to do with water and plants include:

- "I was thinking about collecting things as a child, mostly plants and rocks, and stirring them in water and letting them sit in the water. I remember adding dirt, and it being warm and breezy or crisp and bright. I was thinking then about seasonality, in relation to water and the pond I lived near."
- "I was sitting by a lake or pond in a forest, it was near dusk. The sun filtering through the cedars and pines. I was alone. A creature like a muskrat slithered up and looked at me curiously, then swam around my legs eventually joining me on the rock ledge I was on. We sat there for a while. We weren't holding hands, but it felt like we were. It felt like we were convening and energetically doing something with the water and forest. Like tuning it, almost. There was the buzz of lightning bugs starting up, through the trees, as it darkened."
- "I found myself thinking of my Pisces attributes and left me craving a project based around honoring the sea."
- "There was this repetitive high and low tone pattern that reminded me of the rising and falling of waves."
- "I had feelings of vulnerability or sadness. Also kind of grounding. Deepening, grounding and a certain sadness. Like going down into a watery place."
- "I was walking toward a railroad track by myself through tall grasses."

- "I felt like I was in a cave or forest. Lonely. Awaiting something or someone maybe."[20]

One explanation for the preference for phlegmatic tracks and association with phlegmatic imagery could be that the most common planetary ruler across all charts was Venus, which ruled 24% of participants' charts. In classical astrology, Venus is associated with the phlegmatic temperament. Furthermore, having both the composite Ascendant and Moon in the water sign of Scorpio provided additional weight on water and thus, phlegmatic temperament.

The aesthetic sensibility of Venus and the element of water were also reflected in the art forms that respondents reported being inspired to create. Several participants also reported that listening to the recordings made them want to paint. For example:

- "I enjoyed the feeling I had while focusing so intensely on single notes and the reverberations that they left. It just reminded me of how saturated I often am with noise without giving any of it that much of my attention. It also made me want to paint and use colors, which is weird because I never paint and don't typically enjoy it."[21]
- "I felt motivated to take on a bunch of after work tasks. I also thought about making a watercolor sample board of the new watercolors that I have."[22]

Whereas the Zizia concert feedback survey reflected associations with the music and the environment, the natal chart study focused on the microcosm of the human body. Although I did not expect that many listeners would notice how a note impacted their spleen, for example, the presence of such a question hopefully engaged the listener in a deeper physical meditation. Furthermore, paying attention to subtle changes within the body seemed to enhance the overall listening experience.

The most recurrent body part mentioned was the head, with a total of 24 comments, followed by the chest (17 comments) and throat (16 comments). The head is associated with Aries, the chest with Leo, and the throat with Taurus, three signs that were not emphasized in the multi-composite chart. The heart was the most recurrent organ mentioned, with 22 comments, followed by the lungs with 13 comments. The heart is associated with the Sun, while the lungs are connected to Mercury. The association with the lungs could be due to the fact that my breath determined the tempo of each track. Andrews stated that the harp is the instrument most connected to the crown, brow, throat, and heart chakras.[23] Respondents felt the melody most strongly in the areas of the body and organs associated with the chakra energy centers, suggesting that the choice of instrumentation influenced the physical body more than individual astrology.

The unusual nature of the tuning coupled with a very minimalist performance style resulted in highly idiosyncratic, ambient pieces. Although some respondents were uncomfortable with the amount of silence in the compositions or unfamiliarity of the intervals, they all listened with attention and respect. Many respondents reported that they were anxious or uncomfortable at first, but by the time they reached the last track they felt comfortable and peaceful. The majority had strong emotional responses and/or pictorial imaginations as a result of the compositions.

Forty-four percent of respondents guessed correctly which of the three tracks they listened to corresponded to their own natal chart. Nearly all of the respondents with significant prior experience with astrology guessed correctly, however. Respondents seemed to enjoy the charts of their friends the least, preferring either the chart of a stranger or their own chart to someone that they knew well.

---

20 Natal chart study participants, personal communication, May 24- August 4, 2019

21 Respondent *10 November*, personal communication, June 10, 2019

22 Respondent *22 April*, personal communication, June 18, 2019

23 Andrews, *Sacred Sounds*, p. 39

DISCUSSION

Astrological Indeterminacy

David Tudor initially inspired my explorations of indeterminacy, which emerged as a central compositional methodology for my action research. In the concert study, I applied astrological tunings derived from the work of Schlesinger and Hamilton to apparent movements of the Moon for systems of fixed, cardinal, and mutable indeterminacy. My practice of composing from astrological indeterminacy deepened and became even more specific in the natal chart study. In both studies, fixed indeterminacy helped me emulate natural processes to avoid subjectivity in music composition. Cardinal indeterminacy encouraged interpretation of scores based on intuitions. Mutable indeterminacy offered an important archetypal framework to cultivate opportunities for community engagement through my research.

Fixed indeterminacy functioned in both studies as a chance operation, similar to the I-Ching for John Cage or the Tarot for David Tudor. The employment of fixed indeterminacy helped me to compose in accordance with natural principles rather than from subjective tastes. The importance of this category of astrological indeterminacy, therefore, does not necessarily lie in the predictive aspect of astrology. Instead, chance operation-based compositions allowed for even more transformative listening experiences by buffering the ego of the composer-performer. Furthermore, as both composer and performer, I enjoyed being surprised by the results of each composition. Paying attention to the ways that each piece was congruent or incongruent with my astrological predictions helped me be more engaged with each performance of a melody.

All categories of indeterminacy seemed to allow for more moments of synchronicity or, at the very least, for me to notice moments of synchronicity. Cardinal indeterminacy encouraged Fowler and me to embrace synchronic moments during performance. For example, if a field recording randomly triggered by Fowler was close to the same note as I had played on guitar, then I might choose to slow the rate of my breathing, thus sustaining a microtonal harmony longer than I had sustained previous tones. Performances became greater than my feeling of individual success or failures when I allowed myself to be open to the surprises that arose from intuitive improvisation with cardinal indeterminacy.

Mutable indeterminacy offered flexibility to interpret the archetypal symbolic structure and appreciate the intricate wonders of astrology. Furthermore, the symbolism of astrology provided meaningful experiences for listeners. Because my initial predictions did not correlate with the results of my natal chart study interpretations, I first concluded that astrology would function only as a source of indeterminacy, generating scores and performance cues. However after discovering that the second multi-composite chart was predictively accurate, I realized that I had been minimizing the symbolic power of astrology. Mutable indeterminacy encouraged explorations of the symbolic language of the collective unconscious, expressed through synchronicity.

In describing the fixed indeterminacy of Atlas Elipticalis, Smigel says, "Cage's techniques of chance and indeterminacy, through the lens of sonification, were a way of letting nature speak for itself."[24] Mutable indeterminacy in the natal chart study further situated the human as part of nature, rather than as an observer of natural processes. Mutable indeterminacy honored the symbolic associations that astrology evokes, inspiring meaningful exchanges between composer-performer and participants. The predictive accuracy of the multi-composite chart attests to the power of threefold, astrological indeterminacy in representing archetypes within the collective unconscious.

The buffering of threefold indeterminacy coupled with the interpretive traditions of astrology provided a compelling combination for me as a composer. Composing from fixed indeterminacy kept me from experiencing "composer's block" because inspiration came from a reality larger than my individual experiences and subjective

---

24 Smigel, *Alchemy of the Avant-garde: David Tudor and the New Music of the 1950s.* p. 27.

tastes. Composing with fixed indeterminacy alone could have resulted in a rather detached practice, however. Cardinal indeterminacy provided opportunities to perform with intuition through improvisation. Mutable indeterminacy invited astrological interpretation and incorporation of community feedback as part of an artistic process. Astrological indeterminacy was practiced conceptually throughout my research through the inclusion of the modern planets of Uranus, Pluto, and Neptune.

Cosmic Sound

> *Thus, in using the ancient modes as a new language of music, we have a perfectly open field where no modern laws of melody or harmony need exist to disturb the composer in his own untrammelled inspirations. Who can tell whether they may not lead to a new revelation in the music of the future.*[25]

Uranus, Pluto, and Neptune represent distinct modern approaches to music listening and music creation. In my previous article, I shared that Uranus corresponds to amplification, Neptune corresponds to the capacity to record and edit sound, and Pluto with the ability to perform with electronic musical instruments. I concluded that Uranus symbolizes both the intellectual idealism of sound art and the spiritual idealism of New Age music. Mysterious and confrontational Pluto suits the subversive nature of noise music. Neptune, positioned between the two, best represents my own exploration of a rhythmic tone art practice. In the following section, I will provide examples of how my findings reflected impulses of each of the modern planets.

Uranus represented my utilization of the esoteric and microtonal Planetary Mode frequencies in the natal chart study. Respondents described the tuning of the harp in the natal chart study as simultaneously "eerie," "haunting," and "healing," with musicians identifying the sounds as "microtonal." Although Hamilton and Schlesinger composed and researched prior to the New Age era, their revitalization of the Planetary Modes represented a Uranus approach: an ancient folk tradition was illuminated for a new era through rational thought and extensive research. Furthermore, their compositions were precursors to sound art, highlighting the microtonality of the overtone series. Hamilton hoped that the Modes may "lead to a new revelation in the music of the future."[26] My contribution to the lineage of composition with the Planetary Modes was to link them to current astrology. Thus, I revitalized the esoteric musical language of Hamilton and Schlesinger through site and time specific sound art practices.

Plutonian noise and silence, together with tone, created reverent listening experiences in my action research. Respondents of both the Zizia concert survey and the natal chart study described the listening experience in spiritual terms. One natal chart study respondent remarked that the experience made them wish to meditate more, while another respondent to the Zizia concert survey compared the experience to transcendental meditation. The confrontational impulse of Pluto encouraged me to leave enough silence for discomfort, which eventually made space for deeper listening. Zizia did not make any overt reference to spiritual themes in our concerts. Instead, we discretely followed meditative breathing patterns and focused on cultivating an internally contemplative performance practice. The spiritual reflections that audience members shared were therefore not predetermined by overt spirituality. Overall, findings suggest that listening to pieces that utilize noise and silence has healing potential in the current era of sonic overstimulation.

Attributes of Neptune were most clearly reflected in responses to both studies, leading me to conclude that Neptune corresponded to my practice of tone art. Neptune is associated with the ability to cultivate spiritual love through transcending the sympathies and antipathies of Venus-ruled romantic love. Listeners in the natal chart study experienced musical antipathies and sympathies, but overall, respondents arrived at a degree of objective appreciation of tonal nuance. There did not appear to be any objectively

---

25 Hamilton, 1953, p. 5

26 Hamilton, *The Modes of Ancient Greece*, p. 5.

harmonious or disharmonious tracks; although the harp tuning was unusual and the melodies were sparse, different respondents had markedly distinct reactions to the same track. This finding was a pleasant surprise; I had worried that the unfamiliar musical style would be unapproachable to listeners. Instead, I discovered that my respondents were highly attentive to the subtlety within these unusual compositions, demonstrating the Neptunian transcendence of personal sympathy and antipathy.

Neptune is considered to be a higher octave of the Moon, therefore both correspond to feelings and the unconscious. In the concert and natal chart studies, respondents described a richness of feelings, rather than concrete ideas or desired actions. The Moon reflects the individual unconscious, while Neptune reveals the collective unconscious. Synchronicity revealed through threefold indeterminacy showed the power of Neptune to evoke patterns from the collective unconscious. As ruler of the ocean, Neptune is intimately connected with the element of water. Water-related imagery was the most common theme across all natal chart study responses. Additionally, despite the overall emphasis on sanguinity, respondents in the natal chart study preferred tracks that they perceived as phlegmatic. After water and plants, darkness received the most mentions, affirming the association between Neptune and the symbolism of the goddess Night.

Neptune corresponds to the virtue of inspiration according to Powell.[27] Many respondents in both studies reported being inspired to further their own creative pursuits. Specifically, several natal chart respondents expressed the impulse to paint after listening to the recordings. Neptune is the modern ruler of the sign of Pisces, and one respondent to the natal chart study even said, "I found myself thinking of my Pisces attributes and it left me craving a project based around honoring the sea."[28] Neptune unites the aesthetic sensibility of Venus and the watery impulse of the Moon through the art form of painting. Lastly, while I originally conceived of my research as anthroposophical sound art, the Cosmic Sound of Neptune inspired me to redefine my work as tone art.

Super-nature

He must understand Sub-Nature for what it really is. This he can only do if he rises, in spiritual knowledge, at least as far into extra-earthly Super-Nature as he has descended, in technical Sciences, into Sub-Nature. The age requires a knowledge transcending Nature, because in its inner life it must come to grips with a life content, which has sunk far beneath Nature — a life-content whose influence is perilous. Needless to say, there can be no question here of advocating a return to earlier states of civilization. The point is that man shall find the way to bring the conditions of modern civilization into their true relationship—to himself and to the Cosmos.[29]

Tone art positions the human being as mediator between cosmic and chthonic musical impulses through sounding what Steiner referred to as "extra-earthly Super-Nature."[30] Zizia composed from cosmic principles and performed with both organic instruments and sub-natural forces. Although audience members did not know of the astrological or anthroposophical components of Zizia composition, they nevertheless articulated experiences of an "extra-earthly Super-Nature" in their own manner. The natal chart study did not contain any environmental sounds or explicit references to the natural world, yet numerous respondents reported vivid imaginations of the natural world and strong sensations within their physical bodies. Together, these findings suggest that esoteric musical practices such as astrology and meditative breathing can evoke experiences of super-nature aided by the assistance of sub-nature.

My research led to the realization that sub-nature is equally reflected in the cosmos through the presence of Uranus, Neptune, and Pluto. Pluto

---

27 Powell, *Hermetic Astrology: Volume 2.*
28 Respondent, March 9, personal communication, June 1, 2019

29 Steiner, *Anthroposophical Leading Thoughts,* "From Nature to Sub-nature."
30 Ibid.

in particular, corresponds to sub-nature through the association with Hades, the chthonic god of the underworld. An infamous myth recounts how Hades abducted the goddess of spring, Persephone, forcing her to become his subterranean queen. Demeter, mother of Persephone, mourned the loss of her daughter and thus, the living earth stopped producing food for humans. Eventually, Zeus intervened and an agreement was reached wherein Persephone would spend six months of the year aboveground with her mother, and six months of the year below with her husband. The subterranean negotiation between Hades and Persephone provides an archetype for musical navigations between cosmic, earthly, and chthonic terrains.

Concert study respondents, while impressed with the electronic components, reported many imaginations of being in nature while listening to Zizia. Respondents also expressed the desire to more carefully observe the natural world after listening to Zizia. Several listeners also reported having imaginations of animals moving about the room, or the presence of a supernatural creature. These findings suggest that conscious use of electronic components does not inherently decrease the wisdom of the human being, but rather, extends the imaginative potential of the human outward through time and space. Sub-natural auditory effects enabled city dwellers to feel transported to super-nature through their imaginative capacities.

Natal chart study respondents also reported vivid imaginations of the natural world, which were even more difficult to account for considering the minimalist tones of the harp melodies. The most common themes expressed by natal chart respondents also seemed to demonstrate a feeling for extra-earthly super-nature. In order of most frequent to least, respondents mentioned: water, plants, darkness, animals, and planets. The medium of recorded sound seemingly transported listeners to experiences of extra-earthly super-nature in much the same way that Zizia concerts evoked imaginations of nature.

The etheric body of the human being is associated with the element of water, plants, rhythm, and breath. Steiner associates the art form of painting with the astral body pushing into the "rhythmic and harmonious" etheric body.[31] Three natal chart respondents expressed the desire to paint, one specifically with watercolors. The preference for phlegmatic tracks and the pictorial imaginations of plants and water together suggest that the melodies, although composed according to astral patterns, impacted the etheric body. Natal chart respondents reported feeling melodies in their heart and lungs, both organs within the rhythmic system. Emphasis on the rhythmic system indicates that my usage of the breath as meter, further subdivided by the heartbeat rate of 72 bpm, may have contributed to an etheric awareness.

Music as an art form "contains the laws of our ego... pressed down into the subconscious, into the astral body."[32] Yet tone art, by shifting attention away from a central performer toward an interrelated, shifting ecosystem of ambient sound could be said to correspond more to the steady pulse of the etheric than traditional, melody driven music. The etheric exists on a spiritual level in the Life Spirit, a higher faculty that can only be cultivated through development of the ego. Meditation and awareness of the breath helps to build the collective spiritual love of Life Spirit. Meditative breathing patterns as musical meter, together with attunement to astrological rhythms, provided opportunities for composer-performers and listeners to rise together toward greater spiritual understanding.

The unlikely marriage between the death symbolized by Hades and the rebirth represented by Persephone is a reminder of the ultimate cyclicity of earthly existence. In Zizia concerts, terrestrial stridulations evoked the sound of the insect apocalypse while astral melodies summoned the spiritual potential of the human being. The natal chart compositions embraced the small deaths represented by musical silence in order to make space for the creative hearing of the listener. My research reveals that chthonic sub-nature contains an inherent polarity: the potential to awaken supernatural awareness. The tone artist, like Persephone, cycles

---

31 Steiner, *Art as Seen in the Light of Mystery Wisdom*.
32 Ibid.

between the underworld, the living earth, and the cosmos. Breathing between chthonic and cosmic, winter and spring, death and life, the tone artist embraces the cyclicity of existence.

Tone Art

Action research in the connections between anthroposophy, astrology, and music has inspired my practice of tone art. I will provide an overview of key insights into what characterizes my practice of tone art, again following an elemental schema. Earth introduces physical components of tone art. Fire addresses the spiritual dimension of tone and the creative will of the human. Air situates tone art within a conceptual framework of transdisciplinary creative practice. Water imagines super-natural components of tone art. Lastly, the fifth element of spirit will again be acknowledged with examples of how tone art cultivates the higher faculties of imagination, inspiration, and intuition.

Earth. Tone art is similar to sound art in that tone art begins with the physical properties of sound. Gilmurray posits that sound art is an inherently ecological genre, due the way that sound art can "highlight the vibrant agency of nonhuman matter" and create "an embodied experience of our own ecological interconnectedness with the other things in our environment."[33] He further contends that ecological sound art should be distinguished from sound art, due to the fact that many sound artists explicitly address environmental issues. Tone art as practiced by Zizia shares many similarities with ecological sound art; for example, Zizia explicitly practices habitat restoration to help non-humans in danger of extinction.[34] Observations of the natural world and acoustic characteristics of sound provide a foundation for tone art practice.

Fire. Tone art is distinguishable from sound art in that tone art acknowledges the spirituality of tone. Ecological activism practiced through sound art could be inspired by spiritual values, yet the genre does not explicitly engage with super-natural elements. Tone art, in contrast, acknowledges the soul and spirit in addition to the physical body. Tone art is microcosmic and macrocosmic, recognizing the sacredness of mineral, plant, animal, human, and spirit. Anthroposophy uplifts the wisdom of the human with the conviction that if we understand what makes us unique from animals, plants, and minerals, then we may appreciate what responsibility we have toward nature. Tone art provides one possible pathway toward regenerative environmental activism.

Air. Tone art is always transdisciplinary, working toward holism through art, science, and spirituality. The body of my action research demonstrates a transdisciplinary approach to tone art creation. For example, surveying audience members and creating a case study for listeners in the natal chart study utilized methods from the social sciences within an arts context. The scientific approach to collecting and organizing data from respondents helped me reflect on the relevance of my artistic practice in a unique manner. Furthermore, using a buffered, scientific approach to data collection made space for audience members to express themselves freely. Spirituality guided my use of tone, yet I avoided overtly religious symbolism while performing in secular contexts. Art, science, and spirituality are unified through inspirational tone.

Water. Tone art reveres nature and collaborates with sub-nature to strive toward music creation that reflects extra-earthly super-nature. I revered nature through observation of celestial rhythms and restoration of terrestrial habitats. I embraced sub-nature through performances with electronics and by utilizing the tremendous potential for community engagement provided by the Internet. Spiritual practices such as astrological indeterminacy, explorations of modern planetary archetypes, and meditative breathing practices have been presented as key to creating super-natural listening experiences. Tone art heals imbalances through rhythmic imagination of extra-earthly super-nature.

Spirit. Tone art as a methodology, not a genre, invites transformation of the composer-performer through cultivation of the higher faculties of

---

33 Gilmurray, *Ecology and Environmentalism in Contemporary Sound Art*. pp. 178–179.
34 https://zizia.xyz/plan(e)t_music.html.

imagination, inspiration, and intuition. Spiritual artistic practice has transformed me as a composer-performer. New compositional methods were imagined through my action research, thanks to the illumination of the Planetary Modes by Schlesinger and Hamilton. Regular observation of astral rhythms and attunement to terrestrial environments has inspired the refinement of my performances. Indeterminacy provided by astrology and electronics have created opportunities to perform with intuition.[35] Spiritual cultivation initiates authenticity and beauty within creative practice.

Steiner once stated that he would change the name "Anthroposophy"[36] every day if he could in order to keep the philosophy from becoming dogmatic. Similarly, tone art is a living, mutating term for sound art from Anthroposophy. Tone art has provided a creative framework for my research. In identifying the features of tone art, I have summarized the response to my research question: *How does one create contemporary sound art from Anthroposophy?*

---

35 *Asteraceae* (2020) presents further experiments with astrological indeterminacy: https://zizia.xyz/aster.html

36 Steiner, *The Foundations of Human Experience*.

EVENING MEDITATION

In the evening meditate on the Earth as a great radiant green star shining out into the cosmos, and allow the heart to speak:

May this prayer from my warm heart unite

With the Earth's Light which reveres the Christ–Sun,

That I may find Spirit in the Light of the Spirit,

Breath of the Soul in the World's Breath,

Human Strength in the Life of the Earth.

Given by Rudolf Steiner, March 9, 1924, to Maud B. Monges of Spring Valley, New York (translated by R Powell)

WORKING WITH THE
STAR WISDOM CALENDAR
Robert Powell, PhD

In taking note of the astronomical events listed in the Star Calendar, it is important to distinguish between long- and short-term astronomical events. Long-term astronomical events—for example, Pluto transiting a particular degree of the zodiac—will have a longer period of meditation than would the five days advocated for short-term astronomical events such as the New and Full Moon. The following describes, in relation to meditating on the Full Moon, a meditative process extending over a five-day period.

Sanctification of the Full Moon

As a preliminary remark, let us remind ourselves that the great sacrifice of Christ on the Cross—the Mystery of Golgotha—took place at Full Moon. As Christ's sacrifice took place when the Moon was full in the middle of the sidereal sign of Libra, the Libra Full Moon assumes special significance in the sequence of twelve (or thirteen) Full Moons taking place during the cycle of the year. In following this sequence, the Mystery of Golgotha serves as an archetype for *every* Full Moon, since each Full Moon imparts a particular spiritual blessing. Hence the practice described here as *Sanctification of the Full Moon* applies to every Full Moon. Similarly, there is also the practice of *Sanctification of the New Moon*, as described in *Hermetic Astrology, Volume 2: Astrological Biography*, chapter 10.

During the two days prior to the Full Moon, we can consider the focus of one's meditation to extend over these two days as *preparatory days*, immediately preceding the day of the Full Moon. These two days can be dedicated to spiritual reflection and detachment from everyday concerns as one prepares to become a vessel for the in-streaming light and love one will receive at the Full Moon, something that one can then impart further—for example, to help people in need, or to support Mother Earth in times of catastrophe. During these two days, it is helpful to hold an attitude of dedication and service and try to assume an attitude of receptivity that opens to what one's soul will receive and subsequently impart—an attitude conducive to making one a true *servant of the spirit*.

The day of the Full Moon is itself a day of *holding the sacred space*. In doing so, one endeavors to cultivate inner peace and silence, during which one attempts to contact and consciously hold the in-streaming blessing of the Full Moon for the rest of humanity. One can heighten this silent meditation by visualizing the zodiacal constellation–sidereal sign in which the Moon becomes full, since the Moon serves to reflect the starry background against which it appears.

If the Moon is full in Virgo, for example, it reminds us of the night of the birth of the Jesus child visited by the three magi, as described in the Gospel of St. Matthew. That birth occurred at the Full Moon in the middle of the sidereal sign of Virgo, and the three magi, who gazed up that evening to behold the Full Moon against the background of the stars of the Virgin, witnessed the soul of Jesus emerge from the disk of the Full Moon and descend toward Earth. They participated from afar, via the starry heavens, in the Grail Mystery of the holy birth.

By meditating on the Full Moon and opening oneself to receive the in-streaming blessing from the starry heavens, we can exercise restraint by avoiding the formulation of what will happen or what one might receive from the Full Moon. Moreover, we can also refrain from seeking tangible results or effects connected with our attunement to the Full Moon. Even if we observe only the date but not the exact moment when the Moon is full, it is helpful to find quiet time to reflect alone or to use the opportunity for deep meditation on the day of the Full Moon.

We can think of the two days following the Full Moon as a *time of imparting* what we have received from the in-streaming of the Moon's full disk against the background of the stars. It is now possible to turn our attention toward humanity and the world and endeavor to pass on any spiritual blessing we have received from the starry heavens. Thereby we can assist in the work of the spiritual world by transforming what we have received into goodwill and allowing it to flow wherever the greatest need exists.

It is a matter of *holding a sacred space* throughout the day of the Full Moon. This is an important time to still the mind and maintain inner peace. It is a time of spiritual retreat and contact with the spiritual world, of holding in one's consciousness the archetype of the Mystery of Golgotha as a great outpouring of Divine Love that bridges Heaven and Earth. Prior to the day of the Full Moon, the two preceding days prepare the sacred space as a vessel to receive the heavenly blessing. The two days following the day of the Full Moon are a time to assimilate and distribute the spiritual transmission received into the sacred space we have prepared.

One can apply the process described here as a meditative practice in relation to the Full Moon to any of the astronomical events listed in *Star Wisdom*, especially as most of these *remember* significant Christ Events. Take note, however, whether an event is long-term or short-term and adjust the period of meditative practice accordingly.

"The shadow intellect that is characteristic of all modern culture has fettered human beings to the Earth. They have eyes only for earthly things, particularly when they allow themselves to be influenced by the claims of modern science. In our age it never occurs to someone that their being belongs not to the Earth alone but to the cosmos beyond the Earth. Knowledge of our connection with the cosmos beyond the Earth—that is what we need above all to make our own.... When someone says 'I' to themselves, they experience a force that is working within, and the [ancient] Greek, in feeling the working of this inner force, related it to the Sun;...the Sun and the 'I' are the outer and inner aspects of one being. The Sun out there in space is the cosmic 'I.' What lives within me is the human 'I.'... Human beings are not primarily a creation of Earth. Human beings receive their shape and form from the cosmos. The human being is an offspring of the world of stars, above all of the Sun and Moon.... The Moon forces stream out from a center in the metabolic system.... [The] Moon stimulates reproduction.... Saturn works chiefly in the upper part of the astral body.... Jupiter has to do with thinking...Mars [has] to do with speech.... The Mercury forces work in the part of the human organism that lies below the region of the heart...in the breathing and circulatory functions.... Venus works preeminently in the etheric body of the human being."

—RUDOLF STEINER, *Offspring of the World of Stars*, May 5, 1921

SYMBOLS USED IN CHARTS

	Planets		Zodiacal Signs		Aspects
⊕	Earth	♈	Aries (Ram)	☌	Conjunction 0°
☉	Sun	♉	Taurus (Bull)	✱	Sextile 60°
☽	Moon	♊	Gemini (Twins)	□	Square 90°
☿	Mercury	♋	Cancer (Crab)	△	Trine 120°
♀	Venus	♌	Leo (Lion)	☍	Opposition 180°
♂	Mars	♍	Virgo (Virgin)		
♃	Jupiter	♎	Libra (Scales)		
♄	Saturn	♏	Scorpio (Scorpion)		
♅	Uranus	♐	Sagittarius (Archer)		
♆	Neptune	♑	Capricorn (Goat)		
♇	Pluto	♒	Aquarius (Water Carrier)		
		♓	Pisces (Fishes)		

Other

☊	Ascending (North) Node	☌	Sun Eclipse
☋	Descending (South) Node	☍	Moon Eclipse
P	Perihelion–Perigee	☌	Inferior Conjunction
A	Aphelion–Apogee	☌	Superior Conjunction
	Maximum Latitude	⚷	Chiron
	Minimum Latitude		

TIME

The information relating to daily geocentric and heliocentric planetary positions in the sidereal zodiac is tabulated in the form of an ephemeris for each month, in which the planetary positions are given at 0 hours Universal Time (UT) each day.

Beneath the geocentric and heliocentric ephemeris for each month, the information relating to planetary aspects is given in the form of an aspectarian, which lists the most important aspects—geocentric and heliocentric–hermetic—between the planets for the month in question. The day and the time of occurrence of the aspect on that day are indicated, all times being given in Universal Time (UT), which is identical to Greenwich Mean Time (GMT). For example, zero hours Universal Time is midnight GMT. This time system applies in Britain; however, when summer time is in effect, one hour must be added to all times.

** In other time zones, the time has to be adjusted according to whether it is ahead of or behind Britain. For example, in Germany, where the time is one hour ahead of British time, an hour must be added; when summer time is in effect in Germany, two hours have to be added to all times.

Using the calendar in the United States, do the following subtraction from all time indications according to time zone:

- Pacific Time subtract 8 hours
  (7 hours for daylight saving time);
- Mountain Time subtract 7 hours
  (6 hours for daylight saving time);
- Central Time subtract 6 hours
  (5 hours for daylight saving time);
- Eastern Time subtract 5 hours
  (4 hours for daylight saving time).

This subtraction will often change the date of an astronomical occurrence, shifting it back one day. Consequently, since most of the readers of this calendar live on the American Continent, astronomical occurrences during the early hours of day x are sometimes listed in the Commentaries as occurring on days $x-1/x$. For example, an eclipse occurring at 03:00 UT on the 12th is listed as occurring on the 11–12th since in America it takes place on the 11th.[1]

SIMPLIFYING THE PROCEDURE

The preceding procedure can be greatly simplified. Here is an example for someone wishing to know the zodiacal locations of the planets on Christmas Day, December 25, 2018. Looking at the December ephemeris, it can be seen that Christmas Day falls on a Tuesday. In the upper tabulation, the geocentric planetary positions are given, with that of the Sun indicated in the first column, that of the Moon in the second column, and so on. The position of the Sun is listed as 8°07' Sagittarius.

For someone living in London, 8°07' Sagittarius is the Sun's position at midnight, December 24–25, 2017—noting that in London and all of the United Kingdom, the Time Zone applying there is that of Universal Time–Greenwich Mean Time (UT–GMT).

For someone living in Sydney, Australia, which on Christmas Day is eleven hours ahead of UT–GMT, 8°07' Sagittarius is the Sun's position at 11 a.m. on December 25.

For someone living in California, which is eight hours behind UT–GMT on Christmas Day, 8°07' Sagittarius is the Sun's position at 4 p.m. on **December 24**.

For the person living in California, therefore, it is necessary to look at the entries for **December 26** to know the positions of the planets on December 25. The result is:

For someone living in California, which is eight hours behind UT–GMT on Christmas Day, the Sun's position at 4 p.m. on December 25 is 9°08' Sagittarius and, by the same token, the Moon's

---

1 See *General Introduction to the Christian Star Calendar: A Key to Understanding* for an in-depth clarification of the features of the calendar in *Star Wisdom*, including indications about how to work with it.

position on Christmas Day at 4 p.m. on December 25 is 24°08' Pisces—these are the positions alongside December 26 at midnight UT–GMT—and eight hours earlier equates with 4 p.m. on December 25 in California.

From these examples it emerges that the **planetary positions as given in the ephemeris** can be utilized, but that according to the Time Zone one is in, **the time of day is different** and also for locations West of the United Kingdom **the date changes** (look at the date following the actual date).

Here is a tabulation in relation to the foregoing example of December 25 (Christmas Day).

United Kingdom, Europe, and All Locations With Time Zones East Of Greenwich

Look at what is given alongside December 25—these entries indicate the planetary positions at these times:

- 12:00 a.m. (midnight December 24–25) in London (UT–GMT)
- 01:00 a.m. in Berlin (CENTRAL EUROPEAN TIME, which is one hour ahead of UT–GMT)
- 11:00 a.m. in Sydney (AUSTRALIAN EASTERN DAYLIGHT TIME, which is eleven hours ahead of UT–GMT)

Canada, USA, Central America, South America, and All Locations With Time Zones West Of Greenwich

Look at what is given alongside December 26—these entries indicate the planetary positions at these times:

- 7:00 p.m. in New York (EASTERN STANDARD TIME, which is five hours behind UT–GMT)
- 6:00 p.m. in Chicago (CENTRAL STANDARD TIME, which is six hours behind UT–GMT)
- 5:00 p.m. in Denver (MOUNTAIN STANDARD TIME, which is seven hours behind UT–GMT)
- 4:00 p.m. in San Francisco (PACIFIC STANDARD TIME, which is eight hours behind UT–GMT)
- **IF SUMMER TIME IS IN USE**, add **ONE HOUR**—FOR EXAMPLE:
- 8:00 p.m. in New York (EASTERN DAYLIGHT TIME, which is four hours behind UT–GMT)
- 7:00 p.m. in Chicago (CENTRAL DAYLIGHT TIME, which is five hours behind UT–GMT)
- 6:00 p.m. in Denver (MOUNTAIN DAYLIGHT TIME, which is six hours behind UT–GMT)
- 5:00 p.m. in San Francisco (PACIFIC DAYLIGHT TIME, which is seven hours behind UT–GMT)

Note that in the preceding tabulation, the time given in Sydney on Christmas Day, December 25, is in terms of Daylight Time. Six months earlier, on June 25, for someone in Sydney they would look alongside the entry in the ephemeris for June 25 and would know that this applies (for them) to

- 10:00 a.m. in Sydney (AUSTRALIAN EASTERN TIME, which is ten hours ahead of UT–GMT).

In these examples, it is not just the position of the Sun that is referred to. The same applies to the zodiacal locations given in the ephemeris for *all* the planets, whether geocentric (upper tabulation) or heliocentric (lower tabulation). *All that is necessary to apply this method of reading the ephemeris is to know the Time Zone in which one is and to apply the number of hours difference from UT–GMT.*

The advantage of using the method described here is that it greatly simplifies reference to the ephemeris when studying the **zodiacal positions of the planets**. However, for applying the time indications listed under "Ingresses" or "Aspects" it is still necessary to add or subtract the time difference from UT–GMT as described in the above paragraph denoted.

COMMENTARIES AND EPHEMERIDES
JANUARY–DECEMBER 2022

Commentaries and Ephemerides by Joel Matthew Park, including Monthly Stargazing Previews and Astronomical Sky Watch by Julie Humphreys

COMMENTARIES

From 1991 through 2009, Robert Powell oversaw the publication of the *Christian Star Calendar*, for which he wrote relatively concise commentaries based on his groundbreaking work *Chronicles of the Living Christ*, in which he was able to precisely date the life of Christ based on the visions of Anne Catherine Emmerich (and thereby find the precise astrological phenomena which were occurring during the life of Christ). When the *Christian Star Calendar* evolved into the *Journal for Star Wisdom* in 2010, Claudia McLaren Lainson assumed responsibility for these commentaries. She took on this labor of love for all nine volumes of the *Journal* (2010–2018) and continued to do so for *Cosmology Reborn*, the first volume of *Star Wisdom* (the continuation of Robert Powell's *Journal for Star Wisdom* under my editorship). Over the course of a decade of writing the commentaries, Claudia transformed Robert's concise details into an annual epic—indeed, the length of the commentaries even up through last year's *As Above, So Below* was half the length of an over 200-page volume!

And so it is, and has been, a labor of love. One essentially must write an entire book every year. I took over this task from Claudia in 2019 (for *Saturn–Mary–Sophia: Star Wisdom*, volume 2), and understand very well just how much time, energy, thought, and vision must go into the commentaries in the form into which they had developed. In 2019, I attempted to approach the commentaries somewhat differently by focusing not only on the exact moment of an alignment (conjunction, opposition or square), but also on the whole time period during which two planets were within five degrees of each other. This allowed, on the one hand, for a livelier and more fluid engagement with the planetary alignments—feeling their ebb and flow within one's own biography as well as on the scene of outer social, cultural, and political events; on the other hand, it made an already all-too-complicated task even more complex, as I had to track the movements of all these planets much more precisely than just glancing at the ephemerides!

The next year, for last year's *As Above, So Below: Star Wisdom,* volume 3, I decided to add another level of complexity and challenge to the commentaries—not so much for myself, but for the reader. I decided to focus not so much on the geocentric alignments, but rather on the tychonic alignments. The tychonic perspective, which was resurrected by Robert Powell in his *Hermetic Astrology* series in the late 1980s, is both unfamiliar and unusual. Rather than being Earth-centric (as in classical geocentrism) or Sun-centric (as in modern heliocentrism) it uses both the Earth and Sun and the centers of focus for our Solar System. The Sun and Moon travel around the Earth, while the rest of the planets travel around the Sun. Therefore, one uses a "geocentric lens" to look at the position of the Sun, Moon, and Nodes, while using a "heliocentric lens" for the rest of the planets. Needless to say, this can bring about somewhat confusing planetary alignments—for example, if the Sun is in Aquarius from the *Earth's* perspective while Mars is in Aquarius from the *Sun's* perspective, we would say the Sun and Mars are conjunct tychonically!

This year, I have decided to simplify the process of writing the commentaries. At the same time, this will ask for a bit of an investment of time, money, and spiritual forces from my readers.

I hope I can find understanding and forbearance in the hearts and minds of my readers, as I explain what this entails.

You see, as I wrote the commentaries both in 2019 and 2020, I found myself increasingly borrowing lengthy quotes from the three volumes of *The Visions of Anne Catherine Emmerich*, which were published by my dear friend Jim Wetmore in 2015 after a lifetime of work (talk about a labor of love!). I feel quite strongly that Emmerich's words need no elaboration or editorial input from me—there is a magical power in her visions that is only dampened by my overly complicated rumination. And so a good deal of my time "writing" these commentaries was spent in looking up and transcribing what was already compiled in these three volumes. It began to feel tedious, and a bit silly actually—why was I rewriting what greater personalities had finally compiled so pristinely after 200 years of collective labor?

Adding to this feeling of rewriting what wiser heads and hands had already scribed was a further dilemma. For any given planetary alignment, there are usually several "star memories" from the life of Christ that are called up. For each one, I had to choose which one I would focus on, and which particular quotation from Emmerich would represent the chosen star memory with justice. This was never satisfactory. I always felt like key elements were being left out, and in the end only desired that the reader could experience the fullness of Emmerich's vision rather than the few paragraphs I could copy into the commentaries.

And so, I decided for this year: Why not make that possible for the reader? I set about indexing all of the geocentric, tychonic, and heliocentric alignments in the ministry of Christ (April 29–June AD 33). I then looked through the alignments for 2022, and made reference to *every* star memory in the life of Christ that the particular alignment calls forth, rather than picking only one to focus on. I then direct the reader to the volume and page number of *The Visions of Anne Catherine Emmerich*, where one can read the entirety of the star memory and not just the snippets that I have copied from it.

These are not "commentaries," therefore, and more of an astrological appendix to *The Visions of Anne Catherine Emmerich*. And here is where the investment of the reader comes into play: I leave it up to each of you to purchase for yourselves all three volumes of *The Visions of Anne Catherine Emmeric* (available from Angelico Press). I know this might seem like a somewhat pricey request for some, but I give my word that the one-time cost of these three volumes is well worth the investment. They can and should become a resource to which you can turn for the rest of your days. On the other hand, I also leave it up to each of you to use as you see fit the appendix I have supplied here—you will have to take up the effort of looking up the visionary material, as it will not be contained here in these pages.

For this year, I have been able to index only the planetary alignments from the ministry of Christ. Next year, I hope to provide not only the alignments, but also the positions of the planets in reference to the background of fixed stars. Hypothetically, and ideally, these appendices will have lasting value for the reader, as you will now have listed in perpetuity each time a certain planetary alignment (e.g., heliocentric Mercury opposite Uranus) occurred in the life of Christ. This information will be of value beyond the year 2022 for those who use the star memories of Christ as the ferment of their meditative life; they have the potential to be of use any time and any year a particular alignment occurs.

In what follows, whenever I refer to a volume and page number, I am consistently referring to *The Visions of Anne Catherine Emmerich*, volumes 1–3, Angelico Press, 2015.

STARGAZING

Observing the apparent path of the planets (called *the ecliptic*) before the background of the fixed stars of the zodiac requires denizens of the northern hemisphere to look southward. On the days of our spring and autumn equinoxes, this path will begin directly in the east, arch over the southern horizon, and end directly due west. On the other 363 or 364 days of the year, you'll observe that the planets rise slightly north or south of east, culminate east or west of south, and set south or north of west—however, their east–southwest trajectory remains roughly the same. It is a wonderful exercise throughout the year to simply notice where the planets rise, culminate, and set in reference to your fixed surroundings: trees, mountains, etc.

For readers in the southern hemisphere, who look north to view the passage of the planets before the starry background of the zodiac, references here to left and right (and to south and north) will have to be reversed. This year and henceforth, all phenomena will be reported in UTC alone, in accordance with our ephemerides. An excellent resource for time zone conversion can be found at www.timeanddate.com. This site also provides information on meteor showers, important because peak nights for viewing differ by location.

One final note: Left and right refer to the stargazer's perspective, not that of the angels working within the constellations as they look down upon the Earth.

JANUARY 2022

Stargazing Preview

Once again, New Year's Day brings us the cosmic memory of the birth of the Nathan Jesus—specifically at 1320 UTC—setting a glorious tone for the New Year that we can carry with us until its end.

Two hours before sunrise on the 1st, Mars and the waning crescent Moon rise together; you'll see *Antares*, the star at the center of the Scorpion, above Mars (both have a reddish hue). Venus, eight days shy of her inferior conjunction with the Sun, enters the New Year as an evening star; she'll set an hour after the Sun. Saturn and Jupiter will move below the horizon at 1900 and 2100, leaving the night sky free of visible planets until Mars rises again at 0600.

This month's New Moon occurs on the 2nd at 17° Sagittarius; again, the stars will have the night to themselves between 2100 and 0600. May the skies be clear!

The night of the 3rd marks the peak of the meteor showers known as the Quadrantids, and if the sky is free of clouds, it should be a fine show. These meteors are known to come and go very quickly: look to the northeast after dark to optimize your chances of seeing them.

On the 4th, the waxing Moon zips below Saturn just after they set around 1830. Shortly after midnight on the 6th, the Moon will catch up to Jupiter; both will have set by 2100.

Invisible to our gaze now, retrograde Venus meets the Sun in inferior conjunction on the 9th. She'll continue to move backward through the zodiac—drawing closer to Mars, as she likes to do—until the end of the month. The 9th is also the day of January's First Quarter Moon, at 24° Pisces. This is just a degree from the zodiacal point before which Jupiter and Saturn united in 7 BC; together, they were the "star of the Magi" that drew the three wise kings to the Solomon Jesus. You'll find the Moon high in the south at dusk.

Capricorn greets the Sun just before dawn on the 15th. The Full Moon on the 17th will recall its degree (3° Cancer) at the birth of John the Baptist: *Thou glowing light, become strong!* Just before midnight on Wednesday the 18th, you'll see the Moon high in the southeast as it passes above the *Beehive* at the center of Cancer. On the evening of the 20th, as Jupiter sets at 1900, look to the east to see *Regulus* (the heart of the Lion) and the Moon just above the horizon.

January's Last Quarter Moon shines from 10° Libra on the 25th, as it did as Jesus received the Crown of Thorns. On this night, the rest of the visible planets will be huddled around the Sun in a 65° arc; the Moon will have the sky to itself between moonrise (around 0130) and the entrance of Mars above the horizon at 0600. When Venus stations direct on the 29th, she'll be just 7° from Mars—gearing up for their conjunction in February. It might be worth getting up early on the 30th to see Mars, Venus, and the Moon—all in Sagittarius—rise together around 0600.

By month's end, Orion will be high in the southeast at dusk.

JANUARY COMMENTARIES

2—New Moon Sagittarius:
November 24 AD 29: Temptation in the Wilderness, pp. 365–71, vol. I
December 13 AD 30: Healing of Ctesiphon, pp.179–80, vol. II

3—Jupiter square Node:
January 28 AD 30: The Good Samaritan, pp. 398–99, vol. I

9—Inferior Conjunction Sun and Venus:
January 9 AD 30: Conversation with Virgin Mary, the Place of Baptism, p. 393, vol. I
March 21 AD 33: Cursing of the Fig Tree, Magdalene's Last Anointing, pp. 9–11, vol. III

10—Heliocentric Mercury conjunct Uranus:
July 7 AD 29: Early ministry, p. 300, vol. I
October 3 AD 29: The Inn of Reuben, p. 353, vol. I
December 30 AD 29: End of the Wedding at Cana, p. 390, vol. I
March 29 AD 30: Preparing for Passover, pp. 419–20, vol. I
June 25 AD 30: Saturnin Baptizes, pp. 460–62, vol. I
September 21 AD 30: Gadara, pp. 58–59, vol. II
December 18 AD 30: Kiriathaim, p. 183, vol. II
March 17 AD 31: Cornerstone, p. 325, vol. II
June 13 AD 31: Return to Capernaum, pp. 398–99, vol. II
May 31 AD 32: Zacchaeus's House, p. 472, vol. II
August 27 AD 32: Salathiel, p. 491
February 19 AD 33: Preparing for Death, p. 1, vol. III
May 19 AD 33: The Risen One, pp. 411–12 vol. III

11—Mars square Neptune:
December 8 AD 29: In Dibon, p. 375, vol. I
February 18 AD 31: In Sarepta, p. 313, vol. II
January 24 AD 33: The Prison House, pp. 525–26 ,vol II

13—Heliocentric Mercury opposite Mars:
December 7 AD 29: In Dibon, p. 375, vol. I
March 14 AD 30: At Lazarus's Estate, p. 414, vol. I
June 19 AD 30: Celebrating the New Moon Festival, p. 460, vol. I
September 29 AD 30: Mara the Suphanite, pp. 65–67, vol. II
January 14 AD 31: Grave of Zechariah, p. 211, vol. II
April 30 AD 31: Mercuria, pp. 362–64, vol. II
September 5 AD 32: Salathiel and Nazor, p. 494, vol. II
April 5 AD 33: Resurrection, pp. 387–393, vol. III

Heliocentric Venus opposite Pluto:
December 14 AD 29: In Shiloh, pp. 376–77, vol. I
July 28 AD 30: In Ginea, p. 492, vol. I
March 10 AD 31: In Regaba, pp. 321–22, vol. II
January 15 AD 33: Among the Shepherds, p. 522, vol. III

15—Sun enters Capricorn:
December 20 AD 29: Invited to the Wedding at Cana, p. 379, vol. I
December 20 AD 30—Dispute over the Well, pp. 184–85, vol. II

16—Sun conjunct Pluto:
November 29 AD 29: Ahrimanic Temptation, p. 369, vol. I
December 1 AD 30: Second Raising of Salome, pp. 163–67, vol. II

17—Full Moon Capricorn:
January 8 AD 30: Conversation with Virgin Mary, p. 393, vol. I
January 4 AD 33: Deodatus, p. 519, vol. II

Mars enters Sagittarius:
February 4 AD 30: Fruit Festival, p. 401, vol. I

22—Heliocentric Mercury opposite Pluto:
September 23 AD 29: Baptism in the Jordan, pp. 342–45, vol. I
December 20 AD 29: Invited to the Wedding at Cana, p. 379, vol. I
March 18 AD 30: At an Inn, p. 416, vol. I
September 10 AD 30: Celebration of Gideon, pp. 51–52, vol. II
December 7 AD 30: First Walking on Water, pp. 172–73, vol. II

SIDEREAL GEOCENTRIC LONGITUDES : JANUARY 2022 Gregorian at 0 hours UT

DAY	☉	☽	☊	☿	♀	♂	♃	♄	♅	♆	♇
1 SA	15 ♐ 29	20 ♏ 27	6 ♉ 10R	3 ♑ 8	28 ♐ 15R	18 ♏ 3	5 ♒ 30	16 ♑ 51	15 ♈ 54R	25 ♒ 38	0 ♑ 53
2 SU	16 30	5 ♐ 34	6 7	4 33	27 45	18 46	5 42	16 58	15 53	25 39	0 55
3 MO	17 31	20 44	6 2	5 54	27 13	19 29	5 54	17 4	15 53	25 40	0 57
4 TU	18 32	5 ♑ 45	5 56	7 13	26 40	20 11	6 6	17 11	15 52	25 41	0 59
5 WE	19 34	20 29	5 49	8 29	26 6	20 54	6 18	17 18	15 51	25 42	1 1
6 TH	20 35	4 ♒ 48	5 42	9 40	25 31	21 37	6 30	17 24	15 50	25 43	1 3
7 FR	21 36	18 39	5 36	10 47	24 55	22 20	6 42	17 31	15 50	25 44	1 5
8 SA	22 37	2 ♓ 0	5 32	11 49	24 18	23 3	6 54	17 38	15 49	25 46	1 7
9 SU	23 38	14 54	5 30	12 44	23 41	23 46	7 7	17 44	15 49	25 47	1 9
10 MO	24 39	27 25	5 29D	13 32	23 5	24 29	7 19	17 51	15 48	25 48	1 11
11 TU	25 41	9 ♈ 37	5 30	14 12	22 28	25 11	7 32	17 58	15 48	25 50	1 13
12 WE	26 42	21 35	5 32	14 43	21 52	25 55	7 44	18 5	15 47	25 51	1 15
13 TH	27 43	3 ♉ 25	5 32	15 5	21 17	26 38	7 57	18 12	15 47	25 52	1 17
14 FR	28 44	15 12	5 32R	15 16	20 43	27 21	8 10	18 19	15 47	25 54	1 19
15 SA	29 45	26 59	5 29	15 16R	20 10	28 4	8 22	18 26	15 47	25 55	1 20
16 SU	0 ♑ 46	8 ♊ 50	5 24	15 4	19 38	28 47	8 35	18 33	15 46	25 57	1 22
17 MO	1 47	20 48	5 16	14 41	19 8	29 30	8 48	18 40	15 46	25 58	1 24
18 TU	2 48	2 ♋ 54	5 6	14 5	18 40	0 ♐ 13	9 1	18 47	15 46	26 0	1 26
19 WE	3 49	15 10	4 55	13 19	18 14	0 57	9 14	18 54	15 46D	26 1	1 28
20 TH	4 50	27 36	4 43	12 23	17 50	1 40	9 28	19 1	15 46	26 3	1 30
21 FR	5 51	10 ♌ 13	4 32	11 19	17 29	2 23	9 41	19 8	15 46	26 4	1 32
22 SA	6 53	23 2	4 23	10 8	17 9	3 7	9 54	19 15	15 46	26 6	1 34
23 SU	7 54	6 ♍ 2	4 16	8 53	16 52	3 50	10 7	19 22	15 47	26 8	1 36
24 MO	8 55	19 15	4 12	7 37	16 37	4 34	10 21	19 29	15 47	26 9	1 38
25 TU	9 56	2 ♎ 43	4 10	6 20	16 25	5 17	10 34	19 36	15 47	26 11	1 40
26 WE	10 57	16 27	4 10D	5 6	16 16	6 1	10 48	19 43	15 48	26 13	1 42
27 TH	11 58	0 ♏ 29	4 11	3 57	16 9	6 44	11 1	19 50	15 48	26 14	1 44
28 FR	12 59	14 47	4 10R	2 54	16 4	7 28	11 15	19 57	15 48	26 16	1 46
29 SA	14 0	29 21	4 8	1 58	16 2	8 12	11 29	20 5	15 49	26 18	1 48
30 SU	15 1	14 ♐ 7	4 2	1 10	16 2D	8 55	11 42	20 12	15 50	26 20	1 50
31 MO	16 1	28 58	3 54	0 31	16 5	9 39	11 56	20 19	15 50	26 22	1 52

INGRESSES :

1 ☽ → ♐ 15:10	22 ☽ → ♍ 12:55
3 ☽ → ♑ 14:45	24 ☽ → ♎ 19:11
5 ☽ → ♒ 15:52	26 ☽ → ♏ 23:11
7 ☽ → ♓ 20:20	29 ☽ → ♐ 1: 3
10 ☽ → ♈ 5: 2	31 ☽ → ♑ 1:40
12 ☽ → ♉ 17: 2	
15 ☉ → ♑ 5:52	
☽ → ♊ 6: 7	
17 ♂ → ♐ 16:30	
☽ → ♋ 18:16	
20 ☽ → ♌ 4:34	

ASPECTS & ECLIPSES :

1 ☽ ☌ P 23: 4	☉ □ ☽ 18:10	19 ☽ ☍ ♄ 7:17	☽ ☌ P 7:21
2 ☉ ☌ ☽ 18:32	11 ☽ ☌ ♅ 12:20	20 ☽ N□ ☊ 13:22	☉ □ ♅ 19:29
3 ☽ ☌ ♀ 9:57	♂ □ ♆ 21:55	☽ ☍ ♃ 22:57	31 ☽ ☌ ☿ 2:24
♃ □ ☊ 11:47	13 ☽ ☌ ☊ 4:18	22 ☽ ☍ ♆ 5:43	☽ ☌ ♇ 4:42
☽ ☌ ♇ 16:19	14 ☽ ☌ A 9:36	23 ☉ i☌ ☿ 10:27	
4 ☽ ☌ ☿ 2:35	15 ☽ ☍ ♂ 2:20	25 ☉ □ ☽ 13:39	
☽ ☌ ♄ 18:42	16 ☉ ☌ ♇ 14:44	☽ ☍ ♅ 22:51	
6 ☽ □S ☊ 1:31	☽ ☍ ♀ 20:49	27 ☽ ☌ ☋ 6:15	
☽ ☌ ♃ 2:56	17 ☽ ☍ ♇ 21: 6	29 ☿ ☌ ♇ 4:20	
7 ☽ ☌ ♆ 12:39	☉ ☍ ☽ 23:47	☽ ☌ ♂ 15: 9	
9 ☉ i☌ ♀ 0:46	18 ☽ ☍ ☿ 20:38	30 ☽ ☌ ♀ 3: 7	

SIDEREAL HELIOCENTRIC LONGITUDES : JANUARY 2022 Gregorian at 0 hours UT

DAY	Sid. Time	☿	♀	⊕	♂	♃	♄	♅	♆	♇	Vernal Point
1 SA	6:42:31	28 ♒ 46	10 ♊ 40	15 ♊ 30	0 ♏ 55	14 ♒ 11	19 ♑ 49	18 ♈ 22	27 ♒ 24	1 ♑ 20	4 ♓ 57'11"
2 SU	6:46:28	3 ♓ 24	12 18	16 31	1 26	14 17	19 51	18 23	27 25	1 20	4 ♓ 57'11"
3 MO	6:50:24	8 10	13 55	17 32	1 57	14 22	19 53	18 24	27 25	1 20	4 ♓ 57'11"
4 TU	6:54:21	13 6	15 32	18 33	2 27	14 28	19 55	18 24	27 25	1 21	4 ♓ 57'10"
5 WE	6:58:17	18 10	17 9	19 34	2 58	14 33	19 57	18 25	27 26	1 21	4 ♓ 57'10"
6 TH	7: 2:14	23 24	18 46	20 35	3 29	14 38	19 59	18 26	27 26	1 21	4 ♓ 57'10"
7 FR	7: 6:11	28 47	20 23	21 37	4 0	14 44	20 1	18 26	27 27	1 21	4 ♓ 57'10"
8 SA	7:10: 7	4 ♈ 19	22 0	22 38	4 32	14 49	20 2	18 27	27 27	1 22	4 ♓ 57'10"
9 SU	7:14: 4	9 59	23 38	23 39	5 3	14 55	20 4	18 28	27 27	1 22	4 ♓ 57'10"
10 MO	7:18: 0	15 48	25 15	24 40	5 34	15 0	20 6	18 28	27 28	1 22	4 ♓ 57'10"
11 TU	7:21:57	21 44	26 52	25 41	6 5	15 5	20 8	18 29	27 28	1 23	4 ♓ 57' 9"
12 WE	7:25:53	27 47	28 30	26 42	6 37	15 11	20 10	18 30	27 28	1 23	4 ♓ 57' 9"
13 TH	7:29:50	3 ♉ 56	0 ♋ 7	27 43	7 8	15 16	20 12	18 30	27 29	1 23	4 ♓ 57' 9"
14 FR	7:33:46	10 10	1 44	28 45	7 39	15 22	20 14	18 31	27 29	1 23	4 ♓ 57' 9"
15 SA	7:37:43	16 27	3 22	29 46	8 11	15 27	20 15	18 32	27 29	1 24	4 ♓ 57' 9"
16 SU	7:41:40	22 45	4 59	0 ♋ 47	8 42	15 32	20 17	18 32	27 30	1 24	4 ♓ 57' 9"
17 MO	7:45:36	29 5	6 36	1 48	9 14	15 38	20 19	18 33	27 30	1 24	4 ♓ 57' 9"
18 TU	7:49:33	5 ♊ 23	8 14	2 49	9 46	15 43	20 21	18 34	27 31	1 25	4 ♓ 57' 8"
19 WE	7:53:29	11 39	9 51	3 50	10 17	15 49	20 23	18 34	27 31	1 25	4 ♓ 57' 8"
20 TH	7:57:26	17 51	11 29	4 51	10 49	15 54	20 25	18 35	27 31	1 25	4 ♓ 57' 8"
21 FR	8: 1:22	23 57	13 6	5 52	11 21	16 0	20 27	18 36	27 32	1 26	4 ♓ 57' 8"
22 SA	8: 5:19	29 57	14 44	6 53	11 53	16 5	20 28	18 36	27 32	1 26	4 ♓ 57' 8"
23 SU	8: 9:15	5 ♋ 50	16 21	7 54	12 25	16 10	20 30	18 37	27 32	1 26	4 ♓ 57' 8"
24 MO	8:13:12	11 34	17 59	8 55	12 57	16 16	20 32	18 38	27 33	1 26	4 ♓ 57' 8"
25 TU	8:17: 9	17 9	19 36	9 56	13 29	16 21	20 34	18 38	27 33	1 27	4 ♓ 57' 7"
26 WE	8:21: 5	22 35	21 14	10 57	14 1	16 27	20 36	18 39	27 33	1 27	4 ♓ 57' 7"
27 TH	8:25: 2	27 52	22 51	11 58	14 33	16 32	20 38	18 40	27 34	1 27	4 ♓ 57' 7"
28 FR	8:28:58	2 ♌ 59	24 29	12 59	15 5	16 37	20 40	18 40	27 34	1 28	4 ♓ 57' 7"
29 SA	8:32:55	7 56	26 6	14 0	15 37	16 43	20 41	18 41	27 35	1 28	4 ♓ 57' 7"
30 SU	8:36:51	12 43	27 44	15 1	16 10	16 48	20 43	18 42	27 35	1 28	4 ♓ 57' 7"
31 MO	8:40:48	17 22	29 21	16 2	16 42	16 54	20 45	18 42	27 35	1 28	4 ♓ 57' 7"

INGRESSES :

1 ☿ → ♓ 6:29
7 ☿ → ♈ 5:19
12 ☿ → ♉ 8:40
♀ → ♋ 22:17
15 ⊕ → ♋ 5:38
17 ☿ → ♊ 3:30
22 ☿ → ♋ 0:11
27 ☿ → ♌ 9:55
31 ♀ → ♌ 9:30

ASPECTS (HELIOCENTRIC +MOON(TYCHONIC)) :

1 ☽ □ ♆ 11: 4	7 ☿ □ ♇ 11:15	☽ ☍ ♂ 7:54	19 ☽ □ ♅ 6:36	♀ ☍ ♄ 14:29	30 ☿ □ ♂ 20: 2
☽ □ ☿ 19: 0	☽ ☌ ♆ 15:42	☿ ☍ ♂ 13:29	☽ ☍ ♄ 10: 7	☿ ☍ ♄ 15: 3	☿ ☍ ♃ 21:29
2 ☽ ☍ ♀ 11:53	9 ♀ ☌ ⊕ 0:46	♀ ☍ ♇ 18:51	21 ☽ □ ♂ 2:12	☿ ☌ ♀ 15:18	31 ☽ ☌ ♇ 4: 3
3 ☽ ☌ ♇ 16:54	☽ □ ♀ 19: 9	14 ☽ □ ♃ 0:20	☽ ☍ ♃ 10:56	26 ☽ ☍ ♅ 3:47	♂ □ ♃ 10:29
⊕ ☌ P 17:20	10 ☽ □ ♇ 7:43	☿ □ ♃ 20:10	22 ☿ ☍ ♇ 5:59	☿ N□ ☊ 4:17	
4 ☿ □ ♀ 16:59	☿ ☌ ♅ 10:52	15 ☽ □ ♆ 1: 2	☽ ☍ ♆ 8:22	☽ □ ♄ 7: 9	
☽ □ ♅ 20:35	☿ □ ♄ 17:31	☿ ☌ P 23:58	23 ♀ ☌ P 6:57	☽ □ ♀ 9:18	
☽ ☌ ♄ 23: 6	11 ☿ ☌ ☊ 7:12	16 ⊕ ☍ ♇ 14:44	☿ ☌ ⊕ 10:27	☽ □ ☿ 16:57	
5 ☿ □ ⊕ 8: 3	☽ ☌ ♅ 17:45	☿ □ ♆ 18: 0	24 ♀ □ ♅ 9:37	28 ☽ ☌ ♂ 0:30	
☽ □ ♂ 21:41	☽ □ ♄ 21: 7	17 ☽ ☍ ♇ 21: 3	☽ □ ♇ 21:44	☽ □ ♃ 3: 4	
6 ☽ ☌ ♃ 17: 4	13 ☽ ☌ ☿ 2:12	18 ☽ ☌ ♀ 12: 3	25 ☿ □ ♅ 6:29	☽ □ ♆ 21: 5	

March 5 AD 31: Alms for the Poor, p. 319, vol. II

June 1 AD 31: In Misael, p. 393, vol. II

May 18 AD 32: Healing of Ten Lepers, pp. 468–70, vol. II

August 15 AD 32: Teaching about Marriage, p. 487, vol. II

May 6 AD 33: Increase of the Community, pp. 407–9, vol. III

23—Inferior Conjunction Sun and Mercury:

September 9 AD 29: Jesus and Eliud, p. 317, vol. I

December 24 AD 29: Summons of Phillip, p. 382, vol. I

August 24 AD 30: Herod and John, pp. 28–29, vol. II

December 8 AD 30: Healings in Bethsaida, pp. 173–75, vol. II

April 2 AD 31: Transfiguration, pp. 339–40

November 23 AD 31: Healing of the Man Born Blind, see *Journal for Star Wisdom 2016*

July 20 AD 32: News of Lazarus, p. 477, vol. II

February 23 AD 33: Teaching in the Temple, p. 1, vol. III

25—Heliocentric Venus opposite Saturn:

August 21 AD 29: Pure Love of Truth, p. 307, vol. I

April 9 AD 30: Jesus with the Night Disciples, p. 424, vol. I

November 25 AD 30: Healing of Mary Cleophas, p. 160, vol. II)

Heliocentric Mercury opposite Saturn:

August 13 AD 29: Future Disciples, p. 305, vol. I

November 10 AD 29: Temptation in the Wilderness, pp. 365–69, vol. I

February 7 AD 30: Raising of the Daughter of Jairus the Essene, p. 402, vol. I

August 4 AD 30: Jesus visits the Nobleman's Son, pp. 2–4, vol. II

November 1 AD 30: Teaching at Saul's Well, p. 97, vol. II

January 30 AD 31: Sailing to Tarichea, pp. 301–03, vol. II

April 29 AD 31: At the Home of Jonas's Father, pp. 360–62, vol. II

July 16 AD 32: "Our friend Lazarus has fallen asleep," p. 475, vol. II

October 13 AD 32: Journey to Egypt, p. 517, vol. II

January 10 AD 33: At the Synagogue in Bethain, p. 520, vol. II

April 9 AD 33: The Risen One, pp. 396–98, vol. III

Heliocentric Mercury conjunct Venus:

August 2 AD 29: Whispers and Murmurs, p. 303, vol. I

December 22 AD 29: Healing of a Child at a Distance, pp. 380–82, vol. I

May 29 AD 30: Imprisonment of John the Baptist, p. 459, vol. I

October 4 AD 30: In Akrabis and Shiloh, p. 71, vol. II

March 4 AD 31: In Caesarea-Philippi, pp. 318–19, vol. II

October 12 AD 32: Cursing of the House of Idols, pp. 516–17, vol. II

February 13 AD 33: Healing of an Old Blind Man, p. 530, vol. II

29—Mercury conjunct Pluto:

November 18 AD 29: Temptation in the Wilderness, pp. 365–69, vol. I

November 13 AD 30: Raising of the Youth of Nain, pp. 141–43, vol. II

December 14 AD 30: Healing of Eight Lepers, pp. 180–81, vol. II

December 26 AD 30: Second Conversion of Magdalene, pp. 189–90, vol. II

30—Sun square Uranus:

April 21 AD 29: Passover, p. 292, vol. I

October 31 AD 29: Temptation in the Wilderness, pp. 365–69, vol. I

November 5 AD 30: Journey to Gischala, pp. 102–04, vol. II

May 1 AD 31: Pagan Philosophers, pp. 364–66, vol. II

May 10 AD 33: Days Leading to Ascension, pp. 408–09, vol. III

Heliocentric Mercury opposite Jupiter:

July 12 AD 29: In Sarepta, pp. 301–02, vol. I

October 10 AD 29: Feast of Tabernacles, pp. 359–60, vol. I

January 8 AD 30: Conversation with the Virgin Mary, p. 393, vol. I

April 8 AD 30: Death of Silent Mary and Nighttime Conversation with Nicodemus, p. 424, vol. I

July 8 AD 30: The Unjust Steward, pp. 469–70, vol. I

October 6 AD 30: Healing of Manahem, pp. 72–73, vol. II

January 5 AD 31: Reproached by Pharisees, pp. 203–04, vol. II

April 6 AD 31: The Shekel in the Fish, pp. 342–43, vol. II

July 6 AD 31: The Way of David, p. 465, vol. II

October 2 AD 32: In the House of Azarias, pp. 510–11, vol. II

December 31 AD 32: Egyptian City, p. 518, vol. II

April 1 AD 33: Magdalene's Last Anointing, pp. 19–22, vol. III

31—Heliocentric Mars square Jupiter:

May 31 AD 30: Imprisoning of John the Baptist, p. 459, vol. I

July 6 AD 31: The Way of David, p. 465, vol. II

August 8 AD 32: In Kedar, pp. 484–85, vol. II

FEBRUARY 2022

STARGAZING PREVIEW

A New Moon in Capricorn heralds the new month! All the classical planets are gathered within a 62° arc, between 10° Sagittarius and 12° Aquarius. This means that they'll only appear just before sunrise (Mars and Venus), and just after sunset (only Jupiter is visible now). On the evening of the 2nd—around 1900—the waxing crescent Moon and Jupiter will set together; between them lies 10° Aquarius, the Sun's degree at the Feeding of the Five Thousand and the Walking on the Water.

The First Quarter Moon will occur on the 8th, at 25° of the Ram; once Jupiter sets at 1900, the Moon will be alone in the sky until the following morning, when Mars and Venus appear again. Around 2300 on the 13th, you should have a great view of the Moon below *Pollux*, the lower of the two Gemini stars that mark the heads of the Twins. By this time the Sun will have progressed into Aquarius.

Wednesday the 16th is a big day in the heavens, as Venus and Mars unite in conjunction (22° Sagittarius). This is an aspect that occurred at the births of both the Nathan Mary and the Nathan Jesus. The Full Leo Moon rises at 1800.

Late on the 23rd, the Last Quarter Moon (10° Scorpio) will make an entrance around midnight. At this point, the remaining classical planets will form an even tighter arc of 51°; only Uranus and the Moon are far off from the group. By the 27th, the Moon will have found Mars and Venus; they rise in a cluster at 0510. This is something you will not want to miss! Mars and Venus enter Capricorn on Sunday and Monday (the 27th and 28th); you can watch them rise shortly after 0500.

By the close of February, Orion will be high in the south at sunset.

FEBRUARY COMMENTARIES

1—Mercury enters Sagittarius

November 13 AD 29: Temptation in the Wilderness, pp. 365–71, vol. I

December 28 AD 29: Changing of Water into Wine, pp. 386–89, vol I

November 6 AD 30: Healing of Achias' Son, pp. 104–05

New Moon Capricorn:

December 24 AD 29: Summoning of Philip, p. 382, vol. I

January 12 AD 31: Revelation of the Death of John the Baptist, pp. 209–10, vol. II

January 4 AD 33: Deodatus, p. 519, vol. II

2—Heliocentric Mercury opposite Neptune:

July 5 AD 29: Six New Disciples, p. 300, vol. I

October 29 AD 29: Baptizing through Saturnin, pp. 352–53, vol. I

December 28 AD 29: Changing of Water into Wine, pp. 386–89, vol. I

June 22 AD 30: Teaching in the Fruit Plantation, p. 460, vol. I

September 18 AD 30: Isaac and Elijah, pp. 56–57, vol. II

SIDEREAL GEOCENTRIC LONGITUDES : FEBRUARY 2022 Gregorian at 0 hours UT

DAY	☉	☽	☊	☿	♀	♂	♃	♄	⛢	♆	♇
1 TU	17 ♑ 2	13 ♑ 46	3 ♉ 44R	0 ♑ 0R	16 ♐ 10	10 ♐ 23	12 ♒ 10	20 ♑ 26	15 ♈ 51	26 ♒ 23	1 ♑ 54
2 WE	18 3	28 22	3 32	29 ♐ 38	16 17	11 7	12 24	20 33	15 52	26 25	1 56
3 TH	19 4	12 ♒ 40	3 21	29 25	16 27	11 51	12 38	20 41	15 52	26 27	1 58
4 FR	20 5	26 33	3 10	29 20	16 39	12 35	12 51	20 48	15 53	26 29	2 0
5 SA	21 6	9 ♓ 59	3 2	29 22D	16 53	13 18	13 5	20 55	15 54	26 31	2 2
6 SU	22 7	22 58	2 56	29 32	17 9	14 2	13 19	21 2	15 55	26 33	2 3
7 MO	23 8	5 ♈ 33	2 53	29 48	17 27	14 46	13 34	21 9	15 56	26 35	2 5
8 TU	24 8	17 47	2 52	0 ♑ 10	17 47	15 30	13 48	21 17	15 57	26 37	2 7
9 WE	25 9	29 47	2 52	0 38	18 9	16 14	14 2	21 24	15 58	26 39	2 9
10 TH	26 10	11 ♉ 38	2 51	1 12	18 33	16 58	14 16	21 31	15 59	26 41	2 11
11 FR	27 11	23 25	2 50	1 50	18 58	17 42	14 30	21 38	16 0	26 43	2 13
12 SA	28 11	5 ♊ 14	2 46	2 32	19 25	18 27	14 44	21 45	16 2	26 45	2 15
13 SU	29 12	17 9	2 40	3 18	19 54	19 11	14 58	21 52	16 3	26 47	2 16
14 MO	0 ♒ 13	29 13	2 31	4 8	20 24	19 55	15 13	22 0	16 4	26 49	2 18
15 TU	1 13	11 ♋ 29	2 19	5 2	20 56	20 39	15 27	22 7	16 6	26 51	2 20
16 WE	2 14	23 59	2 5	5 58	21 29	21 23	15 41	22 14	16 7	26 53	2 22
17 TH	3 14	6 ♌ 43	1 51	6 58	22 4	22 8	15 56	22 21	16 9	26 55	2 23
18 FR	4 15	19 40	1 38	8 0	22 40	22 52	16 10	22 28	16 10	26 57	2 25
19 SA	5 15	2 ♍ 50	1 26	9 4	23 18	23 36	16 24	22 35	16 12	27 0	2 27
20 SU	6 16	16 10	1 17	10 11	23 56	24 21	16 39	22 42	16 13	27 2	2 29
21 MO	7 16	29 41	1 12	11 20	24 36	25 5	16 53	22 49	16 15	27 4	2 30
22 TU	8 17	13 ♎ 20	1 9	12 31	25 17	25 50	17 8	22 56	16 17	27 6	2 32
23 WE	9 17	27 8	1 8	13 44	25 59	26 34	17 22	23 3	16 18	27 8	2 34
24 TH	10 18	11 ♏ 6	1 8	14 58	26 42	27 19	17 36	23 10	16 20	27 10	2 35
25 FR	11 18	25 12	1 8	16 15	27 26	28 3	17 51	23 17	16 22	27 13	2 37
26 SA	12 18	9 ♐ 27	1 5	17 32	28 11	28 48	18 5	23 24	16 24	27 15	2 39
27 SU	13 19	23 48	1 0	18 52	28 57	29 32	18 20	23 31	16 26	27 17	2 40
28 MO	14 19	8 ♑ 12	0 53	20 13	29 44	0 ♑ 17	18 34	23 38	16 28	27 19	2 42

INGRESSES :

1 ☿ → ♐ 0: 7
2 ☽ → ♒ 2:42
4 ☽ → ♓ 6: 5
6 ☽ → ♈ 13:20
7 ☿ → ♑ 13:39
9 ☽ → ♉ 0:25
11 ☽ → ♊ 13:22
13 ☉ → ♒ 18:59
14 ☽ → ♋ 1:32
16 ☽ → ♌ 11:23
18 ☽ → ♍ 18:51
21 ☽ → ♎ 0:34
23 ☽ → ♏ 4:56
25 ☽ → ♐ 8: 6
27 ☽ → ♑ 10:19
♂ → ♑ 14:55
28 ♀ → ♑ 7:50

ASPECTS & ECLIPSES :

1 ☉ ☌ ☽ 5:44
☽ ☌ ♄ 11: 0
2 ☽ S ☊ 8:29
☽ ☌ ♃ 23:56
3 ☽ ☌ ♆ 23:53
4 ☉ ☌ ♄ 19: 4
7 ☽ ☌ ⛢ 20:21
8 ☉ □ ☽ 13:49
9 ☽ ☌ ☊ 6:11
11 ☽ ☌ A 2:50
☿ ☌ ♇ 13:56
13 ☽ ☍ ♂ 4:20
☽ ☍ ♀ 5:44
14 ☽ ☍ ♇ 6: 5
☽ ☍ ☿ 10:25
15 ☽ ☍ ♄ 20:37
☉ □ ☊ 21:16
16 ♀ ☌ ♂ 14:30
☽ N ☊ 15: 2
☉ ☍ ☽ 16:55
17 ☽ ☍ ♃ 17:25
18 ☽ ☍ ♆ 13:21
22 ☽ ☍ ⛢ 5: 9
23 ☽ ☌ ☋ 6:54
☉ □ ☽ 22:31
25 ☿ □ ⛢ 2:19
26 ☽ ☌ P 22:38
27 ☽ ☌ ♀ 9: 4
☽ ☌ ♂ 10: 4
☽ ☌ ♇ 14:48
28 ☽ ☌ ☿ 22:10

SIDEREAL HELIOCENTRIC LONGITUDES : FEBRUARY 2022 Gregorian at 0 hours UT

DAY	Sid. Time	☿	♀	⊕	♂	♃	♄	⛢	♆	♇	Vernal Point
1 TU	8:44:44	21 ♌ 51	0 ♌ 59	17 ♋ 3	17 ♏ 14	16 ♒ 59	20 ♑ 47	18 ♈ 43	27 ♒ 36	1 ♑ 29	4 ♓ 57' 7"
2 WE	8:48:41	26 12	2 36	18 4	17 47	17 5	20 49	18 44	27 36	1 29	4 ♓ 57' 6"
3 TH	8:52:38	0 ♍ 25	4 14	19 5	18 19	17 10	20 51	18 44	27 36	1 29	4 ♓ 57' 6"
4 FR	8:56:34	4 30	5 51	20 6	18 52	17 15	20 53	18 45	27 37	1 30	4 ♓ 57' 6"
5 SA	9: 0:31	8 27	7 29	21 7	19 25	17 21	20 54	18 46	27 37	1 30	4 ♓ 57' 6"
6 SU	9: 4:27	12 18	9 6	22 7	19 57	17 26	20 56	18 46	27 37	1 30	4 ♓ 57' 6"
7 MO	9: 8:24	16 2	10 44	23 8	20 30	17 32	20 58	18 47	27 38	1 30	4 ♓ 57' 6"
8 TU	9:12:20	19 40	12 21	24 9	21 3	17 37	21 0	18 48	27 38	1 31	4 ♓ 57' 6"
9 WE	9:16:17	23 12	13 59	25 10	21 36	17 43	21 2	18 48	27 39	1 31	4 ♓ 57' 5"
10 TH	9:20:13	26 40	15 36	26 11	22 9	17 48	21 4	18 49	27 39	1 31	4 ♓ 57' 5"
11 FR	9:24:10	0 ♎ 2	17 14	27 11	22 42	17 53	21 6	18 50	27 39	1 32	4 ♓ 57' 5"
12 SA	9:28: 7	3 20	18 51	28 12	23 15	17 59	21 7	18 50	27 40	1 32	4 ♓ 57' 5"
13 SU	9:32: 3	6 33	20 29	29 13	23 48	18 4	21 9	18 51	27 40	1 32	4 ♓ 57' 5"
14 MO	9:36: 0	9 43	22 6	0 ♌ 13	24 21	18 10	21 11	18 52	27 40	1 33	4 ♓ 57' 5"
15 TU	9:39:56	12 49	23 43	1 14	24 54	18 15	21 13	18 52	27 41	1 33	4 ♓ 57' 5"
16 WE	9:43:53	15 52	25 21	2 14	25 27	18 21	21 15	18 53	27 41	1 33	4 ♓ 57' 5"
17 TH	9:47:49	18 53	26 58	3 15	26 1	18 26	21 17	18 54	27 41	1 33	4 ♓ 57' 4"
18 FR	9:51:46	21 50	28 35	4 16	26 34	18 31	21 19	18 54	27 42	1 34	4 ♓ 57' 4"
19 SA	9:55:42	24 45	0 ♍ 12	5 16	27 8	18 37	21 20	18 55	27 42	1 34	4 ♓ 57' 4"
20 SU	9:59:39	27 39	1 50	6 17	27 41	18 42	21 22	18 56	27 43	1 34	4 ♓ 57' 4"
21 MO	10: 3:36	0 ♏ 30	3 27	7 17	28 15	18 48	21 24	18 56	27 43	1 35	4 ♓ 57' 4"
22 TU	10: 7:32	3 20	5 4	8 17	28 48	18 53	21 26	18 57	27 43	1 35	4 ♓ 57' 4"
23 WE	10:11:29	6 8	6 41	9 18	29 22	18 59	21 28	18 58	27 44	1 35	4 ♓ 57' 4"
24 TH	10:15:25	8 55	8 18	10 18	29 56	19 4	21 30	18 58	27 44	1 35	4 ♓ 57' 3"
25 FR	10:19:22	11 41	9 55	11 19	0 ♐ 30	19 9	21 32	18 59	27 44	1 36	4 ♓ 57' 3"
26 SA	10:23:18	14 27	11 32	12 19	1 3	19 15	21 34	19 0	27 45	1 36	4 ♓ 57' 3"
27 SU	10:27:15	17 12	13 9	13 19	1 37	19 20	21 35	19 0	27 45	1 36	4 ♓ 57' 3"
28 MO	10:31:11	19 57	14 46	14 20	2 11	19 26	21 37	19 1	27 45	1 37	4 ♓ 57' 3"

INGRESSES :

2 ☿ → ♍ 21:36
10 ☿ → ♎ 23:47
13 ⊕ → ♌ 18:45
18 ♀ → ♍ 20:56
20 ☿ → ♏ 19:48
24 ♂ → ♐ 2:59

ASPECTS (HELIOCENTRIC +MOON(TYCHONIC)) :

1 ☽ □ ⛢ 8: 5
☽ ☌ ♄ 11:30
2 ☿ ☍ ♆ 7:53
☽ ☍ ♀ 7:56
⊕ □ ⛢ 15:47
3 ☽ ☌ ♃ 7:45
☽ □ ♂ 10: 5
4 ☽ ☌ ♆ 1:52
⊕ ☍ ♄ 19: 4
☽ ☍ ☿ 20: 4
6 ☽ □ ♇ 16:13
8 ☽ ☌ ⛢ 1:59
☽ □ ♄ 6:23
10 ☽ □ ♀ 9:21
☽ □ ♃ 12:38
☽ ☍ ♂ 22:26
11 ☽ □ ♆ 8:36
♀ ☍ ♃ 10:20
☿ □ ♇ 10:51
13 ♀ N ☊ 20: 2
14 ☽ ☍ ♇ 4:35
15 ☽ □ ☿ 3:25
☽ □ ⛢ 14:14
☽ ☍ ♄ 18:45
16 ♀ □ ♂ 2:35
17 ☿ ☍ ⛢ 0: 8
♀ ☍ ♆ 10:47
☿ □ ♄ 19:40
☽ ☍ ♃ 21:52
18 ☽ □ ♂ 13:10
☿ ☌ ☋ 14: 0
☽ ☍ ♆ 14:40
☽ ☌ ♀ 18:34
20 ♂ □ ♆ 0:59
21 ☽ □ ♇ 3:21
22 ☽ ☍ ⛢ 9:48
☽ □ ♄ 14: 8
23 ☽ ☌ ☿ 19:20
24 ☽ □ ♃ 13:40
☿ □ ⊕ 18:50
25 ☽ □ ♆ 4:17
☽ ☌ ♂ 9:18
26 ☽ □ ♀ 3:56
27 ☽ ☌ ♇ 13: 0
☿ □ ♃ 19:20
28 ☽ □ ⛢ 18: 3
☽ ☌ ♄ 22:27

December 15 AD 30: Close of the Feast of
Lights, pp. 181–82, vol. II

March 13 AD 31: At Matthew's Custom House,
p. 322, vol. II

June 9 AD 31: Healing on the Sabbath,
pp. 396–97, vol. II

August 23 AD 32: On Marriage, p. 490, vol. II

February 15 AD 33: Exhortations of the Virgin,
p. 530, vol. II

May 14 AD 33: Ascension Day, pp. 410–12,
vol. III

Tychonic Sun square Uranus:

April 24 AD 29: John in the Wilderness, p. 292,
vol. I

October 28 AD 29: Temptation in the
Wilderness, pp. 365–71, vol. I

November 2 AD 30: 11/2/30—The Sons of
Jesse, pp. 97–99, vol. II

May 4 AD 31: Family of Barnabas, pp. 368–70,
vol. II

May 14 AD 33: Ascension Day, pp. 410–12,
vol. III

4—**Sun conjunct Saturn:**

May 24 AD 29: Beginning of Jesus's Travels,
p. 292, vol. I

June 23 AD 31: On Samuel, pp. 405–07, vol. II

7—**Mercury enters Capricorn:**

December 2 AD 29: Preparing for Baptism,
p. 373, vol. I

January 11 AD 31: Feast of the Expulsion of
the Sadducees, p. 209, vol. II

11—**Mercury conjunct Pluto:**

November 18 AD 29: Temptation in the
Wilderness, pp. 365–71 vol. I

November 13 AD 30: Raising of the Youth of
Nain, pp. 141–43, vol. II

December 14 AD 30: Healing of Eight Lepers,
pp. 180–81, vol. II

December 26 AD 30: Second Conversion of
Magdalene, pp. 189–90, vol. II

Heliocentric Venus opposite Jupiter:

February 13 AD 30: Teaching in Capernaum,
p. 403, vol. I

October 9 AD 30: In Ophra, pp. 74–75, vol. II

June 4 AD 31: Visiting the Childhood Home of
Elizabeth, p. 394, vol. II

September 21 AD 32: Arrival in the Tent City
of Mensor, pp. 502–04, vol. II

May 16 AD 33: After the Ascension, p. 412,
vol. III

13—**Sun enters Aquarius:**

January 18 AD 30: Valley of the Shepherds,
p. 397, vol. I

January 19 AD 31: Healing of the Paralyzed
Man, pp. 216–18, vol. II

January 18 AD 33: Planning to Meet in
Ephron, p. 523, vol. II

15—**Sun square Node:**

September 9 AD 29: Sanitarium in Endor,
p. 317, vol. I

February 24 AD 30: In Ulama, p. 408, vol. I

August 20 AD 30: At the Baths of Bethulia,
pp. 23–24, vol. II

February 7 AD 31: Conferring Power on the
Disciples, pp. 306–07, vol. II

July 13 AD 32: Teaching on the Good
Samaritan and the Lost Coin, p. 475, vol. II

January 1 AD 33: An Uproar in the City,
p. 518, vol. II

16—**Venus conjunct Mars:**

March 9 AD 31: The Stronghold of Regaba,
p. 321, vol. II

April 12 AD 31: Around the Mount of
Beatitudes, p. 346, vol. II

Full Moon Aquarius:

February 7 AD 30: Raising of the Daughter of
Jairus the Essene, p. 402, vol. I

January 27 AD 31: Report of the Disciples,
p. 297, vol. II

February 3 AD 33: Teaching in Bethany, p. 529,
vol. II

Heliocentric Venus square Mars:

July 25 AD 29: Teaching in Chisloth-Tabor,
pp. 302–03, vol. I

December 29 AD 29: Teaching at the Wedding
House, pp. 389–90, vol. I

June 19 AD 30: Celebrating the New Moon
Festival, p. 460, vol. I

December 16 AD 30: Writing on the Wall,
p. 182, vol. II

May 25 AD 31: In Kyrenia, pp. 387–88, vol. II

October 13 AD 32: Journey to Egypt, p. 517, vol. II

March 24 AD 33: Thy Kingdom Come to Us, p. 12, vol. III

17—Heliocentric Mercury opposite Uranus:

June 4 AD 29: Sabbath in Hebron, p. 296, vol. I

August 31 AD 29: In Chisloth–Tabor, pp. 310–11, vol. I

November 28 AD 29: 38th Day of Temptation, p. 369, vol. I

May 23 AD 30: Imprisonment of John the Baptist, pp. 459–60, vol. I

August 19 AD 30: Healing Peter's Mother-in-law, pp. 21–23, vol. II

November 16 AD 30: 11/16/30—On the Way to Mt. Tabor, pp. 147–48 vol. II

February 12 AD 31: Healing of the Syrophoenician Woman, pp. 308–09, vol. II

May 11 AD 31: On King Djemschid, pp. 374–76, vol. II

July 25 AD 32: Day Before the Raising of Lazarus, pp. 477–78, vol. II

April 16 AD 33: Appearance of the Risen One to the Five Hundred, pp. 404–05, vol. III

Heliocentric Venus opposite Neptune:

May 31 AD 29: Family of Lazarus, pp. 294–96, vol. I

August 25 AD 30: In Gennabris, pp. 30–31, vol. II

April 7 AD 31: Gathering of the Seventy, pp. 343–44, vol. II

20—Heliocentric Mars square Neptune:

February 10 AD 30: In Capernaum, p. 402–03, vol. I

December 15 AD 30: Close of the Feast of Lights, pp. 181–82, vol. II

24—Heliocentric Mars enters Sagittarius:

April 16 AD 30: In Concealment, p. 424, vol. I

27—Mars enters Capricorn:

March 25 AD 30: Chanting and Singing, pp. 418–19, vol. I

July 20 AD 30: Traveling with Lazarus, p. 480, vol. I

28—Venus enters Capricorn:

November 3 AD 29: Temptation in the Wilderness, pp. 365–71, vol. I

December 9 AD 30: Magdalene's Relapse, pp. 175–76, vol. II

MARCH 2022

STARGAZING PREVIEW

At 0500 on our first March morning, Mars will chase Venus above the horizon, shortly followed by Saturn and the waning crescent Moon—all in Capricorn. Saturn and the Moon, just past conjunction, rise at 0600. Jupiter, the only classical planet to set after dusk, will be made invisible by the Sun's radiance. In other words: set your alarms for "early"—you will not be disappointed!

On Wednesday the 2nd we'll be blessed with the Aquarius New Moon (17°): ideal conditions (weather permitting) for stargazing! Venus and Mars will reunite for the second time this year on the 6th; they rise at 0500. On Tuesday the 8th, look to the south at sundown to see the Moon, near its First Quarter, beneath the *Pleiades* (5° Taurus).

Thursday March 10th brings us the First Quarter Moon at 25° Taurus. You'll see it without planetary companions throughout the night. When you look up to the evening sky between the 12th and the 16th, you'll be able to watch the Moon progress beneath Gemini, and above Cancer and Leo as it shines ever brighter. Meanwhile, the Sun will have been welcomed into Pisces on the 15th.

The Full Moon (3° Virgo) on the 18th will be lovely indeed, for it will have the sky to itself until Mars (still close to Venus) rises at 0500. As it travels 12° each day, the Moon will find the last degree of Virgo on the 20th; together, the Virgin with the Moon under her feet will entreat spring to begin! The vernal equinox occurs at 1533.

As we near the end of the month, Mars, Venus, and Saturn will rise close to one another about an hour and a half ahead of the Sun. On the morning of the 23rd, the Moon will be high in the southwest, above and to the right of *Antares*, the tender heart of the Scorpion. The 25th is the day the Moon achieves its Last Quarter, at 10° Sagittarius. By the 28th, it will have caught up with the Mars–Venus–Saturn stellium: stargazers all will see the four rise together (beginning at 0420) on this day and the next.

At the end of the month, Orion will be visible in the western sky for the first four hours of the evening. Venus enters Aquarius during the last moments of March.

March Commentaries

2—**Mercury conjunct Saturn:**

June 15 AD 29: Visiting a Madhouse, p. 297, vol. I

June 10 AD 31: Teaching in Rimon, p. 397, vol. II

June 9 AD 32: Confronting the Pharisees, p. 473, vol. II

New Moon Aquarius:

January 22 AD 30: Feast of the New Moon, pp. 397–98, vol. I

February 10 AD 31: On Fasting, p. 307, vol. II

January 19 AD 33: Reunion in Ephron, p. 523, vol. II

3—**Mars conjunct Pluto:**

February 22 AD 30: Gathering in Shunem, pp. 407–8, vol. I

Venus conjunct Pluto:

November 23 AD 30: Healing on the Shore of the Lake, pp. 157–58, vol. II

5—**Sun conjunct Jupiter:**

April 15 AD 31: Invitation to the Sermon on the Mount, p. 347, vol. II

Heliocentric Mercury conjunct Mars:

July 3 AD 29: Meeting Six of the Baptist's Disciples, p. 300, vol. I

October 7 AD 29: "Behold the Lamb of God," pp. 356–57, vol. I

January 17 AD 30: Visiting the Ruined City of Slaves, pp. 396–97, vol. I

August 21 AD 30: In Bethulia, pp. 24–26, vol. II

November 29 AD 30: The Second Beatitude, p. 163, vol. II

March 5 AD 31: Healing the Sick, p. 319, vol. II

June 8 AD 31: In Maroni's Garden, p. 396, vol. II

July 28 AD 32: Fleeing with Matthew and John, p. 480, vol. II

May 13 AD 33: The Night Before Ascension, p. 410, vol. III

6—**Venus conjunct Mars:**

March 9 AD 31: The Stronghold of Regaba, p. 321, vol. II

April 12 AD 31: Around the Mount of Beatitudes, p. 346, vol. II

Mercury square Node:

August 15 AD 29: Teaching in Two Synagogues, p. 306, vol. I

February 28 AD 30: Feast of Thanksgiving for Rain, pp. 409–10, vol. I

July 26 AD 30: Dinah the Samaritan at Jacob's Well, pp. 486-91, vol. I

August 28 AD 30: Healing in Abel–Mehola, pp. 33–37, vol. II

September 6 AD 30: Festival of Jephthah's Daughter, pp. 45–47, vol. II

February 10 AD 31: On Fasting, p. 307, vol. II

July 8 AD 31: Jephthah's Daughter, p. 467, vol. II

June 18 AD 32: A Shepherd's Wedding, p. 474, vol. II

January 4 AD 33: Leaving Heliopolis, p. 519, vol. II

May 31 AD 33: The First Holy Mass, pp. 416–17

Mercury enters Aquarius:

February 7 AD 30: Raising of the Daughter of Jairus the Essene, p. 402, vol. I

January 31 AD 31: The Bread of Life, p. 303, vol. II

March 1 AD 33: On John the Baptist, p. 2, vol. III

10—**Heliocentric Venus square Pluto:**

June 27 AD 29: "Three months ago…," p. 298, vol. I

October 19 AD 29: Consoling the sick, p. 363, vol. I

September 21 AD 30: In Gadara, pp. 58–59, vol. II

SIDEREAL GEOCENTRIC LONGITUDES : MARCH 2022 Gregorian at 0 hours UT

DAY	☉	☽	☊	☿	♀	♂	♃	♄	⛢	♆	♇
1 TU	15 ♒ 19	22 ♑ 34	0 ♉ 42R	21 ♑ 35	0 ♑ 32	1 ♑ 2	18 ♒ 49	23 ♑ 45	16 ♈ 30	27 ♒ 22	2 ♑ 43
2 WE	16 20	6 ♒ 48	0 31	22 58	1 21	1 46	19 3	23 52	16 32	27 24	2 45
3 TH	17 20	20 47	0 19	24 23	2 10	2 31	19 18	23 59	16 34	27 26	2 46
4 FR	18 20	4 ♓ 28	0 8	25 49	3 1	3 16	19 32	24 5	16 36	27 28	2 48
5 SA	19 20	17 47	29 ♈ 59	27 16	3 51	4 0	19 47	24 12	16 38	27 31	2 49
6 SU	20 20	0 ♈ 44	29 53	28 45	4 43	4 45	20 1	24 19	16 40	27 33	2 51
7 MO	21 20	13 19	29 49	0 ♒ 15	5 35	5 30	20 16	24 26	16 43	27 35	2 52
8 TU	22 20	25 35	29 48	1 46	6 28	6 15	20 30	24 32	16 45	27 37	2 54
9 WE	23 20	7 ♉ 37	29 48D	3 18	7 22	7 0	20 45	24 39	16 47	27 40	2 55
10 TH	24 20	19 30	29 48	4 51	8 16	7 44	21 0	24 46	16 50	27 42	2 56
11 FR	25 20	1 ♊ 19	29 48R	6 26	9 11	8 29	21 14	24 52	16 52	27 44	2 58
12 SA	26 20	13 9	29 46	8 1	10 6	9 14	21 29	24 59	16 55	27 46	2 59
13 SU	27 20	25 6	29 42	9 38	11 2	9 59	21 43	25 5	16 57	27 49	3 0
14 MO	28 20	7 ♋ 14	29 36	11 16	11 58	10 44	21 57	25 12	17 0	27 51	3 2
15 TU	29 20	19 37	29 28	12 55	12 55	11 29	22 12	25 18	17 2	27 53	3 3
16 WE	0 ♓ 20	2 ♌ 18	29 18	14 35	13 52	12 14	22 26	25 24	17 5	27 56	3 4
17 TH	1 19	15 16	29 7	16 17	14 50	12 59	22 41	25 31	17 7	27 58	3 5
18 FR	2 19	28 33	28 57	17 59	15 48	13 44	22 55	25 37	17 10	28 0	3 7
19 SA	3 19	12 ♍ 5	28 48	19 43	16 46	14 29	23 10	25 43	17 13	28 2	3 8
20 SU	4 18	25 50	28 42	21 28	17 45	15 14	23 24	25 49	17 15	28 5	3 9
21 MO	5 18	9 ♎ 46	28 38	23 15	18 45	15 59	23 38	25 55	17 18	28 7	3 10
22 TU	6 18	23 48	28 36	25 2	19 45	16 44	23 53	26 1	17 21	28 9	3 11
23 WE	7 17	7 ♏ 55	28 36D	26 51	20 45	17 30	24 7	26 7	17 24	28 11	3 12
24 TH	8 17	22 3	28 37	28 42	21 45	18 15	24 21	26 13	17 27	28 14	3 13
25 FR	9 16	6 ♐ 12	28 38	0 ♓ 33	22 46	19 0	24 36	26 19	17 29	28 16	3 14
26 SA	10 16	20 20	28 38R	2 26	23 48	19 45	24 50	26 25	17 32	28 18	3 15
27 SU	11 15	4 ♑ 25	28 36	4 20	24 49	20 30	25 4	26 31	17 35	28 20	3 16
28 MO	12 14	18 26	28 31	6 15	25 51	21 16	25 18	26 37	17 38	28 23	3 17
29 TU	13 14	2 ♒ 21	28 25	8 12	26 53	22 1	25 33	26 43	17 41	28 25	3 18
30 WE	14 13	16 6	28 18	10 10	27 56	22 46	25 47	26 48	17 44	28 27	3 19
31 TH	15 12	29 39	28 10	12 9	28 59	23 31	26 1	26 54	17 47	28 29	3 20

INGRESSES :

1	☽ → ♒ 12:30	20	☽ → ♎ 7:11
3	☽ → ♓ 16: 5	22	☽ → ♏ 10:32
4	☊ → ♈ 20:41	24	☽ → ♐ 13:28
5	☽ → ♈ 22:37		☿ → ♓ 16:53
6	☿ → ♒ 20: 4	26	☽ → ♑ 16:27
8	☽ → ♉ 8:45	28	☽ → ♒ 19:55
10	☽ → ♊ 21:19	31	☽ → ♓ 0:36
13	☽ → ♋ 9:44		♀ → ♒ 23:24
15	☉ → ♓ 16: 6		
	☽ → ♌ 19:41		
18	☽ → ♍ 2:36		

ASPECTS & ECLIPSES :

1 ☽ ☌ ♄ 2: 0
☽ □S ☊ 13:30
2 ☿ ☌ ♄ 16:31
☉ ☌ ☽ 17:33
☽ ☌ ♃ 21:22
3 ♂ ☌ ♇ 8:35
☽ ☌ ♆ 11:36
♀ ☌ ♇ 17:48
5 ☉ ☌ ♃ 14: 5
6 ♀ ☌ ♂ 7: 7
☿ □ ☊ 17:21
7 ☽ ☌ ⛢ 6:36
8 ☽ ☌ ☊ 8:20
10 ☉ □ ☽ 10:44
☽ ☌ A 23:29
13 ☉ □ Π 5:50
☉ ☌ ♆ 11:51
☽ ☍ ♇ 15:42
14 ☽ ☍ ♂ 7:16
☽ ☍ ♀ 9:58
15 ☽ ☍ ♄ 10:54
☽ N□ ☊ 18:27
17 ☽ ☍ ☿ 2: 6
☽ ☍ ♃ 13:42
☽ ☍ ♆ 23: 1
18 ☉ ☍ ☽ 7:16
19 ♀ □ ⛢ 11:13
21 ☿ ☌ ♃ 6: 5
☽ ☍ ⛢ 12:56
22 ☽ ☌ ☋ 8: 9
♂ □ ⛢ 20:41
23 ☿ ☌ ♆ 17:47
24 ☽ ☌ P 0:16
25 ☉ □ ☽ 5:36
26 ☽ ☌ ♇ 22: 2
28 ☽ ☌ ♂ 5: 7
☽ ☌ ♀ 13:46
☽ ☌ ♄ 14:10
☽ □S ☊ 17:14
♀ ☌ ♄ 19:26
30 ♀ □ ☊ 7:30
☽ ☌ ♃ 17:23
☉ □ Π 19:55
☽ ☌ ♆ 21:54

SIDEREAL HELIOCENTRIC LONGITUDES : MARCH 2022 Gregorian at 0 hours UT

DAY	Sid. Time	☿	♀	⊕	♂	♃	♄	⛢	♆	♇	Vernal Point
1 TU	10:35: 8	22 ♏ 41	16 ♍ 23	15 ♌ 20	2 ♐ 45	19 ♒ 31	21 ♑ 39	19 ♈ 2	27 ♒ 46	1 ♑ 37	4 ♓ 57' 3"
2 WE	10:39: 5	25 26	18 0	16 20	3 19	19 37	21 41	19 2	27 46	1 37	4 ♓ 57' 3"
3 TH	10:43: 1	28 11	19 37	17 20	3 54	19 42	21 43	19 3	27 47	1 37	4 ♓ 57' 2"
4 FR	10:46:58	0 ♐ 57	21 14	18 21	4 28	19 47	21 45	19 4	27 47	1 38	4 ♓ 57' 2"
5 SA	10:50:54	3 43	22 50	19 21	5 2	19 53	21 47	19 4	27 47	1 38	4 ♓ 57' 2"
6 SU	10:54:51	6 30	24 27	20 21	5 36	19 58	21 48	19 5	27 48	1 38	4 ♓ 57' 2"
7 MO	10:58:47	9 19	26 4	21 21	6 11	20 4	21 50	19 6	27 48	1 39	4 ♓ 57' 2"
8 TU	11: 2:44	12 8	27 40	22 21	6 45	20 9	21 52	19 6	27 48	1 39	4 ♓ 57' 2"
9 WE	11: 6:40	15 0	29 17	23 21	7 20	20 15	21 54	19 7	27 49	1 39	4 ♓ 57' 2"
10 TH	11:10:37	17 53	0 ♎ 54	24 21	7 54	20 20	21 56	19 8	27 49	1 39	4 ♓ 57' 1"
11 FR	11:14:34	20 48	2 30	25 21	8 29	20 25	21 58	19 8	27 49	1 40	4 ♓ 57' 1"
12 SA	11:18:30	23 45	4 7	26 21	9 3	20 31	22 0	19 9	27 50	1 40	4 ♓ 57' 1"
13 SU	11:22:27	26 45	5 43	27 21	9 38	20 36	22 1	19 10	27 50	1 40	4 ♓ 57' 1"
14 MO	11:26:23	29 48	7 19	28 21	10 13	20 42	22 3	19 10	27 51	1 41	4 ♓ 57' 1"
15 TU	11:30:20	2 ♑ 53	8 56	29 20	10 48	20 47	22 5	19 11	27 51	1 41	4 ♓ 57' 1"
16 WE	11:34:16	6 2	10 32	0 ♍ 20	11 23	20 53	22 7	19 12	27 51	1 41	4 ♓ 57' 1"
17 TH	11:38:13	9 15	12 8	1 20	11 57	20 58	22 9	19 12	27 52	1 42	4 ♓ 57' 0"
18 FR	11:42: 9	12 31	13 44	2 20	12 32	21 4	22 11	19 13	27 52	1 42	4 ♓ 57' 0"
19 SA	11:46: 6	15 52	15 20	3 19	13 7	21 9	22 13	19 14	27 52	1 42	4 ♓ 57' 0"
20 SU	11:50: 3	19 17	16 57	4 19	13 43	21 14	22 14	19 14	27 53	1 42	4 ♓ 57' 0"
21 MO	11:53:59	22 47	18 33	5 19	14 18	21 20	22 16	19 15	27 53	1 43	4 ♓ 57' 0"
22 TU	11:57:56	26 22	20 9	6 18	14 53	21 25	22 18	19 16	27 53	1 43	4 ♓ 57' 0"
23 WE	12: 1:52	0 ♒ 3	21 45	7 18	15 28	21 31	22 20	19 16	27 54	1 43	4 ♓ 57' 0"
24 TH	12: 5:49	3 49	23 20	8 17	16 3	21 36	22 22	19 17	27 54	1 44	4 ♓ 57' 0"
25 FR	12: 9:45	7 42	24 56	9 17	16 39	21 42	22 24	19 18	27 55	1 44	4 ♓ 56'59"
26 SA	12:13:42	11 42	26 32	10 16	17 14	21 47	22 26	19 18	27 55	1 44	4 ♓ 56'59"
27 SU	12:17:38	15 48	28 8	11 16	17 50	21 53	22 28	19 19	27 55	1 44	4 ♓ 56'59"
28 MO	12:21:35	20 2	29 44	12 15	18 25	21 58	22 29	19 20	27 56	1 45	4 ♓ 56'59"
29 TU	12:25:32	24 24	1 ♏ 19	13 14	19 1	22 3	22 31	19 20	27 56	1 45	4 ♓ 56'59"
30 WE	12:29:28	28 54	2 55	14 14	19 36	22 9	22 33	19 21	27 56	1 45	4 ♓ 56'59"
31 TH	12:33:25	3 ♓ 32	4 31	15 13	20 12	22 14	22 35	19 22	27 57	1 46	4 ♓ 56'59"

INGRESSES :

3 ☿ → ♐ 15:48
9 ♀ → ♎ 10:40
14 ☿ → ♑ 1:36
15 ⊕ → ♍ 15:52
22 ☿ → ♒ 23:41
28 ♀ → ♏ 4: 5
30 ☿ → ♓ 5:46

ASPECTS (HELIOCENTRIC +MOON(TYCHONIC)) :

1 ☿ ☌ A 0:33
2 ☿ □ ♆ 20:26
☽ ☌ ♃ 22: 6
3 ☽ ☌ ♆ 12:11
☽ □ ☿ 16:10
☽ □ ♂ 23:59
5 ☽ ☍ ♀ 10:36
⊕ ☍ ♃ 14: 5
☿ ☌ ♂ 14:18
6 ☽ □ ♇ 1:42
7 ☽ ☌ ⛢ 11:14
☽ □ ♄ 16:39
10 ☽ □ ♃ 1:42
♀ □ ♇ 11:26
☽ □ ♆ 16:54
11 ☽ ☍ ♂ 15:17
13 ☽ ☍ ☿ 4:22
⊕ ☍ ♆ 11:51
☽ ☍ ♇ 13: 3
14 ☽ □ ♀ 0:11
☿ ☌ ♇ 14:41
☽ □ ⛢ 23: 9
15 ☽ ☍ ♄ 4:43
17 ☽ ☍ ♃ 10:26
☽ ☍ ♆ 22:47
18 ☿ □ ♀ 16:53
19 ☽ □ ♂ 1:54
☿ □ ⛢ 23:40
20 ☽ □ ♇ 10: 8
☿ ☌ ♄ 20:30
21 ☿ □S ☊ 5: 8
♀ ☍ ⛢ 10:38
☽ ☍ ⛢ 16:14
☽ ☌ ♀ 16:56
☽ □ ♄ 21:25
22 ☽ □ ☿ 5:53
23 ♀ □ ♄ 9: 3
☽ □ ♃ 23:13
24 ☽ □ ♆ 9:55
25 ☽ ☌ ♂ 18:30
26 ☽ ☌ ♇ 19:25
28 ☽ □ ⛢ 1:31
☽ ☌ ♄ 6:58
☿ ☌ ♃ 10:55
☽ □ ♀ 21:59
29 ☿ ☌ ♆ 18:56
30 ☽ ☌ ♃ 10:43
☽ ☌ ♆ 20:56
31 ☽ ☌ ☿ 10:46

January 13 AD 31: Joseph of Arimathea, pp. 210–11, vol. II

May 5 AD 31: Teaching at Barnabas's House, pp. 370–71, vol. II

July 29 AD 32: Healing a Blind Shepherd, p. 480, vol. II

March 11 AD 33: Approaching Suffering, p. 4, vol. III

13—**Sun conjunct Neptune:**

January 13 AD 30: Baptizing, pp. 399–401, vol. I

January 15 AD 31: Pilate Holds a Conference, pp. 211–12, vol. II

January 19 AD 33: Reunion in Ephron, p. 523, vol. III

14—**Heliocentric Mercury conjunct Pluto:**

August 14 AD 29: In Mahara's House, pp. 305–06, vol. I

November 10 AD 29: Temptation in the Wilderness, pp. 365–71, vol. I

February 6 AD 30: The Hospitable and Inhospitable, pp. 401–02, vol. I

May 5 AD 30: Many Baptisms, p. 459, vol. I

August 1 AD 30: The Samaritans, pp. 496–97, vol. I

October 28 AD 30: Healing of Issachar of Dothan, pp. 90–92, vol. II

January 25 AD 31: Assembly of Pharisees, p. 223, vol. II

October 3 AD 32: The Wonderful Cure of Two Sick Women, pp. 511–12, vol. II

March 28 AD 33: The Two Gardens, pp. 15–16, vol. III

15—**Sun enters Pisces:**

February 17 AD 30: Healing the Children, p. 406, vol. I

February 18 AD 31: Between Ornithopolis and Rehob, p. 313, vol. II

February 17 AD 33: With Lazarus, p. 530, vol. II

18—**Full Moon Pisces:**

March 8 AD 30: Festival of Purim, p. 414, vol. I

February 25 AD 31: In Nobah, p. 316, vol. II

March 4 AD 33: Passing by the Blind Man, p. 2, vol. III

19—**Venus square Uranus:**

September 17 AD 29: Alone in Prayer, p. 323, vol. I

November 3 AD 30: Naomi of Dabrath, pp. 99–100, vol. II

March 25 AD 31: Roman Soldiers Seize the Galileans, p. 330, vol. II

October 11 AD 32: Teaching the Women by the Fountain, p. 516, vol. II

20—**Heliocentric Mercury conjunct Saturn:**

June 26 AD 29: "Three months ago...," p. 298, vol. I

December 20 AD 29: Invited to the Wedding at Cana, p. 379, vol. I

March 19 AD 30: Jesus and Lazarus in Jerusalem, p. 416, vol. I

September 12 AD 30: The Fishing Lake, pp. 52–53, vol. II

December 9 AD 30: Magdalene's Relapse, pp. 175–76, vol. II

March 8 AD 31: Teaching in Argob, p. 321, vol. II

June 4 AD 31: Elizabeth's Childhood Home, p. 394, vol. II

August 20 AD 32: Washing of Eliud's Feet, p. 488, vol. II

May 13 AD 33: The Night Before Ascension, p. 410, vol. III

21—**Mercury conjunct Jupiter:**

March 6 AD 30: Three Rich Youths, p. 413, vol. I

May 13 AD 31: Baptizing the Bridegrooms, pp. 377–78, vol. II

May 18 AD 32: Healing of Ten Lepers, 469–70, vol. II

May 25 AD 33: The Church at the Pool of Bethesda, pp. 414–16, vol. III

Heliocentric Venus opposite Uranus:

September 28 AD 29: Teaching the Workers in the Fields, pp. 347–49, vol. I

December 26 AD 30: Magdalene's Second Conversion, pp. 189–90, vol. II

22—**Mars square Uranus:**

January 2 AD 30: Two Days' Fasting, p. 390, vol. I

March 11 AD 31: Healing the Sick, p. 322, vol. II

23—Mercury conjunct Neptune:
February 4 AD 30: New Year's Fruit Festival, p. 401, vol. I
January 29 AD 31: Feeding of the 5000 and Walking on Water, pp. 298–301, vol. II

Heliocentric Venus square Saturn:
June 25 AD 29: "Three months ago…," p. 298, vol. I
October 19 AD 29: The Essene Jairus, pp. 362–63, vol. I
February 10 AD 30: In Capernaum, pp. 402–03, vol. I
September 28 AD 30: Healing the Sick, p. 65, vol. II
January 22 AD 31: In Thirza, pp. 219–20, vol. II
May 16 AD 31: Feast of Weeks, pp. 380–81, vol. II
August 18 AD 32: Shepherd Settlement in Kedar, p. 487, vol. II
April 5 AD 33: Resurrection, pp. 387–393, vol. III

24—Mercury enters Pisces:
February 24 AD 30: Teaching in the School, p. 408, vol. I
February 16 AD 31: Visiting the Syrophoenician Woman, pp. 312–13, vol. II
January 31 AD 33: Silvanus, p. 528, vol. II
March 15 AD 33: The Approaching Suffering, p. 5, vol. III

28—Venus conjunct Saturn:
July 10 AD 30: The Baptismal Well, pp. 470–71, vol. I
May 3 AD 31: Teaching in Kythria, pp. 367–68, vol. II

Heliocentric Mercury conjunct Jupiter:
December 5 AD 29: Silencing the Possessed, pp. 374–75, vol. I
March 5 AD 30: Helping in the Storm, pp. 412–13, vol. I
August 30 AD 30: Paralyzed Arms and Hands, p. 38, vol. II
November 28 AD 30: Sermon on the Mount, pp. 162–63, vol. II

February 25 AD 31: In Nobah, p. 316, vol. II
May 25 AD 31: Speaking Against Idolatry, pp. 387–88, vol. II
August 13 AD 32: The Bedridden Married Couple, p. 486, vol. II
February 8 AD 33: Three Secret Disciples, p. 530, vol. II
May 8 AD 33: The Risen One, p. 408, vol. III

29—Heliocentric Mercury conjunct Neptune:
June 1 AD 29: Elizabeth's Cave, p. 296, vol. I
August 28 AD 29: Circumcision and Baptism, pp. 309–10, vol. I
November 24 AD 29: Temptation in the Wilderness, pp. 365–71, vol. I
February 20 AD 30: In Jezreel, p. 406, vol. I
May 19 AD 30: Imprisonment of John the Baptist, p. 459, vol. I
August 16 AD 30: In Peter's House, pp. 17–19, vol. II
November 12 AD 30: On the Way to Nain, p. 141, vol. II
May 7 AD 31: The Prophet Malachi, pp. 372–73, vol. II
July 20 AD 32: News of Lazarus, p. 477, vol. II
April 11 AD 33: The Risen Christ Appears to Thomas, pp. 398–400, vol. III

30—Venus square Node:
April 8 AD 30: Death of Silent Mary and Night-time Conversation with Nicodemus, p. 424, vol. I
September 2 AD 30: Teaching and Healing, pp. 40–41, vol. II
January 18 AD 31: In Bethany with Magdalene, pp. 215–16, vol. II
June 22 AD 31: The Young Pharisee, p. 405, vol. II

April 2022

Stargazing Preview

Another new month, another New Moon! It's a particularly special one, as the Sun is revisiting its degree (16° Pisces) at the birth of the Solomon Jesus as well as the conception of the Nathan Jesus, which occurred four years later—just one of the cosmic indications of their shared destiny. Early on the 5th, Saturn and Mars meet at 28° Capricorn; by the time they rise at 0400, Mars will be in the first degree of Aquarius—the location of the Sun at the Healing of the Paralyzed Man.

The Moon reaches its First Quarter on the 9th (24° Gemini): *O sun life, endure!* The Sun, then, begins its zodiacal journey anew on the 15th as it finds the stars of the Ram shortly after midnight.

April's Full Moon (2° Libra) occurs on the following day, Saturday the 16th. Gemini will be high in the south as the Moon rises at 1900.

Sparks start to fly on the evening of the 22nd: the peak of the Lyrid Meteor Showers! Your best opportunity to see these shooting stars will be before the rising of the waning Moon at 0200; look first to the northeast—and best of luck!. If you happen to be owling that night, you'll want to be awake between 0300 and 0400, when Saturn, Mars, Venus and Jupiter will appear in the east.

The Moon reaches its last Quarter (8° Capricorn) on the 23rd: the Sun's zodiacal degree at the miracle of the Changing of Water into Wine at the Wedding at Cana. Between the 24th and the 28th, those up early will see the waning crescent Moon pass below Saturn, Mars, Venus, and Jupiter.

The New Moon on the 30th (15° Aries—the Sun's position at the Resurrection) will result in a Partial Solar Eclipse over South America and the Antarctic. Any blue whales and Adélie penguins traveling between the Antarctic Peninsula and Tierra del Fuego—the roughest seas on the planet—will experience the eclipse most of all. Blessings on our marine friends!

As the Sun moves closer to Orion, the Hunter will be visible for an hour or so after sunset.

April Commentaries

1—New Moon Pisces:
February 21 AD 30: From Jezreel to Shunem, pp. 406–07, vol. I
March 11 AD 31: Healing the Sick, p. 322, vol. II
February 18 AD 33: With Lazarus and the Holy Women, p. 530, vol. II

2—Superior Conjunction Sun and Mercury:
July 2 AD 29: Meeting Six of the Baptist's Disciples, p. 300, vol. I
October 30 AD 29: Temptation in the Wilderness, pp. 365–69 vol. I
March 4 AD 30: Protecting the Ships at Sea, p. 412, vol. I
October 9 AD 30: Messenger of Cyrinus, pp. 74, vol. II
February 15 AD 31: A Banquet with the Syrophoenician Woman, pp. 310–12, vol. II
June 1 AD 31: In Misael, p. 393, vol. II
September 1 AD 32: Raising of Nazor, pp. 492–94, vol. II
January 10 AD 33: Healing in Bethain, p. 520, vol. II
April 30 AD 33: Days with the Risen One, p. 408, vol. III

5—Mars conjunct Saturn:
April 28 AD 29: John in the Wilderness, p. 292, vol. I
May 22 AD 31: Clothes and Provisions, pp. 385–86, vol. II

Mars square Node:
October 8 AD 29: "The Covenant is fulfilled!," pp. 357–58, vol. I
November 8 AD 30: Magdalene's First Conversion, pp. 107–110, vol. II
May 17 AD 33: Between Ascension and Pentecost, p. 412, vol. III

8—Mars enters Aquarius:
May 26 AD 30: Meeting Bartholomew, pp. 459–60, vol. I
September 20 AD 30: Teaching in the Vineyards, p. 58, vol. II

Mercury enters Aries:

SIDEREAL GEOCENTRIC LONGITUDES :	APRIL 2022 Gregorian at 0 hours UT										
DAY	☉	☽	☊	☿	♀	♂	♃	♄	⛢	♆	♇
1 FR	16 ♓ 12	12 ♓ 58	28 ♈ 3R	14 ♓ 9	0 ♒ 2	24 ♑ 17	26 ♒ 15	26 ♑ 59	17 ♈ 50	28 ♒ 31	3 ♑ 21
2 SA	17 11	25 59	27 58	16 10	1 5	25 2	26 29	27 5	17 53	28 34	3 22
3 SU	18 10	8 ♈ 44	27 54	18 12	2 8	25 47	26 43	27 10	17 56	28 36	3 22
4 MO	19 9	21 12	27 53	20 15	3 12	26 32	26 57	27 16	18 0	28 38	3 23
5 TU	20 8	3 ♉ 25	27 53D	22 19	4 16	27 18	27 11	27 21	18 3	28 40	3 24
6 WE	21 8	15 26	27 54	24 24	5 20	28 3	27 25	27 26	18 6	28 42	3 25
7 TH	22 7	27 19	27 55	26 28	6 25	28 48	27 39	27 31	18 9	28 44	3 25
8 FR	23 6	9 ♊ 9	27 57	28 33	7 29	29 34	27 53	27 36	18 12	28 46	3 26
9 SA	24 5	21 0	27 58	0 ♈ 38	8 34	0 ♒ 19	28 6	27 41	18 15	28 49	3 26
10 SU	25 4	2 ♋ 57	27 58R	2 42	9 39	1 4	28 20	27 46	18 19	28 51	3 27
11 MO	26 3	15 6	27 56	4 46	10 45	1 50	28 34	27 51	18 22	28 53	3 28
12 TU	27 1	27 30	27 53	6 49	11 50	2 35	28 47	27 56	18 25	28 55	3 28
13 WE	28 0	10 ♌ 14	27 49	8 50	12 56	3 20	29 1	28 1	18 29	28 57	3 29
14 TH	28 59	23 20	27 44	10 50	14 1	4 6	29 15	28 5	18 32	28 59	3 29
15 FR	29 58	6 ♍ 48	27 40	12 47	15 7	4 51	29 28	28 10	18 35	29 1	3 29
16 SA	0 ♈ 57	20 37	27 36	14 42	16 13	5 36	29 41	28 15	18 38	29 3	3 30
17 SU	1 55	4 ♎ 44	27 34	16 35	17 20	6 22	29 55	28 19	18 42	29 5	3 30
18 MO	2 54	19 5	27 32	18 24	18 26	7 7	0 ♓ 8	28 23	18 45	29 7	3 31
19 TU	3 53	3 ♏ 35	27 32D	20 10	19 33	7 53	0 21	28 28	18 49	29 9	3 31
20 WE	4 51	18 7	27 33	21 53	20 40	8 38	0 35	28 32	18 52	29 11	3 31
21 TH	5 50	2 ♐ 38	27 34	23 32	21 46	9 23	0 48	28 36	18 55	29 13	3 32
22 FR	6 48	17 2	27 36	25 6	22 53	10 9	1 1	28 40	18 59	29 15	3 32
23 SA	7 47	1 ♑ 16	27 36	26 37	24 1	10 54	1 14	28 44	19 2	29 17	3 32
24 SU	8 45	15 18	27 36R	28 3	25 8	11 39	1 27	28 48	19 6	29 18	3 32
25 MO	9 44	29 8	27 36	29 24	26 15	12 25	1 40	28 52	19 9	29 20	3 32
26 TU	10 42	12 ♒ 43	27 34	0 ♉ 41	27 23	13 10	1 53	28 56	19 12	29 22	3 32
27 WE	11 41	26 5	27 32	1 54	28 31	13 56	2 6	28 59	19 16	29 24	3 33
28 TH	12 39	9 ♓ 13	27 30	3 1	29 39	14 41	2 18	29 3	19 19	29 26	3 33
29 FR	13 37	22 7	27 28	4 3	0 ♓ 46	15 26	2 31	29 6	19 23	29 27	3 33
30 SA	14 36	4 ♈ 48	27 26	5 1	1 55	16 12	2 44	29 10	19 26	29 29	3 33R

INGRESSES :

2	☽ → ♈	7:29
4	☽ → ♉	17:15
7	☽ → ♊	5:26
8	♂ → ♒	13:54
	☿ → ♈	16:42
9	☽ → ♋	18: 6
12	☽ → ♌	4:44
14	☽ → ♍	11:58
15	☉ → ♈	0:54
16	☽ → ♎	16: 0
17	♃ → ♓	9:14
18	☽ → ♏	18: 4
20	☽ → ♐	19:38
22	☽ → ♑	21:51
25	☽ → ♒	1:31
	☿ → ♉	10:55
27	☽ → ♓	7: 6
28	♀ → ♓	7:34
29	☽ → ♈	14:52

ASPECTS & ECLIPSES :

1	☽ ☌ ☿	2:33
	☉ ☌ ☽	6:23
	☉ □ π	6:40
2	☉ ☌S ☿	23: 9
3	☽ ☌ ⛢	17:45
4	☽ ☌ ☊	13: 4
5	♂ ☌ ♄	1:50
	♂ □ ☊	18:55
7	☽ ☌ A	19:29
9	☉ □ ☽	6:46
10	☽ ☍ ♇	0:59
	☿ □ ♇	8:42
11	♄ □ ☊	14:43
12	☽ N ☊	0:42
	☽ ☍ ♄	0:49
	☽ ☍ ♂	10:15
	♃ ☌ ♆	15:29
13	☽ ☍ ♀	5:26
14	☽ ☍ ♆	10:10
	☽ ☍ ♃	10:47
16	☉ ☍ ☽	18:53
17	☽ ☍ ☿	22:41
	☽ ☍ ⛢	23:26
18	☿ ☌ ⛢	4:49
	☽ ☌ ☋	14: 0
	☉ □ ♇	15: 7
19	☽ ☌ P	15:18
23	☽ ☌ ♇	3:51
	☉ □ ☽	11:55
	☿ ☌ ☊	16:32
24	☿ □ ♄	13:48
	☽ S ☊	21:19
	☽ ☌ ♄	23:32
26	☽ ☌ ♂	0:50
27	☽ ☌ ♀	4:48
	☽ ☌ ♆	6: 1
	☽ ☌ ♃	11: 6
	♀ ☌ ♆	19:18
30	☉ ☌ ☽	20:27
	☉ ● P	20:40
	♀ ☌ ♃	21:12

SIDEREAL HELIOCENTRIC LONGITUDES :	APRIL 2022 Gregorian at 0 hours UT										
DAY	Sid. Time	☿	♀	⊕	♂	♃	♄	⛢	♆	♇	Vernal Point
1 FR	12:37:21	8 ♓ 19	6 ♏ 6	16 ♍ 12	20 ♐ 48	22 ♒ 20	22 ♑ 37	19 ♈ 22	27 ♒ 57	1 ♑ 46	4 ♓ 56'58"
2 SA	12:41:18	13 15	7 42	17 12	21 24	22 25	22 39	19 23	27 57	1 46	4 ♓ 56'58"
3 SU	12:45:14	18 19	9 17	18 11	21 59	22 31	22 41	19 24	27 58	1 46	4 ♓ 56'58"
4 MO	12:49:11	23 33	10 53	19 10	22 35	22 36	22 42	19 24	27 58	1 47	4 ♓ 56'58"
5 TU	12:53: 7	28 57	12 28	20 9	23 11	22 42	22 44	19 25	27 59	1 47	4 ♓ 56'58"
6 WE	12:57: 4	4 ♈ 29	14 4	21 8	23 47	22 47	22 46	19 26	27 59	1 47	4 ♓ 56'58"
7 TH	13: 1: 1	10 9	15 39	22 7	24 23	22 52	22 48	19 26	27 59	1 48	4 ♓ 56'58"
8 FR	13: 4:57	15 58	17 14	23 6	24 59	22 58	22 50	19 27	28 0	1 48	4 ♓ 56'57"
9 SA	13: 8:54	21 55	18 49	24 5	25 35	23 3	22 52	19 28	28 0	1 48	4 ♓ 56'57"
10 SU	13:12:50	27 58	20 25	25 4	26 12	23 9	22 54	19 28	28 0	1 48	4 ♓ 56'57"
11 MO	13:16:47	4 ♉ 7	22 0	26 3	26 48	23 14	22 55	19 29	28 1	1 49	4 ♓ 56'57"
12 TU	13:20:43	10 20	23 35	27 2	27 24	23 20	22 57	19 30	28 1	1 49	4 ♓ 56'57"
13 WE	13:24:40	16 37	25 10	28 1	28 0	23 25	22 59	19 30	28 1	1 49	4 ♓ 56'57"
14 TH	13:28:36	22 56	26 45	29 0	28 37	23 31	23 1	19 31	28 2	1 50	4 ♓ 56'57"
15 FR	13:32:33	29 15	28 21	29 58	29 13	23 36	23 3	19 32	28 2	1 50	4 ♓ 56'56"
16 SA	13:36:30	5 ♊ 34	29 56	0 ♎ 57	29 50	23 41	23 5	19 32	28 3	1 50	4 ♓ 56'56"
17 SU	13:40:26	11 49	1 ♐ 31	1 56	0 ♑ 26	23 47	23 7	19 33	28 3	1 51	4 ♓ 56'56"
18 MO	13:44:23	18 1	3 6	2 54	1 3	23 52	23 9	19 34	28 3	1 51	4 ♓ 56'56"
19 TU	13:48:19	24 7	4 41	3 53	1 39	23 58	23 10	19 34	28 4	1 51	4 ♓ 56'56"
20 WE	13:52:16	0 ♋ 7	6 16	4 52	2 16	24 3	23 12	19 35	28 4	1 51	4 ♓ 56'56"
21 TH	13:56:12	6 0	7 51	5 50	2 53	24 9	23 14	19 36	28 4	1 52	4 ♓ 56'56"
22 FR	14: 0: 9	11 44	9 26	6 49	3 29	24 14	23 16	19 36	28 5	1 52	4 ♓ 56'56"
23 SA	14: 4: 5	17 19	11 1	7 47	4 6	24 20	23 18	19 37	28 5	1 52	4 ♓ 56'55"
24 SU	14: 8: 2	22 45	12 36	8 46	4 43	24 25	23 20	19 38	28 5	1 53	4 ♓ 56'55"
25 MO	14:11:59	28 1	14 11	9 44	5 20	24 31	23 22	19 38	28 6	1 53	4 ♓ 56'55"
26 TU	14:15:55	3 ♌ 8	15 46	10 43	5 57	24 36	23 23	19 39	28 6	1 53	4 ♓ 56'55"
27 WE	14:19:52	8 4	17 20	11 41	6 34	24 41	23 25	19 40	28 7	1 53	4 ♓ 56'55"
28 TH	14:23:48	12 52	18 55	12 40	7 10	24 47	23 27	19 40	28 7	1 54	4 ♓ 56'55"
29 FR	14:27:45	17 30	20 30	13 38	7 47	24 52	23 29	19 41	28 7	1 54	4 ♓ 56'55"
30 SA	14:31:41	21 59	22 5	14 36	8 25	24 58	23 31	19 42	28 8	1 54	4 ♓ 56'54"

INGRESSES :

5	☿ → ♈	4:38
10	☿ → ♉	7:59
15	⊕ → ♎	0:39
	☿ → ♊	2:49
16	♀ → ♐	1: 5
	♂ → ♑	6:48
19	☿ → ♋	23:30
25	☿ → ♌	9:13

ASPECTS (HELIOCENTRIC +MOON(TYCHONIC)) :

1	☽ □ ♂	15: 3
2	☽ □ ♇	10:49
	☿ ☍ ⊕	23: 9
3	☿ □ ♂	19: 2
	☽ ☌ ⛢	20:30
4	☽ □ ♄	2:57
5	☿ □ ♇	12:24
	☽ ☍ ♀	20:49
6	☽ □ ♃	14:56
7	☽ □ ♆	1:21
8	☿ ☌ ⛢	14: 8
9	☿ □ ♄	3:49
	☿ ☌ ☊	6:31
	☽ ☍ ♂	9:45
	☽ ☍ ♇	21:43
10	♀ ☌ ☋	21:26
11	☽ □ ⛢	8:32
	☽ ☍ ♄	15:14
	♀ □ ♃	19:51
12	⊕ □ ♂	23:34
13	☽ □ ☿	22:37
	☿ ☌ P	23:18
14	☽ ☍ ♃	0:19
	☿ □ ♃	2:12
	☽ □ ♀	6:59
	☽ ☍ ♆	8:27
	♀ □ ♆	19:20
	☿ □ ♆	19:21
	☿ ☍ ♀	19:21
16	☽ □ ♂	16:24
	☽ □ ♇	19: 7
	⊕ □ ♇	21:49
18	☽ ☍ ⛢	0:47
	☽ □ ♄	6:44
19	♂ ☌ ♇	7:48
20	☿ ☍ ♇	7: 2
	☿ ☍ ♂	9:41
	☽ □ ♃	9:51
	☽ □ ♆	16:26
	☿ □ ⊕	23:12
21	☽ ☌ ♀	9:44
23	☽ ☌ ♇	1: 1
	☽ ☌ ♂	5: 2
	☿ □ ⛢	10: 5
24	☿ ☍ ♄	2:37
	☿ N ☊	3:35
	☽ □ ⛢	7:28
	☽ ☌ ♄	13:55
	☽ ☍ ☿	20:52
26	☽ ☌ ♃	21:27
27	☽ ☌ ♆	3:40
28	☽ □ ♀	20:32
29	☽ □ ♇	18:29
30	☽ □ ♂	7:17
	☿ ☍ ♃	16:42

March 11 AD 30: Last Visit with Eliud, p. 414, vol. I

April 24 AD 30: John returns to Ainon, p. 424, vol. I

March 4 AD 31: In Caesarea-Philippi, pp. 318–19, vol. II

April 10 AD 33: The Holy Eucharist, pp. 397–98, vol III

Heliocentric Mercury conjunct Uranus:

July 7 AD 29: Early ministry, p. 300, vol. I

October 3 AD 29: The Inn of Reuben, p. 353, vol. I

December 30 AD 29: End of the Wedding at Cana, p. 390, vol. I

March 29 AD 30: Preparing for Passover, pp. 419–20, vol. I

June 25 AD 30: Saturnin Baptizes, pp. 460–62, vol. I

September 21 AD 30: Gadara, pp. 58–59, vol. II

December 18 AD 30: Kiriathaim, p. 183, vol. II

March 17 AD 31: Cornerstone, p. 325, vol. II

June 13 AD 31: Return to Capernaum, pp. 398–99, vol. II

May 31 AD 32: Zacchaeus's House, p. 472, vol. II

August 27 AD 32: Salathiel, p. 491

February 19 AD 33: Preparing for Death, p. 1, vol. III

May 19 AD 33: The Risen One, pp. 411–12 vol. III

11—Saturn square Node:

February 24 AD 30: Teaching in the School, p. 408, vol. I

August 6 AD 32: Jesus Departs with Three Shepherd Youths, pp. 482–83, vol. II

Heliocentric Venus square Jupiter:

April 22 AD 29: John in the Wilderness, p. 292, vol. I

August 18 AD 29: The Synagogue and the Madhouse, p. 306, vol. I

December 16 AD 29: On the Way to the Wedding, pp. 377–78, vol. I

August 11 AD 30: Marriage and Divorce, pp. 9–11, vol. II

December 8 AD 30: Healing in Bethsaida, pp. 173–75, vol. II

April 6 AD 31: The Shekel in the Mouth of a Fish, pp. 342–43, vol. II

July 24 AD 32: Rebuke of Mary Salome, p. 477, vol. II

March 17 AD 33: Meeting of Scribes and Pharisees, p. 5, vol. III

12—Jupiter conjunct Neptune: See Editorial Foreword

Tychonic Sun square Mars:

December 17 AD 29: Healing by Word of Command, p. 378, vol. I

February 17 AD 31: In Sarepta, p. 313, vol. II

March 27 AD 33: On the End of Days, pp. 14–15, vol. III

14—Heliocentric Venus square Neptune:

July 25 AD 29: From Mt. Carmel to Mt. Tabor, pp. 302–03, vol. I

November 16 AD 29: Temptation in the Wilderness, pp. 365–69 vol. I

March 8 AD 30: Festival of Purim, p. 414, vol. I

June 30 AD 30: In Simeon's House, p. 464, vol. I

October 20 AD 30: Outside Michmethath, p. 82, vol. II

February 10 AD 31: On Fasting, p. 307, vol. II

August 26 AD 32: In Sichar

April 9 AD 33: With the Risen One, p. 397, vol. III

Heliocentric Mercury opposite Venus:

June 2 AD 29: Alone in Prayer, p. 296, vol. I

October 6 AD 29: Jesus Visits an Inn, p. 356, vol. I

March 12 AD 30: Last Visit with Eliud, p. 414, vol. I

August 7 AD 30: A Home for Lepers, pp. 7–8, vol. II

December 15 AD 30: Close of the Feast of Lights, pp. 181–82, vol. II

May 22 AD 31: Clothes and Provisions, pp. 385–86, vol. II

July 31 AD 32: Beginning the Journey to the Three Kings, pp. 480–81, vol. II

May 5 AD 33: With the Risen One, p. 408, vol. III

15—Sun enters Aries:

March 20 AD 30: Visiting Obed, p. 416, vol. I

March 20 AD 31: Dividing into Groups, p. 327, vol. II

March 20 AD 33: Magdalene's Last Anointing, pp. 9–10, vol. III

16—Full Moon Aries:

April 17 AD 29: John in the Wilderness, p. 292, vol. I

April 6 AD 30: Overturning the Tables in the Temple, p. 423, vol. I

March 27 AD 31: Sharing the Passover Meal, pp. 331–32, vol. II

April 3 AD 33: Passion of Christ, pp. 106–20, 192–224, 300–20, vol. III

Tychonic Sun square Pluto:

August 31 AD 29: The Synagogue and the Madhouse, p. 306, vol. I

February 27 AD 30: Leaving Unnoticed, p. 409, vol. I

September 3 AD 30: Crossing the Jordan, pp. 41–42, vol. II

March 1 AD 31: Teaching and Consoling, p. 318, vol. II

17—Jupiter enters Pisces:

April 20 AD 29: John in the Wilderness, p. 292, vol. I

December 8 AD 29: Andrew and Saturnin, p. 375, vol. I

18—Mercury conjunct Uranus:

July 15 AD 29: In Sarepta, p. 301–02, vol. I

July 10 AD 30: The Baptismal Well, pp. 470–71, vol. I

August 21 AD 32: Beehive and Vineyard, pp. 488–89

Sun square Pluto:

August 29 AD 29: Jesus Among the Publicans, p. 310, vol. I

March 1 AD 30: Elijah and Mt. Carmel, p. 411, vol. I

September 1 AD 30: Teaching the Boys and Girls, pp. 39–40, vol. II

March 3 AD 31: The Lord's Prayer, p. 318, vol. II

September 4 AD 32: Healing in Kedar, p. 494, vol. II

March 7 AD 33: Future Tasks, pp. 2–4, vol. III

19—Heliocentric Mars conjunct Pluto:

May 3 AD 30: The Letter of King Abgar, pp. 458–59, vol. I

20—Heliocentric Mercury opposite Pluto:

September 23 AD 29: Baptism in the Jordan, pp. 342–45, vol. I

December 20 AD 29: Invited to the Wedding at Cana, p. 379, vol. I

March 18 AD 30: At an Inn, p. 416, vol. I

September 10 AD 30: Celebration of Gideon, pp. 51–52, vol. II

December 7 AD 30: First Walking on Water, pp. 172–73, vol. II

March 5 AD 31: Alms for the Poor, p. 319, vol. II

June 1 AD 31: In Misael, p. 393, vol. II

May 18 AD 32: Healing of Ten Lepers, pp. 468–70, vol. II

August 15 AD 32: Teaching about Marriage, p. 487, vol. II

May 6 AD 33: Increase of the Community, pp. 407–9, vol. III

Heliocentric Mercury opposite Mars:

December 7 AD 29: In Dibon, p. 375, vol. I

March 14 AD 30: At Lazarus's Estate, p. 414, vol. I

June 19 AD 30: Celebrating the New Moon Festival, p. 460, vol. I

September 29 AD 30: Mara the Suphanite, pp. 65–67, vol. II

January 14 AD 31: Grave of Zechariah, p. 211, vol. II

April 30 AD 31: Mercuria, pp. 362–64, vol. II

September 5 AD 32: Salathiel and Nazor, p. 494, vol. II

April 5 AD 33: Resurrection, pp. 387–93, vol. III

23—Mercury conjunct Node:

May 20 AD 31: Jesus Visits the Mines near Kythria, pp. 384–85, vol. II

April 14 AD 33: The Night before the Communion of Fish, pp. 400–01, vol. III

24—Heliocentric Mercury opposite Saturn:

August 13 AD 29: Future Disciples, p. 305, vol. I

November 10 AD 29: Temptation in the Wilderness, pp. 365–69, vol. I

February 7 AD 30: Raising of the Daughter of Jairus the Essene, p. 402, vol. I

August 4 AD 30: Jesus visits the Nobleman's Son, pp. 2–4, vol. II

November 1 AD 30: Teaching at Saul's Well, p. 97, vol. II

January 30 AD 31: Sailing to Tarichea, pp. 301–03, vol. II

April 29 AD 31: At the Home of Jonas's Father, pp. 360–62, vol. II

July 16 AD 32: "Our friend Lazarus has fallen asleep," p. 475, vol. II

October 13 AD 32: Journey to Egypt, p. 517, vol. II

January 10 AD 33: At the Synagogue in Bethain, p. 520, vol. II

April 9 AD 33: The Risen One, pp. 396–98, vol. III

25—Mercury enters Taurus:

April 3 AD 29: Death of Joseph, p. 292, vol. I

March 30 AD 30: From Jutta to Hebron, p. 420, vol. I

May 13 AD 30: Controversy around Baptism, p. 459, vol. I

May 12 AD 31: Sabbath Year and Jubilee, pp. 376–77, vol. II

April 25 AD 33: Days with the Risen One, p. 408, vol. III

27—Venus conjunct Neptune:

December 2 AD 29: Preparing the Pool for Baptism, p. 373, vol. I

January 2 AD 30: Two Days' Fasting, p. 390, vol. I

March 28 AD 30: In the Home of Joseph of Arimathea, p. 419, vol. I

December 29 AD 30: Visiting Jonadab, p. 193–94, vol. II

30—New Moon Aries:

April 2 AD 29: Death of Joseph, p. 292, vol. I

March 22 AD 30: Feast of the New Moon, p. 418, vol. I

April 10 AD 31: The Son of the Vineyard Owner, pp. 345–46, vol. II

March 19 AD 33: Triumphant Entry into Jerusalem, pp. 6–9

Venus conjunct Jupiter:

May 4 AD 30: Controversy around Baptism, p. 459, vol. I

March 4 AD 31: In Caesarea-Philippi, pp. 318–19, vol. II

May 24 AD 32: Walking through the Pharisees, p. 470, vol. II

Heliocentric Mercury opposite Jupiter:

July 12 AD 29: In Sarepta, pp. 301–02, vol. I

October 10 AD 29: Feast of Tabernacles, pp. 359–60, vol. I

January 8 AD 30: Conversation with the Virgin Mary, p. 393, vol. I

April 8 AD 30: Death of Silent Mary and Nighttime Conversation with Nicodemus, p. 424, vol. I

July 8 AD 30: The Unjust Steward, pp. 469–70, vol. I

October 6 AD 30: Healing of Manahem, pp. 72–73, vol. II

January 5 AD 31: Reproached by Pharisees, pp. 203–04, vol. II

April 6 AD 31: The Shekel in the Fish, pp. 342–43, vol. II

July 6 AD 31: The Way of David, p. 465, vol. II

October 2 AD 32: In the House of Azarias, pp. 510–11, vol. II

December 31 AD 32: Egyptian City, p. 518, vol. II

April 1 AD 33: Magdalene's Last Anointing, pp. 19–22, vol. III

MAY 2022

STARGAZING PREVIEW

During the first moments of May, the Sun joyously recalls it zodiacal degree at the Resurrection. There's a celebration in the heavens on the night of the 5th; this is the time of the peak of the Eta Aquariid Meteor Showers, known for their speed. As the waxing crescent Moon doesn't set until midnight, you're more likely to see the showers after this time. Look to the northeast for your best chance of seeing these shooting stars streak across the night sky.

Over the next few days, the Moon will wind below *Castor* and *Pollux*, and above the Beehive on its way to its First Quarter (23° Cancer) on the 9th. On the 13th, look in the southeast after sunset for the Moon, now above *Spica*, the brightest star of Virgo—you can always find *Spica* by extending the arc of the handle of the Big Dipper through bright *Arcturus* (of Boötes), and on to Virgo.

The Bull welcomes the Sun on the 15th; may we all attune our "horns" to cosmic thoughts! On the following day, the Full Moon will shine from the first degree of Scorpio (known to initiates of the past as the Eagle)—resulting in a Total Lunar Eclipse over the Americas and West Africa. The greatest eclipse will be experienced very near Lake Titicaca, where it might be possible to see the silhouette of a condor fly before the darkened Moon.

On Sunday the 22nd, the Moon conjoins Saturn; they rise the following morning—Saturn first—at 0100. Also on Sunday, the Last Quarter Moon glows before the backdrop of the stars of the Waterman. As it rises the following morning at 0100, it will recall the Sun's position at the Feeding of the Five Thousand and the Walking on the Water.

If you find yourself unable to sleep during the wee hours of the 25th, take a peek at Mars, the Moon, and Jupiter as they rise in unison at 0200. The precise conjunction of Mars and Jupiter (at nearly the same declination, meaning that they will be very close indeed) occurs on the 29th; you'll only have two hours to see them before sunrise. A great night for stargazing for those who can stay up!

The Sun and Moon find each other at 14° Taurus on the 30th. That evening, after sunset, all ten planets will be below the horizon. You'll find the Lion, high in the south, ruling over all that he sees.

Orion is now veiled by the radiance of the Sun.

MAY COMMENTARIES

1—Heliocentric Mercury opposite Neptune:
    July 5 AD 29: Six New Disciples, p. 300, vol. I
    October 29 AD 29: Baptizing through Saturnin, pp. 352–53, vol. I
    December 28 AD 29: Changing of Water into Wine, pp. 386–89, vol. I
    June 22 AD 30: Teaching in the Fruit Plantation, p. 460, vol. I
    September 18 AD 30: Isaac and Elijah, pp. 56–57, vol. II
    December 15 AD 30: Close of the Feast of Lights, pp. 181–82, vol. II
    March 13 AD 31: At Matthew's Custom House, p. 322, vol. II
    June 9 AD 31: Healing on the Sabbath, pp. 396–97, vol. II
    August 23 AD 32: On Marriage, p. 490, vol. II
    February 15 AD 33: Exhortations of the Virgin, p. 530, vol. II
    May 14 AD 33: Ascension Day, pp. 410–12, vol. III

5—Sun conjunct Uranus:
    July 28 AD 29: The Sanhedrin Send Spies, p. 303, vol. I
    August 3 AD 30: Healing of the Nobleman's Son, pp. 1–2, vol. II
    August 12 AD 32: Healing a Bedridden Couple, p. 486, vol. II

6—Heliocentric Venus conjunct Pluto:
    August 23 AD 29: In the Valley of Zebulon, p. 307, vol. I
    April 5 AD 30: Passover Meal in Lazarus's Castle, pp. 422–23, vol. I
    November 17 AD 30: Healing of Lepers, pp. 148–50, vol. II
    June 30 AD 31: Interpreting Numbers and Judges, p. 409, vol. II
    September 23 AD 32: Visiting Theokeno with Mensor, p. 504, vol. II

SIDEREAL GEOCENTRIC LONGITUDES : MAY 2022 Gregorian at 0 hours UT

DAY	☉	☽	☊	☿	♀	♂	♃	♄	♅	♆	♇
1 SU	15 ♈ 34	17 ♈ 15	27 ♈ 26R	5 ♉ 53	3 ♓ 3	16 ♒ 57	2 ♓ 56	29 ♑ 13	19 ♈ 30	29 ♒ 31	3 ♑ 33R
2 MO	16 32	29 31	27 26D	6 40	4 11	17 42	3 9	29 16	19 33	29 33	3 33
3 TU	17 30	11 ♉ 36	27 26	7 22	5 19	18 27	3 21	29 20	19 37	29 34	3 32
4 WE	18 29	23 33	27 27	7 59	6 28	19 13	3 33	29 23	19 40	29 36	3 32
5 TH	19 27	5 ♊ 24	27 28	8 30	7 36	19 58	3 46	29 26	19 43	29 38	3 32
6 FR	20 25	17 14	27 28	8 56	8 45	20 43	3 58	29 29	19 47	29 39	3 32
7 SA	21 23	29 5	27 29	9 17	9 54	21 28	4 10	29 31	19 50	29 41	3 32
8 SU	22 21	11 ♋ 2	27 29	9 33	11 2	22 14	4 22	29 34	19 54	29 42	3 32
9 MO	23 19	23 10	27 29R	9 43	12 11	22 59	4 34	29 37	19 57	29 44	3 31
10 TU	24 17	5 ♌ 32	27 29	9 48	13 20	23 44	4 45	29 39	20 1	29 45	3 31
11 WE	25 15	18 14	27 29	9 48R	14 29	24 29	4 57	29 42	20 4	29 47	3 31
12 TH	26 13	1 ♍ 18	27 29	9 43	15 38	25 14	5 9	29 44	20 8	29 48	3 30
13 FR	27 11	14 48	27 29	9 33	16 47	25 59	5 20	29 46	20 11	29 50	3 30
14 SA	28 9	28 42	27 29D	9 19	17 57	26 44	5 32	29 49	20 15	29 51	3 30
15 SU	29 7	13 ♎ 1	27 29	9 1	19 6	27 29	5 43	29 51	20 18	29 53	3 29
16 MO	0 ♉ 5	27 39	27 29	8 39	20 15	28 14	5 54	29 53	20 21	29 54	3 29
17 TU	1 3	12 ♏ 31	27 29R	8 13	21 25	28 59	6 6	29 54	20 25	29 55	3 28
18 WE	2 0	27 28	27 29	7 45	22 34	29 44	6 17	29 56	20 28	29 56	3 28
19 TH	2 58	12 ♐ 23	27 28	7 14	23 44	0 ♓ 29	6 28	29 58	20 32	29 58	3 27
20 FR	3 56	27 8	27 28	6 41	24 54	1 14	6 39	0 ♒ 0	20 35	29 59	3 27
21 SA	4 54	11 ♑ 38	27 27	6 8	26 4	1 59	6 49	0 1	20 39	0 ♓ 0	3 26
22 SU	5 51	25 48	27 26	5 33	27 13	2 44	7 0	0 3	20 42	0 1	3 26
23 MO	6 49	9 ♒ 37	27 26D	4 59	28 23	3 29	7 11	0 4	20 45	0 3	3 25
24 TU	7 47	23 5	27 26	4 25	29 33	4 13	7 21	0 5	20 49	0 4	3 24
25 WE	8 44	6 ♓ 14	27 27	3 52	0 ♈ 43	4 58	7 32	0 6	20 52	0 5	3 24
26 TH	9 42	19 4	27 28	3 21	1 53	5 43	7 42	0 7	20 55	0 6	3 23
27 FR	10 40	1 ♈ 39	27 29	2 52	3 3	6 28	7 52	0 8	20 59	0 7	3 22
28 SA	11 37	14 1	27 30	2 25	4 14	7 12	8 2	0 9	21 2	0 8	3 22
29 SU	12 35	26 13	27 31	2 2	5 24	7 57	8 12	0 10	21 5	0 9	3 21
30 MO	13 32	8 ♉ 16	27 30R	1 42	6 34	8 41	8 22	0 10	21 8	0 10	3 20
31 TU	14 30	20 13	27 29	1 26	7 45	9 26	8 32	0 11	21 12	0 11	3 19

INGRESSES :

2 ☽ → ♉ 0:57
4 ☽ → ♊ 13: 2
7 ☽ → ♋ 1:50
9 ☽ → ♌ 13:19
11 ☽ → ♍ 21:38
14 ☽ → ♎ 2:11
15 ☉ → ♉ 22: 2
16 ☽ → ♏ 3:48
18 ☽ → ♐ 4: 3
♂ → ♓ 8:25
20 ☽ → ♑ 4:41
♄ → ♒ 6:15
♆ → ♓ 19:16
22 ☽ → ♒ 7:13
24 ♀ → ♈ 9:10
☽ → ♓ 12:33
26 ☽ → ♈ 20:49
29 ☽ → ♉ 7:30
31 ☽ → ♊ 19:46

ASPECTS & ECLIPSES :

1 ☽ ☌ ♅ 4:23
☽ ☌ ☊ 19:53
2 ☽ ☌ ☿ 15: 4
5 ☉ ☌ ♅ 7:19
☽ ☌ A 13: 6
7 ☽ ☍ ♇ 8:57
9 ☉ □ ☽ 0:20
☽ ⚺ ☊ 8:27
☽ ☍ ♄ 12:37
11 ☽ ☍ ♂ 12:16
☽ ☍ ♆ 21:16
12 ☽ ☍ ♃ 7: 0
13 ☽ ☍ ♀ 3:48
☉ ☌ ☊ 7:20
15 ☽ ☍ ♅ 12: 3
☉ □ ♄ 18:48
☽ ☌ ☋ 23:43
16 ☽ ☍ T 4:10
☉ ☍ ☽ 4:13
☽ ☍ ☿ 17:17
17 ☽ ☌ P 15:28
18 ♂ ☌ ♆ 6:44
20 ☽ ☌ ♇ 10:22
21 ☉ ⚻ ☿ 19:16
22 ☽ ⚼ ☊ 2:48
☽ ☌ ♄ 7:18
☉ □ ☽ 18:42
24 ☽ ☌ ♆ 12:41
☽ ☌ ♂ 21:32
25 ☽ ☌ ♃ 2:26
27 ☽ ☌ ♀ 2:59
♀ □ ♇ 6:23
28 ☽ ☌ ♅ 13:49
29 ☽ ☌ ☊ 2:33
♂ ☌ ♃ 10:29
☽ ☌ ☿ 11:13
30 ☉ ☌ ☽ 11:29

SIDEREAL HELIOCENTRIC LONGITUDES : MAY 2022 Gregorian at 0 hours UT

DAY	Sid. Time	☿	♀	⊕	♂	♃	♄	♅	♆	♇	Vernal Point
1 SU	14:35:38	26 ♌ 20	23 ♐ 40	15 ♎ 35	9 ♑ 2	25 ♒ 3	23 ♑ 33	19 ♈ 42	28 ♒ 8	1 ♑ 55	4 ♓ 56'54"
2 MO	14:39:34	0 ♍ 32	25 15	16 33	9 39	25 9	23 35	19 43	28 8	1 55	4 ♓ 56'54"
3 TU	14:43:31	4 37	26 50	17 31	10 16	25 14	23 37	19 44	28 9	1 55	4 ♓ 56'54"
4 WE	14:47:28	8 34	28 24	18 29	10 53	25 20	23 38	19 44	28 9	1 55	4 ♓ 56'54"
5 TH	14:51:24	12 25	29 59	19 27	11 30	25 25	23 40	19 45	28 9	1 56	4 ♓ 56'54"
6 FR	14:55:21	16 9	1 ♑ 34	20 26	12 8	25 31	23 42	19 46	28 10	1 56	4 ♓ 56'54"
7 SA	14:59:17	19 47	3 9	21 24	12 45	25 36	23 44	19 46	28 10	1 56	4 ♓ 56'53"
8 SU	15: 3:14	23 19	4 44	22 22	13 22	25 41	23 46	19 47	28 11	1 57	4 ♓ 56'53"
9 MO	15: 7:10	26 46	6 19	23 20	14 0	25 47	23 48	19 48	28 11	1 57	4 ♓ 56'53"
10 TU	15:11: 7	0 ♎ 8	7 54	24 18	14 37	25 52	23 50	19 48	28 11	1 57	4 ♓ 56'53"
11 WE	15:15: 3	3 26	9 28	25 16	15 14	25 58	23 51	19 49	28 12	1 57	4 ♓ 56'53"
12 TH	15:19: 0	6 39	11 3	26 14	15 52	26 3	23 53	19 50	28 12	1 58	4 ♓ 56'53"
13 FR	15:22:57	9 49	12 38	27 12	16 29	26 9	23 55	19 50	28 12	1 58	4 ♓ 56'53"
14 SA	15:26:53	12 55	14 13	28 10	17 7	26 14	23 57	19 51	28 13	1 58	4 ♓ 56'52"
15 SU	15:30:50	15 58	15 48	29 7	17 44	26 20	23 59	19 52	28 13	1 59	4 ♓ 56'52"
16 MO	15:34:46	18 58	17 23	0 ♏ 5	18 22	26 25	24 1	19 52	28 13	1 59	4 ♓ 56'52"
17 TU	15:38:43	21 56	18 58	1 3	19 0	26 31	24 3	19 53	28 14	1 59	4 ♓ 56'52"
18 WE	15:42:39	24 51	20 33	2 1	19 37	26 36	24 5	19 54	28 14	2 0	4 ♓ 56'52"
19 TH	15:46:36	27 44	22 8	2 59	20 15	26 42	24 6	19 54	28 15	2 0	4 ♓ 56'52"
20 FR	15:50:32	0 ♏ 36	23 43	3 56	20 53	26 47	24 8	19 55	28 15	2 0	4 ♓ 56'52"
21 SA	15:54:29	3 25	25 17	4 54	21 30	26 52	24 10	19 56	28 15	2 0	4 ♓ 56'52"
22 SU	15:58:26	6 14	26 52	5 52	22 8	26 58	24 12	19 56	28 16	2 1	4 ♓ 56'51"
23 MO	16: 2:22	9 1	28 27	6 50	22 46	27 3	24 14	19 57	28 16	2 1	4 ♓ 56'51"
24 TU	16: 6:19	11 47	0 ♒ 2	7 47	23 24	27 9	24 16	19 58	28 16	2 1	4 ♓ 56'51"
25 WE	16:10:15	14 32	1 37	8 45	24 1	27 14	24 18	19 58	28 17	2 2	4 ♓ 56'51"
26 TH	16:14:12	17 17	3 12	9 43	24 39	27 20	24 19	19 59	28 17	2 2	4 ♓ 56'51"
27 FR	16:18: 8	20 2	4 47	10 40	25 17	27 25	24 21	20 0	28 17	2 2	4 ♓ 56'51"
28 SA	16:22: 5	22 47	6 22	11 38	25 55	27 31	24 23	20 0	28 18	2 2	4 ♓ 56'51"
29 SU	16:26: 1	25 32	7 58	12 35	26 33	27 36	24 25	20 1	28 18	2 3	4 ♓ 56'50"
30 MO	16:29:58	28 17	9 33	13 33	27 11	27 42	24 27	20 2	28 19	2 3	4 ♓ 56'50"
31 TU	16:33:55	1 ♐ 2	11 8	14 31	27 49	27 47	24 29	20 2	28 19	2 3	4 ♓ 56'50"

INGRESSES :

1 ☿ → ♍ 20:52
5 ♀ → ♑ 0: 9
9 ☿ → ♎ 23: 0
15 ⊕ → ♏ 21:48
19 ☿ → ♏ 18:59
23 ♀ → ♒ 23:23
30 ☿ → ♐ 14:58

ASPECTS (HELIOCENTRIC +MOON(TYCHONIC)) :

1 ☽ ☌ ♅ 4:46
☿ ☍ ♆ 10:11
☽ □ ♄ 12:18
4 ☽ □ ♃ 3:37
☽ □ ♆ 9:18
5 ⊕ ☍ ♅ 7:19
☽ □ ☿ 20:48
6 ♀ ☌ ♇ 5:32
7 ☽ ☍ ♇ 5:45
☽ ☍ ♀ 9:26
8 ☽ ☍ ♂ 4:54
☽ □ ♅ 17:22
9 ☽ ☍ ♄ 1:14
⊕ □ ♄ 11:56
10 ☿ □ ♇ 13:11
11 ☽ ☍ ♃ 14:22
☽ ☍ ♆ 18:21
14 ☽ □ ♇ 5:32
☿ □ ♀ 21: 8
15 ☽ □ ♀ 5:10
☽ ☌ ☿ 6:10
☽ □ ♂ 8: 9
☽ ☍ ♅ 11:17
♀ ☌ A 15:33
☿ □ ♂ 17:48
☽ □ ♄ 18: 4
16 ☿ ☍ ♅ 7:16
17 ♀ ☌ ♂ 0:45
☿ ☌ ☋ 13:12
♀ □ ♅ 14: 3
☿ □ ♄ 17:30
☽ □ ♃ 22:36
18 ☽ □ ♆ 1:14
♂ □ ♅ 10:38
20 ♀ ☌ ♄ 6:38
☽ ☌ ♇ 7:59
21 ☽ □ ♅ 13:58
☽ ☌ ♂ 17:25
☿ ☌ ⊕ 19:16
☽ ☌ ♄ 21:14
22 ☽ ☌ ♀ 2: 3
☽ □ ☿ 22:38
24 ☽ ☌ ♃ 7:24
☽ ☌ ♆ 9:24
25 ♂ ☌ ♄ 10:52
26 ♂ ⚼ ☊ 0:58
27 ☽ □ ♇ 0:44
☿ ☌ A 23:44
28 ☽ ☌ ♅ 11:44
☽ □ ♄ 20:25
29 ☽ □ ♂ 0:41
☿ □ ♃ 18:43
30 ☿ □ ♆ 0:16
☽ □ ♀ 2:56
31 ☽ □ ♃ 15:24
☽ □ ♆ 16:22

May 7 AD 33: Days with the Risen One, p. 408, vol. III

9—Tychonic Sun square Saturn:

August 29 AD 29: Jesus Among the Publicans, p. 310, vol. I

March 3 AD 30: The Doctors of the Synagogue, p. 412, vol. I

September 13 AD 30: Harsh Interpretation of the Law, p. 53, vol. II

March 18 AD 31: Peter Receives the Keys of the Kingdom of Heaven, pp. 325–27, vol. II

October 10 AD 32: The Birthplace of Abraham, pp. 515–16, vol. II

April 15 AD 33: Communion of Fish, pp. 401–04, vol. III

13—Sun conjunct Node:

May 24 AD 30: Imprisonment of John the Baptist, p. 459, vol. I

May 5 AD 31: Teaching at Barnabas's House, pp. 370–71, vol. II

March 27 AD 33: On the End of Days, pp. 14–15, vol. III

15—Sun square Saturn:

September 5 AD 29: Jesus in a Shepherd Village near Nazareth, pp. 312–13, vol. I

February 24 AD 30: Teaching in the School, p. 408, vol. I

September 19 AD 30: The Pillar of Elijah, pp. 57–58, vol. II

March 11 AD 31: Curing on the Way to Chorazin, p. 322, vol. II

April 8 AD 33: Days with the Risen One, pp. 396–97, vol. III

Sun enters Taurus:

April 19 AD 29: John in the Wilderness, p. 292, vol. I

April 20 AD 30: John returns to Ainon, p. 424, vol. I

April 20 AD 31: Warnings of Herod, pp. 349–50, vol. II

April 20 AD 33: Increase of the Community, pp. 407–08, vol. III

16—Full Moon Taurus:

May 6 AD 30: Controversy around Baptism, p. 459, vol. I

April 25 AD 31: Sailing to Cyprus by Starlight, pp. 353–54, vol. II

May 3 AD 33: Days with the Risen One, p. 408, vol. III

Heliocentric Mercury opposite Uranus:

June 4 AD 29: Sabbath in Hebron, p. 296, vol. I

August 31 AD 29: In Chisloth-Tabor, pp. 310–11, vol. I

November 28 AD 29: 38th Day of Temptation, p. 369, vol. I

May 23 AD 30: Imprisonment of John the Baptist, pp. 459–60, vol. I

August 19 AD 30: Healing Peter's Mother-in-law, pp. 21–23, vol. II

November 16 AD 30: 11/16/30—On the Way to Mt. Tabor, pp. 147–48 vol. II

February 12 AD 31: Healing of the Syrophoenician Woman, pp. 308–09, vol. II

May 11 AD 31: On King Djemschid, pp. 374–76, vol. II

July 25 AD 32: Day Before the Raising of Lazarus, pp. 477–78, vol. II

April 16 AD 33: Appearance of the Risen One to the Five Hundred, pp. 404–05, vol. III

17—Heliocentric Venus square Uranus:

August 2 AD 29: Whispers and Murmurs, p. 303, vol. I

November 24 AD 29: Temptation in the Wilderness, pp. 365–71, vol. I

March 17 AD 30: The Samarian Orphan, p. 415, vol. I

July 9 AD 30: Inviting the People of Adama, p. 470, vol. I

October 29 AD 30: The Sacred Fountain, pp. 92–94, vol. II

February 20 AD 31: Spending the Night with Tax Collectors, pp. 313–14, vol. II

June 13 AD 31: Ships from Cyprus, pp. 398–99, vol. II

May 18 AD 32: Healing of Ten Lepers, pp. 468–70, vol. II

September 8 AD 32: Jesus Reaches the Tent City, pp. 495–96, vol. II

December 31 AD 32: The First Egyptian City, p. 518, vol. II

April 22 AD 33: Days with the Risen One,
p. 408, vol. III

Heliocentric Venus conjunct Mars:

March 21 AD 30: Fulfilling of the Prophecies,
pp. 416–18, vol. I

January 5 AD 33: A Small Desert Town, p. 520,
vol. II

18—**Heliocentric Mars square Uranus:**

March 8 AD 30: Festival of Purim, p. 414,
vol. I

January 14 AD 31: The Grave of Zechariah,
p. 211, vol. II

Mars conjunct Neptune:

August 15 AD 30: Healing the Possessed
Widow, pp. 16–17, vol. II

August 24 AD 30: Herod Interrogates John,
pp. 28–30, vol. II

Mars enters Pisces:

November 19 AD 30: Teaching Aboard Ship,
pp. 152–54, vol. II

May 14 AD 32: Jesus Walks through the
Pharisees, p. 470, vol. II

Heliocentric Venus conjunct Saturn:

April 29 AD 29: Jesus and Mary move from
Nazareth to Capernaum, p. 292, vol. I

December 15 AD 29: Honoring the Aged,
p. 377, vol. I

August 2 AD 30: Meeting the Widow Maroni
in Nain, p. 497, vol. I

March 20 AD 31: Dividing into Groups, p. 327,
vol. II

June 22 AD 32: Come to Bring a Sword, p. 475,
vol. II

21—**Inferior Conjunction Sun and Mercury:**

September 9 AD 29: Jesus and Eliud, p. 317,
vol. I

December 24 AD 29: Summons of Phillip,
p. 382, vol. I

August 24 AD 30: Herod and John, pp. 28–29,
vol. II

December 8 AD 30: Healings in Bethsaida,
pp. 173–75, vol. II

April 2 AD 31: Transfiguration, pp. 339–40

November 23 AD 31: Healing of the Man Born
Blind, see *Journal for Star Wisdom*
2016

July 20 AD 32: News of Lazarus, p. 477, vol. II

February 23 AD 33: Teaching in the Temple,
p. 1, vol. III

24—**Venus enters Aries:**

May 2 AD 30: Concealed in Lazarus's Castle,
p. 424, vol. I

February 19 AD 31: Mount Hermon, p. 313,
vol. II

February 3 AD 33: Healing a Man with Edema,
p. 529, vol. II

25—**Heliocentric Mars conjunct Saturn:**

April 4 AD 29: Death of Joseph, p. 292, vol. I

April 21 AD 31: The Lost Sheep and Lost Coin,
p. 350, vol. II

May 9 AD 33: Days with the Risen One,
p. 408, vol. III

27—**Venus square Pluto:**

July 27 AD 29: The Sanhedrin Send Spies,
p. 303, vol. I

April 15 AD 30: In Concealment, p. 424, vol. I

September 11 AD 30: Gideon's Victory and the
Prodigal Son, p. 52, vol. II

February 5 AD 31: Revealing the Character of
the Twelve, p. 306, vol. II

August 15 AD 32: Teaching on Marriage,
p. 487, vol. II

January 18 AD 33: Three "Silent Disciples,"
p. 523, vol. II

29—**Mars conjunct Jupiter:**

January 17 AD 31: Recovery and Burial of
John's Remains, pp. 212–15, vol. II

30—**New Moon Taurus:**

May 2 AD 29: Jesus and Mary move from
Nazareth to Capernaum, p. 292, vol. I

April 21 AD 30: John Returns to Ainon, p. 424,
vol. I

May 10 AD 31: Three Blind Boys, p. 374,
vol. II

April 17 AD 33: Majesty and Dignity of the
Virgin Mary, pp. 406–07, vol. III

May 17 AD 33: Between Ascension and
Pentecost, p. 412, vol. III

JUNE 2022

STARGAZING PREVIEW

Throughout the entire month of June, all of the planets, visible and transcendent—with the exception of the Moon, which is always rushing about—are "morning stars," meaning that they cannot be seen in the evening at all. This presents a wonderful opportunity to seek a deeper understanding of the zodiac, in the absence of planetary interpreters.

The First Quarter Moon will shine from Leo on the 7th, very close to its degree at the birth of Steiner. Who can fail to admire the compassionate warmth of the Lion! Saturn, the leader of the rising classical planets, appears on the eastern horizon around 2230, before the 0100 moonset on the following morning.

The week that follows offers no change for stargazers other than finding the waxing Moon higher in the sky at sunset each day. By the evening of the 12th, the Moon, nearing Full, will have crossed the cusp into Scorpio. As it reaches 28° on the 14th—the zodiacal longitude of the Scorpion's stinger, *Lesotho*—it will be directly opposite the Sun, bearing the secrets of transformation and rebirth. This is the first of *three* Supermoons this year, during which the Moon's closeness to the Earth makes it appear larger than it usually does. Prepare to be awed!

Moments after sunrise (0400) on the 16th, the Sun will bid farewell to the Bull as it hails the Twins. Late on the 18th, Venus, now in Taurus, squares Saturn (Aquarius)—but you won't be able to see them before 0200, when Venus makes herself visible in the night sky. At this time, Saturn will be high in the south, and the 90° that separate them will be easy to see.

By the 20th, retrograde Saturn will have backed itself into Capricorn—for the duration of the year. June's Last Quarter Moon (5° Pisces) comes up just after midnight on the 21st. This is also the day of the summer solstice (at 0914), when the Sun reaches its highest latitude of the year—making evident the power granted to the Sun at this point of its yearly journey.

Around 0200 on the 26th, the Moon, Venus, and the *Pleiades* will rise arm in arm as the Scorpion sets. By this time, Saturn will be high in the southwest, Jupiter and Mars, both still in Pisces, in the southeast. Mars, ruler of Aries, gets a boost on Tuesday the 28th as he crosses the cusp into the Ram.

Saturn, Jupiter, Mars, Venus and Mercury will have risen before the New Moon (12° Gemini) on the 29th. The Sun today bears the memory of the birth of John the Baptist.

JUNE COMMENTARIES

3—Heliocentric Mars enters Aquarius:
July 23 AD 30: Lazarus and the Holy Women Support Christ, pp. 483–84, vol. I
June 9 AD 32: Confronted by One Hundred Pharisees, p. 473, vol. II

5—Tychonic Sun square Venus:
March 24 AD 31: Magdalene Follow Christ, pp. 329–30, vol. II

6—Heliocentric Jupiter conjunct Neptune: See Editorial Foreword

10—Heliocentric Mercury conjunct Pluto:
August 14 AD 29: In Mahara's House, pp. 305–06, vol. I
November 10 AD 29: Temptation in the Wilderness, pp. 365–71, vol. I
February 6 AD 30: The Hospitable and Inhospitable, pp. 401–02, vol. I
May 5 AD 30: Many Baptisms, p. 459, vol. I
August 1 AD 30: The Samaritans, pp. 496–97, vol. I
October 28 AD 30: Healing of Issachar of Dothan, pp. 90–92, vol. II
January 25 AD 31: Assembly of Pharisees, p. 223, vol. II
October 3 AD 32: The Wonderful Cure of Two Sick Women, pp. 511–12, vol. II
March 28 AD 33: The Two Gardens, pp. 15–16, vol. III

Heliocentric Venus conjunct Neptune:
September 21 AD 29: The Village Giah and Lazarus's Castle, pp. 326–28, vol. I

SIDEREAL GEOCENTRIC LONGITUDES : JUNE 2022 Gregorian at 0 hours UT

DAY	☉	☽	☊	☿	♀	♂	♃	♄	♅	♆	♇
1 WE	15 ♉ 28	2 ♊ 5	27 ♈ 27R	1 ♉ 14R	8 ♈ 55	10 ♓ 10	8 ♓ 41	0 ♒ 11	21 ♈ 15	0 ♓ 12	3 ♑ 18R
2 TH	16 25	13 55	27 24	1 6	10 5	10 55	8 51	0 12	21 18	0 13	3 18
3 FR	17 23	25 45	27 21	1 2	11 16	11 39	9 0	0 12	21 21	0 13	3 17
4 SA	18 20	7 ♋ 37	27 18	1 3D	12 26	12 24	9 9	0 12	21 25	0 14	3 16
5 SU	19 18	19 35	27 15	1 8	13 37	13 8	9 18	0 12R	21 28	0 15	3 15
6 MO	20 15	1 ♌ 42	27 13	1 18	14 48	13 52	9 27	0 12	21 31	0 16	3 14
7 TU	21 12	14 3	27 12	1 32	15 58	14 36	9 36	0 12	21 34	0 16	3 13
8 WE	22 10	26 41	27 11D	1 51	17 9	15 20	9 45	0 12	21 37	0 17	3 12
9 TH	23 7	9 ♍ 40	27 12	2 14	18 20	16 4	9 53	0 11	21 40	0 18	3 11
10 FR	24 5	23 4	27 13	2 41	19 31	16 48	10 2	0 11	21 43	0 18	3 10
11 SA	25 2	6 ♎ 54	27 15	3 13	20 41	17 32	10 10	0 10	21 46	0 19	3 9
12 SU	25 59	21 11	27 15	3 49	21 52	18 16	10 18	0 10	21 49	0 19	3 8
13 MO	26 57	5 ♏ 52	27 15R	4 29	23 3	19 0	10 26	0 9	21 52	0 20	3 7
14 TU	27 54	20 53	27 14	5 13	24 14	19 44	10 34	0 8	21 55	0 20	3 6
15 WE	28 51	6 ♐ 5	27 11	6 1	25 25	20 27	10 42	0 7	21 58	0 21	3 5
16 TH	29 48	21 18	27 7	6 53	26 36	21 11	10 50	0 6	22 1	0 21	3 3
17 FR	0 ♊ 46	6 ♑ 22	27 2	7 49	27 48	21 55	10 57	0 5	22 4	0 22	3 2
18 SA	1 43	21 9	26 58	8 48	28 59	22 38	11 4	0 4	22 7	0 22	3 1
19 SU	2 40	5 ♒ 32	26 54	9 52	0 ♉ 10	23 22	11 12	0 2	22 10	0 22	3 0
20 MO	3 38	19 28	26 52	10 59	1 21	24 5	11 19	0 1	22 13	0 23	2 59
21 TU	4 35	2 ♓ 58	26 51	12 9	2 32	24 48	11 25	29 ♑ 59	22 15	0 23	2 58
22 WE	5 32	16 2	26 52D	13 23	3 44	25 31	11 32	29 58	22 18	0 23	2 56
23 TH	6 29	28 44	26 53	14 40	4 55	26 15	11 39	29 56	22 21	0 23	2 55
24 FR	7 27	11 ♈ 9	26 54	16 1	6 7	26 58	11 45	29 54	22 23	0 23	2 54
25 SA	8 24	23 20	26 55	17 26	7 18	27 41	11 51	29 53	22 26	0 24	2 53
26 SU	9 21	5 ♉ 21	26 55R	18 53	8 30	28 24	11 58	29 51	22 29	0 24	2 51
27 MO	10 18	17 15	26 53	20 24	9 41	29 7	12 3	29 49	22 31	0 24	2 50
28 TU	11 16	29 6	26 49	21 59	10 53	29 49	12 9	29 46	22 34	0 24	2 49
29 WE	12 13	10 ♊ 55	26 43	23 36	12 4	0 ♈ 32	12 15	29 44	22 36	0 24R	2 47
30 TH	13 10	22 45	26 35	25 17	13 16	1 15	12 20	29 42	22 39	0 24	2 46

INGRESSES :

3	☽ → ♋	8:36
5	☽ → ♌	20:38
8	☽ → ♍	6:12
10	☽ → ♎	12: 8
12	☽ → ♏	14:28
14	☽ → ♐	14:25
16	☉ → ♊	4:49
	☽ → ♑	13:48
18	☽ → ♒	14:40
	♀ → ♉	20:40
20	♄ → ♑	15:43
	☽ → ♓	18:39
23	☽ → ♈	2:25
25	☽ → ♉	13:17
28	☽ → ♊	1:49
	♂ → ♈	5:59
30	☽ → ♋	14:39

ASPECTS & ECLIPSES :

2	☽ ☌ A	1:44
3	☽ ☍ ♇	15:13
5	☽ N□ ☊	15:10
	☽ ☍ ♄	21: 2
7	☉ □ ☽	14:47
8	☽ ☍ ♆	6:44
9	☽ ☍ ♃	0:24
	☽ ☍ ♂	12:14
11	♀ ☌ ♅	22:55
12	☽ ☍ ♅	1: 3
	☽ ☍ ♀	1:14
	☽ ☌ ☋	10: 0
	☽ ☍ ☿	21:38
14	☉ ☍ ☽	11:50
	☽ ☌ P	23:29
16	♀ ☌ ☊	9:43
	☉ □ ♆	13:50
	☽ ☌ ♇	18:40
18	☽ S□ ☊	9:34
	☽ ☌ ♄	14:45
	♀ □ ♄	21:31
20	☽ ☌ ♆	19:20
21	☉ □ ☽	3: 9
	☽ ☌ ♃	15:35
22	☽ ☌ ♂	18:57
24	☽ ☌ ♅	22:13
25	☽ ☌ ☊	7: 9
26	☽ ☌ ♀	7: 1
27	☽ ☌ ☿	7:20
29	☉ □ ♃	0:58
	☉ ☌ ☽	2:51
	☽ ☌ A	6:25
30	☽ ☍ ♇	20:12

SIDEREAL HELIOCENTRIC LONGITUDES : JUNE 2022 Gregorian at 0 hours UT

DAY	Sid. Time	☿	♀	⊕	♂	♃	♄	♅	♆	♇	Vernal Point
1 WE	16:37:51	3 ♐ 49	12 ♒ 43	15 ♏ 28	28 ♑ 27	27 ♒ 53	24 ♑ 31	20 ♈ 3	28 ♒ 19	2 ♑ 4	4 ♓ 56'50"
2 TH	16:41:48	6 36	14 18	16 26	29 4	27 58	24 33	20 4	28 20	2 4	4 ♓ 56'50"
3 FR	16:45:44	9 24	15 53	17 23	29 42	28 3	24 34	20 4	28 20	2 4	4 ♓ 56'50"
4 SA	16:49:41	12 14	17 28	18 21	0 ♒ 20	28 9	24 36	20 5	28 20	2 4	4 ♓ 56'50"
5 SU	16:53:37	15 5	19 4	19 18	0 58	28 14	24 38	20 6	28 21	2 5	4 ♓ 56'49"
6 MO	16:57:34	17 59	20 39	20 16	1 36	28 20	24 40	20 6	28 21	2 5	4 ♓ 56'49"
7 TU	17: 1:30	20 54	22 14	21 13	2 14	28 25	24 42	20 7	28 21	2 5	4 ♓ 56'49"
8 WE	17: 5:27	23 51	23 49	22 10	2 52	28 31	24 44	20 8	28 22	2 6	4 ♓ 56'49"
9 TH	17: 9:24	26 51	25 25	23 8	3 31	28 36	24 46	20 8	28 22	2 6	4 ♓ 56'49"
10 FR	17:13:20	29 54	27 0	24 5	4 9	28 42	24 48	20 9	28 23	2 6	4 ♓ 56'49"
11 SA	17:17:17	3 ♑ 0	28 35	25 2	4 47	28 47	24 49	20 10	28 23	2 6	4 ♓ 56'49"
12 SU	17:21:13	6 9	0 ♓ 10	26 0	5 25	28 53	24 51	20 10	28 23	2 7	4 ♓ 56'48"
13 MO	17:25:10	9 21	1 46	26 57	6 3	28 58	24 53	20 11	28 24	2 7	4 ♓ 56'48"
14 TU	17:29: 6	12 38	3 21	27 54	6 41	29 4	24 55	20 12	28 24	2 7	4 ♓ 56'48"
15 WE	17:33: 3	15 59	4 57	28 52	7 19	29 9	24 57	20 12	28 24	2 8	4 ♓ 56'48"
16 TH	17:36:59	19 24	6 32	29 49	7 57	29 15	24 59	20 13	28 25	2 8	4 ♓ 56'48"
17 FR	17:40:56	22 54	8 8	0 ♐ 46	8 35	29 20	25 1	20 14	28 25	2 8	4 ♓ 56'48"
18 SA	17:44:53	26 29	9 43	1 44	9 13	29 26	25 2	20 14	28 25	2 8	4 ♓ 56'48"
19 SU	17:48:49	0 ♒ 10	11 18	2 41	9 51	29 31	25 4	20 15	28 26	2 9	4 ♓ 56'48"
20 MO	17:52:46	3 57	12 54	3 38	10 29	29 36	25 6	20 16	28 26	2 9	4 ♓ 56'47"
21 TU	17:56:42	7 50	14 30	4 35	11 8	29 42	25 8	20 16	28 27	2 9	4 ♓ 56'47"
22 WE	18: 0:39	11 50	16 5	5 33	11 46	29 47	25 10	20 17	28 27	2 10	4 ♓ 56'47"
23 TH	18: 4:35	15 57	17 41	6 30	12 24	29 53	25 12	20 18	28 27	2 10	4 ♓ 56'47"
24 FR	18: 8:32	20 11	19 16	7 27	13 2	29 58	25 14	20 18	28 28	2 10	4 ♓ 56'47"
25 SA	18:12:28	24 33	20 52	8 24	13 40	0 ♓ 4	25 16	20 19	28 28	2 11	4 ♓ 56'47"
26 SU	18:16:25	29 3	22 28	9 22	14 18	0 9	25 17	20 20	28 28	2 11	4 ♓ 56'47"
27 MO	18:20:22	3 ♓ 41	24 3	10 19	14 56	0 15	25 19	20 20	28 29	2 11	4 ♓ 56'46"
28 TU	18:24:18	8 28	25 39	11 16	15 34	0 20	25 21	20 21	28 29	2 11	4 ♓ 56'46"
29 WE	18:28:15	13 24	27 15	12 13	16 12	0 26	25 23	20 22	28 29	2 12	4 ♓ 56'46"
30 TH	18:32:11	18 29	28 51	13 11	16 50	0 31	25 25	20 22	28 30	2 12	4 ♓ 56'46"

INGRESSES :

3	♂ → ♒	11: 6
10	☿ → ♑	0:47
11	♀ → ♓	21:21
16	⊕ → ♐	4:35
18	☿ → ♒	22:53
24	♃ → ♓	7:14
26	☿ → ♓	4:59
30	♀ → ♈	17:23

ASPECTS (HELIOCENTRIC +MOON(TYCHONIC)) :

1	☽ ☍ ☿	4:33
3	☽ ☍ ♇	12:48
5	☽ □ ♅	1: 0
	♀ □ ⊕	9:16
	☽ ☍ ♄	10: 4
	☽ ☍ ♂	23:47
6	♃ ☌ ♆	5:42
	♀ S□ ☊	17:53
7	☽ ☍ ♀	17:50
8	☽ ☍ ♆	3: 9
	☽ ☍ ♃	3:27
10	☽ □ ☿	15:23
	☽ □ ♇	15:46
	☿ ☌ ♇	17: 9
	♀ ☌ ♆	20:54
11	♀ ☌ ♃	3:13
	☽ ☍ ♅	22:19
12	☽ □ ♄	6: 4
13	☽ □ ♂	0:17
14	☽ □ ♆	11:53
	⊕ □ ♆	12:27
	☽ □ ♃	13: 0
	☽ □ ♀	22: 0
15	⊕ □ ♃	8: 2
16	☿ □ ♅	5:39
	☽ ☌ ♇	17:13
17	☿ S□ ☊	4:20
	☿ ☌ ♄	14:17
	☽ □ ♅	22:30
18	☽ ☌ ♄	6:26
	☽ ☌ ☿	11:49
19	☽ ☌ ♂	7:42
20	☽ ☌ ♆	15:52
	☽ ☌ ♃	18: 5
21	♂ ☌ P	11: 6
	☿ ☌ ♂	23:30
22	☽ ☌ ♀	0: 7
23	☽ □ ♇	6:34
24	☽ ☌ ♅	18: 1
25	☽ □ ♄	3:51
	☿ ☌ ♆	20:58
26	☿ ☌ ♃	5:55
	☽ □ ♂	19: 3
27	☽ □ ♆	22:45
28	☽ □ ♃	2:32
	☿ □ ⊕	16:57
29	☽ □ ☿	8:47
30	☽ □ ♀	14:14
	☽ ☍ ♇	19: 6

May 4 AD 30: Controversy around Baptism, p. 459, vol. I

December 16 AD 30: Writing on the Wall, p. 182, vol. II

11—Venus conjunct Uranus:

June 30 AD 29: Building on John's Foundation, pp. 298–99, vol. I

August 20 AD 30: At the Baths of Bethulia, pp. 23–24, vol. II

June 20 AD 31: A Feast of Remembrance, pp. 403–04, vol. II

Heliocentric Venus conjunct Jupiter:

October 17 AD 29: Dining with the Essenes, p. 362, vol. I

February 6 AD 31: Joseph Barsabbas, p. 306, vol. II

May 26 AD 32: Christ Baptizes Fifty People, pp. 388–89, vol. II

January 18 AD 33: Three "Silent Disciples," p. 523, vol. II

14—Full Moon Taurus:

May 6 AD 30: Controversy around Baptism, p. 459, vol. I

April 25 AD 31: Sailing to Cyprus by Starlight, pp. 353–54, vol. II

May 3 AD 33: Days with the Risen One, p. 408, vol. III

Tychonic Sun square Neptune:

October 16 AD 29: John's Baptism Soon to Cease, p. 362, vol. I

April 14 AD 30: In Concealment, p. 424, vol. I

October 18 AD 30: The Family of Obed, pp. 80–81, vol. II

April 17 AD 31: Visiting the Sanatorium, pp. 347–48, vol. II

April 21 AD 33: Days with the Risen One, p. 408, vol. III

15—Tychonic Sun square Jupiter:

November 30 AD 29: Ministered unto by Angels, pp. 370–71, vol. I

June 20 AD 30: Celebration of the New Moon Festival, p. 460, vol. I

January 5 AD 31: Dining with Pharisees, pp. 203–04, vol. II

September 1 AD 32: Raising of Nazor, pp. 492–94, vol. II

March 15 AD 33: The Disciples are Downcast, p. 5, vol. III

16—Sun enters Gemini:

May 21 AD 30: Imprisonment of John the Baptist, p. 459–60, vol. I

May 21 AD 31: Jesus Visits the Mines near Kythria, pp. 384–85, vol. II

May 21 AD 33: Between Ascension and Pentecost, p. 412, vol. III

Venus conjunct Node:

May 26 AD 29: Jesus Begins His Travels, p. 292, vol. I

June 24 AD 30: Healing in the Bathing Garden, pp. 460–62, vol. I

March 28 AD 31: The Rich Glutton and Poor Lazarus, pp. 333–35, vol. II

May 27 AD 32: Walking Through the Pharisees, p. 470, vol. II

February 18 AD 33: With Lazarus, p. 530, vol. II

March 10 AD 33: Centurion Cornelius, p. 4, vol. III

May 11 AD 33: Days Immediately Preceding the Ascension, p. 409, vol. III

Sun square Neptune:

October 14 AD 29: Mother Mary and the Holy Women, p. 360, vol. I

April 16 AD 30: In Concealment, p. 424, vol. I

October 16 AD 30: Feast of the New Moon, pp. 78–79, vol. II

April 19 AD 31: Recovery of the Head of the Baptist, pp. 348–49, vol. II

April 23 AD 33: Days with the Risen One, p. 408, vol. III

17—Heliocentric Mercury conjunct Saturn:

June 26 AD 29: "Three months ago…," p. 298, vol. I

December 20 AD 29: Invited to the Wedding at Cana, p. 379, vol. I

March 19 AD 30: Jesus and Lazarus in Jerusalem, p. 416, vol. I

September 12 AD 30: The Fishing Lake, pp. 52–53, vol. II

December 9 AD 30: Magdalene's Relapse, pp. 175–76, vol. II

March 8 AD 31: Teaching in Argob, p. 321, vol. II

June 4 AD 31: Elizabeth's Childhood Home, p. 394, vol. II

August 20 AD 32: Washing of Eliud's Feet, p. 488, vol. II

May 13 AD 33: The Night Before Ascension, p. 410, vol. III

18—Venus enters Taurus:

March 16 AD 31: Teaching on Board Peter's Ship, pp. 324–25, vol. II

Venus square Saturn:

July 30 AD 29: Jacob's Well, p. 303, vol. I

April 14 AD 30: In Concealment, p. 424, vol. I

September 26 AD 30: Feast of Atonement, pp. 62–63, vol. II

February 12 AD 31: Healing of the Syrophoenician Woman, pp. 308–09, vol. II

September 17 AD 32: Journey to the Tent City, pp. 499–500, vol. II

May 30 AD 33: The Church at the Pool of Bethesda, pp. 414–16, vol. III

21—Heliocentric Mercury conjunct Mars:

July 3 AD 29: Meeting Six of the Baptist's Disciples, p. 300, vol. I

October 7 AD 29: "Behold the Lamb of God," pp. 356–57, vol. I

January 17 AD 30: Visiting the Ruined City of Slaves, pp. 396–97, vol. I

August 21 AD 30: In Bethulia, pp. 24–26, vol. II

November 29 AD 30: The Second Beatitude, p. 163, vol. II

March 5 AD 31: Healing the Sick, p. 319, vol. II

June 8 AD 31: In Maroni's Garden, p. 396, vol. II

July 28 AD 32: Fleeing with Matthew and John, p. 480, vol. II

May 13 AD 33: The Night Before Ascension, p. 410, vol. III

24—Heliocentric Jupiter enters Pisces:

August 10 AD 29: On the Shores of Galilee, p. 305, vol. I

25—Heliocentric Mercury conjunct Neptune:

June 1 AD 29: Elizabeth's Cave, p. 296, vol. I

August 28 AD 29: Circumcision and Baptism, pp. 309–10, vol. I

November 24 AD 29: Temptation in the Wilderness, pp. 365–71, vol. I

February 20 AD 30: In Jezreel, p. 406, vol. I

May 19 AD 30: Imprisonment of John the Baptist, p. 459, vol. I

August 16 AD 30: In Peter's House, pp. 17–19, vol. II

November 12 AD 30: On the Way to Nain, p. 141, vol. II

May 7 AD 31: The Prophet Malachi, pp. 372–73, vol. II

July 20 AD 32: News of Lazarus, p. 477, vol. II

April 11 AD 33: The Risen Christ Appears to Thomas, pp. 398–400, vol. III

26—Heliocentric Mercury conjunct Jupiter:

December 5 AD 29: Silencing the Possessed, pp. 374–75, vol. I

March 5 AD 30: Helping in the Storm, pp. 412–13, vol. I

August 30 AD 30: Paralyzed Arms and Hands, p. 38, vol. II

November 28 AD 30: Sermon on the Mount, pp. 162–63, vol. II

February 25 AD 31: In Nobah, p. 316, vol. II

May 25 AD 31: Speaking Against Idolatry, pp. 387–88, vol. II

August 13 AD 32: The Bedridden Married Couple, p. 486, vol. II

February 8 AD 33: Three Secret Disciples, p. 530, vol. II

May 8 AD 33: The Risen One, p. 408, vol. III

28—Mars enters Aries:

January 6 AD 31: The Two Debtors, p. 204, vol. II

29—Sun square Jupiter:

May 26 AD 29: Jesus Begins His Travels, p. 292, vol. I

November 18 AD 29: Temptation in the Wilderness, pp. 365–69, vol. I

July 4 AD 30: In Adama, pp. 465–66, vol. I

December 24 AD 30: A Cool Reception, p. 187, vol. II

September 13 AD 32: Shepherds Create a Throne, pp. 497–98, vol. II

New Moon Gemini:
May 31 AD 29: The Family of Lazarus,
pp. 294–96, vol. I
June 19 AD 30: Celebration of the New Moon Festival, p. 460, vol. I
June 8 AD 31: In Maroni's Garden, p. 396, vol. II
May 27 AD 32: Walking Through the Pharisees, p. 470, vol. II

JULY 2022

STARGAZING PREVIEW

Welcome to the month of another Supermoon! As midnight chimes on the 1st, Mars will be ready to join Saturn and Jupiter in the southeastern sky. At 0200, Venus and *Aldebaran*, the determined eye of the Bull, rise together. Thursday the 7th is the day of July's First Quarter Moon at 20° Virgo; by dusk, the Moon will be at the top of the zodiacal arc, now at 29° Virgo. This is the zodiacal longitude of both *Spica* and *Arcturus*, which together form a star path to Ursa Major.

The Supermoon (26° Sagittarius) comes our way on the 13th. Like all opposites, Gemini and Sagittarius can teach each other a great deal: Gemini benefits from the intense focus of the Archer, while Sagittarius can watch in awe as Gemini reveals the art of cooperation. When the Moon rises, there will be no other planets in view—a powerful entrance onto an empty stage! Venus joins the Sun and Mercury in Gemini later that evening. Mercury and the Sun say hello to the Crab on the 17th: *Warm soul life; Thou resting, glowing light!*

Before sunrise on Tuesday the 19th, the Moon and Jupiter will be together, high in the southwest, at 13°30' Pisces—the Moon's position as Jesus stilled the storm on the Sea of Galilee. The fearsome storm is depicted by Rembrandt in "The Storm on the Sea of Galilee," whereabouts unknown, unfortunately, following the 1990 heist at the Gardner Museum. The Moon (3°Aries) reaches its Last Quarter on Wednesday the 20th; you'll see it midway between Jupiter and Mars at midnight.

Venus and Jupiter form a square aspect on the 25th: Jupiter will be at culmination (high in the south) as Venus rises; Mars and the Moon will be between them. The Moon will join the Sun for July's New Moon (10° Cancer) on Thursday the 28th; the Ram rules the sky from the high point of the zodiacal band as they rise together at 0400. Later that same day, we're going to be treated to another meteor show, and the absence of moonlight is a very hopeful sign! The Delta Aquariids peak tonight—after the late sunset at 2000, look to the northeast for your best shot at seeing them. If you're up later still, keep an eye on Saturn and Jupiter: when you cast your gaze between them, you'll be looking in the direction of Aquarius, whence these showers appear to originate.

On the final day of the month, though invisible to the human eye, Uranus joins the North Node of the Moon in conjunction (23° Aries). This is worth attending to, for the nodal axis identifies a portal to the angelic realm; revelations streaming from Uranus might find us more easily today. Fortunately, helpful Mars (at the same degree), rising just before midnight, shows us where they are!

Orion now rises three hours before the Sun.

JULY COMMENTARIES

2—Mercury enters Gemini:
May 27 AD 31: The Approach of the Kingdom, p. 389, vol. II
May 18 AD 32: Healing of Ten Lepers, pp. 468–70, vol. II
May 9 AD 33: Days with the Risen One, p. 408, vol. III
Mars square Pluto:
September 27 AD 29: Retracing the Steps of Mary and Joseph, pp. 346–47, vol. I
December 7 AD 30: First Walking on the Water, pp. 172–73, vol. II
June 4 AD 32: Dining with the Pharisees, p. 472, vol. II
Heliocentric Venus square Pluto:
June 27 AD 29: "Three months ago...," p. 298, vol. I
October 19 AD 29: Consoling the sick, p. 363, vol. I

SIDEREAL GEOCENTRIC LONGITUDES : JULY 2022 Gregorian at 0 hours UT

DAY	☉	☽	☊	☿	♀	♂	♃	♄	♅	♆	♇
1 FR	14 ♊ 7	4 ♋ 38	26 ♈ 26R	27 ♉ 1	14 ♉ 28	1 ♈ 57	12 ♓ 26	29 ♑ 40R	22 ♈ 41	0 ♓ 24R	2 ♑ 45R
2 SA	15 4	16 34	26 17	28 48	15 39	2 40	12 31	29 37	22 44	0 23	2 43
3 SU	16 2	28 37	26 9	0 ♊ 38	16 51	3 22	12 36	29 35	22 46	0 23	2 42
4 MO	16 59	10 ♌ 48	26 2	2 30	18 3	4 4	12 40	29 32	22 49	0 23	2 41
5 TU	17 56	23 11	25 57	4 26	19 15	4 46	12 45	29 29	22 51	0 23	2 39
6 WE	18 53	5 ♍ 48	25 54	6 23	20 27	5 28	12 49	29 26	22 53	0 23	2 38
7 TH	19 51	18 43	25 53	8 24	21 39	6 10	12 54	29 24	22 55	0 22	2 36
8 FR	20 48	2 ♎ 0	25 53D	10 26	22 51	6 52	12 58	29 21	22 58	0 22	2 35
9 SA	21 45	15 41	25 54	12 30	24 3	7 34	13 2	29 18	23 0	0 22	2 34
10 SU	22 42	29 48	25 54R	14 36	25 15	8 15	13 5	29 15	23 2	0 21	2 32
11 MO	23 39	14 ♏ 21	25 53	16 43	26 27	8 57	13 9	29 11	23 4	0 21	2 31
12 TU	24 36	29 17	25 49	18 51	27 39	9 38	13 12	29 8	23 6	0 21	2 29
13 WE	25 34	14 ♐ 27	25 43	21 0	28 51	10 19	13 15	29 5	23 8	0 20	2 28
14 TH	26 31	29 44	25 36	23 9	0 ♊ 3	11 1	13 18	29 1	23 10	0 20	2 27
15 FR	27 28	14 ♑ 56	25 27	25 18	1 15	11 42	13 21	28 58	23 12	0 19	2 25
16 SA	28 25	29 52	25 18	27 27	2 28	12 23	13 24	28 55	23 14	0 19	2 24
17 SU	29 23	14 ♒ 26	25 10	29 36	3 40	13 4	13 26	28 51	23 16	0 18	2 22
18 MO	0 ♋ 20	28 30	25 4	1 ♋ 43	4 52	13 44	13 28	28 47	23 17	0 17	2 21
19 TU	1 17	12 ♓ 5	25 1	3 51	6 5	14 25	13 30	28 44	23 19	0 17	2 19
20 WE	2 14	25 12	24 59	5 57	7 17	15 5	13 32	28 40	23 21	0 16	2 18
21 TH	3 11	7 ♈ 54	24 59D	8 2	8 29	15 46	13 34	28 36	23 23	0 15	2 17
22 FR	4 9	20 15	24 59	10 5	9 42	16 26	13 35	28 32	23 24	0 15	2 15
23 SA	5 6	2 ♉ 22	24 59R	12 7	10 54	17 6	13 36	28 28	23 26	0 14	2 14
24 SU	6 3	14 18	24 58	14 8	12 7	17 46	13 37	28 25	23 27	0 13	2 12
25 MO	7 1	26 9	24 54	16 7	13 20	18 26	13 38	28 21	23 29	0 12	2 11
26 TU	7 58	7 ♊ 57	24 47	18 5	14 32	19 6	13 39	28 16	23 30	0 12	2 9
27 WE	8 55	19 47	24 38	20 0	15 45	19 45	13 39	28 12	23 32	0 11	2 8
28 TH	9 53	1 ♋ 40	24 26	21 55	16 58	20 25	13 40	28 8	23 33	0 10	2 7
29 FR	10 50	13 39	24 13	23 47	18 11	21 4	13 40R	28 4	23 34	0 9	2 5
30 SA	11 47	25 43	24 0	25 38	19 23	21 43	13 40	28 0	23 36	0 8	2 4
31 SU	12 45	7 ♌ 56	23 47	27 27	20 36	22 22	13 39	27 56	23 37	0 7	2 2

INGRESSES :

2 ☿ → ♊ 15:52
3 ☽ → ♌ 2:44
5 ☽ → ♍ 13: 2
7 ☽ → ♎ 20:26
10 ☽ → ♏ 0:19
12 ☽ → ♐ 1: 9
13 ♀ → ♊ 22:59
14 ☽ → ♑ 0:25
16 ☽ → ♒ 0:12
17 ☿ → ♋ 4:34
☉ → ♋ 15:43
18 ☽ → ♓ 2:35
20 ☽ → ♈ 8:59
22 ☽ → ♉ 19:16
25 ☽ → ♊ 7:49
27 ☽ → ♋ 20:38
30 ☽ → ♌ 8:26

ASPECTS & ECLIPSES :

2 ♂ □ ♇ 2: 5
☽ N ☊ 19: 8
☿ □ ♆ 20:56
3 ☽ ☍ ♄ 1:53
5 ☽ ☍ ♆ 13:45
6 ☽ ☍ ♃ 13:11
7 ☉ □ ☽ 2:13
8 ☽ ☍ ♂ 9: 5
9 ☿ □ ♃ 6:12
☽ ☍ ♅ 12:32
☽ ☌ ☋ 17:26
11 ☽ ☍ ♀ 21:10
13 ☽ ☌ P 9:10
☽ ☍ ☿ 11:57
☉ ☍ ☽ 18:36
14 ☽ ☌ ♇ 4:15
♀ □ ♆ 5:30
15 ☽ S ☊ 16:40
☽ ☌ ♄ 22:26
16 ☉ S☋ ☿ 19:36
18 ☽ ☌ ♆ 3: 6
☿ ☍ ♇ 6:57
19 ☽ ☌ ♃ 2:33
20 ☉ ☍ ♇ 1:32
☉ □ ☽ 14:17
21 ☽ ☌ ♂ 16: 5
22 ☽ ☌ ♅ 6:12
☽ ☌ ☊ 9:19
25 ♀ □ ♃ 6:11
26 ☽ ☌ A 10:24
☽ ☌ ♀ 14:53
☿ □ ♂ 19:11
28 ☽ ☍ ♇ 0:52
☉ ☌ ☽ 17:53
☿ □ ♅ 21:14
29 ☿ □ ☊ 4:57
☽ N ☊ 20:38
☽ ☌ ☿ 23:47
30 ☽ ☍ ♄ 4:28
31 ☿ ☍ ♄ 6: 4
♅ ☌ ☊ 20:21

SIDEREAL HELIOCENTRIC LONGITUDES : JULY 2022 Gregorian at 0 hours UT

DAY	Sid. Time	☿	♀	⊕	♂	♃	♄	♅	♆	♇	Vernal Point
1 FR	18:36: 8	23 ♓ 44	0 ♈ 26	14 ♐ 8	17 ♒ 29	0 ♓ 37	25 ♑ 27	20 ♈ 23	28 ♒ 30	2 ♑ 12	4 ♓ 56'46"
2 SA	18:40: 4	29 7	2 2	15 5	18 7	0 42	25 29	20 24	28 31	2 13	4 ♓ 56'46"
3 SU	18:44: 1	4 ♈ 39	3 38	16 2	18 45	0 48	25 31	20 24	28 31	2 13	4 ♓ 56'46"
4 MO	18:47:57	10 20	5 14	16 59	19 23	0 53	25 32	20 25	28 31	2 13	4 ♓ 56'45"
5 TU	18:51:54	16 9	6 50	17 57	20 1	0 59	25 34	20 26	28 32	2 13	4 ♓ 56'45"
6 WE	18:55:51	22 6	8 26	18 54	20 39	1 4	25 36	20 26	28 32	2 14	4 ♓ 56'45"
7 TH	18:59:47	28 9	10 2	19 51	21 17	1 10	25 38	20 27	28 32	2 14	4 ♓ 56'45"
8 FR	19: 3:44	4 ♉ 18	11 38	20 48	21 55	1 15	25 40	20 28	28 33	2 14	4 ♓ 56'45"
9 SA	19: 7:40	10 32	13 14	21 45	22 33	1 20	25 42	20 28	28 33	2 15	4 ♓ 56'45"
10 SU	19:11:37	16 49	14 50	22 43	23 11	1 26	25 44	20 29	28 33	2 15	4 ♓ 56'45"
11 MO	19:15:33	23 8	16 26	23 40	23 49	1 31	25 46	20 30	28 34	2 15	4 ♓ 56'45"
12 TU	19:19:30	29 27	18 2	24 37	24 27	1 37	25 47	20 30	28 34	2 15	4 ♓ 56'44"
13 WE	19:23:26	5 ♊ 45	19 38	25 34	25 5	1 42	25 49	20 31	28 35	2 16	4 ♓ 56'44"
14 TH	19:27:23	12 1	21 14	26 31	25 43	1 48	25 51	20 32	28 35	2 16	4 ♓ 56'44"
15 FR	19:31:20	18 12	22 50	27 29	26 20	1 53	25 53	20 32	28 35	2 16	4 ♓ 56'44"
16 SA	19:35:16	24 18	24 26	28 26	26 58	1 59	25 55	20 33	28 36	2 17	4 ♓ 56'44"
17 SU	19:39:13	0 ♋ 18	26 3	29 23	27 36	2 4	25 57	20 34	28 36	2 17	4 ♓ 56'44"
18 MO	19:43: 9	6 10	27 39	0 ♑ 20	28 14	2 10	25 59	20 34	28 36	2 17	4 ♓ 56'44"
19 TU	19:47: 6	11 54	29 15	1 17	28 52	2 15	26 1	20 35	28 37	2 17	4 ♓ 56'43"
20 WE	19:51: 2	17 29	0 ♉ 52	2 15	29 30	2 21	26 2	20 36	28 37	2 18	4 ♓ 56'43"
21 TH	19:54:59	22 54	2 28	3 12	0 ♓ 7	2 26	26 4	20 36	28 37	2 18	4 ♓ 56'43"
22 FR	19:58:55	28 10	4 4	4 9	0 45	2 32	26 6	20 37	28 38	2 18	4 ♓ 56'43"
23 SA	20: 2:52	3 ♌ 16	5 41	5 7	1 23	2 37	26 8	20 38	28 38	2 19	4 ♓ 56'43"
24 SU	20: 6:49	8 13	7 17	6 4	2 1	2 43	26 10	20 38	28 39	2 19	4 ♓ 56'43"
25 MO	20:10:45	13 0	8 54	7 1	2 38	2 48	26 12	20 39	28 39	2 19	4 ♓ 56'43"
26 TU	20:14:42	17 38	10 30	7 58	3 16	2 54	26 14	20 40	28 39	2 19	4 ♓ 56'42"
27 WE	20:18:38	22 7	12 7	8 56	3 53	2 59	26 16	20 40	28 40	2 20	4 ♓ 56'42"
28 TH	20:22:35	26 27	13 43	9 53	4 31	3 5	26 17	20 41	28 40	2 20	4 ♓ 56'42"
29 FR	20:26:31	0 ♍ 39	15 20	10 51	5 9	3 10	26 19	20 42	28 40	2 20	4 ♓ 56'42"
30 SA	20:30:28	4 44	16 56	11 48	5 46	3 16	26 21	20 42	28 41	2 21	4 ♓ 56'42"
31 SU	20:34:24	8 41	18 33	12 45	6 24	3 21	26 23	20 43	28 41	2 21	4 ♓ 56'42"

INGRESSES :

2 ☿ → ♈ 3:52
7 ☿ → ♉ 7:14
12 ☿ → ♊ 2: 5
16 ☿ → ♋ 22:47
17 ⊕ → ♑ 15:30
19 ♀ → ♉ 11: 9
20 ♂ → ♓ 19:19
22 ☿ → ♌ 8:32
28 ☿ → ♍ 20:12

ASPECTS (HELIOCENTRIC +MOON(TYCHONIC)) :

2 ♀ □ ♇ 2:35
☽ □ ♅ 7:39
☿ □ ♇ 13:29
☽ ☍ ♄ 17:48
☿ ☌ ♀ 17:52
4 ☽ ☍ ♂ 17:34
5 ⊕ ☌ A 8:12
☽ ☍ ♆ 10:14
☽ ☍ ♃ 14:59
☿ ☌ ♅ 17:20
6 ☿ ☌ ☊ 5:46
☿ □ ♄ 14: 1
8 ☽ □ ♇ 0:25
☽ ☍ ♀ 19:11
9 ☽ ☍ ♅ 8:13
☽ □ ♄ 17: 7
10 ☿ ☌ P 22:34
11 ☿ □ ♂ 2:53
☽ □ ♂ 15:56
☿ □ ♆ 20:39
☽ □ ♆ 22:52
12 ☽ ☍ ☿ 0:28
☽ □ ♃ 3:44
☿ □ ♃ 8:21
13 ♀ ☌ ♅ 13:20
14 ☽ ☌ ♇ 3:59
15 ☽ □ ♅ 8:57
☽ □ ♀ 14: 9
☽ ☌ ♄ 17:34
16 ☿ ☍ ⊕ 19:36
♀ □ ♄ 22:29
17 ☿ ☍ ♇ 8: 3
☽ ☌ ♂ 23:30
18 ☽ ☌ ♆ 0:10
☽ ☌ ♃ 6:25
♂ ☌ ♆ 14:21
20 ⊕ ☌ ♇ 1:15
☽ □ ♇ 13:19
☿ □ ♅ 13:44
21 ☿ N ☊ 2:53
☿ ☍ ♄ 14:27
22 ☽ ☌ ♅ 0:42
☽ □ ♄ 11:33
23 ☽ □ ☿ 3: 6
☽ ☌ ♀ 7:39
☿ □ ♀ 17:12
25 ☽ □ ♆ 5: 4
♂ ☌ ♃ 7:23
☽ □ ♃ 13:37
☽ □ ♂ 13:55
28 ☽ ☍ ♇ 1:20
☿ ☍ ♆ 12:34
29 ☽ □ ♅ 14: 3
☿ ☍ ♃ 15: 2
30 ☽ ☍ ♄ 1:14
☿ ☍ ♂ 7:24
31 ☽ □ ♀ 23:44

September 21 AD 30: In Gadara, pp. 58–59, vol. II

January 13 AD 31: Joseph of Arimathea, pp. 210–11, vol. II

May 5 AD 31: Teaching at Barnabas's House, pp. 370–71, vol. II

July 29 AD 32: Healing a Blind Shepherd, p. 480, vol. II

March 11 AD 33: Approaching Suffering, p. 4, vol. III

Heliocentric Mercury conjunct Venus:

August 2 AD 29: Whispers and Murmurs, p. 303, vol. I

December 22 AD 29: Healing of a Child at a Distance, pp. 380–82, vol. I

May 29 AD 30: Imprisonment of John the Baptist, p. 459, vol. I

October 4 AD 30: In Akrabis and Shiloh, p. 71, vol. II

March 4 AD 31: In Caesarea–Philippi, pp. 318–19, vol. II

October 12 AD 32: Cursing of the House of Idols, pp. 516–17, vol. II

February 13 AD 33: Healing of an Old Blind Man, p. 530, vol. II

5—Heliocentric Mercury conjunct Uranus:

July 7 AD 29: Early ministry, p. 300, vol. I

October 3 AD 29: The Inn of Reuben, p. 353, vol. I

December 30 AD 29: End of the Wedding at Cana, p. 390, vol. I

March 29 AD 30: Preparing for Passover, pp. 419–20, vol. I

June 25 AD 30: Saturnin Baptizes, pp. 460–62, vol. I

September 21 AD 30: Gadara, pp. 58–59, vol. II

December 18 AD 30: Kiriathaim, p. 183, vol. II

March 17 AD 31: Cornerstone, p. 325, vol. II

June 13 AD 31: Return to Capernaum, pp. 398–99, vol. II

May 31 AD 32: Zacchaeus's House, p. 472, vol. II

August 27 AD 32: Salathiel, p. 491

February 19 AD 33: Preparing for Death, p. 1, vol. III

May 19 AD 33: The Risen One, pp. 411–12 vol. III

13—Venus enters Gemini:

May 8 AD 29: Jesus and Mary move from Nazareth to Capernaum, p. 292, vol. I

April 11 AD 31: Massacre of the Galileans, p. 346, vol. II

May 23 AD 32: Healing of a Crippled Woman, p. 470, vol. II

Full Moon Gemini:

June 14 AD 29: Visiting a Madhouse, p. 297, vol. I

May 25 AD 31: Speaking Against Idolatry, pp. 387–88, vol. II

June 12 AD 32: Raising the Daughter of a Shepherd, pp. 473–74, vol. II

Heliocentric Venus conjunct Uranus:

June 7 AD 29: Helping Men Repair Boats, p. 297, vol. I

January 19 AD 30: Casting Out Evil Spirits, p. 397, vol. I

September 3 AD 30: Crossing the Jordan, pp. 41–42, vol. II

April 17 AD 31: Visiting the Sanatorium, pp. 347–48, vol. II

July 13 AD 32: The Good Samaritan and the Lost Coin, p. 475, vol. II

February 25 AD 33: Overgrown with Weeds, p. 1, vol. III

14—Venus square Neptune:

September 3 AD 29: Healing a Woman of Edema, pp. 311–12, vol. I

May 25 AD 30: Meeting Bartholomew, pp. 459–60, vol. I

October 17 AD 30: Consider the Lilies, pp. 79–80, vol. II

March 15 AD 31: Feeding of the 4000, pp. 323–24, vol. II

September 21 AD 32: Jesus Meet with Mensor, pp. 502–04, vol. II

16—Superior Conjunction Sun and Mercury:

July 2 AD 29: Meeting Six of the Baptist's Disciples, p. 300, vol. I

October 30 AD 29: Temptation in the Wilderness, pp. 365–69 vol. I

March 4 AD 30: Protecting the Ships at Sea, p. 412, vol. I

October 9 AD 30: Messenger of Cyrinus, pp. 74, vol. II

February 15 AD 31: A Banquet with the Syrophoenician Woman, pp. 310–12, vol. II

June 1 AD 31: In Misael, p. 393, vol. II

September 1 AD 32: Raising of Nazor, pp. 492–94, vol. II

January 10 AD 33: Healing in Bethain, p. 520, vol. II

April 30 AD 33: Days with the Risen One, p. 408, vol. III

Heliocentric Venus square Saturn:

June 25 AD 29: "Three months ago…," p. 298, vol. I

October 19 AD 29: The Essene Jairus, pp. 362–63, vol. I

February 10 AD 30: In Capernaum, pp. 402–03, vol. I

September 28 AD 30: Healing the Sick, p. 65, vol. II

January 22 AD 31: In Thirza, pp. 219–20, vol. II

May 16 AD 31: Feast of Weeks, pp. 380–81, vol. II

August 18 AD 32: Shepherd Settlement in Kedar, p. 487, vol. II

April 5 AD 33: Resurrection, pp. 387–393, vol. III

17—Sun enters Cancer:

June 21 AD 29: Herod Wishes to Visit John the Baptist, pp. 297–98, vol. I

June 22 AD 30: Reunited with the Disciples, p. 460, vol. I

June 22 AD 31: The Young Pharisee, p. 405, vol. II

June 21 AD 32: No Man Can Serve Two Masters, p. 475, vol. II

Heliocentric Mercury opposite Pluto:

September 23 AD 29: Baptism in the Jordan, pp. 342–45, vol. I

December 20 AD 29: Invited to the Wedding at Cana, p. 379, vol. I

March 18 AD 30: At an Inn, p. 416, vol. I

September 10 AD 30: Celebration of Gideon, pp. 51–52, vol. II

December 7 AD 30: First Walking on Water, pp. 172–73, vol. II

March 5 AD 31: Alms for the Poor, p. 319, vol. II

June 1 AD 31: In Misael, p. 393, vol. II

May 18 AD 32: Healing of Ten Lepers, pp. 468–70, vol. II

August 15 AD 32: Teaching about Marriage, p. 487, vol. II

May 6 AD 33: Increase of the Community, pp. 407–9, vol. III

18—Mercury opposite Pluto:

June 16 AD 29: Wedding in Dothan, p. 297, vol. I

June 2 AD 31: Samson as Forerunner, pp. 393–94, vol. II

May 25 AD 32: Walking through the Pharisees, p. 470, vol. II

May 18 AD 33: Between Ascension and Pentecost, p. 412, vol. III

Heliocentric Mars conjunct Neptune:

July 16 AD 30: Sowing of the Seed, pp. 473–77, vol. I

June 9 AD 32: Confronted by One Hundred Pharisees, p. 473, vol. II

20—Sun opposite Pluto:

May 29 AD 29: Jesus Begins His Travels, p. 292–94, vol. I

June 3 AD 31: Judas and Thomas Make Arrangements, p. 394, vol. II

June 4 AD 32: Dining with the Pharisees, p. 472, vol. II

Heliocentric Mars enters Pisces:

September 9 AD 30: Baptizing the Pagans, pp. 50–51, vol. II

July 27 AD 32: Christ and Lazarus in Hiding, pp. 479–80, vol. II

21—Heliocentric Mercury opposite Saturn:

August 13 AD 29: Future Disciples, p. 305, vol. I

November 10 AD 29: Temptation in the Wilderness, pp. 365–69, vol. I

February 7 AD 30: Raising of the Daughter of Jairus the Essene, p. 402, vol. I

August 4 AD 30: Jesus visits the Nobleman's Son, pp. 2–4, vol. II

November 1 AD 30: Teaching at Saul's Well, p. 97, vol. II

January 30 AD 31: Sailing to Tarichea, pp. 301–03, vol. II

April 29 AD 31: At the Home of Jonas's Father, pp. 360–62, vol. II

July 16 AD 32: "Our friend Lazarus has fallen asleep," p. 475, vol. II

October 13 AD 32: Journey to Egypt, p. 517, vol. II

January 10 AD 33: At the Synagogue in Bethain, p. 520, vol. II

April 9 AD 33: The Risen One, pp. 396–98, vol. III

25—Venus square Jupiter:

October 3 AD 29: Healing Reuben's Grandchildren, pp. 353–54, vol. I

July 28 AD 30: Celebrating the Sabbath, p. 492, vol. I

December 11 AD 30: A Blind Man by the Well, p. 177, vol. II

June 16 AD 31: Scarlet Fever, pp. 400–01, vol. II

August 19 AD 32: Eliud's Wife Confesses, pp. 487–88, vol. II

Heliocentric Mars conjunct Jupiter:

November 19 AD 30: Teaching Aboard Ship, pp. 152–54, vol. II

February 25 AD 33: Overgrown with Weeds, p. 1, vol. III

28—New Moon Cancer:

June 30 AD 29: Building on John's Foundation, pp. 298–99, vol. I

July 19 AD 30: John the Baptist's Arrest, pp. 477–80, vol. I

July 8 AD 31: Jephthah's Daughter, p. 467, vol. II

Heliocentric Mercury opposite Neptune:

July 5 AD 29: Six New Disciples, p. 300, vol. I

October 29 AD 29: Baptizing through Saturnin, pp. 352–53, vol. I

December 28 AD 29: Changing of Water into Wine, pp. 386–89, vol. I

June 22 AD 30: Teaching in the Fruit Plantation, p. 460, vol. I

September 18 AD 30: Isaac and Elijah, pp. 56–57, vol. II

December 15 AD 30: Close of the Feast of Lights, pp. 181–82, vol. II

March 13 AD 31: At Matthew's Custom House, p. 322, vol. II

June 9 AD 31: Healing on the Sabbath, pp. 396–97, vol. II

August 23 AD 32: On Marriage, p. 490, vol. II

February 15 AD 33: Exhortations of the Virgin, p. 530, vol. II

May 14 AD 33: Ascension Day, pp. 410–12, vol. III

29—Mercury square Node:

August 15 AD 29: Teaching in Two Synagogues, p. 306, vol. I

February 28 AD 30: Feast of Thanksgiving for Rain, pp. 409–10, vol. I

July 26 AD 30: Dinah the Samaritan at Jacob's Well, pp. 486–91, vol. I

August 28 AD 30: Healing in Abel–Mehola, pp. 33–37, vol. II

September 6 AD 30: Festival of Jephthah's Daughter, pp. 45–47, vol. II

February 10 AD 31: On Fasting, p. 307, vol. II

July 8 AD 31: Jephthah's Daughter, p. 467, vol. II

June 18 AD 32: A Shepherd's Wedding, p. 474, vol. II

January 4 AD 33: Leaving Heliopolis, p. 519, vol. II

May 31 AD 33: The First Holy Mass, pp. 416–17

Heliocentric Mercury opposite Jupiter

July 12 AD 29: In Sarepta, pp. 301–02, vol. I

October 10 AD 29: Feast of Tabernacles, pp. 359–60, vol. I

January 8 AD 30: Conversation with the Virgin Mary, p. 393, vol. I

April 8 AD 30: Death of Silent Mary and Nighttime Conversation with Nicodemus, p. 424, vol. I

July 8 AD 30: The Unjust Steward, pp. 469–70, vol. I

October 6 AD 30: Healing of Manahem, pp. 72–73, vol. II

January 5 AD 31: Reproached by Pharisees, pp. 203–04, vol. II

April 6 AD 31: The Shekel in the Fish, pp. 342–43, vol. II

July 6 AD 31: The Way of David, p. 465, vol. II

October 2 AD 32: In the House of Azarias, pp. 510–11, vol. II

December 31 AD 32: Egyptian City, p. 518, vol. II

April 1 AD 33: Magdalene's Last Anointing, pp. 19–22, vol. III

30—Heliocentric Mercury opposite Mars:

December 7 AD 29: In Dibon, p. 375, vol. I

March 14 AD 30: At Lazarus's Estate, p. 414, vol. I

September 29 AD 30: Mara the Suphanite, pp. 65–67, vol. II

June 19 AD 30: Celebrating the New Moon Festival, p. 460, vol. I

January 14 AD 31: Grave of Zechariah, p. 211, vol. II

April 30 AD 31: Mercuria, pp. 362–64, vol. II

September 5 AD 32: Salathiel and Nazor, p. 494, vol. II

April 5 AD 33: Resurrection, pp. 387–393, vol. III

31—Mercury opposite Saturn (G):

November 20 AD 29: Temptation in the Wilderness, pp. 365–69, vol. I

November 28 AD 30: Sermon on the Mount, pp. 162–63, vol. II

December 1 AD 30: Second Raising of Salome, pp. 164–67, vol. II

January 5 AD 31: Reproached by Pharisees, pp. 203–04, vol. II

January 10 AD 33: Healing the Sick in Bethain, p. 520, vol. II

Uranus conjunct Node: See Editorial Foreword

AUGUST 2022

STARGAZING PREVIEW

You guessed it—we have another Super-moon coming!

After sunset on the 3rd, you'll find the Moon high in the southwest, just above *Spica*; in the year AD 29, this same Moon shone over Jesus as he arrived at Mount Attarus. It's as if Mary (*Spica*) accompanied him to his destiny to endure the Temptations, knowing that she could not be of service to him until the ordeal was over. On Friday the 5th, the Moon reaches its First Quarter, recalling its degree (18° Libra) as Mary was taken into heaven.

You'll be able to observe Mars and Saturn on the 7th as they stand 90° apart. As Mars rises at 2230, Saturn will be overhead while the waxing gibbous Moon will be low in the west, above the red-hued heart of the Scorpion, *Antares*.

Though the Full Moon will happen during the small hours of the 12th, start looking on the evening of the 11th for the third and last Supermoon of 2022! Saturn rises just after the Moon, though you likely won't be able to see it in the presence of all that radiant glory! And speaking of glory: our Moon (24° Capricorn) stirs the memory of the Transfiguration.

However, this poses a problem for the mighty Perseid Meteor Showers, which peak the night of the 12th. Will it be possible to see them when the outsized, Full Moon will be out all night? If you'd like to give it a try anyway, keep an eye on Mars, which is now in the general direction of Perseus. Mars rises just before midnight and will be high in the south before dawn. Best of luck, and remember—visible or not, our blood will be fortified by the ferric blessing of the Perseids!

On Sunday the 14th, Saturn will be opposite the Sun, and therefore very bright indeed. Saturn's nighttime schedule will be exactly that of a Full Moon: up at sunset, down at dawn.

The Sun enters its kingdom, Leo, on Wednesday the 17th. On the 19th, the Last Quarter Moon (first degree of Taurus) rises below Mars and the *Pleiades* at 2300. The early morning hours of the

24th will reveal the waning Moon, now below and to the right of *Pollux* on its approach to Venus and the Sun.

Saturday the 27th is the day of August's New Moon, now at 9° Leo. Can we hear the roar?

Orion rises shortly before midnight.

AUGUST COMMENTARIES

1—Mercury enters Leo:
July 12 AD 29: In Sarepta, pp. 301–02, vol. I
July 5 AD 30: A Great Banquet, pp. 466–67, vol. I
June 28 AD 31: Taking Leave of Many, pp. 408–09, vol. II

Mars conjunct Node:
May 31 AD 29: The Family of Lazarus, pp. 294–96, vol. I
March 17 AD 31: The True Doctrine, p. 325, vol. II
August 22 AD 32: An Open-Air Wedding, pp. 489–90, vol. II
September 7 AD 32: On Melchizedek, pp. 494–95, vol. II

Mars Conjunct Uranus:
August 10 AD 29: On the Shores of Galilee, p. 305, vol. I

6—Heliocentric Venus square Neptune:
July 25 AD 29: From Mt. Carmel to Mt. Tabor, pp. 302–03, vol. I
November 16 AD 29: Temptation in the Wilderness, pp. 365–69 vol. I
March 8 AD 30: Festival of Purim, p. 414, vol. I
June 30 AD 30: In Simeon's House, p. 464, vol. I
October 20 AD 30: Outside Michmethath, p. 82, vol. II
February 10 AD 31: On Fasting, p. 307, vol. II
August 26 AD 32: In Sichar
April 9 AD 33: With the Risen One, p. 397, vol. III

7—Venus enters Cancer:
June 2 AD 29: Alone in the Wilderness, p. 296, vol. I
July 18 AD 30: Discussing John's Imprisonment, p. 477, vol. I
May 7 AD 31: The Prophet Malachi, pp. 372–73, vol. II
June 17 AD 32: Healing the Shepherds, Attending a Wedding, p. 474, vol. II

Mars square Saturn:
October 7 AD 29: "Behold the Lamb of God," pp. 356–57, vol. I
February 14 AD 30: Healing the Possessed, p. 403, vol. I
December 26 AD 30: Second Conversion of Mary Magdalene, pp. 189–90, vol. II
January 7 AD 33: Retracing the Flight to Egypt, p. 520, vol. II

8—Tychonic Sun square Uranus:
April 24 AD 29: John in the Wilderness, p. 292, vol. I
October 28 AD 29: Temptation in the Wilderness, pp. 365–69, vol. I
April 29 AD 30: In Concealment, p. 424, vol. I
November 2 AD 30: Cousin Jesse, pp. 97–9, vol. II
May 4 AD 31: Family of Barnabas, pp. 368–70, vol. II
May 14 AD 33: Ascension, pp. 410–12, vol. III

9—Venus opposite Pluto:
June 30 AD 30: In Simeon's House, p. 464, vol. I
April 22 AD 31: In the Mountains of Garisima, p. 350, vol. II
June 4 AD 32: Dining with the Pharisees, p. 472, vol. II

Heliocentric Venus square Jupiter:
April 22 AD 29: John in the Wilderness, p. 292, vol. I
August 18 AD 29: The Synagogue and the Madhouse, p. 306, vol. I
December 16 AD 29: On the Way to the Wedding, pp. 377–78, vol. I
August 11 AD 30: Marriage and Divorce, pp. 9–11, vol. II
December 8 AD 30: Healing in Bethsaida, pp. 173–75, vol. II
April 6 AD 31: The Shekel in the Mouth of a Fish, pp. 342–43, vol. II
July 24 AD 32: Rebuke of Mary Salome, p. 477, vol. II

SIDEREAL GEOCENTRIC LONGITUDES : AUGUST 2022 Gregorian at 0 hours UT

DAY	☉	☽	☊	☿	♀	♂	♃	♄	♅	♆	♇
1 MO	13 ♋ 42	20 ♌ 17	23 ♈ 36R	29 ♋ 15	21 ♊ 49	23 ♈ 1	13 ♓ 39R	27 ♑ 51R	23 ♈ 38	0 ♓ 6R	2 ♑ 1R
2 TU	14 40	2 ♍ 48	23 28	1 ♌ 1	23 2	23 40	13 38	27 47	23 39	0 5	1 59
3 WE	15 37	15 31	23 23	2 45	24 15	24 18	13 37	27 43	23 40	0 4	1 58
4 TH	16 34	28 29	23 20	4 27	25 28	24 56	13 36	27 38	23 41	0 3	1 57
5 FR	17 32	11 ♎ 44	23 20	6 8	26 41	25 34	13 35	27 34	23 42	0 2	1 55
6 SA	18 29	25 19	23 20	7 47	27 54	26 12	13 33	27 30	23 43	0 1	1 54
7 SU	19 27	9 ♏ 16	23 19	9 25	29 7	26 50	13 31	27 25	23 44	29 ♒ 59	1 53
8 MO	20 24	23 35	23 17	11 1	0 ♋ 21	27 28	13 30	27 21	23 45	29 58	1 51
9 TU	21 22	8 ♐ 15	23 13	12 36	1 34	28 5	13 27	27 16	23 46	29 57	1 50
10 WE	22 19	23 11	23 5	14 8	2 47	28 43	13 25	27 12	23 47	29 56	1 49
11 TH	23 17	8 ♑ 15	22 56	15 39	4 0	29 20	13 23	27 7	23 47	29 55	1 47
12 FR	24 14	23 19	22 45	17 9	5 14	29 57	13 20	27 3	23 48	29 53	1 46
13 SA	25 12	8 ♒ 12	22 34	18 37	6 27	0 ♉ 33	13 17	26 58	23 49	29 52	1 45
14 SU	26 9	22 45	22 24	20 3	7 40	1 10	13 14	26 54	23 49	29 51	1 43
15 MO	27 7	6 ♓ 52	22 16	21 27	8 54	1 46	13 11	26 49	23 50	29 50	1 42
16 TU	28 5	20 30	22 11	22 50	10 7	2 22	13 7	26 45	23 50	29 48	1 41
17 WE	29 2	3 ♈ 41	22 8	24 11	11 21	2 58	13 4	26 40	23 50	29 47	1 40
18 TH	0 ♌ 0	16 25	22 7	25 31	12 34	3 34	13 0	26 36	23 51	29 46	1 38
19 FR	0 58	28 49	22 7	26 48	13 48	4 10	12 56	26 31	23 51	29 44	1 37
20 SA	1 55	10 ♉ 56	22 7	28 4	15 1	4 45	12 52	26 27	23 51	29 43	1 36
21 SU	2 53	22 52	22 5	29 17	16 15	5 20	12 48	26 22	23 52	29 41	1 35
22 MO	3 51	4 ♊ 43	22 1	0 ♍ 29	17 29	5 55	12 43	26 18	23 52	29 40	1 34
23 TU	4 49	16 32	21 55	1 39	18 42	6 30	12 38	26 14	23 52	29 38	1 32
24 WE	5 47	28 25	21 46	2 46	19 56	7 4	12 34	26 9	23 52	29 37	1 31
25 TH	6 45	10 ♋ 23	21 35	3 51	21 10	7 38	12 29	26 5	23 52R	29 35	1 30
26 FR	7 42	22 29	21 23	4 54	22 24	8 12	12 23	26 0	23 52	29 34	1 29
27 SA	8 40	4 ♌ 44	21 10	5 54	23 38	8 46	12 18	25 56	23 52	29 32	1 28
28 SU	9 38	17 10	20 58	6 52	24 52	9 19	12 13	25 52	23 52	29 31	1 27
29 MO	10 36	29 47	20 47	7 47	26 6	9 52	12 7	25 47	23 51	29 29	1 26
30 TU	11 34	12 ♍ 34	20 39	8 39	27 20	10 25	12 1	25 43	23 51	29 28	1 25
31 WE	12 32	25 33	20 34	9 28	28 34	10 58	11 55	25 39	23 51	29 26	1 24

INGRESSES :

1 ☿ → ♌ 10:12	16 ☽ → ♈ 17:13
☽ → ♍ 18:39	17 ☉ → ♌ 23:59
4 ☽ → ♎ 2:45	19 ☽ → ♉ 2:19
6 ☽ → ♏ 8: 7	21 ☿ → ♍ 14:12
♆ → ♒ 13:21	☽ → ♊ 14:25
7 ♀ → ♋ 17:15	24 ☽ → ♋ 3:12
8 ☽ → ♐ 10:33	26 ☽ → ♌ 14:45
10 ☽ → ♑ 10:51	29 ☽ → ♍ 0:24
12 ♂ → ♉ 2:10	31 ☽ → ♎ 8: 9
☽ → ♒ 10:43	
14 ☽ → ♓ 12:14	

ASPECTS & ECLIPSES :

1 ♂ ☌ ☊ 18: 7	☉ □ ☊ 16:32	18 ☽ ☌ ☊ 10:57	27 ♀ □ ♅ 4:31
☽ ☍ ♆ 18:49	☽ ☍ ♀ 16:38	☽ ☌ ♅ 14:18	☉ □ ♂ 5:26
♂ ☌ ♅ 23:50	☽ ☌ P 17:14	19 ☉ □ ☽ 4:35	☉ ☌ ☽ 8:16
2 ☽ ☍ ♃ 20:26	11 ☉ □ ♅ 12:51	☽ ☌ ♂ 11: 4	28 ♀ ☍ ♄ 18:26
5 ☉ □ ☽ 11: 5	☽ S ☊ 23: 6	21 ☿ ☍ ♆ 7:47	☽ ☍ ♆ 23:26
☽ ☌ ☋ 20:30	12 ☉ ☍ ☽ 1:34	22 ☽ ☌ A 22: 0	29 ☽ ☌ ☿ 16: 9
☽ ☍ ♅ 21:11	☽ ☌ ♄ 5:57	24 ☽ ☍ ♇ 6:15	☽ ☍ ♃ 22:58
6 ☽ ☍ ♂ 1:36	13 ☽ ☍ ☿ 19: 0	25 ♀ □ ☊ 7: 6	
7 ♂ □ ♄ 19:56	14 ☽ ☌ ♆ 11:57	☽ N ☊ 21:52	
9 ♀ ☍ ♇ 5:12	☉ ☍ ♄ 17: 9	☽ ☌ ♀ 23:49	
10 ☽ ☌ ♇ 13:43	15 ☽ ☌ ♃ 10:58	26 ☽ ☍ ♄ 6:53	

SIDEREAL HELIOCENTRIC LONGITUDES : AUGUST 2022 Gregorian at 0 hours UT

DAY	Sid. Time	☿	♀	⊕	♂	♃	♄	♅	♆	♇	Vernal Point
1 MO	20:38:21	12 ♍ 31	20 ♉ 10	13 ♑ 43	7 ♓ 1	3 ♓ 26	26 ♑ 25	20 ♈ 44	28 ♒ 41	2 ♑ 21	4 ♓ 56'42"
2 TU	20:42:18	16 15	21 46	14 40	7 39	3 32	26 27	20 44	28 42	2 21	4 ♓ 56'41"
3 WE	20:46:14	19 53	23 23	15 38	8 16	3 37	26 29	20 45	28 42	2 22	4 ♓ 56'41"
4 TH	20:50:11	23 25	25 0	16 35	8 53	3 43	26 31	20 46	28 43	2 22	4 ♓ 56'41"
5 FR	20:54: 7	26 52	26 37	17 32	9 31	3 48	26 32	20 46	28 43	2 22	4 ♓ 56'41"
6 SA	20:58: 4	0 ♎ 14	28 13	18 30	10 8	3 54	26 34	20 47	28 43	2 23	4 ♓ 56'41"
7 SU	21: 2: 0	3 31	29 50	19 27	10 45	3 59	26 36	20 48	28 44	2 23	4 ♓ 56'41"
8 MO	21: 5:57	6 45	1 ♊ 27	20 25	11 23	4 5	26 38	20 48	28 44	2 23	4 ♓ 56'41"
9 TU	21: 9:53	9 54	3 4	21 22	12 0	4 10	26 40	20 49	28 44	2 24	4 ♓ 56'41"
10 WE	21:13:50	13 0	4 41	22 20	12 37	4 16	26 42	20 50	28 45	2 24	4 ♓ 56'40"
11 TH	21:17:47	16 3	6 18	23 17	13 14	4 21	26 44	20 50	28 45	2 24	4 ♓ 56'40"
12 FR	21:21:43	19 3	7 55	24 15	13 51	4 27	26 46	20 51	28 45	2 24	4 ♓ 56'40"
13 SA	21:25:40	22 1	9 32	25 12	14 28	4 32	26 47	20 52	28 46	2 25	4 ♓ 56'40"
14 SU	21:29:36	24 56	11 9	26 10	15 5	4 38	26 49	20 52	28 46	2 25	4 ♓ 56'40"
15 MO	21:33:33	27 49	12 46	27 8	15 42	4 43	26 51	20 53	28 47	2 25	4 ♓ 56'40"
16 TU	21:37:29	0 ♏ 40	14 23	28 5	16 19	4 49	26 53	20 54	28 47	2 26	4 ♓ 56'40"
17 WE	21:41:26	3 30	16 0	29 3	16 56	4 54	26 55	20 54	28 47	2 26	4 ♓ 56'39"
18 TH	21:45:22	6 18	17 37	0 ♒ 1	17 33	5 0	26 57	20 55	28 48	2 26	4 ♓ 56'39"
19 FR	21:49:19	9 5	19 15	0 58	18 10	5 5	26 59	20 56	28 48	2 26	4 ♓ 56'39"
20 SA	21:53:16	11 52	20 52	1 56	18 47	5 11	27 1	20 56	28 48	2 27	4 ♓ 56'39"
21 SU	21:57:12	14 37	22 29	2 54	19 23	5 16	27 2	20 57	28 49	2 27	4 ♓ 56'39"
22 MO	22: 1: 9	17 22	24 6	3 52	20 0	5 22	27 4	20 58	28 49	2 27	4 ♓ 56'39"
23 TU	22: 5: 5	20 7	25 44	4 49	20 37	5 27	27 6	20 58	28 49	2 28	4 ♓ 56'39"
24 WE	22: 9: 2	22 52	27 21	5 47	21 13	5 33	27 8	20 59	28 50	2 28	4 ♓ 56'38"
25 TH	22:12:58	25 36	28 58	6 45	21 50	5 38	27 10	21 0	28 50	2 28	4 ♓ 56'38"
26 FR	22:16:55	28 21	0 ♋ 35	7 43	22 26	5 44	27 12	21 0	28 51	2 28	4 ♓ 56'38"
27 SA	22:20:51	1 ♐ 7	2 13	8 41	23 3	5 49	27 14	21 1	28 51	2 29	4 ♓ 56'38"
28 SU	22:24:48	3 53	3 50	9 39	23 39	5 55	27 16	21 2	28 51	2 29	4 ♓ 56'38"
29 MO	22:28:45	6 41	5 28	10 37	24 16	6 0	27 17	21 2	28 52	2 29	4 ♓ 56'38"
30 TU	22:32:41	9 29	7 5	11 35	24 52	6 6	27 19	21 3	28 52	2 30	4 ♓ 56'38"
31 WE	22:36:38	12 19	8 42	12 33	25 28	6 11	27 21	21 4	28 52	2 30	4 ♓ 56'37"

INGRESSES :

5 ☿ → ♎ 22:21
7 ♀ → ♊ 2:25
15 ☿ → ♏ 18:20
17 ⊕ → ♒ 23:45
25 ♀ → ♋ 15:15
26 ☿ → ♐ 14:17

ASPECTS (HELIOCENTRIC +MOON(TYCHONIC)) :

1 ☽ ☍ ♆ 16:10	⊕ □ ♅ 9:58	14 ☽ ☌ ♆ 10: 9	20 ☽ ☍ ☿ 2:24	28 ☿ □ ♃ 17:58
2 ♀ ☌ ☊ 0:51	☽ ☍ ♀ 14:31	☿ □ ⊕ 15:20	21 ☽ □ ♆ 12: 1	☽ ☍ ♆ 22:15
☽ ☍ ♃ 1:24	☽ □ ♃ 17:19	☿ □ ♄ 15:51	22 ☽ □ ♃ 1:19	29 ☽ ☍ ♃ 11:47
☽ ☍ ♂ 9:39	9 ☽ □ ♂ 6:18	⊕ ☌ ♄ 16:54	23 ☽ □ ♂ 8:42	☽ □ ☿ 16:37
3 ☽ ☌ ☿ 11:11	♀ □ ♃ 17:25	☽ ☌ ♃ 20:17	☽ ☌ ♀ 21:31	30 ☽ ☍ ♂ 23:51
4 ☽ □ ♇ 7: 5	10 ☽ ☌ ♇ 14:41	15 ☽ □ ♀ 11:39	☿ ☌ A 23: 4	31 ☽ □ ♇ 12:43
5 ☽ ☍ ♅ 16: 2	11 ☽ □ ☿ 15:30	☽ ☌ ♂ 16:11	24 ☽ ☍ ♇ 8: 9	
6 ☽ □ ♄ 2:10	☽ □ ♅ 20: 3	16 ☽ □ ♇ 21:41	25 ☽ □ ♅ 21: 5	
♀ □ ♆ 7:26	12 ☽ ☌ ♄ 5:31	17 ♀ □ ♂ 22:15	26 ☿ □ ♆ 4:14	
☿ □ ♇ 15:37	☿ ☍ ♅ 14:35	18 ☽ ☌ ♅ 8:38	☽ ☍ ♄ 9:17	
8 ☽ □ ♆ 8:28	13 ☿ ☌ ☋ 12:32	☽ □ ♄ 20:23	27 ♀ ☍ ♇ 3:55	

March 17 AD 33: Meeting of Scribes and Pharisees, p. 5, vol. III

10—Sun square Node:

September 9 AD 29: Sanatorium in Endor, p. 317, vol. I

February 24 AD 30: In Ulama, p. 408, vol. I

August 20 AD 30: At the Baths of Bethulia, pp. 23–24, vol. II

February 7 AD 31: Conferring Power on the Disciples, pp. 306–07, vol. II

July 13 AD 32: Teaching on the Good Samaritan and the Lost Coin, p. 475, vol. II

January 1 AD 33: An Uproar in the City, p. 518, vol. II

11—Sun square Uranus:

April 21 AD 29: Passover, p. 292, vol. I

October 31 AD 29: Temptation in the Wilderness, pp. 365–69, vol. I

November 5 AD 30: Journey to Gischala, pp. 102–04, vol. II

May 1 AD 31: Pagan Philosophers, pp. 364–66, vol. II

May 10 AD 33: Days Leading to Ascension, pp. 408–09, vol. III

12—Mars enters Taurus:

February 21 AD 31: Great Uncle of Bartholomew, p. 314, vol. II

January 22 AD 33: Healing of a Sick Girl, p. 525, vol. II

Full Moon Cancer:

July 14 AD 29: In Sarepta, p. 301, vol. I

July 3 AD 30: In the Court of Simeon's Mansion, p. 465, vol. I

June 23 AD 31: The Coming of the Son of Man, pp. 405–07, vol. II

July 11 AD 32: With the Three Holy Women, p. 475, vol. II

Heliocentric Mercury opposite Uranus:

June 4 AD 29: Sabbath in Hebron, p. 296, vol. I

August 31 AD 29: In Chisloth–Tabor, pp. 310–11, vol. I

November 28 AD 29: 38th Day of Temptation, p. 369, vol. I

May 23 AD 30: Imprisonment of John the Baptist, pp. 459–60, vol. I

August 19 AD 30: Healing Peter's Mother-in-law, pp. 21–23, vol. II

November 16 AD 30: 11/16/30—On the Way to Mt. Tabor, pp. 147–48 vol. II

February 12 AD 31: Healing of the Syrophoenician Woman, pp. 308–09, vol. II

May 11 AD 31: On King Djemschid, pp. 374–76, vol. II

July 25 AD 32: Day Before the Raising of Lazarus, pp. 477–78, vol. II

April 16 AD 33: Appearance of the Risen One to the Five Hundred, pp. 404–05, vol. III

14—Sun opposite Saturn: (G, T)

November 30 AD 29: Ministered unto by Angels, pp. 370–71, vol. I

December 14 AD 30: Malachi's Prophecy, pp. 180–81, vol. II

January 10 AD 33: Healing in Bethain, p. 520, vol. II

17—Sun enters Leo:

July 23 AD 29: From Sarepta to Mt. Carmel, p. 302, vol. I

July 23 AD 30: Lazarus and the Holy Women Support Christ, pp. 483–84, vol. I

July 22 AD 32: Events of Matthew 20, p. 477, vol. II

Heliocentric Venus square Mars:

July 25 AD 29: Teaching in Chisloth–Tabor, pp. 302–03, vol. I

December 29 AD 29: Teaching at the Wedding House, pp. 389–90, vol. I

June 19 AD 30: Celebrating the New Moon Festival, p. 460, vol. I

December 16 AD 30: Writing on the Wall, p. 182, vol. II

May 25 AD 31: In Kyrenia, pp. 387–88, vol. II

October 13 AD 32: Journey to Egypt, p. 517, vol. II

March 24 AD 33: Thy Kingdom Come to Us, p. 12, vol. III

21—Mercury opposite Neptune:

July 9 AD 29: The Widow Who Fed Elijah, pp. 300–01, vol. I

July 2 AD 30: Healing the Pagans, pp. 464–65, vol. I

June 27 AD 31: Preaching to a Jubilant Crowd, p. 408, vol. II

July 17 AD 32: Traveling to the Dead Lazarus, p. 475, vol. II

August 9 AD 32: Teaching in Kedar, pp. 485–86, vol. II

Mercury enters Virgo:

July 30 AD 29: Visiting Jacob's Well, p. 303, vol. I

July 26 AD 30: Dinah the Samaritan Woman, pp. 486–91, vol. I

September 10 AD 30: Gideon's Victory, pp. 51–52, vol. II

August 27 AD 32: Salathiel, p. 491, vol. II

25—**Venus square Node:**

April 8 AD 30: Death of Silent Mary and Nighttime Conversation with Nicodemus, p. 424, vol. I

September 2 AD 30: Teaching and Healing, pp. 40–41, vol. II

January 18 AD 31: In Bethany with Magdalene, pp. 215–16, vol. II

June 22 AD 31: The Young Pharisee, p. 405, vol. II

27—**Venus square Uranus:**

September 17 AD 29: Alone in Prayer, p. 323, vol. I

November 3 AD 30: Naomi of Dabrath, pp. 99–100, vol. II

March 25 AD 31: Roman Soldiers Seize the Galileans, p. 330, vol. II

October 11 AD 32: Teaching the Women by the Fountain, p. 516, vol. II

Sun square Mars:

March 12 AD 30: Last Visit with Eliud the Essene, p. 414, vol. I

November 23 AD 30: Meeting the Virgin, Maroni, and Martialis, pp. 157–58, vol. II

June 5 AD 32: Tax Collectors, p. 472, vol. II

January 14 AD 33: Reunion at Jacob's Well, p. 522, vol. II

New Moon Leo:

July 29 AD 29: Visiting Jacob's Well, p. 303, vol. I

August 17 AD 30: Healing Many in Bethsaida, pp. 19–20, vol. II

July 26 AD 32: Raising of Lazarus, pp. 478–79, vol. II

Heliocentric Venus opposite Pluto:

December 14 AD 29: In Shiloh, pp. 376–77, vol. I

July 28 AD 30: In Ginea, p. 492, vol. I

March 10 AD 31: In Regaba, pp. 321–22, vol. II

January 15 AD 33: Among the Shepherds, p. 522, vol. III

28—**Venus opposite Saturn:**

October 18 AD 29: Visiting the Essene Jairus, p. 362–63, vol. I

December 5 AD 30: Healing Two Possessed Youths, p. 169, vol. II

SEPTEMBER 2022

STARGAZING PREVIEW

The Scorpion will rule the evening sky at sunset on the 3rd, when you'll find our First Quarter Moon above *Antares* (15° Scorpio). Venus stood before this zodiacal degree as the Christ "I" united with the Nathan Jesus at the Baptism: the cosmos proclaiming that through the work of Christ Jesus, death becomes life.

On Tuesday the 6th, Mars and *Aldebaran* (15° Taurus) rise together at 2130. Plan on some stargazing after sunset (1830) on the 8th to witness Saturn and the waxing Moon meet in the last few degrees of the Goat. They'll begin the evening low in the east.

The Aquarius Full Moon (23°) appears on the 10th! As it rises, Saturn will be its only visible companion in the night sky—but not for long. By the time you put the kids to sleep, Jupiter and Mars will have followed.

The Moon's rise (2100) on the 16th draws Mars into the night sky. This will set the stage for the ascent of Orion shortly thereafter (weather permitting!). If you're up at 0500 the following morning, you'll see the Moon and Mars high in the south, before the stars of Taurus.

The Last Quarter Moon rises at 2200 on Saturday the 17th; watch for the stars of the belt of

Orion directly beneath the waning orb. Just before midnight, the Sun moves before the stars of the Virgin: *Behold worlds, O soul!*

Nature begins her long rest on the 23rd, as the fall equinox is upon us at 0104 UTC.

The morning of the 25th begins as the waning Moon, Venus, Mercury, and the Sun crest the horizon as one, bathed in the glory of the Sun. The Moon will pass Venus and Mercury before lunch is over, and by the time some of us are ready for bed, the Moon and Sun will stand together before 8° Virgo. Monday the 26th will feature the first of three conjunctions of Mercury and Venus this year. As far as I know, these always occur too close to the Sun to be visible, but it's important to acknowledge them, for the weaving forces of these two planets allows us to better understand the arts of healing and of peacemaking. This conjunction shone over humanity at the Crucifixion, Descent, and Resurrection of Jesus. Later this evening, Jupiter (8° Pisces), now opposite the Sun, will be "Full"—it rises at dusk.

By month's end, Orion and Mars crest the eastern horizon at 2100.

September Commentaries

1—Venus enters Leo:

June 27 AD 29: "Three months ago...," p. 298, vol. I

August 11 AD 30: Marriage and Divorce, pp. 9–11, vol. II

June 6 AD 31: The Carpenter's Workshop, pp. 394–95, vol. II

July 11 AD 32: With the Three Holy Women, p. 475, vol. II

3—Mercury opposite Jupiter:

August 2 AD 29: Whispers and Murmurs, p. 303, vol. I

October 3 AD 30: Talking with Mara the Suphanite, pp. 70–71, vol. II

6—Heliocentric Mercury conjunct Pluto:

August 14 AD 29: In Mahara's House, pp. 305–06, vol. I

November 10 AD 29: Temptation in the Wilderness, pp. 365–71, vol. I

February 6 AD 30: The Hospitable and Inhospitable, pp. 401–02, vol. I

May 5 AD 30: Many Baptisms, p. 459, vol. I

August 1 AD 30: The Samaritans, pp. 496–97, vol. I

October 28 AD 30: Healing of Issachar of Dothan, pp. 90–92, vol. II

January 25 AD 31: Assembly of Pharisees, p. 223, vol. II

October 3 AD 32: The Wonderful Cure of Two Sick Women, pp. 511–12, vol. II

March 28 AD 33: The Two Gardens, pp. 15–16, vol. III

7—Heliocentric Mars enters Aries:

October 29 AD 30: The Sacred Fountain, pp. 92–94, vol. II

September 15 AD 32: Abolition of Idol Worship, p. 499, vol. II

Heliocentric Venus square Uranus:

August 2 AD 29: Whispers and Murmurs, p. 303, vol. I

November 24 AD 29: Temptation in the Wilderness, pp. 365–71, vol. I

March 17 AD 30: The Samarian Orphan, p. 415, vol. I

July 9 AD 30: Inviting the People of Adama, p. 470, vol. I

October 29 AD 30: The Sacred Fountain, pp. 92–94, vol. II

February 20 AD 31: Spending the Night with Tax Collectors, pp. 313–14, vol. II

June 13 AD 31: Ships from Cyprus, pp. 398–99, vol. II

May 18 AD 32: Healing of Ten Lepers, pp. 468–70, vol. II

September 8 AD 32: Jesus Reaches the Tent City, pp. 495–96, vol. II

December 31 AD 32: The First Egyptian City, p. 518, vol. II

April 22 AD 33: Days with the Risen One, p. 408, vol. III

10—Full Moon Leo:

August 12 AD 29: Future Disciples, p. 305, vol. I

August 2 AD 30: Meeting the Widow Maroni in Nain, p. 497, vol. I

SIDEREAL GEOCENTRIC LONGITUDES : SEPTEMBER 2022 Gregorian at 0 hours UT

DAY	☉	☽	☊	☿	♀	♂	♃	♄	⛢	♆	♇
1 TH	13 ♌ 30	8 ♎ 43	20 ♈ 32R	10 ♍ 13	29 ♋ 48	11 ♉ 30	11 ♓ 49R	25 ♑ 35R	23 ♈ 50R	29 ♒ 25R	1 ♑ 23R
2 FR	14 28	22 6	20 31	10 55	1 ♌ 2	12 2	11 43	25 31	23 50	29 23	1 22
3 SA	15 26	5 ♏ 43	20 32D	11 33	2 16	12 34	11 37	25 27	23 50	29 21	1 21
4 SU	16 25	19 36	20 32R	12 8	3 30	13 6	11 30	25 23	23 49	29 20	1 20
5 MO	17 23	3 ♐ 44	20 31	12 37	4 44	13 37	11 23	25 19	23 49	29 18	1 19
6 TU	18 21	18 7	20 28	13 3	5 58	14 8	11 17	25 15	23 48	29 17	1 18
7 WE	19 19	2 ♑ 42	20 22	13 23	7 12	14 38	11 10	25 11	23 47	29 15	1 17
8 TH	20 17	17 24	20 15	13 38	8 27	15 8	11 3	25 7	23 47	29 13	1 17
9 FR	21 15	2 ♒ 5	20 6	13 48	9 41	15 38	10 56	25 3	23 46	29 12	1 16
10 SA	22 14	16 39	19 57	13 52	10 55	16 8	10 49	24 59	23 45	29 10	1 15
11 SU	23 12	0 ♓ 58	19 48	13 50R	12 10	16 37	10 42	24 56	23 44	29 8	1 14
12 MO	24 10	14 56	19 42	13 41	13 24	17 6	10 34	24 52	23 43	29 7	1 13
13 TU	25 9	28 31	19 38	13 26	14 38	17 35	10 27	24 48	23 42	29 5	1 13
14 WE	26 7	11 ♈ 40	19 36	13 4	15 53	18 3	10 19	24 45	23 42	29 4	1 12
15 TH	27 5	24 26	19 35D	12 36	17 7	18 31	10 12	24 41	23 40	29 2	1 11
16 FR	28 4	6 ♉ 52	19 36	12 1	18 22	18 59	10 4	24 38	23 39	29 0	1 11
17 SA	29 2	19 1	19 37	11 19	19 36	19 26	9 56	24 35	23 38	28 59	1 10
18 SU	0 ♍ 1	1 ♊ 0	19 38R	10 31	20 51	19 53	9 48	24 31	23 37	28 57	1 10
19 MO	0 59	12 52	19 37	9 38	22 5	20 19	9 41	24 28	23 36	28 55	1 9
20 TU	1 58	24 43	19 34	8 40	23 20	20 45	9 33	24 25	23 35	28 54	1 8
21 WE	2 57	6 ♋ 38	19 29	7 38	24 34	21 11	9 25	24 22	23 33	28 52	1 8
22 TH	3 55	18 40	19 23	6 34	25 49	21 36	9 17	24 19	23 32	28 50	1 7
23 FR	4 54	0 ♌ 53	19 15	5 29	27 4	22 0	9 9	24 16	23 31	28 49	1 7
24 SA	5 53	13 19	19 7	4 25	28 18	22 25	9 1	24 13	23 29	28 47	1 6
25 SU	6 52	25 59	19 0	3 22	29 33	22 49	8 53	24 11	23 28	28 45	1 6
26 MO	7 50	8 ♍ 54	18 53	2 24	0 ♍ 48	23 12	8 45	24 8	23 26	28 44	1 6
27 TU	8 49	22 2	18 49	1 31	2 3	23 35	8 37	24 6	23 25	28 42	1 5
28 WE	9 48	5 ♎ 23	18 46	0 45	3 17	23 57	8 29	24 3	23 23	28 40	1 5
29 TH	10 47	18 55	18 45	0 7	4 32	24 19	8 21	24 1	23 22	28 39	1 5
30 FR	11 46	2 ♏ 37	18 45D	29 ♌ 38	5 47	24 41	8 13	23 58	23 20	28 37	1 4

INGRESSES :

1 ♀ → ♌ 4: 1
2 ☽ → ♏ 13:58
4 ☽ → ♐ 17:41
6 ☽ → ♑ 19:34
8 ☽ → ♒ 20:35
10 ☽ → ♓ 22:21
13 ☽ → ♈ 2:40
15 ☽ → ♉ 10:40
17 ☽ → ♊ 21:59
☉ → ♍ 23:38
20 ☽ → ♋ 10:39
22 ☽ → ♌ 22:15
25 ☽ → ♍ 7:30
♀ → ♍ 8:36
27 ☽ → ♎ 14:22
29 ☿ → ♌ 5: 0
☽ → ♏ 19:25

ASPECTS & ECLIPSES :

1 ☽ ☌ ☋ 21:11
2 ☽ ☍ ⛢ 3: 4
3 ☿ ☍ ♃ 1:48
☽ ☍ ♂ 12:21
☉ □ ☽ 18: 6
6 ☽ ☌ ♇ 21:41
7 ☽ ☌ P 18:20
8 ☽ ⚼ ☊ 4:36
☽ ☌ ♄ 12:32
9 ☽ ☍ ♀ 13:38
10 ☉ ☍ ☽ 9:57
☽ ☌ ♆ 20:55
11 ☽ ☌ ♃ 16:29
☽ ☍ ☿ 21:51
14 ☽ ☌ ☊ 14:47
☽ ☌ ⛢ 22:32
16 ♀ □ ♂ 18:47
☉ ☍ ♆ 22:29
17 ☽ ☌ ♂ 0:50
☉ □ ☽ 21:50
18 ☿ ☍ ♃ 22:32
19 ☽ ☌ A 14:51
20 ☽ ☍ ♇ 12:57
22 ☽ ⚻ ☊ 1:23
☽ ☍ ♄ 11: 5
23 ☉ ☌ ☿ 6:48
24 ♀ ☍ ♆ 8:57
25 ☽ ☍ ♆ 5:10
☽ ☌ ♀ 7:23
☽ ☌ ☿ 12:48
☉ ☌ ☽ 21:53
☽ ☍ ♃ 23:43
26 ☿ ☌ ♀ 17:57
☉ ☍ ♃ 19:32
28 ☽ ☌ ☋ 23:42
29 ☽ ☍ ⛢ 7:48

SIDEREAL HELIOCENTRIC LONGITUDES : SEPTEMBER 2022 Gregorian at 0 hours UT

DAY	Sid. Time	☿	♀	⊕	♂	♃	♄	⛢	♆	♇	Vernal Point
1 TH	22:40:34	15 ♐ 10	10 ♋ 20	13 ♒ 31	26 ♓ 5	6 ♓ 17	27 ♑ 23	21 ♈ 4	28 ♒ 53	2 ♑ 30	4 ♓ 56'37"
2 FR	22:44:31	18 4	11 57	14 29	26 41	6 22	27 25	21 5	28 53	2 30	4 ♓ 56'37"
3 SA	22:48:27	20 59	13 35	15 27	27 17	6 27	27 27	21 6	28 53	2 31	4 ♓ 56'37"
4 SU	22:52:24	23 57	15 12	16 25	27 53	6 33	27 29	21 6	28 54	2 31	4 ♓ 56'37"
5 MO	22:56:20	26 57	16 50	17 23	28 29	6 38	27 31	21 7	28 54	2 31	4 ♓ 56'37"
6 TU	23: 0:17	29 59	18 27	18 21	29 5	6 44	27 32	21 8	28 55	2 32	4 ♓ 56'37"
7 WE	23: 4:13	3 ♑ 5	20 5	19 19	29 41	6 49	27 34	21 8	28 55	2 32	4 ♓ 56'37"
8 TH	23: 8:10	6 15	21 42	20 18	0 ♈ 17	6 55	27 36	21 9	28 55	2 32	4 ♓ 56'36"
9 FR	23:12: 7	9 27	23 20	21 16	0 53	7 0	27 38	21 10	28 56	2 32	4 ♓ 56'36"
10 SA	23:16: 3	12 44	24 57	22 14	1 29	7 6	27 40	21 11	28 56	2 33	4 ♓ 56'36"
11 SU	23:20: 0	16 5	26 35	23 12	2 5	7 11	27 42	21 11	28 56	2 33	4 ♓ 56'36"
12 MO	23:23:56	19 31	28 12	24 11	2 40	7 17	27 44	21 12	28 57	2 33	4 ♓ 56'36"
13 TU	23:27:53	23 1	29 50	25 9	3 16	7 22	27 46	21 13	28 57	2 34	4 ♓ 56'36"
14 WE	23:31:49	26 36	1 ♌ 27	26 8	3 51	7 28	27 47	21 13	28 57	2 34	4 ♓ 56'36"
15 TH	23:35:46	0 ♒ 17	3 5	27 6	4 27	7 33	27 49	21 14	28 58	2 34	4 ♓ 56'35"
16 FR	23:39:42	4 4	4 42	28 4	5 3	7 39	27 51	21 15	28 58	2 34	4 ♓ 56'35"
17 SA	23:43:39	7 58	6 20	29 3	5 38	7 44	27 53	21 15	28 59	2 35	4 ♓ 56'35"
18 SU	23:47:36	11 58	7 57	0 ♓ 1	6 13	7 50	27 55	21 16	28 59	2 35	4 ♓ 56'35"
19 MO	23:51:32	16 5	9 35	1 0	6 49	7 55	27 57	21 17	28 59	2 35	4 ♓ 56'35"
20 TU	23:55:29	20 19	11 12	1 59	7 24	8 1	27 59	21 17	29 0	2 36	4 ♓ 56'35"
21 WE	23:59:25	24 41	12 50	2 57	7 59	8 6	28 1	21 18	29 0	2 36	4 ♓ 56'35"
22 TH	0: 3:22	29 12	14 27	3 56	8 34	8 12	28 2	21 19	29 0	2 36	4 ♓ 56'34"
23 FR	0: 7:18	3 ♓ 51	16 5	4 55	9 10	8 17	28 4	21 19	29 1	2 37	4 ♓ 56'34"
24 SA	0:11:15	8 38	17 42	5 53	9 45	8 23	28 6	21 20	29 1	2 37	4 ♓ 56'34"
25 SU	0:15:11	13 34	19 20	6 52	10 20	8 28	28 8	21 21	29 1	2 37	4 ♓ 56'34"
26 MO	0:19: 8	18 40	20 57	7 51	10 55	8 34	28 10	21 21	29 2	2 37	4 ♓ 56'34"
27 TU	0:23: 5	23 54	22 34	8 50	11 30	8 39	28 12	21 22	29 2	2 38	4 ♓ 56'34"
28 WE	0:27: 1	29 18	24 12	9 49	12 4	8 45	28 14	21 23	29 3	2 38	4 ♓ 56'34"
29 TH	0:30:58	4 ♈ 50	25 49	10 47	12 39	8 50	28 16	21 23	29 3	2 38	4 ♓ 56'33"
30 FR	0:34:54	10 32	27 26	11 46	13 14	8 56	28 18	21 24	29 3	2 39	4 ♓ 56'33"

INGRESSES :

6 ☿ → ♑ 0: 4
7 ♂ → ♈ 12:34
13 ♀ → ♌ 2:28
14 ☿ → ♒ 22: 7
17 ⊕ → ♓ 23:25
22 ☿ → ♓ 4:12
28 ☿ → ♈ 3: 4

ASPECTS (HELIOCENTRIC +MOON(TYCHONIC)) :

1 ☽ □ ♀ 3:19
☽ ☍ ⛢ 22:11
2 ☽ □ ♄ 9:26
4 ☽ □ ♆ 15:50
♀ ☌ P 23:56
5 ☽ □ ♃ 4:54
☿ □ ♂ 15:11
6 ☽ □ ♂ 18:50
☿ ☌ ♇ 19:42
☽ ☌ ♇ 23:43
7 ☽ ☌ ☿ 0:48
♀ □ ⛢ 15:47
8 ☽ □ ⛢ 6: 8
☽ ☍ ♀ 7:54
☽ ☌ ♄ 16:42
10 ☽ ☌ ♆ 20:34
11 ☽ ☌ ♃ 10:40
♀ ☍ ♄ 16:47
♂ □ ♇ 19:19
12 ☿ □ ⛢ 11:40
13 ☿ ⚼ ☊ 3:34
☽ □ ♇ 7:18
☽ ☌ ♂ 8:59
14 ☿ ☌ ♄ 7:50
☽ ☌ ⛢ 17:53
15 ☽ □ ♄ 6:29
☽ □ ☿ 16: 7
☽ □ ♀ 19: 9
16 ☿ ☍ ♀ 6:49
⊕ ☌ ♆ 22:13
17 ☽ □ ♆ 19:56
18 ☽ □ ♃ 13:54
20 ☽ ☍ ♇ 15:53
21 ☽ □ ♂ 2:51
☿ ☌ ♆ 23: 0
22 ☽ □ ⛢ 5:13
☽ ☍ ♄ 18:29
23 ☿ ☌ ⊕ 6:48
☿ ☌ ♃ 22:43
24 ☽ ☌ ♀ 9:35
25 ☽ ☍ ♆ 5:41
☽ ☍ ♃ 23:22
26 ♀ ⚻ ☊ 12:57
⊕ ☌ ♃ 19:17
27 ☽ ☍ ☿ 5:40
☽ □ ♇ 19: 5
28 ☽ ☍ ♂ 12:26
☿ □ ♇ 14:31
29 ☽ ☍ ⛢ 4:21
☽ □ ♄ 16:26
30 ☿ ☌ ♂ 12:27
♀ ☍ ♆ 23:59

August 9 AD 32: Teaching in Kedar, pp. 485–86, vol. II

11—Heliocentric Venus opposite Saturn:

August 21 AD 29: Pure Love of Truth, p. 307, vol. I

April 9 AD 30: Jesus with the Night Disciples, p. 424, vol. I

November 25 AD 30: Healing of Mary Cleophas, p. 160, vol. II)

Heliocentric Mars square Pluto:

November 8 AD 29: Temptation in the Wilderness, pp. 365–71, vol. I

September 26 AD 30: Feast of Atonement, pp. 62–63, vol. II

August 20 AD 32: Washing of Eliud's Feet, p. 488, vol. II

14—Heliocentric Mercury conjunct Saturn:

June 26 AD 29: "Three months ago…," p. 298, vol. I

December 20 AD 29: Invited to the Wedding at Cana, p. 379, vol. I

March 19 AD 30: Jesus and Lazarus in Jerusalem, p. 416, vol. I

September 12 AD 30: The Fishing Lake, pp. 52–53, vol. II

December 9 AD 30: Magdalene's Relapse, pp. 175–76, vol. II

March 8 AD 31: Teaching in Argob, p. 321, vol. II

June 4 AD 31: Elizabeth's Childhood Home, p. 394, vol. II

August 20 AD 32: Washing of Eliud's Feet, p. 488, vol. II

May 13 AD 33: The Night Before Ascension, p. 410, vol. III

16—Venus square Mars:

November 6 AD 29: Temptation in the Wilderness, pp. 365–71, vol. I

December 16 AD 29: On the Way to the Wedding, pp. 377–78, vol. I

November 11 AD 30: The Hands of Your Heart, pp. 139–41, vol. II

Sun opposite Neptune:

July 16 AD 29: In Sarepta, p. 301–02, vol. I

July 18 AD 30: Discussing John's Imprisonment, p. 477, vol. I

July 22 AD 32: July 22 AD 32: Events of Matthew 20, p. 477, vol. II

Heliocentric Mercury opposite Venus:

June 2 AD 29: Alone in Prayer, p. 296, vol. I

October 6 AD 29: Jesus Visits an Inn, p. 356, vol. I

March 12 AD 30: Last Visit with Eliud, p. 414, vol. I

August 7 AD 30: A Home for Lepers, pp. 7–8, vol. II

December 15 AD 30: Close of the Feast of Lights, pp. 181–82, vol. II

May 22 AD 31: Clothes and Provisions, pp. 385–86, vol. II

July 31 AD 32: Beginning the Journey to the Three Kings, pp. 480–81, vol. II

May 5 AD 33: With the Risen One, p. 408, vol. III

17—Sun enters Virgo:

August 23 AD 29: In the Valley of Zebulon, p. 307, vol. I

August 23 AD 30: In the Harvest Field of Dothaim, pp. 27–28, vol. II

August 22 AD 32: August 22 AD 32: An Open-Air Wedding, pp. 489–90, vol. II

18—Mercury opposite Jupiter:

August 2 AD 29: Whispers and Murmurs, p. 303, vol. I

October 3 AD 30: Talking with Mara the Suphanite, pp. 70–71, vol. II

21—Heliocentric Mercury conjunct Neptune:

June 1 AD 29: Elizabeth's Cave, p. 296, vol. I

August 28 AD 29: Circumcision and Baptism, pp. 309–10, vol. I

November 24 AD 29: Temptation in the Wilderness, pp. 365–71, vol. I

February 20 AD 30: In Jezreel, p. 406, vol. I

May 19 AD 30: Imprisonment of John the Baptist, p. 459, vol. I

August 16 AD 30: In Peter's House, pp. 17–19, vol. II

November 12 AD 30: On the Way to Nain, p. 141, vol. II

May 7 AD 31: The Prophet Malachi, pp. 372–73, vol. II

July 20 AD 32: News of Lazarus, p. 477, vol. II

April 11 AD 33: The Risen Christ Appears to Thomas, pp. 398–400, vol. III

23—Inferior Conjunction Sun and Mercury:
September 9 AD 29: Jesus and Eliud, p. 317, vol. I
December 24 AD 29: Summons of Phillip, p. 382, vol. I
August 24 AD 30: Herod and John, pp. 28–29, vol. II
December 8 AD 30: Healings in Bethsaida, pp. 173–75, vol. II
April 2 AD 31: Transfiguration, pp. 339–40
November 23 AD 31: Healing of the Man Born Blind, see *Journal for Star Wisdom 2016*
July 20 AD 32: News of Lazarus, p. 477, vol. II
February 23 AD 33: Teaching in the Temple, p. 1, vol. III

Heliocentric Mercury conjunct Jupiter:
December 5 AD 29: Silencing the Possessed, pp. 374–75, vol. I
March 5 AD 30: Helping in the Storm, pp. 412–13, vol. I
August 30 AD 30: Paralyzed Arms and Hands, p. 38, vol. II
November 28 AD 30: Sermon on the Mount, pp. 162–63, vol. II
February 25 AD 31: In Nobah, p. 316, vol. II
May 25 AD 31: Speaking Against Idolatry, pp. 387–88, vol. II
August 13 AD 32: The Bedridden Married Couple, p. 486, vol. II
February 8 AD 33: Three Secret Disciples, p. 530, vol. II
May 8 AD 33: The Risen One, p. 408, vol. III

24—Venus opposite Neptune:
June 22 AD 29: Herod Wishes to Visit John the Baptist, pp. 297–98, vol. I
August 7 AD 30: A Home for Lepers, pp. 7–8, vol. II
June 5 AD 31: The Pharisee of Thaanach, p. 394, vol. II
July 11 AD 32: With the Three Holy Women, p. 475, vol. II

25—Venus enters Virgo:
July 21 AD 29: Naomi and Ruth, p. 302, vol. I
September 4 AD 30: Mara the Suphanite, pp. 42–44, vol. II
August 4 AD 32: Planning the Journey, p. 482, vol. II

New Moon Virgo:
August 28 AD 29: Circumcision and Baptism, pp. 309–10, vol. I
September 16 AD 30: Gifts from Abigail, p. 54, vol. II
August 24 AD 32: A House by Beehives, p. 490, vol. II

26—Mercury conjunct Venus:
May 4 AD 29: Jesus and Mary move from Nazareth to Capernaum, p. 292, vol. I
January 26 AD 30: Where the "Good Samaritan" Occurred, pp. 398–99, vol. I
August 31 AD 30: Meeting in Bezek, pp. 38–39, vol. II
October 1 AD 30: Confession of an Adulteress, pp. 68–70, vol. II
December 4 AD 30: Authority to the Twelve, pp. 168–69, vol. II
July 13 AD 32: Teaching on the Good Samaritan and the Lost Coin, p. 475, vol. II
April 6 AD 33: On the Road to Emmaus, pp. 393–96, vol. III

Sun opposite Jupiter:
August 24 AD 29: In the Valley of Zebulon, p. 307, vol. I
September 30 AD 30: Feast of Tabernacles, pp. 67–68, vol. II

29—Mercury enters Leo:
July 12 AD 29: In Sarepta, pp. 301–02, vol. I
July 5 AD 30: A Great Banquet, pp. 466–67, vol. I
June 28 AD 31: Taking Leave of Many, pp. 408–09, vol. II

30—Heliocentric Mercury conjunct Mars:
July 3 AD 29: Meeting Six of the Baptist's Disciples, p. 300, vol. I
October 7 AD 29: "Behold the Lamb of God," pp. 356–57, vol. I
January 17 AD 30: Visiting the Ruined City of Slaves, pp. 396–97, vol. I
August 21 AD 30: In Bethulia, pp. 24–26, vol. II

November 29 AD 30: The Second Beatitude, p. 163, vol. II

March 5 AD 31: Healing the Sick, p. 319, vol. II

June 8 AD 31: In Maroni's Garden, p. 396, vol. II

July 28 AD 32: Fleeing with Matthew and John, p. 480, vol. II

May 13 AD 33: The Night Before Ascension, p. 410, vol. III

Heliocentric Venus opposite Neptune:

May 31 AD 29: Family of Lazarus, pp. 294–96, vol. I

August 25 AD 30: In Gennabris, pp. 30–31, vol. II

April 7 AD 31: Gathering of the Seventy, pp. 343–44, vol. II

OCTOBER 2022

STARGAZING PREVIEW

As the Sun dips below the horizon on Monday the 3rd, the First Quarter Moon will be high in the south in the center of Sagittarius; Jupiter, still bright from its opposition to the Sun, will have just risen. As the Moon speeds toward Full, it passes beneath both Saturn and Jupiter on the 5th and the 8th, respectively.

Sunday the 9th will bless us with a Pisces Full Moon (21°) beneath the head of *Andromeda*, representative of the soul of humanity. Will we, too, be freed of our chains? Mars and the Moon rise in unison on the 15th (at 2000) as Jupiter shines from the top of the zodiacal circle.

October's Last Quarter Moon will occur on the 17th as the Moon moves below *Pollux*, the immortal twin of Gemini. By now, the Sun, Mercury, and Venus are in Virgo, and the other planets are spread widely around the circle.

The night of Friday the 21st will be the peak of the Orionid meteor showers, which appear to radiate from—you guessed it—Orion. These shooting stars, which have their genesis in stardust from Comet Halley, have a fine night to show off, as the waning crescent Moon (nearing New) doesn't rise until 0300. At this time, Orion will be due south.

The New Moon on the 25th, at 7° Libra, will result in a Partial Solar Eclipse over Europe, Asia, and the Middle East. The Moon's position recalls its degree as Jesus was sadistically tried by Caiaphas—one of the most egregious examples of judicial kabuki theater across the centuries, of which tyrants never tire.

By the end of the month, Mars will be our only morning star; he'll be in the northwest at dawn, between the Bull and the Twins. Orion rises at 1900, and disappears into the sunlight at dawn.

OCTOBER COMMENTARIES

1—Venus opposite Jupiter:

July 25 AD 29: From Mt. Carmel to Mt. Tabor, pp. 302–03, vol. I

October 4 AD 30: In Akrabis and Shiloh, p. 71, vol. II

Heliocentric Mercury conjunct Uranus:

July 7 AD 29: Early ministry, p. 300, vol. I

October 3 AD 29: The Inn of Reuben, p. 353, vol. I

December 30 AD 29: End of the Wedding at Cana, p. 390, vol. I

March 29 AD 30: Preparing for Passover, pp. 419–20, vol. I

June 25 AD 30: Saturnin Baptizes, pp. 460–62, vol. I

September 21 AD 30: Gadara, pp. 58–59, vol. II

December 18 AD 30: Kiriathaim, p. 183, vol. II

March 17 AD 31: Cornerstone, p. 325, vol. II

June 13 AD 31: Return to Capernaum, pp. 398–99, vol. II

May 31 AD 32: Zacchaeus's House, p. 472, vol. II

August 27 AD 32: Salathiel, p. 491

February 19 AD 33: Preparing for Death, p. 1, vol. III

May 19 AD 33: The Risen One, pp. 411–12 vol. III

5—Mercury enters Virgo:

July 30 AD 29: Visiting Jacob's Well, p. 303, vol. I

SIDEREAL GEOCENTRIC LONGITUDES : OCTOBER 2022 Gregorian at 0 hours UT

DAY	☉	☽	☊	☿	♀	♂	♃	♄	♅	♆	♇
1 SA	12 ♍ 45	16 ♏ 29	18 ♈ 47	29 ♌ 18R	7 ♍ 2	25 ♉ 1	8 ♓ 5R	23 ♑ 56R	23 ♈ 18R	28 ♒ 36R	1 ♑ 4R
2 SU	13 44	0 ♐ 29	18 48	29 9	8 17	25 22	7 57	23 54	23 17	28 34	1 4
3 MO	14 43	14 36	18 49R	29 11D	9 32	25 42	7 49	23 52	23 15	28 32	1 4
4 TU	15 42	28 49	18 48	29 22	10 46	26 1	7 41	23 50	23 13	28 31	1 4
5 WE	16 41	13 ♑ 5	18 46	29 44	12 1	26 20	7 33	23 48	23 11	28 29	1 4
6 TH	17 40	27 22	18 42	0 ♍ 15	13 16	26 38	7 25	23 47	23 9	28 28	1 3
7 FR	18 39	11 ♒ 35	18 38	0 56	14 31	26 55	7 17	23 45	23 7	28 26	1 3
8 SA	19 38	25 41	18 33	1 45	15 46	27 13	7 10	23 43	23 6	28 25	1 3
9 SU	20 38	9 ♓ 36	18 29	2 42	17 1	27 29	7 2	23 42	23 4	28 23	1 3D
10 MO	21 37	23 14	18 26	3 47	18 16	27 45	6 55	23 41	23 2	28 22	1 3
11 TU	22 36	6 ♈ 34	18 25	4 57	19 31	28 0	6 47	23 39	23 0	28 20	1 3
12 WE	23 35	19 35	18 24D	6 13	20 46	28 15	6 40	23 38	22 58	28 19	1 3
13 TH	24 35	2 ♉ 17	18 25	7 34	22 1	28 29	6 32	23 37	22 55	28 17	1 4
14 FR	25 34	14 41	18 26	8 59	23 16	28 42	6 25	23 36	22 53	28 16	1 4
15 SA	26 34	26 51	18 28	10 28	24 31	28 54	6 18	23 35	22 51	28 14	1 4
16 SU	27 33	8 ♊ 51	18 29	11 59	25 46	29 6	6 11	23 34	22 49	28 13	1 4
17 MO	28 32	20 44	18 30	13 34	27 1	29 18	6 4	23 34	22 47	28 12	1 4
18 TU	29 32	2 ♋ 36	18 30R	15 10	28 16	29 28	5 58	23 33	22 45	28 10	1 5
19 WE	0 ♎ 32	14 32	18 30	16 47	29 31	29 38	5 51	23 33	22 42	28 9	1 5
20 TH	1 31	26 35	18 28	18 26	0 ♎ 47	29 47	5 45	23 32	22 40	28 8	1 5
21 FR	2 31	8 ♌ 51	18 26	20 6	2 2	29 55	5 38	23 32	22 38	28 6	1 5
22 SA	3 30	21 22	18 24	21 47	3 17	0 ♊ 3	5 32	23 32	22 36	28 5	1 6
23 SU	4 30	4 ♍ 12	18 22	23 28	4 32	0 9	5 26	23 32	22 33	28 4	1 6
24 MO	5 30	17 20	18 21	25 9	5 47	0 15	5 20	23 32D	22 31	28 3	1 7
25 TU	6 30	0 ♎ 48	18 19	26 50	7 2	0 20	5 14	23 32	22 29	28 1	1 7
26 WE	7 30	14 32	18 19	28 32	8 17	0 24	5 8	23 32	22 26	28 0	1 8
27 TH	8 29	28 32	18 19D	0 ♎ 13	9 33	0 28	5 3	23 33	22 24	27 59	1 8
28 FR	9 29	12 ♏ 42	18 20	1 54	10 48	0 31	4 58	23 33	22 21	27 58	1 9
29 SA	10 29	26 59	18 20	3 35	12 3	0 32	4 52	23 34	22 19	27 57	1 9
30 SU	11 29	11 ♐ 18	18 21	5 16	13 18	0 33	4 47	23 34	22 17	27 56	1 10
31 MO	12 29	25 37	18 21	6 56	14 33	0 33R	4 43	23 35	22 14	27 54	1 10

INGRESSES :

1 ☽ → ♐ 23:11
4 ☽ → ♑ 2: 0
5 ☿ → ♍ 13: 9
6 ☽ → ♒ 4:26
8 ☽ → ♓ 7:23
10 ☽ → ♈ 12: 6
12 ☽ → ♉ 19:39
15 ☽ → ♊ 6:16
17 ☽ → ♋ 18:44
18 ☉ → ♎ 11:17
19 ♀ → ♎ 9: 8
20 ☽ → ♌ 6:43
21 ♂ → ♊ 15:32
22 ☽ → ♍ 16:12
24 ☽ → ♎ 22:35
26 ☿ → ♎ 20:52
27 ☽ → ♏ 2:30
29 ☽ → ♐ 5: 3
31 ☽ → ♑ 7:22

ASPECTS & ECLIPSES :

1 ☽ ☍ ♂ 15: 2
♀ ☍ ♃ 18:10
3 ☉ □ ☽ 0:12
4 ☽ ☌ ♇ 3:47
☽ ☌ P 16:24
5 ☽ S ☊ 9:30
☽ ☌ ♄ 17:58
8 ☽ ☌ ♆ 4:39
☽ ☍ ☿ 11: 9
☽ ☌ ♃ 19:35
9 ☽ ☍ ♀ 14:18
☉ ☍ ☽ 20:53
11 ☽ ☌ ☊ 21:48
12 ☽ ☌ ♅ 6:18
♂ □ ♆ 6:21
☿ ☍ ♃ 7:22
15 ☽ ☌ ♂ 4: 9
16 ☉ □ Π 1:58
17 ☽ ☌ A 10:19
☉ □ ☽ 17:14
☽ ☍ ♇ 20:54
19 ☽ N ☊ 7:55
☉ □ ♇ 13:27
☽ ☍ ♄ 17:58
20 ♀ □ ♇ 5:57
22 ☽ ☍ ♆ 12:37
☉ S☋ ♀ 21:16
23 ☽ ☍ ♃ 2:15
24 ☽ ☌ ☿ 16: 0
25 ☉ ☌ ☽ 10:47
☉ ● P 10:58
☽ ☌ ♀ 12: 3
26 ☽ ☌ ☋ 6:30
☽ ☍ ♅ 13:33
27 ☿ □ ♇ 13: 4
29 ☽ ☍ ♂ 5:58
☽ ☌ P 14:35
31 ☽ ☌ ♇ 9:21

SIDEREAL HELIOCENTRIC LONGITUDES : OCTOBER 2022 Gregorian at 0 hours UT

DAY	Sid. Time	☿	♀	⊕	♂	♃	♄	♅	♆	♇	Vernal Point
1 SA	0:38:51	16 ♈ 21	29 ♌ 4	12 ♓ 45	13 ♈ 49	9 ♓ 1	28 ♑ 19	21 ♈ 25	29 ♒ 4	2 ♑ 39	4 ♓ 56'33"
2 SU	0:42:47	22 18	0 ♍ 41	13 44	14 23	9 7	28 21	21 25	29 4	2 39	4 ♓ 56'33"
3 MO	0:46:44	28 21	2 18	14 43	14 58	9 12	28 23	21 26	29 4	2 39	4 ♓ 56'33"
4 TU	0:50:40	4 ♉ 30	3 55	15 42	15 32	9 18	28 25	21 27	29 5	2 40	4 ♓ 56'33"
5 WE	0:54:37	10 44	5 33	16 42	16 7	9 23	28 27	21 27	29 5	2 40	4 ♓ 56'33"
6 TH	0:58:34	17 1	7 10	17 41	16 41	9 29	28 29	21 28	29 5	2 40	4 ♓ 56'33"
7 FR	1: 2:30	23 20	8 47	18 40	17 16	9 34	28 31	21 29	29 6	2 41	4 ♓ 56'32"
8 SA	1: 6:27	29 39	10 24	19 39	17 50	9 40	28 33	21 29	29 6	2 41	4 ♓ 56'32"
9 SU	1:10:23	5 ♊ 57	12 1	20 38	18 24	9 45	28 34	21 30	29 7	2 41	4 ♓ 56'32"
10 MO	1:14:20	12 13	13 38	21 37	18 58	9 51	28 36	21 31	29 7	2 41	4 ♓ 56'32"
11 TU	1:18:16	18 24	15 15	22 37	19 32	9 56	28 38	21 31	29 7	2 42	4 ♓ 56'32"
12 WE	1:22:13	24 30	16 52	23 36	20 7	10 2	28 40	21 32	29 8	2 42	4 ♓ 56'32"
13 TH	1:26: 9	0 ♋ 29	18 29	24 35	20 41	10 7	28 42	21 33	29 8	2 42	4 ♓ 56'32"
14 FR	1:30: 6	6 21	20 5	25 35	21 15	10 13	28 44	21 33	29 8	2 43	4 ♓ 56'31"
15 SA	1:34: 3	12 4	21 42	26 34	21 48	10 18	28 46	21 34	29 9	2 43	4 ♓ 56'31"
16 SU	1:37:59	17 39	23 19	27 34	22 22	10 24	28 48	21 35	29 9	2 43	4 ♓ 56'31"
17 MO	1:41:56	23 4	24 56	28 33	22 56	10 29	28 49	21 35	29 9	2 43	4 ♓ 56'31"
18 TU	1:45:52	28 20	26 32	29 33	23 30	10 35	28 51	21 36	29 10	2 44	4 ♓ 56'31"
19 WE	1:49:49	3 ♌ 26	28 9	0 ♈ 32	24 3	10 40	28 53	21 37	29 10	2 44	4 ♓ 56'31"
20 TH	1:53:45	8 22	29 45	1 32	24 37	10 46	28 55	21 37	29 11	2 44	4 ♓ 56'31"
21 FR	1:57:42	13 9	1 ♎ 22	2 31	25 11	10 51	28 57	21 38	29 11	2 45	4 ♓ 56'30"
22 SA	2: 1:38	17 46	2 58	3 31	25 44	10 57	28 59	21 39	29 11	2 45	4 ♓ 56'30"
23 SU	2: 5:35	22 15	4 35	4 31	26 18	11 2	29 1	21 39	29 12	2 45	4 ♓ 56'30"
24 MO	2: 9:32	26 35	6 11	5 30	26 51	11 8	29 3	21 40	29 12	2 45	4 ♓ 56'30"
25 TU	2:13:28	0 ♍ 47	7 48	6 30	27 24	11 13	29 5	21 41	29 12	2 46	4 ♓ 56'30"
26 WE	2:17:25	4 51	9 24	7 30	27 58	11 19	29 6	21 41	29 13	2 46	4 ♓ 56'30"
27 TH	2:21:21	8 48	11 0	8 30	28 31	11 24	29 8	21 42	29 13	2 46	4 ♓ 56'30"
28 FR	2:25:18	12 38	12 36	9 30	29 4	11 30	29 10	21 43	29 13	2 47	4 ♓ 56'30"
29 SA	2:29:14	16 22	14 13	10 30	29 37	11 35	29 12	21 43	29 14	2 47	4 ♓ 56'29"
30 SU	2:33:11	19 59	15 49	11 30	0 ♉ 10	11 41	29 14	21 44	29 14	2 47	4 ♓ 56'29"
31 MO	2:37: 7	23 31	17 25	12 30	0 43	11 46	29 16	21 45	29 15	2 47	4 ♓ 56'29"

INGRESSES :

1 ♀ → ♍ 13:53
3 ☿ → ♉ 6:27
8 ☿ → ♊ 1:18
12 ☿ → ♋ 22: 1
18 ☿ → ♌ 7:47
⊕ → ♈ 11: 4
20 ♀ → ♎ 3:37
24 ☿ → ♍ 19:28
29 ♂ → ♉ 16:39

ASPECTS (HELIOCENTRIC +MOON(TYCHONIC)) :

1 ☿ ☌ ♅ 20:29
☽ □ ♆ 21:35
2 ☽ □ ♀ 0:23
☿ ☌ ☊ 4:58
☽ □ ♃ 14:47
3 ☿ □ ♄ 0: 7
4 ☽ ☌ ♇ 6:29
5 ☽ □ ♂ 5:18
☽ □ ♅ 14: 4
6 ☽ ☌ ♄ 1:52
☿ ☌ P 21:47
7 ♀ ☍ ♃ 12:26
☿ □ ♆ 21:53
8 ☽ ☌ ♆ 5:51
☽ □ ☿ 12:26
9 ☽ ☌ ♃ 0:16
☽ ☍ ♀ 4:47
☿ □ ♃ 14:45
10 ☿ □ ♀ 7:23
☽ □ ♇ 16:57
11 ☿ □ ⊕ 19:44
12 ☽ ☌ ♂ 1: 2
☽ ☌ ♅ 3:39
☽ □ ♄ 17: 9
13 ☿ ☍ ♇ 9: 1
14 ♂ ☌ ♅ 13:31
15 ☽ □ ♆ 4:34
16 ☽ □ ♃ 3: 8
☿ □ ♅ 17:21
☿ □ ♂ 23:19
17 ☿ N ☊ 2: 8
☽ □ ♀ 9:48
18 ☽ ☍ ♇ 0:15
☿ ☍ ♄ 2:28
19 ☽ □ ♅ 14: 9
☽ □ ♂ 19:55
20 ♂ ☌ ☊ 2:28
☽ ☍ ♄ 4:36
21 ⊕ □ ♇ 5:20
☽ ☌ ☿ 13:13
♀ □ ♇ 20:36
22 ☽ ☍ ♆ 14:42
♀ ☍ ⊕ 21:16
23 ☽ ☍ ♃ 12:39
24 ☿ ☍ ♆ 14:53
25 ☽ □ ♇ 3:27
☽ ☌ ♀ 13:54
26 ☽ ☍ ♅ 12:19
☽ ☍ ♂ 23:58
27 ☽ □ ♄ 1: 2
☿ ☍ ♃ 16:36
28 ♂ □ ♄ 4:46
29 ☽ □ ♆ 3:46
30 ☽ □ ♃ 0:37
☽ □ ☿ 19:19
31 ☽ ☌ ♇ 12: 4

July 26 AD 30: Dinah the Samaritan Woman, pp. 486–91, vol. I

September 10 AD 30: Gideon's Victory, pp. 51–52, vol. II

August 27 AD 32: Salathiel, p. 491, vol. II

7—**Heliocentric Venus opposite Jupiter:**

February 13 AD 30: Teaching in Capernaum, p. 403, vol. I

October 9 AD 30: In Ophra, pp. 74–75, vol. II

June 4 AD 31: Visiting the Childhood Home of Elizabeth, p. 394, vol. II

September 21 AD 32: Arrival in the Tent City of Mensor, pp. 502–04, vol. II

May 16 AD 33: After the Ascension, p. 412, vol. III

9—**Full Moon Virgo:**

September 11 AD 29: Teaching the Pharisees, p. 318, vol. I

August 31 AD 30: Meeting in Bezek, pp. 38–39, vol. II

September 8 AD 32: Jesus Reaches the Tent City, pp. 495–96, vol. II

12—**Mars square Neptune:**

December 8 AD 29: In Dibon, p. 375, vol. I

February 18 AD 31: In Sarepta, p. 313, vol. II

January 24 AD 33: The Prison House, pp. 525–26, vol II

Mercury opposite Jupiter:

August 2 AD 29: Whispers and Murmurs, p. 303, vol. I

October 3 AD 30: Talking with Mara the Suphanite, pp. 70–71, vol. II

13—**Heliocentric Mercury opposite Pluto:**

September 23 AD 29: Baptism in the Jordan, pp. 342–45, vol. I

December 20 AD 29: Invited to the Wedding at Cana, p. 379, vol. I

March 18 AD 30: At an Inn, p. 416, vol. I

September 10 AD 30: Celebration of Gideon, pp. 51–52, vol. II

December 7 AD 30: First Walking on Water, pp. 172–73, vol. II

March 5 AD 31: Alms for the Poor, p. 319, vol. II

June 1 AD 31: In Misael, p. 393, vol. II

May 18 AD 32: Healing of Ten Lepers, pp. 468–70, vol. II

August 15 AD 32: Teaching about Marriage, p. 487, vol. II

May 6 AD 33: Increase of the Community, pp. 407–9, vol. III

14—**Heliocentric Mars conjunct Uranus:**

August 25 AD 29: Jesus Doesn't Yet Heal the Possessed, pp. 307–08, vol. I

18—**Sun enters Libra:**

September 22 AD 29: Jesus Prepares for His Baptism, pp. 328–42, vol. I

September 22 AD 30: On Baal and Elijah, p. 59, vol. II

September 22 AD 32: Christ Visits Theokeno with Mensor, p. 504, vol. II

Heliocentric Mercury opposite Saturn:

August 13 AD 29: Future Disciples, p. 305, vol. I

November 10 AD 29: Temptation in the Wilderness, pp. 365–69, vol. I

February 7 AD 30: Raising of the Daughter of Jairus the Essene, p. 402, vol. I

August 4 AD 30: Jesus visits the Nobleman's Son, pp. 2–4, vol. II

November 1 AD 30: Teaching at Saul's Well, p. 97, vol. II

January 30 AD 31: Sailing to Tarichea, pp. 301–03, vol. II

April 29 AD 31: At the Home of Jonas's Father, pp. 360–62, vol. II

July 16 AD 32: "Our friend Lazarus has fallen asleep," p. 475, vol. II

October 13 AD 32: Journey to Egypt, p. 517, vol. II

January 10 AD 33: At the Synagogue in Bethain, p. 520, vol. II

April 9 AD 33: The Risen One, pp. 396–98, vol. III

19—**Venus enters Libra:**

August 15 AD 29: Teaching in Two Synagogues, p. 306, vol. I

September 28 AD 30: Healing the Sick, p. 65, vol. II

August 29 AD 32: On Marriage, pp. 491–92, vol. II

Sun square Pluto:
August 29 AD 29: Jesus Among the Publicans, p. 310, vol. I
March 1 AD 30: Elijah and Mt. Carmel, p. 411, vol. I
September 1 AD 30: Teaching the Boys and Girls, pp. 39–40, vol. II
March 3 AD 31: The Lord's Prayer, p. 318, vol. II
September 4 AD 32: Healing in Kedar, p. 494, vol. II
March 7 AD 33: Future Tasks, pp. 2–4, vol. III

20—**Venus square Pluto:**
July 27 AD 29: The Sanhedrin Send Spies, p. 303, vol. I
April 15 AD 30: In Concealment, p. 424, vol. I
September 11 AD 30: Gideon's Victory and the Prodigal Son, p. 52, vol. II
February 5 AD 31: Revealing the Character of the Twelve, p. 306, vol. II
August 15 AD 32: Teaching on Marriage, p. 487, vol. II
January 18 AD 33: Three "Silent Disciples," p. 523, vol. II

21—**Mars enters Gemini:**
April 29 AD 29: Jesus and Mary move from Nazareth to Capernaum, p. 292, vol. I
April 9 AD 31: Returning to Leccum, p. 345, vol. II
March 17 AD 33: Meeting of Scribes and Pharisees, p. 5, vol. III

Tychonic Sun square Pluto:
August 31 AD 29: The Synagogue and the Madhouse, p. 306, vol. I
February 27 AD 30: Leaving Unnoticed, p. 409, vol. I
September 3 AD 30: Crossing the Jordan, pp. 41–42, vol. II
March 1 AD 31: Teaching and Consoling, p. 318, vol. II

Heliocentric Venus square Pluto:
June 27 AD 29: "Three months ago...," p. 298, vol. I
October 19 AD 29: Consoling the sick, p. 363, vol. I
September 21 AD 30: In Gadara, pp. 58–59, vol. II
January 13 AD 31: Joseph of Arimathea, pp. 210–11, vol. II
May 5 AD 31: Teaching at Barnabas's House, pp. 370–71, vol. II
July 29 AD 32: Healing a Blind Shepherd, p. 480, vol. II
March 11 AD 33: Approaching Suffering, p. 4, vol. III

22—**Superior Conjunction Sun and Venus:**
October 22 AD 30: Parable of the Talents, pp. 82–83, vol. II
June 1 AD 32: Lazarus Falls Ill, p. 472, vol. II

24—**Heliocentric Mercury opposite Neptune:**
July 5 AD 29: Six New Disciples, p. 300, vol. I
October 29 AD 29: Baptizing through Saturnin, pp. 352–53, vol. I
December 28 AD 29: Changing of Water into Wine, pp. 386–89, vol. I
June 22 AD 30: Teaching in the Fruit Plantation, p. 460, vol. I
September 18 AD 30: Isaac and Elijah, pp. 56–57, vol. II
December 15 AD 30: Close of the Feast of Lights, pp. 181–82, vol. II
March 13 AD 31: At Matthew's Custom House, p. 322, vol. II
June 9 AD 31: Healing on the Sabbath, pp. 396–97, vol. II
August 23 AD 32: On Marriage, p. 490, vol. II
February 15 AD 33: Exhortations of the Virgin, p. 530, vol. II
May 14 AD 33: Ascension Day, pp. 410–12, vol. III

25—**New Moon Libra:**
September 26 AD 29: A Warm Welcome in Ensemes, p. 346, vol. I
October 15 AD 30: Outer Form and Inner Spirit, p. 78, vol. II
September 23 AD 32: Visiting Theokeno with Mensor, p. 504, vol. II

26—**Mercury enters Libra:**
October 6 AD 29: Jesus Visits an Inn, p. 356, vol. I

27—Heliocentric Mercury opposite Jupiter:
  September 29 AD 30: Mara the Suphanite, pp. 65–67, vol. II
  September 13 AD 32: Shepherds Create a Throne, pp. 497–98, vol. II

27—Heliocentric Mercury opposite Jupiter:
  July 12 AD 29: In Sarepta, pp. 301–02, vol. I
  October 10 AD 29: Feast of Tabernacles, pp. 359–60, vol. I
  January 8 AD 30: Conversation with the Virgin Mary, p. 393, vol. I
  April 8 AD 30: Death of Silent Mary and Nighttime Conversation with Nicodemus, p. 424, vol. I
  July 8 AD 30: The Unjust Steward, pp. 469–70, vol. I
  October 6 AD 30: Healing of Manahem, pp. 72–73, vol. II
  January 5 AD 31: Reproached by Pharisees, pp. 203–04, vol. II
  April 6 AD 31: The Shekel in the Fish, pp. 342–43, vol. II
  July 6 AD 31: The Way of David, p. 465, vol. II
  October 2 AD 32: In the House of Azarias, pp. 510–11, vol. II
  December 31 AD 32: Egyptian City, p. 518, vol. II
  April 1 AD 33: Magdalene's Last Anointing, pp. 19–22, vol. III

28—Heliocentric Mars square Saturn:
  November 8 AD 29: Temptation in the Wilderness, pp. 365–71, vol. I
  October 15 AD 30: Outer Form and Inner Spirit, p. 78, vol. II

29—Heliocentric Mars enters Taurus:
  December 21 AD 30: Pharisees Treat Him with Respect, p. 185, vol. II

NOVEMBER 2022

STARGAZING PREVIEW

November begins with some awesome evening stargazing, starting with the First Quarter Moon on the 1st, shining from the center of the Goat. What from the past must be preserved so that it might serve the future?—this is the question posed by the Capricorn Moon. By sunset, the Moon will be nearly conjunct Saturn as they summit the zodiacal circle; you'll find Saturn slightly above and to the left of the Moon. The peak of the Southern Taurid Meteor Showers occurs on the 5th, but the Moon, closing in on Full, will make viewing suboptimal. If you'd like to give it a try just the same, Taurus (the apparent origin of the showers) will move between the eastern and western horizons between 1800 and 0600.

November's Full Moon, at 21° Aries, happens on Tuesday the 8th, and will create a Total Lunar Eclipse over the Pacific; the greatest eclipse will be experienced very near the Hawaiian Islands. *E ho'i koke ke kukui*! By the 11th, the Moon will have just passed Mars as they appear in the east at 1800.

Mars's ascent over the eastern horizon on the 11th (1800) will be followed quickly by that of the Moon, now in Gemini. November's Last Quarter Moon, in the last degree of Cancer, occurs early on the 16th. When it rises shortly before midnight, it will do so alongside *Regulus*, the star of the Lion's heart; Saturn will have just set, and Jupiter, Mars, and the Moon will form a bridge across the starry vault. On the following day, the Sun moves into Scorpio.

The Leonid Meteor Showers peak on the evening of the 17th; as the name implies, they appear to radiate from the Lion, though they can be seen anywhere in the night sky. Leo will be due north after dusk, as will the waning Moon, simultaneously diminishing our chances of seeing the shooting stars while showing us where to look! For those who wish to meditate on the year's second conjunction of Mercury and Venus, be aware that it happens on the Monday the 21st, at 11° Scorpio.

The Moon joins the Sun (6° Scorpio) on Wednesday the 23rd, with Mercury and Venus now aligned with the heart of Scorpio. When the Scorpion sets at 1600, we'll be left with a gloriously dark sky for stargazing! Mars, still above Orion, rises at 1700, joining Saturn (due southwest) and Jupiter (due south).

November closes with a second First Quarter Moon, this one at 13° Aquarius. You'll find it between Saturn and Jupiter as the evening begins, shining from the Sun's zodiacal degree at the births of both Rudolf Steiner and Valentin Tomberg. Hallelujah!

November Commentaries

2—Heliocentric Venus opposite Uranus:
September 28 AD 29: Teaching the Workers in the Fields, pp. 347–49, vol. I
December 26 AD 30: Magdalene's Second Conversion, pp. 189–90, vol. II

3—Venus opposite Node:
October 18 AD 29: Visiting the Essene Jairus, p. 362–63, vol. I
November 10 AD 30: Valley of the Doves, pp. 136–39, vol. II
September 11 AD 32: Jesus Encounters a Pastoral Tribe, p. 497, vol. II

5—Sun opposite Node:
December 2 AD 29: Preparing the Pool for Baptism, p. 373, vol. I
November 14 AD 30: Day after the Raising of the Youth of Nain, pp. 143–44, vol. II
October 8 AD 32: Reprimanding Mozian's Idolatry, p. 515, vol. II

Venus opposite Uranus:
March 12 AD 30: Last Visit with Eliud, p. 414, vol. I
January 12 AD 31: Revelation of the Death of John the Baptist, pp. 209–10, vol. II

6—Mercury opposite Node:
November 20 AD 29: Temptation in the Wilderness, pp. 365–69, vol. I
November 2 AD 30: Cousin Jesse, pp. 97–99, vol. II
September 24 AD 32: Visiting Theokeno with Mensor, p. 504, vol. II

7—Venus square Saturn:
July 30 AD 29: Jacob's Well, p. 303, vol. I
April 14 AD 30: In Concealment, p. 424, vol. I
September 26 AD 30: Feast of Atonement, pp. 62–63, vol. II
February 12 AD 31: Healing of the Syrophoenician Woman, pp. 308–09, vol. II
September 17 AD 32: Journey to the Tent City, pp. 499–500, vol. II
May 30 AD 33: The Church at the Pool of Bethesda, pp. 414–16, vol. III

Heliocentric Venus square Saturn:
June 25 AD 29: "Three months ago...," p. 298, vol. I
October 19 AD 29: The Essene Jairus, pp. 362–63, vol. I
February 10 AD 30: In Capernaum, pp. 402–03, vol. I
September 28 AD 30: Healing the Sick, p. 65, vol. II
January 22 AD 31: In Thirza, pp. 219–20, vol. II
May 16 AD 31: Feast of Weeks, pp. 380–81, vol. II
August 18 AD 32: Shepherd Settlement in Kedar, p. 487, vol. II
April 5 AD 33: Resurrection, pp. 387–393, vol. III

8—Mars enters Taurus:
February 21 AD 31: Great Uncle of Bartholomew, p. 314, vol. II
January 22 AD 33: Healing of a Sick Girl, p. 525, vol. II

Full Moon Libra:
October 11 AD 29: The Sick Brought on Litters, p. 360, vol. I
September 30 AD 30: Feast of Tabernacles, pp. 67–68, vol. II
October 7 AD 32: Crossing the River Tigris, pp. 514–15, vol. II

Superior Conjunction Sun and Mercury:
July 2 AD 29: Meeting Six of the Baptist's Disciples, p. 300, vol. I
October 30 AD 29: Temptation in the Wilderness, pp. 365–69 vol. I

SIDEREAL GEOCENTRIC LONGITUDES : NOVEMBER 2022 Gregorian at 0 hours UT

DAY	☉	☽	☊	☿	♀	♂	♃	♄	⛢	♆	♇
1 TU	13 ♎ 29	9 ♑ 52	18 ♈ 21	8 ♎ 36	15 ♎ 49	0 ♊ 32R	4 ♓ 38R	23 ♑ 36	22 ♈ 12R	27 ♒ 53R	1 ♑ 11
2 WE	14 29	24 0	18 21R	10 16	17 4	0 31	4 34	23 37	22 9	27 52	1 12
3 TH	15 29	7 ♒ 59	18 21	11 55	18 19	0 28	4 29	23 38	22 7	27 51	1 12
4 FR	16 29	21 49	18 21	13 34	19 34	0 25	4 25	23 39	22 4	27 50	1 13
5 SA	17 29	5 ♓ 27	18 21	15 12	20 50	0 20	4 21	23 40	22 2	27 49	1 14
6 SU	18 29	18 53	18 21D	16 50	22 5	0 15	4 18	23 42	21 59	27 49	1 15
7 MO	19 30	2 ♈ 6	18 21	18 27	23 20	0 9	4 14	23 43	21 57	27 48	1 16
8 TU	20 30	15 5	18 21	20 4	24 35	0 2	4 11	23 45	21 54	27 47	1 16
9 WE	21 30	27 49	18 21R	21 41	25 50	29 ♉ 54	4 7	23 46	21 52	27 46	1 17
10 TH	22 30	10 ♉ 20	18 20	23 17	27 6	29 46	4 5	23 48	21 49	27 45	1 18
11 FR	23 30	22 39	18 20	24 53	28 21	29 36	4 2	23 50	21 47	27 44	1 19
12 SA	24 31	4 ♊ 46	18 19	26 29	29 36	29 26	3 59	23 52	21 44	27 44	1 20
13 SU	25 31	16 44	18 18	28 4	0 ♏ 51	29 15	3 57	23 54	21 42	27 43	1 21
14 MO	26 31	28 38	18 17	29 39	2 7	29 2	3 55	23 56	21 39	27 42	1 22
15 TU	27 32	10 ♋ 29	18 16	1 ♏ 14	3 22	28 49	3 53	23 58	21 37	27 42	1 23
16 WE	28 32	22 23	18 16	2 48	4 37	28 36	3 51	24 1	21 35	27 41	1 24
17 TH	29 33	4 ♌ 25	18 16D	4 22	5 53	28 21	3 49	24 3	21 32	27 40	1 25
18 FR	0 ♏ 33	16 38	18 16	5 56	7 8	28 6	3 48	24 6	21 30	27 40	1 26
19 SA	1 34	29 8	18 17	7 30	8 23	27 50	3 47	24 8	21 27	27 39	1 28
20 SU	2 34	11 ♍ 58	18 18	9 3	9 38	27 33	3 46	24 11	21 25	27 39	1 29
21 MO	3 35	25 11	18 20	10 37	10 54	27 15	3 45	24 14	21 22	27 38	1 30
22 TU	4 35	8 ♎ 49	18 21	12 10	12 9	26 57	3 45	24 17	21 20	27 38	1 31
23 WE	5 36	22 50	18 21R	13 43	13 24	26 38	3 44	24 20	21 17	27 38	1 32
24 TH	6 37	7 ♏ 13	18 20	15 15	14 40	26 19	3 44D	24 23	21 15	27 37	1 34
25 FR	7 37	21 50	18 18	16 48	15 55	25 59	3 44	24 26	21 13	27 37	1 35
26 SA	8 38	6 ♐ 37	18 16	18 20	17 10	25 38	3 45	24 30	21 10	27 37	1 36
27 SU	9 39	21 25	18 13	19 52	18 25	25 17	3 45	24 33	21 8	27 36	1 38
28 MO	10 40	6 ♑ 6	18 10	21 24	19 41	24 55	3 46	24 37	21 6	27 36	1 39
29 TU	11 40	20 35	18 8	22 56	20 56	24 34	3 47	24 40	21 3	27 36	1 40
30 WE	12 41	4 ♒ 48	18 7	24 28	22 11	24 11	3 48	24 44	21 1	27 36	1 42

INGRESSES :

2	☽ → ♒	10:16
4	☽ → ♓	14:22
6	☽ → ♈	20:10
8	♂ → ♉	7:16
9	☽ → ♉	4: 8
11	☽ → ♊	14:31
12	♀ → ♏	7:35
14	☽ → ♋	2:46
	☿ → ♏	5:15
16	☽ → ♌	15:13
17	☉ → ♏	10:50
19	☽ → ♍	1:38
21	☽ → ♎	8:33
23	☽ → ♏	12: 1
25	☽ → ♐	13:16
27	☽ → ♑	14: 0
29	☽ → ♒	15:50

ASPECTS & ECLIPSES :

1	☉ □ ☽	6:36
	☽ S ☊	14:23
	☽ ☌ ♄	23:21
3	♀ ☍ ☊	0:35
4	☽ ☌ ♆	10:33
	☽ ☌ ♃	22: 4
5	☉ ☍ ☊	20:28
	♀ ☍ ⛢	22:20
6	☿ ☍ ☊	22:23
7	♀ □ ♄	7:32
8	☽ ☌ ☊	6: 6
	☽ ☍ ☿	10:42
	☽ •–• T	10:57
	☉ ☍ ☽	11: 1
	☽ ☌ ⛢	12:45
	☉ S☌ ☿	16:41
	☽ ☍ ♀	19:49
9	☿ ☍ ⛢	2:38
	☉ ☍ ⛢	8:24
10	☿ □ ♄	7:50
11	☉ □ ♄	8: 3
	☽ ☌ ♂	13:33
14	☽ ☍ ♇	5:33
	☽ ☌ A	6:48
15	☽ N ☊	15:41
16	☽ ☍ ♄	3:16
	☉ □ ☽	13:25
18	☽ ☍ ♆	21:11
19	☽ ☍ ♃	8:45
	♂ □ ♆	15: 8
21	☿ ☌ ♀	22:53
22	☽ ☌ ☋	16:22
	☽ ☍ ⛢	21:23
23	☉ ☌ ☽	22:56
24	☽ ☌ ♀	13:24
	☽ ☌ ☿	14:47
25	☽ ☍ ♂	6:34
26	☽ ☌ P	1:46
27	☽ ☌ ♇	16:41
28	☽ S ☊	19:54
29	☽ ☌ ♄	6:52
	☿ ☍ ♂	20:29
30	☉ □ ☽	14:35

SIDEREAL HELIOCENTRIC LONGITUDES : NOVEMBER 2022 Gregorian at 0 hours UT

DAY	Sid. Time	☿	♀	⊕	♂	♃	♄	⛢	♆	♇	Vernal Point
1 TU	2:41: 4	26 ♍ 58	19 ♎ 1	13 ♈ 30	1 ♉ 16	11 ♓ 52	29 ♑ 18	21 ♈ 45	29 ♒ 15	2 ♑ 48	4 ♓ 56'29"
2 WE	2:45: 1	0 ♎ 20	20 37	14 30	1 49	11 57	29 20	21 46	29 15	2 48	4 ♓ 56'29"
3 TH	2:48:57	3 37	22 13	15 30	2 22	12 3	29 21	21 47	29 16	2 48	4 ♓ 56'29"
4 FR	2:52:54	6 50	23 49	16 30	2 54	12 8	29 23	21 47	29 16	2 49	4 ♓ 56'29"
5 SA	2:56:50	10 0	25 25	17 30	3 27	12 14	29 25	21 48	29 16	2 49	4 ♓ 56'28"
6 SU	3: 0:47	13 6	27 0	18 30	4 0	12 19	29 27	21 49	29 17	2 49	4 ♓ 56'28"
7 MO	3: 4:43	16 9	28 36	19 30	4 32	12 25	29 29	21 49	29 17	2 49	4 ♓ 56'28"
8 TU	3: 8:40	19 9	0 ♏ 12	20 30	5 5	12 30	29 31	21 50	29 17	2 50	4 ♓ 56'28"
9 WE	3:12:36	22 6	1 48	21 30	5 37	12 35	29 33	21 51	29 18	2 50	4 ♓ 56'28"
10 TH	3:16:33	25 1	3 23	22 31	6 10	12 41	29 35	21 51	29 18	2 50	4 ♓ 56'28"
11 FR	3:20:30	27 54	4 59	23 31	6 42	12 46	29 37	21 52	29 19	2 51	4 ♓ 56'28"
12 SA	3:24:26	0 ♏ 45	6 34	24 31	7 14	12 52	29 38	21 53	29 19	2 51	4 ♓ 56'27"
13 SU	3:28:23	3 35	8 10	25 32	7 47	12 57	29 40	21 53	29 19	2 51	4 ♓ 56'27"
14 MO	3:32:19	6 23	9 45	26 32	8 19	13 3	29 42	21 54	29 20	2 51	4 ♓ 56'27"
15 TU	3:36:16	9 10	11 21	27 32	8 51	13 8	29 44	21 55	29 20	2 52	4 ♓ 56'27"
16 WE	3:40:12	11 56	12 56	28 33	9 23	13 14	29 46	21 55	29 20	2 52	4 ♓ 56'27"
17 TH	3:44: 9	14 42	14 32	29 33	9 55	13 19	29 48	21 56	29 21	2 52	4 ♓ 56'27"
18 FR	3:48: 5	17 27	16 7	0 ♉ 34	10 27	13 25	29 50	21 57	29 21	2 53	4 ♓ 56'27"
19 SA	3:52: 2	20 11	17 42	1 34	10 59	13 30	29 52	21 57	29 21	2 53	4 ♓ 56'26"
20 SU	3:55:59	22 56	19 18	2 35	11 31	13 36	29 53	21 58	29 22	2 53	4 ♓ 56'26"
21 MO	3:59:55	25 41	20 53	3 35	12 3	13 41	29 55	21 59	29 22	2 53	4 ♓ 56'26"
22 TU	4: 3:52	28 26	22 28	4 36	12 34	13 47	29 57	21 59	29 23	2 54	4 ♓ 56'26"
23 WE	4: 7:48	1 ♐ 12	24 3	5 37	13 6	13 52	29 59	22 0	29 23	2 54	4 ♓ 56'26"
24 TH	4:11:45	3 58	25 38	6 37	13 38	13 58	0 ♒ 1	22 1	29 23	2 54	4 ♓ 56'26"
25 FR	4:15:41	6 45	27 14	7 38	14 9	14 3	0 3	22 1	29 24	2 55	4 ♓ 56'26"
26 SA	4:19:38	9 34	28 49	8 39	14 41	14 9	0 5	22 2	29 24	2 55	4 ♓ 56'26"
27 SU	4:23:34	12 24	0 ♐ 24	9 39	15 12	14 14	0 7	22 3	29 24	2 55	4 ♓ 56'25"
28 MO	4:27:31	15 15	1 59	10 40	15 44	14 20	0 9	22 3	29 25	2 55	4 ♓ 56'25"
29 TU	4:31:28	18 8	3 34	11 41	16 15	14 25	0 10	22 4	29 25	2 56	4 ♓ 56'25"
30 WE	4:35:24	21 4	5 9	12 42	16 47	14 31	0 12	22 5	29 25	2 56	4 ♓ 56'25"

INGRESSES :

1	☿ → ♎	21:39
7	♀ → ♏	21: 1
11	☿ → ♏	17:39
17	⊕ → ♉	10:36
22	☿ → ♐	13:37
23	♄ → ♒	10:48
26	♀ → ♐	18: 0

ASPECTS (HELIOCENTRIC +MOON(TYCHONIC)) :

1	☽ □ ♀	17:30
	☽ □ ⛢	20:12
2	☽ ☌ ♄	9: 8
	☽ □ ♂	13:55
	♀ ☍ ⛢	17:25
	☿ □ ♇	18: 1
4	☽ ☌ ♆	13: 4
5	☽ ☌ ♃	12: 8
7	☽ □ ♇	1:20
	♀ □ ♄	13:31
8	☽ ☍ ☿	9:54
	☽ ☌ ⛢	12:40
	☿ ☍ ⊕	16:41
	☿ ☍ ⛢	21:55
9	☽ □ ♄	3:17
	⊕ ☌ ⛢	8: 8
	☽ ☍ ♀	8:40
	☿ ☌ ☋	11:50
	☽ ☌ ♂	15:34
11	☽ □ ♆	13: 9
	☿ □ ♄	14:31
12	♀ ☍ ♂	15:13
	☽ □ ♃	16:20
14	☽ ☍ ♇	8:33
	☿ ☍ ♂	20:37
15	☽ □ ⛢	23: 3
16	☽ ☍ ♄	14:47
	☿ ☌ ♀	20:32
17	⊕ □ ♄	5:58
	☽ □ ♂	11:21
	☽ □ ♀	22:50
18	☽ □ ☿	2: 0
19	☽ ☍ ♆	0:25
	☿ ☌ A	22:24
20	☽ ☍ ♃	3: 1
21	☽ □ ♇	13:39
	♀ ☌ ☋	14:18
22	☿ □ ♆	8:13
	☽ ☍ ⛢	22:34
23	☽ □ ♄	12: 1
24	☽ ☍ ♂	10:58
25	☽ ☌ ♀	9:49
	☽ □ ♆	12:17
26	☽ ☌ ☿	5:54
	♀ □ ♆	8:57
	☽ □ ♃	12:17
27	☿ □ ♃	16: 2
	☽ ☌ ♇	18:47
29	☽ □ ⛢	2:28
	☽ ☌ ♄	16:10
30	☽ □ ♂	21:25

March 4 AD 30: Protecting the Ships at Sea, p. 412, vol. I

October 9 AD 30: Messenger of Cyrinus, pp. 74, vol. II

February 15 AD 31: A Banquet with the Syrophoenician Woman, pp. 310–12, vol. II

June 1 AD 31: In Misael, p. 393, vol. II

September 1 AD 32: Raising of Nazor, pp. 492–94, vol. II

January 10 AD 33: Healing in Bethain, p. 520, vol. II

April 30 AD 33: Days with the Risen One, p. 408, vol. III

Heliocentric Mercury opposite Uranus:

June 4 AD 29: Sabbath in Hebron, p. 296, vol. I

August 31 AD 29: In Chisloth-Tabor, pp. 310–11, vol. I

November 28 AD 29: 38th Day of Temptation, p. 369, vol. I

May 23 AD 30: Imprisonment of John the Baptist, pp. 459–60, vol. I

August 19 AD 30: Healing Peter's Mother-in-law, pp. 21–23, vol. II

November 16 AD 30: 11/16/30—On the Way to Mt. Tabor, pp. 147–48 vol. II

February 12 AD 31: Healing of the Syrophoenician Woman, pp. 308–09, vol. II

May 11 AD 31: On King Djemschid, pp. 374–76, vol. II

July 25 AD 32: Day Before the Raising of Lazarus, pp. 477–78, vol. II

April 16 AD 33: Appearance of the Risen One to the Five Hundred, pp. 404–05, vol. III

9—Mercury opposite Uranus:

February 12 AD 30: In His Mother's House, p. 403, vol. I

February 24 AD 30: Teaching in the School, p. 408, vol. I

February 7 AD 31: Conferring Power on the Disciples, pp. 306–07, vol. II

January 27 AD 33: Silencing a Devil, p. 526, vol. II

Sun opposite Uranus:

January 26 AD 30: Where the "Good Samaritan" Occurred, pp. 398–99, vol. I

January 31 AD 31: The Bread of Life, p. 303, vol. II

February 9 AD 33: Lazarus Opens the Gate, p. 530, vol. II

11—Sun square Saturn:

September 5 AD 29: Jesus in a Shepherd Village near Nazareth, pp. 312–13, vol. I

February 24 AD 30: Teaching in the School, p. 408, vol. I

September 19 AD 30: The Pillar of Elijah, pp. 57–58, vol. II

March 11 AD 31: Curing on the Way to Chorazin, p. 322, vol. II

April 8 AD 33: Days with the Risen One, pp. 396–97, vol. III

12—Venus enters Scorpio:

September 10 AD 29: The Goddess Astarte, pp. 317–18, vol. I

October 22 AD 30: Parable of the Talents, pp. 82–83, vol. II

September 22 AD 32: Christ Visits Theokeno with Mensor, p. 504, vol. II

Heliocentric Venus opposite Mars:

October 11 AD 29: The Sick Brought on Litters, p. 360, vol. I

September 18 AD 30: Isaac and Elijah, pp. 56–57, vol. II

July 15 AD 32: Death of Lazarus, p. 475, vol. II

14—Mercury enters Scorpio:

October 25 AD 29: Temptation in the Wilderness, pp. 365–69 vol. I

October 17 AD 30: Consider the Lilies, pp. 79–80, vol. II

October 3 AD 32: The Wonderful Cure of Two Sick Women, pp. 511–12, vol. II

Heliocentric Mercury opposite Mars:

December 7 AD 29: In Dibon, p. 375, vol. I

March 14 AD 30: At Lazarus's Estate, p. 414, vol. I

June 19 AD 30: Celebrating the New Moon Festival, p. 460, vol. I

September 29 AD 30: Mara the Suphanite, pp. 65–67, vol. II

January 14 AD 31: Grave of Zechariah, p. 211, vol. II

April 30 AD 31: Mercuria, pp. 362–64, vol. II

September 5 AD 32: Salathiel and Nazor, p. 494, vol. II

April 5 AD 33: Resurrection, pp. 387–393, vol. III

16—**Heliocentric Mercury opposite Venus:**

June 2 AD 29: Alone in Prayer, p. 296, vol. I

October 6 AD 29: Jesus Visits an Inn, p. 356, vol. I

March 12 AD 30: Last Visit with Eliud, p. 414, vol. I

August 7 AD 30: A Home for Lepers, pp. 7–8, vol. II

December 15 AD 30: Close of the Feast of Lights, pp. 181–82, vol. II

May 22 AD 31: Clothes and Provisions, pp. 385–86, vol. II

July 31 AD 32: Beginning the Journey to the Three Kings, pp. 480–81, vol. II

May 5 AD 33: With the Risen One, p. 408, vol. III

17—**Sun enters Scorpio:**

October 22 AD 29: Preparing to Enter the Wilderness, p. 364, vol. I

October 22 AD 30: Parable of the Talents, pp. 82–83, vol. II

Tychonic Sun square Saturn:

August 29 AD 29: Jesus Among the Publicans, p. 310, vol. I

March 3 AD 30: The Doctors of the Synagogue, p. 412, vol. I

September 13 AD 30: Harsh Interpretation of the Law, p. 53, vol. II

March 18 AD 31: Peter Receives the Keys of the Kingdom of Heaven, pp. 325–27, vol. II

October 10 AD 32: The Birthplace of Abraham, pp. 515–16, vol. II

April 15 AD 33: Communion of Fish, pp. 401–04, vol. III

19—**Mars square Neptune:**

December 8 AD 29: In Dibon, p. 375, vol. I

February 18 AD 31: In Sarepta, p. 313, vol. II

January 24 AD 33: The Prison House, pp. 525–26, vol II

21—**Mercury conjunct Venus:**

May 4 AD 29: Jesus and Mary move from Nazareth to Capernaum, p. 292, vol. I

January 26 AD 30: Where the "Good Samaritan" Occurred, pp. 398–99, vol. I

August 31 AD 30: Meeting in Bezek, pp. 38–39, vol. II

October 1 AD 30: Confession of an Adulteress, pp. 68–70, vol. II

December 4 AD 30: Authority to the Twelve, pp. 168–69, vol. II

July 13 AD 32: Teaching on the Good Samaritan and the Lost Coin, p. 475, vol. II

April 6 AD 33: On the Road to Emmaus, pp. 393–96, vol. III

23—**New Moon Scorpio:**

October 25 AD 29: Temptation in the Wilderness, pp. 365–69 vol. I

November 14 AD 30: Day after the Raising of the Youth of Nain, pp. 143–44, vol. II

26—**Heliocentric Venus square Neptune:**

July 25 AD 29: From Mt. Carmel to Mt. Tabor, pp. 302–03, vol. I

November 16 AD 29: Temptation in the Wilderness, pp. 365–69 vol. I

March 8 AD 30: Festival of Purim, p. 414, vol. I

June 30 AD 30: In Simeon's House, p. 464, vol. I

October 20 AD 30: Outside Michmethath, p. 82, vol. II

February 10 AD 31: On Fasting, p. 307, vol. II

August 26 AD 32: In Sichar

April 9 AD 33: With the Risen One, p. 397, vol. III

29—**Mercury opposite Mars:**

July 6 AD 30: The Evil of Obstinancy, pp. 467–69, vol. I

September 21 AD 32: Arrival in the Tent City of Mensor, pp. 502–04, vol. II

DECEMBER 2022

STARGAZING PREVIEW

The month begins with a bit of tension in the skies, as Venus and Mars stand at opposition. Though it won't be possible to see Venus (as she's still clothed in sunlight), Mars will rise shortly after sunset. Five of the seven classical planets—Sun, Moon, Mercury, Venus, and Mars—are now in fixed signs of the zodiac (Taurus, Leo, Scorpio, and Aquarius). Associated with this "cross" in space is the mantra: *To will, to dare, to be silent, to know.*

The Full Moon on Thursday the 8th will shine from 21° Taurus, just a degree from the celestial longitude of *Rigel* (the left foot of Orion): the Sun's position at the Ascension. By daybreak, the Moon's voyage above Mars announces the opposition between the Sun and Mars, an aspect in the natal chart of Beethoven. *Freude!*

The evening of Wednesday the 13th is the peak of the Geminids! Follow the zodiacal arc from Saturn, to Jupiter, and through Mars to find Gemini, which will be rising just after sunset. You'll have a better chance of seeing the shooting stars before Taurus is overhead (due south) at 2200, for this is when the Leo Moon will rise. Then, on the 16th, the Moon squares the Sun (29° Scorpio): the year's last Last Quarter Moon! The Sun crosses the cusp into Sagittarius on the following day.

We'll have fewer than eight hours of daylight on the 21st as the Sun reaches its lowest point on its yearly voyage around the Earth: the winter solstice. This will also be an evening of shooting stars, as today marks the peak of the Ursids, the last meteor showers of the calendar year. Appearing to radiate from Ursa Minor, this is generally thought of as a minor meteor shower, but with the cooperation of the phase of the Moon (almost New), it could be a wonderful night for viewing! Because Polaris is part of the Little Dipper, all you'll need to know is to look straight up! *Buona fortuna a tutti!*

The final New Moon (7° Sagittarius) of the year recalls the Sun's degree at the First Temptation, during which Jesus was offered limitless power if he would only bow to the prince of this world. We know how that worked out! December closes with a First Quarter Moon on the 30th, at 13° Pisces: its degree as Jesus stilled the Sea of Galilee. As the storm was swamping the boat, the disciples were afraid, saying, "Master, Master, we are perishing." Jesus awoke and rebuked the wind and the raging waves (they ceased), then said to the disciples, "Where is your faith?"

May we approach the New Year with faithfulness and love.

DECEMBER COMMENTARIES

1—**Venus opposite Mars:**
August 8 AD 30: Different Ways of Curing the Sick, p. 8, vol. II
September 11 AD 32: Jesus Encounters a Pastoral Tribe, p. 497, vol. II

3—**Mercury enters Sagittarius:**
November 13 AD 29: Temptation in the Wilderness, pp. 365–71, vol. I
December 28 AD 29: Changing of Water into Wine, pp. 386–89, vol I
November 6 AD 30: Healing of Achias' Son, pp. 104–05

Heliocentric Mercury conjunct Pluto:
August 14 AD 29: In Mahara's House, pp. 305–06, vol. I
November 10 AD 29: Temptation in the Wilderness, pp. 365–71, vol. I
February 6 AD 30: The Hospitable and Inhospitable, pp. 401–02, vol. I
May 5 AD 30: Many Baptisms, p. 459, vol. I
August 1 AD 30: The Samaritans, pp. 496–97, vol. I
October 28 AD 30: Healing of Issachar of Dothan, pp. 90–92, vol. II
January 25 AD 31: Assembly of Pharisees, p. 223, vol. II
October 3 AD 32: The Wonderful Cure of Two Sick Women, pp. 511–12, vol. II
March 28 AD 33: The Two Gardens, pp. 15–16, vol. III

4—**Venus square Neptune:**
September 3 AD 29: Healing a Woman of Edema, pp. 311–12, vol. I

May 25 AD 30: Meeting Bartholomew, pp. 459–60, vol. I

October 17 AD 30: Consider the Lilies, pp. 79–80, vol. II

March 15 AD 31: Feeding of the 4000, pp. 323–24, vol. II

September 21 AD 32: Jesus Meet with Mensor, pp. 502–04, vol. II

6—Venus enters Sagittarius:

October 6 AD 29: Jesus Visits an Inn, p. 356, vol. I

November 15 AD 30: Healing the Sick in Megiddo, pp. 144–47, vol. II

Heliocentric Venus square Jupiter:

April 22 AD 29: John in the Wilderness, p. 292, vol. I

August 18 AD 29: The Synagogue and the Madhouse, p. 306, vol. I

December 16 AD 29: On the Way to the Wedding, pp. 377–78, vol. I

August 11 AD 30: Marriage and Divorce, pp. 9–11, vol. II

December 8 AD 30: Healing in Bethsaida, pp. 173–75, vol. II

April 6 AD 31: The Shekel in the Mouth of a Fish, pp. 342–43, vol. II

July 24 AD 32: Rebuke of Mary Salome, p. 477, vol. II

March 17 AD 33: Meeting of Scribes and Pharisees, p. 5, vol. III

8—Full Moon Scorpio:

November 10 AD 29: Temptation in the Wilderness, pp. 365–69, vol. I

October 30 AD 30: Meeting with Elderly Relatives, pp. 94–95, vol. II

Sun opposite Mars:

July 22 AD 30: Praying Alone on the Mount of Olives, pp. 482–83, vol. I

October 1 AD 32: A Hut of Earth and Moss, p. 510, vol. II

9—Venus square Jupiter:

October 3 AD 29: Healing Reuben's Grandchildren, pp. 353–54, vol. I

July 28 AD 30: Celebrating the Sabbath, p. 492, vol. I

December 11 AD 30: A Blind Man by the Well, p. 177, vol. II

June 16 AD 31: Scarlet Fever, pp. 400–01, vol. II

August 19 AD 32: Eliud's Wife Confesses, pp. 487–88, vol. II

12—Heliocentric Mercury conjunct Saturn:

June 26 AD 29: "Three months ago…," p. 298, vol. I

December 20 AD 29: Invited to the Wedding at Cana, p. 379, vol. I

March 19 AD 30: Jesus and Lazarus in Jerusalem, p. 416, vol. I

September 12 AD 30: The Fishing Lake, pp. 52–53, vol. II

December 9 AD 30: Magdalene's Relapse, pp. 175–76, vol. II

March 8 AD 31: Teaching in Argob, p. 321, vol. II

June 4 AD 31: Elizabeth's Childhood Home, p. 394, vol. II

August 20 AD 32: Washing of Eliud's Feet, p. 488, vol. II

May 13 AD 33: The Night Before Ascension, p. 410, vol. III

14—Sun square Neptune:

October 14 AD 29: Mother Mary and the Holy Women, p. 360, vol. I

April 16 AD 30: In Concealment, p. 424, vol. I

October 16 AD 30: Feast of the New Moon, pp. 78–79, vol. II

April 19 AD 31: Recovery of the Head of the Baptist, pp. 348–49, vol. II

April 23 AD 33: Days with the Risen One, p. 408, vol. III

16—Tychonic Sun square Neptune:

October 16 AD 29: John's Baptism Soon to Cease, p. 362, vol. I

April 14 AD 30: In Concealment, p. 424, vol. I

October 18 AD 30: The Family of Obed, pp. 80–81, vol. II

April 17 AD 31: Visiting the Sanatorium, pp. 347–48, vol. II

April 21 AD 33: Days with the Risen One, p. 408, vol. III

17—Sun enters Sagittarius:

SIDEREAL GEOCENTRIC LONGITUDES : DECEMBER 2022 Gregorian at 0 hours UT

DAY	☉	☽	☊	☿	♀	♂	♃	♄	♅	♆	♇
1 TH	13 ♏ 42	18 ♒ 43	18 ♈ 6	26 ♏ 0	23 ♏ 27	23 ♉ 49R	3 ♓ 49	24 ♑ 48	20 ♈ 59R	27 ♒ 36R	1 ♑ 43
2 FR	14 43	2 ♓ 20	18 7	27 31	24 42	23 26	3 51	24 51	20 57	27 36	1 45
3 SA	15 43	15 39	18 9	29 2	25 57	23 3	3 53	24 55	20 55	27 36	1 46
4 SU	16 44	28 42	18 11	0 ♐ 33	27 13	22 40	3 55	24 59	20 52	27 36	1 48
5 MO	17 45	11 ♈ 32	18 12	2 3	28 28	22 17	3 57	25 3	20 50	27 36D	1 49
6 TU	18 46	24 9	18 12R	3 34	29 43	21 54	3 59	25 8	20 48	27 36	1 51
7 WE	19 47	6 ♉ 36	18 10	5 3	0 ♐ 58	21 31	4 2	25 12	20 46	27 36	1 52
8 TH	20 48	18 53	18 7	6 33	2 14	21 8	4 5	25 16	20 44	27 36	1 54
9 FR	21 49	1 ♊ 1	18 2	8 2	3 29	20 45	4 8	25 20	20 42	27 36	1 55
10 SA	22 50	13 3	17 55	9 30	4 44	20 22	4 11	25 25	20 40	27 36	1 57
11 SU	23 51	24 59	17 48	10 57	5 59	19 59	4 14	25 30	20 38	27 36	1 58
12 MO	24 52	6 ♋ 51	17 41	12 24	7 15	19 37	4 18	25 34	20 36	27 37	2 0
13 TU	25 52	18 42	17 35	13 49	8 30	19 15	4 22	25 39	20 34	27 37	2 2
14 WE	26 53	0 ♌ 36	17 30	15 13	9 45	18 53	4 26	25 44	20 32	27 37	2 3
15 TH	27 54	12 35	17 27	16 36	11 1	18 32	4 30	25 49	20 30	27 38	2 5
16 FR	28 56	24 44	17 25	17 57	12 16	18 11	4 34	25 53	20 29	27 38	2 7
17 SA	29 57	7 ♍ 8	17 25D	19 16	13 31	17 50	4 39	25 58	20 27	27 38	2 8
18 SU	0 ♐ 58	19 52	17 27	20 33	14 46	17 30	4 43	26 4	20 25	27 39	2 10
19 MO	1 59	3 ♎ 0	17 28	21 47	16 2	17 11	4 48	26 9	20 23	27 39	2 12
20 TU	3 0	16 35	17 29R	22 57	17 17	16 52	4 53	26 14	20 22	27 40	2 14
21 WE	4 1	0 ♏ 38	17 28	24 4	18 32	16 34	4 58	26 19	20 20	27 40	2 15
22 TH	5 2	15 9	17 25	25 7	19 47	16 16	5 4	26 25	20 19	27 41	2 17
23 FR	6 3	0 ♐ 2	17 20	26 4	21 3	15 59	5 10	26 30	20 17	27 42	2 19
24 SA	7 4	15 10	17 13	26 56	22 18	15 43	5 15	26 35	20 16	27 42	2 21
25 SU	8 5	0 ♑ 23	17 5	27 41	23 33	15 27	5 21	26 41	20 14	27 43	2 23
26 MO	9 7	15 29	16 56	28 18	24 48	15 12	5 27	26 47	20 13	27 44	2 24
27 TU	10 8	0 ♒ 21	16 49	28 47	26 3	14 58	5 34	26 52	20 11	27 45	2 26
28 WE	11 9	14 49	16 44	29 7	27 19	14 45	5 40	26 58	20 10	27 45	2 28
29 TH	12 10	28 53	16 41	29 17	28 34	14 33	5 47	27 4	20 9	27 46	2 30
30 FR	13 11	12 ♓ 30	16 40	29 16R	29 49	14 21	5 54	27 10	20 7	27 47	2 32
31 SA	14 12	25 43	16 40D	29 3	1 ♑ 4	14 10	6 1	27 16	20 6	27 48	2 34

INGRESSES :

- 1 ☽ → ♓ 19:51
- 3 ☿ → ♐ 15:18
- 4 ☽ → ♈ 2:24
- 6 ♀ → ♐ 5:22
- ☽ → ♉ 11:14
- 8 ☽ → ♊ 21:58
- 11 ☽ → ♋ 10: 8
- 13 ☽ → ♌ 22:48
- 16 ☽ → ♍ 10:16
- 17 ☉ → ♐ 1:21
- 18 ☽ → ♎ 18:36
- 20 ☽ → ♏ 22:55
- 22 ☽ → ♐ 23:56
- 24 ☽ → ♑ 23:23
- 26 ☽ → ♒ 23:26
- 29 ☽ → ♓ 1:56
- 30 ♀ → ♑ 3:30
- 31 ☽ → ♈ 7:54

ASPECTS & ECLIPSES :

- 1 ♀ ☍ ♂ 5:27
- ☽ ☌ ♆ 15:35
- 2 ☿ □ ♆ 1:13
- ☽ ☌ ♃ 2:43
- 4 ♀ □ ♆ 7:18
- 5 ☽ ☌ ☊ 12:37
- ☽ ☌ ♅ 17:36
- 6 ☿ □ ♃ 7: 4
- 8 ☉ ☍ ☽ 4: 7
- ☽ ☌ ♂ 4:17
- ☉ ☍ ♂ 5:40
- 9 ☽ ☍ ♀ 5:27
- ♀ □ ♃ 12:53
- ☽ ☍ ☿ 15:54
- 11 ☽ ☍ ♇ 14: 9
- 12 ☽ ☌ A 0:31
- ☽ N ☊ 21:44
- 13 ☽ ☍ ♄ 14: 7
- 14 ☉ □ ♆ 17:18
- 16 ☽ ☍ ♆ 5:40
- ☉ □ ☽ 8:55
- ☽ ☍ ♃ 19:11
- 20 ☽ ☌ ☋ 1:33
- ☽ ☍ ♅ 6:31
- 22 ☉ □ ♃ 0:49
- ☽ ☍ ♂ 1:47
- 23 ☉ ☌ ☽ 10:15
- 24 ☽ ☌ P 8:31
- ☽ ☌ ♀ 12:14
- ☽ ☌ ☿ 19:31
- 25 ☽ ☌ ♇ 3: 9
- 26 ☽ S ☊ 2:17
- ☽ ☌ ♄ 18:18
- 28 ☽ ☌ ♆ 22: 4
- 29 ☽ ☌ ♃ 12:10
- ☿ ☌ ♀ 13:56
- 30 ☉ □ ☽ 1:19

SIDEREAL HELIOCENTRIC LONGITUDES : DECEMBER 2022 Gregorian at 0 hours UT

DAY	Sid. Time	☿	♀	⊕	♂	♃	♄	♅	♆	♇	Vernal Point
1 TH	4:39:21	24 ♐ 1	6 ♐ 44	13 ♉ 42	17 ♉ 18	14 ♓ 36	0 ♒ 14	22 ♈ 5	29 ♒ 26	2 ♑ 56	4 ♓ 56'25"
2 FR	4:43:17	27 2	8 19	14 43	17 49	14 42	0 16	22 6	29 26	2 57	4 ♓ 56'25"
3 SA	4:47:14	0 ♑ 4	9 54	15 44	18 20	14 47	0 18	22 7	29 27	2 57	4 ♓ 56'25"
4 SU	4:51:10	3 10	11 29	16 45	18 51	14 53	0 20	22 7	29 27	2 57	4 ♓ 56'24"
5 MO	4:55: 7	6 20	13 4	17 46	19 22	14 58	0 22	22 8	29 27	2 57	4 ♓ 56'24"
6 TU	4:59: 3	9 33	14 39	18 47	19 53	15 4	0 24	22 9	29 28	2 58	4 ♓ 56'24"
7 WE	5: 3: 0	12 50	16 14	19 47	20 24	15 9	0 26	22 9	29 28	2 58	4 ♓ 56'24"
8 TH	5: 6:57	16 11	17 48	20 48	20 55	15 15	0 27	22 10	29 28	2 58	4 ♓ 56'24"
9 FR	5:10:53	19 36	19 23	21 49	21 26	15 20	0 29	22 11	29 29	2 59	4 ♓ 56'24"
10 SA	5:14:50	23 7	20 58	22 50	21 57	15 26	0 31	22 11	29 29	2 59	4 ♓ 56'24"
11 SU	5:18:46	26 42	22 33	23 51	22 28	15 31	0 33	22 12	29 29	2 59	4 ♓ 56'23"
12 MO	5:22:43	0 ♒ 24	24 8	24 52	22 58	15 37	0 35	22 13	29 30	3 0	4 ♓ 56'23"
13 TU	5:26:39	4 11	25 43	25 53	23 29	15 42	0 37	22 13	29 30	3 0	4 ♓ 56'23"
14 WE	5:30:36	8 4	27 18	26 54	23 59	15 48	0 39	22 14	29 31	3 0	4 ♓ 56'23"
15 TH	5:34:32	12 4	28 53	27 55	24 30	15 53	0 41	22 15	29 31	3 0	4 ♓ 56'23"
16 FR	5:38:29	16 12	0 ♑ 27	28 56	25 1	15 59	0 43	22 15	29 31	3 1	4 ♓ 56'23"
17 SA	5:42:26	20 26	2 2	29 57	25 31	16 4	0 44	22 16	29 32	3 1	4 ♓ 56'23"
18 SU	5:46:22	24 49	3 37	0 ♊ 58	26 1	16 10	0 46	22 17	29 32	3 1	4 ♓ 56'22"
19 MO	5:50:19	29 19	5 12	1 59	26 32	16 15	0 48	22 17	29 32	3 2	4 ♓ 56'22"
20 TU	5:54:15	3 ♓ 58	6 47	3 0	27 2	16 21	0 50	22 18	29 33	3 2	4 ♓ 56'22"
21 WE	5:58:12	8 46	8 22	4 1	27 32	16 26	0 52	22 19	29 33	3 2	4 ♓ 56'22"
22 TH	6: 2: 8	13 43	9 57	5 3	28 2	16 32	0 54	22 19	29 33	3 2	4 ♓ 56'22"
23 FR	6: 6: 5	18 49	11 31	6 4	28 33	16 37	0 56	22 20	29 34	3 3	4 ♓ 56'22"
24 SA	6:10: 1	24 3	13 6	7 5	29 3	16 43	0 58	22 21	29 34	3 3	4 ♓ 56'22"
25 SU	6:13:58	29 27	14 41	8 6	29 33	16 48	1 0	22 22	29 35	3 3	4 ♓ 56'22"
26 MO	6:17:55	5 ♈ 0	16 16	9 7	0 ♊ 3	16 54	1 1	22 22	29 35	3 4	4 ♓ 56'21"
27 TU	6:21:51	10 42	17 51	10 8	0 33	16 59	1 3	22 23	29 35	3 4	4 ♓ 56'21"
28 WE	6:25:48	16 31	19 26	11 9	1 3	17 5	1 5	22 24	29 36	3 4	4 ♓ 56'21"
29 TH	6:29:44	22 28	21 1	12 11	1 32	17 10	1 7	22 24	29 36	3 4	4 ♓ 56'21"
30 FR	6:33:41	28 32	22 36	13 12	2 2	17 16	1 9	22 25	29 36	3 5	4 ♓ 56'21"
31 SA	6:37:37	4 ♉ 42	24 11	14 13	2 32	17 21	1 11	22 26	29 37	3 5	4 ♓ 56'21"

INGRESSES :

- 2 ☿ → ♑ 23:25
- 11 ☿ → ♒ 21:28
- 15 ♀ → ♑ 17: 3
- 17 ⊕ → ♊ 1: 8
- 19 ☿ → ♓ 3:32
- 25 ☿ → ♈ 2:22
- ♂ → ♊ 21:50
- 30 ☿ → ♉ 5:43

ASPECTS (HELIOCENTRIC +MOON(TYCHONIC)) :

- 1 ☽ ☌ ♆ 18:51
- 2 ☽ □ ♀ 12:10
- ☽ ☌ ♃ 22:25
- 3 ☿ ☌ ♇ 22:18
- 4 ☽ □ ♇ 7:54
- ☽ □ ☿ 11: 0
- 5 ☽ ☌ ♅ 20: 9
- 6 ♀ □ ♃ 6:47
- ☽ □ ♄ 12: 1
- 8 ☽ ☌ ♂ 4:11
- ⊕ ☌ ♂ 5:29
- ☽ □ ♆ 20:56
- 9 ☿ □ ♅ 17:44
- 10 ☿ S ☊ 2:55
- ☽ □ ♃ 4:49
- ☽ ☍ ♀ 18:21
- 11 ☽ ☍ ♇ 16:10
- 12 ☿ ☌ ♄ 1:14
- ♃ S ☊ 6: 3
- 13 ☽ □ ♅ 7: 7
- 14 ☽ ☍ ♄ 0: 6
- ☽ ☍ ☿ 22:29
- 16 ☽ □ ♂ 0:34
- ☽ ☍ ♆ 9:20
- ⊕ □ ♆ 13:56
- 17 ♀ ☌ ♇ 14:53
- ☽ ☍ ♃ 17: 3
- 18 ☿ □ ♂ 7:20
- 19 ☽ □ ♇ 0: 3
- ☿ ☌ ♆ 1: 8
- ☽ □ ♀ 4:29
- ☿ □ ⊕ 17:42
- 20 ☽ ☍ ♅ 9:52
- 21 ☽ □ ♄ 0:23
- 22 ☿ ☌ ♃ 13:36
- ☽ ☍ ♂ 21:31
- ☽ □ ♆ 23:14
- 24 ☽ □ ♃ 2:27
- ☽ □ ☿ 21:42
- 25 ♂ □ ♆ 1:31
- ☽ ☌ ♇ 4:13
- ☿ □ ♇ 15:39
- 26 ☽ ☌ ♀ 1:23
- ♀ ☌ A 8:27
- ☽ □ ♅ 11: 3
- 27 ☽ ☌ ♄ 1:10
- 28 ☿ □ ♀ 16: 2
- ☿ ☌ ♅ 23:42
- 29 ☽ ☌ ♆ 1:15
- ☿ ☌ ☊ 4:15
- ☽ □ ♂ 4:48
- ♀ □ ♅ 21:13
- 30 ☽ ☌ ♃ 8:37
- ☿ □ ♄ 10:16
- 31 ☽ □ ♇ 13:39

November 20 AD 29: Temptation in the Wilderness, pp. 365–69, vol. I

November 21 AD 30: The Stilling of the Storm, pp. 155–57, vol. II

Heliocentric Venus conjunct Pluto:

August 23 AD 29: In the Valley of Zebulon, p. 307, vol. I

April 5 AD 30: Passover Meal in Lazarus's Castle, pp. 422–23, vol. I

November 17 AD 30: Healing of Lepers, pp. 148–50, vol. II

June 30 AD 31: Interpreting Numbers and Judges, p. 409, vol. II

September 23 AD 32: Visiting Theokeno with Mensor, p. 504, vol. II

May 7 AD 33: Days with the Risen One, p. 408, vol. III

19—Heliocentric Mercury conjunct Neptune:

June 1 AD 29: Elizabeth's Cave, p. 296, vol. I

August 28 AD 29: Circumcision and Baptism, pp. 309–10, vol. I

November 24 AD 29: Temptation in the Wilderness, pp. 365–71, vol. I

February 20 AD 30: In Jezreel, p. 406, vol. I

May 19 AD 30: Imprisonment of John the Baptist, p. 459, vol. I

August 16 AD 30: In Peter's House, pp. 17–19, vol. II

November 12 AD 30: On the Way to Nain, p. 141, vol. II

May 7 AD 31: The Prophet Malachi, pp. 372–73, vol. II

July 20 AD 32: News of Lazarus, p. 477, vol. II

April 11 AD 33: The Risen Christ Appears to Thomas, pp. 398–400, vol. III

22—Sun square Jupiter:

May 26 AD 29: Jesus Begins His Travels, p. 292, vol. I

November 18 AD 29: Temptation in the Wilderness, pp. 365–69, vol. I

July 4 AD 30: In Adama, pp. 465–66, vol. I

December 24 AD 30: A Cool Reception, p. 187, vol. II

September 13 AD 32: Shepherds Create a Throne, pp. 497–98, vol. II

Heliocentric Mercury conjunct Jupiter:

December 5 AD 29: Silencing the Possessed, pp. 374–75, vol. I

March 5 AD 30: Helping in the Storm, pp. 412–13, vol. I

August 30 AD 30: Paralyzed Arms and Hands, p. 38, vol. II

November 28 AD 30: Sermon on the Mount, pp. 162–63, vol. II

February 25 AD 31: In Nobah, p. 316, vol. II

May 25 AD 31: Speaking Against Idolatry, pp. 387–88, vol. II

August 13 AD 32: The Bedridden Married Couple, p. 486, vol. II

February 8 AD 33: Three Secret Disciples, p. 530, vol. II

May 8 AD 33: The Risen One, p. 408, vol. III

23—New Moon Sagittarius:

November 24 AD 29: Temptation in the Wilderness, pp. 365–71, vol. I

December 13 AD 30: Healing of Ctesiphon, pp. 179–80, vol. II

25—Heliocentric Mars enters Gemini:

April 2 AD 29: Death of Joseph, p. 292, vol. I

February 18 AD 31: In Sarepta, p. 313, vol. II

January 5 AD 33: A Small Desert Town, p. 520, vol. II

Heliocentric Mars square Neptune:

February 10 AD 30: In Capernaum, p. 402–03, vol. I

December 15 AD 30: Close of the Feast of Lights, pp. 181–82, vol. II

28—Heliocentric Mercury conjunct Uranus:

July 7 AD 29: Early ministry, p. 300, vol. I

October 3 AD 29: The Inn of Reuben, p. 353, vol. I

December 30 AD 29: End of the Wedding at Cana, p. 390, vol. I

March 29 AD 30: Preparing for Passover, pp. 419–20, vol. I

June 25 AD 30: Saturnin Baptizes, pp. 460–62, vol. I

September 21 AD 30: Gadara, pp. 58–59, vol. II

December 18 AD 30: Kiriathaim, p. 183, vol. II

March 17 AD 31: Cornerstone, p. 325, vol. II

June 13 AD 31: Return to Capernaum, pp. 398–99, vol. II

May 31 AD 32: Zacchaeus's House, p. 472, vol. II

August 27 AD 32: Salathiel, p. 491

February 19 AD 33: Preparing for Death, p. 1, vol. III

May 19 AD 33: The Risen One, pp. 411–12 vol. III

29—Mercury conjunct Venus:

May 4 AD 29: Jesus and Mary move from Nazareth to Capernaum, p. 292, vol. I

January 26 AD 30: Where the "Good Samaritan" Occurred, pp. 398–99, vol. I

August 31 AD 30: Meeting in Bezek, pp. 38–39, vol. II

October 1 AD 30: Confession of an Adulteress, pp. 68–70, vol. II

December 4 AD 30: Authority to the Twelve, pp. 168–69, vol. II

July 13 AD 32: Teaching on the Good Samaritan and the Lost Coin, p. 475, vol. II

April 6 AD 33: On the Road to Emmaus, pp. 393–96, vol. III

Heliocentric Venus square Uranus:

August 2 AD 29: Whispers and Murmurs, p. 303, vol. I

November 24 AD 29: Temptation in the Wilderness, pp. 365–71, vol. I

March 17 AD 30: The Samarian Orphan, p. 415, vol. I

July 9 AD 30: Inviting the People of Adama, p. 470, vol. I

October 29 AD 30: The Sacred Fountain, pp. 92–94, vol. II

February 20 AD 31: Spending the Night with Tax Collectors, pp. 313–14, vol. II

June 13 AD 31: Ships from Cyprus, pp. 398–99, vol. II

May 18 AD 32: Healing of Ten Lepers, pp. 468–70, vol. II

September 8 AD 32: Jesus Reaches the Tent City, pp. 495–96, vol. II

December 31 AD 32: The First Egyptian City, p. 518, vol. II

April 22 AD 33: Days with the Risen One, p. 408, vol. III

30—Venus enters Capricorn:

November 3 AD 29: Temptation in the Wilderness, pp. 365–71, vol. I

December 9 AD 30: December 9 AD 30: Magdalene's Relapse, pp. 175–76, vol. II

"The stars are the expression of love in the cosmic ether.... To see a star means to feel a caress that has been prompted by love.... To gaze at the stars is to become aware of the love proceeding from divine spiritual beings.... The stars are signs and tokens of the presence of gods in the universe."
—Rudolf Steiner (*Karmic Relationships,* vol. 7, June 8, 1924)

"We must see in the shining stars the outer signs of colonies of spirits in the cosmos. Wherever a star is seen in the heavens, there—in that direction—is a colony of spirits."
—Rudolf Steiner (*Karmic Relationships,* vol. 6, June 1, 1924)

"They looked up above all to what is represented by the zodiac. And they regarded what the human being bears within as the spirit in connection with the constellations, the glory of the fixed stars, the spiritual powers whom they knew to be there in the stars."
—Rudolf Steiner (*Karmic Relationships,* vol. 4, Sept. 12, 1924)

SOPHIA STAR CALENDAR 2022

Kathleen Baiocchi

This Calendar is dedicated to Holy Mary Sophia and Archangel Michael.
The Sophia Star Calendar 2022 highlights the beautiful Stars that shine directly overhead our Sun, for every day during 2022.
May the Sophia Star Calendar serve to awaken Humanity to the Love that holds All.

Contents:

Acknowledgements and Prayers	191
Introduction	192
Sophia Star Calendar 2022 Charts	193
Sophia Star Calendar 2022 Lists	205
Sophia Star Calendar 2022 Mega Star Index *for Mega Stars 1-200*	234
Sophia Star Calendar 2022 Index *for 700 stars*	237
Sophia Star Calendar 2022 Constellations Index *with Abbreviations*	241
References and Sources	243

Acknowledgements and Prayers

The Sophia Star Calendar stands on the research, love and sacrifices of those who have come before and of those who are here now.

First, deepest gratitude is offered to Dr. Robert Powell and his extraordinary research on the Megastars, the Meridians of the Stars and "Finding One's Birth Star". Robert's outstanding work inspired and planted the seeds for an overlighting star project that evolved into this calendar.

Second, I am profoundly grateful to Peter Treadgold and his remarkable Astrofire Database for over 4000 Stars. His tremendous research and compilations provided precise measurements for longitude and luminosity ratings of megastars.

Next, there is much thankfulness for Jon Fox and authors, Fred Rubenfeld and Michael Smulkis, for their book, *Starlight Elixirs and Cosmic Vibrational Healing* and for originating the Starlight Elixirs. The *Starlight* book first inspired me to pray to the Stars, starting about 30 years ago. Special appreciation is given to Stan Deland at Pegasus, for his kind support and selfless service for the Stars.

Heartfelt gratitude to all friends who have shared their love of the magnificent Stars, including our beloved Choreo/Eurythmy teacher, Audrey Wiebe, and all our dear friends who gather weekly to pray Eurythmy in the meadow, and especially, Kathleen Thompson and Leah Knudsen, for their beautiful hearts, support and encouragement to complete this project. Sincere appreciation is offered to Nick Fiorenza for his inspiring Sidereal Map of the Cosmos in JSW 2017. Gratitude is given for Doug Zimmerman who provided invaluable editorial and technical support at just the right time for the calendar. Finally, the Sophia Star Calendar has been made possible because of the infinite love, patience and perseverance of dear spiritual helpers. Thank You All!

Prayer to Holy Mary Sophia:
O Holy Mary-Sophia, Daughter of God,
Extend to us now Thy bounteous mercy,
Envelop us in Thy loving embrace,
That we may know Thy love and the love of Thy Son.
Vanquish every foe; subdue the evil serpent.
Protect us in Thy starry mantle
And keep us in Thy Immaculate Heart
Until that day comes
When a new Heaven and a new Earth
Shall rise together in glory.
Watch over Thy servants,
O Holy Mary-Sophia.
Amen.
Prayer given to Estelle Isaacson by Mary-Sophia on December 11, 2009.
Powell and Issacson, *The Mystery of Sophia*, p 100.

Prayer to Archangel Michael:
Oh Michael!
I entrust myself to your protection.
I unite myself with your guidance,
With all the strength of my heart.
That this day may become
The reflection of your
Destiny ordering will.
Verse attributed to Rudolf Steiner.

Valentine Tomberg writes about **Faithfulness to the Star**, MOT pp. 533-535.

"But those who follow the "star" must learn a lesson once and for all: not to consult Herod and the "chief priests and scribes of the people" at Jerusalem, but to follow the "star" that they have seen "in the East" and which "goes before them", without seeking for indications and confirmation on the part of Herod and his people. The gleam of the "star" and the effort to understand its message ought to suffice. Because Herod, representing the anti-revelatory force and principle, is also eternal. The time of Christmas is not that of the nativity of the Child alone; it is also the time of the massacre of the children of Bethlehem —the time where autonomous intelligence is driven to kill, i.e. to strangle and push back into the unconscious, all the tender flowers of spirituality which threaten the absolute autonomy arrogated to itself by intelligence.

May those who follow the "star" do so completely and without reserve! May they not seek—once having the "star" before their eyes — scientific confirmation, approval or sanction. . .or, what would be still worse, direction on the part of science! May they follow the "star" above them and nothing else'. Noblesse oblige".

Daily Prayer for Working with the Sophia Star Calendar
Dearest Holy Mary Sophia and Archangel Michael,
We pray for Clarity.

Cosmic Communion: Star Wisdom, Volume 4

May this calendar be a blessing and inspire us to know, love and serve You better.
May this calendar remind us to take responsibility for the beautiful, radiant Light that You always stream.
May this calendar and our efforts serve only the Highest Good.
Please help our hearts to be open and clear to receive and discern Your true inspirations most accurately.
Please help us to honor the holy Star Beings with our love, devotion and gratitude.
Please raise us up to do Christ's and Sophia's work in this world.
And if it is possible, may we become instruments of Love in this world and in the Cosmos.
Thank You All, dear Holy Angels and Saints, Holy Teachers and Masters, dear Spiritual Ancestors, Holy Bodhisattvas, Holy Rishis, beloved Spiritual Hierarchies, Holy Mary Sophia, Archangel Michael and Christ Jesus for Your profound Love and Sacrifice, for all gifts and blessings, for Your loving patience, guidance and support.
Michael-Sophia in Nomine Christi.

Introduction

The Sophia Star Calendar 2022 highlights the beautiful Stars that shine directly overhead our Sun, for every day during 2022.

This Sophia Star Calendar is an evolving spiritual project that was first inspired by Robert Powell's research on Overlighting Stars and Mega Stars, which I most gratefully learned about in the *Journal for Star Wisdom 2016*.

The purpose of the Calendar is to bring attention to the beautiful Stars on a daily basis. There is hope that the Calendar will provide a simple, clear and convenient reference to know the Stars who overlight our Sun on any given day. When we focus our gaze and attention on Stars directly overhead the Sun, this invites a more straightforward way to meet the holy Stars, especially the unnamed Mega Stars, during the daytime hours.

With sincere hearts and focused attention, it becomes easier to connect, to develop and deepen relationships, and to receive and feel the profound love and blessings of the overlighting Stars. It is also a great blessing to call the Star by name, who shines overhead our Divine Christ Sun on any given day. The Sophia Star Calendar makes this possible. And it is wonderful to share these blessings with others. Thank you, dearest Stars!

Part 1**: **Process for Choosing the Overlighting Stars of the sidereal Sun for any particular day, follows.

First, there was a "combing through" the Astrofire Database of approximately 4000 Stars, per zodiac sign, per degree, for well known and named Stars.

Second, there was a search for Stars whose sidereal longitudes were **within a *30 minute range prior to* and *30 minute range following*** the Sun's sidereal longitude as recorded at midnight UT, within the daily 2022 sidereal ephemeris. There was careful calculation in order to include all time zones for any particular day.

Next, the Stars' luminosity measurements (intrinsic brightness) were assessed for selecting the Stars to be included in the "Star Calendar List".

Then, the Holy Angels and the Holy Spiritual World were called upon, consulted with, and trusted for each Star to be chosen and named in the Calendar, to ensure that it was for the HIghest Good that each Star be named in the Calendar. The following questions and corresponding statements were posed to the Spiritual World to discern the most beneficent and luminous Stars who were interested to support our mission of Love.

"Is there genuine interest and willingness for this Star to be part of the Sophia Calendar project?"/ "This Star has genuine interest and willingness to be a part of the Sophia Calendar project."

"Does this Star support the spiritual mission of our Divine Christ Sun, Earth and Humanity at this time?"/ "This Star supports the spiritual mission of our Divine Christ Sun, the Earth and Humanity, at this time."

"Is it for the Highest Good that this Star be named and listed on the Sophia Star Calendar?"/" It is for the Highest Good that this Star be named and listed on the Sophia Star Calendar."

Thus, through spiritual discernment, Stars were chosen to be named on the "Calendar Chart" and "Calendar List".

Stars named on the "Calendar Chart" and "Calendar List" continue to always stream the most beautiful and luminous light, love and blessings through Christ Sun to Earth and Humanity for the Highest Good. Yet, it also appears for the Highest Good that some Stars were not included on the Calendar at this time.

All of the above spiritual imaginations and inspirations were tested and retested many times for accuracy, as best as the author was able, in order to avoid and be protected from "any fantasy or illusion" as we are warned of by Rudolf Steiner. All of the above spiritual imaginations and inspirations will continue to be tested and updated in the future.

Part 2**: **Process for Calculating the Overlighting Stars that are on the "*Calendar Chart*" and "*Calendar List*" follows.

An example for calculating the Overlighting Stars is given for Thursday, 2/24/22.

On 2/24/22, the Sun's sidereal geographic longitude is given as 10Aqr18, at midnight UT.

To find the 30 minute range prior to Sun's sidereal geographic longitude, one subtracts: Sun's sidereal geographic longitude is 10Aqr18 *minus* 30 minutes = 09Aqr48.

To find the 30 minute range following Sun's sidereal geographic longitude, one adds: Sun's sidereal geographic longitude is 10Aqr18 *plus* 30 minutes = 10Aqr48.

The **sidereal longitude range** for all Stars overlighting the Sun on 2/24/22 = **09Aqr48** through **10Aqr48.**

Three Stars were calculated to be within the **sidereal longitude range** for 2/24/22 and they were chosen to be Overlighting Stars on the "Calendar List" for 2/24/22:

9 Pegasi (10Aqr16) with luminosity/intrinsic brightness of 1221.
Deneb (10Aqr35) with luminosity/intrinsic brightness of almost 270,000.
Eta Phoenices (10Aqr36) with luminosity/intrinsic brightness of 85.

Deneb was selected to be the Overlighting Star on the "Calendar Chart" for 2/24/22 because it is the beloved Alpha Star of Cygnus the Swan and it is considered a *Super Mega Star*, above 100,000 luminosity.

Deneb has a very beautiful and loving relationship with Christ, Earth and Humanity. Robert Powell's truly remarkable research indicates that Deneb was in accord with and overlighted the Sun at the precise time when Christ performed the miracles of the "Feeding of the 5000" and the "Walking on the Water".

In conclusion, I am honored to offer this Sophia Star Calendar 2022 as a gift to the Sophia Foundation and, especially, to Robert and Lucky for dedicating their most beautiful and inspiring lives to serve Christ and Sophia, Earth and Humanity. They have brought so much Joy into this world through all of their magnificent research, teachings and writings. There are no words for the deep love and gratitude that is within my heart for each of them.

It is because of the mercy and grace of Christ and Sophia that this project has been completed.

SOPHIA STAR CALENDAR 2022 CHARTS

January 2022

Sun's *Sidereal Geocentric Longitude* is given at Midnight UT.
Star's *Sidereal Longitude* designates it as the Overlighting **Star** for the day.
Star's *Luminosity* indicates its intrinsic brightness as compared with **Sun's** *Luminosity*: **Sun** L=1.
Mega Stars are identified by an assigned numerical ranking according to their *Luminosity*, as recorded in AstroFire Database.
Mega Stars may or may not have proper names, but all are identified by assigned *Luminosity* numerical ranking.
This calendar identifies all **Stars** over 1000 *Luminosity* as **Mega Stars,** as recorded in AstroFire Database.
Please refer to "**Mega Star Index** for **Mega Stars 1 - 200**" for ranked *Luminosity* ratings.
Please refer to "**Sophia Star Calendar 2022 List**" for additional **Stars**, designated for overlighting our **Sun** per day.

Archai, the Spirits of Personality, dwell in the region of the Archer, ♐, Sagittarius / Sgr. (Dec 16 - Jan 15)   Virtue to develop is Self Discipline.
Archangels, the Spirits of Fire, dwell in the region of the Goat, ♑, Capricorn / Cap. (Jan 15 - Feb 13)   Virtue to develop is Courage.

Day of Resurrection Sunday	Day of Holy Trinity Monday	Day of Archangel Michael Tuesday	Day of Human Pastors Wednesday	Day of Holy Spirit Thursday	Day of Cavalry, Christ Crucified Friday	Day of Holy Virgin Saturday
						1 Mega 252. Phi Sagittarii. ☉ 15 ♐ 29 *Mary, Holy Mother of God*
2 Epsilon Scuti. ☉ 16 ♐ 30	3 Mega 14. Ainalrami. Nunki. ☉ 17 ♐ 31	4 Xi 1 Sagittarii. Ascella. ☉ 18 ♐ 32	5 Alphecca. ☉ 19 ♐ 34	6 Vega. Arkab. ☉ 20 ♐ 35 *Epiphany*	7 Albaldah. Rukbat. ☉ 21 ♐ 36	8 Althalimin. ☉ 22 ♐ 37
9 Mega 269. ☉ 23 ♐ 38	10 Sheliak. Upsilon Sagittarii. ☉ 24 ♐ 39	11 21 Aquilae. ☉ 25 ♐ 41	12 Sulaphat. ☉ 26 ♐ 42	13 Iota Sagittarii. ☉ 27 ♐ 43	14 Nu Aquilae. Peacock Star. ☉ 28 ♐ 44	15 Kappa Aquilae. Theta 1 Sagittarii. ☉ 29 ♐ 45
16 Terebellum. Al Thalimain. ☉ 00 ♑ 46	17 Iota Lyrae. ☉ 01 ♑ 47	18 Mega 84. Sigma Aquilae. ☉ 02 ♑ 48	19 Mega 462. ☉ 03 ♑ 49	20 Aladfar. ☉ 04 ♑ 50	21 Mega 97. Tarazed. ☉ 05 ♑ 51	22 Albireo. Altair. ☉ 06 ♑ 53
23 Mega 8. ☉ 07 ♑ 54 ——— 30 Alpha Tucanae. ☉ 15 ♑ 01	24 Giedi. Dabih. ☉ 08 ♑ 55 *Our Lady of Peace* ——— 31 70 Aquilae. ☉ 16 ♑ 01	25 9 Sagittae. Theta Aquilae. ☉ 09 ♑ 56	26 Mega 238. 10 Sagittae. ☉ 10 ♑ 57	27 Gamma Sagittae. ☉ 11 ♑ 58	28 Omega Capricorni. ☉ 12 ♑ 59	29. Mega 254. Tau Capricorni. ☉ 14 ♑ 00

Oh, Holy Mary Sophia, pray for us.

Cosmic Communion: Star Wisdom, Volume 4

February 2022

Sun's *Sidereal Geocentric Longitude* is given at Midnight UT.
Star's *Sidereal Longitude* designates it as the Overlighting **Star** for the day.
Star's *Luminosity* indicates its intrinsic brightness as compared with **Sun's** *Luminosity*: **Su**n L=1.
Mega Stars are identified by an assigned numerical ranking according to their *Luminosity*, as recorded in AstroFire Database.
Mega Stars may or may not have proper names, but all are identified by assigned *Luminosity* numerical ranking.
This calendar identifies all **Stars** over 1000 *Luminosity* as **Mega Stars,** as recorded in AstroFire Database.
Please refer to "**Mega Star Index** for **Mega Stars 1 - 200**" for ranked *Luminosity* ratings.
Please refer to "**Sophia Star Calendar 2022 List**" for additional **Stars,** designated for overlighting our **Sun** per day.

Archangels, the Spirits of Fire, dwell in the region of the Goat, ♑ *,* **Capricorn** */ Cap. (Jan 15 - Feb 13)*   *Virtue to develop is Courage.*

Angels, the Sons of Life, dwell in the region of the Waterman, ♒*,* **Aquarius** */ Aqr. (Feb 13 - Mar 15)*   *Virtue to develop is Discernment.*

Day of Resurrection Sunday	Day of Holy Trinity Monday	Day of Archangel Michael Tuesday	Day of Human Pastors Wednesday	Day of Holy Spirit Thursday	Day of Cavalry, Christ Crucified Friday	Day of Holy Virgin Saturday
		1 Mega 21. ☉ 17 ♑ 02	2 Mega 297. Armus. ☉ 18 ♑ 03	3 Mega 34. Epsilon Delphini. ☉ 19 ♑ 04	4 25 Cygni. ☉ 20 ♑ 05	5 Theta Delphini. Delta Cygni. ☉ 21 ♑ 06
6 Mega 561. ☉ 22 ♑ 07	7 Sualocin. ☉ 23 ♑ 08	8 Theta Piscis Austrini. ☉ 24 ♑ 08	9 35 Cygni. Castra. ☉ 25 ♑ 09	10 Mega 33. ☉ 26 ♑ 10	11 34 Cygni. Nashira. ☉ 27 ♑ 11 Our Lady of Lourdes	12 Sadalsuud. ☉ 28 ♑ 11
13 Mega 371. Deneb Algedi. ☉ 29 ♑ 12	14 Sadr. ☉ 00 ♒ 13	15 Mega 553. ☉ 01 ♒ 13	16 Beta Piscis Austrini. ☉ 02 ♒ 14	17 35 Aquarii. Gienah. ☉ 03 ♒ 14	18 Mega 509. ☉ 04 ♒ 15	19 32 Cygni. ☉ 05 ♒ 15
20 Epsilon Piscis Austrini. ☉ 06 ♒ 16	21 Enif. ☉ 07 ♒ 16	22 Sadalmelik. ☉ 08 ♒ 17	23 Fomalhaut. ☉ 09 ♒ 17	24 Deneb. ☉ 10 ♒ 18	25 Ruchba. ☉ 11 ♒ 18	26 Sadachbia. Upsilon Cygni. ☉ 12 ♒ 18
27 55 Cygni. ☉ 13 ♒ 19	28 Mega 218. Situla. ☉ 14 ♒ 19					

Oh, Holy Mary Sophia, pray for us.

Sophia Star Calendar 2022 Charts

March 2022

Sun's *Sidereal Geocentric Longitude* is given at Midnight UT.
Star's *Sidereal Longitude* designates it as the Overlighting **Star** for the day.
Star's *Luminosity* indicates its intrinsic brightness as compared with **Sun's** *Luminosity*: **Sun** L=1.
Mega Stars are identified by an assigned numerical ranking according to their *Luminosity*, as recorded in AstroFire Database.
Mega Stars may or may not have proper names, but all are identified by assigned *Luminosity* numerical ranking.
This calendar identifies all **Stars** over 1000 *Luminosity* as **Mega Stars**, as recorded in AstroFire Database.
Please refer to "**Mega Star Index** for **Mega Stars 1 - 200**" for ranked *Luminosity* ratings.
Please refer to "**Sophia Star Calendar 2022 List**" for additional **Stars**, designated for overlighting our **Sun** per day.

*Angels, the Sons of Life, dwell in the region of the Waterman, ≈, **Aquarius** / Aqr. (Feb13 - Mar 15)*   *Virtue to develop is Discernment.*
Humanity dwells in the region of the Fish, ♓, Pisces / Psc. (Mar 15 - April 15)   *Virtue to develop is Magnanimity.*

Day of Resurrection Sunday	Day of Holy Trinity Monday	Day of Archangel Michael Tuesday	Day of Human Pastors Wednesday	Day of Holy Spirit Thursday	Day of Cavalry, Christ Crucified Friday	Day of Holy Virgin Saturday
		1 Sigma Cygni. ☉ 15 ≈ 19	2 Mega 117. ☉ 16 ≈ 20	3 Mega 61. Lambda Aquarii ☉ 17 ≈ 20	4 59 Cygni. ☉ 18 ≈ 20	5 68 Cygni. ☉ 19 ≈ 20
6 Mega 308. Achernar. ☉ 20 ≈ 20	7 Homam. ☉ 21 ≈ 20	8 Situla. ☉ 22 ≈ 20	9 103 Aquarii. ☉ 23 ≈ 20	10 Beta Piscium. ☉ 24 ≈ 20	11 Mega 105. ☉ 25 ≈ 20	12 Gamma Piscium. ☉ 26 ≈ 20
13 57 Pegasi. ☉ 27 ≈ 20	14 Mega 142. Markab. ☉ 28 ≈ 20	15 Sadalbari. ☉ 29 ≈ 20	16 Theta Piscium. ☉ 00 ♓ 20	17 Matar. ☉ 01 ♓ 19	18 Pi 2 Cygni. ☉ 02 ♓ 19	19 Azelfafage. ☉ 03 ♓ 19
20 Scheat. ☉ 04 ♓ 18	21 77 Pegasi. ☉ 05 ♓ 18	22 Schemali. ☉ 06 ♓ 18	23 Upsilon Pegasi. ☉ 07 ♓ 17	24 Diphda. ☉ 08 ♓ 17	25 Mega 181. ☉ 09 ♓ 16 The Annunciation	26 Mega 181. ☉ 10 ♓ 16
27 Mega 60. ☉ 11 ♓ 15	28 Mega 141. ☉ 12 ♓ 14	29 Mega 315. Omega Andromedae. ☉ 13 ♓ 14	30 Algenib. ☉ 14 ♓ 13	31 Garnet Star. ☉ 15 ♓ 12		

Oh, Holy Mary Sophia, pray for us.

April 2022

Sun's *Sidereal Geocentric Longitude* is given at Midnight UT.
Star's *Sidereal Longitude* designates it as the Overlighting **Star** for the day.
Star's *Luminosity* indicates its intrinsic brightness as compared with **Sun's** *Luminosity*: **Sun** L=1.
Mega Stars are identified by an assigned numerical ranking according to their *Luminosity*, as recorded in AstroFire Database.
Mega Stars may or may not have proper names, but all are identified by assigned *Luminosity* numerical ranking.
This calendar identifies all **Stars** over 1000 *Luminosity* as **Mega Stars**, as recorded in AstroFire Database.
Please refer to "**Mega Star Index** for **Mega Stars 1 - 200**" for ranked *Luminosity* ratings.
Please refer to "**Sophia Star Calendar 2022 List**" for additional **Stars**, designated for overlighting our **Sun** per day.

Humanity dwells in the region of the Fish, ♓, Pisces / Psc. (Mar 15 - April 15)   *Virtue to develop is Magnanimity.*
Son of God dwells in the region of the Ram, ♈, Aries / Ari. (April 15 - May 15)   *Virtue to develop is Devotion.*

Day of Resurrection Sunday	Day of Holy Trinity Monday	Day of Archangel Michael Tuesday	Day of Human Pastors Wednesday	Day of Holy Spirit Thursday	Day of Cavalry, Christ Crucified Friday	Day of Holy Virgin Saturday
					1 42 Piscium. ☉ 16 ♓ 12	2 14 Cephei. ☉ 17 ♓ 11
3 Mega 329. Alderamin. ☉ 18 ♓ 10	4 Nu Cephei. Alpheratz. ☉ 19 ♓ 09	5 9 Cephei. ☉ 20 ♓ 08	6 Lambda Cephei. ☉ 21 ♓ 08	7 Mega 83. ☉ 22 ♓ 07	8 Delta Cephei. ☉ 23 ♓ 06	9 6 Cephei. ☉ 24 ♓ 05
10 19 Cephei. ☉ 25 ♓ 04	11 Mega 18. Mega 51. ☉ 26 ♓ 03	12 Baten Kaitos. Pi Andromedae. ☉ 27 ♓ 01	13 Pi Andromedae. ☉ 28 ♓ 00	14 Acamar. ☉ 28 ♓ 59	15 Chi Piscium. ☉ 29 ♓ 58	16 2 Cassiopeiae. ☉ 00 ♈ 57
17 Alpherg. ☉ 01 ♈ 55 The Resurrection	18 101 Piscium. ☉ 02 ♈ 54	19 26 Cephei. ☉ 03 ♈ 53	20 Mega 143. Alrisha. ☉ 04 ♈ 51	21 Rho Cassiopeiae Mirach. ☉ 05 ♈ 50	2 Rho Cassiopeiae Mira. ☉ 06 ♈ 48	23 Omicron Cassiopeiae. ☉ 07 ♈ 47
24 Mesarthim. Sheraton. ☉ 08 ♈ 45 Divine Mercy Sunday	25 Lambda Cassiopeiae. ☉ 09 ♈ 44	26 6 Cassiopeiae. Alfirk. ☉ 10 ♈ 42 Our Lady of Good Counsel	27 Mega 184. ☉ 11 ♈ 41	28 9 Cassiopeiae. Schedar. Hamal. ☉ 12 ♈ 39	29 Nu Ceti. ☉ 13 ♈ 37	30 Mega 310. ☉ 14 ♈ 36

Oh, Holy Mary Sophia, pray for us.

Sophia Star Calendar 2022 Charts

May 2022

Sun's *Sidereal Geocentric Longitude* is given at Midnight UT.
Star's *Sidereal Longitude* designates it as the Overlighting **Star** for the day.
Star's *Luminosity* indicates its intrinsic brightness as compared with **Sun's** *Luminosity*: **Sun** L=1.
Mega Stars are identified by an assigned numerical ranking according to their *Luminosity*, as recorded in AstroFire Database.
Mega Stars may or may not have proper names, but all are identified by assigned *Luminosity* numerical ranking.
This calendar identifies all **Stars** over 1000 *Luminosity* as **Mega Stars**, as recorded in AstroFire Database.
Please refer to "**Mega Star Index** for Mega Stars 1 - 200" for ranked *Luminosity* ratings.
Please refer to "**Sophia Star Calendar 2022 List**" for additional **Stars**, designated for overlighting our **Sun** per day.

Son of God dwells in the region of the Ram, ♈, Aries / Ari. (April 15 - May 15) — Virtue to develop is Devotion.

Holy Spirit dwells in the region of the Bull, ♉, Taurus / Tau. (May 15 - June 16.) — Virtue to develop is Inner Balance.

Day of Resurrection Sunday	Day of Holy Trinity Monday	Day of Archangel Michael Tuesday	Day of Human Pastors Wednesday	Day of Holy Spirit Thursday	Day of Cavalry, Christ Crucified Friday	Day of Holy Virgin Saturday
1 Mega 245. ☉ 15 ♈ 34	2 Mega 36. ☉ 16 ♈ 32	3 Kappa Cassiopeiae. ☉ 17 ♈ 30	4 Omicron Arietis. ☉ 18 ♈ 29	5 Tsih. Almach. ☉ 19 ♈ 27	6 Phi Cassiopeiae. ☉ 20 ♈ 25	7 2 Persei. ☉ 21 ♈ 23
8 60 Andromedae. ☉ 22 ♈ 21	9 15 Trianguli. Ruchbah. ☉ 23 ♈ 19	10 1 Persei. ☉ 24 ♈ 17	11 Delta Caeli. ☉ 25 ♈ 15	12 Mega 115. ☉ 26 ♈ 13	13 Beta Doradus. ☉ 27 ♈ 11 Our Lady of Fatima	14 5 Persei. ☉ 28 ♈ 09
15 Mega 274. Zaurak. ☉ 29 ♈ 07	16 10 Persei. Segin. ☉ 00 ♉ 05	17 Mega 171. Algol. ☉ 01 ♉ 03	18 53 Cassiopeiae. ☉ 02 ♉ 07	19 Mega 38. ☉ 02 ♉ 58	20 Mega 127. Miram. ☉ 03 ♉ 56	21 Pleiades Stars. Alcyone. ☉ 04 ♉ 54
22 Atlas. ☉ 05 ♉ 51	23 Atik. ☉ 06 ♉ 49	24 Mirfak. ☉ 07 ♉ 47	25 Zeta Persei. ☉ 08 ♉ 44	26 Delta Persei. ☉ 09 ♉ 42 The Ascension	27 Menkib. ☉ 10 ♉ 40	28 Mega 73. ☉ 11 ♉ 37
29 Hyadum II. ☉ 12 ♉ 35	30 Mega 19. Ain. ☉ 13 ♉ 32	31 Mu Eridani. ☉ 14 ♉ 30 The Visitation of Blessed Virgin Mary				

Oh, Holy Mary Sophia, pray for us.

Cosmic Communion: Star Wisdom, Volume 4

June 2022

Sun's *Sidereal Geocentric Longitude* is given at Midnight UT.
Star's *Sidereal Longitude* designates it as the Overlighting **Star** for the day.
Star's *Luminosity* indicates its intrinsic brightness as compared with **Sun's** *Luminosity*: **Sun** L=1.
Mega Stars are identified by an assigned numerical ranking according to their *Luminosity*, as recorded in AstroFire Database.
Mega Stars may or may not have proper names, but all are identified by assigned *Luminosity* numerical ranking.
This calendar identifies all **Stars** over 1000 *Luminosity* as **Mega Stars**, as recorded in AstroFire Database.
Please refer to "**Mega Star Index** for **Mega Stars 1 - 200**" for ranked *Luminosity* ratings.
Please refer to "**Sophia Star Calendar 2022 List**" for additional **Stars**, designated for overlighting our **Sun** per day.

Holy Spirit dwells in the region of the Bull, ♉, Taurus / Tau. (May 15 - June 16)   *Virtue to develop is Inner Balance.*

Seraphim, Spirits of Universal Love, dwell in the region of the Twins, ♊, Gemini/ Gem. (June 16 - July 17)   *Virtue to develop is Perseverance.*

Day of Resurrection Sunday	Day of Holy Trinity Monday	Day of Archangel Michael Tuesday	Day of Human Pastors Wednesday	Day of Holy Spirit Thursday	Day of Cavalry, Christ Crucified Friday	Day of Holy Virgin Saturday
			1 Aldebaran. ☉ 15 ♉ 28	2 Mega 328. ☉ 16 ♉ 25	3 Pi 5 Orionis. ☉ 17 ♉ 23	4 Psi Eridani. ☉ 18 ♉ 20
5 Pi 6 Orionis. ☉ 19 ♉ 18 Pentecost	6 Lambda Eridani. ☉ 20 ♉ 15	7 Kappa Leporis. ☉ 21 ♉ 12 The Blessed Virgin Mary, Mother of the Church	8 Rigel. Mega 55. ☉ 22 ♉ 10	9 103 Tauri. ☉ 23 ♉ 07	10 Al Maaz. ☉ 24 ♉ 05	11 Eta Orionis. Nihal. ☉ 25 ♉ 02
12 Alpha Camelopardalis. Bellatrix. ☉ 25 ♉ 59	13 Arneb. Thabit. Capella. ☉ 26 ♉ 57	14 Mega 103. Hatysa. Mintaka. ☉ 27 ♉ 54	15 Alnilam. Meissa. ☉ 28 ♉ 51	16 Chi Aurigae. Alnitak. ☉ 29 ♉ 48	17 Mega 411. ☉ 00 ♊ 46	18 Saiph. ☉ 01 ♊ 43
19 55 Orionis. ☉ 02 ♊ 40	20 Betelgeuse. Polaris. ☉ 03 ♊ 38	21 Mega 44. ☉ 04 ♊ 35	22 Mega 187. Menkalinan. ☉ 05 ♊ 32	23 Chi 2 Orionis. ☉ 06 ♊ 29	24 3 Geminorium. Mega 122. ☉ 07 ♊ 27 Sacred Heart of Jesus	25 6 Geminorum. Propus. ☉ 08 ♊ 24 Immaculate Heart of Mary
26 Psi 1 Aurigae. ☉ 09 ♊ 21	27 Tejat. ☉ 10 ♊ 18 Our Lady of Perpetual Help	28 Mega 508. ☉ 11 ♊ 16	29 Mega 106. Mirzam. ☉ 12 ♊ 13	30 Mega 152. ☉ 13 ♊ 10		

Oh, Holy Mary Sophia, pray for us.

Sophia Star Calendar 2022 Charts

July 2022

Sun's *Sidereal Geocentric Longitude* is given at Midnight UT.
Star's *Sidereal Longitude* designates it as the Overlighting **Star** for the day.
Star's *Luminosity* indicates its intrinsic brightness as compared with **Sun's** *Luminosity*: **Sun** L=1.
Mega Stars are identified by an assigned numerical ranking according to their *Luminosity*, as recorded in AstroFire Database.
Mega Stars may or may not have proper names, but all are identified by assigned *Luminosity* numerical ranking.
This calendar identifies all **Stars** over 1000 *Luminosity* as **Mega Stars**, as recorded in AstroFire Database.
Please refer to "**Mega Star Index** for **Mega Stars 1 - 200**" for ranked *Luminosity* ratings.
Please refer to "**Sophia Star Calendar 2022 List**" for additional **Stars**, designated for overlighting our **Sun** per day.

Seraphim, Spirits of Universal Love, dwell in the region of the Twins, ♊, Gemini / Gem .(June 16 - July 17)   *Virtue to develop is Perseverance.*
Cherubim, Spirits of Harmony, dwell in the region of the Crab, ♋ , Cancer / Can. (July 17 - Aug 17)   *Virtue to develop is Selflessness.*

Day of Resurrection Sunday	Day of Holy Trinity Monday	Day of Archangel Michael Tuesday	Day of Human Pastors Wednesday	Day of Holy Spirit Thursday	Day of Cavalry, Christ Crucified Friday	Day of Holy Virgin Saturday
					1 Mega 114. Alhena. ☉ 14 ♊ 07	2 Mega 182. Mebsuta. ☉ 15 ♊ 04
3 Mega 16. Xi 1 Canis Majoris. ☉ 16 ♊ 02	4 Mega 23. ☉ 16 ♊ 59	5 35 Geminorium. ☉ 17 ♊ 56	6 Sirius. ☉ 18 ♊ 53	7 41 Geminorum. Canopus. Mekbuda. ☉ 19 ♊ 51	8 Mega 214. ☉ 20 ♊ 48	9 10 Canis Majoris. ☉ 21 ♊ 45
10 Iota Canis Majoris. ☉ 22 ♊ 42	11 Omicron 1 Canis Majoris. ☉ 23 ♊ 39	12 Mega 241. ☉ 24 ♊ 36	13 Mega 157. Adhara. Castor. ☉ 25 ♊ 34	14 Mega 15. Omicron 2 Canis Majoris. ☉ 26 ♊ 31	15 Mega 148. Gomeisa. ☉ 27 ♊ 28	16 Wezen. Pollux. ☉ 28 ♊ 25 Our Lady of Mount Carmel
17 Mega 286. ☉ 29 ♊ 23	18 Mega 63. Mega 96. ☉ 00 ♋ 20	19 Tau Canis Majoris. Procyon. ☉ 01 ♋ 17	20 Omega 1 Cancri. ☉ 02 ♋ 14	21 Mega 137. ☉ 03 ♋ 11	22 Mega 144. ☉ 04 ♋ 09	23 Aludra. ☉ 05 ♋ 06
24 Pi Puppis. ☉ 06 ♋ 03 ——— 31 Praesepe. Asellus Borealis. ☉ 12 ♋ 45	25 Mega 17. Tegmine. ☉ 07 ♋ 01	26 Mega 294. Pherkad Minoris. ☉ 07 ♋ 58	27 Talitha Australis. ☉ 08 ♋ 55	28 El Tarf. ☉ 09 ♋ 53	29 3 Puppis. Asmidiske. ☉ 10 ♋ 50	30 Omicron Puppis. ☉ 11 ♋ 47

Oh, Holy Mary Sophia, pray for us.

Cosmic Communion: Star Wisdom, Volume 4

August 2022

Sun's *Sidereal Geocentric Longitude* is given at Midnight UT.
Star's *Sidereal Longitude* designates it as the Overlighting **Star** for the day.
Star's *Luminosity* indicates its intrinsic brightness as compared with **Sun's** *Luminosity*: **Sun** L=1.
Mega Stars are identified by an assigned numerical ranking according to their *Luminosity*, as recorded in AstroFire Database.
Mega Stars may or may not have proper names, but all are identified by assigned *Luminosity* numerical ranking.
This calendar identifies all **Stars** over 1000 *Luminosity* as **Mega Stars**, as recorded in AstroFire Database.
Please refer to "**Mega Star Index** for **Mega Stars 1 - 200**" for ranked *Luminosity* ratings.
Please refer to "**Sophia Star Calendar 2022 List**" for additional **Stars**, designated for overlighting our **Sun** per day.

Cherubim, Spirits of Harmony, dwell in the region of the Crab, ♋, Cancer / Can. (July 17 - Aug 17)   *Virtue to develop is Selflessness.*

Thrones, Spirits of Will, dwell in the region of the Lion, ♌, Leo/ Leo. (Aug 18 - Sept 17)   *Virtue to develop is Compassion.*

Day of Resurrection Sunday	Day of Holy Trinity Monday	Day of Archangel Michael Tuesday	Day of Human Pastors Wednesday	Day of Holy Spirit Thursday	Day of Cavalry, Christ Crucified Friday	Day of Holy Virgin Saturday
	1 Asellus Australis. ☉ 13 ♋ 42	2 Mega 136. ☉ 14 ♋ 40	3 20 Puppis. ☉ 15 ♋ 37	4 Mega 212. ☉ 16 ♋ 34	5 Alpha Lyncis. ☉ 17 ♋ 32	6 Kochab. Acubens. ☉ 18 ♋ 29
7 Mega 285. ☉ 19 ♋ 27	8 Mega 300. Dubhe. ☉ 20 ♋ 24	9 Kappa Cancri. ☉ 21 ♋ 22	10 Mega 12. ☉ 22 ♋ 19	11 Alterf. ☉ 23 ♋ 17	12 Naos. Merak. ☉ 24 ♋ 14	13 Mega 524. ☉ 25 ♋ 12
14 Mega 215 Algenubi. ☉ 26 ♋ 09	15 Pherkad. ☉ 27 ♋ 07 Assumption of Mary	16 Mega 174. ☉ 28 ♋ 05	17 Mega 86. Mega 140. ☉ 29 ♋ 02	18 Subra. ☉ 00 ♌ 00	19 Mega 447. ☉ 00 ♌ 58	20 Sumut. ☉ 01 ♌ 55
21 Eta Leonis. Gamma 2 Velorum. Alphard. ☉ 02 ♌ 53	22 Psi Ursae Majoris. ☉ 03 ♌ 51 Queenship of Mary	23 Algieba. Regulus. ☉ 04 ♌ 49	24 Chi Carinae. Phecda. ☉ 05 ♌ 47	25 Mega 64. Megrez. ☉ 06 ♌ 45	26 Mega 271. ☉ 07 ♌ 42	27 Mega 384 Chi Ursae Majoris. ☉ 08 ♌ 40
28 Alpha Sextantis. ☉ 09 ♌ 38	29 Mega 221. ☉ 10 ♌ 36	30 Rho Leonis. Mega 79. Alula Borealis. ☉ 11 ♌ 34	31 Mega 194. Thuban. ☉ 12 ♌ 32			

Oh, Holy Mary Sophia, pray for us.

Sophia Star Calendar 2022 Charts

September 2022

Sun's *Sidereal Geocentric Longitude* is given at Midnight UT.
Star's *Sidereal Longitude* designates it as the Overlighting **Star** for the day.
Star's *Luminosity* indicates its intrinsic brightness as compared with **Sun's** *Luminosity*: **Sun** L=1.
Mega Stars are identified by an assigned numerical ranking according to their *Luminosity*, as recorded in AstroFire Database.
Mega Stars may or may not have proper names, but all are identified by assigned *Luminosity* numerical ranking.
This calendar identifies all **Stars** over 1000 *Luminosity* as **Mega Stars**, as recorded in AstroFire Database.
Please refer to "**Mega Star Index** for **Mega Stars 1 - 200**" for ranked *Luminosity* ratings.
Please refer to "**Sophia Star Calendar 2022 List**" for additional **Stars**, designated for overlighting our **Sun** per day.

Thrones, Spirits of Will, dwell in the region of the Lion, ♌, Leo/ Leo. (Aug 18 - Sept 17)   *Virtue to develop is Compassion.*

Kyriotetes, Spirits of Wisdom, dwell in the region of the Virgin, ♍, Virgo/ Vir. (Sept 17 - Oct 18)   *Virtue to develop is Courtesy.*

Day of Resurrection Sunday	Day of Holy Trinity Monday	Day of Archangel Michael Tuesday	Day of Human Pastors Wednesday	Day of Holy Spirit Thursday	Day of Cavalry, Christ Crucified Friday	Day of Holy Virgin Saturday
				1 Mega 211. ☉ 13 ♌ 30	2 Mega 213. Alioth. ☉ 14 ♌ 28	3 72 Leo. ☉ 15 ♌ 26
4 Mega 111. Suhail. Zosma. ☉ 16 ♌ 25	5 36 Sextantis. ☉ 17 ♌ 23	6 Mega 30. Chort. ☉ 18 ♌ 21	7 Mega 126. ☉ 19 ♌ 19	8 Mega 192. ☉ 20 ♌ 17 The Nativity of BVM	9 Alcor. Mizar. ☉ 21 ♌ 15	10 90 Leonis. ☉ 22 ♌ 14
11 90 Leonis. ☉ 23 ♌ 12	12 Mega 363. Sigma Leonis. ☉ 24 ♌ 10 Most Holy Name of Mary	13 75 Leonis. ☉ 25 ♌ 09	14 Nu Hydrae. ☉ 26 ♌ 07	15 Denebola. Tau Leonis. ☉ 27 ♌ 05 Our Lady of Sorrows	16 Mega 29. Avior. ☉ 28 ♌ 04	17 Alkes. ☉ 29 ♌ 02
18 Mega 138. Cor Caroli. ☉ 00 ♍ 01	19 Mega 540. ☉ 00 ♍ 59	20 Alkaid. Zavijava. ☉ 01 ♍ 58	21 Pi Virginis. ☉ 02 ♍ 57	22 Mega 239. Markeb. ☉ 03 ♍ 55	23 37 Coma Berenices. ☉ 04 ♍ 54	24 24 Coma Berenices. ☉ 05 ♍ 53 Our Lady of Mercy
25 Mega 229. ☉ 06 ♍ 52	26 Asellus Primus. ☉ 07 ♍ 50	27 Mega 293. ☉ 08 ♍ 49 Our Lady, Star of the Sea	28 Zaniah. ☉ 09 ♍ 48	29 Tseen Ke. Aspidiske. ☉ 10 ♍ 47	30 Mega 134. ☉ 11 ♍ 46	

Oh, Holy Mary Sophia, pray for us.

Cosmic Communion: Star Wisdom, Volume 4

October 2022

Sun's *Sidereal Geocentric Longitude* is given at Midnight UT.
Star's *Sidereal Longitude* designates it as the Overlighting **Star** for the day.
Star's *Luminosity* indicates its intrinsic brightness as compared with **Sun's** *Luminosity*: **Sun** L=1.
Mega Stars are identified by an assigned numerical ranking according to their *Luminosity*, as recorded in AstroFire Database.
Mega Stars may or may not have proper names, but all are identified by assigned *Luminosity* numerical ranking.
This calendar identifies all **Stars** over 1000 *Luminosity* as **Mega Stars**, as recorded in AstroFire Database.
Please refer to "**Mega Star Index** for **Mega Stars 1 - 200**" for ranked *Luminosity* ratings.
Please refer to "**Sophia Star Calendar 2022 List**" for additional **Stars**, designated for overlighting our **Sun** per day.

Kyriotetes, Spirits of Wisdom, dwell in the region of the Virgin, ♍, Virgo/ Vir. (Sept 17 - Oct 18)   *Virtue to develop is Courtesy.*
Dynamis, Spirits of Movement, dwell in region of the Scales, ♎, Libra / Lib. (Oct 18 - Nov 17)   *Virtue to develop is Contentment.*

Day of Resurrection Sunday	Day of Holy Trinity Monday	Day of Archangel Michael Tuesday	Day of Human Pastors Wednesday	Day of Holy Spirit Thursday	Day of Cavalry, Christ Crucified Friday	Day of Holy Virgin Saturday
						1 32 Virginis. ☉ 12 ♍ 45
2 Mega 172. ☉ 13 ♍ 44	3 Vindemiatrix. ☉ 14 ♍ 43	4 Gienah. ☉ 15 ♍ 42	5 Mega 351. Minelauva. ☉ 16 ♍ 41	6 Mega 350. ☉ 17 ♍ 40	7 Zeta Corvi. ☉ 18 ♍ 39 Our Lady of the Rosary	8 33 Bootis. ☉ 19 ♍ 38
9 Mega 327. Sigma Virginis. ☉ 20 ♍ 38	10 Mega 1. ☉ 21 ♍ 37	11 Mega 190. Kraz. ☉ 22 ♍ 36	12 Mega 46. Mega 56. ☉ 23 ♍ 35	13 Mega 7. Mega 68. ☉ 24 ♍ 35	14 Mega 80. ☉ 25 ♍ 34	15 Mega 77. ☉ 26 ♍ 34
16 Eta Carinae. ☉ 27 ♍ 33	17 Mega 2. Upsilon Carinae. ☉ 28 ♍ 32	18 Mega 10. Spica. Arcturus. ☉ 29 ♍ 32	19 Mega 39. ☉ 00 ♎ 32	20 Mega 518. ☉ 01 ♎ 31	21 Mega 25. Delta Centauri. ☉ 02 ♎ 31	22 Izar. ☉ 03 ♎ 30
23 Mega 87. Omicron 2 Centauri. ☉ 04 ♎ 30	24 Sigma Centauri. ☉ 05 ♎ 30	25 Mega 205. ☉ 06 ♎ 30	26 Mega 228. Muhlifain. Miaplacidus. ☉ 07 ♎ 30	27 Alkalurops. ☉ 08 ♎ 29	28 Mega 207. Lambda Centauri. ☉ 09 ♎ 29	29 Mega 202. Delta Crucis. ☉ 10 ♎ 29
30 Mega 259. ☉ 11 ♎ 29	31 Mega 88. Omega Carinae. ☉ 12 ♎ 29					

Oh, Holy Mary Sophia, pray for us.

Sophia Star Calendar 2022 Charts

November 2022

Sun's *Sidereal Geocentric Longitude* is given at Midnight UT.
Star's *Sidereal Longitude* designates it as the Overlighting **Star** for the day.
Star's *Luminosity* indicates its intrinsic brightness as compared with **Sun's** *Luminosity*: **Sun** L=1.
Mega Stars are identified by an assigned numerical ranking according to their *Luminosity*, as recorded in AstroFire Database.
Mega Stars may or may not have proper names, but all are identified by assigned *Luminosity* numerical ranking.
This calendar identifies all **Stars** over 1000 *Luminosity* as **Mega Stars**, as recorded in AstroFire Database.
Please refer to "**Mega Star Index** for **Mega Stars 1 - 200**" for ranked *Luminosity* ratings.
Please refer to "**Sophia Star Calendar 2022 List**" for additional **Stars**, designated for overlighting our **Sun** per day.

Dynamis, Spirits of Movement, dwell in region of the Scales, ♎, Libra / Lib. (Oct 18 - Nov 17)   *Virtue to develop is Contentment.*
Exusiai, Spirits of Form, dwell in the region of the Scorpion, ♏, Scorpio /Sco. (Nov 17 - Dec 17)   *Virtue to develop is Patience.*

Day of Resurrection Sunday	Day of Holy Trinity Monday	Day of Archangel Michael Tuesday	Day of Human Pastors Wednesday	Day of Holy Spirit Thursday	Day of Cavalry, Christ Crucified Friday	Day of Holy Virgin Saturday
		1 Epsilon Crucis. ☉ 13 ♎29	2 Mega 158 b. Theta 2 Crucis. ☉ 14 ♎29	3 Mu 1 Crucis. ☉ 15 ♎29	4 Mega 32. Mimosa. ☉ 16 ♎29	5 Mega 101. Acrux. Alphecca. ☉ 17 ♎29
6 Mega 178. Kappa Crucis. ☉ 18 ♎29	7 Tau Herculis. ☉ 19 ♎30	8 Epsilon Centauri Alnair. ☉ 20 ♎30	9 Mega 121. ☉ 21 ♎30	10 Mega 437. ☉ 22 ♎30	11 Mega 6. Mega 71. ☉ 23 ♎30	12 Zubeneschamali. Nu Librae. ☉ 24 ♎31
13 Theta Muscae. Eta Centauri. ☉ 25 ♎31	14 Mega 282. ☉ 26 ♎31	15 Mega 448. ☉ 27 ♎32	16 Mega 13. Mega 74. ☉ 28 ♎32	17 Hadar(Agena). KeKwan. ☉ 29 ♎33	18 Ke Kouan. Zubenelakrab. ☉ 00 ♏33	19 Mega 448. ☉ 01 ♏34
20 Mega 57. Pi Lupi. ☉ 02 ♏34	21 Delta Lupi. ☉ 03 ♏35 Presentation of Mary	22 Tau Librae. ☉ 04 ♏35	23 Epsilon Lupi. ☉ 05 ♏36	24 Gamma Lupi. Kornephoros. ☉ 06 ♏37	25 Mega 53. Dschubba. ☉ 07 ♏37	26 Graffias. ☉ 08 ♏38
27 Jabbah. ☉ 09 ♏39	28 Mega 3. Delta Circini. ☉ 10 ♏40	29 Theta Lupi. ☉ 11 ♏40	30 Mega 110. AlNiyat. ☉ 12 ♏41			

Oh, Holy Mary Sophia, pray for us.

Cosmic Communion: Star Wisdom, Volume 4

December 2022

Sun's *Sidereal Geocentric Longitude* is given at Midnight UT.
Star's *Sidereal Longitude* designates it as the Overlighting **Star** for the day.
Star's *Luminosity* indicates its intrinsic brightness as compared with **Sun's** *Luminosity*: **Sun** L=1.
Mega Stars are identified by an assigned numerical ranking according to their *Luminosity*, as recorded in AstroFire Database.
Mega Stars may or may not have proper names, but all are identified by assigned *Luminosity* numerical ranking.
This calendar identifies all **Stars** over 1000 *Luminosity* as **Mega Stars,** as recorded in AstroFire Database.
Please refer to "**Mega Star Index** for **Mega Stars 1 - 200**" for ranked *Luminosity* ratings.
Please refer to "**Sophia Star Calendar 2022 List**" for additional **Stars,** designated for overlighting our **Sun** per day.

Exusiai, Spirits of Form, dwell in the region of the Scorpion, ♏ *, Scorpio /Sco.* (Nov 17 - Dec 17)   *Virtue to develop is Patience.*

Archai, Spirits of Personality, dwell in the region of the Archer, ♐ *, Sagittarius / Sgr.* (Dec 17 - Jan 15)   *Virtue to develop is Self Discipline.*

Day of Resurrection Sunday	Day of Holy Trinity Monday	Day of Archangel Michael Tuesday	Day of Human Pastors Wednesday	Day of Holy Spirit Thursday	Day of Cavalry, Christ Crucified Friday	Day of Holy Virgin Saturday
				1 Mega 200. Chi Ophiuchi. ☉ 13 ♏42	2 Antares. Han. ☉ 14 ♏43	3 Mega 260. ☉ 15 ♏43
4 Mega 161. Alniyat. ☉ 16 ♏44	5 Mega 52. ☉ 17 ♏45	6 Mu Normae. Kappa Trianguli Australis. ☉ 18 ♏46	7 Delta Trianguli Australis. ☉ 19 ♏47	8 Mega 41. ☉ 20 ♏48 Immaculate Conception of Blessed Virgin Mary	9 Mega 72. Mega 94. Rasalgethi. ☉ 21 ♏49	10 Mega 31. Mega 45. Mega 65. ☉ 22 ♏50
11 Mega 50. ☉ 23 ♏51	12 Mega 224. ☉ 24 ♏52 Our Lady of Guadalupe	13 Mega 146. Sigma Ophiuchi. Alpha Trianguli Australis. ☉ 25 ♏52	14 Mega 242. Theta Ophiuchi. ☉ 26 ♏53	15 Mega 404. Rasalhague. ☉ 27 ♏54	16 Lesath. ☉ 28 ♏56	17 Shaula. Gamma Arae. ☉ 29 ♏57
18 Mega 414. Sargas. ☉ 00 ♐58	19 Gertab. Galactic Center. ☉ 01 ♐59	20 Iota 1 Scorpii. Eta Pavonis. ☉ 03 ♐00	21 Mega 95. 89 Herculis. ☉ 04 ♐01	22 67 Ophiuchi. Nu Herculis. ☉ 05 ♐02	23 Mega 22. 9 Sagittarii. Gamma Sagittarii. ☉ 06 ♐03	24 Mega 75. ☉ 07 ♐04
25 Polis. ☉ 08 ♐05 The Nativity	26 16 Sagittarii. 15 Sagittarii. ☉ 09 ♐07	27 Mega 163. Media. ☉ 10 ♐08	28 Mega 303. ☉ 11 ♐09	29 Mega 307. 105 Herculis. ☉ 12 ♐10	30 24 Sagittarii. Lambda Pavonis. ☉ 13 ♐11	31 Omega Pavonis. ☉ 14 ♐12

Oh, Holy Mary Sophia, pray for us.

Thank you, Holy Mary Sophia, for a most beautiful year.

SOPHIA STAR CALENDAR 2022 LISTS

January 2022

Sun's *Sidereal Geocentric Longitude* is given at Midnight UT.
Star's *Sidereal Longitude* designates it as the Overlighting **Star** for the day.
Star's *Luminosity* indicates its intrinsic brightness as compared with **Sun's** *Luminosity*: **Sun** L=1.
Mega Stars are identified by an assigned numerical ranking according to their *Luminosity*, as recorded in AstroFire Database.
Mega Stars may or may not have proper names, but all are identified by assigned *Luminosity* numerical ranking.
This calendar identifies all **Stars** over 1000 *Luminosity* as **Mega Stars**, as recorded in AstroFire Database.

Archai, the Spirits of Personality, dwell in the region of the Archer, Sagittarius / Sgr. (Dec 16 - Jan 15)   *Virtue is Self Discipline.*
Archangels, the Spirits of Fire, dwell in the region of the Goat, Capricorn / Cap. (Jan 15 - Feb 13)   *Virtue is Courage.*

Midnight UT Date, Sun Sidereal Geocentric Longitude		Overlighting Star	Star's Sidereal Longitude	Star's Sidereal Latitude	Luminosity (Sun L = 1)
01 SA	15Sgr29	Lambda Telescopii	15Sgr22	30S	
		Phi Sagittarii	15Sgr26	03S	
		Mega 252	15Sgr28	08N	4759
02 SU	16Sgr30	NGC6752. Pavo, Globular C.	16Sgr17	37S	
		Epsilon Scuti	16Sgr24	14N	
		M26. Scutum, Open C.	16Sgr44	13N	
03 MO	17Sgr31	Mega 14	17Sgr03	12N	941464
		Mega 604	17Sgr38	17N	1140
		Beta Scuti	17Sgr38	18N	
		Sigma Sgr/ Nunki	17Sgr39	03S	
		Nu1Sgr/AinAlRami/Mega316	17Sgr44	00N	3199
		33 Sgr/ Mega 593	17Sgr49	01N	1317
04 TU	18Sgr32	M11. Scutum, Wild Duck	18Sgr31	16N	
		Mega 380	18Sgr32	07N	2106
		Xi 1 Sgr/ Mega 90	18Sgr40	02N	20238
		Xi 2 Sagittarii	18Sgr43	01N	
		Zeta Sgr/ Ascella	18Sgr54	07S	
05 WE	19Sgr34	Beta Coronae Australis	19Sgr19	16S	
		Alpha CrA/ Alphecca	19Sgr24	15S	
		Mega 473	19Sgr34	16S	1649
06 TH	20Sgr35	Alpha Lyr/ Vega	20Sgr35	61N	
		Beta 1 Sgr/ Arkab	21Sgr02	22S	
07 FR	21Sgr36	Pi Sgr/ Albaldah/ Mega 595	21Sgr31	01N	1118
		Mega 453	21Sgr42	03S	1774
		Mega 482	21Sgr49	13S	1615
		Alpha Sgr/ Rukbat	21Sgr54	18S	
08 SA	22Sgr37	Alpha Octantis	22Sgr15	56S	
		Psi Sagittarii	22Sgr18	02S	
		Lambda Aql/ Althalimin	22Sgr36	17N	
		Iota Telescopii	22Sgr44	26S	
09 SU	23Sgr38	Mega 269	23Sgr29	39N	3689
		20 Aquilae	23Sgr51	14N	
		Nu 1 Lyrae	23Sgr53	55N	
10 MO	24Sgr39	Beta Lyr/Sheliak/ Mega 366	24Sgr09	65N	2487
		Chi 3 Sagittarii	24Sgr44	01S	
		Upsilon Sagittarii/ Mega 295	24Sgr59	06N	3564
		Zeta Aql/ Deneb el Okab	25Sgr03	36N	
11 TU	25Sgr41	21 Aquilae	25Sgr34	24N	
12 WE	26Sgr42	Delta 2 Lyr/ Mega 537	26Sgr56	59N	1356
		Upsilon Pavonis	27Sgr03	46S	
		Gamma Lyr/ Sulaphat	27Sgr11.	55N	1652
13 TH	27Sgr43	Xi Tel/ Mega 516	27Sgr17	31S	1374
		Lambda Lyr/ Mega 418	27Sgr24	54N	2048
		Beta Pavonis	27Sgr45	45S	
		Iota Sagittarii	27Sgr49	20S	
14 FR	28Sgr44	Omega 1 Aquilae	28Sgr17	33N	
		Nu Aql/ Mega 27	28Sgr41	22N	154769
		Delta Aql/ Deneb Okab	28Sgr54	24N	

Day	Sun	Star	Position	Lat	Dist
15 SA	29Sgr45	Alpha Pav/ Peacock Star	29Sgr05	36S	
		Kappa Aql/ Mega 434	00Cap07	14N	1851
		Theta 1 Sagittarii	00Cap08	14S	
16 SU	00Cap46	Eta Mensae	00Cap19	80S	
		2 Vul/ Mega 424	00Cap48	44N	1973
		45 Dra/ Mega 158 (a)	00Cap56	79N	8430
		Iota Aql/ AlThalimain	01Cap06	20N	
		59 Sgr/ Terebellum	01Cap11	06S	1825
17 MO	01Cap47	Iota Lyrae	01Cap28	58N	
		Mu Aquilae	02Cap04	28N	
18 TU	02Cap48	Mega 84	02Cap33	24N	22855
		Beta Ind/ Mega 658	03Cap03	39S	1013
		Sigma Aquilae	03Cap04	26N	
		Kappa 2 Sagittarii	03Cap14	22S	
19 WE	03Cap49	Mega 462	03Cap53	75N	1674
20 TH	04Cap50	Alpha Indi	04Cap22	27S	
		Alpha Vul/ Anser	04Cap46	45N	
		Epsilon Sagittae	05Cap05	37N	
		Eta Lyr/ Aladfar/ Mega 503	05Cap18	60N	1503
21 FR	05Cap51	Chi Aquilae	05Cap27	32N	
		Eta Aquilae/ Mega 322	05Cap42	21N	3191
		Mega 554	05Cap44	37N	1223
		Theta Lyrae	05Cap47	59N	
		Mega 97	06Cap06	24N	16428
		Gamma Aql/ Tarazed	06Cap12	31N	1419
		Alpha Sagittae	06Cap20	38N	
22 SA	06Cap53	Beta Sagittae	06Cap28	38N	
		Beta 1 Cyg/ Albireo	06Cap31	48N	
		Alpha Aql/ Altair	07Cap02	29N	
		Pi Aquilae	07Cap11	32N	
23 SU	07Cap54	Beta Aql/ Alshain	07Cap41	26N	
		Sigma Capricorni	07Cap56	00N	
		Mega 8	08Cap17	10N	2690033
24 MO	08Cap55	Delta Sagittae	08Cap39	38N	
		Alpha 1 Capricorni	09Cap02	06N	
		Alpha 2 Cap/ Giedi	09Cap07	06N	
		Phi Aquilae	09Cap12	31N	
		Beta Cap/ Dabih	09Cap18	04N	
25 TU	09Cap56	Nu Cap/ Alshat	09Cap42	06N	
		Mega 646	09Cap50	58N	1054
		Pi Capricorni	09Cap58	00N	
		9 Sagittae/ Mega 47	10Cap10	38N	52547
		Theta Aquilae	10Cap10	18N	
26 WE	10Cap57	Mega 238	10Cap28	47N	4807
		10 Sagittae/ Mega 165	10Cap37	36N	7841
		Alpha Microscopii	10Cap53	15S	
27 TH	11Cap58	Beta Microsopii	11Cap29	14S	
		NGC2070.Dorado,Tarantula N.	11Cap43	86S	
		Eta Microscopii	11Cap48	23S	
		Mega 507	12Cap12	44N	1582
		Gamma Sagittae	12Cap18	39N	
		Mega 429	12Cap19	52N	1759
28 FR	12Cap59	Omega Capricorni	13Cap13	08S	
29 SA	14Cap00	Tau Cap/ Mega 415	13Cap33	03N	2018
		M27.Vulpecula, Dumbbell N.	13Cap40	42N	
		Mega 254	14Cap06	35N	4083
		Mega 335	14Cap17	41N	2762
30 SU	15Cap01	Mega 639	14Cap50	53N	1090
		Alpha Tucanae	14Cap56	45S	
31 MO	16Cap01	Gamma Hydri	15Cap44	76S	
		Beta Mensae	16Cap00	83S	
		70 Aql/ Mega 264	16Cap11	15N	4320
		NGC104.Tucana,47 TucanaeC.	16Cap31		

Oh, Holy Mary Sophia, pray for us.

Sophia Star Calendar 2022 Lists

February 2022

Sun's *Sidereal Geocentric Longitude* is given at Midnight UT.
Star's *Sidereal Longitude* designates it as the Overlighting *Star* for the day.
Star's *Luminosity* indicates its intrinsic brightness as compared with **Sun's** *Luminosity*: **Sun** L=1.
Mega Stars are identified by an assigned numerical ranking according to their *Luminosity*, as recorded in AstroFire Database.
Mega Stars may or may not have proper names, but all are identified by assigned *Luminosity* numerical ranking.
This calendar identifies all **Stars** over 1000 *Luminosity* as **Mega Stars**, as recorded in AstroFire Database.

Archangels, the Spirits of Fire, dwell in the region of the Goat, Capricorn / Cap. (Jan 15 - Feb 13)   *Virtue is Courage.*
Angels, the Sons of Life, dwell in the region of the Waterman, Aquarius / Aqr.   (Feb13 - Mar 15)   *Virtue is Discernment.*

Midnight UT Date,	Sun Sidereal Geocentric Longitude	Overlighting Star	Star's Sidereal Longitude	Star's Sidereal Latitude	Luminosity (Sun L = 1)
01 TU	17Cap02	**Mega 21**	16Cap50	40N	229728
		Epsilon Aqr/ **AlBali**	16Cap59	08N	
02 WE	18Cap03	**Mega 297**	17Cap58	57N	3338
		Eta Cap/ **Armus**	18Cap00	03S	
		Eta Cygni	18Cap11	54N	
		Mu Aquarii	18Cap19	08N	
03 TH	19Cap04	**22 Vul**/ Mega 120	18Cap42	41N	13118
		19 Vul / Mega 536	18Cap58	45N	1334
		Theta Cap/ **Dorsum**	19Cap06	00S	
		Epsilon Delphini	19Cap18	20N	
		Mega 34	19Cap19	51N	85424
		Mega 549	19Cap29	43N	1428
04 FR	20Cap05	**Mega 332**	19Cap48	59N	2887
		22 Cyg/ Mega 585	20Cap08	57N	1242
		Phi Capricorni	20Cap17	04S	
		25 Cyg/ Mega 454	20Cap34	55N	1770
05 SA	21Cap06	**25 Vul**/ Mega 472	21Cap00	42N	1677
		Alpha Gru/ **Al Na'ir**	21Cap10	32S	
		Theta Delphini	21Cap29	30N	
		Delta Cygni	21Cap31	64N	
		Mega 616	21Cap31	52N	1183
		Beta Delphini	21Cap36	31N	
06 SU	22Cap07	**Mega 561**	21Cap55	59N	1257
		Zeta Capriconi	22Cap12	06S	
		Iota Piscis Austrini	22Cap31	18S	
07 MO	23Cap08	Alpha Del/ **Sualocin**	22Cap38	33N	
		Gamma Gru/ **Al Dhanab**	22Cap41	23S	
		Iota Capricorni	22Cap57	01S	
		Delta Delphini	23Cap23	31N	
08 TU	24Cap08	**Theta Piscis Austrini**	23Cap52	16S	
		Eta Gruis	24Cap03	41S	
		Mu Mensae	24Cap27	81S	
09 WE	25Cap09	**35 Cyg**/ Mega 333	25Cap19	52N	2882
		NGC6888.Cygnus, CrescentN.	25Cap24	56N	
		Mega 543	25Cap26	40N	1384
		Epsilon Cap/ **Castra**	25Cap28	04S	
10 TH	26Cap10	**41 Cyg**/ Mega 624	25Cap59	47N	1172
		Mega 33	26Cap02	65N	103551
		Theta Hydri	26Cap30	73S	
11 FR	27Cap11	Kappa Capricorni	26Cap54	04S	
		Upsilon Piscis Austrini	26Cap58	21S	
		34 Cyg/ Mega 62	27Cap02	55N	39810
		Gamma Cap/ **Nashira**	27Cap03	02S	
		Mega 385	27Cap07	66N	2162
		Mega 399	27Cap18	66N	2255
		Eta Piscis Austrini	27Cap32	15S	
		Mega 535	27Cap32	51N	1389
		Beta Gruis	27Cap35	35S	
12 SA	28Cap11	**Mega 548**	28Cap07	56N	1358
		Alpha Equ/ **Kitalpha**	28Cap23	20N	
		Beta Aqr/ **Sadalsuud**	28Cap39	08N	2121
13 SU	29Cap12	Delta Cap/ **Deneb Algedi**	28Cap48	02S	
		M29. Cygnus, Open C.	29Cap20	55N	
		42 Cyg/ Mega 644	29Cap34	53N	1021

		Mega 371	29Cap42	08S	2481
14 MO	00Aqr13	Gamma Cyg /**Sadr**/ Mega78	00Aqr06	57N	24388
		47 Cyg/ Mega 662	00Aqr10	51N	1012
		Lambda Capricorni	00Aqr16	01N	
		Beta Equulei	00Aqr42	21N	
15 TU	01Aqr13	**Mu Capricorni**	01Aqr06	00S	
		Mega 553	01Aqr16	43N	1247
16 WE	02Aqr14	**Beta Piscis Austrini**	02Aqr26	21S	
17 TH	03Aqr14	**35 Aqr**/ Mega 92	02Aqr55	06S	18093
		Epsilon Cyg/ **Gienah**	03Aqr00	49N	
		Mega 679	03Aqr13	51N	1031
		31 Cyg/ Mega 249	03Aqr20	63N	4529
		26 Aqr/ Mega 603	03Aqr31	14N	1118
18 FR	04Aqr15	**Iota Aquarii**	03Aqr59	02S	
		M15. Pegasus, Globular C.	04Aqr28	25N	
		Mega 509	04Aqr35	62N	1500
		Psi Cygni	04Aqr39	69N	
19 SA	05Aqr15	**Lambda Cygni**	05Aqr00	51N	
		32 Cyg/ Mega 352	05Aqr03	64N	2626
		38 Aquarii	05Aqr45	00S	
20 SU	06Aqr16	**Epsilon Piscis Austrini**	06Aqr35	17S	
21 MO	07Aqr16	**Mega 512**	07Aqr05	45N	1449
		Epsilon Peg/ **Enif**/ Mega 261	07Aqr09	22N	4135
		Sigma Phoenicis	07Aqr21	43S	
		Omicron Aquarii	07Aqr22	09N	
22 TU	08Aqr17	**Zeta Cygni**	08Aqr18	43N	
		Mega 459	08Aqr27	43N	1636
		Alpha Aqr/ **Sadalmelik**	08Aqr37	10N	3112
23 WE	09Aqr17	Alpha PsA/ **Fomalhaut**	09Aqr07	21S	
		Rho Aquarius	09Aqr17	02N	
24 TH	10Aqr18	**9 Peg**/ Mega 591	10Aqr16	29N	1221
		Alpha Cyg/ **Deneb** /Mega 20	10Aqr35	59N	269996
		Eta Phoenices	10Aqr36	54S	
25 FR	11Aqr18	Omega 1 Cyg/ **Ruchba**	11Aqr17	64N	
		Nu Cygni	11Aqr24	54N	
26 SA	12Aqr18	Gamma Aqr/ **Sadachbia**	11Aqr58	08N	
		Theta Peg/ **Bihan**	12Aqr06	16N	
		Beta Sculptoris	12Aqr30	31S	
		Upsilon Cyg/ Mega 605	12Aqr31	47N	1144
27 SU	13Aqr19	**55 Cyg**/ Mega 233	13Aqr41	59N	4935
28 MO	14Aqr19	Pi Aqr/ **Seat**/ Mega 614	13Aqr51	10N	1195
		Delta Aqr/ **Skat**	14Aqr08	08S	
		Mega 218	14Aqr40	58N	5222
		Kappa Aqr/ **Situla**	14Aqr41	04N	
		NGC7000.Cygnus,NAmerican N.	14Aqr43		

Oh, Holy Mary Sophia, pray for us.

Sophia Star Calendar 2022 Lists

March 2022

Sun's *Sidereal Geocentric Longitude* is given at Midnight UT.
Star's *Sidereal Longitude* designates it as the Overlighting **Star** for the day.
Star's *Luminosity* indicates its intrinsic brightness as compared with **Sun's** *Luminosity*: **Sun** L=1.
Mega Stars are identified by an assigned numerical ranking according to their *Luminosity*, as recorded in AstroFire Database.
Mega Stars may or may not have proper names, but all are identified by assigned *Luminosity* numerical ranking.
This calendar identifies all **Stars** over 1000 *Luminosity* as **Mega Stars**, as recorded in AstroFire Database.

Angels, the Sons of Life, dwell in the region of the Waterman, Aquarius / Aqr. (Feb13 - Mar 15)   *Virtue is Discernment.*
Humanity dwells in the region of the Fish, Pisces / Psc. (Mar 15- April 15)   *Virtue is Magnanimity.*

Midnight UT Date,	Sun Sidereal Geocentric Longitude	Overlighting Star	Star's Sidereal Longitude	Star's Sidereal Latitude	Luminosity (Sun L = 1)
01 TU	15Aqr19	Epsilon Phoenicis	14Aqr54	41S	
		Mega 253	15Aqr15	50N	4436
		Sigma Cyg/ Mega 66	15Aqr36	51N	34462
		Eta Aquarii	15Aqr40	08N	
02 WE	16Aqr20	69 Cyg/ Mega 349	15Aqr50	48N	2656
		Xi Cyg/ Mega 267	16Aqr04	56N	3690
		70 Cyg/ Mega 410	16Aqr35	48N	1951
		Mega 117	16Aqr45	65N	14374
		Lambda Aquarii	16Aqr50	00S	
03 TH	17Aqr20	Lambda Aquarii	16Aqr50	00S	
		Mega 61	17Aqr06	60N	38007
		60 Cyg/ Mega 654	17Aqr14	58N	1074
04 FR	18Aqr20	59 Cyg/ Mega 584	18Aqr21	60N	1316
		33 Cygni	18Aqr40	71N	
05 SA	19Aqr20	Mega 531	19Aqr18	45N	1329
		68 Cyg/ Mega 5	19Aqr46	55N	3357841
06 SU	20Aqr20	Mega 375	19Aqr59	01N	2422
		63 Cyg/ Mega 634	20Aqr22	59N	1185
		NGC55. Sculptor	20Aqr24	36S	
		Alpha Eri/ Achernar	20Aqr34	59S	1119
		Mega 308	20Aqr44	33N	3113
		Alpha Phe/ Ankaa	20Aqr45	40S	
07 MO	21Aqr20	Zeta Pegasi/ Homam	21Aqr25	17N	
		Beta Horologii	21Aqr36	71S	
08 TU	22Aqr20	Psi 2 Aquarii	21Aqr59	04S	
		Chi Aqr/ Situla	22Aqr19	02S	
		Phi Aquarii	22Aqr24	01S	
09 WE	23Aqr20	77 Cygni	23Aqr30	50N	
		103 Aquarii	23Aqr44	14S	
10 TH	24Aqr20	Beta Piscium	23Aqr51	09N	
		Mega 580	24Aqr29	05S	1317
		Pi 2 Pegasi	24Aqr49	40N	
11 FR	25Aqr20	Mega 105	25Aqr24	49N	15432
		Omega 2 Aquarii	25Aqr27	11S	
		Beta Phoenicis	25Aqr42	48S	
		NGC7469. Pegasus, Seyfert C.	25Aqr44	13N	
12 SA	26Aqr20	Mega 519	26Aqr07	02S	1348
		Beta Reticuli	26Aqr39	76S	
		Gamma Piscium	26Aqr43	07N	
13 SU	27Aqr20	Eta Sculptoris	26Aqr51	32S	
		57 Pegasi	27Aqr07	12N	
		Iota Sculptoris	27Aqr35	28S	
14 MO	28Aqr20	M39. Cygnus, Open C.	27Aqr55	57N	
		Lambda Pegasi	28Aqr19	28N	
		Mega 142	28Aqr21	69N	9375
		Alpha Peg/ Markab	28Aqr45	19N	
15 TU	29Aqr20	Mu Peg/ Sadalbari	29Aqr39	29N	
16 WE	00Psc20	Theta Piscium	00Psc27	09N	
		Xi Sculptoris	00Psc36	41S	

Cosmic Communion: Star Wisdom, Volume 4

Day	Sun	Star	Longitude	Latitude	Distance
17 TH	01Psc19	Eta Peg/ **Matar**	00Psc58	35N	
		Chi Eridani	01Psc30	57S	
18 FR	02Psc19	**Lambda Piscium**	01Psc51	03N	
		3 Cet/ Mega 398	02Psc04	10S	2133
		Pi 2 Cyg/ Mega 395	02Psc27	56N	2226
19 SA	03Psc19	**Gamma Phoenicis**	03Psc24	47S	
		19 Piscium	03Psc32	04N	
		Pi 1Cyg/**Azelfafage**/Mega 311	03Psc32	58N	3079
20 SU	04Psc18	**22 Piscium**	04Psc35	03N	
		Beta Peg/ **Scheat**	04Psc38	31N	
21 MO	05Psc18	NGC253. Sculptor/ Spiral G.	05Psc20	27S	
		77 Pegasi	05Psc36	11N	
		Alpha Sculptoris	05Psc45	32S	
22 TU	06Psc18	**Mega 642**	05Psc59	30S	1023
		Iota Cet/ **Schemali**	06Psc11	10S	
		Phi Eridani	06Psc16	58S	
		Psi Phoenicis	06Psc35	52S	
		6 **Lac**/ Mega 370	06Psc42	47N	2392
23 WE	07Psc17	**Upsilon Pegasi**	07Psc14	24N	
24 TH	08Psc17	Beta Cet/ **Diphda**	07Psc51	20S	
		Omega Piscium	07Psc51	06N	
		71 Pegasi	08Psc39	23N	
25 FR	09Psc16	**Mega 181**	09Psc46	66N	6874
26 SA	10Psc16	**Mega 181**	09Psc46	66N	6874
		Eta Cephei	09Psc56	71N	
		Phi Phoenicis	10Psc07	73N	
27 SU	11Psc15	**Mega 60**	10Psc57	68N	37273
		4 **Lac**/ Mega 209	11Psc08	53N	5559
		Phi Pegasi	11Psc25	18N	
28 MO	12Psc14	**Mega 141**	11Psc48	57N	9801
29 TU	13Psc14	**Alpha Reticuli**	12Psc46	78S	
		Mega 315	12Psc55	49N	3126
		Omega And /Mega 544	13Psc02	43N	1399
29 TU	13Psc14	**Alpha Reticuli**	12Psc46	78S	
		Mega 315	12Psc55	49N	3126
		Omega And /Mega 544	13Psc02	43N	1399
		Kappa Eridani	13Psc12	57S	
		Alpha Lacertae	13Psc24	53N	
		13 **Cep**/ Mega 359	13Psc43	61N	2647
30 WE	14Psc13	13 **Cep**/ Mega 359	13Psc43	61N	2647
		Gamma Peg/ **Algenib**	14Psc25	12N	
31 TH	15Psc12	Mu Cep/**Garnet Star**/Mega 54	14Psc58	64N	46049
		Psi Pegasi	15Psc20	23N	
		Mega 433	15Psc41	64N	1761
		Mega 342	15Psc41	66N	2890

Oh, Holy Mary Sophia, pray for us.

Sophia Star Calendar 2022 Lists

April 2022

Sun's *Sidereal Geocentric Longitude* is given at Midnight UT.
Star's *Sidereal Longitude* designates it as the Overlighting **Star** for the day.
Star's *Luminosity* indicates its intrinsic brightness as compared with **Sun's** *Luminosity*. **Sun** L=1.
Mega Stars are identified by an assigned numerical ranking according to their *Luminosity*, as recorded in AstroFire Database.
Mega Stars may or may not have proper names, but all are identified by assigned *Luminosity* numerical ranking.
This calendar identifies all **Stars** over 1000 *Luminosity* as **Mega Stars**, as recorded in AstroFire Database.

Humanity dwells in the region of the Fish, Pisces / Psc. (Mar 15- April 15)   *Virtue is Magnanimity.*
Son of God dwells in the region of the Ram, Aries / Ari. (April 15 - May 15)   *Virtue is Devotion.*

Midnight UT Date,	Sun Sidereal Geocentric Longitude	Overlighting Star	Star's Sidereal Longitude	Star's Sidereal Latitude	Luminosity (Sun L = 1)
01 FR	16Psc12	42 Piscium	15Psc47	10N	
02 SA	17Psc11	Chi Pegasi	16Psc52	17N	
		Mega 542	16Psc54	72N	1420
		Eta Ceti	17Psc02	16S	
		14 Cep/ Mega 139	17Psc16	61N	10710
03 SU	18Psc10	Alpha Cep/ **Alderamin**	18Psc02	68N	
		Mega 329	18Psc03	50N	2903
		Mega 479	18Psc23	58N	1633
04 MO	19Psc09	Zeta Cep/ Mega 445	19Psc13	61N	1903
		Delta Piscium	19Psc24	02N	
		Alpha And/ **Alpheratz**	19Psc34	25N	
		Nu Cep/ Mega 58	19Psc36	65N	42427
05 TU	20Psc08	9 Cep/ Mega 85	20Psc14	66N	20957
06 WE	21Psc08	Lambda Cep/ Mega 391	21Psc14	61N	2122
		Iota Andromedae	21Psc21	41N	
07 TH	22Psc07	Mega 83	22Psc06	64N	22877
		Mega 514	22Psc10	66N	1396
08 FR	23Psc06	Epsilon Piscium	22Psc47	01N	
		Delta Cep/ Mega 432	22Psc52	59N	1861
		Lambda Andromedae	23Psc33	43N	
09 SA	24Psc05	6 Cephei	23 Psc48	69N	
		Iota Eridani	24Psc02	51S	
10 SU	25Psc04	Upsilon Ceti	24Psc41	31S	
		19 Cep/ Mega 81	25Psc05	64N	22683
		Zeta Psc/ **Revati**	25Psc08	00S	
		Psi And/ Mega 528	25Psc12	42N	1444
11 MO	26Psc03	Sigma Andromedae	25Psc40	31N	
		Epsilon Andromedae	26Psc11	23N	
		Mega 51	26Psc24	65N	51745
		Mega 18	26Psc26	55N	353035
12 TU	27Psc01	Delta Andromedae	27Psc04	24N	
		Zeta Cet/ **Baten Kaitos**	27Psc13	20S	
13 WE	28Psc00	Eta Andromedae	27Psc38	15N	
		Mega 572	27Psc41	13S	1208
		Pi Andromedae	27Psc56	27N	
		Mu Piscium	28Psc24	03S	
14 TH	28Psc59	Theta 1 Eri/ **Acamar**	28Psc32	53S	
		Psi 2 Piscium	28Psc54	12N	
		Xi Cep/ **Kurhah**	29Psc29	65N	
15 FR	29Psc58	Xi Cep/ **Kurhah**	29Psc29	65N	
		22 Andromedae	29Psc43	40N	
		Omega Fornacis	29Psc46	40S	
		Chi Piscium	29Psc48	12N	
16 SA	00Ari57	1 Cas/ Mega 631	00Ari38	56N	1160
		Nu Piscium	00Ari46	04S	
		2 Cas/ Mega 465	01Ari02	56N	1710
		NGC7023.Cepheus,ReflectiveN.	01Ari15	72N	
17 SU	01Ari55	Beta Fornaci	01Ari30	45S	
		Phi Piscium	01Ari43	15N	
		Eta Psc/ **Alpherg**	02Ari05	05N	

Cosmic Communion: Star Wisdom, Volume 4

		Star	Longitude	Latitude	Distance
		Pi Piscium	02Ari10	01N	
18 MO	02Ari54	Sigma Piscium	02Ari28	23N	
		101 Psc/ Mega 532	02Ari48	04N	1391
		Omicron Piscium	03Ari00	01S	
19 TU	03Ari53	26 Cep/ Mega 319	03Ari38	63N	3242
		Upsilon Piscium	04Ari03	17N	
		Mega 652	04Ari06	55N	1074
20 WE	04Ari51	Nu Andromedae	04Ari25	32N	
		Alpha Psc/ **Alrisha**	04Ari38	09S	
		Rho Ceti	04Ari59	25S	
		Mega 143	05Ari00	44N	9644
		Mega 547	05Ari02	51N	1380
		NGC7635.Cassiopeia,BubbleN.	05Ari11	56N	
21 TH	05Ari50	Sigma Cas/ Mega 377	05Ari23	49N	2124
		Beta And/ **Mirach**	05Ari40	25N	
		NGC147.Cas,Dwarf Elliptic G.	05Ari44	40N	
		Rho Cas/ Mega 24	06Ari19	51N	174455
22 FR	06Ari48	Rho Cas/ Mega 24	06Ari19	51N	174455
		Mega 175	06Ari25	51N	6506
		NGC185.Cas,DwarfSphericG.	06Ari42	39N	
		Omicron Cet/ **Mira**	06Ari47	15S	
		4 Cassiopeiae	07Ari14	57N	
23 SA	07Ari47	Omicron Cas/ Mega 668	07Ari43	39N	1085
24 SU	08Ari45	Gamma 2 Ari/ **Mesarthim**	08Ari27	07N	
		M33.Triangulum,Pinwheel G.	08Ari30	19N	
		69 Cet/ Mega 673	08Ari35	12S	1075
		Xi Cas/ Mega 562	08Ari44	41N	1211
		Iota Arietis	08Ari47	05N	
		Pi Ceti	09Ari01	28S	
		Beta Ari/ **Sheraton**	09Ari14	08N	
25 MO	09Ari44	Beta Ari/ **Sheraton**	09Ari14	08N	
		Lambda Cassiopeiae	09Ari56	45N	
26 TU	10Ari42	Zeta Cassiopeiae	10Ari20	44N	
		Beta Cas/ **Caph**	10Ari23	51N	
		6 Cas/ Mega 28	10Ari41	55N	146535
		Beta Cep/ **Alfirk**/ Mega 497	10Ari48	71N	1481
		Lambda Arietis	10Ari57	10N	
27 WE	11Ari41	Mega 184	11Ari25	53N	6902
		Phi Andromedae	11Ari41	36N	
		Alpha Tri/ **Mothallah**	12Ari07	16N	
28 TH	12Ari39	Delta Ceti	12Ari50	14S	
		Alpha Ari/ **Hamal**	12Ari55	09N	
		9 Cas/ Mega 223	13Ari01	53N	4800
		Alpha Cas/ **Schedar**	13Ari03	46N	
		Alpha Doradus	13Ari05	74S	
29 FR	13Ari37	M77. Cetus, Spiral G.	13Ari31	15S	
		Nu Ceti	13Ari39	09S	
		Eta Eridani	4Ari01	24S	
30 SA	14Ari36	Theta Arietis	14Ari08	05N	
		Tau Andromedae	14Ari10	27N	
		Mega 310	14Ari30	55N	3214
		Gamma Ceti	14Ari42	12S	

Oh, Holy Mary Sophia, pray for us.

Sophia Star Calendar 2022 Lists

May 2022

Sun's *Sidereal Geocentric Longitude* is given at Midnight UT.
Star's *Sidereal Longitude* designates it as the Overlighting **Star** for the day.
Star's *Luminosity* indicates its intrinsic brightness as compared with **Sun's** *Luminosity*:Sun L=1.
Mega Stars are identified by an assigned numerical ranking according to their *Luminosity*, as recorded in AstroFire Database.
Mega Stars may or may not have proper names, but all are identified by assigned *Luminosity* numerical ranking.
This calendar identifies all **Stars** over 1000 *Luminosity* as **Mega Stars**, as recorded in AstroFire Database.

Son of God dwells in the region of the Ram,   Aries / Ari.   (April 15 - May 15)   Virtue is Devotion.
The Holy Spirit dwells in the region of the Bull, Taurus / Tau (May 15 - June 16)   Virtue is Inner Balance.

Midnight UT Date,	Sun Sidereal Geocentric Longitude	Overlighting Star	Star's Sidereal Longitude	Star's Sidereal Latitude	Luminosity (Sun L = 1)
01 SU	15Ari34	10 Cassiopeiae	15Ari35	55N	
		Epsilon Trianguli	15Ari36	19N	
		Mega 245	15Ari46	50N	4513
02 MO	16Ari32	Mega 640	16Ari27	58N	1027
		Mega 36	16Ari39	48N	82244
03 TU	17Ari30	Theta Cas/ **Marfak**	17Ari 03	43N	
		Mega 481	17Ari30	43N	1586
		Beta Trianguli	17Ari37	20N	
		Kappa Cas/ Mega 76	17Ari52	52N	29974
04 WE	18Ari29	**Omicron Arietis**	18Ari40	00S	
		Gamma Trianguli	18Ari47	18N	
05 TH	19Ari27	Gamma Cas/ **Tsih** /Mega 257	19Ari11	48N	4248
		Mega 409	19Ari23	50N	1947
		Gamma 1 And / **Almach**	19Ari29	27N	1491
		Alpha Cet/ **Menkar**	19Ari35	12S	
		Phi Per/ Mega 643	19Ari51	36N	1047
06 FR	20Ari25	**M76.** Perseus,Little Dumbell	20Ari07	37N	
		Sigma Arietis	20Ari12	01S	
		Lambda Ceti	20Ari21	07S	
		Pi Arietis	20Ari24	01N	
		Phi Cas/ Mega 240	20Ari46	45N	4653
07 SA	21Ari23	**Alpha Horologii**	21Ari05	61S	
		2 Persei	21Ari25	36N	
		13 Cassiopeiae	21Ari41	55N	
08 SU	22Ari21	**60 Andromedae**	22Ari06	28N	
09 MO	23Ari19	**15 Tri**/ Mega 98	22Ari52	18N	17049
		Mega 478	22Ari57	44N	1654
		Mega 326	23Ari07	62N	3035
		Delta Cas/ **Ruchbah**	23Ari11	46N	
		Epsilon Arietis	23Ari46	04N	
10 TU	24Ari17	**1 Persei**	23Ari52	40N	
		Kappa 2 Ceti	24Ari07	24N	
		Lambda Pictoris	24Ari30	71S	
		53 Arietis	24Ari39	00N	
11 WE	25Ari15	**4 Persei**	25Ari12	39N	
		Delta Caeli	25Ari15	65S	
12 TH	26Ari13	Delta Ari/ **Botein**	26Ari07	01N	
		Pi Eridani	26Ari14	31S	
		Mega 115	26Ari20	37N	14384
13 FR	27Ari11	**M34.** Perseus,Open C.	27Ari00	25N	
		Zeta Arietis	27Ari12	02N	
		Beta Dor/ Mega 339	27Ari23	85S	2768
14 SA	28Ari09	**6 Tauri**	28Ari24	09S	
		5 Per/ Mega 496	28Ari32	41N	1491
		Mega 506	28Ari34	42N	1480
		Mega 456	28Ari35	49N	1825
15 SU	29Ari07	Mega 274	28Ari40	33S	3759
		Mega 610	29Ari03	40N	1187
		Gamma Eri/ **Zaurak**	29Ari08	33S	
		Pi Per/ **Gorgonea Secunda**	29Ari10	21N	
		Mega 648	29Ari17	38N	1012
		9 Per/ Mega 340	29Ari17	39N	2973

		Mega 455	29Ari26	41N	1827
16 MO	00Tau05	**Mega 407**	29Ari59	40N	1947
		Epsilon Cas/ **Segin**	00Tau01	47N	
		10 Per/ Mega 304	00Tau10	39N	3254
		Rho Per/ **Gorgonea Tertia**	00Tau10	20N	
		62 Arietis	00Tau32	08N	
17 TU	01Tau03	**Mega 171**	01Tau19	30N	7068
		Alpha Caeli	01Tau24	62S	
		Beta Per/ **Algol**	01Tau26	22N	
18 WE	02Tau00	**Mega 416**	01Tau34	15N	2047
		Omega Per/**GorgoneaQuarto.**	01Tau37	20N	
		53 Cas/ Mega 199	01Tau46	47N	5725
		31 Tauri	02Tau30	13S	
19 TH	02Tau58	**31 Tauri**	02Tau30	13S	
		Kappa Per/ **Misam**	02Tau57	26N	
		Mega 38	03Tau08	56N	80752
		Tau Persei	03Tau10	34N	
20 FR	03Tau56	Eta Per/ **Miram**/ Mega 244	03Tau58	37N	4505
		Mega 127	04Tau20	38N	11017
		Omega Cassiopeiae	04Tau25	51N	
21 SA	04Tau54	**Omega Cassiopeiae**	04Tau25	51N	
		17 Tau/ **Electra**	04Tau40	04N	
		Omicron 1 Eri/ **Beid**	04Tau42	27S	
		16 Tau/ **Celaeno**	04Tau42	04N	
		19 Tau/**Taygeta**	04Tau50	04N	
		20 Tau/ **Maia**	04Tau56	04N	
		23 Tau/ **Merope**	04Tau56	03N	
		21 Tau/ **Asterope**	05Tau00	04N	
		Taurus, **Pleiades Stars**	05Tau09	04N	
		Eta Tau/ **Alcyone**	05Tau16	04N	
		Gamma Persei	05Tau17	34N	
22 SU	05Tau51	27 Tau/ **Atlas**	05Tau37	00N	
		28 Tau/ **Pleione**	05Tau38	04N	
		Lambda Tauri	05Tau54	07S	
23 MO	06Tau49	Omicron Per/ **Atik**/Mega 235	06Tau24	12N	5191
24 TU	07Tau47	Alpha Per/ **Mirfak**/ Mega 208	07Tau20	30N	5517
		Kappa Pictoris	07Tau38	78S	
		Sigma Persei	07Tau52	28N	
		Mega 598	08Tau08	34S	1159
25 WE	08Tau44	Zeta Per/ **Mega 191**	08Tau23	11N	5777
		Mega 672	08Tau32	29N	1029
		Mu Tauri	08Tau50	12S	
		Psi Persei	09Tau00	27N	
		Nu Persei	09Tau05	22N	
26 TH	09Tau42	**Delta Per**/ Mega 539	10Tau04	27N	1426
27 FR	10Tau40	Xi Per/ **Menkib** / Mega 186	10Tau14	14N	6582
		Epsilon Per /Mega 471	10Tau56	19N	1641
		Gamma Tau/**Primus Hyadum**	11Tau04	05S	
28 SA	11Tau37	**45 Eridani**	11Tau27	21S	
		Mega 173	11Tau33	38N	7566
		Mega 73	11Tau50	39N	31216
		Nu Eridani	12Tau04	25S	
29 SU	12Tau35	Delta 1 Tau/ **Hyadum II**	12Tau08	03S	
		Mega 653	12Tau32	00S	1089
		Pi Tauri	12Tau33	06S	
30 MO	13Tau32	**Phi Tauri**	13Tau10	05N	
		Theta 2 Tauri	13Tau13	05S	
		Mega 597	13Tau16	44N	1134
		Mega 19	13Tau22	60N	325087
		Epsilon Tau/ **Ain**	13Tau44	02S	
		Mega 422	13Tau57	39N	2011
31 TU	14Tau30	**Mu Eridani**	14Tau36	25S	

Oh, Holy Mary Sophia, pray for us.

Sophia Star Calendar 2022 Lists

June 2022

Sun's *Sidereal Geocentric Longitude* is given at Midnight UT.
Star's *Sidereal Longitude* designates it as the Overlighting **Star** for the day.
Star's *Luminosity* indicates its intrinsic brightness as compared with **Sun's** *Luminosity*: **Sun** L=1.
Mega Stars are identified by an assigned numerical ranking according to their *Luminosity*, as recorded in AstroFire Database.
Mega Stars may or may not have proper names, but all are identified by assigned *Luminosity* numerical ranking.
This calendar identifies all **Stars** over 1000 *Luminosity* as **Mega Stars,** as recorded in AstroFire Database.

The Holy Spirit dwells in the region of the Bull, Taurus / Tau. (May 15 - June 16)   *Virtue is Inner Balance.*
Seraphim, Spirits of Universal Love, dwell in the region of the Twins, Gemini / Gem. (June 16 - July 17)   *Virtue is Perseverance.*

Midnight UT Date,	Sun Sidereal Geocentric Longitude	Overlighting Star	Star's Sidereal Longitude	Star's Sidereal Latitude	Luminosity (Sun L = 1)
01 WE	15Tau28	**Lambda Persei**	15Tau01	28N	
		Alpha Tau/ **Aldebaran**	15Tau03	05S	
		Sigma 1 Tauri	15Tau43	06S	
		NGC1851.Columba,Globe C.	15Tau51	62S	
02 TH	16Tau25	**Mu Persei**	16Tau03	26N	
		Omega Eridani	16Tau18	27S	
		Mega 328	16Tau34	39N	2838
03 FR	17Tau23	**Mega 374**	17Tau04	37N	2464
		Pi 3 Ori/ **Tabit**	17Tau11	15S	
		Epsilon Leporis	17Tau19	44S	
		Pi 4 Ori/ Mega 247	17Tau22	16S	4379
		Tau Tauri	17Tau25	00N	
		Pi 5 Ori/ Mega 234	17Tau45	20S	4839
04 SA	18Tau20	**Psi Eridani**	18Tau28	29S	
		Omicron 1 Orion	18Tau45	08S	
		Pi 6 Ori/ Mega 577	18Tau48	20S	1213
05 SU	19Tau18	**Pi 6 Ori**/ Mega 577	18Tau48	20S	1213
06 MO	20Tau15	**Gamma Camelopardalis**	19Tau54	49N	
		Mega 345	19Tau57	25S	2974
		Mega 637	20Tau23	57S	1119
		Lambda Eri/ Mega 231	20Tau28	31S	5023
		Beta Eri/ **Cursa**	20Tau32	27S	
		Mu Leporis	20Tau39	39S	
07 TU	21Tau12	**Kappa Leporis**	21Tau10	35S	
		2 Aurigae	21Tau24	14N	
08 WE	22Tau10	Iota Aur/ **Hassaleh**/Mega 450	21Tau54	10N	1802
		Beta Ori/ **Rigel**/ Mega 59	22Tau05	31S	41436
		Mega 55	22Tau06	13N	40335
09 TH	23Tau07	**Lambda Lep**/ Mega 449	23Tau02	36S	1824
		Tau Orionis	23Tau06	29S	
		103 Tau/ Mega 198	23Tau27	01N	5387
10 FR	24Tau05	Zeta Aur/ **Haedus I**	23Tau54	18N	1698
		Epsilon Columbae	23Tau57	58S	
		Mega 558	24Tau06	18N	1224
		Epsilon Aur/**Al Maaz**/ Mega91.	24Tau06	20N	20881
		8 Lep/ Mega 378	24Tau09	37S	2135
11 SA	25Tau02	Eta Aur/ **Haedus II**	24Tau42	18N	
		22 Ori/ Mega 441	24Tau50	23S	1761
		Beta Lep/ **Nihal**	24Tau56	43S	
		Mega 520	25Tau05	14N	1346
		Eta Ori/ Mega 299	25Tau25	25S	3038
12 SU	25Tau59	**Psi 1 Ori**/ Mega 602	25Tau48	21S	1115
		Gamma Ori/ **Bellatrix**	26Tau12	16S	1068
		Alpha Cam/ Mega 37	26Tau14	43N	77948
		Psi 2 Ori/ Mega 368	26Tau26	20S	2402
13 MO	26Tau57	**Beta Cam**/ Mega 408	26Tau32	37N	1990
		Alpha Lep/ **Arneb**/ Mega 123	26Tau38	41S	12541
		19 Aur/ Mega 169	26Tau50	10N	7403
		Alpha Aur/ **Capella**	27Tau07	22N	
		Upsilon Ori/ **Thabit**/ Mega343	27Tau10	30S	2776
		Alpha Col/ **Phact**	27Tau26	57S	
14 TU	27Tau54	Alpha Col/ **Phact**	27Tau26	57S	
		Delta Ori/ **Mintaka**/ Mega160	27Tau37	23S	8652

		Mega 275	27Tau44	24S	3948
		Beta Tau/ El Nath	27Tau50	05N	
		Mega 413	27Tau59	24S	2018
		Mega 373	28Tau07	06N	2320
		Mega 103	28Tau08	29S	15534
		Mega 288	28Tau09	29S	3483
		Theta 1 Ori/ **Trapezium**	28Tau14	28S	2592
		Theta 1 Ori/ Mega 392	28Tau14	28S	2258
		Iota Ori/**Hatsya**/ Mega128	28Tau15	28S	11432
		Theta 2 Ori/ **Trapezium**	28Tau16	28S	2999
		M42. Orion, Orion N.	28Tau16	28S	
15 WE	28Tau51	**Mega 494**	28Tau27	26S	1535
		Mega 495	28Tau35	29S	1567
		119 Tau/ Mega 206	28Tau39	04S	5638
		Epsilon Ori/ **Alnilam**/ Mega69	28Tau43	24S	31102
		M38. Auriga, Open C.	28Tau46	12N	
		Phi 1 Ori/ Mega 530	28Tau52	13S	1394
		120 Tau/ Mega 489	28Tau58	04S	1552
		Lambda Ori/**Meissa**/ Mega 263	28Tau58	13S	4019
		Mega 669	29Tau00	13S	1008
		Sigma Ori/ Mega 287	29Tau21	25S	3352
		M1. Taurus, Crab N.	29Tau21	01S	
16 TH	29Tau48	Sigma Ori/ Mega 287	29Tau21	25S	3352
		M1. Taurus, Crab N.	29Tau21	01S	
		Mega 439	29Tau23	39N	1774
		Chi Aur/ Mega 93	29Tau25	08N	17775
		Omega Ori/ Mega 298	29Tau46	19S	3417
		Zeta Ori/ **Alnitak**/ Mega 131	29Tau56	25S	11017
		Mega 268	00Gem00	24S	3748
		Mu Col/ Mega 615	00Gem01	55S	1162
		Zeta Tauri/ **Alheckla**	00Gem03	02S	
		M36. Auriga, Open C.	00Gem14	10N	
		NGC2024.Orion, Flame N.	00Gem16	25S	
17 FR	00Gem46	NGC2024.Orion, Flame N.	00Gem16	25S	
		Mega 411	00Gem39	16N	1966
		17 Camelopardalis	00Gem53	39N	
18 SA	01Gem43	Kappa Ori/ **Saiph**/ Mega 180	01Gem40	33S	6335
		Beta Col/ **Wezn**	01Gem41	59S	
19 SU	02Gem40	**Delta Leporis**	02Gem26	44S	
		Lambda Col/ **Tsze**	02Gem37	57S	
		55 Ori/ Mega 480	02Gem46	30S	1661
20 MO	03Gem38	**56 Ori**/ Mega 586	03Gem14	21S	1266
		M37. Auriga, Open C.	03Gem38	09N	
		Alpha UMi/**Polaris**/Mega 369	03Gem50	66N	2483
		Sigma Col/ Mega 670	03Gem54	54S	1085
		AlphaOri/**Betelgeuse**/Mega145	04Gem01	16S	9884
21 TU	04Gem35	**Gamma Col**/ Mega 651	04Gem18	58S	1076
		Mega 324	04Gem30	05N	3101
		Mega 44	04Gem34	00N	58557
		139 Tau/ Mega 265	04Gem49	02N	4319
		Eta Columbae	04Gem52	66S	
22 WE	05Gem32	**Beta Aur**/ **Menkalinan**	05Gem10	21N	
		Delta Aur/ **Prijipati**	05Gem11	30N	
		Theta Aur/ **Mahasim**	05Gem12	13N	
		Pi Aur/ Mega 617	05Gem15	22N	1102
		Mega 187	05Gem29	04N	6820
		Lambda Ursae Minoris	05Gem44	67N	
		3 Monocerotis	05Gem48	34S	
23 TH	06Gem29	**Chi 2 Ori**/ Mega 11	06Gem11	03S	1213388
		Delta UMi/ **Yildun**	06Gem28	69N	
		66 Ori/ Mega 336	06Gem34	19S	2841
		17 Lep/ Mega 655	06Gem49	39S	1008
24 FR	07Gem27	**Nu Orionis**	07Gem07	08S	
		Mega 348	07Gem08	27S	2646
		M35. Gemini, Open C.	07Gem17	00N	
		Mega 122	07Gem28	01S	13166
		3 Gem/ Mega 99	07Gem30	00S	16783
		Mega 487	07Gem54	05S	1630
25 SA	08Gem24	Mega 487	07Gem54	05S	1630
		6 Gem/ Mega 272	08Gem06	00S	3753
		Theta Columbae	08Gem19	65S	

Sophia Star Calendar 2022 Lists

		Star	Position	Dec	Dist
		Mega 625	08Gem40	29S	1122
		Eta Gem/ **Propus**	08Gem42	00S	
26 SU	09Gem21	**9 Gem**/ Mega 622	09Gem09	00N	1142
		73 Ori/ Mega 671	09Gem10	10S	1070
		Gamma Monocerotis	09Gem31	29S	
		Psi 1 Aur/ Mega 119	09Gem46	25N	12977
27 MO	10Gem18	Mu Gem/ **Tejat**	10Gem34	00S	
28 TU	11Gem16	**7 Monocerotis**	10Gem58	31S	
		7 Lynx	11Gem03	32N	
		Mega 522	11Gem27	44S	1343
		Mega 508	11Gem40	35S	1472
29 WE	12Gem13	**Mega 106**	11Gem47	16S	15470
		16 Geminorum	11Gem49	02S	
		Nu Geminorum	12Gem04	03S	
		Mega 574	12Gem13	33S	1239
		Beta CMa/**Mirzam**/ Mega 323	12Gem27	41S	3297
29 WE	12Gem13	**Mega 106**	11Gem47	16S	15470
		16 Geminorum	11Gem49	02S	
		Nu Geminorum	12Gem04	03S	
		Mega 574	12Gem13	33S	1239
		Beta CMa/**Mirzam**/ Mega 323	12Gem27	41S	3297
		Delta Pic/ Mega 346	12Gem35	78S	2904
		Mega 641	12Gem37	36S	1074
		Zeta CMa/ **Furud**	12Gem38	53S	
		Mega 431	12Gem40	15N	1860
30 TH	13Gem10	**Mega 431**	12Gem40	15N	1860
		Mega 152	13Gem04	11S	8517
		10 Mon/ Mega 550	13Gem09	28S	1419
		Mega 405	13Gem12	57S	2000
		Beta Mon/ Mega 579	13Gem33	30S	1225

Oh, Holy Mary Sophia, pray for us.

Cosmic Communion: Star Wisdom, Volume 4

July 2022

Sun's Sidereal Geocentric Longitude is given at Midnight UT.
Star's Sidereal Longitude designates it as the Overlighting **Star** for the day.
Star's Luminosity indicates its intrinsic brightness as compared with Sun's Luminosity : **Sun** L=1.
Mega Stars are identified by an assigned numerical ranking according to their *Luminosity*, as recorded in AstroFire Database.
Mega Stars may or may not have proper names, but all are identified by assigned *Luminosity* numerical ranking.
This calendar identifies all **Stars** over 1000 *Luminosity* as **Mega Stars**, as recorded in AstroFire Database.

Seraphim, Spirits of Universal Love, dwell in the region of the Twins, Gemini / Gem. (June 16 - July 17)   *Virtue is Perseverance.*
Cherubim, Spirits of Harmony, dwell in the region of the Crab, Cancer / Can. (July 17 - Aug 17)   *Virtue is Selflessness.*

Midnight UT Date, Sun Sidereal Geocentric Longitude		Overlighting Star	Star's Sidereal Longitude	Star's Sidereal Latitude	Luminosity (Sun L = 1)
01 FR	14Gem07	13 Mon/ Mega 321	13Gem45	15S	3042
		Mega 114	14Gem10	33S	13804
		Gamma Gem/ Alhena	14Gem22	06S	
		Epsilon Ursae Minoris	14Gem24	73N	
02 SA	15Gem04	Mega 325	14Gem47	22S	3267
		Mega 197	14Gem59	16S	6047
		Mega 182	15Gem12	18S	6591
		EpsilonGem/ Mebsuta	15Gem12	02N	3990
03 SU	16Gem02	Mega 442	15Gem37	12S	1777
		15 Mon/ Mega 261	15Gem38	13S	1171
		Mega 320	15Gem39	21S	3044
		Lambda Canis Majoris	15Gem50	55S	
		Psi 9 Aurigae	15Gem51	23N	
		Xi 1 CMa/ Mega 183	15Gem55	46S	6327
		Mega 16	16Gem09	16S	388884
		Theta Geminorum	16Gem23	11N	
		Xi Gem/ Alzirr	16Gem28	10S	
04 MO	16Gem59	Mega 23	16Gem47	19S	197580
		Mega 362	17Gem14	37S	2399
		33 Geminorum	17Gem18	06S	
05 TU	17Gem56	35 Geminorum	17Gem41	09S	
06 WE	18Gem53	Mega 618	18Gem30	21S	1099
		40 Geminorum	18Gem37	03N	
		Psi 1Dra/ Dziban	19Gem04	84N	
		Mega 559	19Gem08	31S	1305
		Alpha CMa/ Sirius	19Gem20	39S	
07 TH	19Gem51	Omega Gem/ Mega 443	19Gem28	01N	1867
		Mega 135	19Gem34	10S	10916
		Mega 438	19Gem44	60N	1841
		41 Gem/ Mega 113	19Gem49	06S	14178
		M41.Canis Major, Open C.	20Gem11	43S	
		Mega 629	20Gem13	59S	1156
		AlphaCar/Canopus/Mega112	20Gem13	75S	14172
		Zeta Gem/ Mekbuda	20Gem15	02S	2785
		Mega 546	20Gem19	05S	1365
		Mega 214	20Gem19	24S	5721
08 FR	20Gem48	Mega 546	20Gem19	05S	1365
		Mega 214	20Gem19	24S	5721
		Tau Geminorum	20Gem42	07N	
09 SA	21Gem45	Theta Canis Majoris	21Gem27	34S	
		10 CMa/ Mega 250	21Gem32	53S	4510
		Mega 633	21Gem53	53S	1159
10 SU	22Gem42	Mu Canis Majoris	22Gem18	36S	
		Nu Puppis	22Gem24	66S	
		15 CMa/ Mega 358	22Gem30	42S	2519
		Iota CMa/ Mega 116	22Gem47	39S	13976
		Mega 452	22Gem56	31S	1792
11 MO	23Gem39	Omicron 1 CMa/ Mega 149	23Gem25	46S	8893
		M50. Monoceros, Heart C.	23Gem32	30S	
		Mega 331	23Gem43	45S	2924
		Delta Gem/ Wasat	23Gem47	00S	
		Kappa CMa/ Mega 427	23Gem50	55S	2033
		Lambda Geminorum	24Gem02	05S	
12 TU	24Gem36	Iota Geminorium	24Gem13	05N	
		Mega 357	24Gem39	33S	2585

Sophia Star Calendar 2022 Lists

Day		Star	Position	Dec	Dist
		Gamma CMa/ **Muliphein**	24Gem52	38S	
		Mega 241	25Gem00	33S	4514
13 WE	25Gem34	**Mega 216**	25Gem09	34S	5116
		Alpha Gem/ **Castor**	25Gem30	10N	
		Mega 157	25Gem37	32S	8946
		Mega 230	25Gem42	06S	5010
		EpsilonCMa/ **Adhara**	26Gem01	51S	3818
14 TH	26Gem31	EpsilonCMa/ **Adhara**	26Gem01	51S	3818
		Omicron 2 CMa/ Mega 67	26Gem16	46S	33450
		Mega 15	26Gem44	38S	428070
		Sigma CMa /Mega 227	26Gem49	50S	4872
		Epsilon Canis Minoris	26Gem55	12S	
		Mega 421	26Gem58	32S	1968
15 FR	27Gem28	**Mega 421**	26Gem58	32S	1968
		Mega 451	27Gem05	32S	1896
		Mega 246	27Gem06	75S	4631
		Mega 148	27Gem25	21S	9405
		Beta CMi/ **Gomeisa**	27Gem27	13S	
		Gamma Canis Minoris	27Gem36	12S	
		Mega 283	27Gem41	45S	3608
		Eta Canis Minoris	27Gem53	14S	
		Pi Geminorum	27Gem57	12N	
16 SA	28Gem25	**Pi Geminorum**	27Gem57	12N	
		Omicron UMa/ **Muscida**	28Gem15	40N	
		Beta Gem/ **Pollux**	28Gem29	06N	
		Delta CMa/ **Wezen**/ Mega 49	28Gem39	48S	48737
		Mega 499	28Gem47	47S	1456
17 SU	29Gem23	**Mega 286**	29Gem00	30S	3589
		Mega 630	29Gem28	27S	1194
		Mega 570	29Gem43	23S	1253
		Delta 1 Canis Minoris	29Gem46	19S	
18 MO	00Cnc20	**Mega 102**	00Cnc17	41S	16947
		Sigma 1 Ursae Majoris	00Cnc28	47N	
		Mega 63	00Cnc31	45S	37670
		27 CMa/ Mega 281	00Cnc35	48S	3468
		Mega 167	00Cnc40	49S	7822
		Mega 96	00Cnc45	26S	18276
19 TU	01Cnc17	Omega CMa/ Mega436	00Cnc53	48S	1740
		Alpha CMi/ **Procyon**	01Cnc03	16S	
		29 CMa/ Mega166	01Cnc31	46S	8187
		Tau CMa/ Mega 107	01Cnc39	46S	14955
20 WE	02Cnc14	**Mega 623**	02Cnc10	48S	1148
		Omega 1 Cancri	02Cnc25	04N	
		Chi Geminorum	02Cnc30	07N	
		Zeta Ursae Minoris	02Cnc40	75N	
21 TH	03Cnc11	**31 Lyncis**	02Cnc49	23N	
		Mega 313	02Cnc55	43S	3150
		Mega 665	02Cnc58	48S	1058
		Tau Puppis	02Cnc59	72S	
		Mega 301	03Cnc32	08N	3265
		Mega 137	03Cnc34	35S	10926
22 FR	04Cnc09	**Mega 258**	03Cnc53	46S	4124
		Mega 569	04Cnc14	35S	1222
		M47. Puppis, Open C.	04Cnc23	35S	
		Alpha Monocerotis	04Cnc32	30S	
		Mega 144	04Cnc38	44S	9803
23 SA	05Cnc06	**Mega 144**	04Cnc38	44S	9803
		M81. Ursa Major, Bodes G.	04Cnc45	51N	
		Eta CMa/ **Aludra**/ Mega 35	04Cnc48	50S	87660
		Zeta Canis Minoris	04Cnc54	18S	
		Theta Ursae Minoris	05Cnc23	74N	
		Mega 627	05Cnc24	53S	1159
		Pi Puppis/ Mega 168	05Cnc34	58S	8083
24 SU	06Cnc03	Pi Puppis/ Mega 168	05Cnc34	58S	8083
		Mega 557	05Cnc47	40S	1251
		M46. Puppis, Open C.	05Cnc59	35S	
25 MO	07Cnc01	Zeta 1 Cnc/ **Tegmine**	06Cnc36	02S	
		Mega 17	07Cnc12	44S	396114

– 219 –

26 TU	07Cnc58	Mega 294	07Cnc39	51S	3475
		Mega 555	07Cnc59	36S	1274
		Mega 526	08Cnc02	36S	1321
		Iota UMa/ Talitha Borealis	08Cnc04	29N	
		4 UMi/ Pherkad Minor	08Cnc04	70N	
		Mega 394	08Cnc18	22S	2156
27 WE	08Cnc55	10 Puppis	09Cnc01	35S	
		Kappa UMa/Talitha Australis	09Cnc12	28N	
28 TH	09Cnc53	Beta Cnc/ El Tarf	09Cnc31	10S	
		Mega 657	09Cnc45	39S	1035
		Mega 483	09Cnc46	45S	1607
		Upsilon 2 Cancri	09Cnc50	05N	
29 FR	10Cnc50	Zeta Monocerotis	10Cnc24	22S	5070
		Eta Cancri	10Cnc40	01N	
		Theta Cancri	10Cnc59	00S	
		3 Pup/ Mega 26	11Cnc09	49S	168887
		Xi Pup/ Asmidiske /Mega 185	11Cnc18	44S	6861
		Omicron Pup/ Mega 153	11Cnc19	46S	8687
30 SA	11Cnc47	Xi Pup/ Asmidiske /Mega 185	11Cnc18	44S	6861
		Omicron Pup/ Mega 153	11Cnc19	46S	8687
		Upsilon Ursae Majoris	11Cnc32	42N	
		Iota Cancri	11Cnc36	10N	
31 SU	12Cnc45	Theta Ursae Majoris	12Cnc31	34N	
		M44. Epsilon Cnc/ Praesepe	12Cnc39	01N	
		GammaCnc/Asellus Borealis	12Cnc48	03N	
		11 Puppis	12Cnc54	42S	
		53 Cancri	12Cnc59	10N	

Oh, Holy Mary Sophia, pray for us.

Sophia Star Calendar 2022 Lists

August 2022

Sun's Sidereal Geocentric Longitude is given at Midnight UT.
Star's Sidereal Longitude designates it as the Overlighting **Star** for the day.
Star's Luminosity indicates its intrinsic brightness as compared with Sun's Luminosity: **Sun** L=1.
Mega Stars are identified by an assigned numerical ranking according to their *Luminosity*, as recorded in AstroFire Database.
Mega Stars may or may not have proper names, but all are identified by assigned *Luminosity* numerical ranking.
This calendar identifies all **Stars** over 1000 *Luminosity* as **Mega Stars**, as recorded in AstroFire Database.

Cherubim, Spirits of Harmony, dwell in the region of the Crab, Cancer / Can. (July 17 - Aug 17) Virtue is Selflessness.
Thrones, Spirits of Will, dwell in the region of the Lion, Leo/ Leo. (Aug 18 - Sept 17) Virtue is Compassion.

Midnight UT Date,	Sun Sidereal Geocentric Longitude	Overlighting Star	Star's Sidereal Longitude	Star's Sidereal Latitude	Luminosity (Sun L = 1)
01 MO	13Cnc42	**12 Puppis**	13Cnc44	42S	
		Sigma Puppis	13Cnc57	63S	
		Delta Cnc/ **Asellus Australis**	13Cnc59	00N	
		14 Puppis	14Cnc07	39S	
02 TU	14Cnc40	**Phi Ursae Majoris**	14Cnc37	38N	
		Mega 136	14Cnc51	13S	10659
03 WE	15Cnc37	**20 Pup**/ Mega 571	15Cnc18	34S	1252
		Delta Hydrae	15Cnc34	12S	
		Lambda Dra/ **Giausar**	15Cnc36	57N	
		Tau Cancri	15Cnc54	12N	
04 TH	16Cnc34	**Mega 212**	16Cnc09	57S	5622
		Mega 393	16Cnc11	49S	2127
		Nu Cancri	16Cnc18	07N	
		Sigma Hya/ **Minchir**	16Cnc28	14S	
		Mega 302	16Cnc41	00S	3308
05 FR	17Cnc32	**Alpha Lyncis**	17Cnc06	17N	
		Mega 607	17Cnc15	58S	1181
		Eta Hydrae	17Cnc34	14S	
		Epsilon Hydrae	17Cnc36	11S	
06 SA	18Cnc29	**Xi Cancri**	18Cnc28	05N	
		Beta UMi/ **Kochab**	18Cnc35	72N	
		Alpha Cnc/ **Acubens**	18Cnc54	05S	
07 SU	19Cnc27	**Mega 285**	19Cnc27	51S	3581
		Zeta Hydrae	19Cnc50	10S	
08 MO	20Cnc24	**Mega 300**	20Cnc25	52S	3277
		Alpha UMa/ **Dubhe**	20Cnc27	49N	
		42 Ursae Majoris	20Cnc42	46N	
09 TU	21Cnc22	**Kappa Cancri**	21Cnc26	05S	
		Kappa Draconis	21Cnc31	61N	
10 WE	22Cnc19	**Pi 2 Cancri**	21Cnc55	00S	
		Mega 12	22Cnc04	44S	1075715
		Mega 130	22Cnc36	68S	11020
		Omega Hya/ **Mega 592**	22Cnc39	11S	1215
		Mega 270	22Cnc40	27S	3919
11 TH	23Cnc17	Lambda Leo/ **Alterf**	23Cnc08	07N	
12 FR	24Cnc14	Zeta Puppis/ **Naos**/ Mega 82	23Cnc49	58S	20955
		Mega 170	24Cnc20	65S	7241
		Mega 521	24Cnc22	55S	1331
		Mega 667	24Cnc41	54S	1045
		Beta UMa/ **Merak**	24Cnc42	45N	
13 SA	25Cnc12	Beta UMa/ **Merak**	24Cnc42	45N	
		Lambda UMa/ **Tania Borealis**	24Cnc46	29N	
		Mega 524	24Cnc50	65S	1416
		Mega 575	25Cnc02	62S	1254
		Mega 649	25Cnc03	53S	1021
14 SU	26Cnc09	**Mega 262**	25Cnc43	53S	4077
		Epsilon Leo/ **Algenubi**	25Cnc58	09N	
		Mega 215	26Cnc06	57S	4818
		Mu UMa/ **Tania Australis**	26Cnc30	29N	
15 MO	27Cnc07	Mu Leo/ **Rasalas**	26Cnc41	12N	
		Omega Leonis	26Cnc48	05S	
		Gamma UMi/ **Pherkad**	26Cnc51	75N	1192
		Xi Leonis	26Cnc54	03S	
		Mega 446	27Cnc07	53S	1845
		6 Leonis	27Cnc25	04S	

— 221 —

16 TU	28Cnc05	Mega 174	27Cnc45	66S	6330
		M97. Ursa Major, Owl N.	27Cnc55	45N	
17 WE	29Cnc02	Psi Leonis	28Cnc45	00N	
		Mega 86	28Cnc52	60S	22793
		Alpha Pictoris	29Cnc23	83S	
		Mega 566	29Cnc24	62S	1214
		Mega 140	29Cnc28	60S	9672
		Omicron Leo/ **Subra**	29Cnc30	03S	
18 TH	00Leo00	Omicron Leo/ **Subra**	29Cnc30	03S	
		Beta Leonis Minoris	29Cnc48	25N	
		Mega 594	00Leo19	09N	1097
19 FR	00Leo58	Gamma Pyxidis	00Leo44	43S	
		Mega 663	00Leo46	64S	1029
		Mega 447	00Leo58	67S	1810
		Tau 2 Hya/ **Ukdah**	01Leo00	14S	
20 SA	01Leo55	Alpha Pyx/**Sumut**/ Mega 419	01Leo46	48S	1972
		Omega Ursae Majoris	01Leo47	33N	
		Beta Pyxidis	2Leo04	51S	
21 SU	02Leo53	Alpha Hya/ **Alphard**	02Leo32	22S	
		Nu Leonis	02Leo36	00N	
		Gamma2Velorum/ Mega125	02Leo37	64S	11543
		Zeta Leo/ **Adhafera**	02Leo50	11N	
		Iota Hydrae	02Leo54	14S	
		Mega 318	03Leo05	59S	3233
		Eta Leonis/ Mega 104	03Leo10	04N	15087
22 MO	03Leo51	Psi Ursae Majoris	04Leo04	35N	
23 TU	04Leo49	Pi Leonis	04Leo34	03S	
		Gamma 1 Leo/ **Algieba**	04Leo53	08N	
		Alpha Leo/ **Regulus**	05Leo05	00N	
24 WE	05Leo47	NGC 3227. Leo, Seyfert G.	05Leo39	09N	
		Gamma UMa/ **Phecda**	05Leo44	47N	
		Chi Carinae	05Leo59	70S	
		46 Leo Minor/ **Praecipua**	06Leo08	24N	
25 TH	06Leo45	Delta UMa/ **Megrez**	06Leo19	51N	
		Mega 64	06Leo21	60S	38353
		Mega 565	06Leo44	60S	1234
		46 Ursae Majoris	06Leo58	24N	
		Mega 271	07Leo14	58S	3837
26 FR	07Leo42	Mega 271	07Leo14	58S	3837
		NGC6543. Draco, Cat'sEyeN.	07Leo31	89N	
		Kappa Hydrae	07Leo56	26S	
27 SA	08Leo40	Mega 384	08Leo18	64S	2265
		Theta Pyxidis	08Leo19	39S	
		Mega 541	08Leo31	61S	1407
		Mega 533	08Leo31	54S	1344
		Chi Ursae Majoris	08Leo55	41N	
28 SU	09Leo38	Alpha Sextantis	09Leo23	11S	
		Mega 469	09Leo43	63S	1623
		Mega 576	09Leo49	73S	1268
		Mega 645	09Leo59	62S	1012
		44 Leonis	10Leo06	01S	
29 MO	10Leo36	44 Leonis	10Leo06	01S	
		Mega 612	10Leo13	56S	1186
		54 Leonis	10Leo46	16N	
		Mega 221	10Leo53	59S	4948
		Upsilon 1 Hydrae	10Leo57	26S	
30 TU	11Leo34	NGC3115.Sextans, Spindle G.	11Leo28	18S	
		Rho Leo/ Mega 40	11Leo39	00N	78028
		Mega 79	11Leo48	61S	24526
		Nu UMa/ **Alula Borealis**	11Leo55	26N	
31 WE	12Leo32	Xi UMa/ **Alula Australis**	12Leo36	26N	
		Alpha Dra/ **Thuban**	12Leo43	66N	
		Mega 266	12Leo44	61S	3741
		Mega 210	12Leo45	60S	5592
		Mega 194	12Leo46	59S	5980

Oh, Holy Mary Sopha, pray for us.

Sophia Star Calendar 2022 Lists

September 2022

Sun's Sidereal Geocentric Longitude is given at Midnight UT.
Star's Sidereal Longitude designates it as the Overlighting Star for the day.
Star's Luminosity indicates its intrinsic brightness as compared with Sun's Luminosity: **Sun** L=1
Mega Stars are identified by an assigned numerical ranking according to their *Luminosity*, as recorded in AstroFire Database.
Mega Stars may or may not have proper names, but all are identified by assigned *Luminosity* numerical ranking.
This calendar identifies all **Stars** over 1000 *Luminosity* as **Mega Stars**, as recorded in AstroFire Database.

Thrones, Spirits of Will, dwell in the region of the Lion, Leo/ Leo. (Aug 18 - Sept 17)   *Virtue is Compassion.*
Kyriotetes, Spirits of Wisdom, dwell in the region of the Virgin, Virgo/ Vir. (Sept 17 - Oct 18)   *Virtue is Courtesy.*

Midnight UT Date,	Sun Sidereal Geocentric Longitude	Overlighting Star	Star's Sidereal Longitude	Star's Sidereal Latitude	Luminosity (Sun L = 1)
01 TH	13Leo30	Mega 211	13Leo15	60S	5591
		M105. Leo, Elliptical G.	13Leo50	04N	
		Mega 504	13Leo57	62S	1503
02 FR	14Leo28	Epsilon UMa/ Alioth	14Leo12	54N	
		Ursa Major, Seyfert G.	14Leo31	40N	
		Mega 213	14Leo36	60S	5476
		Beta Sextantis	14Leo46	09S	
03 SA	15Leo26	Theta Antliae	15Leo12	38S	
		Delta Sextantis	15Leo22	11S	
		72 Leo/ Mega 48	15Leo44	16N	54401
04 SU	16Leo25	Epsilon Antliae	16Leo16	47S	
		Lambda Vel/ Suhail	16Leo27	55S	3450
		Delta Leo/ Zosma	16Leo35	14N	
		Mega 111	16Leo51	40S	15062
05 MO	17Leo23	36 Sextantis	17Leo03	05S	
06 TU	18Leo21	Mega 30	18Leo40	56S	130033
		Theta Leo/ Chort	18Leo41	09N	
07 WE	19Leo19	Canes Venatici, Quasar G.	19Leo21	36N	
		Mega 126	19Leo31	55S	11886
		Chi Leonis	19Leo46	01N	
08 TH	20Leo17	Mega 192	20Leo03	56S	6052
		Mu Hydrae	20Leo18	24S	
		NGC3242.Hydra, GhostJupiter	20Leo46	26S	
09 FR	21Leo15	NGC3242.Hydra, GhostJupiter	20Leo46	26S	
		Zeta UMa/ Mizar	20Leo58	56N	
		86 Leonis	21Leo06	13N	
		80 UMa/ Alcor	21Leo08	56N	
10 SA	22Leo14	Phi 2 Hydrae	22Leo31	23S	
		90 Leo/ Mega 525	22Leo43	12N	1350
11 SU	23Leo12	90 Leo/ Mega 525	22Leo43	12N	1350
		Iota Leo/Tsze Tseang	22Leo50	06N	
		Phi 3 Hydrae	23Leo19	23S	
12 MO	24Leo10	Sigma Leonis	23Leo58	01N	
		Delta Velorum	24Leo12	67S	
		Mega 420	24Leo12	71S	1917
		Mega 363	24Leo21	36S	2398
13 TU	25Leo09	75 Leonis	24Leo39	02S	
		Nu Hydrae	25Leo38	21S	
14 WE	26Leo07	Nu Hydrae	25Leo38	21S	
		Vela, Nebula	26Leo25	55S	
15 TH	27Leo05	Phi Leonis	26Leo45	07S	
		Tau Leonis	26Leo46	00S	
		Beta Leo/ Denebola	26Leo53	12N	
		4 Coma Berenices	26Leo58	24N	
		Omega Virginis	27Leo05	05N	
16 FR	28Leo04	Alpha Antliae	27Leo42	37S	
		Delta Antliae	28Leo01	36S	
		Mega 29	28Leo20	61S	140314
		Epsilon Car/ Avior/ Mega195	28Leo23	72S	5898

17 SA	29Leo02	Alpha Crt/ **Alkes**	28Leo57	22S	
		Nu Virginis	29Leo25	04N	
18 SU	00Vir01	Alpha 2 CVn/ **Cor Caroli**	29Leo50	40N	
		Mega 138	29Leo53	61S	10192
		Upsilon Leonis	00Vir18	03S	
		M51. CanesVenatici,Whirlpool	00Vir23	50N	
19 MO	00Vir59	**Mega 540**	00Vir43	54S	1415
		NGC3132.Vela, SouthernRing	00Vir51	49S	
20 TU	01Vir58	**Epsilon Crateris**	01Vir30	13S	
		M63. CanesVenatici,Sunflower	01Vir36	45N	
		Delta Crateris	01Vir57	17S	
		Eta UMa/ **Alkaid**	02Vir12	54N	
		Beta Vir/ **Zavijava**	02Vir25	00N	
21 WE	02Vir57	**Pi Virginis**	02Vir49	06N	
		Omicron Virginis	02Vir57	08N	
22 TH	03Vir55	**M85.** Com, Lenticular G.	03Vir35	19N	
		Mega 309	03Vir35	71S	3082
		Beta Crateris	03Vir49	25S	
		Mega 334	03Vir50	64S	2969
		Mega 239	04Vir02	55S	4436
		KappaVel/ **Markeb**/ Mega361	04Vir09	63S	2446
23 FR	04Vir54	**Chi 2 Hydrae**	04Vir43	30S	
		Kappa 2Boo/ **Asellus Tertius**	05Vir13	58N	
		37 Coma Berenices	05Vir21	33N	
24 SA	05Vir53	24 Com/ **Mega 551**	05Vir43	20N	1334
		M84. Virgo, Lenticular G.	05Vir48	14N	
		M86. Virgo, Lenticular G.	06Vir01	14N	
		Iota Boo/ **Asellus Secundus**	06Vir22	58N	
25 SU	06Vir52	Iota Boo/ **Asellus Secundus**	06Vir22	58N	
		Mega 229	06Vir59	57S	4941
		M87. Virgo, Elliptical G.	07Vir19	14N	
26 MO	07Vir50	Theta Boo/ **Asellus Primus**	07Vir52	60N	
27 TU	08Vir49	**Mega 305**	08Vir26	52S	3239
		Zeta Dra/ **Aldhibah**	08Vir38	84N	
		Mega 293	08Vir45	58S	3408
		Mega 367	08Vir54	61S	2390
		M49. Virgo, Elliptical G.	08Vir54	10N	
		M64. Com, Sleep Beauty G.	09Vir11	25N	
28 WE	09Vir48	Eta Vir/ **Zaniah**	10Vir06	01N	
		M59. Virgo, Elliptical G.	10Vir13	14N	
29 TH	10Vir47	**Mega 601**	10Vir19	56S	1104
		Iota Car/ **Aspidiske**/Mega 236	10Vir35	67S	5128
		M60. Virgo, Elliptical G.	10Vir36	15N	
		Phi Vel/ **Tseen Ke**/ Mega 129	11Vir12	59S	11919
30 FR	11Vir46	**Eta Crateris**	11Vir21	16S	
		Mega 134	11Vir31	60S	10339
		Lambda Bootis	12Vir13	54N	

Oh, Holy Mary Sophia, pray for us.

Sophia Star Calendar 2022 Lists

October 2022

Sun's Sidereal Geocentric Longitude is given at Midnight UT.
Star's Sidereal Longitude designates it as the Overlighting **Star** for the day.
Star's Luminosity indicates its intrinsic brightness as compared with Sun's Luminosity: **Sun** L=1.
Mega Stars are identified by an assigned numerical ranking according to their *Luminosity*, as recorded in AstroFire Database.
Mega Stars may or may not have proper names, but all are identified by assigned *Luminosity* numerical ranking.
This calendar identifies all *Stars* over 1000 *Luminosity* as **Mega Stars**, as recorded in AstroFire Database.

Kyriotetes, Spirits of Wisdom, dwell in the region of the Virgin, Virgo/ Vir. (Sept 17 - Oct 18)   *Virtue is Courtesy.*
Dynamis, Spirits of Movement, dwell in the region of the Scales, Libra / Lib. (Oct 18 - Nov 17)   *Virtue is Contentment.*

Midnight UT Date,	Sun Sidereal Geocentric Longitude	Overlighting Star	Star's Sidereal Longitude	Star's Sidereal Latitude	Luminosity (Sun L = 1)
01 SA	12Vir45	41 Virginis	12Vir38	16N	
		32 Virginis	12Vir41	11N	
		Xi Hydrae	13Vir15	31S	
02 SU	13Vir44	Xi Hydrae	13Vir15	31S	
		Mega 400	13Vir32	17S	1945
		Mega 556	13Vir56	67S	1268
		Mega 172	14Vir00	65S	7465
		Alpha Com/ Diadem	14Vir13	22N	
03 MO	14Vir43	Alpha Com/ Diadem	14Vir13	22N	
		Epsilon Vir/ Vindemiatrix	15Vir12	16N	
04 TU	15Vir42	Epsilon Vir/ Vindemiatrix	15Vir12	16N	
		Gamma Vir/ Porrima	15Vir24	02N	
		Mu Velorum	15Vir47	51S	
		37 Virginis	15Vir56	07N	
		Gamma Crv/ Gienah	15Vir59	14S	
05 WE	16Vir41	Omicron Hydrae	16Vir26	33S	
		Mega 351	16Vir28	58S	2649
		Delta Vir/ Minelauva	16Vir43	08N	
		Epsilon Crv/ Minkar	16Vir56	19S	
06 TH	17Vir40	Chi Virginis	17Vir25	03S	
		Alpha Crv/ Alchibah	17Vir30	21S	
		Mega 560	17Vir42	57S	1227
		Mega 354	18Vir04	58S	2521
		Mega 350	18Vir04	41S	2738
07 FR	18Vir39	Beta Hydrae	18Vir42	31S	
		Delta Crv/ Algorab	18Vir43	12S	
		M104. Virgo, Sombrero G.	19Vir01	06S	
		Zeta Corvi	19Vir04	18S	
08 SA	19Vir38	33 Bootis	19Vir36	55N	
09 SU	20Vir38	70 Virginis	20Vir14	21N	
		Beta Volantis	20Vir26	75S	
		9 Bootis	20Vir37	36N	
		Mega 327	20Vir59	63S	2880
		Mega 564	21Vir00	56S	1278
		Sigma Virginis	21Vir03	12N	
10 MO	21Vir37	Mega 290	21Vir14	63S	3555
		Mega 1	21Vir27	59S	120226400
		Psi Virginis	21Vir28	03S	
11 TU	22Vir36	Mega 599	22Vir18	62S	1194
		Mega 190	22Vir20	66S	6239
		Beta Crv/ Kraz	22Vir38	18S	
		Mega 353	22Vir50	58S	2573
		Gamma Boo/ Seginus	22Vir55	49N	
		Mega 356	23Vir06	59S	2660
12 WE	23Vir35	Mega 356	23Vir06	59S	2660
		Mega 46	23Vir19	58S	55409
		Theta Virginis	23Vir30	01N	
		Mega 56	23Vir52	59S	41996
13 TH	24Vir35	Upsilon Bootis	24Vir28	25N	
		Mega 474	24Vir29	64S	1707
		Eta Boo/ Muphrid	24Vir36	28N	
		Mega 7	24Vir38	55S	2545411
		Mega 68	24Vir47	58S	35309

Cosmic Communion: Star Wisdom, Volume 4

		Mega 403	24Vir52	57S	1906
14 FR	25Vir34	Mega 425	25Vir20	62S	1955
		Mega 80	25Vir27	56S	23508
		Mega 276	25Vir38	59S	3741
		Mega 470	25Vir51	33S	1674
		Alpha Volantis	25Vir51	72S	
15 SA	26Vir34	Mega 379	26Vir18	36S	2237
		Mega 77	26Vir21	58S	27134
		65 Virginis	26Vir21	03N	
		Mega 151	26Vir38	28N	8535
		Mega 177	26Vir46	59S	6751
16 SU	27Vir33	NGC5548. Bootes,Seyfert G.	27Vir16	36N	
		Zeta Vir/ Heze	27Vir24	08N	
		Eta Carinae	27Vir25	58S	4600000
		Pi Centauri	27Vir27	51S	
		NGC3372. Carina, Keyhole N.	27Vir28	59S	
		Mega 484	27Vir45	59S	1707
		Mega 147	27Vir50	59S	9163
		Rho Bootis	28Vir03	42N	
17 MO	28Vir32	Rho Bootis	28Vir03	42N	
		Upsilon Car/ Mega 108	28Vir09	67S	14642
		Mega 2	28Vir15	58S	35318290
		Mega 376	28Vir21	55S	2473
		Mega 527	28Vir26	59S	1369
18 TU	29Vir32	Alpha Vir/ Spica/ Mega 387	29Vir06	02S	2282
		54 Virginis	29Vir22	10S	
		Epsilon Volantis	29Vir26	77S	
		Alpha Boo/ Arcturus	29Vir30	30N	
		Beta Boo/ Nekkar	29Vir31	54N	
		Mega 10	29Vir36	57S	1555535
19 WE	00Lib32	Mega 39	00Lib23	56S	77139
20 TH	01Lib31	Centaurus, SuperGalCentre	01Lib06	35S	
		NGC5886. Bootes, SpindleG.	01Lib57	55N	
		Mega 518	02Lib01	56S	1375
21 FR	02Lib31	Mega 518	02Lib01	56S	1375
		Mega 189	02Lib06	63S	6280
		Gamma Hydrae	02Lib17	13S	
		Delta Cen/ Mega 606	02Lib45	44S	1189
		Mega 25	02Lib46	56S	187955
		Tau Virginis	03Lib01	13N	
22 SA	03Lib30	Tau Virginis	03Lib01	13N	
		Epsilon Boo/ Izar	03Lib22	40N	
23 SU	04Lib30	Mega 87	04Lib21	58S	22610
		Theta Car/ Mega 581	04Lib27	62S	1265
		Rho Centauri	04Lib39	45S	
		Omicron 1 Cen/ Mega 164	04Lib44	54S	8005
		Omicron 2 Cen/ Mega 156	04Lib50	54S	8462
24 MO	05Lib30	Mega 486	05Lib58	56S	1613
		Sigma Centauri	05Lib59	42S	
25 TU	06Lib30	Mega 289	06Lib15	55N	3437
		Tau Centauri	06Lib35	40S	
		Mega 205	06Lib54	55S	5468
26 WE	07Lib30	Pi 1 Bootis	07Lib07	30N	
		Pi 2 Bootis	07Lib07	30N	
		Beta Car/ Miaplacidus	07Lib14	72S	
		Gamma Cen/ Muhlifain	07Lib35	40S	
		Mega 228	07Lib35	55S	5123
		Nu 1 Bootis	07Lib48	57N	
27 TH	08Lib29	Nu 2 Bootis	08Lib01	57N	
		Zeta Bootis	08Lib18	27N	
		Mu 1 Boo/ Alkalurops	08Lib26	53N	
		Delta Boo/ Princeps	08Lib27	48N	
		Upsilon Virginis	08Lib38	11N	
		Psi Bootis	08Lib46	42N	
28 FR	09Lib29	Iota Vir/ Syrma	09Lib03	07N	
		Omega Bootis	09Lib04	40N	

Sophia Star Calendar 2022 Lists

		Mega 563	09Lib30	73S	1306
		Mega 207	09Lib36	57S	5259
		Lambda Centauri	09Lib48	56S	
		Mega 674	09Lib50	47S	1077
		Mega 423	09Lib55	56S	1919
29 SA	10Lib29	**Mega 202**	10Lib14	55S	5400
		Chi Bootis	10Lib28	45N	
		Mu Coronae Borealis	10Lib34	55N	
		Mega 676	10Lib38	56S	1095
		Delta Crucis	10Lib55	50S	
30 SU	11Lib29	**Mega 259**	11Lib27	55S	4144
		Mega 292	11Lib44	27S	3549
		Omicron Coronae Borealis	11Lib52	45N	
		Mega 458	11Lib56	29S	1758
31 MO	12Lib29	Gamma Cru/ **Gacrux**	12Lib00	47S	
		Mega 578	12Lib02	52S	1242
		Lambda Vir/ **Khambalia**	12Lib13	00N	
		Kappa 1 Volantis	12Lib39	76S	
		Omega Carinae	12Lib42	67S	
		Xi 2 Centauri	12Lib49	38S	
		Mega 365	12Lib52	55S	2379
		Mega 88	12Lib57	54S	19561

Oh, Holy Mary Sophia, pray for us.

COSMIC COMMUNION: STAR WISDOM, VOLUME 4

November 2022

Sun's Sidereal Geocentric Longitude is given at Midnight UT.
Star's Sidereal Longitude designates it as the Overlighting Star for the day.
Star's Luminosity indicates its intrinsic brightness as compared with Sun's Luminosity: Sun L=1.
Mega Stars are identified by an assigned numerical ranking according to their *Luminosity*, as recorded in AstroFire Database.
Mega Stars may or may not have proper names, but all are identified by assigned *Luminosity* numerical ranking.
This calendar identifies all **Stars** over 1000 *Luminosity* as **Mega Stars,** as recorded in AstroFire Database.

Dynamis, Spirits of Movement, dwell in region of the Scales, Libra / Lib. (Oct 18 - Nov 17)   *Virtue is Contentment.*
Exusiai, Spirits of Form, dwell in the region of the Scorpion, Scorpio /Sco. (Nov 17 - Dec 17)   *Virtue is Patience.*

Midnight UT Date, Sun Sidereal Geocentric Longitude		Overlighting Star	Star's Sidereal Longitude	Star's Sidereal Latitude	Luminosity (Sun L = 1)
01 TU	13Lib29	Zeta 1 Coronae Borealis	13Lib32	53N	
		Epsilon Crucis	13Lib32	51S	
		Upsilon Herculis	13Lib39	64N	
		Pi Hydrae	13Lib53	13S	
02 WE	14Lib29	Theta 2 Crucis	14Lib03	54S	
		Mega 513	14Lib11	49S	1474
		Beta CrB/ Nusakan	14Lib23	46N	
		Theta Coronae Borealis	14Lib43	48N	
		Mega 278	14Lib43	55S	3825
		Mega 680	14Lib51	69S	1040
		Mega 158 (b)	14Lib57	53S	8392
03 TH	15Lib29	Mu Vir/ Rijl AsAwa	15Lib23	09N	
		Mega 389	15Lib49	45S	2128
		Mu 1 Crucis	15Lib52	46S	
04 FR	16Lib29	Mega 523	16Lib12	36S	1360
		Mega 338	16Lib21	74S	2981
		Nu Centauri	16Lib25	28S	
		Mu Muscae	16Lib42	58S	
		Mu Centauri	16Lib48	28S	
		Beta Cru/ Mimosa/ Mega 306	16Lib54	48S	3219
		Mega 32	16Lib55	54S	112658
		Mega 133	16Lib59	39S	10407
05 SA	17Lib29	Mega 133	16Lib59	39S	10407
		Alpha 1 Cru/ Acrux/Mega 256	17Lib08	52S	4143
		Mega 101	17Lib12	56S	17293
		Lambda Crucis	17Lib31	47S	
		Alpha CrB/ Alphecca	17Lib33	44N	
		Theta Cen/ Menkent	17Lib34	22S	
06 SU	18Lib29	Mega 279	18Lib02	48S	3812
		Phi Centauri	18Lib18	28S	
		Mega 178	18Lib20	48S	6653
		Kappa Crucis	18Lib27	48S	
07 MO	19Lib30	Chi Centauri	19Lib24	26S	
		Mu Librae	19Lib26	02N	
		Tau 1 Serpentis	19Lib32	32N	
		Tau Herculis	19Lib39	65N	
08 TU	20Lib30	Zeta Cen/ Alnair/ Mega 613	20Lib13	32S	1157
		Alpha 2 Lib/Zubenelgenubi	20Lib21	00N	
		Xi 2 Librae	20Lib22	05N	
		Delta Lib/ ZubenElakribi	20Lib33	08N	
		Upsilon 2 Centauri	20Lib33	30S	
		Epsilon Cen/ Mega 545	20Lib49	39S	1403
09 WE	21Lib30	Mega 121	21Lib03	46N	13159
		Mega 664	21Lib04	04S	1081
		Epsilon Muscae	21Lib49	57S	
10 TH	22Lib30	Mega 437	22Lib07	60S	1768
		Delta Coronae Borealis	22Lib17	44N	
		Iota Serpentis	22Lib26	38N	
		Zeta 1 Muscae	22Lib50	56S	
11 FR	23Lib30	Mega 312	23Lib24	42S	3029
		Mega 6	23Lib25	55S	3145991
		Delta Serpentis	23Lib36	28N	
		Mega 71	23Lib44	49S	30705
12 SA	24Lib31	Nu Librae	24Lib02	01N	
		Iota Lupi	24Lib03	30S	

Sophia Star Calendar 2022 Lists

		Iota Coronae Borealis	24Lib16	49N	
		Epsilon Coronae Borealis	24Lib23	46N	
		Iota Volantis	24Lib31	83S	
		Beta Lib/ Zubeneschamali	24Lib38	08N	
		Tau 1Lup/ Mega 568	24Lib57	28S	1316
13 SU	25Lib31	Kappa Serpentis	25Lib02	37N	
		Theta Mus/ Mega 4	25Lib07	51S	6452938
		Mega 364	25Lib21	31S	2330
		Beta Muscae	25Lib25	55S	
		Eta Centauri	25Lib31	25S	
		Alpha Muscae	25Lib38	56S	
		Mega 466	25Lib39	32S	1735
		Sigma Lib/ Zubenelgubi	25Lib57	07S	
14 MO	26Lib31	Mega 650	26Lib09	55S	1060
		Epsilon Librae	26Lib36	08N	
		Mega 282	26Lib36	37S	3421
		30 Herculis	26Lib49	62N	
15 TU	27Lib32	Alpha Ser/ Unuk	27Lib20	25N	
		Mega 660	27Lib25	29S	1021
		Mega 448	27Lib35	66S	1549
		Mega 588	27Lib47	52S	1310
16 WE	28Lib32	Mega 74	28Lib10	47S	30597
		Sigma Lupi	28Lib24	33S	
		Alpha Lup/ Men/ Mega 347	28Lib46	30S	2958
		Mega 13	29Lib01	43S	968412
17 TH	29Lib33	Beta Cen/Hadar/Mega 124	29Lib03	44S	12877
		Zeta 1 Librae	29Lib10	02N	
		Mega 388	29Lib15	39S	2194
		Nu 1 Coronae Borealis	29Lib17	54N	
		Gamma Muscae	29Lib17	58S	
		Nu 2 Coronae Borealis	29Lib22	54N	
		Upsilon Coronae Borealis	29Lib28	49N	
		1 Lup/ Mega 638	29Lib57	13S	1157
		Kappa Cen / KeKwan	00Sco03	24S	1332
18 FR	00Sco33	Kappa Cen / KeKwan	00Sco03	24S	1332
		Zeta 4 Librae	00Sco17	02N	
		Beta Lup/KeKouan/ Mega 430.	00Sco17	25S	1901
		Gamma Lib/ Zubenelakrab	00Sco24	04N	
		Kappa Her/ Marsic	00Sco59	37N	
19 SA	01Sco34	Mega 448	01Sco43	34S	1784
20 SU	02Sco34	Mega 57	02Sco09	41S	42909
		Eta Lib/ Zubenhakrabi	02Sco37	04N	
		Phi 1 Lupi	02Sco45	17S	
		Pi Lupi	02Sco54	28S	
		Kappa Librae	03Sco01	00S	
21 MO	03Sco35	Mega 600	03Sco08	22S	1176
		Phi 2 Lupi	03Sco12	17S	
		Upsilon Librae	03Sco52	08S	
		Delta Lup/ Mega 619	03Sco55	21S	1099
		Eta Herculis	04Sco03	60N	
22 TU	04Sco35	Gamma Herculis	04Sco28	40N	
		Kappa Chamaeleontis	04Sco29	62S	
		Alpha Chamaeleontis	04Sco34	75S	
		Tau Librae	04Sco37	10S	
23 WE	05Sco36	Mega 383	05Sco16	48S	2225
		Epsilon Lupi	05Sco23	25S	
		Gamma Chamaeleontis	05Sco41	68S	
24 TH	06Sco37	Mega 656	06Sco15	20S	1055
		Beta Her/ Kornephoros	06Sco21	42N	
		Zeta Herculis	06Sco43	53N	
		Gamma Lup/ Mega 428	06Sco45	21S	1998
		Mega 390	07Sco07	35S	2220
25 FR	07Sco37	Mega 390	07Sco07	35S	2220
		Delta Ophiuchi	07Sco34	17N	
		Mega 196	07Sco35	49S	6012
		Mega 53	07Sco35	52S	44594
		Alpha Circini	07Sco37	46S	
		Delta Sco/ Dschubba	07Sco50	01S	1603

26 SA	08Sco38	**Pi Sco**/ Mega 573	08Sco12	05S	1206
		Theta Circini	08Sco21	43S	
		Rho Scorpii	08Sco24	08S	
		Beta 1 Sco/ **Graffias**	08Sco27	01N	2179
		Beta 2 Sco/ Mega 611	08Sco27	01N	1151
		Omega 1Sco/**Jabhat alAkrab**	08Sco56	00N	
27 SU	09Sco39	Nu Sco/ **Jabbah**	09Sco54	01N	
		Zeta Circini	09Sco55	46S	
28 MO	10Sco40	**Mega 109**	10Sco13	41S	14624
		Mega 502	10Sco21	40S	1524
		Delta Cir/ Mega 70	10Sco26	40S	32275
		Mega 3	10Sco31	40S	14653460
		Beta Chamaeleontis	10Sco42	63S	
		Gamma Circini	10Sco42	39S	
		Lambda Ophiuchi/ **Marfik**	10Sco51	23N	
		Eta Lupi	11Sco02	17S	
29 TU	11Sco40	**Epsilon Circini**	11Sco47	43S	
		Theta Lupi	12Sco00	15S	
30 WE	12Sco41	**Mega 589**	12Sco18	60S	1312
		Mega 110	12Sco31	46S	14832
		Omicron Sco/ Mega 461	12Sco42	02S	1718
		Zeta Chamaeleontis	12Sco51	70S	
		Sigma Sco/**AlNiyat** /Mega317	13Sco04	04S	3057

Oh, Holy Mary Sophia, pray for us.

Sophia Star Calendar 2022 Lists

December 2022

Sun's Sidereal Geocentric Longitude is given at Midnight UT.
Star's Sidereal Longitude designates it as the Overlighting **Star** for the day.
Star's Luminosity indicates its intrinsic brightness as compared with Sun's Luminosity: **Sun** L=1.
Mega Stars are identified by an assigned numerical ranking according to their *Luminosity*, as recorded in AstroFire Database.
Mega Stars may or may not have proper names, but all are identified by assigned *Luminosity* numerical ranking.
This calendar identifies all **Stars** over 1000 *Luminosity* as **Mega Stars**, as recorded in AstroFire Database.

Exusiai, Spirits of Form, dwell in the region of the Scorpion, Scorpio / Sco.   (Nov 17 - Dec 17)   *Virtue is Patience.*
Archai, Spirits of Personality, dwell in the region of the Archer, Sagittarius / Sgr.   (Dec 17 - Jan 15)   *Virtue is Self Discipline.*

Midnight UT Date, Sun Sidereal Geocentric Longitude		Overlighting Star	Star's Sidereal Longitude	Sttar's Sidereal Latitude	Luminosity (Sun L = 1)
01 TH	13Sco42	**Chi Ophiuchi**	13Sco14	03N	
		Epsilon Herculis	13Sco35	53N	
		Mega 200	13Sco38	34S	5562
		Rho Ophiuchi	13Sco42	01S	
		Phi Ophiuchi	13Sco56	05N	
		Eta Normae	14Sco08	27S	
02 FR	14Sco43	**Zeta Oph/ Han/** Mega 485	14Sco29	11N	1656
		Gamma Trianguli Australis	14Sco39	48S	
		Alpha Sco/**Antares/**Mega 132	15Sco01	04S	11252
03 SA	15Sco43	**Epsilon Trianguli Australis**	15Sco44	45S	
		Mega 609	15Sco46	58S	1170
		Mega 260	15Sco49	45N	4029
04 SU	16Sco44	**Tau Sco/Alniyat /** Mega 626	16Sco43	06S	1126
		Gamma 1 Nor/ Mega 468	16Sco48	28S	1738
		Mega 161	17Sco00	31S	7743
		Mega 511	17Sco01	37S	1511
		Kappa Ophiuchi	17Sco05	31N	
		Beta Dra/ **Rastaban**	17Sco14	75N	
05 MO	17Sco45	**Pi Herculis**	17Sco20	59N	
		Mega 52	17Sco57	19S	45335
06 TU	18Sco46	**Mu Nor/** Mega 89	18Sco47	21S	20221
		Kappa 1 Apodis	18Sco58	52S	
		NGC6087. Norma, Open C.	19Sco00	35S	
		Mega 220	19Sco02	20S	4980
		Epsilon Apodis	19Sco09	59S	
		Kappa TrA/ Mega 188	19Sco14	46S	6624
07 WE	19Sco47	**Alpha Apodis**	19Sco41	58S	
		Delta Her/ **Sarin**	20Sco01	47N	
		Delta Trianguli Australis	20Sco07	41S	
08 TH	20Sco48	Epsilon Sco/ **Wei**	20Sco36	11S	
		Rho Her/ Mega 284	20Sco38	60N	3062
		Mega 41	20Sco49	23S	70785
		Mega 498	20Sco56	26S	1489
		Mega 222	21Sco09	27S	4920
09 FR	21Sco49	Alpha 1 Her/ **Rasalgethi**	21Sco25	37N	
		Alpha 2 Her/ Mega 501	21Sco25	37N	1374
		Mu 1 Sco/ Mega 280	21Sco25	15S	3487
		Mu 2 Scorpii	21Sco30	15S	
		Mega 72	21Sco46	18S	30586
		Mega 330	21Sco59	19S	2878
		Mega 94	22Sco19	19S	18848
10 SA	22Sco50	**Mega 162**	22Sco20	19S	7964
		Mega 475	22Sco21	19S	1732
		Zeta 1Sco/ Mega 155	22Sco23	19S	8992
		Mega 65	22Sco25	18S	36732
		Mega 45	22Sco29	19S	55115
		Mega 31	22Sco33	19S	116901
		Mega 273	22Sco42	18S	3972
		Eta Oph/ **Sabik**	23Sco14	07N	
11 SU	23Sco51	**Mega 382**	23Sco39	35S	2157
		Mega 179	23Sco39	11S	6844
		Mega 50	23Sco51	14S	50531
		Eta Arae	24Sco10	36S	
		Delta Octantis	24Sco17	62S	
12 MO	24Sco52	**Zeta Ara/** Mega 490	25Sco05	33S	1525

		Iota Herculis	25Sco09	69N	
		Lambda Herculis/ **Maasim**	25Sco10	49N	
		Mega 224	25Sco13	09S	4797
		Pi 2 Oct/ Mega 515	25Sco15	61S	1354
13 TU	25Sco52	**Mega 146**	25Sco49	10S	9405
		Sigma Oph/ Mega 412	25Sco51	27N	2070
		Mega 538	26Sco03	35S	1335
		Mega 176	26Sco09	16S	6542
		Alpha TrA/ Mega 372	26Sco09	46S	2434
14 WE	26Sco53	Theta Oph/ Mega 583	26Sco39	01S	1278
		Delta 2 Apodis	26Sco46	55S	
		Delta 1 Apodis	26Sco46	56S	
		Mega 242	27Sco05	21S	4768
15 TH	27Sco54	**Mega 404**	27Sco39	14S	1935
		Alpha Oph/ **Rasalhague**	27Sco43	35N	
		Gamma Apodis	27Sco58	56S	
		Beta Apodis	28Sco13	54S	
16 FR	28Sco56	Iota Arae	28Sco28	24S	
		Mega 510	28Sco53	36S	1463
		UpsilonSco/ **Lesath**	29Sco16	14S	1831
		Mega 701	29Sco25	27S	1000
17 SA	29Sco57	**Beta Ara**/ Mega 396	29Sco28	32S	2176
		Gamma Ara/ Mega 226	29Sco33	33S	5015
		Mu Ophiuchi	29Sco35	15N	
		Mega 360	29Sco49	07N	2462
		Lambda Sco/**Shaula**/Mega154	29Sco51	13S	9098
		Mega 225	29Sco52	09S	5006
		Mega 243	29Sco57	54N	4424
		Mega 628	29Sco57	39S	1165
		Mega 590	29Sco58	22S	1273
		Alpha Ara/ **Tchou**	00Sgr12	26S	
18 SU	00Sgr58	**Mega 491**	00Sgr35	33S	1515
		Beta Oph/ **Cheleb**	00Sgr36	27N	
		Mega 414	00Sgr40	14S	2063
		Delta Arae	00Sgr49	37S	
		Theta Sco / **Sargas**	00Sgr52	19S	1092
		M6. Scorpio, Butterfly C.	01Sgr00	08S	
19 MO	01Sgr59	**Mega 401**	01Sgr33	04S	1947
		Mega 493	01Sgr40	09S	1553
		Kappa Sco / **Gertab**	01Sgr44	15S	1950
		Gamma Ophiuchi	01Sgr54	26N	
		Mega 464	01Sgr59	27N	1625
		Ophiuchus, **Galactic Center**	02Sgr06	05S	
20 TU	03Sgr00	**3 Sgr**/ Mega 492	02Sgr30	04S	1463
		Iota 1 Sco/ Mega 100	02Sgr47	16S	16744
		Eta Pavonis	03Sgr14	41S	
		Iota 2 Sco/ Mega 118	03Sgr18	16S	13773
		Mega 381	03Sgr21	17N	2260
21 WE	04Sgr01	**89 Her**/ Mega 204	03Sgr41	49N	5430
		Theta Her/ Mega 675	03Sgr44	60N	1049
		M7. Scorpio, Ptolemy's C.	03Sgr59	11S	
		Mega 95	04Sgr06	01S	18360
		M23. Sagittarius, Open C.	04Sgr30	04N	
22 TH	05Sgr02	Nu Herculis	04Sgr43	53N	
		Nu Ophiuchi	05Sgr01	13N	
		67 Oph/ Mega 248	05Sgr26	26N	4411
23 FR	06Sgr03	**Mega 22**	05Sgr42	00N	228952
		M20. Sagittarius, Trifid N.	05Sgr51	00N	
		M8. Sagittarius, Lagoon N.	06Sgr08	00S	
		9 Sgr/ Mega 150	06Sgr09	00S	8809
		M21. Sagittarius, Open C.	06Sgr19	00N	
		Gamma 1 Sgr/ Mega 217	06Sgr21	06S	4833
		Theta Ara/ Mega 344	06Sgr27	26S	2913
		Gamma 2Sgr/ **Al Nasal**	06Sgr31	06S	
		Mega 201	06Sgr32	25N	5277
24 SA	07Sgr04	Hercules, **Solar Apex**	06Sgr43	53N	
		Mega 251	06Sgr56	01N	4775
		Mega 402	07Sgr16	01N	2019
		Epsilon Telescopii	07Sgr22	22S	

Sophia Star Calendar 2022 Lists

Day		Star	Position	Lat	Mag
		Mega 75	07Sgr34	10S	32009
25 SU	08Sgr05	**Mega 500**	07Sgr52	17S	1456
		Omicron Herculis	07Sgr57	52N	
		102 Her/ Mega 296	08Sgr07	44N	3398
		Mu Sgr/ **Polis**/ Mega 9	08Sgr28	02N	2095148
26 MO	09Sgr07	**15 Sgr**/ Mega 43	08Sgr49	02N	61231
		16 Sgr/ Mega 42	08Sgr50	03N	74328
		Eta Sagittarii	08Sgr53	13S	
		Mega 237	08Sgr55	18S	4803
		Mega 232	08Sgr57	04N	4807
		Mega 596	09Sgr32	14S	1110
27 TU	10Sgr08	**Mega 163**	09Sgr38	45N	7679
		Delta Sgr/ **Media**	09Sgr50	06S	
		M16. Serpens,Eagle QueenC.	09Sgr53	09N	
		Nu Pavonis	09Sgr57	38S	
		M18. Sagittarius, Open C.	10Sgr03	06N	
		M17. Sagittarius, Swan N.	10Sgr18	07N	
		Epsilon Sgr/ **Kaus Australis**	10Sgr20	11S	
		Alpha Telescopii	10Sgr20	22S	
		NGC6624. Sagittarius,Glob C.	10Sgr25	07S	
28 WE	11Sgr09	**Mega 303**	11Sgr22	28N	3239
		Lambda Sgr/ **Kaus Borealis**	11Sgr35	02S	
29 TH	12Sgr10	**105 Her**/ Mega 647	11Sgr46	47N	1016
		Theta Coronae Australis	11Sgr48	19S	
		Kappa 1 CrA/ Mega 587	12Sgr00	15S	1302
		Gamma Scuti	12Sgr24	08N	
		Mega 307	12Sgr29	09S	3157
30 FR	13Sgr11	**M25**. Sagittarius, Open C.	12Sgr44	03N	
		Kappa Pavonis	12Sgr53	44S	
		24 Sgr/ Mega 193	13Sgr00	00S	6145
		Lambda Pavonis/ Mega 203	13Sgr04	39S	5514
		25 Sgr/ Mega 406	13Sgr08	01S	2086
		M22. Sagittarius, Facies C.	13Sgr30	00S	
31 SA	14Sgr12	**Alpha Scuti**	14Sgr17	14N	
		Omega Pavonis	14Sgr21	37S	
		Kappa Telescopii	14Sgr28	29S	

Oh, Holy Mary Sophia, pray for us.

SOPHIA STAR CALENDAR 2022 MEGA-STAR INDEX

Midnight UT Overlights Sun Date, 2022	Star Name	Star's Sidereal Longitude	Star's Sidereal Latitude	Luminosity (Sun L = 1)
10/10	Mega 1	21Vir27	59S	120226400
10/16	Mega 2	28Vir15	58S	35318290
11/28	Mega 3	10Sco31	40S	14653460
11/13	Mega 4 (Theta Mus)	25Lib07	51S	6452938
10/16	Mega 4.1 (Eta Carinae)	27Vir25	58S	4600000
03/05	Mega 5 (68 Cyg)	19Aqr46	55N	3357841
11/11	Mega 6	23Lib25	55S	3145991
10/13	Mega 7	24Vir38	55S	2545411
01/23	Mega 8	08Cap17	10N	2690033
12/25	Mega 9 (Mu Sgr/ Polis)	08Sgr28	02N	2095148
10/18	Mega 10	29Vir36	57S	1555535
06/23	Mega 11 (Chi 2 Ori)	06Gem11	03S	1213388
08/10	Mega 12	22Cnc04	44S	1075715
11/16	Mega 13	29Lib01	43S	968412
01/03	Mega 14	17Sgr03	12N	941464
07/14	Mega 15	26Gem44	38S	428070
07/03	Mega 16	16Gem09	16S	388884
07/25	Mega 17	07Cnc12	44S	396114
04/11	Mega 18	26Psc26	55N	353035
05/30	Mega 19	13Tau22	60N	325087
02/24	Mega 20 (Alpha Cyg/ Deneb)	10Aqr35	59N	269996
02/01	Mega 21	16Cap50	40N	229728
12/23	Mega 22	05Sgr42	00N	228952
07/04	Mega 23	16Gem47	19S	197580
04/21	Mega 24 (Rho Cas)	06Ari19	51N	174455
10/21	Mega 25	02Lib46	56S	187955
07/29	Mega 26 (3 Pup)	11Cnc09	49S	168887
01/14	Mega 27 (Nu Aql)	28Sgr41	22N	154769
04/26	Mega 28 (6 Cas)	10Ari41	55N	146535
09/16	Mega 29	28Leo20	61S	140314
09/06	Mega 30	18Leo40	56S	130033
12/10	Mega 31	22Sco33	19S	116901
11/04	Mega 32	16Lib55	54S	112658
02/10	Mega 33	26Cap02	65N	103551
02/03	Mega 34	19Cap19	51N	85424
07/23	Mega 35 (Eta CMa/ Aludra)	04Cnc48	50S	87660
05/02	Mega 36	16Ari39	48N	82244
06/12	Mega 37 (Alpha Cam)	26Tau14	43N	77948
05/19	Mega 38	03Tau08	56N	80752
10/19	Mega 39	00Lib23	56S	77139
08/30	Mega 40 (Rho Leo)	11Leo39	00N	78028
12/08	Mega 41	20Sco49	23S	70785
12/26	Mega 42 (16 Sgr)	08Sgr50	03N	74328
12/26	Mega 43 (15 Sgr)	08Sgr49	02N	61231
06/21	Mega 44	04Gem34	00N	58557
12/10	Mega 45	22Sco29	19S	55115
10/12	Mega 46	23Vir19	58S	55409
01/25	Mega 47 (9 Sge)	10Cap10	38N	52547
09/03	Mega 48 (72 Leo)	15Leo44	16N	54401
07/16	Mega 49 (Delta CMa/ Wezen)	28Gem39	48S	48737
12/11	Mega 50	23Sco51	14S	50531
04/11	Mega 51	26Psc24	65N	51745
12/05	Mega 52	17Sco57	19S	45335
11/25	Mega 53	07Sco35	52S	44594
03/31	Mega 54 (MuCep/Garnet Star)	14Psc58	64N	46049
06/08	Mega 55	22Tau06	13N	40335
10/12	Mega 56	23Vir52	59S	41996
11/20	Mega 57	02Sco09	41S	42909
04/04	Mega 58 (Nu Cep)	19Psc36	65N	42427
06/08	Mega 59 (Beta Ori/Rigel)	22Tau05	31S	41436
03/27	Mega 60	10Psc57	68N	37273
03/03	Mega 61	17Aqr06	60N	38007
02/11	Mega 62 (34 Cyg)	27Cap02	55N	39810
07/18	Mega 63	00Cnc31	45S	37670
08/25	Mega 64	06Leo21	60S	38353
12/10	Mega 65	22Sco25	18S	36732
03/01	Mega 66 (Sigma Cyg)	15Aqr36	51N	34462
07/14	Mega 67 (Omicron 2CMa)	26Gem16	46S	33450
10/13	Mega 68	24Vir47	58S	35309
06/15	Mega 69 (Epsilon Ori/Alnilam)	28Tau48	24S	31102
11/28	Mega 70 (Delta Cir)	10Sco26	40S	32275
11/11	Mega 71	23Lib44	49S	30705

Sophia Star Calendar 2022 Mega-Star Index

Date	Mega	Position	Lat	Value
12/09	Mega 72	21Sco46	18S	30586
05/28	Mega 73	11Tau50	39N	31216
11/16	Mega 74	28Lib10	47S	30597
12/24	Mega 75	07Sgr34	10S	32009
05/03	Mega 76 (Kappa Cas)	17Ari52	52N	29974
10/15	Mega 77	26Vir21	58S	27134
02/14	Mega 78 (Gamma Cyg/Sadr)	00Aqr06	57N	24388
08/30	Mega 79	11Leo48	61S	24526
10/14	Mega 80	25Vir27	56S	23508
04/10	Mega 81 (19 Cep)	25psc05	64N	22683
08/12	Mega 82 (Zeta Pup/ Naos)	23Cnc49	58S	20955
04/07	Mega 83	22Psc06	64N	22877
01/18	Mega 84	02Cap33	24N	22855
04/05	Mega 85 (9 Cep)	20Psc14	66N	20957
08/17	Mega 86	28Cnc52	60S	22793
10/23	Mega 87	04Lib21	58S	22610
10/31	Mega 88	12Lib57	54S	19561
12/06	Mega 89 (Mu Nor)	18Sco47	21S	20221
01/04	Mega 90 (Xi 1 Sgr)	18Sgr40	02N	20238
06/10	Mega 91 (Epsilon Aur/ Maaz)	24Tau06	20N	20881
02/17	Mega 92 (35 Aqr)	02Aqr55	06S	18093
06/16	Mega 93 (Chi Aur)	29Tau25	08N	17775
12/09	Mega 94	22Sco19	19S	18848
12/21	Mega 95	04Sgr06	01S	18360
07/18	Mega 96	00Cnc45	26S	18276
01/21	Mega 97	06Cap06	24N	16428
05/09	Mega 98 (15 Tri)	22Ari52	18N	17049
06/24	Mega 99 (3 Gem)	07Gem30	00S	16783
12/20	Mega 100 (Iota 1Sco)	02Sgr47	16S	16744
11/05	Mega 101	17Lib12	56S	17293
07/18	Mega 102	00Cnc17	41S	16947
06/14	Mega 103	28Tau08	29S	15534
08/21	Mega 104 (Eta Leo)	03Leo10	04N	15087
03/11	Mega105	25Aqr24	49N	15432
06/29	Mega 106	11Gem47	16S	15470
07/19	Mega 107 (Tau CMa)	01Cnc39	46S	14955
10/17	Mega 108 (Upsilon Car)	28Vir09	67S	14642
11/27	Mega 109	10Sco13	41S	14624
11/30	Mega 110	12Sco31	46S	14832
09/04	Mega 111	16Leo51	40S	15062
07/07	Mega 112(AlphaCar/Canopus)	)20Gem13	75S	14172
07/07	Mega 113 (41 Gem)	19Gem49	06S	14178
07/01	Mega 114	14Gem19	33S	13804
05/12	Mega 115	26Ari20	37N	14384
07/10	Mega 116 (Iota CMa)	22Gem47	39S	13976
03/02	Mega 117	16Aqr45	65N	14374
12/20	Mega 118 (Iota 2 Sco)	03Sgr18	16S	13773
06/26	Mega 119 (Psi 1 Aur)	09Gem46	25N	12977
02/03	Mega 120 (22 Vul)	18Cap42	41N	13118
11/09	Mega 121	21Lib03	46N	13159
06/24	Mega 122	07Gem28	01S	13166
06/13	Mega 123(Alpha Lep/ Arneb)	26Tau38	41S	12541
11/17	Mega 124(BetaCen/Hadar/Agena)	29Lib03	44S	12877
08/21	Mega 125(Gamma 2 Vel/Suhail)	02Leo37	64S	11543
09/07	Mega 126	19Leo31	55S	11886
05/20	Mega 127	04Tau20	38N	11017
06/14	Mega 128(IotaOri/ Na'irAlSaif)	28Tau15	28S	11432
09/29	Mega 129(Phi Vel /Tseen Ke)	11Vir12	59S	11919
08/10	Mega 130	22Cnc36	68S	11020
06/16	Mega 131 (Zeta Ori/ Alnitak)	29Tau56	25S	11017
12/02	Mega 132(Alpha Sco/ Antares)	15Sco01	04S	11252
11/04	Mega 133	16Lib59	39S	10407
09/30	Mega 134	11Vir31	60S	10339
07/07	Mega 135	19Gem34	10S	10916
08/02	Mega 136	14Cnc51	13S	10659
07/21	Mega 137	03Cnc34	35S	10926
09/18	Mega 138	29Leo53	61S	10192
04/02	Mega 139 (14 Cep)	17Psc16	61N	10710
08/17	Mega 140	29Cnc28	60S	9672
03/28	Mega 141	11Psc48	57N	9801
03/14	Mega 142	28Aqr21	69N	9375
04/20	Mega 143	05Ari00	44N	9644
07/22	Mega 144	04Cnc38	44S	9803
06/20	Mega 145(AlphaOri /Betelgeuse)	04Gem01	16S	9884
12/13	Mega 146	25Sco49	10S	9405
10/16	Mega 147	27Vir50	59S	9163
07/15	Mega 148	27Gem25	21S	9405
07/11	Mega 149 (Omicron 1 CMa)	23Gem25	46S	8893

12/23	**Mega 150** (9 Sgr)	06Sgr09	00S	8809
10/15	**Mega 151**	26Vir38	28N	8535
06/30	**Mega 152**	13Gem04	11S	8517
07/30	**Mega 153** (Omicron Pup)	11Cnc19	46S	8687
12/17	**Mega 154**(Lambda Sco/Shaula)	29Sco51	13S	9098
12/10	**Mega 155** (Zeta 1 Sco)	22Sco23	19S	8992
10/23	**Mega 156** (Omicron 2 Cen)	04Lib50	54S	8462
07/13	**Mega 157**	25Gem37	32S	8946
01/16	**Mega 158 a.** (45 Dra)	00Cap56	79N	8430
11/02	**Mega 158 b.**	14Lib57	53S	8392
	Mega 159			
06/14	**Mega 160** (DeltaOri/Mintaka)	27Tau37	23S	8652
12/04	**Mega 161**	17Sco00	31S	7743
12/10	**Mega 162**	22Sco20	19S	7964
12/27	**Mega 163**	09Sgr38	45N	7679
10/23	**Mega 164** (Omicron 1 Cen)	04Lib44	54S	8005
01/26	**Mega 165** (10 Sge)	10Cap37	36N	7841
07/19	**Mega 166** (29 CMa)	01Cnc31	46S	8187
07/18	**Mega 167**	00Cnc40	49S	7822
07/23	**Mega 168** (Pi Pup)	05Cnc34	58S	8083
06/13	**Mega 169** (19 Aur)	26Tau50	10N	7403
08/12	**Mega 170**	24Cnc20	65S	7241
05/17	**Mega 171**	01Tau19	30N	7068
10/02	**Mega 172**	14Vir00	65S	7465
05/28	**Mega 173**	11Tau33	38N	7566
08/16	**Mega 174**	27Cnc45	66S	6330
04/22	**Mega 175**	06Ari25	51N	6506
12/13	**Mega 176**	26Sco09	16S	6542
10/15	**Mega 177**	26Vir26	59S	6751
11/06	**Mega 178**	18Lib20	48S	6653
12/11	**Mega 179**	23Sco39	11S	6844
06/18	**Mega 180** (Kappa Ori/ Saiph)	01Gem40	33S	6335
03/25	**Mega 181**	09Psc46	66N	6874
07/02	**Mega 182**	15Gem12	18S	6591
07/03	**Mega 183** (Xi 1 CMa)	15Gem55	46S	6327
04/27	**Mega 184**	11Ari25	53N	6902
07/29	**Mega 185** (XiPup/ Asmidiske)	11Cnc18	44S	6861
05/27	**Mega 186** (XiPer/ Menkib)	0Tau14	14N	6582
06/22	**Mega 187**	05Gem29	04N	6820
12/06	**Mega 188** (Kappa TrA)	19Sco14	46S	6624
10/21	**Mega 189**	02Lib06	63S	6280
10/11	**Mega 190**	22Vir20	66S	6239
05/25	**Mega 191** (Zeta Per)	08Tau23	11N	5777
09/08	**Mega 192**	20Leo03	56S	6052
12/30	**Mega 193** (24 Sgr)	13Sgr00	00S	6145
08/31	**Mega 194**	12Leo46	59S	5980
09/16	**Mega 195**(Epsilon Car/Avior)	28Leo23	72S	5898
11/25	**Mega 196**	07Sco35	49S	6012
07/02	**Mega 197**	14Gem59	16S	6047
06/09	**Mega 198** (103 Tau)	23Tau27	01N	5387
05/18	**Mega 199** (53 Cas)	01Tau46	47N	5725
12/01	**Mega 200**	13Sco38	34S	5562

Oh, Holy Mary Sophia, pray for us.

SOPHIA STAR CALENDAR 2022 INDEX FOR 700 STARS

Sophia Star Calendar 2022 Index

Star Name	Sidereal Longitude	Overlighting Date
1 Cassiopeiae	00Ari38	04/16
1 Persei	23Ari52	05/10
2 Cassiopeiae	01Ari02	04/16
2 Persei	21Ari25	05/07
3 Ceti	02Psc04	03/18
3 Geminorium/ Mega 99	07Gem30	06/24
3 Puppis/ Mega 26	11Cnc09	07/29
4 Lacertae	11Psc08	03/27
4 Persei	25Ari12	05/11
5 Persei	28Ari32	05/14
6 Cassiopeiae/ Mega 28	10Ari41	04/26
6 Cephei	23Psc48	04/09
6 Geminorum/ Mega 272	08Gem06	06/25
6 Lacertae	06 Psc42	03/22
9 Cassiopeiae	13Ari01	04/28
9 Cephei/ Mega 85	20Psc14	04/05
9 Persei	29Ari17	05/15
9 Sagittae/ Mega 47	10Cap10	01/25
9 Sagittarii/ Mega 150	06Sgr09	12/23
10 Canis Majoris	21Gem32	07/09
10 Persei	00Tau10	05/16
10 Sagittae	10Cap37	01/26
11 Puppis	12Cnc54	07/31
13 Cephei	13Psc43	03/29
14 Cephei	17Psc16	04/02
15 Trianguli/ Mega 98	22Ari52	05/09
15 Sagittarii Mega 43	08Sgr49	12/26
16 Sagittarii Mega 42	08Sgr50	12/26
17 Camelopardalis	00Gem53	06/17
19 Aurigae	26Tau50	06/13
19 Cephei/ Mega 81	25Psc05	04/10
20 Puppis/Mega 571	15Cnc18	08/03
21 Aquilae	25Sgr34	01/11
22 Vulpeculae	18Cap42	02/03
24 Coma Berenices	05Vir43	09/24
24 Sagittarii Mega 193	13Sgr00	12/30
25 Cygni/ Mega 454	20Cap34	02/04
26 Cephei	03Ari38	04/19
29 Canis Majoris	01Cnc31	07/19
30 Herculis	26Lib49	11/14
31 Cygni	03Aqr20	02/17
31 Lyncis	02Cnc49	07/21
32 Cygni	05Aqr03	02/19
32 Virginis	12Vir41	10/01
33 Bootis	19Vir36	10/08
33 Cygni	18Aqr40	03/04
34 Cygni/ Mega 62	27Cap02	02/11
35 Aquarii/Mega 92	02Aqr55	02/17
35 Cygni	25Cap19	02/09
35 Geminorum	17Gem41	07/05
36 Sextantis	17Leo03	09/05
37 Coma Berenices	05Vir21	09/23
41 Geminorum	19Gem49	07/07
42 Piscium	15Psc47	04/01
45 Draconis/ Mega 158	00Cap56	01/16
53 Cassiopeiae	01Tau46	05/18
55 Orionis	02Gem46	06/19
55 Cygni	13Aqr41	02/27
57 Pegasi	27Aqr07	03/13
59 Cygni	18Aqr21	03/04
60 Andromedae	22Ari06	05/08
62 Ursae Majoris	17Leo28	09/05
65 Virginis	26Vir21	10/15
66 Orionis	06Gem34	06/23
67 Ophiuchi	05Sgr26	12/22
68 Cygni/ Mega 5	19Aqr46	03/05
70 Aquilae	16Cap31	01/31
71 Pegasi	08Psc39	03/24
72 Leonis/ Mega 48	15Leo44	09/03
75 Leonis	24Leo39	08/13
77 Pegasi	05Psc36	03/21
89 Herculis/Mega 204	03Sgr41	12/20
90 Leonis	22Leo43	09/10
101 Piscium/ Mega532	02Ari48	04/18
103 Aquarii	23Aqr44	03/09
103 Tauri	23Tau27	06/09
105 Herculis	11Sgr46	12/29
139 Tauri	04Gem49	06/21
Acamer (Theta 1Eri)	28Psc32	04/14
Achernar (Alpha Eri)	20Aqr34	03/06
Acrux (Alpha 1 Cru)	17Lib08	11/05
Acubens (Alpha Cnc)	18Cnc54	08/06
Adhafera (Zeta Leo)	02Leo50	08/21

Star Name	Sidereal Longitude	Overlighting Date
Adhara (Epsilon CMa)	26Gem01	07/13
Agena/Hadar(BetaCen)Mega124	.29Lib03	11/16
Ain (Epsilon Tau)	13Tau44	05/30
Ainalrami (Nu1Sgr)	17 Sgr44	01/03
Aladfar (Eta Lyr)	05Cap18	01/20
AlBali (Epsilon Aqr)	16Cap59	02/01
Albaldah (Pi Sgr)	21Sgr31	01/07
Albireo (Beta Cyg)	06Cap31	01/22
Alchibah (Alpha Crv)	17Vir30	10/06
Alcor (80 UMa)	21Leo08	09/09
Alcyone (Eta Tau)	05Tau16	05/21
Aldebaran (Alpha Tau)	15Tau03	06/01
Alderamin (Alpha Cep)	18Psc02	04/03
Aldhibah (Zeta Dra)	08Vir38	09/27
Alfirk (Beta Cep)	10Ari48	04/26
Algenib (Gamma Peg)	14Psc25	03/30
Algenubi (Epsilon Leo)	25Cnc58	08/14
Algieba (Gamma 1 Leo)	04Leo53	08/23
Algol (Beta Per)	01Tau26	05/17
Algorab (Delta Crv)	18Vir43	10/07
AlHaud (Theta UMa)	12Cnc31	07/31
Alheckla (Zeta Tau)	00Gem03	06/16
Alhena (Gamma Gem)	14Gem22	07/01
Alioth (Epsilon UMa)	14Leo10	09/02
Alkaid (Eta UMa)	02Vir12	09/20
Alkalurops (Mu Boo)	08Lib26	10/27
Alkes (Alpha Crt)	28Leo57	09/17
AlMa'az(Epsilon Aur)/Mega 91	24Tau06	06/10
Almach (Gamma 1 And)	19Ari29	05/05
Alnair (Zeta Cen)	20Lib13	11/08
Al Nasl (Gamma 2 Sgr)	06Sgr31	12/23
Alnilam(Epsilon Ori)/Mega 69	28Tau43	06/15
Alnitak (Zeta Ori)	29Tau56	06/16
Al Niyat (Sigma Sco)	13Sco00	11/30
Alniyat (Tau Sco)	16Sco43	12/04
Alpha Apodis	19Sco41	12/07
Alpha Arae (Tchou)	00Sgr12	12/17
Alpha Camelopardalis/Mega 37	26Tau14	06/12
Alpha Centauri	04Sco44	11/22
Alpha Fornacis	09Ari52	04/25
Alpha Indi	04Cap22	01/20
Alpha Lupi (Men)	28Lib46	11/16
Alpha Lyncis	17Cnc06	08/05
Alpha Microscopii	10Cap53	01/26
Alpha Pavonis (Peacock Star)	29Sgr05	01/14
Alpha Sagittae	06Cap20	01/21
Alpha Sculptoris	05Psc45	03/21
Alpha Scuti	14Sgr17	12/31
Alpha Sextantis	09Leo23	08/28
Alpha Telescopii	10Sgr20	12/27
Alpha Trianguli (Mothallah)	12Ari07	04/27
Alpha Trianguli Australis	26Sco09	12/13
Alpha Tucanae	14Cap56	01/30
Alpha Volantis	25Vir51	10/14
Alphard (Alpha Hya)	02Leo32	08/21
Alphecca (Alpha CrA)	19Sgr24	01/05
Alphecca (Alpha CrB)	17Lib33	11/05
Alpheratz (Alpha And)	19Psc34	04/04
Alpherg (Eta Psc)	02Ari05	04/17
Alrisha (Alpha Pis)	04Ari38	04/20
Alshain (Beta Aql)	07Cap41	01/23
Altair (Alpha Aql)	07Cap02	01/22
Alterf (Lambda Leo)	23Cnc08	08/11
AlThalimain (Iota Aql)	01Cap06	01/16
Althalimin (Lambda Aql)	22Sgr36	01/08
Aludra (Alpha CMa)/ Mega 35	04Cnc48	07/23
Alula Australis (Xi UMa)	12Leo36	08/31
Alula Borealis (Nu UMa)	11Leo55	08/30
Ankaa (Alpha Phe)	20Aqr45	03/06
Antares (Alpha Sco)Mega132	15Sco01	12/02
Arcturus (Alpha Boo)	29Vir30	10/18
Arkab (Beta 1 Sgr)	21Sgr02	01/06
Armus (Eta Cap)	18Cap00	02/02
Arneb (Alpha Lep)	26Tau38	06/13
Ascella (Zeta Sgr)	18Sgr54	01/04
Asellus Australis (Delta Cnc)	13Cnc59	08/01
Asellus Borealis (Gamma Cnc)	12Cnc48	07/31
Asellus Secundus (Iota Bootis)	06Vir22	09/24
Asellus Primus (Theta Boo)	07Vir52	09/26
Asellus Tertius (Kappa 2 Boo)	05Vir13	09/23
Asmidiske (Xi Pup)	11Cnc18	07/29
Aspidiske (Iota Car)	10Vir35	09/29
Asterope (Pleiades)	05Tau00	05/21
Atik (Omicron Per)	06Tau24	05/23
Atlas (Pleiades)	05Tau37	05/22
Avior (Epsilon Car)	28Leo23	09/16
Azelfafage (Pi 1 Cyg)	03Psc32	03/19

Cosmic Communion: Star Wisdom, Volume 4

Star	Position	Date
Baten Kaitos (Zeta Cet)	27Psc13	04/12
Bellatrix (Gamma Ori)	26Tau12	06/12
Beta Corvi (Kraz)	22Vir38	10/11
Beta Crucis (Mimosa)	16Lib54	11/04
Beta Delphini	21Cap36	02/05
Beta Doradus	27Ari23	05/13
Beta Leonis Minoris	29Cnc48	08/18
Beta Lupi	00Sco17	11/18
Beta Monocerotis	13Gem33	06/30
Beta Piscium	23Aqr51	03/10
Beta Piscis Austrini	02Aqr26	02/16
Beta Trianguli	17Ari37	05/03
Betelgeuse (Alpha Ori)	04Gem01	06/20
Bihan (Theta Peg)	12Aqr13	02/26
Bogardus(Theta Aur)	05Gem12	06/22
Botein (Delta Ari)	26Ari07	05/12
Canopus (Alpha Car)	20Gem13	07/07
Capella (Alpha Aur)	27Tau07	06/13
Caph (Beta Cas)	10Ari23	04/26
Castor (Alpha Gem)	25Gem30	07/13
Castra (Epsilon Cap)	25Cap28	02/09
Celaeno (Pleiades)	04Tau42	05/21
CentaurusSuperGalacticCen	01Lib06	10/19
Center of Galaxy (Oph)	02Sgr06	12/19
Cheleb (Beta Oph)	00Sgr36	12/18
Chi Aquilae	05Cap27	01/21
Chi Aurigae/ Mega 93	29Tau25	06/16
Chi Carinae	05Leo59	08/24
Chi Leonis	19Leo46	09/07
Chi Ophiuchi	13Sco14	12/01
Chi 2 Orionis/ Mega 11	06Gem11	06/23
Chi Pegasi	16Psc52	04/02
Chi Piscium	29Psc48	04/15
Chi Ursae Majoris	08Leo55	08/27
Chort (Theta Leo)	18Leo41	09/06
Cor Caroli (Alpha 2 CVn)	29Leo50	09/18
Cursa (Beta Eri)	20Tau32	06/06
Dabih (Beta Cap)	09Cap18	01/24
Delta Andromedae	27Psc04	04/12
Delta Bootis (Princeps)	08Lib27	10/27
Delta Caeli	25Ari15	05/11
Delta 1 Canis Minoris	29Gem46	07/17
Delta Centauri	02Lib45	10/21
Delta Cephei	22Psc52	04/08
Delta Circini/ Mega70	10Sco26	11/28
Delta Coronae Borealis	22Lib17	11/10
Delta Crucis	10Lib55	10/29
Delta Cygni	21Cap31	02/05
Delta Lupi	03Sco55	11/21
Delta Ophiuchi	07Sco34	11/25
Delta Persei	10Tau04	05/26
Delta Pictoris	12Gem35	06/29
Delta Sagittae	08Cap39	01/24
Delta Serpentis (Two Stars)	23Lib36	11/11
Delta 1Tauri (Hyadum II)	12Tau08	05/28
Delta Trianguli Australis	20Sco07	12/07
Delta Virginis (Minelauva)	16Vir43	10/05
Deneb (Alpha Cyg)/ Mega 20	10Aqr35	02/24
Deneb Algedi (Delta Cap)	28Cap48	02/13
Deneb el Okab (Zeta Aql)	25Sgr03	01/10
Deneb Okab (Delta Aql)	28Sgr54	01/14
Denebola (Beta Leo)	26Leo53	09/15
Diadem (Alpha Com)	14Vir13	10/02
Diphda (Beta Cet)	07Psc51	03/24
Dschubba (Delta Sc)	07Sco50	11/25
Dubhe (Alpha UMa)	20Cnc27	08/08
El Nath (Beta Tau)	27Tau50	06/14
El Tarf (Beta Cnc)	09Cnc31	07/28
Electra (Pleiades)	04Tau40	05/21
Enif (Epsilon Peg)	07Aqr09	02/21
Epsilon Centauri	20Lib49	11/08
Epsilon Crateris	01Vir30	09/20
Epsilon Crucis	13Lib32	11/01
Epsilon Delphini	19Cap18	02/03
Epsilon Hydrae	17Cnc36	08/05
Epsilon Leonis (Algenubi)	25Cnc58	08/14
Epsilon Lupi	05Sco23	11/23
Epsilon Muscae	21Lib49	11/09
Epsilon Persei	10Tau56	05/27
Epsilon Phoenicis	14Aqr54	03/01
Epsilon Piscis Austrini	06Aqr35	02/20
Epsilon Scuti	16Sgr24	01/02
Epsilon Telescopii	07Sgr22	12/24
Epsilon Trianguli	15Ari36	05/01
Epsilon Trianguli Australis	15Sco44	12/03
Eta Aquilae	05Cap42	01/21
Eta Arae	24Sco10	12/11
Eta Aurigae (Haedus II)	24Tau42	06/11
Eta Carinae	27Vir25	10/16
Eta Centauri	25Lib31	11/13
Eta Cephei	09Psc56	03/26
Eta Ceti	17Psc02	04/02
Eta Herculis	04Sco03	11/21
Eta Hydrae	17Cnc34	08/05
Etamin (Gamma Dra)	03Sgr14	12/20
Eta Leonis	03Leo10	08/21
Eta Orionis	25Tau25	06/11
Eta Pavonis	03Sgr14	12/20
Eta Sagittarii	08Sgr53	12/26
Eta Serpentis	10Sgr56	12/28
Fomalhaut (Alpha PsA)	09Aqr07	02/23
Furud (Zeta CMa)	12Gem38	06/29
Gacrux (Gamma Cru)	12Lib00	10/31
Galactic Center	02Sgr06	12/19
Gamma Arae	29Sco33	12/17
Gamma Camelopardalis	19Tau54	06/06
Gamma Ceti	14Ari42	04/30
Gamma Herculis	04Sco28	11/22
Gamma Hydrae	02Lib17	10/21
Gamma Lupi	06Sco45	11/24
Gamma Persei	05Tau17	05/21
Gamma Piscium	26Aqr43	03/12
Gamma Sagittae	12Cap18	01/27
Gamma 1 Sagittarii	06Sgr21	12/23
Gamma Trianguli	18Ari47	05/04
Gamma 2 Velorum	02Leo37	08/21
Garnet Star (Mu Cep)/Mega54	14Psc58	03/31
Gertab (Kappa Sco)	01Sgr44	12/19
Giausar (Lambda Dra)	15Cnc36	08/03
Giedi (Alpha Cap)	09Cap07	01/24
Gienah (Epsilon Cyg)	03Aqr00	02/17
Gienah (Gamma Crv)	15Vir59	10/04
Gomeisa (Beta CMi)	27Gem27	07/15
Graffias (Beta Sco)	08Sco27	11/26
Hadar/Agena(Beta Cen)	29Lib03	11/17
Haedus I (Zeta Aur)	23Tau54	06/10
Haedus II (Eta Aur)	24Tau42	06/11
Hamal (Alpha Ari)	12Ari55	04/28
Han (Zeta Oph)	14Sco29	12/02
Hassaleh (Iota Aur)	21Tau54	06/08
Hatysa (Iota Ori)	28Tau15	06/14
Heze (Zeta Vir)	27Vir24	10/16
Homam (Zeta Peg)	21Aqr25	03/07
Hyadum II (Delta 1 Tau)	12Tau08	05/29
Iota Aurigae (Hassaleh)	21Tau54	06/08
Iota Cancri	11Cnc36	07/30
Iota Canis Majoris	22Gem47	07/10
Iota Capricorni	22Cap57	02/07
Iota Geminorum	24Gem13	07/12
Iota Herculis	25Sco09	12/12
Iota Lyrae	01Cap28	01/17
Iota Orionis (Hatysa)	28Tau15	06/14
Iota Sagittarii	27Sgr49	01/13
Iota 1 Scorpii Mega100	02Sgr47	12/20
Iota 2 Scorpii Mega 118	03Sgr18	12/20
Izar (Epsilon Boo)	03Lib22	10/22
Jabbah (Nu Sco)	09Sco54	11/27
Kappa Aquilae	00Cap07	01/15
Kappa Cancri	21Cnc26	08/09
Kappa Canis Majoris	23Gem50	07/11
Kappa Cassiopeiae/ Mega 76	17Ari52	05/03
Kappa 1 Coronae Australis	2Sgr00	12/29
Kappa Crucis	18Lib27	11/06
Kappa Draconis	21Cnc31	08/09
Kappa Herculis (Marsic)	00Sco59	11/18
Kappa Hydrae	07Leo56	08/26
Kappa Leporis	21Tau10	06/07
Kappa Librae	03Sco01	11/20
KappaTriA Mega188	19Sco14	12/06
Kaus Australis (Epsilon Sgr)	10Sgr20	12/27
Kaus Borealis (Lambda Sgr)	11Sgr35	12/28
Ke Kouan (Beta Lupi)	00Sco17	11/18
Ke Kwan (Kappa Cen)	00Sco03	11/17
Khambalia (Lambda Vir)	12Vir13	10/31
Kochab (Beta UMi)	18Cnc35	08/06
Kornephoros (Beta Her)	06Sco21	11/24
Kraz (Beta Crv)	22Vir38	10/11
Kurhah (Xi Cep)	29Psc29	04/14
Lambda Aquarii	16Aqr50	03/03
Lambda Capricorni	00Aqr16	02/14
Lambda Cassiopeiae	09Ari56	04/25
Lambda Centauri	09Lib48	10/28
Lambda Cephei	21Psc14	04/06
Lambda Cygni	05Aqr00	02/19
Lambda Eridani	20Tau28	06/06
Lambda Herculis (Maasim)	25Sco10	12/12
Lambda Ophiuchi	10Sco51	11/28
Lambda Pavonis	13Sgr04	12/30

Sophia Star Calendar 2022 Index for 700 Stars

Name	Position	Date
Lambda Pictoris	24Ari30	05/10
Lesath (Upsilon Sco)	29Sco16	12/16
M1 (Taurus Crab Nebula)	29Tau21	06/16
M2 (Aquarius Globular Cluster)		
M3 (Canes Venatici Globular Cluster)		
M4 (Scorpio Globular Cluster)		
M5 (Serpens Globular Cluster)		
M6 (Scorpio Butterfly Cluster)	01Sgr00	12/18
M7 (Scorpio Ptolemy's Cluster)	03Sgr59	12/21
M8 (Sagittarius Lagoon Nebula)	06Sgr08	12/23
M9 (Ophiuchus GlobularCluster)		
M10 (Ophiuchus GlobularCluster)		
M11 (Scutum Wild Duck Cluster)	18Sgr31	01/04
M12 (Ophiuchus GlobularCluster)		
M13 (Hercules Globular Cluster)		
M14 (Ophiuchus Globular Cluster)		
M15 (Pegasus Globular Cluster)	04Aqr28	02/18
M16 (Serpens Eagle QueenCl)	09Sgr53	12/27
M17 (Sagittarius Swan Nebula)	10Sgr18	12/27
M18 (Sagittarius Open Cluster)	10Sgr03	12/27
M19 (Ophiuchus Globular Cluster)		
M20 (Sagittarius Trifid Nebula)	05Sgr51	12/23
M21 (Sagittarius Open Cluster)	06Sgr19	12/23
M22 (Sagittarius Facies Cluster)	13Sgr30	12/30
M23 (Sagittarius Open Cluster)	04Sgr30	12/21
M25 (Sagittarius Open Cluster)	12Sgr44	12/30
M26 (Scutum Open Cluster)	16Sgr44	01/02
M27 (Vulpecula Dumbbell N.)	13Cap40	01/28
M28(Sagittarius Globular Cluster)		
M29 (Cygnus Open Cluster)	29Cap20	02/13
M30 (Capricorn Globular Cluster)		
M32 (Andromeda Elliptical Galaxy)		
M33 (Triangulum Pinwheel G)	08Ari30	04/24
M34 (Perseus Open Cluster)	27Ari00	05/13
M35 (Gemini Open Cluster)	07Gem17	06/24
M36 (Auriga Open Cluster)	00Gem14	06/16
M37 (Auriga Open Cluster)	03Gem38	06/20
M38 (Auriga Open Cluster)	28Tau46	06/15
M39 (Cygnus Open Cluster)	27Aqr55	03/14
M41 (CanisMajor Open Cluster)	20Gem11	07/07
M42 (Orion Orion Nebula)	28Tau16	06/14
M44 (Cancer Beehive Cluster)	12Cnc39	07/31
M45 (Taurus Pleiades Stars)	05Tau09	05/21
M46 (Puppis Open Cluster)	05Cnc59	07/24
M47 (Puppis Open Cluster)	04Cnc23	07/22
M49 (Virgo Elliptical Galaxy)	08Vir54	09/27
M50 (Monoceros Heart Cluster)	23Gem32	07/11
M51 (CVn Whirlpool Galaxy)	00Vir23	09/18
M52 (Cassiopeia Open Cluster)		
M53 (Coma Globular Cluster)		
M54 (Sagittarius Globular Cluster)		
M55 (Sagittarius Globular Cluster)		
M56 (Lyra Globular Cluster)		
M57 (Lyra Ring Nebula)		
M59 (Virgo Elliptical Galaxy)	10Vir13	09/28
M60 (Virgo Elliptical Galaxy)	10Vir36	09/29
M62 (Scorpius Globular Cluster)		
M63 (CVn Sunflower Galaxy) 01Vir36	09/20	
M64 (Coma Sleeping BeautyG)	09Vir11	09/27
M65 (Leo Spiral Galaxy)		
M66 (Leo Spiral Galaxy)		
M67 (Cancer Open Cluster)		
M68 (Hydra Globular Cluster)		
M69 (Sagittarius Globular Cluster)		
M71 (Sagitta Star Cluster)		
M74 (Pisces Spiral Galaxy)		
M75 (Sagittarius Globular Cluster)		
M76 (Perseus Little Dumbbell)	20Ari07	05/06
M77 (Cetus Spiral Galaxy)	13Ari31	04/29
M78 (Orion Reflection Nebula)		
M79 (Lepus Globular Cluster)		
M80 (Scorpio Globular Cluster)		
M81 (Ursa Major BodesGalaxy)	04Cnc45	07/23
M82 (Ursa Major Starburst Galaxy)		
M83 (Hydra/Centaurus Spiral Galaxy)		
M84 (Virgo Lenticular Galaxy)	05Vir48	09/24
M85 (Coma Lenticular Galaxy)	03Vir35	09/21
M86 (Virgo Lenticular Galaxy)	06Vir01	09/24
M87 (Virgo Elliptical Galaxy) 07Vir19	09/25	
M92 (Hercules Globular Cluster)		
M93 (Puppis Open Cluster)		
M96 (Leo Spiral Galaxy)		
M97 (Ursa Major Owl Nebula)	27Cnc55	08/16
M100 (Coma Spiral Galaxy)		
M101 (Ursa Major Pinwheel Galaxy)		
M103 (Cassiopeia Star Cluster)		
M104 (Virgo Sombrero Galaxy)	19Vir01	10/07
M105 (Leo Elliptical Galaxy)	13Leo50	09/01
M110 (Andromeda Elliptical Galaxy)		

Name	Position	Date
Maasim (Lambda Her)	25Sco10	12/12
Maia (Pleiades)	04Tau56	05/21
Markab (Alpha Peg)	28Aqr45	03/14
Markeb (Kappa Vela)	04Vir09	09/22
Marfak (Theta Cas)	17Aqr03	05/03
Marfik (Lambda Oph)	10Sco51	11/28
Marsic (Kappa Her)	00Sco59	11/18
Matar (Eta Peg)	00Psc58	03/17
Mebsuta (Epsilon Gem)	15Gem37	07/02
Media (Delta Sgr)	09Sgr50	12/26
Megrez (Delta UMa)	06Leo19	08/25
Meissa (Lambda Ori)	28Tau58	06/15
Mekbuda (Zeta Gem)	20Gem15	07/07
Menkalinan (Beta Aur)	05Gem10	06/22
Menkar (Alpha Cet)	19Ari35	05/05
Menkent (Theta Cen)	17Lib34	11/05
Menkib (Xi Per)	10Tau14	05/27
Merak (Beta UMa)	24Cnc42	08/12
Merope (Pleiades)	04Tau56	05/21
Mesarthim (Gamma 2Ari)	08Ari27	04/24
Miaplacidus (Beta Car)	07Lib14	10/26
Mimosa (Beta Cru)	16Lib54	11/04
Minelauva (Delta Vir)	16Vir43	10/05
Minkar (Epsilon Crv)	16Vir56	10/05
Mintaka (Delta Ori)	27Tau37	06/14
Mira (Omicron Cet)	06Ari47	04/22
Mirach (Beta And)	05Ari40	04/21
Miram (Eta Per)	03Tau58	05/20
Mirfak (Alpha Per)	07Tau20	05/24
Mirzam (Beta CMa)	12Gem27	06/29
Misam (Kappa Per)	02Tau57	05/19
Mizar (Zeta UMa)	20Leo58	09/09
Mothallah (Alpha Tri)	12Ari07	04/27
Mu Cephei(Garnet Star)Mega54	14Psc58	03/31
Mu 1 Crucis	15Lib52	11/03
Mu Eridani	14Tau36	05/31
Mu Mensae	24Cap27	02/08
Mu Normae Mega 89	18Sco47	12/06
Mu Persei	16Tau03	06/02
Mu Tauri	08Tau50	05/25
Mu Virginis	15Lib23	11/03
Muhlifain (Gamma Cen)	07Lib35	10/26
Muliphein (Gamma CMa)	24Gem52	07/12
Muphrid (Eta Boo)	24Vir36	10/13
Muscida (Omicron UMa)	28Gem15	07/16
Naos (Zeta Pup)/ Mega 82	23Cnc49	08/12
Nashira (Gamma Cap)	27Cap03	02/11
Nekkar (Beta Boo)	29Vir31	10/18
Nihal (Beta Lep)	24Tau56	06/11
Nu Aquilae /Mega 27	28Sgr41	01/14
Nu Cephei/Mega 58	19Psc36	04/04
Nu Ceti	13Ari39	04/29
Nu Eridani	12Tau08	05/28
Nu Herculis	04Sgr43	12/22
Nu Hydrae	25Leo38	09/14
Nu Librae	24Lib02	11/12
Nu Ophiuchi	05Sgr01	12/22
Nu Orionis	07Gem07	06/24
Nu Piscium	00Ari46	04/16
Nu Puppis	22Gem24	07/10
Nunki (Sigma Sgr)	17Sgr39	01/03
Nusakan (Beta CrB)	14Lib23	11/02
Omega Andromedae	13Psc02	03/29
Omega Bootis	09Lib04	10/28
Omega 1 Cancri	02Cnc25	07/20
Omega Canis Majoris	00Cnc53	07/18
Omega Carinae	12Lib42	10/31
Omega Capricorni	13Cap13	01/28
Omega Eridani	16Tau18	06/02
Omega Hydrae	22Cnc39	08/10
Omega Orionis	29Tau46	06/16
Omega Pavonis	14Sgr21	12/31
Omega Piscium	07Psc51	03/24
Omicron Arietis	18Ari40	05/04
Omicron 1 CMa/ Mega 149	23Gem25	07/11
Omicron 2 CMa/ Mega 67	26Gem16	07/14
Omicron Cassiopeiae	07Ari43	04/23
Omicron 1 Centauri	04Lib44	10/24
Omicron 2 Centauri	04Lib50	10/23
Omicron Herculis	07Sgr57	12/25
Omicron 1 Orionis	18Tau45	06/04
Omicron Piscium	03Ari00	04/18
Omicron Puppis/ Mega 153	11Cnc19	07/30
Peacock Star (Alpha Pav)	29Sgr05	01/14
Phact (Alpha Col)	27Tau26	06/13
Phecda (Gamma UMa)	05Leo44	08/24
Pherkad (Gamma UMi)	26Cnc51	08/15
Pherkad Minoris	08Cnc04	07/26
Phi Andromedae	11Ari41	04/27

Cosmic Communion: Star Wisdom, Volume 4

Star	Position	Date
Phi Capricorni	20Cap17	02/04
Phi Cassiopeiae	20Ari46	05/06
Phi 3 Hydrae	23Leo19	09/11
Phi Piscium	01Ari43	04/17
Phi Sagittarii	15Sgr26	01/01
Phi Ursae Majoris	14Cnc37	08/02
Pi Andromedae	27Psc56	04/13
Pi 2 Cygni	02Psc27	03/18
Pi Herculis	17Sco20	12/05
Pi Hydrae	13Lib53	11/01
Pi Leonis	04Leo34	08/23
Pi Lupi	02Sco54	11/20
Pi 4 Orionis	17Tau22	06/03
Pi 5 Orionis	17Tau45	06/03
Pi 6 Orionis	18Tau48	06/05
Pi Puppis	05Cnc34	07/23
Pi Sagittarii (Albaldah)	21Sgr31	01/07
Pi Virginis	02Vir49	09/21
Pleiades Stars (Taurus)	05Tau09	05/21
Pleione (Pleiades)	05Tau38	05/22
Polaris (Alpha UMi)	03Gem50	06/20
Polis (MuSgr) Mega 9	08Sgr28	12/25
Pollux (Beta Gem)	28Gem29	07/16
Porrima (Gamma Vir)	15Vir24	10/04
Praecipua (46 LMi)	06Leo08	08/24
Praesepe (Epsilon Cnc)	12Cnc39	07/31
Primus Hyadum	11Tau04	05/27
Procyon (Alpha CMi)	01Cnc03	07/19
Propus (Eta Gem)	08Gem42	06/25
Psi Andromedae	25Psc12	04/10
Psi 1 Aurigae	09Gem46	06/26
Psi Eridani	18Tau28	06/04
Psi Leonis	28Cnc45	08/17
Psi Persei	09Tau00	05/25
Psi Ursae Majoris	04Leo04	08/22
Psi Virginis	21Vir28	10/10
Rasalas (Mu Leo)	26Cnc41	08/15
Rasalgethi (Alpha 1 Her)	21Sco25	12/09
Rasalhague (Alpha Oph)	27Sco43	12/15
Rastaban (Beta Dra)	17Sco14	12/04
Regulus (Alpha Leo)	05Leo05	08/23
Revati (Zeta Psc)	25Psc08	04/10
Rho Cassiopeiae/ Mega24	06/Ari19	04/21
Rho Herculis	20Sco38	12/08
Rho Leonis/ Mega 40	11Leo39	08/30
Rho Ophiuchi	13Sco42	12/01
Rigel (Beta Ori)/ Mega 59	22Tau05	06/08
Rijl AsAwwa (Mu Vir)	15Lib23	11/03
Ruchba (Omega 1 Cyg)	11Aqr17	02/25
Ruchbah (Delta Cas)	23Ari11	05/09
Rukbat (Alpha Sgr)	21Sgr54	01/07
Sabik (Eta Oph)	23Sco14	12/10
Sadachbia (Gamma Aqr)	11Aqr58	02/26
Sadalbari (Mu Peg)	29Aqr39	03/15
Sadalmelik (Alpha Aqr)	08Aqr37	02/22
Sadalsuud (Beta Aqr)	28Cap39	02/12
Sadr (Gamma Cyg)/Mega 78	00Aqr06	02/14
Saiph (Kappa Ori)	01Gem40	06/18
Sargas (Theta Sco)	00Sgr52	12/18
Sarin (Delta Her)	20Sco01	12/07
Scheat (Beta Peg)	04Psc38	03/20
Schedar (Alpha Cas)	13Ari03	04/28
Schemali (Iota Cet)	06Psc11	03/22
Segin (Epsilon Cas)	00Tau01	05/16
Seginus (Gamma Boo)	22Vir55	10/11
Seyfert Galaxy (Ursa Major)	14Leo31	09/02
Shaula (Lambda Sco)Mega154	29Sco51	12/17
Sheliak (Beta Lyr)	24Sgr09	01/10
Sheraton (Beta Ari)	09Ari14	04/24
Sigma Aquilae	03Cap04	01/18
Sigma Cassiopeiae	05Ari23	04/21
Sigma Centauri	05Lib59	10/24
Sigma Cygni/ Mega 66	15Aqr36	03/01
Sigma Leonis	23Leo58	09/12
Sigma Ophiuchi	25Sco51	12/13
Sigma Orionis	29Tau21	06/15
Sigma Scorpii (Alniyat)	13Sco04	11/30
Sigma Virginis	21Vir03	10/09
Sirius (Alpha CMa)	19Gem20	07/06
Situla (Chi Aqr)	22Aqr19	03/08
Situla (Kappa Aqr)	14Aqr41	02/28
Skat (Delta Aqr)	14Aqr08	02/28
Spica (Alpha Vir)	29Vir06	10/18
Sualocin (Alpha Del)	22Cap38	02/07
Subra (Omicron Leo)	29Cnc30	08/18
Suhail (Lambda Vel)	16Leo27	09/04
Sulaphat (Gamma Lyr)	27Sgr11	01/12
Sumut (Alpha Pyx)	01Leo46	08/20
Syrma (Iota Vir)	09Lib03	10/28
Tabit (Pi 3Ori)	17Tau11	06/03
Talitha (Iota UMa)	08Cnc04	07/26
Talitha Australis (Kappa UMa)	09Cnc12	07/27
Talitha Borealis (Iota UMa)	08Cnc04	07/26
Tania Australis (Mu UMa)	26Cnc30	08/14
Tania Borealis (Lambda UMa)	24Cnc46	08/13
Tarazed (Gamma Aql)	06Cap12	01/21
Tau Andromedae	14Ari10	04/30
Tau Canis Majoris	01Cnc39	07/19
Tau Capricorni	13Cap33	01/29
Tau Herculis	19Lib39	11/07
Tau Leonis	26Leo46	09/15
Tau Librae	04Sco37	11/22
Tau Orionis	23Tau06	06/09
Tau Puppis	02Cnc58	07/21
Tau Scorpii (Alniyat)	16Sco43	12/04
Taygeta (Pleiades)	04Tau50	05/21
Tegmine (Zeta Cnc)	06Cnc36	07/25
Tejat (Mu Gem)	10Gem34	06/27
Terebellum (59 Sgr)	01Cap11	01/16
Thabit (Upsilon Orionis)	27Tau10	06/13
Theta Aquilae	10Cap10	01/25
Theta Aurigae (Mahasim)	05Gem12	06/22
Theta Bootis(Asellus Primus)	07Vir52	09/26
Theta Canis Majoris	21Gem27	07/09
Theta 2 Crucis	14Lib03	11/02
Theta Delphini	21Cap29	02/05
Theta Herculis	03Sgr44	12/21
Theta Lupi	12Sco00	11/29
Theta Muscae/ Mega 4	25Lib07	11/13
Theta Ophiuchi	26Sco39	12/14
Theta Pegasi (Bihan)	12Aqr13	02/26
Theta Piscis Austrini	23Cap52	02/08
Theta Piscium	00Psc27	03/16
Theta 1 Sagittarii	00Cap08	01/15
Theta 2 Tauri	13Tau13	05/29
Theta Ursae Majoris (AlHaud)	12Cnc31	07/31
Theta Virginis	23Vir30	10/12
Thuban (Alpha Dra)	12Leo43	08/31
Tseen Ke (Phi Vel)	11Vir12	09/29
Tsih (Gamma Cas)	19Ari11	05/05
Tsze (Lambda Col)	02Gem37	06/19
Tsze Tseang (Iota Leo)	22Leo50	09/11
Ukdah (Tau 2 Hya)	01Leo00	08/19
Unuk (Alpha Ser)	27Lib20	11/15
Upsilon Carinae	28Vir09	10/17
Upsilon Ceti	24Psc41	04/10
Upsilon Cygni	12Aqr31	02/26
Upsilon 1 Hydrae	10Leo57	08/29
Upsilon Pegasi	07Psc14	03/23
Upsilon Sagittarii	24Sgr59	01/10
Vega (Alpha Lyr)	20Sgr35	01/06
Vindemiatrix (Epsilon Vir)	15Vir12	10/03
Wasat (Delta Gem)	23Gem47	07/11
Wezn (Beta Col)	01Gem41	06/18
Wei (Epsilon Sco)	20Sco36	12/08
Wezen (Delta CMa)/Mega 49	28Gem39	07/16
Xi 1 Canis Majoris	15Gem55	07/03
Xi Cassiopeiae	08Ari44	04/24
Xi Cygni	16Aqr04	03/02
Xi Leonis	26Cnc54	08/15
Xi 1 Sagittarii/ Mega 90	18Sgr40	01/04
Xi 2 Sagittarii	18Sgr43	01/04
Yildun (Delta UMi)	06Gem28	06/23
Zaniah (Eta Vir)	10Vir06	09/28
Zaurak (Gamma Eri)	29Ari08	05/15
Zavijava (Beta Vir)	02Vir25	09/20
Zeta Aquilae (Deneb el Okab)	25Sgr03	01/10
Zeta Arae	25Sco05	12/12
Zeta Cassiopeiae	10Ari20	04/26
Zeta Corvi	19Vir04	10/07
Zeta Cygni	08Aqr18	02/22
Zeta Herculis	06Sco43	11/24
Zeta Hydrae	19Cnc50	08/07
Zeta Monocerotis	10Cnc24	07/29
Zeta Pegasi	21Aqr25	03/07
Zeta Persei	08Tau23	05/25
Zeta Puppis (Naos)/Mega 82	23Cnc49	08/12
Zeta 1 Scorpii Mega155	22Sco23	12/10
Zeta Tauri (Alheckla)	00Gem03	06/16
Zosma (Delta Leo)	16Leo35	09/04
Zubenelakrab (Gamma Lib)	00Sco24	11/18
Zuben Elakribi (Delta Lib)	20Lib33	11/08
Zubenelgenubi (Alpha 2 Lib)	20Lib33	11/08
Zubenelgubi (Sigma Lib)	25Lib57	11/13
Zubeneschamali (Beta Lib)	24Lib38	11/12
Zubenhakrabi (Eta Lib)	02Sco37	11/20

SOPHIA STAR CALENDAR CONSTELLATION INDEX WITH ABBREVIATIONS

Sophia Star Calendar 2022 Constellation Index with Abbreviations Used in Calendar

Constellation	Abbreviation	Meaning	Alpha Star	Sidereal Longitude	Beta Star	Sidereal Longitude
Andromeda	And	Princess Daughter	Alpheratz	19Psc34	Mirach	05Ari40
Antlia	Ant	Pump	Alpha Ant	27Leo42	Epsilon Ant.	16Leo16
Apus	Aps	Bird of Paradise	Alpha Aps	19Sco41	Beta Aps	28Sco13
Aquarius	Aqr	Water Carrier	Sadalmelik	08Aqr37	Sadalsuud	28Cap39
Aquila	Aql	Eagle	Altair	07Cap02	Alshain	07Cap41
Ara	Ara	Altar	Alpha Ara	00Sgr12	Beta Ara	29Sco28
Aries	Ari	Ram	Hamal	12Ari55	Sheraton	09Ari14
Auriga	Aur	Charioteer	Capella	27Tau07	Menkalinan.	05Gem10
Bootes	Boo	Herdsman	Arcturus	29Vir30	Nekkar	29Vir31
Caelum	Cae	Sculptor's Chisel	Alpha Cae	01Tau24	Beta Cae	04Tau38
Camelopardalis	Cam	Giraffe	Alpha Cam	26Tau14	Beta Cam	26Tau32
Cancer	Cnc	Crab	Acubens	18Cnc54	ElTarf	09Cnc31
Canes Venatici	CVn	Hunting Dogs	Cor Caroli	29Leo50	Chara	22Leo58
Canis Major	CMa	Greater Dog	Sirius	19Gem20	Mirzam	12Gem27
Canis Minor	CMi	Lesser Dog	Procyon	01Cnc03	Gomeisa	27Gem27
Capricornus	Cap	Sea Goat	Geidi	09Cap07	Dabih	09Cap18
Carina	Car	Keel	Canopus	20Gem13	Miaplacidus.	07Lib14
Cassiopeia	Cas	Queen	Schedar	13Ari03	Caph	10Ari23
Centaurus	Cen	Centaur	Rigel Kent	04Sco44	Hadar	29Lib03
Cepheus	Cep	King	Alderamin	18Psc02	Alfirk	10Ari48
Cetus	Cet	Whale	Menkar	19Ari35	Diphda	07Psc51
Chamaeleon	Cha	Lizard	Alpha Cha	04Sco34	Beta Cha	10Sco42
Circinus	Cir	Compass	Alpha Cir	07Sco37	Beta Cir	09Sco34
Columba	Col	Dove	Phact	27Tau26	Wezn	01Gem41
Coma Berenices	Com	Lock of Hair	Diadem	14Vir13	Beta Com	09Vir38
Corona Australis	CrA	Southern Crown	Alphecca	19Sgr24	Beta CrA	19Sgr19
Corona Borealis	CrB	Northern Crown	Alphecca	17Lib33	Nusakan	14Lib23
Corvus	Crv	Crow	Alchibah	17Vir30	Kraz	22Vir38
Crater	Crt	Cup	Alkes	28Leo57	Beta Crt	03Vir49
Crux	Cru	Cross	Acrux	17Lib08	Mimosa	16Lib54
Cygnus	Cyg	Swan	Deneb	10Aqr35	Albireo	06Cap31
Delphinus	Del	Dolphin	Sualocin	22Cap38	Beta Del	21Cap36
Dorado	Dor	Dolphin Fish	Alpha Dor	13Ari05	Beta Dor	27Ari23
Draco	Dra	Dragon	Thuban	12Leo43	Rastaban	17Sco14
Equuleus	Equ	Little Horse	Kitalpha	28Cap23	Beta Equ	00Aqr42
Eridanus	Eri	River	Achernar	20Aqr34	Cursa	20Tau32
Fornax	For	Furnace	Alpha For	09Ari52	Beta For	01Ari30
Gemini	Gem	Twins	Castor	25Gem30	Pollux	28Gem29
Grus	Gru	Crane	Alnair	21Cap10	Beta Gru	27Cap35
Hercules	Her	Hero	Rasalgethi	21Sco25	Kornephoros.	06Sco21
Horologium	Hor	Clock	Alpha Hor	21Ari05	Beta Hor	21Aqr36
Hydra	Hya	Water Snake, F.	Alphard	02Leo32	Beta Hya	18Vir42
Hydrus	Hyi	Water Snake, M	Alpha Hyi	17Aqr23	Beta Hyi	06Cap14
Indus	Ind	Indian	Alpha Ind	04Cap22	Beta Ind	03Cap03
Lacerta	Lac	Lizard	Alpha Lac	13Psc24	Beta Lac	13Psc54
Leo	Leo	Lion	Regulus	05Leo05	Denebola	26Leo53
Leo Minor	LMi	Lesser Lion	Praecipua	06Leo08	Beta LMi	29Cnc48
Lepus	Lep	Hare	Arneb	26Tau38	Nihal	24Tau56
Libra	Lib	Scales	Zubenelgenubi	20Lib17	Zubeneschamali.	24Lib38
Lupus	Lup	Wolf	Alpha Lup	28Lib46	Beta Lup	00Sco17
Lynx	Lyn	Lynx	Alpha Lyn	17Cnc06	38 Lyn	15Cnc50
Lyra	Lyr	Lyre	Vega	20Sgr35	Sheliak	24Sgr09
Mensa	Men	Table	Alpha Men	00Sgr33	Beta Men	16Cap00
Microscopium	Mic	Microscope	Alpha Mic	10Cap53	Beta Mic	11Cap29
Monoceros	Mon	Unicorn	Alpha Mon	04Cnc32	Beta Mon	13Gem33
Musca	Mus	Fly	Alpha Mus	25Lib38	Beta Mus	25Lib25
Norma	Nor	Carpenter Tool	Gamma1Nor.	16Sco48	Epsilon Nor.	18Sco08

Cosmic Communion: Star Wisdom, Volume 4

Constellation	Abbreviation	Meaning	Alpha Star	Sidereal Longitude	Beta Star	Sidereal Longitude
Octans	Oct	Navigation Tool	Alpha Oct	22Sgr15	Beta Oct	23Sgr17
Ophiuchus	Oph	Snake Holder	Rasalhague	27Sco43	Cheleb	00Sgr36
Orion	Ori	Hunter	Betelgeuse	04Gem01	Rigel	22Tau05
Pavo	Pav	Peacock	Peacock	29Sgr05	Beta Pav	27Sgr45
Pegasus	Peg	Winged Horse	Markab	28Aqr45	Scheat	04Psc38
Perseus	Per	Hero	Mirfak	07Tau20	Algol	01Tau26
Phoenix	Phe	Phoenix	Ankaa	20Aqr45	Beta Phe	25Aqr42
Pictor	Pic	Painter/easel	Alpha Pic	29Cnc23	Beta Pic	27Tau48
Pisces	Psc	Fish	Alrisha	04Ari38	Beta Psc	23Aqr51
Piscis Austrinus	PsA	Southern Fish	Fomalhaut	09Aqr07	Beta PsA	02Aqr26
Puppis	Pup	Poop deck/stern	Naos(Zeta Pup)	23Cnc49	Asmidiske(Xi Pup)	11Cnc18
Pyxis	Pyx	Compass	Alpha Pyx	01Leo46	Beta Pyx	02Leo04
Reticulum	Ret	Optical Device	Alpha Ret	12Psc46	Beta Ret	26Aqr39
Sagitta	Sge	Arrow	Alpha Sge	06Cap20	Beta Sge	06Cap28
Sagittarius	Sgr	Archer	Rukbat	21Sgr54	Arkab	21Sgr02
Scorpius	Sco	Scorpion	Antares	15Sco01	Graffias	08Sco27
Sculptor	Scl	Sculptor	Alpha Scl	05Psc45	Beta Scl	12Aqr30
Scutum	Sct	Shield	Alpha Sct	14Sgr17	Beta Sct	17Sgr38
Serpens	Ser	Serpent	Unuk	27Lib20	Beta Ser	25Lib13
Sextans	Sex	Sextant	Alpha Sex	09Leo23	Beta Sex	14Leo46
Taurus	Tau	Bull	Aldebaran	15Tau03	Elnath	27Tau50
Telescopium	Tel	Telescope	Alpha Tel	10Sgr20	Zeta Tel	10Sgr30
Triangulum	Tri	Triangle	Mothallah	12Ari07	Beta Tri	17Ari37
Triangulum Australe	TrA	Southern Triangle	Atria	26Sco09	Beta TrA	17Sco06
Tucana	Tuc	Toucan	Alpha Tuc	14Cap56	Beta Tuc	01Aqr51
Ursa Major	UMa	Greater Bear	Dubhe	20Cnc27	Merak	24Cnc42
Ursa Minor	UMi	Lesser Bear	Polaris	03Gem50	Kochab	18Cnc35
Vela	Vel	The Sails	Gamma2Vel	02Leo37	Delta Vel	24Leo12
Virgo	Vir	Virgin	Spica	29Vir06	Zavijava	02Vir25
Volans	Vol	Flying Fish	Alpha Vol	25Vir51	Beta Vol	20Vir26
Vulpecula	Vul	Little Fox	Anser	04Cap46	23 Vul	20Cap37

Other:
Cluster — C.
Galaxy — G.
Nebula — N.
Messier Object — M

REFERENCES AND SOURCES

www.constellation-guide.com
www.constellationsofwords.com/
www.constellationsofwords.com/stars/
Gibson, Steven, Star Names: www.naic.edu/~gibson/starnames/
www.naic.edu/~gibson/starnames/starnames.html
IAU (International Astronomical Union): www.iau.org/public/themes/constellations/
Kaler, James, Stars: stars.astro.illinois.edu/sow/sowlist.html
www.rapidtables.com/math/symbols/greek_alphabet.html
www.seasky.org/constellations/constellations.html
www.seasky.org/astronomy/astronomy-messier.html
www.theskylive.com/sky/constellations
www.universeguide.com/constellation
www.en.wikipedia.org/wiki/Bayer_designation

SOURCES

Anon. *Meditations on the Tarot,* pp. 458, 533–552.
Fiorenza, Nick Anthony. "Sidereal Heavens Star Map." *Journal for Star Wisdom 2017,* pp. 76–77.
——. "The Star Catalog: Sidereal Longitudes and Latitudes of the Fixed Stars and Deep Space Objects," 1992–2015: https://www.lunarplanner.com/SkyChart/SkyChart.html (Nick Fiorenza crossed the threshold October 2020 ,and his website is no longer accessible.)
McLaren Lainson, Claudia. "Behold, We are to Make All Things New." *Journal for Star Wisdom 2017,* pp. 119–120.
Powell, Robert. *Astrogeography,* pp. 42–43.
——. "Finding One's Birth Star," in "The Stars New Perspectives" (http://www.astrogeographia.org/the_stars).
——. "The Healing of the Man Born Blind and the Central Sun: Foundations of Star Wisdom (Astrosophy)," *Journal for Star Wisdom 2016,* pp. 29–30.
——. *Hermetic Astrology: Vol. 2,* pp.346–371, 391–396.
Tomberg, Valentin. *Christ and Sophia,* pp. 302–314.

Other relevant sources can be found in the bibliography for this volume

Oh, Holy Sophia, Purest, Most Luminous Divine Light, pray for us.

Please know that the Sophia Star Calendar 2022 is a "living draft" of overlighting Stars, subject to revision, updates, and always in progress, evolving for Truth and Highest Good. —KB

Oh, Holy Mary Sophia, pray for us.

GLOSSARY

This glossary of entries relating to Esoteric Christianity lists only some of the specialized terms used in the articles and commentaries of *Star Wisdom*. Owing to limited space, the entries are very brief, and the reader is encouraged to study the foundational works of Rudolf Steiner for a more complete understanding of these terms.

Ahriman: An adversarial being identified by the great prophet Zarathustra during the ancient Persian cultural epoch (5067–2907 BC) as an opponent to the Sun God *Ahura Mazda* (obs.; "Aura of the Sun"). Also called Satan, Ahriman represents one aspect of the Dragon. Ahriman's influence leads to materialistic thinking devoid of feeling, empathy, and moral conscience. Ahriman helps inspire science and technology, and works through forces of sub-nature such as gravity, electricity, magnetism, radioactivity—forces that are antithetical to life. The influence of Ahriman's activity upon the human being limits human cognition to what is derived from sense perception, hardens thinking (materialistic thoughts), attacks the etheric body by way of modern technology (electromagnetic radiation, etc.), and hardens hearts (cold and calculating).

ahrimanic beings: Spiritual beings who have become agents of Ahriman's influences.

Angel Jesus: A pure immaculate Angelic being who sacrifices himself so that the Christ may work through him. This Angelic being is actually of the status of an Archangel, who has descended to work on the Angelic level to be closer to human beings and to assist them on the path of confrontation with evil.

Ascension: An unfathomable process at the start of which, on May 14 AD 33, Christ united with the etheric realm that surrounds and permeates the Earth with Cosmic Life. Thus began his cosmic ascent to the realm of the heavenly Father, with the goal of elevating the Earth spiritually and opening pathways between the Earth and the spiritual world for the future.

astral body: Part of the human being that is the bearer of consciousness, passion, and desires, as well as idealism and the longing for perfection.

Asuras: Fallen Archai (Time Spirits) from the time of Old Saturn, whose opposition to human evolution comes to expression through promoting debauched sexuality and senseless violence among human beings. So low is the regard that the Asuras have for the sacredness of human life, that as well as promoting extreme violence and debauchery (for example, through the film industry), they do not hold back from the destruction of the physical body of human beings. In particular, the activity of the Asuras retards the development of the consciousness soul.

bodhisattva: On the human level a bodhisattva is a human being far advanced on the spiritual path, a human being belonging to the circle of twelve great teachers surrounding the Cosmic Christ. One who incarnates periodically to further the evolution of the Earth and humanity, working on the level of an angelic, archangelic, or higher being in relation to the rest of humanity. Every 5,000 years, one of these great teachers from the circle of bodhisattvas takes on a special mission, incarnating repeatedly to awake a new human faculty and capacity. Once that capacity has been imparted through its human bearer, this bodhisattva then incarnates upon the Earth for the last time, ascending to the level of a Buddha to serve humankind from spirit realms. See also Maitreya Bodhisattva.

Central Sun: Heart of the Milky Way, also called the Galactic Center. Our Sun orbits this Central Sun over a period of approximately 225 million years.

chakra: One of seven astral organs of perception through which human beings develop higher

Glossary

levels of cognition such as clairvoyance, telepathy, and so on.

Christ: The eternal being who is the second member of the Trinity. Also called the "Divine 'I AM,'" the Son of God, the Cosmic Christ, and the Logos–Word. Christ began to fully unite with the human vessel (Jesus) at the Baptism in the Jordan, and for 3½ years penetrated as the *Divine I AM* successively into the astral body, etheric body, and physical body of Jesus, spiritualizing each member. Through the Mystery of Golgotha Christ united with the Earth, kindling the spark of Christ consciousness (*Not I, but Christ in me*) in all human beings.

consciousness soul: The portion of the human soul in which "I" consciousness is awaking not only to its own sense of individuality and to the individualities of others, but also to its higher self—spirit self (Sanskrit: *manas*). Within the consciousness soul, the "I" perceives truth, beauty, and goodness; within the spirit self, the "I" becomes truth, beauty, and goodness.

crossing the threshold: a term applicable to our time, as human beings are increasingly encountering the spiritual world—in so doing, crossing the threshold between the sense-perceptible realm and non-physical realms of existence. To the extent that spiritual capacities have not been cultivated, this encounter with non-physical realms beyond the sense world signifies a descent into the subconscious (for example, through drugs) rather than an ascent to knowledge of higher worlds through the awaking of higher levels of consciousness.

decan: The zodiac of 360° is divided into twelve signs, each of 30°. A decan is 10°, thus one third of one sign or $1/36$ of the zodiac.

devil: Another term for Lucifer.

dragon: As used in the Apocalypse of John, there are different appearances of the dragon, each one representing an adversarial being opposed to Michael, Christ, and Sophia. For example, the great red dragon of chapter 12 opposes Sophia, the woman clothed with the Sun (Sophia is the pure Divine-Cosmic Feminine Soul of the World). The imagery from chapter 12 of Revelation depicts the woman clothed with the Sun as pregnant and that the great red dragon attempts to devour her child as soon as it is born. The child coming to birth from the woman clothed with the Sun represents the Divine-Cosmic "I AM" born through the assistance of the pure Divine Feminine Soul of the World. The dragon is cast down from the heavenly realm by the mighty Archangel Michael. Cast down to the Earth, the dragon continues with attempts to devour the cosmic child (the Divine-Cosmic "I AM") coming to birth among humankind.

ego: The soul sheath through which the "I" begins to incarnate and to experience life on Earth (to be distinguished from the term *ego* used in Freudian and Jungian psychology). The terms "I," and *soul* are sometimes used interchangeably in Spiritual Science. The ego maintains threads of integrity and continuity through memory, while experiencing new sensations and perceptions through observation and thinking, feeling, and willing. The ego is capable of moral discernment and also experiences temptation. Thus, it is often stated that the "I" comprises both a higher nature and the lower nature ("ego").

Emmerich, Anne Catherine (also "Sister Emmerich"): A Catholic stigmatist (1774–1824) whose visions depicted the daily life of Jesus, beginning some weeks before the event of the descent of Christ into the body of Jesus at the Baptism in the River Jordan and extending for a period of several weeks after the Crucifixion.

Ephesus: The area in Asia Minor (now Turkey) to which the Apostle John (also called John Zebedee, the brother of James the Greater) accompanied the Virgin Mary approximately three years after the death of Jesus Christ. Ephesus was a very significant ancient mystery center where cosmic mysteries of the East found their way into the West. Initiates at Ephesus were devoted to the goddess Artemis, known as "Artemis of Ephesus," whose qualities are more those of a Mother goddess than is the case with the Greek goddess Artemis, although there is a certain degree of overlap between Artemis and Artemis of Ephesus with regard to many of their respective characteristics. A magnificent Ionic mystery temple was built in honor of Artemis of Ephesus at a location close to the Aegean Sea. Mary's house, built by John, was located high up above, on the nearby hill known as Mount Nightingale, about six miles from the temple of Artemis at Ephesus.

etheric body: The body of life forces permeating and animating the physical body. The etheric body was formed during ancient Sun evolution. The etheric body's activity is expressed in the seven life processes permeating the seven vital organs. The etheric body is related to the movements of the seven visible planets.

Fall, The: A fall from oneness with spiritual worlds. The Fall, which took place during the Lemurian period of Earth evolution, was a time of dramatic transition in human evolution when the soul descended from "Paradise" into earthly existence. Through the Fall the human soul began to incarnate into a physical body upon the Earth and experience the world from "within" the body, perceiving through the senses.

Fifth Gospel: The writings and lectures of Rudolf Steiner based on new spiritual perceptions and insights into the mysteries of Christ's life on Earth, including the Second Coming of Christ—his appearance in the etheric realm in our time, beginning in the twentieth century.

Golgotha, Mystery of: Rudolf Steiner's designation for the entire mystery of the coming of Christ to the Earth. Sometimes this term is used more specifically to refer to the events surrounding the Crucifixion and Resurrection. In particular, the Crucifixion—the sacrifice on the cross—marked the birth of Christ's union with the Earth. Also referred to as the "Turning Point of Time," whereby at the Crucifixion Christ descended from the sphere of the Sun and became the "Spirit of the Earth."

Grail: An etheric chalice into which Christ can work to transform earthly substance into spiritual substance. The term *Grail* has many deep levels of meaning and refers on the one hand to a spiritual stream in service of Christ, and on the other hand to the means by which the human "I" penetrates and transforms evil into good. The power of transubstantiation expresses something of this process of transformation of evil into good.

Grail Knights: Those trained to confront evil and transform it into something good, in service of Christ. Members of a spiritual stream that existed in the past and continues to exist—albeit in metamorphosed form—in the present. Every human being striving for the good can potentially become a Grail Knight.

I AM: One's true individuality, that—with few exceptions—never fully incarnates but works into the developing "I" and its lower bodies (astral, etheric, and physical). The **Cosmic I AM** is the "I AM" of Christ, through which—on account of the Mystery of Golgotha—we are all graced with the possibility of receiving a divine spark therefrom.

Jesus (see Nathan Jesus and Solomon Jesus): The pure human being who received the Christ at the Baptism in the River Jordan.

Jesus Christ: The Divine-Human being; the God-Man; the union of the Divine with the Human. The presence of the Cosmic Christ in the physical body of the human being called the Nathan Jesus during the 3½ years of the ministry.

Jesus of Nazareth: The name of the human being whose birth is celebrated in the Gospel of Luke, also referred to as the Nathan Jesus. When Jesus of Nazareth reached the age of twelve, the spirit of the Solomon Jesus (Gospel of Matthew) united with the body and sheaths of the pure Nathan Jesus. This union lasted for about 18 years, until the Baptism in the River Jordan. During these eighteen years, Jesus of Nazareth was a composite being comprising the Nathan Jesus and the spirit ("I") of the Solomon Jesus. Just before the Baptism, the spirit of the Solomon Jesus withdrew, and at the Baptism Jesus became known as "Jesus Christ" through the union of Christ with the sheaths of Jesus.

Jezebel: Wife of King Ahab, approximately 900 BC, who worked through the powers of black magic against the prophet Elijah.

Kali Yuga: Yugas are ages of influence referred to in Hindu cosmography, each yuga lasting a certain numbers of years in length (always a multiple of 2,500). The Kali Yuga is also known as the Dark Age, which began with the death of Krishna in 3102 BC (-3101). Kali Yuga lasted 5,000 years and ended in AD 1899.

Kingly Stream: Biblically, the line of heredity from King David into which the Solomon Jesus (Gospel of Matthew) was born. The kings (the three magi) were initiates who sought to bring the cosmic will of the heavenly Father to expression on the Earth through spiritual forces working from spiritual beings dwelling in the stars. The minds of the wise kings were enlightened by the coming of Jesus Christ.

Krishna: A cosmic-human being, the sister soul of Adam that over-lighted Arjuna as described in the Bhagavad Gita. The over-lighting by Krishna of Arjuna could be described as an incorporation of Krishna into Arjuna. An incorporation is a partial incarnation. The cosmic-human being known as Krishna later fully incarnated as Jesus of Nazareth (Nathan Jesus—Gospel of Luke).

Lazarus: The elder brother of Mary Magdalene, Martha, and Silent Mary. At his raising from the dead, Lazarus became the first human being to be fully initiated by Christ (see Lazarus–John).

Lazarus–John: At the raising of Lazarus from the dead by Christ, the spiritual being of John the Baptist united with Lazarus. The higher spiritual members of John (spirit body, life spirit, spirit self) entered into the members of Lazarus, which were developed to the level of the consciousness soul.

Lucifer: The name of a fallen spiritual being, also called the Light-Bearer, who acts as a retarding force within the human astral body and also in the sentient soul. Lucifer inflames egoism and pride within the human being, often inspiring genius and supreme artistry. Arrogance and self-importance are stimulated, without humility or sacrificial love. Lucifer stirs up forces of rebellion, but cannot deliver true freedom—just its illusion.

luciferic beings: Spiritual beings who have become agents of Lucifer's influences.

magi: Initiates in the mystery school of Zarathustra, the Bodhisattva who incarnated as Zoroaster (Zaratas, Nazaratos) in the sixth century BC and who, after he came to Babylon, became a teacher of the Chaldean priesthood. At the time of Jesus, the magi were still continuing the star-gazing tradition of the school of Zoroaster. The task of the magi was to recognize when their master would reincarnate. With their visit to the newborn Jesus child in Bethlehem (Gospel of Matthew), to this child who was the reincarnated Zarathustra–Zoroaster, they fulfilled their mission. The three magi are the "priest kings from the East" referred to in the Gospel of Matthew.

Maitreya Bodhisattva: The bodhisattva individuality that is preparing to become the successor of Gautama Buddha and will be known as the Bringer of the Good. This bodhisattva was incarnated in the second century BC as Jeshu ben Pandira, the teacher of the Essenes, who died about 100 BC. Rudolf Steiner indicated that Jeshu ben Pandira reincarnated at the beginning of the twentieth century as a great bodhisattva individuality to fulfill the lofty mission of proclaiming Christ's coming in the etheric realm, beginning around 1933: "He will be the actual herald of Christ in his etheric form" (lecture about Jeshu ben Pandira held in Leipzig on November 4, 1911). There are differing points of view as to who this individuality actually was in his twentieth century incarnation.

manas: Also called the spirit self; the purified astral body, lifted into full communion with truth and goodness by becoming the true and the good within the essence of the higher self of the human being. Manas is the spiritual source of the "I," and as it is the eternal part of the human being that goes from life to life, manas bears the human being's true "eternal name" through its union with the Holy Spirit. The "eternal name" expresses the human being's true mission from life to life.

Mani: The name of a lofty initiate who lived in Babylon in the third century AD. The founder of the Manichean stream, whose mission is the transformation of evil into goodness through compassion and love. Mani reincarnated as Parzival in the ninth century AD. Mani–Parzival is one of the leading initiates of our present age—the age of the consciousness soul (AD 1414–3574). One of the highest beings ever to incarnate upon the Earth, he will become the future Manu beginning in the astrological Age of Sagittarius. This future Manu will oversee the spiritual evolution of a sequence of seven ages, comprising the seven cultural epochs of the Sixth Great Age of Earth evolution from the Age of Sagittarius to the Age of Gemini—lasting a total of 7 x 2,160 years (15,120 years), since each zodiacal age lasts 2,160 years.

Manu: Like the word Buddha, the word Manu is a title. A Manu has the task of spiritually overseeing one Great Age of Earth evolution, comprising seven astrological ages (seven cultural epochs)—lasting a total of 7 x 2,160 years (15,120 years), since each zodiacal age lasts 2,160 years. The present Age of Pisces (AD 215–2375)—with its corresponding cultural epoch (AD 1414–3574)—is the fifth epoch during the Fifth Great Age of

Earth evolution. (Lemuria was the Third Great Age, Atlantis the Fourth Great Age, and since the great flood that destroyed Atlantis, we are now in the Fifth Great Age.) The present Manu is the exalted Sun-initiate who guided humanity out of Atlantis during the ancient flooding that destroyed the continent of Atlantis formerly in the region of the Atlantic Ocean—the Flood referred to in the Bible in connection with Noah. He is the overseer of the seven cultural epochs corresponding to the seven astrological ages from the Age of Cancer to the Age of Capricorn, following the sequence: Cancer, Gemini, Taurus, Aries, Pisces, Aquarius, Capricorn. The present Manu was the teacher of the Seven Holy Rishis who were the founders of the ancient Indian cultural epoch (7227–5067 BC) during the Age of Cancer. He is known in the Bible as Noah, and in the Flood story belonging to the Gilgamesh epic he is called Utnapishtim. Subsequently this Manu appeared to Abraham as Melchizedek and offered Abraham an agape ("love feast") of bread and wine. Jesus "was designated by God to be high priest in the order of Melchizedek" (Heb. 5:10).

Mary: Rudolf Steiner distinguishes between the Nathan Mary and the Solomon Mary (see corresponding entries). The expression "Virgin Mary" refers to the Solomon Mary, the mother of the child Jesus whose birth is described in the Gospel of Matthew.

Mary Magdalene: Sister of Lazarus, whose soul was transformed and purified as Christ cast out seven demons who had taken possession of her. Christ thus initiated Mary Magdalene. Later, she anointed Jesus Christ. And she was the first to behold the Risen Christ in the Garden of the Holy Sepulcher on the morning of his resurrection.

megastar: Stars with a luminosity greater than 10,000 times that of our Sun.

Nain, Youth of: Referred to in the Gospel of Luke as the son of the widow of Nain. The Youth of Nain—at the time he was twelve years old—was raised from the dead by Jesus. The Youth of Nain later reincarnated as the Prophet Mani (third century AD) and subsequently as the Grail King Parzival (ninth century AD).

Nathan Jesus: From the priestly line of David, as described in the Gospel of Luke. An immaculate and pure soul whose one and only physical incarnation was as Jesus of Nazareth (Nathan Jesus).

Nathan Mary: A pure being who was the mother of the Nathan Jesus. The Nathan Mary died in AD 12, but her spirit united with the Solomon Mary at the time of the Baptism of Jesus in the River Jordan. From this time on, the Solomon Mary—spiritually united with the Nathan Mary—was known as the Virgin Mary.

New Jerusalem: A spiritual condition denoting humanity's future existence that will come into being as human beings free themselves from the *maya* of the material world and work together to bring about a spiritualized Earth.

Osiris: *Osiris* and *Isis* are names given by the Egyptians to the preincarnatory forms of the spiritual beings who are now known as Christ and Sophia.

Parzival: Son of Gahmuret and Herzeloyde in the epic *Parzival* by Wolfram von Eschenbach. Although written in the thirteenth century, this work refers to actual people and events in the ninth century AD, one of whom (the central figure) bore the name Parzival. After living a life of dullness and doubt, Parzival's mission was to seek the Castle of the Grail and to ask the question "What ails thee?" of the Grail King, Anfortas—moreover, to ask the question without being bidden to do so. Parzival eventually became the new Grail King, the successor of Anfortas. Parzival was the reincarnated prophet Mani. In the incarnation preceding that of Mani, he was incarnated as the Youth of Nain (Luke 7:11–15). Parzival is a great initiate responsible for guiding humanity during the Age of Pisces, which has given birth to the cultural epoch of the development of the consciousness soul (AD 1414–3574).

Pentecost: Descent of the Holy Spirit fifty days after Easter, whereby the cosmic "I AM" was birthed among the disciples and those individuals close to Christ. They received the capacity to develop manas, or spirit self, within the community of striving human individuals, whereby the birth of the spirit self is facilitated through the soul of the Virgin Mary. See also World Pentecost.

phantom body: The pure spiritual form of the human physical body, unhindered by matter. The far-distant future state of the human physical body when it has become purified and spiritualized into a body of transformed divine will.

Glossary

Presbyter John: Refers to Lazarus–John who moved to Ephesus about twenty years after the Virgin Mary had died there. In Ephesus he became a bishop. He is the author of the book of Revelation, the Gospel of St. John, and the Letters of John.

Risen One: The initial appearance of Christ in his phantom body (resurrection body), beginning with his appearance to Mary Magdalene on Easter Sunday morning. Christ frequently appeared to the disciples in his phantom body during the forty days leading from Easter to Ascension.

Satan: The traditional Christian name for Ahriman.

Serpent: Another name for Lucifer, but sometimes naming a combination of Lucifer and Ahriman: "The great dragon was hurled down—that ancient serpent called the devil, or Satan, who leads the whole world astray" (Rev. 12:9).

Shepherd Stream: Biblically, the genealogical line from David the shepherd through his son Nathan. It was into this line that the Nathan Jesus was born, whose birth is described in the Gospel of Luke. Rudolf Steiner describes the shepherds, who—according to Luke—came to pay homage to the newborn child, as those servants of pure heart who perceive the goodwill streaming up from Mother Earth. The hearts of the shepherds were kindled with the fire of Divine Love by the coming of the Christ. The shepherds can be regarded as precursors of the heart stream of humanity that now intuits the being of Christ as the spirit of the Earth.

Solomon Jesus: Descended from the genealogical line from David through his son Solomon. This line of descent is described in the Gospel of Matthew. The Solomon Jesus was a reincarnation of Zoroaster (sixth century BC). In turn, Zoroaster was a reincarnation of Zarathustra (6000 BC), the great prophet and founder of the ancient Persian religion of Zoroastrianism. He was a bodhisattva who, as the founder of this new religion that focused on the Sun Spirit Ahura Mazda, helped prepare humanity for the subsequent descent into incarnation of Ahura Mazda, the cosmic Sun Spirit, as Christ.

Solomon Mary: The wise mother of the Solomon Jesus, who adopted the Nathan Jesus after the death of the Nathan Mary. At the time of the Baptism of Jesus in the River Jordan, the spirit of the Nathan Mary united with the Solomon Mary. Usually referred to as the Virgin Mary or Mother Mary, the Solomon Mary bore witness at the foot of the cross to the Mystery of Golgotha. She died in Ephesus eleven years after Christ's Ascension.

Sophia: Part of the Divine Feminine Trinity comprising the Mother (counterpart of the Father), the Daughter (counterpart of the Son), and the Holy Soul (counterpart of the Holy Spirit). Sophia, also known as the Bride of the Lamb, is the Daughter aspect of the threefold Divine Feminine Trinity. To the Egyptians Sophia was known as Isis, who was seen as belonging to the starry realm surrounding the Earth. In the Book of Proverbs, attributed to King Solomon, Sophia's temple has seven pillars (Proverbs 9:1). The seven pillars in Sophia's temple represent the seven great stages of Earth evolution (from ancient Saturn to future Vulcan).

Sorath: The great enemy of Christ who works against the "I" in the human being. Sorath is identified with the two-horned beast that rises up from the depths of Earth, as described in the book of Revelation. Sorath is the Sun Demon, and is identified by Rudolf Steiner as the Antichrist. According to the book of Revelation, his number is 666.

Sun Demon: Another name for Sorath.

Transfiguration: The event on Mt. Tabor where Jesus Christ was illumined with Divine Light raying forth from the purified etheric body of Jesus, which the Divine "I AM" of Christ had penetrated. The Gospels of Matthew and Luke describe the Transfiguration. The Sun-like radiance that shone forth from Jesus Christ on Mt. Tabor was an expression of the purified etheric body that had its origin during the Old Sun period of Earth evolution.

Transubstantiation: Sacramental transformation of physical substance—for example, the transubstantiation of bread and wine during the Mass to become the body and blood of Christ. During the Holy Eucharist the bread and wine are transformed in such a way that the substances of bread and wine are infused with the life force (body) and light (blood) of Christ. Thereby the bread and wine are reunited with their divine archetypes and are no longer "merely" physical substances, but are bearers on the physical level of a spiritual reality.

Turning Point of Time: Transition between involution and evolution, as marked by the Mystery of Golgotha. The descending stream of involution culminated with the Mystery of Golgotha. With the descent of the Cosmic Christ into earthly evolution, through his sacrifice on Golgotha an ascending stream of evolution began. This sacrifice of Christ was followed by the events of his Resurrection and Ascension, which were followed in turn by Whitsun (Pentecost)—all expressing the ascending stream of evolution. This path of ascent was also opened up to all human beings by way of the power of the divine "I AM" bestowed—at least, potentially—on all humanity by Christ through his sacrifice on the cross.

Union in the Temple: The event of the union of the spirit of the Solomon Jesus with the twelve-year-old Nathan Jesus. This union of the two Jesus children signified the uniting of the priestly (Nathan) line and the kingly (Solomon) line—both lines descended from King David.

Whitsun: "White Sunday"; Pentecost.

World Pentecost is the gradual event of cosmic revelation becoming human revelation as a signature of the end of the Dark Age (Kali Yuga). Anthroposophy (Spiritual Science) is a language of spiritual truth that could awake a community of striving human beings to the presence of the Holy Spirit and the founding of the New Jerusalem.

Zarathustra: The great teacher of the ancient Persians in the sixth millennium BC (around 6000 BC). In the sixth century BC, Zarathustra reincarnated as Zoroaster. He then reincarnated as the Solomon Jesus (6 BC–AD 12), whose birth is described in the Gospel of Matthew.

Zoroaster: An incarnation of Zarathustra. Zarathustra–Zoroaster was a Bodhisattva. Zoroaster lived in the sixth century BC. He was a master of wisdom. Among his communications as a teacher of wisdom was his specification as to how the zodiac of living beings in the heavens comes to expression in relation to the stars comprising the twelve zodiacal constellations. Zoroaster subsequently incarnated as the Solomon Jesus, whose birth is described in the Gospel of Matthew, to whom the three magi came from the East bearing gifts of gold, frankincense, and myrrh.

"It became clearer and clearer to me—as the outcome of many years of research—that in our epoch there is really something like a resurrection of the astrology of the third epoch [the Egyptian–Babylonian period], but permeated now with the Christ Impulse. Today, we must search among the stars in a way different from the old ways. The stellar script must once more become something that speaks to us."
—Rudolf Steiner (*Christ and the Spiritual World and the Search for the Holy Grail*, p. 106)

"In Palestine during the time that Jesus of Nazareth walked on Earth as Jesus Christ—during the three years of his life, from his thirtieth to his thirty-third year—the entire being of the cosmic Christ was acting uninterruptedly upon him, and was working into him. The Christ stood always under the influence of the entire cosmos; he made no step without this working of the cosmic forces into and in him.... It was always in accordance with the collective being of the whole universe with whom the Earth is in harmony that all that Jesus Christ did took place."
—Rudolf Steiner (*Spiritual Guidance of Man and Humanity*, p. 66)

BIBLIOGRAPHY AND RELATED READING

See "Literature" on page 10 for an annotated list of books on Astrosophy.

Andreev, Daniel. *The Rose of the World*. Great Barrington, MA: Lindisfarne Books, 1997.

Anonymous. *Meditations on the Tarot: A Journey into Christian Hermeticism*. New York: Putman, 2002.

Bailey, Alice. *A Treatise on the Seven Rays, vol. 3: Esoteric Astrology*. New York: Lucis, 2002.

Bauval, Robert, and Thomas Brophy. *Black Genesis: The Prehistoric Origins of Ancient Egypt*. Rochester, VT: Bear, 2011.

Bondarev, G. A. *Events in the Ukraine and a Possible Future Scenario*, book 1. Self-published, 2016.

Bradeen Spannaus, Nancy. *Hamilton Versus Wall Street: The Core Principles of the American System of Economics*. Self-published, 2019.

Cage, John. *Branches*, 1976 (https://johncage.org/pp/John-Cage-Work-Detail.cfm?work_ID=34).

——. *Child of Tree*, 1975 (https://johncage.org/pp/John-Cage-Work-Detail.cfm?work_ID=40).

——. *Concert for Piano and Orchestra*, 1958 (https://johncage.org/pp/John-Cage-Work-Detail.cfm?work_ID=48).

——. *Music of Changes*, 1952 (https://johncage.org/pp/John-Cage-Work-Detail.cfm?work_ID=134).

Dionysius the Areopagite, *Mystical Theology and the Celestial Hierarchies*. Fintry, UK: Shrine of Wisdom, 1965.

Dorsan, Jacques. *The Clockwise House System: A True Foundation for Sidereal and Tropical Astrology*. Great Barrington, MA: Lindisfarne Books, 2011.

Emmerich, Anne Catherine. *Visions of the Life of Christ* (3 vols.). Kettering, OH: Angelico Press, 2015.

Genge, Heinze. "Versuch einer Abraham-Datierung," in *Memoriam Eckhard Unger, Beitrage zu Geschichte, Kultur und Religion des alten Orients*, Baden-Baden, 1971.

Gilmurray, Jonathan. *Ecology and Environmentalism in Contemporary Sound Art*, 2017 (http://ualresearchonline.arts.ac.uk/13705/1/Jonathan%20Gilmurray_PhD%20Thesis_FINAL%20SUBMISSION.pdf).

Grosse, Rudolf. *The Christmas Foundation: Beginning of a New Cosmic Age*. North Vancouver, BC: Steiner Book Centre, 1984.

Hamilton, E. *The Modes of Ancient Greece*, 1953 (http://www.anaphoria.com/lee/2modes.pdf).

Ingraham, Robert. *The Modern Anglo-Dutch Empire: Its Origins, Evolution, and Anti-human Outlook*. Self-published, 2021.

Isaacson, Estelle. *Through the Eyes of Mary Magdalene*, 3 vols. Taos, NM: LogoSophia, 2012–2015.

Kennedy, E. S., and David Pingree, *The Astrological History of Masha'allah*. Cambridge, MA: Harvard Univsersity Press, 1971.

Kirchner-Bockholt, Margarete and Erich Kirchner-Bockholt. *Rudolf Steiner's Mission and Ita Wegman*. Forest Row, UK: Rudolf Steiner Press, 2016.

Lessing, Gotthold Ephraim *The Education of the Human Race: The Harvard Classics*, vol. 32. (Tr. F. W. Robertson). New York: Harvard Univsersity Press, 1910.

Marshall, S. *John Cage's I-Ching Chance Operations* (https://www.biroco.com/yijing/cage.htm).

McLaren Lainson, Claudia. *The Circle of Twelve and the Legacy of Valentin Tomberg*. Boulder: Windrose Academy, 2015.

Nakai, Y. *David Tudor and the Occult Passage of Music* (https://www.academia.edu/35233758/David_Tudor_and_The_Occult_Passage_of_Music).

Powell, Robert. *The Christ Mystery*. Fair Oaks, CA: Rudolf Steiner College, 1999.

——. *Christian Hermetic Astrology: The Star of the Magi and the Life of Christ*. Great Barrington, MA: Lindisfarne Books, 2009.

——. *Chronicle of the Living Christ: The Life and Ministry of Jesus Christ: Foundations of Cosmic Christianity*. Hudson, NY: Anthroposophic Press, 1996.

——. *Cultivating Inner Radiance and the Body of Immortality: Awakening the Soul through Modern Etheric Movement*. Great Barrington, MA: Lindisfarne Books, 2012.

——. *Elijah Come Again: A Prophet for Our Time: A Scientific Approach to Reincarnation*. Great Barrington, MA: Lindisfarne Books, 2009.

——. *Hermetic Astrology*, vols. 1 and 2. San Rafael, CA: Sophia Foundation Press, 2006.

——. *History of the Zodiac*. San Rafael, CA: Sophia Academic Press, 2007.

——. *The Most Holy Trinosophia: The New Revelation of the Divine Feminine*. Great Barrington, MA: SteinerBooks, 2000.

———. *The Mystery, Biography, and Destiny of Mary Magdalene: Sister of Lazarus–John and Spiritual Sister of Jesus*. Great Barrington, MA: Lindisfarne Books, 2008.

———. *Prophecy-Phenomena-Hope: The Real Meaning of the year 2012*. Great Barrington, MA: SteinerBooks, 2011.

———. *The Sign of the Son of Man in Heaven*. San Rafael, CA: Sophia Foundation, 2007.

———. *The Sophia Teachings: The Emergence of the Divine Feminine in Our Time*. Great Barrington, MA: Lindisfarne Books, 2007.

Powell, Robert, and David Bowden. *Astrogeographia: Correspondences between the Stars and Earthly Locations: Earth Chakras and the Bible of Astrology*. Great Barrington, MA: SteinerBooks, 2012.

Powell, Robert, and Kevin Dann. *The Astrological Revolution: Unveiling the Science of the Stars as a Science of Reincarnation and Karma*. Great Barrington, MA: SteinerBooks, 2010.

———. *Christ and the Maya Calendar: 2012 and the Coming of the Antichrist*. Great Barrington, MA: SteinerBooks, 2009.

Powell, Robert, and Estelle Isaacson. *Gautama Buddha's Successor: A Force for Good in our Time*. Great Barrington, MA: SteinerBooks, 2013.

———. *The Mystery of Sophia: Bearer of the New Culture: The Rose of the World*. Great Barrington, MA: SteinerBooks, 2014.

Powell, Robert, and Lacquanna Paul. *Cosmic Dances of the Planets*. San Rafael, CA: Sophia Foundation Press, 2006.

Powell, Robert, and Peter Treadgold. *The Sidereal Zodiac*. Tempe, AZ: AFA, 1985.

Pye, Michael, and Kirsten Dalley. *Lost Cities and Forgotten Civilizations: Mysteries Uncovered, Secrets Declassified*. New York: Rosen, 2012.

Renold, Maria. *Intervals, Scales, Tones: And the Concert Pitch c = 128 Hz*. Forest Row, UK: Temple Lodge, 2015.

Robbins, Michael D. *The Tapestry of the Gods, vol 1: The Seven Rays: An Esoteric Key to Understanding Human Nature*. University of the Seven Rays, 1996.

Schlesinger, Kathleen. *The Greek Aulos: A Study of Its Mechanism and of Its Relation to the Modal System of Ancient Greek Music*. N. Yorkshire, UK: Methuen, 1939.

Smigel, Eric. *Alchemy of the Avant-garde: David Tudor and the New Music of the 1950s* (doctoral disertation). Los Angeles: USC, 2003.

Smulkis, Michael, and Fred Rubenfeld. *Starlight Elixirs and Cosmic Vibrational Healing*. UK: C. W. Daniel, 1992.

Steiner, Rudolf. *According to Matthew: The Gospel of Christ's Humanity*. Great Barrington, MA: Anthroposophic Press, 2002.

———. *Agriculture: Spiritual Foundations for the Renewal of Agriculture*. Kimberton, PA: BFGA, 1993.

———. *Anthroposophical Leading Thoughts: Anthroposophy as a Path of Knowledge: The Michael Mystery*. London: Rudolf Steiner Press, 1973.

———. *Anthroposophy and the Inner Life: An Esoteric Introduction*. Forest Row, UK: Rudolf Steiner Press, 1983.

———. *Approaching the Mystery of Golgotha*. Great Barrington, MA: SteinerBooks, 2018.

———. *Art as Seen in the Light of Mystery Wisdom*. London: Rudolf Steiner Press, 1984.

———. *Artistic Sensitivity as a Spiritual Approach to Knowing Life and the World*. Great Barrington, MA: SteinerBooks, 2006.

———. *The Arts and Their Mission*. Hudson, NY: Anthroposophic Press, 1986.

———. *Astronomy and Astrology: Finding a Relationship to the Cosmos*. Forest Row, UK: Rudolf Steiner Press, 2009.

———. *Autobiography: Chapters in the Course of my Life, 1861–1907*. Great Barrington, MA: SteinerBooks, 2000.

———. *Background to the Gospel of St. Mark*. Hudson, NY: Anthroposophic Press, 1986.

———. *Building Stones for an Understanding of the Mystery of Golgotha: Human Life in a Cosmic Context*. Forest Row, UK: Rudolf Steiner Press, 2015.

———. *Christ and the Spiritual World and the Search for the Holy Grail*. Forest Row, UK: Rudolf Steiner Press, 1963.

———. *The Christmas Conference: For the Foundation of the General Anthroposophical Society 1923/1924*. Hudson, NY: SteinerBooks, 2020.

———. *The Christmas Conference for the Foundation of the General Anthroposophical Society 1923/1924: The Laying of the Foundation Stone, Lectures and Addresses, Discussions of the Statutes*. Hudson, NY: Anthroposophic Press, 1990.

———. *Constitution of the School of Spiritual Science* (G. Adams, ed.). Forest Row, UK: Rudolf Steiner Press, 2013.

———. *Death as Metamorphosis of Life: Including "What Does the Angel Do in our Astral Body?" and "How Do I Find Christ?"* Great Barrington, MA: SteinerBooks, 2008.

———. *From Jesus to Christ*. Forest Row, UK: Rudolf Steiner Press, 2005.

———. *The Foundations of Human Experience*. Hudson, NY: Anthroposophic Press, 1996.

Bibliography and Related Reading

———. *Freemasonry and Ritual Work: The Misraim Service.* Great Barrington, MA: SteinerBooks, 2007.

———. *The Inner Nature of Music and the Experience of Tone.* Hudson, NY: Anthroposophic Press, 1983.

———. *Interdisciplinary Astronomy: Third Scientific Course.* Great Barrington, MA: SteinerBooks, 2003.

———. *The Karma of Untruthfulness: Secret Societies, the Media, and Preparations for the Great War,* 2 vols. Forest Row, UK: Rudolf Steiner Press, 2005.

———. *Karmic Relationships: Esoteric Studies,* vol. 1. Forest Row, UK: Rudolf Steiner Press, 2012.

———. *Karmic Relationships: Esoteric Studies,* vol. 4. Forest Row, UK: Rudolf Steiner Press, 2017.

———. *The Occult Movement in the Nineteenth Century and Its Relation to Modern Culture.* London: Rudolf Steiner Press, 1973.

———. *Occult Science, an Outline.* London: Rudolf Steiner Press, 1969.

———. *An Outline of Esoteric Science.* Hudson, NY: Anthroposophic Press, 1997.

———. *The Reappearance of Christ in the Etheric.* Great Barrington, MA: SteinerBooks, 2003.

———. *Riddles of Philosophy: Presented in an Outline of Its History.* Great Barrington, MA: SteinerBooks, 2009

———. *The Second Coming of Christ* (audio CD). Forest Row, UK: Rudolf Steiner Press, 2010.

———. *The Secret Stream: Christian Rosenkreutz and Rosicrucianism.* Great Barrington, MA: Anthroposophic Press, 2000.

———. *Spiritual Beings in the Heavenly Bodies and in the Kingdoms of Nature.* Great Barrington, MA: SteinerBooks, 2011.

———. *The Spiritual Guidance of the Individual and Humanity: Some Results of Spiritual–Scientific Research into Human History and Development.* Hudson, NY: 1992.

———. *The Temple Legend: Freemasonry and Related Occult Movements: From the Contents of the Esoteric School.* Forest Row, UK: Rudolf Steiner Press, 2002.

———. *Theosophy: An Introduction to the Spiritual Processes in Human Life and in the Cosmos.* Hudson, NY: Anthroposophic Press, 1994.

———. *Truth and Knowledge: Introduction to the Philosophy of Spiritual Activity.* Spring Valley, NY: Anthroposophic Press, 1981.

———. *Twelve Moods.* Spring Valley, NY: Mercury Press, 1984.

Sucher, Willi. *Cosmic Christianity and the Changing Countenance of Cosmology: An Introduction to Astrosophy: A New Wisdom of the Stars.* Hudson, NY: Anthroposophic Press, 1993.

———. *The Drama of the Universe.* Larkfield, UK: Landvidi Research Centre, 1958.

———. *Isis Sophia I: Introducing Astrosophy.* Meadow Vista, CA: Astrosophy Research Center, 1999.

———. *Isis Sophia II: An Outline of a New Star Wisdom.* Meadow Vista, CA: Astrosophy Research Center, 1985.

———. *Star Journals II: Toward New Astrosophy.* Meadow Vista, CA: Astrosophy Research Center, 2006.

Sullivan, Erin. *Retrograde Planets: Traversing the Inner Landscape.* York, ME: Samuel Weiser, 2000.

Tarnas, Richard. *Cosmos and Psyche: Intimations of a New World View.* New York: Penguin, 2007.

Tomberg, Valentin. *The Art of the Good: On the Regeneration of Fallen Justice.* Brooklyn, NY: Angelico Press, 2021.

———. *Christ and Sophia: Anthroposophic Meditations on the Old Testament, New Testament, and Apocalypse.* Great Barrington, MA: SteinerBooks, 2006.

———. *Inner Work.* Hudson, NY: Anthroposophic Press, 1992.

———. *Lazarus, Come Forth! Meditations of a Christian Esotericist on the Mysteries of the Raising of Lazarus, the Ten Commandments, the Three Kingdoms & the Breath of Life.* Great Barrington, MA: Lindisfarne Books, 2006.

———. *Studies on the Foundation Stone Meditation.* San Rafael, CA: LogoSophia, 2010.

Tommasini, Anthony. *The Indispensable Composers: A Personal Guide.* New York: Penguin, 2018.

Tresemer, David, and Robert Schiappacasse. *Star Wisdom and Rudolf Steiner: A Life Seen through the Oracle of the Solar Cross.* Great Barrington, MA: SteinerBooks, 2006.

Vaid, Vashist. *The Secrets of Astrology.* The Global Movement, 2012.

von Eschenbach, Wolfram. *Parzival: A Romance of the Middle Ages* (trans. H. Mustard and C. Passage). New York: Vintage Classics, 1961.

Vreede, Elisabeth. *Astronomy and Spiritual Science: The Astronomical Letters of Elisabeth Vreede.* Great Barrington, MA: SteinerBooks, 2007.

ABOUT THE CONTRIBUTORS

KATHLEEN BAIOCCHI, MPS, Loyola, is a graduate student in the Anthroposophic Counseling Psych Program (AAP). She has worked with flowers, gems and stars for inner healing since 1989. Kathleen was a student of Zen and Quantum Shiatsu for more than ten years. Kathleen met Anthroposophy in 2013 and is most grateful to be a student of Choreocosmos Eurythmy in Boulder, Colorado.

KRISZTINA CSERI graduated as an economist and worked in the production and financial controlling field at various companies for twelve years. She started to work with astrology in 2002 and attended a course from 2004 until 2007. She became a student of Anthroposophy at Pentecost 2009, when a friend invited her to the anniversary celebration of Rudolf Steiner's "Budapest-lectures." Owing to the impact of that event, she soon left her financial career. She first encountered the work of Willi Sucher and Robert Powell in 2010. In 2012, with her husband she founded the Hungarian Sophia Foundation (www.szofia-magyarorszag.hu). They have a small publishing company and translate and distribute books on spiritual themes. Krisztina translated six books written by Robert Powell (and Kevin Dann) into Hungarian and finished translating *Meditations on the Tarot* into Hungarian in 2020. She is a mother of two little children and lives with her family in a village near Budapest.

JULIE HUMPHREYS is a graduate of Stanford and a former pediatric nurse and Waldorf mom. An early interest in astrology lay dormant for more than three decades until she was introduced to the sidereal system, the works of Robert Powell, and the visions of Anne Catherine Emmerich. She has taken great joy in researching astrological phenomena for the *Journal for Star Wisdom*. Julie lives in Carmel, California, where shooting stars and the Milky Way are often visible.

JOEL MATTHEW PARK is a husband, father, and Christian Hermeticist based in Copake, New York. From 2011 to 2019 he was a life-sharing coworker at Plowshare Farm (a Camphill affiliate), farming and candlemaking with people from a variety of countries, ages, and developmental backgrounds. During this time, he earned a certification in Social Therapy from the School of Spiritual Science through the Camphill Academy. He has been living and working in Camphill Village Copake since 2019. After a time devoted to elder care, he has become increasingly involved in teaching in the Camphill Academy, on topics such as Stargazing, the Karma of Vocation, Theosophy, the Human Soul, the Festival Year, and Philosophical Perspectives. Joel has been a student of Anthroposophy since 2008 and a Christian Hermeticist since 2010. In 2014, he met Phillip Malone; together, the two of them have been investigating the Tarot of Marseilles since 2016. Since then, Joel has led two retreats on "Tarot and the Art of Hermetic Conversation" (2017 and 2019). The fruits of Joel and Phillip's collaboration in this realm can be found at www.the-unknown-friends.com. In 2015, he joined the Grail Knighthood, a group-spiritual practice offered through the Sophia Foundation. Through this, he met Robert Powell, whose work he had been studying since 2009. Since then, Joel has been working actively with him to continue the karma research Robert began in 1977 and exemplifies in works such as *Hermetic Astrology*, volumes I and II, and *Elijah, Come Again*. Joel's first contribution was to the *Journal for Star Wisdom* 2018 (published Nov. 2017), after which he became editor for the journal's continuation, the Star Wisdom series. The first volume of this series was published in November 2018. A selection of Joel's writings can be found on his website, TreeHouse: www.treehouse.live.

About the Contributors

ROBERT POWELL, PhD, is an internationally known lecturer, author, eurythmist, and movement therapist. He is founder of the Choreocosmos School of Cosmic and Sacred Dance, and cofounder of the Sophia Foundation of North America. He received his doctorate for his thesis *The History of the Zodiac*, available as a book from Sophia Academic Press. His published works include *The Sophia Teachings*, a six-tape series (Sounds True Recordings), as well as *Elijah Come Again: A Prophet for Our Time*; *The Mystery, Biography, and Destiny of Mary Magdalene*; *Divine Sophia—Holy Wisdom*; *The Most Holy Trinosophia and the New Revelation of the Divine Feminine*; *Chronicle of the Living Christ*; *Christian Hermetic Astrology*; *The Christ Mystery*; *The Sign of the Son of Man in the Heavens*; *Cultivating Inner Radiance and the Body of Immortality*; and the yearly *Journal for Star Wisdom* (previously *Christian Star Calendar*). He translated the spiritual classic *Meditations on the Tarot* and co-translated Valentin Tomberg's *Lazarus, Come Forth!* Robert is coauthor with David Bowden of *Astrogeographia: Correspondences between the Stars and Earthly Locations* and coauthor with Estelle Isaacson of *Gautama Buddha's Successor* and *The Mystery of Sophia*. Robert is also coauthor with Kevin Dann of *The Astrological Revolution: Unveiling the Science of the Stars as a Science of Reincarnation and Karma* and *Christ and the Maya Calendar: 2012 and the Coming of the Antichrist*; and coauthor with Lacquanna Paul of *Cosmic Dances of the Zodiac* and *Cosmic Dances of the Planets*. He teaches a gentle form of healing movement: the sacred dance of eurythmy, as well as the Cosmic Dances of the Planets and signs of the zodiac. Through the Sophia Grail Circle, Robert facilitates sacred celebrations dedicated to the Divine Feminine. He offers workshops in Europe and Australia, and with Karen Rivers, cofounder of the Sophia Foundation, leads pilgrimages to the world's sacred sites: Turkey, 1996; the Holy Land, 1997; France, 1998; Britain, 2000; Italy, 2002; Greece, 2004; Egypt, 2006; India, 2008; Turkey, 2009; the Grand Canyon, 2010; South Africa, 2012; Peru, 2014; the Holy Land, 2016; and Bali, 2018. Visit www.sophiafoundation.org and www.astrogeographia.org.

AMBER WOLFE ROUNDS is a second-generation astrologer with 15 years of experience. She provides astrology services, including predictive forecasting, natal charts for individuals, composite readings for couples or groups, and workshops. Amber composes and performs musical scores from astrology with Zizia. She earned a Waldorf Certificate and an MEd from Antioch University New England after submitting her thesis, *Tone Art: Anthroposophy, Astrology, Music*.

Lightning Source UK Ltd.
Milton Keynes UK
UKHW051149021121
393246UK00001B/4